Roy Thomas - Cream Crackers (E5,5c) Ogmore
(Page 258) Photo: Carl Ryan

Adrian Berry - Masterpiece (E6,6b) Giants Cave
(Page 64) Photo: Carl Ryan

Gower & South East Wales Guide

Goi Ashmore & Roy Thomas

Guidebook Team

Adrian Berry	Nic O'Neill
John Harwood	Ed Rees
Ren Hoek	Andy Sharp
Myles Jordan	Chris Shorrock
Pete Lewis	James Tracey
Danny McCarroll	

Action Shots by Carl Ryan unless credited otherwise

Front Cover: Gwyn Evans on Osiris (VS,4c) Fall Bay Buttress (Page 60)
Photo: Carl Ryan

Rear Cover: Goi Ashmore & James Tracey on pitch 2 of The Caerphilly Contract (Fr7b+) Llanbradach (Page 437)
Photo: Carl Ryan

For detailed maps to the area, OS sheet 159 Covers Gower and the rest is covered by 170 & 171

Produced by South Wales Mountaineering Club

Previous Publications

Gower (West Col 1970)
By J.O.Talbot

Gower Peninsula Supplement (West Col 1973)
By J.O.Talbot

South East Wales (SWMC 1973)
By J.C.Horsfield

South East Wales (SWMC 1978)
By J.Harwood

Gower And Sourh East Wales (SWMC 1983)
By M.Danford and T.Penning

Gower & South East Wales (SWMC 1991)
By A.E.Richardson

South East Wales Sanstone (JDMEL 1991)
By G.Ashmore and A.Senior

South East Wales Sandstone (JDMEL 1995)
By G.Ashmore

Gower Sports Climbs (A.Berry 1997)
By A.Berry

South East Wales Sandstone, Limestone & Gower Sports Topos (Climb High 1997)
By G.Gibson

Dedicated to 'Bridgend' Steve James, who sadly passed away in 2001. Ogmore can never be the same again.

Note that all second ascents in this guidebook were by Eddie Yates and Alec Trench.

(c) South Wales Mountaineering Club & Authors 2003

Ashmore, Goi Thomas, Roy   Gower And South East Wales Guide

ISBN 1 871890 94 2

Typeset by Goi Ashmore

Produced by: HI-TEC PRINT, Units 9&10, Houghton Road
North Anston Trading Estate, North Anston, SHEFFIELD S25 4JJ

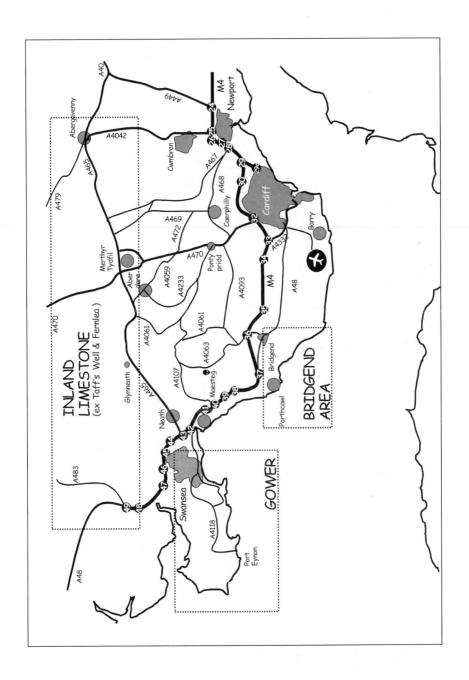

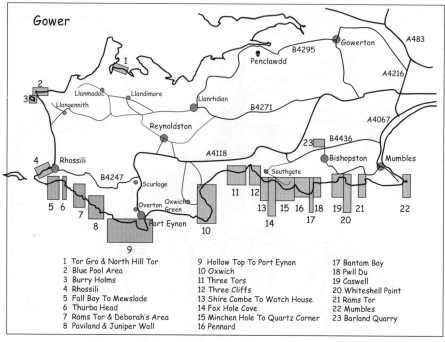

Gower

Penclawdd
B4295
Gowerton
A483
A4216

Llanmadoc
Llandimore
Llanrhidian
B4271
A4067

Llangennith

Reynoldston
A4118

23 B4436
Bishopston
Mumbles

Rhossili
B4247
Scurlage
Southgate

Overton
Oxwich Green
Port Eynon

1 Tor Gro & North Hill Tor
2 Blue Pool Area
3 Burry Holms
4 Rhossili
5 Fall Bay To Mewslade
6 Thurba Head
7 Rams Tor & Deborah's Area
8 Paviland & Juniper Wall

9 Hollow Top To Port Eynon
10 Oxwich
11 Three Tors
12 Three Cliffs
13 Shire Combe To Watch House
14 Fox Hole Cove
15 Minchen Hole To Quartz Corner
16 Pennard

17 Bantam Bay
18 Pwll Du
19 Caswell
20 Whiteshell Point
21 Rams Tor
22 Mumbles
23 Barland Quarry

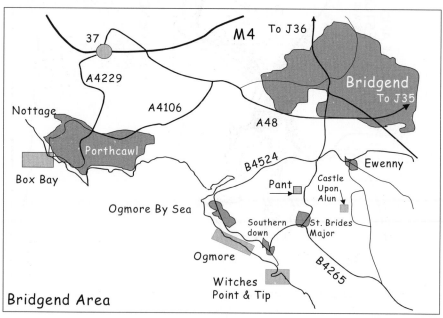

M4
To J36
37
A4229
Bridgend
To J35
Nottage
A4106
A48
Porthcawl
B4524
Ewenny
Box Bay
Pant
Castle Upon Alun
Ogmore By Sea
Southern down
St. Brides Major
Ogmore
B4265
Witches Point & Tip

Bridgend Area

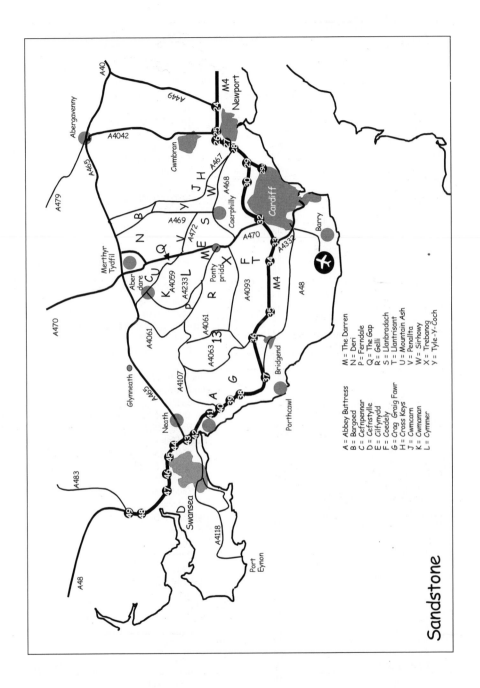

Sandstone

Contents

PHOTOGRAPHS

TOPOS

GUIDEBOOK DISCLAIMER

This guidebook attempts to provide a definitive record of all existing climbs and is compiled from information from a variety of sources. The inclusion of any route does not imply that it remains in the condition described. Climbs can change unpredictably. Rock can deteriorate and the condition of in-situ gear may alter or it may have been stolen. All climbers must rely on their own ability and experience to gauge the difficulty and seriousness of any climb. Climbing is an inherently dangerous activity.

Neither SWMC nor the authors and editors of this guidebook accept any liability whatsoever for injury or damage caused to (or by) climbers, third parties, or property arising from its use. Whilst the content of the guide is believed to be accurate, no responsibility is accepted for any error, omission or mis-statement. Users must rely on their own judgement and are recommended to insure against injury to person and property or third party risks.

The inclusion in this guidebook of a crag or routes upon it does not mean that any member of the public has a right of access to the crag or the right to climb upon it.

Information on all climbing in the area is made available regardless of the access position; for historical purposes; for the sake of completeness; and so that facts are available if access is permitted in the future.

Before climbing on any crag in this guidebook, please read all the introductory section and the crag notes and stick to any stated access rules.

PUBLICATION DATE

This guidebook is in fact out ahead of schedule as we are using the Islamic Calender.

ACKNOWLEDGEMENTS

A fair number of people who are not part of the guidebook team have contributed in someway or other to the publication of this guidebook or climbing in the area. They are:

Proof reading was supplied by Gwyn Evans, Haydn Griffiths, Bill Gregory and Dave Gregory. It's a good job because the rest of the editorial team am total illiterate. Candy Jewell helped us out with the type setting and put us up when we all went down to North Devon to climb and got smashed instead. Pete Bennett helped us with the legal stuff.

More accurate first ascent dates or old route information, or help with researching the historical section came from Jim Birch, John Brailsford, Martin Crocker, Harold Drasdo, Bob Griffiths, Pat Littlejohn, Tony Penning and Jeremy Talbot.

Wayne Gladwin and Stuart Thompson for (respectively) chairing and being secretary to the 1999-2000 bolt forum and for some balanced input from staff from the CCW (Michael Williams) and RSPB (David Painter).

A large number of other people have helped either by providing information on repeats or holding our ropes, re-bolting or re-cleaning things: Bob Brewer, John Bullock, Si Coles, Stefan Doerr, Chris Evans, Iain Fisher, Gary Gibson, Gareth Griffiths, Paul Hadley, Dee Herbert, Alice Howe, Duncan Irving, Steve James, Ceri Jones, Andy Meek, Dave Meek, Rich Phillips, Duncan Powell, Bryce Rea, Gringo Rich, Martyn Richards, Smithy, Tom Starke, Eugene Travers-Jones, Trudi Veenstra (Ashmore) and Big Neil White.

Support has also been forthcoming over the years from Up & Under in Cardiff. We'd particularly like to thank Norman Carter for help and support starting right back in 1992 with the Sandstone Guide and also Caerwyn Bridges. The other staff are too numerous to mention, but cheers for the brews.

During the work one of the editors broke his back and heel in a nasty tumble, whilst the other one decked out from 65ft. up (and a month later had another accident involving a wall and a plate glass door). In terms of the contributors at least one of them managed to get arrested, several withdrew for a time due to the bolt forum, one got in big trouble with the Ministry of Defence, one of them was expelled from university and one of them thought he was going to die in a curious incident involving the door of plane when trying to get out of Libya. There were no typesetting problems other than those caused by Famke The Monkey. Only a few animals were hurt during the making of this guidebook.

ETHICS AND STYLE

'I still remember the days when climbers didn't pull their ropes through if they fell off.' Make sure that you red-point first ascents if you fall off or declare rests and points of aid honestly. Chipping or gluing back on holds that were not there in the first place is naughty.

PROJECTS

Please leave bolted projects alone in South East Wales and Gower. We do not steal visitors projects and we prefer to receive the same level of courtesy from visitors.

GRADING SYSTEM

Two grading systems are in use in this guidebook. All routes receive the traditional UK grades and sports routes receive a Sports (French) grade as well. Sports routes are those where the gear is in-situ, although this does not imply that the gear on these routes is in good condition or properly placed and so does not imply that there is no danger involved.

UK GRADES

UK grades consist of two parts, an adjectival grade and a technical grade. Technical grades do theoretically exist below 4a, but it is genuinely difficult to differentiate between easier grades and so none are given.

TECHNICAL GRADES

Technical grades describe only the hardest move on a particular route or pitch. A succession of moves at one grade does not lead to a higher technical grade. That is to say, a succession of 6a moves does not get a 6b technical grade. Certain factors, particularly height/reach mean that some climbers are going to find some moves technically easier than they are graded. Short of standardising everyone's height, which we feel is better done by the EU, there is nothing we can do about this, except to say that they are graded for the climber of average stature (about 5'10"). Technical grades are open-ended and have the following progression from easier to harder:

4a,4b,4c,5a,5b,5c,6a,6b,6c,7a etc.

ADJECTIVAL GRADES

Adjectival grades describe a combination of factors and are intended to give an indication of the overall difficulty of a route. The factors generally taken into account are the overall physical difficulty of a route, the quality and quantity of protection and the exposure. It is assumed that the leader carries a full modern rack of climbing protection for traditional routes and so does not apply to Roy Thomas who still uses John Syrrett's hexes and the rest of whose kit came out of the sea at Ogmore.

It is really the combination of technical and adjectival grades that is important. There are no real hard and fast rules about combinations, grades of VS,6a are perfectly possible, if for instance there is a superbly protected crack line with easy climbing but one desperate move. Adjectival grades for sports routes are included to give a rough measure of difficulty for those unfamiliar with the French grading system. However, there are a number of combinations that account for the vast majority of route grades shown below. If the route has a low technical grade for its adjectival class, then it is either badly protected but with relatively easy technical moves or adequately protected but with a lot of moves at one technical standard. Routes with a high technical grade relative to their adjectival grades either have excellent protection, or more likely have one very hard move.

Normal Adjectival and Technical Combinations

HS 4a,4b	E1,5b,5c	E4,6a,6b
VS 4b,4c	E2,5b,5c	E5,6b
HVS 5a,5b	E3,5c,6a	E6,6b,6c

If all guidebooks moved to a three parameter system, where the E-Grade accounted for only overall difficulty and there was a P-Grade for protection, then there would be no ambiguity between say sustained routes and bold routes of their respective technical grade. This has been done for the Yorkshire Gritstone guide, but other than that, it has not really caught on. Perhaps that is just because there are too many thick climbers around. Until such a happy day arrives, look carefully at your chosen route before climbing it, keep an eye out for words like 'bold', 'death' or 'Bridgend Steve' and consider sacrificing the on-sight by checking out gear on abseil first, because in our experience decking out hurts.

Note that in theory the adjectival grade assumes an 'on-sight' style of ascent, i.e. turning up at a crag the first time and climbing the route straight off from bottom to top with no falls. This is obviously difficult for traverses. Abseil inspections, pre-placing gear etc. reduce the adjectival grade for this reason, but not the technical grade. Confused? Well never mind, so are most Americans.

SPORTS GRADES

As Kasper Martin said 'Loose rock, plants, self-placed gear, nothing for continentals in this country!' Fortunately that was in England and this is Wales.

Sports grades are much more straightforward because the sports grade simply takes into account the overall physical difficulty of the climbing, with protection, exposure etc. deemed to be irrelevant. We have chosen to interpret sports grades as that applying to a 'worked' i.e. pre-practised ascent, although an on-sight ascent is still far more of an achievement. The sports grades are denoted by 'Fr' as they were originally developed in France, probably by Eric Lenoir.

Sports Grades are also open ended, from easier to harder:

Fr1, Fr1+, Fr2, Fr2+, Fr3, Fr3+, Fr4, Fr4+, Fr5, Fr5+, Fr6a, Fr6a+, Fr6b, Fr6b+, Fr6c, Fr6c+, Fr7a etc.

However, do not assume that sports routes are safe. Bolts may be in bad places to clip, may not have been placed correctly, rot over time etc. etc. Both the editors of this guide have had nasty injuries sports climbing. (One of them has also has a nasty injury traditional climbing, whilst the other had a bad injury involving a lamp).

ABBREVIATIONS

Once upon a time one of the guidebook editors, who had just purchased the famous 1985 "rkshi mestone" guide, was very confused about the abbreviation "TR (not in situ)". Do you have to carry a tree with you and plant it? To avoid future ambiguity, please refer to the section below. Note that sports routes do not have all fixed protection listed individually.

PR = Peg Runner
BR = Bolt Runner
TR = Thread Runner
Bristol PR = one that has been removed by the first ascensionist who expects subsequent ascensionists to place their own. Sometimes this has been done for a good reason (to stop sea corrosion).
Bristol BR = one where the hanger has been removed by the first ascensionist to save expense and local climbers are expected to place the hangers (cheeky monkey).

PB = Peg Belay
BB = Bolt Belay
TB = Thread Belay

1pt = An aid or rest point
2pt = 2 aid or rest points etc.

♇ = A route subject to a seasonal bird restriction detailed in the crag descriptions

☹ = A route subject to a permanent ban detailed in the crag descriptions
\ = A route that has not had enough ascents for the grade/quality to be considered accurate

FFA = First Free Ascent of an aid route
ALCH = A route re-climbed after loss of significant holds

QUALITY

We reject the line taken in some guidebooks that stars for quality should not be used as they result in the abandonment/under-utilisation of some routes and over-utilisation of others. This is for three reasons. Firstly in the absence of stars, routes are often selected on a 'word-of-mouth' basis, meaning that some routes are going to get even more trashed. Secondly, it seems sad to assume that most climbers are so shallow that they only do the three-starred routes. Finally and by far the most important, if we did not put stars on things then we would have no fun in misdirecting people to routes that are given three stars in this guidebook, but are really tottering heaps of choss.

Quality is often thought of as subjective and what pleases one does not please another. To overcome this people have written long-winded essays in new routes books and the like saying that to have three stars (the best) a route must have an outstanding line, exceptional climbing, superb position and probably a picture of Andy Pollitt on it in Extreme Rock. A route with two stars must have at least n of these attributes (say a picture of Sophia Gardens in it in On The Edge or some other nonsense). You get the picture.

We, by contrast, do not like these rules. Instead we have chosen a totally objective method of scoring quality. We impose a pareto distribution on the stars in the guidebook, so that the mean is no stars and the maximum number of three star routes is .01 on the right-hand tail of the distribution. Obviously what is really needed is an empirical study of stars throughout guidebooks in the UK, so that we can set absolute values. So we have commissioned one from the team of Bert Hof, Anthony Hams, Richard Nibbering, Martina Brueck, Ron Porath, Mark London, (Phil) Brock, Deckert & Sheinkmann. We are lying of course, but about 30% of the routes in the guidebook get 1 star or better and about 2.5% get three stars. The best routes get ***, good routes get *, the rest of the routes are OK, except for the really horrid ones, which get the black spot (●).

NEW ROUTES

Details of new routes, dates of ascents and new crags should be sent to Roy Thomas, 90 Robins Close, Brackla, BRIDGEND, CF31 2PS. Please do not assume that routes written up elsewhere will be located by Roy or any other future guidebook writers. There is also a new routes book in Up & Under in Cardiff. In the future SWMC plan to set up something on their website too. Note we cannot be held responsible for names given to routes by first ascensionists, we just record them, not name them, so you can just....

HISTORICAL INFORMATION

We have tried to include information on dates of first ascents for this guidebook. This information is patchy to say the least, so please do send in more accurate information to the same address as new routes.

AREA BOLTING POLICY

South East Wales and Gower has a bolt policy agreed at a series of Open Meetings at WICC in 1999-2000, chaired by Wayne Gladwin (brave man) and minuted by Stuart Thompson. The bolting policy is listed seperately for each crag, except for the sandstone, where it is noted at the start of the section. The following aspects of the policy are more general. Please keep to the policy, which reflects the wishes of local climbers.

1. Bolting will be defined as the placement of any 'drilled gear' assumed to be bolts.
2. De-bolting/smashing/spoiling of bolts is totally condemned.
3. New sports routes should avoid interfering with existing traditional routes.
4. Where (3) might occur, the first ascensionist of the traditional route should be consulted. It is left to the conscience of the leader to consult with the others on first ascent.

5. Retro-bolting, where permissible, requires the permission of the first ascensionist. Retro-bolting for the purposes of this policy, means making a route into a clip up, rather than replacing worn placements with bolts.

6. Replacement of worn placements with bolts should be on a 'point for point' basis and only at specified crags.

7. Bolting at crags discovered in the future should assume the following:

Natural Sandstone – No Bolting
Gower – No Bolting
Quarried Sandstone – Sports routes allowed.
Quarried Limestone – Sports routes allowed.
Other rock types – Apply common sense, i.e. do not bolt up adequately protected cracks on natural limestone, for instance.

Bolts should be at least 8.8mm or staples and for sea-cliffs should always be BS316 stainless steel.

Those of you who have climbed on the fabulous South East Wales sandstone and other bolted crags will no doubt have thought about the time and expense that has gone into bolting and equipping. Put your hand in your pocket and make a donation the South East Wales Bolt Fund. Without it and your contributions, there will be no quality sports routes or quality bolts for you to fall on. Please send your vital contributions c/o, Roy Thomas, 90 Robins Hill, Brackla, BRIDGEND CF31 2PS.

It would be a good idea to bring any future problems to the attention of the correct forum of discussion, namely the BMC Committee of Wales area meetings. Your input is vital and welcomed.

ACCESS
Access notes appear at the beginning of each crag section, so there are only a few general points to make here. Remember that most of the South Gower coast is owned by the NT and/or managed by the Countryside Council for Wales where there is natural or ecological interest. Tread carefully and consult where necessary. There are bird-bans in place for some cliffs; The Worm (permanent), Thurba and Yellow Wall although they are variable and should be checked with either the NT (01792 390636) or the BMC. Deri Crag and Llangattock have special conditions attached to them, especially for groups at Llangattock, so please check the individual crag notes. There are a couple of banned quarries, but this may change at some stage in the future.

HOSPITALS
For injuries that you are going to get seen to yourself (as opposed to 999 calls), but are too urgent to wait for a visit to your GP, there are casualty departments at the following local hospitals:

1. Gower Area
Morriston Hospital, Heol Maes Eglwys, Morriston, SWANSEA (Tel: 01792 702222)

2. Bridgend Area
Princess of Wales Hospital, Coity Road, BRIDGEND (Tel: 01656 720371)

3. South East Wales Limestone
Prince Charles Hospital, Gurnos Estate, MERTHYR TYDFIL (Tel: 01685 721721)

4. South East Wales Sandstone
University of Wales Hospital, Heath Park, CARDIFF (Tel: 02920 747747)
Royal Glamorgan Hospital, Ynys Maerdy, LLANTRISANT (Tel: 01443 443443)

FIRST AID

IF YOU HAVE A LIFE THREATENING INJURY AT OGMORE WITH AN INCOMING TIDE YOU STAND A VERY HIGH CHANCE OF DROWNING. TAKE THIS WARNING VERY SERIOUSLY.

1. IF SPINAL INJURIES or HEAD INJURIES are suspected, DO NOT MOVE THE PATIENT without skilled help, except to maintain breathing.

2. IF BREATHING HAS STOPPED, clear airways and commence artificial respiration. DO NOT STOP UNTIL EXPERT OPINION DIAGNOSES DEATH.

3. STOP BLEEDING BY APPLYING DIRECT PRESSURE AND NOT A TOURNIQUET.

4. KEEP THE PATIENT WARM.

5. SUMMON HELP.

REACHING SOUTH EAST WALES AND GOWER

There is an International Airport at Cardiff, with flights from various European destinations. There is a sort of Airport at Swansea and you could fly there from Ireland. Cardiff, Bridgend and Swansea are on the main London to Swansea railway line and the area is connected to the national motorway network by the M4 and the Severn (Toll) Bridges.

PUBLIC TRANSPORT

The following information services are available 0845 7484950 for Rail Enquiries or 0870 6082608 for buses. Also try http://www.pti.org.uk.

1.Gower

Swansea itself is on the main London to Swansea railway line (surprisingly enough). There are number of buses running from Swansea Town Centre. Bus #18 runs along the South Gower as far as Oxwich and Bus #18A and #18D run all the way to Rhossili. Bus #16 runs to Llangennith.

2.Bridgend Area

Bridgend itself is on the main London to Swansea railway line. To get to Ogmore or Witches Point use the #145 bus from Bridgend. For Castle Upon Alun take the #145 to the Ogmore turn off and walk. For Box Bay take the #61 or # 63 buses from Bridgend to Porthcawl.

3. South East Wales Limestone

The South East Wales Limestone crags are not the easiest to reach by public transport and are going to require some walking. The current best place to check out timetables seems to be http://www.stagecoachbus.com. For the crags near to Merthyr, trains run up from Cardiff Central Station to Methyr station itself. Bus #40 runs from the centre close to Pant Industrial Estate. Walk from here for Morlais, Cefn Coed, Taf Fechan or Twynau Gwynion. For Taff's Well take the train from Cardiff Central to Taff's Well Station and walk back down the road. Dinas can be reached by taking the train to Aberdare from Cardiff and then the X55 to the Lamb And Flag in Glynneath, or by taking the X75 Swansea-Merthyr bus. The nearest bus route to Llangattock is the #21 from Abergavenny (reached by train) to Brecon. For Dinas Fach, Dinas Fawr and Fernlea, just forget it.

4. South East Wales Sandstone

The sandstone valleys north of Cardiff are served pretty well by the rail network so most of the crags in this area have detailed approaches from the nearest railway station. The rail network runs straight out of Cardiff Central and Queen Street Stations. For train timetables use the following information services:

National Rail Enquiries (Tel: 0845 7484950)   or: www.railtrack.co.uk

PUBS

There are a wealth of pubs in the area, not all of which are dangerous. If you want to go out big time go to Cardiff town centre or the Mumbles, Kingsway and Wind Street in Swansea. Do not do this in The Valleys. The following pubs are handy due to their proximity to climbing areas.

The Gower Inn (Parkmill)
This is the obvious pub on the main A4118 Gower road.

The Joiners Arms (Bishopston)
The pub is reached by turning off the B4436 into Bishopston at Barland Quarry. It is about 250m up the road on the right-hand side. This is where we always end up because of the fine own-brewed beer.

Three Golden Cups (Southerndown)
The pub is on the corner of the B4524, opposite the turn off down to Southerndown and Witches Point.

The Pelican (Ogmore)
The pub is about 2 miles down the B4524 after leaving the B4265 from Bridgend. It is on the left.

Lewis Arms (Tongwynlais)
Leave the A470 at Taff's Well and follow the flyover into Tongwynlais. The pub is in the centre of the village on the left hand side.

Fagin's (Taff's Well)
Leave the A470 at Taff's Well and follow the B4262 towards Morganstown. The pub is on the right after about 1 mile.

The Glyntaff Arms (Quaker's Yard)
The pub is on the right of the A4054 in an offshoot of the road. It is opposite the left turning over the bridge described in the access notes for The Gap.

CAMPSITES AND ACCOMMODATION

For accommodation other than campsites, contact the Wales Tourist Board:

Wales Tourist Board, Brunel House, 2 Fitzalan Road, CARDIFF CF24 OUY
(Tel: 02920 499909, http://www.tourist information.co.uk)

There are a lot of campsites on the Gower, but moving further east, things get more tricky. Here is a non-exhaustive list under the four main areas, it is strongly recommended that you make telephone enquiries first, as they are not all open all year round.

1.Gower
Hillend Caravan and Camping, Hillend, Llangennith, Gower, SWANSEA SA3 1AU (Tel: 01792391195)
Kennexstone Farm Caravan and Camping Site, Kennexstone Farm, Llangennith, Gower, SWANSEA SA3 1HS (Tel: 01792 386311)
Pitton Cross Caravan and Camping Park, Rhossili, Gower, SWANSEA SA3 2HB (Tel: 01792 390593)
Three Cliffs Camping, North Hills Farm, Penmaen, SWANSEA SA3 2HB (01792 371218)

2.Bridgend Area
Acorn Camping and Caravaning, Rose Dew Farm, Ham Lane South, LLANTWIT MAJOR CF61 1RP (Tel: 01446 794527)

General Notes

Llandow Touring Caravan Park, Llandow, COWBRIDGE CF7 7PB (Tel: 01446 794527)

3.South East Wales Limestone
South East Wales Limestone is fairly starved of campsites. However, the Welsh International Climbing Centre does bunkhouse style accommodation and is handy for the cluster of crags round Merthyr Tydfil. Alternatively use the campsites as for sandstone below.

WICC, Taff Bargoed Centre, Trelewis, MERTHR TYDFIL CF46 6RA (Tel: 01443 710749)

The following campsite is useful for Llangattock:

Riverside Camping and Caravan Park, New Road, CRICKHOWELL NP8 1AY (Tel: 01873 810397)

4.South East Wales Sandstone
Cwmcarn Forest Drive Campsite, Nantcarn Road, Cwmcarn, CROSSKEYS NP1 7FA (Tel: 01495 272001)
Dare Valley Country Park, ABERDARE (CF44 7RG) (Tel: 01685 874672)
Parc Cwm Darran, Deri, BARGOED CF8 9AB (Tel: 01656 880505)
Also see WICC above.

CLIMBING WALLS
There are several small walls in the area. For details of these it is best to refer to the BMC website http://www.thebmc.co.uk.

The main climbing wall is WICC, Taff Bargoed Centre, Trelewis, MERTHR TYDFIL CF46 6RA (Tel: 01443 710749).

Other smaller walls are:

Centre For Sport And Physical Recreation, University of Glamorgan, Llantwit Road, Treforest, PONTYPRIDD CF37 1DL (Tel: 01443 482681)

Clyne Farm Activity Centre, Westport Avenue, Mayals, SWANSEA SA3 5AR (Tel: 01792 403333)

Port Talbot YMCA, Talbot Road, PORT TALBOT SA13 1HU (Tel: 01639 887034)

GEOLOGY
By Danny McCarroll

Rock climbing in South Wales, as elsewhere in Britain, owes much to the events of the Carboniferous Period, between 355 and 325 million years ago. At that time much of Britain was covered in a shallow tropical sea, similar to the Bahamas area today, with coral reefs teeming with life and laying down great masses of limey mud and shell debris that would eventually become the Carboniferous limestone. In the Upper Carboniferous, great river deltas spread across the area, depositing layers of gravel and sand that would become gritstone and sandstone. Lush vegetation in this wet environment decayed to peat and was eventually compressed into coal. In South Wales these Carboniferous rocks were squeezed to form a great basin, or syncline, with the sandstones and coal in the middle and the limestone peeping out around the edges. It is the folding, and therefore stretching of the limestone at the bottom of the pile, that accounts for the regular jointing and thus the frequency of vertical cracks.

The Carboniferous limestone provides climbing all around the coalfield. On the north side it forms the majestic cliffs of south Pembrokeshire, to the east the delights of Dinas and Llangattock and on the south the more subtle, and more varied climbing of Gower. It is the intricate folding and faulting of the limestone on Gower that accounts for the great variety of climbing to be found on this single rock type in such a small area. Where the bedding dips towards the coast there are beautiful crack-seamed slabs, as at Three Cliffs and Tor Bay, and where the bedding dips away from the coast there are steep walls with overhangs and roofs, as around Mewslade, the Sisters and Pennard. Old quarries dotted around the coast, where the rock could be removed by boat, provide wonderful steep wall climbing, as at Trial Wall. At Barland the quarrying has revealed a pristine bedding surface, providing the best slab climbs in the area, marred only by the loose bowl-shaped depressions that mark the bottom of blast holes. Some of the steeper walls on Gower follow large faults. Hairy Dog Wall, for example, is the overhanging wall of one of a number of faults that have chewed-up the back of Great Boulder Cove. There will be scope for many more routes on it when Yellow Wall eventually falls down (look in the cave behind it!). The uncompromising overhanging wall at Oxwich Quarry also follows a fault, as does the magnificent main wall at Pant. Water percolating through these faults accounts for the cave-like features, including tufa and the subtle scalloping that makes Pant so special.

The mining villages of the South Wales Valleys are built mainly of upper coal measures Pennant Sandstone and quarries, with rock of widely varying quality, are widespread. The sand was laid down in meandering river channels and weathering of the iron-rich cement gives it the characteristic rusty colour and brittle nature. The rivers carried plant debris which, when turned to coal, easily weathers out to form incut pockets. Plant fossils, including giant horsetails, can be found on the floor of many of the quarries and are particularly common along the path to Navigation Quarry.

The Carboniferous limestone extends east of Swansea and forms the rock platform at Ogmore, but the climbing in this area is on rocks that are much younger, formed also in shallow tropical seas but this time in the Jurassic (205-195 million years ago). Most of the Jurassic limestone of South Wales is thinly bedded with layers of mud and is not suitable for climbing, but at the shallow edges of the sea a much more solid limestone, known locally as the Sutton Stone was deposited. When you stand at the bottom of Ogmore, or Witches Point, your feet are on Carboniferous limestone, with beautiful fossil corals, but your hands are on the Jurassic. The basal layers of Sutton Stone contain lots of fragments of hard flinty chert left over from the erosion of the rocks beneath. The Jurassic rocks are less folded than the older Carboniferous rocks and thus there are fewer vertical cracks. As you climb up the cliff at Ogmore the rocks become less coastal and so more thinly bedded, so that the breaks get closer together but more fragile (beware when you place a camming device!). This, and weathering at the top of the cliff, explains the bold lower sections and the terrifying top-outs.

More typical Jurassic rocks form the cliffs at Dunraven Bay, Southerndown, and fossil ammonites and 'Devil's Toenails' (curled relatives of oysters) are common on the beach and fallen blocks, but at the southern end of the bay the Sutton Stone is dragged up along a fault. The overhanging bolted wall taken by Stone Wings is the fault itself and if you look to your left you can see the contortion of the softer 'Blue Lias' Jurassic limestones and muds.

During the last Ice Age, about 22 thousand years ago, glacier ice moved down the South Wales Valleys and also impinged on the north side of Gower, but the south side was untouched, so bays and particularly the caves contain a wonderful record of changing climate. Cemented raised beach deposits, formed during the last interglacial, about

Geology

125 thousand years ago, cling to the rock platform in many areas but are particularly clear at Foxhole, beneath the calcite lined fault taken by 'Hypnotic Groove'. Here, as elsewhere, the beach is overlain by angular limestone breccia, formed by freeze-thaw of the cliffs during the last ice age. The cave would have been half full of this breccia and a former floor level forms the odd 'collar' and bits of breccia form crucial but terrifying holds on most of the routes. There are lots of animal bones in the cave sediments and breccias of Gower, including woolly rhino, reindeer, mammoth, bear and wolf, as well as archaeological remains of international importance. Please resist the urge to poke about, but if you spot anything just leave it alone and contact the National Museum in Cardiff.

History

This history section draws on the previous work of Gwyn Evans and John Harwood, expanded with the benefits of extensive date research and an interviewing programme carried out in 1999-2002. The current historical development leaves us with just shy of 3,500 routes.

1937-1972
No doubt the odd route on Gower was climbed during the pre-history of the sport, but the development of the area has essentially been a post-war phenomenon. Only one of the currently recorded routes had a definite pre-war ascent, East Ridge on Great Tor, traditionally described as being first climbed by Vaughan-Thomas in the 1930s, although there is a counter-claim from an unknown mountaineer putting the first ascent date in 1937 and Jeremy Talbot now believes that it was probably climbed in the twenties.

During the war, several of Gower's beaches were used for rehearsals for the D-Day landings by American troops and commando parties. Jeremy Talbot clearly remembers Lewes Castle being used for this purpose, but feels it unlikely that any routes were climbed, the major objective being grappling practice. However, the Americans did create several crags such as Goonland, through the liberal use of explosives.

The first recorded ascents were those of Alan Osbourne and Brian Taylor on Boiler Slab in 1949 and its likely that some of the other ridges on the Gower were also climbed in the period 1949-1952, since Alan Osbourne had a keen interest in finding mountaineering-style routes. This development, however, came to a dead end after the obvious ridge lines were climbed, as Osbourne's interest did not extend to outcrop/sea-cliff climbing. However, Osbourne mentioned some of his ascents to Donald Thomas, a close friend of Jeremy Talbot and probably to John Brailsford too.

John Brailsford was working as a blacksmith at RAF St. Athan. On the rare occasions when they were granted passes in 1954-1955, they would make lightning visits to Gower. Three Cliffs, Pobbles and Caswell were developed in this way and probably many of the 'Unknown' ascent routes should be credited to Brailsford and the St. Athan's Mountain Rescue Team. The highlights of this period are clearly Scavenger and Inverted V at Three Cliffs, the former being graced with a fair amount of grass at the time and the latter seeing the use of one of Brailsford's fine home made

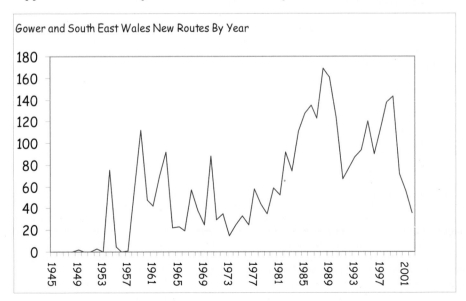

Gower and South East Wales New Routes By Year

pegs. These were the first routes of real substance to be established and have become firm favourites. More obscure and often forgotten are routes like Insanity and Limpet Route at Pobbles East, which are pretty stiff boulder problems for their era, especially impressive given that they were climbed in big boots.

There seems to have been little contact between the few groups active in the area and virtually no contact with climbers outside the area at this time. Jeremy Talbot, who started to establish his first routes at about the same time as Brailsford, describes the situation:

'At that time in North Wales if you were an outsider, there was no information. We didn't even know where the crags were. We turned up at the Mot once looking for routes that were on the Grochan, to be told that Brown and Whillians were in the pass. This meant nothing to us, we'd never heard of them; the only thing we managed to find out was that it seemed to be important to wear a flat cap if you wanted to be regarded as a hard man. It was a waste of time climbing there as everyone drank too much beer in Dolgellau on the way up, so no-one was in a fit state to climb the next day. The weather was poor and the rock was always greasy. The weather was much better on Gower, but the information was hardly any better; Donald had some information from Alan Osbourne about Boiler Slab, so we tried to find that, but often we found a totally different crag instead.'

Talbot and friends started to develop new routes at places like Caswell in 1954-1955, since this was the easiest place to get to without a car. Further explorations revealed hosts of crags, with the sea-level crags being preferred due to the better rock quality. The modus operandi was to find a crag and work out all the lines there before moving on, rather than climbing the obvious and best lines on a number of crags, so wholesale developments occurred on crags like King Wall (named after Kingspitzer wall in the Kaisergebirge) in 1959 and 1962-3.

At this time Talbot was very active in the Alps and this backdrop determined the style and ethics of an ascent. The objective was to climb ground up, gardening as necessary, with the use of direct aid where there was a move that might slow down the climbing or interfere with the flow. Talbot and friends had no interest in returning to free routes climbed with aid, even though Talbot himself could certainly have climbed routes like South East Wall on Third Sister (1963) free by about 1969, judging by his repeats of Eryl Pardoe's later routes.

By the mid 1960s Talbot, in conjunction with friends like Donald Thomas, Peter Hinder and Derrick Jones had extensively developed much of the lower tiers of Fall Bay to Mewslade and either developed, or knew about virtually all the crags in the Gower section of this Guidebook. There were over 500 routes on the Gower, although these climbers knew little about anything recorded in the rest of South East Wales. This group knew about cliffs like Ogmore and by about 1967 had certainly heard about the quarries at Morlais, although chose not to visit because of car security concerns. Shortly afterwards Talbot and Chris Connick visited Dinas, although Talbot did not think it was worthwhile developing the crag.

Several aid-extravaganzas like Twm-Schon-Catti and Deborah's Overhang were developed in the mid to late 1960s, the latter taking about sixty hours to drill by hand. Talbot and friends were never averse to the use of bolts, normally hand-drilled rawl-bolts which were removed only to prevent corrosion of the bolt. Perhaps the most impressive of these aid routes was Yellow Wall, which involved some free climbing. Deborah's Overhang nearly featured in a BBC documentary set up with John Cleare to star Jeremy Talbot and Pete Crew, but for various reasons, the project was abandoned. A more successful project that started in the late 1960s was the compilation of the first climbing guide to Gower with the encouragement of Robin Collomb.

In the mid 1960s a new group of climbers started to get involved – Swansea University Mountaineering Club. There were three catalysts for the development of the club's new routing activity. The first, was Eryl Pardoe an exceptionally talented climber from Aberdare, who knew Jeremy and Beryl Talbot and so had full knowledge of the routes that existed on Gower. The second factor was the arrival of Bob Griffiths in 1965. Whilst Eryl was the stronger climber, Bob had been a habituee of Stoney Middleton in the early 1960s and immediately saw the potential of the near virgin rock above sea level, like Pennard, High Pennard and Castle Lewes. The only serious attacks on these buttress had been by Harold Insley, who had established the impressive, but loose lines of Alpha and South East Edge – Gower's first extreme - in 1959. The final factor was the foot and mouth outbreak of 1966/7, which meant that the club was unable to go away climbing and so concentrated on developing its own backyard.

An early trip to Pennard to repeat Alpha and some of the shorter routes, ended up with Bob spotting High Pennard. He coaxed over the sceptical Eryl and the result was a rapid ascent of Skive in November 1966. Lewes Castle was the first significant target of 1967 on which the pair shared leads for Osiris and Isis. However, as Eryl's confidence grew and the new stopper nuts became available, the level of difficulty jumped a notch. Between 1966 and 1969 routes like V-Groove (almost certainly done without aid) and Phreatic Line (one point) were established, which were Gower's first true hard routes of any length. Soon after Eryl emigrated to Canada and sadly died on a rescue attempt.

There were some other climbers from SUMC around at about the same time. One of the most forceful being Martyn 'Captain' Hogge, a climber notorious for huge lobs. Martyn and a few other members discovered Juniper Wall in about 1968 and established what is now the Jackal Finish, with one point of aid. These details were only half recorded and so there was some confusion about later ascents. However, various climbers such as Trevor Smith, Richard Leigh and Martyn Hogge accounted for several of the routes at Juniper Wall. Jeremy Talbot was still very active during this period and contributed the fine and awkward Isis.

All these ascents were brought together Jeremy Talbot's fine 1970 West Col Gower guide, which was to soon to attract some forceful climbers to the area.

Climbing in South East Wales probably started even later than on Gower. However, there was certainly some activity during the late fifties and early sixties. Much of this information has been lost and is not particularly partial to being rediscovered. Some of the earlier ascents were aid routes climbed on sandstone. Some of the quarries, notably Deri and The Gap were more than twice their current height and provided some interesting A1 and A2 pegging. Trebanog was certainly discovered by the early sixties as shown by Peter Leyshon's climbing artwork although the records have been tucked away.

The records for limestone are better preserved and virtually all the large inland limestone cliffs were discovered and explored in this period. Unsurprisingly given its proximity to Cardiff and its visibility, Taffs Well Main was one of the first cliffs fto receive attention, with Barry Powell finding Pine Tree and Ken Hughes climbing Nero as early as 1960. However, the focus of attention in the early sixties was clearly Morlais Middle Tier. This was extensively developed by Barry Powell, Harold Insley and some other members of SWMC. Later on Mike Danford, Pat Wood and Taff Ellis also contributed. Llangattock must have also received an early visit from Harold Insley and friends judging by the eponymous route there, whilst John Bradley, Alan Barney and Tom Dodd were active at Pant-Y-Rhiw at about the same time.

Over 1967-1968 one of the first concentrated attacks, which have later characterised South East Wales development, was made by a large group of climbers on Taf Fechan. The principal climbers were Cled Jones, Dave Parsons, Peter Leyshon, Phil Watkin and Derek Taff Ellis (sadly killed in a fishing accident in 1974) and Les Ainsworth. A supplement was published to Taf Fechan in 1969 as well as some publicity in Rocksport. One of the climbs, Monument To Insanitary appeared with the following text: 'A hangover, wet rock, cold feet, a watch stopping at the start of the climb, the nearby sheep carcass, the flight of a large black bird and the erection of a large memorial cairn by watching friends defeated another party.' Another route 'The Coffin' had written below it 'A block fell onto Dave Parsons head' although the block probably had the worst of it as Dave is is very much alive and well. Probably the most concerned person was Peter Leyshon, a good Catholic who made sure the telephone number of the nearest priest was included in case of the necessity for last rites.

By 1969, Cefn Coed had been discovered by Clive Horsfield and Phill Thomas and the usual suspects moved on from Taf Fechan, operating with remarkable productivity during 1969-1971. A new comer on the scene was John Kerry, one of the first new routing climbers operating between Gower and South East Wales. Jim Perrin made early visits to the crag and tried to set an example to some local climbers by not gardening the routes there and climbing them on sight, much to John Kerry's annoyance on one occaison. Amongst these Cefn Coed routes were the first extremes in the area, but the pace was still clearly behind that on the Gower and it was to stay so until the eighties.

Finally Dinas was located by at least two parties. Chris Connick had visited there in either the late sixties or early seventies and left the line of drilled rawl bolt holes up what was later to become the Big Time. This is probably pre-dated by Cled Jones, Dave Parsons and Phil Watkin's early aid routes. The first free route of any significance was Phill Thomas' Strider and Phil Watkin's Jeepers Creepers after which the crag was virtually abandoned for free climbing until the other end of the 1970s.

This phase of exploration came to a close with the amazing (re) discovery of Ogmore by John Mothersele in 1970. Another rush of exploration kicked off. Mothersele climbed parts of what was later to become Exposure Explosion and then John Kerry quickly got in on the act. Some of the lines being attempted were adventurous to say the least, like Gremlin and Arrow. Several of these early routes involved a pegged escape. Jim Birch from SUMC was understandably displeased when John Kerry hammered most of his gear into the crag and promptly left. All these developments were pulled together a little later with the publication of the 1973 guide.

The climbing scene at the start of the seventies right across the South East Wales area was pretty active, adventurous by national standards, but lagging in terms of difficulty. This was about to change.

1972-1984
The catalyst for this change was Pat Littlejohn, who brought the same forceful style to the area that he had already demonstrated elsewhere in the South West. The earliest significant route was Pat's free ascent of Yellow Wall on Gower in February 1972. This was quickly followed by Transformer in 1973, both clearly more going into more sustained territory than Eryl Pardoe's routes of the late sixties.

Over in South East Wales, development at Ogmore was being spearheaded by the likes of Phill Thomas. Many of his routes, like Nyth and Fool's Fantasy started off as free attempts as did Wipeout, which nearly was. These were pretty bold undertakings despite the use of aid and provided a ready source of semi-free routes for Pat Littlejohn to try, which he did, freeing all three in 1977. (These ascents were almost as historically important as Norm Carter's opening of Up And Under in Cardiff in the same year). However, virgin rock was also found, resulting in stunning lines like Spellbinder and later Sorcery, which in 1979 was the cutting edge in terms of British Sea Cliff climbing. Clearly Ogmore had some lure for Pat, hence the move to Cardiff.

Some locals slowly started to catch up. One local in fact caught up very quickly and has been a significant presence ever since. Andy Sharp, together with long standing climbing partner Pete Lewis, got out of trouble in school with their mentor, Peter Leyshon – by being climbers. By the mid-seventies, Andy has already established himself as a climber with potential, making for instance the fifth ascent of Great Wall (Cloggy) free. Clearly Andy soon realised that Cloggy simply couldn't compete with South East Wales and chose to put up bouldery routes like Fingerprint in 1977, and bold routes like Promises at Taff's Well in 1979, of similar difficulty to Pat Littlehjohn's Diamonds and Skywalker of the same year.

The star routes of Littlejohn should not detract from the steady exploration being done by other climbers at the same time. John Harwood, Clive Horsfield and others were putting up some fine routes at many crags in the mid seventies, whilst Jeremy Talbot and Chris Connick developed Paviland between 1976 and 1978. Jeremy, contrary to popular belief has not faded away and still continues to climb up and down the Gower, although not recording his new routes. One local entrant in the tail end of the seventies was John Bullock, who started off a tendency to undergrade almost everything he touched, Dan Dare, graded HVS in 1981 being an obvious example. Another temporary local active at this time (and since) was Tony Penning, who mostly with John Harwood kicked off a long running development campaign at Llangattock.

Llangattock had already seen some development in this period, with Pat Liitlejohn's Cold Snatch and Hangman, which Tony and John Harwood repeated. Many visits ensued sometimes in the company of Dennis Hillier, Pete Cresswell and Andy Sharp and resulted in leads like Johnny Cum Lately (John being a week late for the first ascent). Andy's contribution Acid Rain was considered the hardest lead on inland limestone when it was first established.

John Harwood has been influential in bringing the right person to the right place at the right time over the years and in 1981 got Andy Sharp to visit Rhossili. Loz Francombe had whittled down the aid on Crime And Punishment to one point, which was soon dispensed with by Andy, who also freed Blackman's Pinch and the Adultress at around the same time. These technical, fingery routes were to become widespread in a few years time, but in a different context. They were also extended to the old inland limestone quarries like Morlais and Cefn Coed which had something of a renaissance in the early to mid eighties and Andy, Tony Penning and a few others added or freed routes like Blade

Runner, Exile and Partners In Crime.

From 1981-1984 everyone seemed to be down in Pembroke and there was a slight lull, interrupted by the odd big number from Littlejohn, like a free ascent of Tony Penning's Thurba aid pitch Earthly Powers and the first really big route at Dinas, the impressive Giant Killer, with one rest at the lip. Andy Sharp continued to grab the odd gem up and down Gower like Barracuda. However, things got moving again in 1984 when Pat climbed Thriller and brought Gower up to date with his Ogmore contributions of five years previously, with the stunning Masterpiece. Andy Sharp and team produced a mauler with Hairy Dog and John Bullock produced the now popular Desperate Dan. Meanwhile at Ogmore, Roy Thomas started to produce some harder routes, massively undergraded at the time and only now is it becoming clear that things like Black Looks are seriously serious undertakings.

Pat Littlejohn's interest now started to move away from the area, as did he, but not before an almost free ascent of the Big Time at Dinas in 1985 and finally Astrobrain at Ogmore in 1986. However, as the 1983 guide hit the press, a new combination of factors was about to propel development much further forward.

1984-1987
The first factor was Andy Sharp climbing extremely well, witnessed by free climbing the top part of Skull Attack in 1985, the current start arriving in 1986. This includes most of the hard climbing and was the hardest technical outing on Gower or South East Wales at the time. More brutal pitches in the form of King Swing and Hound Of Hell were added to Hairy Dog wall and a really fun E6 arrived in the form of Resisting Arrest.

However, it was Dinas where the most impressive pitches were climbed. Angel Heart weighed in at E6,6c with one point (as for The Big Time), with far less gear than it currently has. Cautious Lip was an impressive E6 too. Equally impressive, although using a point of aid was Harlem and most impressive of all Salem's Lot. This started up what is now Crock Of Gold and finished up what is now the top of Sharp Cereal Professor. The bottom was hard and the top virtually unprotected and to be honest, most people who repeat the sports versions of the current routes, would probably agree that in its trad form, the route would be a good E7. Andy's routes, some with the odd aid point, clealy showed what potential for harder routes existed in the area.

Just a little earlier, an active SWMC composed of climbers like Gary Lewis, Tony Penning, the late Giles Barker, Haydn Griffiths and later Mick Learoyd were starting to explore the sandstone quarries of South East Wales. As already mentioned, several of the crags had had aid routes climbed on them in the sixties. One or two had received the odd free route, notably Trebanog, Llwynypia and obviously Penallta. From about 1981 the SWMC team had developed the odd route at the Darren, but in 1982-1985 a more serious onslaught brought some good long routes at Cilfynydd like Fly Me To The Moon, Let Me Play Amongst The Stars, Let Me Know What Life Is Like and The Owl And The Antelope. Frank Sinatra had clearly bowed out on the last one. The hardest of these earlier routes was Mick Learoyd's peg protected Western Front. A little later in 1986, Roy Thomas, Graham Royle and friends eventually did what many kept saying they would do on the way back from the Gower and walked up to inspect Abbey Buttress. The resulting routes of Crack Basher and Restrictive Practice remain amongst the best traditionally protected routes on sandstone. Roy had previously done Sign Of The Times and Urban Development with a rest point a piece and offered to share attempts with Martin Crocker on freeing them, a different approach than would probably prevail now. The second factor about to play a role was then, the opening up of sandstone.

The third factor, that had in fact already arisen before the 1984 guide, was the use of bolts for protection. Bolts were obviously not new to the area given Talbot's activities in the fifties and sixties and some of, say Andy Sharp's free routes on Trial Wall relied on old bolts. A new bolt seems to have appeared in an old bolt hole at Dinas around the time the Big Time was done. But these were not really bolts placed 'new new' for an ascent. The mysterious bolt in the wall left of Expansionist was placed 'new new' for an ascent that never happened, so certainly Gary Gibson's placement of a bolt on Rogues Gallery at Morlais in 1984 was hardly the first. Probably it seemed controversial at the time, because some climbers wanted to leave that particular line for others to do without the bolt and could have done it themselves with it. A year later Gary geared up Berlin at Dinas, which although it had only a couple of bolts was mostly protected with in situ gear and so perhaps the first proper sports route in South East Wales.

The final factor was the arrival of Martin Crocker onto the scene. By 1986 he had repeated everything in Tiger Bay at Ogmore, no mean feat, added Twenty First Century, Delirious and The Uncanny to the cliff and established his first big routes on Gower with Thurba Pillar, Heroin and in 1987 Divine Guiding Light. Things were set for an intensive burst of activity for the second part of the eighties.

However, before that burst of energy, the Gower again produced some more amenable extremes from John Bullock, with the superb Samurai and Alun Richardson's mysterious King Rat, Alan Price's free version of Sisters Of Mercy and Steve Lewis The Steal – from under most people's noses. Slightly more tricky was Roy Thomas' acclaimed Plot 13.

Similarly at Llangattock an extensive phase of development was underway. Chris Court developed Chwar Pant Y Rhiw and Craig Y Castell with Gold Rush and Julia Andrea and White Tiger being notable as was Liberator a little later. .Tony Penning added a large number of climbs including Winning and Gary Gibson came down to add Mad Hatter and Martin Crocker added Vendetta and The Roaring Eighties.

1988-1991

Things really started moving in 1988 with a wet Easter. Martin Crocker, who was obviously impressed with the place when he seconded Gary Gibson on the first ascent of Berlin. Seeing what could be done with bolts and peg protection he added a string of high quality routes, pushing the grade up from what was effectively Fr7b+ on Angel Heart to mild Fr7c+ with Powers That Be. Other additions were Crock Of Gold, placing some bolts on the almost free Harlem and freeing it as well as freeing the aid point from Giant Killer (although not retro-placing that bolt). Gary Gibson turned up and impressed everyone by on-sighting almost to the top of Subversive Body Pumping, before unfortunately pulling a block off. Roy Thomas' special and Hazel saved the day.

As the weather cleared up in summer, Martin added a big line to Yellow Wall with Yellow Regeneration, added Chilean Flame Flower and the clip up of Flaming Fingers to Third Sister, whilst Andy Sharp added Wide Eyed And Legless and the heinous Popped In Souled Out to the same area. Bizarrely for such a bold and experienced climber Martin failed to spot a thread placement under the roof of Five Years To Live and placed possibly the first protection bolt on Gower. It was quickly chopped and the route lead without, something still not yet done for Gibson's Rogues Gallery.

However, volume wise, the action was elsewhere than the Gower or Dinas. The sandstone boom, tentatively sparked off in the mid-eighties was about to take over. An early crag to be reported in the magazines was Mountain Ash. This has been climbed on and known for many years, for example Alun Richardson's inappropriately named A Load Of Rubbish. Martin Crocker and Roy Thomas established full sports routes with Outspan, Ripe And Ready, Whiter Than White Wall and A Certain Peace. Despite Mountain Magazine's editorial comment 'Bolts on Grit – it had to happen' bolts in sandstone quarries seemed to be acceptable to more climbers than those on natural limestone. More followed. Cilfynydd got Western Front Direct and Eastern Bloc Rock. Andy Sharp and Pete Lewis developed Cwmaman with a string of real finger rippers in Mother Of Pearl and Le Rage and some less painful alternatives with Propaganda and Science Friction. Martin Crocker and Roy Thomas then took on the monster of Llanbradach and walked out with the huge prizes of The Caerphilly Contract, Little White Lies and what is still regarded as the hardest route on sandstone - Contraband.

In the middle of this frantic activity, locals found the time to be impressed by Martin Crocker and Roy Thomas' ascent of Davy Jones's Locker at Ogmore, the huge 22m roof originally aided by G.Andrews and Charlie Heard. Even during the sandstone boom, Roy Thomas had been beavering away at the biscuit routes, with Takes The Biscuit and Information Received, whilst Martin added Worn Out Superman and Pete Oxley added a direct start to Martin's 1985 The Uncanny in 1988. Roofs continued to be fashionable in 1989, when Oxley added Jesus Wept to Giant's Cave.

The following three years were even more manic. Andy Sharp's routes got even more fingery with the hardly ever repeated Loctite, the Sport For All routes at Mountain Ash and Anything You Can Do at the Gap, where Pete Lewis added Salmon Running Bear Cunning and Martin Crocker added two gems with Encore Magnifique and Mad At The Sun. Andy and Pete developed The Darren, Martin and Roy developed Treherbert and the excellent Sirhowy. More or less everyone got in on the act in the rediscovered eldorado of Cwm Dimbath, where Roy added the tricky Sucking Eggs, Pete found Haven't A Clue and Andy found the yosemite routes of Coming On Strong and Where The Power Lies. Older crags were not forgotten, as shown by Giles' Barker's Elastic Retreat. In the midst of all the sandstone action and frantic bolting, the same treatment was handed out by Gary, Martin, Andy, Pete and Roy to

Taff's Well West. Martin Crocker handed out similar fare to Taffs Well Main with Talk About False Gods and Scram and just after the 1991 guidebook hit the shelf Gary added the outstanding and under-rated Sugar Bullets.

Gower was not quite forgotten during this period by one of its more durable devotees and John Bullock found a crag that was to come to prominence later when he found Fox Hole and with Roy Thomas added Foxy Lady and The Hooker.

Such was the state of play when the 1991 guide was published and one pundit declared that all the sports climbing and the sandstone was a blind alley that would never catch on. Poor Roy Thomas then, beavering away at the Gap bolting up loads of Fr6a+s in 1992, that would never catch on.

1992-1997

At the time of the 1991 guide most bolts and most sports climbs in the area were in the quarries or at Dinas. Gower, had seen only a handful of bolts newly placed for protection and most of these were quickly removed. The harder routes on the Gower tended to be things like Martin Crocker's new Skyhedral Wall (1991), or Gary Gibson's Man Of The Earth (1989), protected with a fair amount of in situ gear, but not bolts.

A test case at about the time the guide was published was Pete Oxley's Sistine Ceiling in Giant's Cave. This was a pretty run out Fr7c+ through a roof, on 'mix and match' ethics (i.e. no bolts where wires can be placed). Clearly it upset some local climbers (and non-climbers) and was more important in sparking off the 1993/4 bolt debates than were the bolted routes climbed at Ramstor. The other piece of bolting that brought on the 1994 bolt forum was the development of full sports routes at Witches Point by Gary Gibson and Roy Thomas. Routes climbed over 1993-4, like Roy's Five O'Clock Shadow, or his retro-bolted 1985 route Hanging By A Thread and Gary's Staple Diet, Edge Hog and This God Is Mine quickly became (and have stayed) amongst the most popular in the area. A couple of other contributed, like Eugene Jones with the amusingly named Help, Help Me Rhondda. Opposition and criticism was delivered in the superb witticism of 'even the walk ins are bolted at Witches Point.'

The SWMC and BMC organised a debate held in Channel View Sports Centre in Cardiff in January 1994, where a paper was presented by Eugene Jones arguing for a small number of Gower cliffs to be bolted and the rest to remain bolt free. The paper was generally accepted by consensus rather than vote. Although the policy was almost immediately broken when someone pulled the bolts out of The Sistine Ceiling, the policy was generally adhered to for the next four years.

Immediately a very small group of climbers started to re-gear sandstone and Dinas with stainless staples all at their own expense. Be aware that if you are sports climbing in S.E.Wales, then less than half-a-dozen people have contributed to the work, three are responsible for over 75 percent and only £230 has ever gone through the bolt fund.

Quick off the mark to take advantage of bolting possibilities on Gower was Martin Crocker, who established the first proper sports route there with Power Struggle. Soon afterwards, Martin and Roy Thomas were busy down at Pwll Du, with Roy's amusingly named Crock Block and Martin's Senser. Originally claimed as the first Fr8a in the area, it quickly settled down to Fr7c+, but gained almost universal acclaim as a three star route. Shortly afterwards Adrian Berry established the first of his hard Gower sports routes with Fin, possibly still unrepeated.

Although the climbing fraternity had agreed on a bolt policy, the National Trust and CCW now wanted to be involved and there were a couple of access problems that emerged, both with Foxhole and Oxwich. Some of these were quickly solved by Eugene Jones, Roy Thomas and the CCW. Oxwich took longer. The result was a delay in the development of these crags, but the situation was resolved and in the period 1994-1997 a large number of sports routes were established, to the almost exclusion of traditional climbing by most of the new routers in the area.

At Dinas, things were less problematic on the access front and Gary Gibson added some fine routes, the most memorable being Still Life. Roy Thomas, his climbing partner added the classy El Camino Del Roy. Someone who was busy in 1994 taking advantage of all the regeared routes at Dinas was sandstone addict Goi Ashmore, who jackled in to make the first free ascents of Kennelgarth and Angel Heart.

In 1995 Gary Gibson stunned everyone by not only freeing the Big Time at Dinas easily, but also adding a much harder finish. However, the biggest event of the mid-nineties was Eugene Jones ascent of Masada at Witches Point. Also claimed as the areas first Fr8a, it has since been upgraded to Fr8a+ and also worth three stars. It's worth noting that both the first and the third ascensionist completed the route on a freak high tide and in a thunderstorm. Roy Thomas who belayed both ended up stood on a rock 10ft out from the crag and both lower offs were memorable. Towards the middle of the year, the access situation at Oxwich had stabilised enough to allow development, which kicked off on an industrial scale, with half the routes now listed at the crag put up that summer. Amongst the best were Gary Gibson's Red With Rage, For Sportsmen Of The Epoxy Clips from Roy Thomas and Eugene Jones' Kissin' The Pink.

On sandstone things were fairly quiet apart from Martin Crocker's quick raid to pick off a sandstone 'last great problem' at Mountain Ash, which produced the excellent Cointreau at a surprisingly amenable grade. The following year, sandstone was rediscovered and the amount of routes at Llanbradach tripled in the course of a few months. The active team was Gary Gibson and Roy Thomas, who produced some very fine routes around Sinister Walls, Sinister and Abbatoir and Costello from Gary and The Host, Parasite, Dream In Colour and Shadow Of The Sun from Roy. The same team blitzed the upper tier a little later.

Meanwhile on limestone, Adrian Berry and Goi Ashmore were both bolting up projects. Goi, who was off to France, got paranoid that someone would steal his line and ended up establishing the first route of note when it was soaking wet – Pioneers Of The Hypnotic Groove. When it turned out to be wet in Buoux, he drove back to South Wales and freed the old aid route Deborah's Overhang, possibly the first true Fr8a on Gower, when this was also wet (which Deborah's almost always is). The rest of the routes did need to dry out, which they had by mid summer and Roy Thomas put up many good routes like Goose In Lucy around the walls of Fox Hole waiting for Goi to complete Palace Of Swords Reversed. At about the same time, Adrian succeded on one of his projects to give the bouldery Sansarete at Oxwich, a foretaste of things to come. The only significant route round Bridgend that year was Roy Thomas' Evil Kneeful.

In 1997 it started to rain and rained until mid-June, so the obvious choice for new routing was Dinas. Roy Thomas and Gary Gibson wore out many drill bits and came away from the roadside crags with some good lines, like Gary's Cujo and some awful ones, like Morticia. The Regulators was added at the same time and at Fr7b proved a major sandbag. Goi Ashmore was lured back by these new routes and by a desire to finish off an old project, which became Durbin Two, Watson Nil. He walked away with another 'never go free' in the form of Bloody Spore Climbers and severely inflamed elbows. The elbow problems did have a positive side effect in terms of the search for slabby rock. Acting on a tip off from Adrian Berry, on the verge of moving away, Goi and Roy Thomas visited Barland and over 1997-1998, established most of the routes on the main slab.

During the same monsoon, Andy Sharp and Pete Lewis, with the Rhondda Social Services and Glamorgan Uni team in tow made a welcome comeback and added a number of steep overhanging pitches on The Terminal Overhanging Wall. For years this wall had been thought of as too loose for development – anyone who has had the misfortune to repeat Tony Penning's appalling Alive And Kicking can see why. However, Andy persisted and by avoiding the obvious cracks established some of the best routes on sandstone with Capstan and Sharpy Unplugged being truly outstanding.

As things dried out during the summer, Gary Gibson and Roy returned to Oxwich for another monster new routing session. Gary added considerably to the sports E6 range with The Morgue The Merrier, Bitchin and Milkier Way whilst Roy added some fillers in and a little later the tricky Before The Beak. These sessions marked the end of a 'mass sports climbing development era' for both Gower and South East Wales, as interests either shifted elsewhere (Gary), injuries took hold (Goi, Roy) or people moved away (Adrian). However, someone else was about to make a comeback, as were traditional lines.

1997-1999
Just before Martin Crocker started his wholesale development of traditional lines and just before Adrian Berry moved away, Adrian put up an outstanding and virtually unreported line up the wall to the right of Masterpiece in Giant's Cave, Napalm In The Morning. This was the first unambiguous traditional E7 on Gower and deserves more recognition,

especially as it is hard for the grade.

Martin's 1997-1998 crusade, normally accompanied by John Harwood, was notable for the volume of routes put up, usually on the more remote areas of Gower like Ram Grove Crag, The Second Sister, The Tooth Fairy Area and the worthless Seaspit Small Cove. Amongst this large number of routes were some high quality, impressive lines, like Cool Britannia, an impressive, albeit partial solution, to the east arete of Thurba Head and Fire In Their Eyes at Third Sister. The most significant discovery of this period was Stallion Cove. Judging by Martin's find of some old jammed nuts and slings, there was some previous development of this huge crag, but it had never been recorded anywhere and was probably one of Jeremy Talbot's later discoveries. Amazingly, given its proximity to Paviland the crag was therefore virgin of harder lines and Martin came away with a number of fine ones, especially Machine Gun Kelly. Almost no-one else appeared to be active on Gower at all during this period, but this was deceptive. Adrian Berry was making occasional visits during 1998 and was about to make a big impression the following year. Goi Ashmore managed one new route with the obscure and vicious Gower Kut.

Martin's exploration continued into 1999, this time teasing out a notable 'last great problem' from the superb but diversionary Earthly Powers, Unearthly Power. However his main interests at this time were elsewhere in South East Wales. Gary Gibson made a welcome return to tidy up some old problems at Oxwich with Red Letter Day and Red Snapper, but the big numbers on the Gower fell to Adrian Berry, who slew two old projects with Inferno, bringing the Fr8a+ to Gower and the horrendous Route Of All Evil, bringing hard Fr8b to the area in a convincing fashion. Elsewhere on the Gower, Andy Sharp, Pete Lewis, Martyn Richards, Jon Williams, Chris Evans and friends developed Stallion Cove in a through fashion, producing some good long routes, the hardest and most significant being Devolution.

At Ogmore Roy Thomas added the first signifcant new route for some time with Implausible Suggestion. Then came the major event of the summer when Martin Crocker used his intimate knowledge of Ogmore to make perhaps the most significant day's worth of deep water soloing ever seen anywhere. Warming up with solos of Sorcery and the new routes Buzzarena and Enchanted, he went on to make the awesome traverse of Total Eclipse Of The Sun, bringing trad E8 to the area. He came back a few days later to add the decidedly difficult Totality and an attempt on Tereus with Eugene Travers-Jones which had to be abandoned due to an incoming tide and had to wait until 2001 for an ascent.

Equally impressive in the traditional sphere, for being physically harder if not quite so death defying, was Adrian Berry's Chasing The Dragon on Yellow Wall, which brought E8 to the Gower a month later than to South East Wales. This period of history in the area was brought to a close with the kick off of another bolt debate. Although it may appear from the story so far that new routers had bolted little up during 1998-1999, this was not the case and matters came to a head in 1999-2000 as a result of a number of developments.

Gary Gibson and Roy Thomas had developed a new venue in Minchen Hole and established some long, quality sports routes, of which Jump The Sun and The Raven stand out. Minchen was not known about when the 1994 policy was developed, so could not be included in the list of possible sports crags. On the other hand, Gower was to be bolt free unless stated in the policy. Some local climbers were annoyed at the bolting in Minchen and alerted the NT, one official of which was far from happy. The far from happy result was that the crag was banned for all climbing an unfortunate side effect.

A second development was Goi Ashmore's retro-bolting of Skull Attack at Trial Wall. This was prompted by annoyance that every time he turned up to do it, the pegs had been stolen. Andy Sharp was more than happy to see the route retro bolted to get round this problem, but John Harwood, who had been on the first ascent of the upper section was not happy to learn Goi had bolted it. Unlike the other two events a fairly good natured series of discussions went on about whether this was inside or outside the scope of the 1994 policy. Clearly there was some ambiguity that needed resolving.

The final development was the placement of some bolt lower offs on some traditional routes at the new Bosco's Wall crag by Roy Thomas and Gary Gibson. This clearly annoyed a local group of friends and the bolts were removed. Parties unknown then slashed the threads and persons unknown made some ridiculous report to the National Trust that weed killer had been tipped down on the vegetation at the top of the cliff.

Access somehow got mixed up with bolting in the ensuing pantomime and as a result SWMC and the BMC decided a general debate would have to be held on fixed gear which was held over three sessions at WICC. Wayne Gladwin chaired and the NT and CCW attended. Goi Ashmore, ironically the person who was least in favour of a replacement of the 1994 policy, drew up a list of crags stating what bolting had or had not gone on and the meeting eventually thrashed out another compromise, which marginally extended the number of bolting permissible cliffs on the Gower, but kept the ban on Minchen Hole.

2000-2003
After the 1999-2000 bolting forums, there was a feeling of lethargy when it came to Gower. However, locals Roy Thomas, Steve James and Rich Phillipps had just got their hands on Pant Quarry, which was developed by various climbers in 2000-2001 and doubled the number of Fr8as in South East Wales with Dai Laffin' Maesteg-A-Sawrus and Three Turd Slab. One of the most outstanding routes in this period was Welsh Fargo, acclaimed as an instant classic and unusual for the area being more than 30m long. At the end of this period of development Steve McLure's team visited from Sheffield and made impressive on-sights of all the routes over a weekend. This team behaved impeccably, unlike a certain visitor, who ignored the finger-tape on Iain Fisher's project and grabbed 'Too Good To Leave' Fr8a. Locals who had left the route alone due to Iain's finger injury were unimpressed but had the last laugh when the second ascensionist found it to be easy Fr7c and the route was renamed Theiving Little Scrote by popular demand. Unfortunately development of Pant has come to an indefinite pause, with the quarry being re-activated.

One exception to quietness on the Gower was the almost simultaneous development of Blue Pool. Adrian Berry and Jason Brown had added a couple of lines there in 1996, followed by Stefan Doerr's The Thing in 1997. Adrian Berry made a flying visit with Shane Ohly to put up some classy lines like Refugee. More significant were Martin Crocker's deep water solos including No Ya Limits and Jetski Gobsmacksi

Elsewhere in 2001-2002, the main new routing activity was again focussed on Martin Crocker's deep water solos, this time being concentrated around the caves of Davy Jones' Locker and as well as deep water solos of older routes like Twenty First Century, routes like Mindfuck and AFA (Absolutely Fucking Awesome) were established.

Andy Sharp made one of his occasional comebacks and added a number of routes around Fall Bay, the best of which was Monkey See And Monkey Do. Sharp also accompanied Martyn Richards on his on-sight of A Rush Of Blood To The Head.

Just before the guide went to print, Tony Penning and friends rounded off a good couple of years activity at Llangattock with some big routes like Heart Bypass and Maggie's Gate, which look worthy of a visit. Then at the eleventh hour Martyn Richards returned to Gower and established the impressive Shock And Awe at Jacky's Tor. Climbed on the second go, this last great problem is almost certain to be undergraded.

So what of the future. Well we can confidently say that there is a hell of a lot of unclimbed rock around in the area. Things have slowed down, but all that is needed for a new wave of new routes is someone with determination and time on their hands. That someone could come armed with a drill to take advantage of the acres of rock at Taff's Well Main or the many unexplored sandstone quarries that have hardly been touched east of Newport which have started to yield up excellent rock like the main wall of Tyle-Y-Coch recently developed by John James, Wayne Gladwin, Gary Gibson and Gordon Jenkins. That someone could realise that Ogmore still has vast potential and yields more adventure per square foot than most other adventure crags in the South West. Or they could go and ferret out yet more new routes in the gullies east of Thurba Head. You could even go to Llangattock, it would make a nice change if Tony Penning and John Harwood could have some new routes cleaned up for them to do.

Two things are clearer now than when the last guide was written. South East Wales has enough route volume to be considered as an area to be visited in its own right. Secondly, sports climbing and traditional climbing co-exist well and complement each other all over the area, but best typified by the nearby Ogmore and Witches Point, that share the same devotees. This has been achieved mostly by luck and accident and not in the slightest by preaching. Which is handy as we can avoid the usual sermon at the end of a historical section and bugger off down the pub to watch the Rugby.

Gower

TOR GRO

GR457937
By Goi Ashmore & Chris Shorrock

TIDAL STATUS: Non-Tidal.

BOLTING POLICY: No bolting.

PREAMBLE
This cliff is formed by large north-facing slabs on the north coast overlooking the Landimore and Llanrhidian Marshes. Unfortunately, the routes are often without the benefit of natural line, but they are still worthwhile, providing a shady venue on hot days.

ACCESS
Follow the B4271 through Llanrhidian, then follow the unmarked road towards Llanmadoc to reach the village of Landimore (GR465930). At the start of Landimore village is a village signpost. Turn right here into the village proper. Turn right at the next T-junction, then follow this lane to its end at a parking spot and gate, where a track continues along the edge of the marshes. From the parking area, follow the track to reach the foot of the Main Slab after about 10 minutes. Note that the access track may be underwater during spring tides.

DESCENTS: The most practical descent for all routes is by abseil.

THE ROUTES

Overhang Slab
This is the undercut slab up and left of the Main Slab. The routes are vegetated and have not been climbed for many years.

1. **Overhang Direct**   15m   VS,4b   ⌁
    The central line up the slab. The exit is unpleasant.
    D.Jones, R.Owen 00.00.1959

2. **Overhang Traverse**   22m   VS,4b   ⌁
    Start at the right-hand end of the slab and climb directly to the overhang. Move left and finish up Overhang Direct.
    D.Jones, R.Owen 00.00.1959

Main Slab
The old line of Broken Slab (HS D.Jones, R.Owen, C.Edwards, C.Andrews 1958) has been superseded by other routes hereabouts. The first route starts just right of the left edge of the slab.

3. **Central Slab**   45m   VS,4b   *
    Climb the shallow groove right of the left edge of the slab. Where it peters out, bear slightly right to pass some small overlaps. Continue directly up, keeping right of the arete of the slab.
    D.Jones, R.Owen, C.Edwards, C.Andrews 00.00.1958

4. **Sycamore**   45m   VS,4b
    Start just right of Central Slab below a small sycamore at 18m. Climb a vague scoop to the tree and move left to finish up a shallow depression, 1m right of the overlap on Central Slab.
    D.Jones, R.Owen, C.Edwards, C.Andrews 00.00.1958

5. **Sycamore Direct**   45m   HVS,4b
    As for Sycamore to the tree. Continue delicately up the slab above.
    J.Aylward solo 14.08.1995

*Pete Lewis - Blackman's Pinch (E4,6a) Trial Wall
(Page 42) Photo: Carl Ryan*

Andy Sharp & Pete Lewis - Black Wall (Fr8a+) Trial Wall
(Page 43) Photo: Carl Ryan

6. **Marsh Dance**   50m   E1,5a   \
Start 4m right of Sycamore, below a shallow scoop just right of a black streak. Gain the scoop, move up and trend left for 4m to a point above a black streak. Continue to the top on the clean rock between patches of vegetation. Bold.
J.Aylward solo 14.08.1995

7. **Altered Images**   55m   VS,4c
Climb the slab 8m right of Marsh Dance.
A.Foster, D.Gregan 00.00.1985

Hidden Slab

About 100m right of the Main Slab, is a smaller sheet of rock bounded on its right by a col formed by a lower slab. In the centre is a cluster of trees.

8. **Left Slab**   28m   VS,4b
Start just right of the centre of the slab left of the trees, below a protruding PR at 15m. Climb to the PR on scoops, then up for another 5m before moving right to the arete of Tree Edge. Follow this to finish.
D.Jones, R.Owen, C.Edwards, C.Andrews 00.00.1958

9. **Tree Edge**   28m   S
Climb the arete just left of the trees in the centre of the slab.
D.Jones, R.Owen, C.Edwards, C.Andrews 00.00.1958

10. **Central Tower**   14m   M   \
This takes the lower slab running up to the col.
D.Jones, R.Owen, C.Edwards, C.Andrews 00.00.1958

Bone Buttress

This is the much larger slab down and right of Hidden Slab. The old route The Right Slab (VS,4b D.Jones, R.Owen, C.Edwards, C.Andrews 1958) has been superseded by more recent offerings.

11. **The Sorcerer**   35m   VS,4b
Fine climbing up the centre of the slab. Start 5m left of the right arete. Ascend trending slightly right via a series of depressions that peter out at half-height. Continue up the slab above, finishing 2m right of the arete.
J.Aylward solo 15.08.1995

12. **Rowan Slab**   35m   VD
The right arete of the slab.
J.Aylward solo 15.08.1995

NORTH HILL TOR

GR453938
By Chris Shorrock

TIDAL STATUS: Non-Tidal.

BOLTING POLICY: No bolting.

PREAMBLE

This is the steeper north-facing crag further up the track from Tor Gro. It consists of some slab routes and an area of steeper rock, with more testing fare. It is better to avoid North Hill Tor in the summer due to nettles and brambles at the base.

ACCESS
As for Tor Gro, but continue along the path for another 5 minutes. There have been some access problems with one of the farmers in the past, but there is no official ban.

DESCENTS: Descent is either side of the crag.

THE ROUTES

Main Slab
In the centre of the larger slab is a grassy y-shaped crack.

1. **Slimline**   27m   VD
    Start 5m left of the y-shaped crack. Take a direct line just right of two low horizontal cracks.
    D.Williams, A.Roche 00.00.1982

2. **White Slab**   27m   VD
    Start 2m right of Slimline and climb the slab directly, following a white mark.
    D.Jones, R.Owen, C.Edwards, C.Andrews 00.00.1958

3. **Clean Cut**   36m   VD
    Climb just left of the y-shaped crack, finishing up some grassy steps.
    D.Jones, R.Owen 00.00.1958

4. **Central Slab**   36m   VD
    Start in the centre of the slab by a deep cut in the rock. Climb the slab past two grassy ledges. Now trend right, following three distinct hollows to the top.
    D.Jones, R.Owen, C.Edwards, C.Andrews 00.00.1958

5. **Slab and Rib**   36m   VD
    Start 8m right of the y-shaped crack, below a short crack at 6m. Gain the short crack, step right and climb to a ledge below a corner. Finish up the right edge.
    D.Jones, R.Owen, C.Edwards, C.Andrews 00.00.1958

6. **Groove**   36m   VD
    Start 12m right of the y-shaped crack. Climb to a slight hollow, then up to a slight indentation with a narrow chiselled groove. Wander up to a flake handhold, then join West Slab to finish.
    D.Jones, R.Owen, C.Edwards, C.Andrews 00.00.1958

7. **West Slab**   36m   D   *
    Start 14m right of the y-shaped crack, but left of the right edge of the Main Slab. Gain a hollow at 8m, then a ledge, before going left to another ledge below an overhang. Step left and climb to a large ledge at a corner. A series of steps leads to the top.
    D.Jones, R.Owen, C.Edwards, C.Andrews 00.00.1958

8. **Girdle Traverse**   36m   VD   \
    Take the right edge of West Slab to a sloping ledge with a shot hole (possible TB). Move across left for 18m to a wide crack. Continue left, descending slightly, to exit in a gully with an obvious tree. Abseil or scramble easily to the top.
    P.Hinder, C.Manison 00.00.1971

West Recessed Slab
The smooth slab just to the right of the Main Slab. The climbs are marred by unpleasant exits onto turf and grass, so a lower off rope might be useful.

9. **Black Slab**   15m   HS,4a
    Climb the left side of the slab to a small grassy ledge. Use a thin crack to gain the corner separating West Recessed and Main Slabs. Finish up this corner.
    J.Talbot, D.Thomas 00.00.1959

10. **Flake Route**   15m   HVS,4b
    As for Black Slab, but go right to a raised slab. Gain the narrow ledge, then move up left to exit as for Black Slab.
    J.Talbot, D.Thomas 00.00.1959

11. **Holes**   22m   VS,4b
    Start at the right side of the slab, just left of a little tree. Climb the slab directly in line with some small round solution holes, to reach a tiny corner crack above. Finish up this.
    J.Talbot, B.Talbot 00.00.1966

Round towards the back of the tor is an obvious central groove.

12. **Naughty But Nice**   24m   E3,5c,6a
    Takes the acutely overhanging wall left of the obvious central groove. Start at a rib just left of a blackberry bush.
    1. 12m Climb the rib and continue to a TB below the overhanging wall.
    2. 12m Follow a discontinuous crack left up the wall with difficulty. Finish more easily.
    D.Jones, R.Owen, C.Edwards, C.Andrews - South Wall 00.00.1959
    FFA A.Sharp, P.Lewis, J.Harwood 20.11.1982

13. **Windy City**   24m   E2,5c,5b
    Start at the blackberry bush below the obvious central groove.
    1. 12m Surmount the overhang and continue to a belay below the groove. Alternatively, gain the obvious bore-hole more directly via a slot from the corner on the right.
    2. 12m Climb the steep groove.
    P. Hinder - South Wall Crack 00.00.1970
    FFA A.Sharp, P.Lewis, J.Harwood 20.11.1982, G.Evans, J.Bullock - Alternative Start 27.11.1982

CWM IVY TOR

GR436939
By Goi Ashmore

TIDAL STATUS: Non-Tidal.

BOLTING POLICY: No bolting.

PREAMBLE
Cwm Ivy is a substantial slab of about 18m, overlooking Forestry Commission plantations. There is apparently scope for new routing, but note that the area has not been checked for the guidebook.

ACCESS
From Llanmadoc, follow the minor road into the hamlet of Cwm Ivy (GR438936). From the end of the road, follow the continuation path for about 10 minutes until the crag is seen up on the left.

DESCENTS: Unknown.

THE ROUTES

1. **Unnamed**   15m   HVS,5a
    Start a few metres left of a small tree and finish at an ant hill.
    R.Bennett, S.Chapman 00.00.1995

BLUE POOL AREA

GR404927 to 406929
By Goi Ashmore

TIDAL STATUS: Extremely Tidal. 1 hour either side of low water on Spring Tides. Danny's Buttress 2 hours either side of low water.

BOLTING POLICY: Retro-bolting permissible with first ascensionist's permission. Replacement of worn fixed gear on a point for point basis with bolts is permissible. New sports routes allowed.

PREAMBLE
A major new development of an area of 25m high cliffs on the north side of the ridge running from Llangennith to Burry Holms. The best time to visit is in high summer, when the crag is generally seepage free. Although the crag is extremely tidal, it is well worth a visit for its steep rock and uncompromising lines. There are also some easier routes on Danny's Buttress, which is worth a visit and is considerably less tidal.

ACCESS
The best approach is from Llangennith village. Follow the minor road signposted to Llangennith Burrows, which ends at a car park (GR415925). Follow the footpath leading from the playground into the dunes to eventually reach the beach. To the north (right) is a tidal causeway leading out to Burry Holms island. Cross the causeway to a small bay on the north side containing Danny's Buttress. To get to the main cliff of Living Wall, contour rightwards around the rocks for 150m, to reach the obvious bowl-shaped crag, which blocks further progress along the beach. Note that some of the conventional routes on Living Wall can be started from a non-tidal platform. This platform and the deep water solos, are gained from abseil points above the crag. The abseil points are reached by reversing the descent route described below.

DESCENTS: For Danny's Buttress, scramble down to the left back to the beach. For Living Wall, descent is by walking down the raised banking leading back down to the causeway. There are some stakes at the top. It is probably best to pre-place a lower-off rope, due to the sloping grassy banking at the top of the cliff.

THE ROUTES

Danny's Buttress

1. **Al'Hambra**   11m   E2,5b   \
   A deep water solo. The grade for a conventional ascent is not yet known. From the seaward (left) end of the face, traverse right and climb an obvious crack.
   M.Crocker solo 17.06.2001

2. **Left Route**   9m   E1,5b
   The left-hand groove on the main face of the crag.
   J.Mothersele, D.McCarroll 00.04.1997

3. **Right Route**   9m   E2,6a   *
   The groove to the right of Left Route.
   J.Mothersele, S.Doerr 00.08.1997

Living Wall
Note that there is another route in this area, but its location is unfathomable. It could be the offwidth about 100m east of Living Wall (Chimney Route E1,5c J.Mothersele, D.McCarroll 1997).

Living Wall has a gently sloping left-hand (north) flank. Descend this to gain the start of Astral Slide.

1. **Astral Slide**   28m   E4,6a   **   \
   The grade is given for a solo ascent at high tide. In normal conditions it would be much bolder. From the sloping shelf at the left end of the wall, traverse right, then down the rectangular slab (Living Wall). Drop down under the bulge to gain a traverse line leading right to finish up the chimney of Refugee.
   M.Crocker solo 07.05.2001

2. **Living Wall**   20m   E5,5c   \
   This route is characterised by a recessed slab positioned high on the left-hand side of the wall. Gain the slab, then move out right and finish up a short groove. Steep climbing, with spaced protection.
   A.Berry, J.Bullock 06.07.1997

3. **Refugee**   25m   E4,6a   **
   Right of Living Wall is an obvious chimney high up on the crag. Start down and left of the chimney. Climb the lower wall directly to gain an obvious handhold. Use this to pass an overlap, then up to the obvious finishing chimney.
   A.Berry, S.Ohly 04.05.2001

The next routes start from a large ledge to the right of the angle of the crag. At low water, this can be reached by an easy scramble. When the tide is in, the ledge can be gained via an abseil point on the pillar above the crag.

4. **Anybody Who's Anybody**   21m   E4,6a   *   \
   Graded for a deep water solo at high water. More serious for a conventional ascent. From the left of the belay ledge move up to pockets and follow these to the base of the chimney on Refugee. Traverse left, keeping low for 4m. Finish up the exciting flake-crack in the bulges above.
   M.Crocker solo 07.05.2001

Living Wall

Photo: Adrian Berry

5. **Astral Sidle** 20m E2,5b *

A surprisingly amenable climb. Move up from the large belay ledge to gain a break. Follow the break leftward to a corner system. Follow the corner system to an overhang (junction with Refugee) and cross it on large rounded holds. Move left to gain a bridging position, then pull out right to finish.
M.Crocker, J.Harwood 07.03.2001

6. **Into The Blue** 20m E5,6a * \

A serious route. From the large belay ledge, follow the leftward-slanting crack up the right side of the recessed wall to an arched roof. Pass this to reach easier ground.
M.Crocker, J.Harwood 07.05.2001

7. **Buccaneer** 18m HVS,4c

Follow the corner crack above the large belay ledge, taking care with a rocking block.
S.Ohly, A.Berry 25.05.2001

8. **Privateer** 18m E1,5b *

From a few metres up Buccaneer, make a rising traverse rightwards across the pillar of Open, to gain the finish of The Thing.
A.Berry, S.Ohly 25.05.2001

To the right of the large belay ledge is a prominent pillar, bounding the left-hand side of a large recess.

9. **Open** 18m E2,5a

Take a fairly direct line up the prominent pillar. The protection is spaced.
J.Brown, A.Berry 00.00.1996

Living Wall

Photo: Adrian Berry

Right of the pillar of Open is a large recess, the right-hand side of which is bounded by a prominent leftward-slanting groove, taken by The Thing.

10. **Blue Pool Cool**   27m   E6,6a   *   \
   Strenuous, run-out and damp. Start right of the pillar of Open. Climb a pillar then trend right to a recess and gear. Traverse right into a verdant niche below a roof. Leave this to the right, gaining slopers and gear slots. Trend left up the wall to a pocket, pull up to a second pocket, then follow the left-trending crack left of the Thing. Finish direct. M.Crocker 07.05.2001

11. **The Thing**   28m   E5,6a   **   \
   Follows the obvious left-trending groove at the right side of the recess. Make unprotected, but reasonable moves up the lower wall to gain the strenuous groove. From the top of the groove walk right and up to stakes. S.Doerr, J.Mothersele 21.07.1997

The next routes are deep water solos up the protruding wall to the right of The Thing. They are reached by abseil from the top and would be very serious if done ground up at low water. The 50m abseil starts from a small outcrop at the top of the grass slope. Aim for small ledges in a hollow left of the tongue at the right end of the wall. In the event of a fall, jump out as far as possible, since there is a toe of rock directly below No Ya Limits.

12. **No Ya Limits**   12m   E6,6b   ***   \
   The overhanging groove right of The Thing. Traverse left for 3m from the end of the abseil to gain the groove. Move up to a projecting hold. Lurch up the wall past a jug on the arete at 8m. Pull through a white bulge to finish. M.Crocker solo 17.06.2001

13. **Jetski Gobsmacksy**   12m   E5,6b   ***   \
   From the end of the abseil, traverse left for 2m to gain the rib right of No Ya Limits. Follow the rib to a long stretch for a pocket, then extend left to a small white scoop. Finish more easily. M.Crocker solo 17.06.2001

14. **Fulmar Halo**   12m   E3,5b   \
   From the end of the abseil ledge, go left to gain a slot up and left. Climb direct and exit up left up a pocketed ramp. M.Crocker solo 17.06.2001

BURRY HOLMS

GR397926 to 399925
By Goi Ashmore

TIDAL STATUS: 2½ hours either side of low water. Note the tidal nature of the island.

BOLTING POLICY: No bolting.

PREAMBLE
There are three areas of climbing on Burry Holms, which is itself a tidal island accessible until about half-tide. The climbing areas consist of the Southern Area, with pleasant easy routes on excellent rock, the overhanging Littlejohn Legacy Area, and Pincers Cove Area on the far side of the island. The crags dry very quickly except for Pincers Cove, which is almost always sea damp.

ACCESS
As for Blue Pool Area to the beach, from where the island of Burry Holms is clearly visible, as is a tidal causeway leading out to it. The Southern Area of Burry Holms is reached by skirting round the island to the south (left). Pincers Cove is reached by following the path which leads up from the tidal causeway to the west side of the island. The Littlejohn Legacy Area is reached by starting up the same path, but contouring south (left) down the first gully.

DESCENTS: Descent is by walking off. For the Southern Area, walk leftwards (west) down a sloping platform. For the Littlejohn Legacy Area, walk rightwards (landwards) and skirt back out to sea down the gully. For the Pincers Cove Area, walk down the Northern Pincer (right when looking out to sea from the top).

THE ROUTES

Southern Area
About 200m west of the start of the island is a gully. It contains a very prominent cave crack (Promontory Crack).

1. **Left Wall**   15m   M
    The buttress left of the obvious crack of Promontory Crack, taken by a vague central scoop.
    D.Jones, R.Edwards Pre-1960

2. **Promontory Crack**   25m   S   **
    Bridge into the crack from the seaward end. Climb the crack with a brief detour onto the left wall at half-height.
    D.Jones, R.Edwards Pre-1960

3. **Right Wall**   20m   VD
    As for Promontory Crack, but 5m in, break out onto the right wall. Climb this by a series of scoops.
    D.Jones, R.Edwards Pre-1960

The Littlejohn Legacy Area
These routes are below the prominent roof towards the seaward end of the gully, 100m on from the Southern Area.

1. **The Littlejohn Legacy**   28m   HVS,5a
    Climb the prominent groove below the left side of the prominent roof. Pass the roof on the left.
    J.Mothersele, D.McCarroll 00.07.1997

2. **Gower Reality**   28m   E5 6b 1pt   **   \
    Climb the wall to the right of the Littlejohn Legacy to gain thin cracks in the roof. Cross the roof with difficulty.
    S.Doerr, J.Mothersele 1pt (rest) 00.08.1997

3. **The Right Hand One**   25m   HS,4b   *
    Climb the centre of the wall to the right of Gower Reality
    J.Mothersele, D.McCarroll 00.04.1997

4. **The Sissy Traverse**   45m   HVS,5a
    Start about 5m right of The Right Hand One. Traverse the crag at high tide level, to finish as for The Littlejohn Legacy.
    J.Mothersele, S.Doerr 00.00.1997

Pincer Cove
The cove at the west end of the island contains some routes on the north (right when viewed from the top) pincer. These are centred around a prominent open corner. To gain the routes walk down the top of the pincer to a platform and traverse in to gain the wall (on the Pincer Cove side).

1. **Great Corner**   15m   D
    Traverse into the prominent open corner and climb it, turning the overlap on its left.
    D.Jones, R.Edwards Pre-1960

2. **West Wall**   15m   HS,4a
    As for Great Corner, but traverse out on the right wall of the corner to finish up cracks. Alternatively, finish up a groove 1m further on.
    D.Jones, R.Edwards Pre-1960

RHOSSILI

GR407877 to 403875
By Goi Ashmore & Andy Sharp

TIDAL STATUS: The Upper Crags are Non-Tidal. The Lower Crags are accessible between 1 and 3 hours either side of low water.

BOLTING POLICY: See individual crags.

PREAMBLE
The crags overlook the beautiful Rhossili Bay and the Worms Head itself. They contain a good mixture of easy and hard routes. The sea level crags look small when the tide is, but this view proves decpetive as the tide recedes. The upper crags face west, whilst the sea-level crags are mainly north facing. The best area of the upper crags is the solid quarried wall of Trial Wall, containing mostly semi-equipped routes. At sea level there are a number of pleasant areas the best being The Platform area and Poser Buttress.

ACCESS
Climbing on the Worms Head itself is STRICTLY FORBIDDEN. To ignore this ban could jeopardise access to many other cliffs on Gower and it should be strictly adhered to. Climbing on the Worms Head Inn probably would not go down too well with the landlord. Worse still you might disturb Turbo, Fester, Ronnie or worst of all, Chris Davies.

For a small fee it is possible to park in the farmers field at the end of the roading leading into Rhossili village (GR 415881). Walk south along the narrow private road past the National Trust Shop and coastguard cottages, in the direction of the Worms Head. Just before the end of the road, where the stone wall and cliff edge are closest, cut down and right. The path, obvious once one has gone over the rim of the grassy plateau, passes beneath a steep south-west facing wall on the right (Trial Wall). The rest of the upper cliffs are reached by striking off south (left when facing

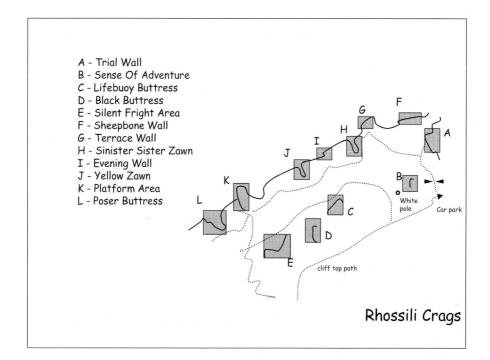

A - Trial Wall
B - Sense Of Adventure
C - Lifebuoy Buttress
D - Black Buttress
E - Silent Fright Area
F - Sheepbone Wall
G - Terrace Wall
H - Sinister Sister Zawn
I - Evening Wall
J - Yellow Zawn
K - Platform Area
L - Poser Buttress

Rhossili Crags

seaward). The sea level cliffs can be reached by following the path down below Trial Wall and walking along the beach or from the short cuts noted below.

Sheepbone Wall is directly below Trial Wall.

Sinister Sister Zawn lies directly below the white pole halfway between Trial Wall and Lifebuoy Butress.

Evening Wall lies directly below Lifebuoy Buttress.

Yellow Zawn is down and south from Lifebuoy Buttress.

The Secret is almost directly below the arete of An Audience of Sheep.

The Platform is below and south of An Audience Of Sheep on Silent Fright Buttress.

Rhossili Bay Crag is reached by continuing the walk along the beach. Kitchen Corner is reached by contouring from the end of the upper crags to drop down onto the beach by some rocky steps.

DESCENTS: Are obvious and just by walking off.

THE ROUTES

Upper Crags

Trial Wall

BOLTING POLICY: Retro-bolting permissible with first ascensionist's permission. Replacement of worn fixed gear on a point for point basis with bolts is permissible. No new sports routes allowed.

This is the steep quarried wall passed on the descent to sea-level. Many of the routes are old aid routes so some of the in-situ gear is dubious. Some of it has been replaced. Some of the routes are chipped. It can be sheltered in winter and dries relatively quickly. To the left of the obvious main face, the seaward face has two corners separated by an undercut v-groove.

1. **Laughing Spam Fritter**   27m   VS,4b
   Climb the v-groove and ramp to a grass ledge. Traverse rightwards into the cave. Scramble off to the right.
   T.Penning, P.Cresswell et al 08.11.1981

2. **Somme Mothers**   27m   HVS,5a
   The name is not a misprint as it was climbed on Remembrance Sunday. This climbs the groove just right of Laughing Spam Fritter, joining it to finish.
   A.Sharp, J.Harwood 08.11.1981

3. **The Adulteress**   24m   E2,5c   **
   Climb the crack just right of the left arete of the main face, through an overhang, then traverse right along an obvious break and climb the wide crack to the top.
   S.Padfield, D.Thomas - Worm Variation 00.00.1965
   FFA A.Sharp, J.Harwood 08.11.1981

4. **Blackman's Pinch**   24m   E4,6a   **
   A popular test piece, sadly now chipped. Start just right of the arete. Climb a rightward-slanting crack to the overlap. Surmount this, BR, and gain the break above. Finish as for The Adulteress.
   S.Padfield, D.Thomas - Worm 00.00.1965, FFA A.Sharp, J.Harwood 05.12.1981

Trial Wall

Photo: Adrian Berry

The story of Skull Attack

Skull Attack is a route with a compli-cated history. It was originally climbed by Andy Sharp in 1983, coming out of Crime And Punishment's ramp and climbing the top wall with 1pt. The protection was 4PRs and a wire or two. Andy returned the year after with John Harwood again and removed the aid point. The lower section was added by Andy with Pete Lewis two year later in 1986 with an extra PR in the bottom wall. The route received as-cents from various climbers like Mar-tin Crocker and Andy Swann before the pegs were stolen. Pegs were spo-radically placed by climbers such as Andy Long and Stefan Doerr, but kept going missing.

Andy said he thought the route should be bolted up instead, which Goi Ashmore did in 1998. Various people got rather annoyed about 5PRs being replaced with 6BRs.

Andy on the other hand still reckons there should be another bolt in it.

For the enlightenment of non-locals, Skull Attack is the famous Brains SA Bitter.

5. **Skull Attack**   24m   E6,6b   Fr7b+   ***
A stunningly technical wall climb, currently fully bolted. Start right of Blackman's Pinch and left of the Crime and Punishment groove below an overlap. Climb to and surmount the overlap to a ledge. Move left to a thin crack. Moving slightly right at a good thin break, make a baffling sequence on non-existent flakes to gain a prominent groove. Mantle awkwardly into this, topping out to good in situ thread belays.
A.Sharp, J.Harwood 1pt – Top Section 29.05.1983, A.Sharp, J.Harwood – Top Section 15.04.1984, A.Sharp, P.Lewis 00.00.1986

6. **Crime and Punishment**   23m   E5,6b   ***
Fine sustained climbing. Start below a scoop and PRs and BRs in the middle of the wall. Gain the scoop, then follow the shallow groove to its top. Move right to a thin crack and climb this to the overhang. Move past this and reach the top.
G.Hicks, S.Padfield, D.Thomas – Trial 00.00.1966, L.Francombe 1pt 00.00.1980, FFA A.Sharp, J.Harwood 18.10.1981

7. **Black Wall**   21m   E7,7a   Fr8a+   *   \
A vicious, fingery problem, especially when the direct finish is taken. Start 3m right of Crime and Punishment at a line of rusting BRs. Make a series of difficult moves to below the bulge. Desperate moves past the remains of an edge lead over the overlap to the top. The route has lost a hold at the top and it is not known if it has been successfully redpointed since. The grade is estimated from 'the dog'.
J.Talbot, B.Talbot 00.00.1961, A.Sharp, J.Harwood 3pt 22.11.1981, A.Forster, A.Sharp – Direct 00.00.1988

8. **Inch Pinch** 18m E4,6b
A trivial pitch, up a short crack on the right side of the crag. Boulder up directly to a PR. Gain a crack with difficulty and climb it. Continue more easily to the top.
A.Sharp, P.Lewis, J.Harwood 29.05.1983

9. **The Hant** 15m E4,6b
Follow Inch Pinch to a good lay-away hold, then move right and over the overlap with difficulty. Follow a shallow groove and crack to the top.
A.Sharp, P.Lewis 00.04.1987

10. **Tribulations** 12m E4,6a Fr7a
The right arete of the buttress, moving left at the top. PRs, BRs.
R.Thomas 20.09.1998

11. **Shakeout** 27m E3,6a **
A girdle of Trial Wall from right to left. Start at the right edge of the wall, at the obvious breakline below the bulges. Follow the break past 2PRs to join Crime and Punishment. Move up for 2m and continue leftwards, PR, to finish up The Adulteress. A hanging stance can be taken on on Crime And Punishment.
A.Sharp, J.Harwood 23.10.1982

The Sense Of Adventure Area

BOLTING POLICY: Retro-bolting permissible with first ascensionist's permission. Replacement of worn fixed gear on a point for point basis with bolts is permissible. New sports routes allowed.

The Sense of Adventure area lies well above sea level 100m on from Trial Wall and before Lifebuoy Buttress. There is some atrocious rock.

1. **The Edge** 5m E4,6a \
A perfect square-cut arete at the left end of the crag. Unprotected.
A.Berry 00.00.1997

2. **The Beautiful People** 12m E1,5b \
The clean arete at the far right side of the crag.
G.Morris, A.Berry 00.00.1997

Lifebuoy Buttress

BOLTING POLICY: Retro-bolting permissible with first ascensionist's permission. Replacement of worn fixed gear on a point for point basis with bolts is permissible. New sports routes allowed.

About 30m right of The Sense Of Adventure Area is a white pole and 30m further right is a buttress in the upper cliff.

1. **The Axe** 14m E1,5a
The left-hand arete.
T.Penning, A.Sharp, J.Harwood 26.05.1985

2. **Blockbuster** 14m E1,5a
The wall 3m right of The Axe. Climb from ledge to ledge parallel with the arete, finishing up a short scoop. PRs missing.
N.Williams, P.Williams 00.00.1978

3. **Pulpit**   14m   HVS,5a
    Not a route to preach about! Climb a stepped corner 9m right of Blockbuster to a pulpit, move left and up a smooth curving crack for 1m then left and up a wall into a scoop to the top.
    N.Williams, P.Williams 00.00.1978
    G.Evans, J.Bullock – Direct 00.00.1982

4. **Crunch**   24m   VS,4c
    Some 6m right of Pulpit is a corner with a grassy ledge. Climb this and the central crack in the upper buttress.
    A.Tyas, J.Pratt, G.Evans 00.00.1981

Black Buttress

BOLTING POLICY: Retro-bolting permissible with first ascensionist's permission. Replacement of worn fixed gear on a point for point basis with bolts is permissible. New sports routes allowed.

About 60m right of Lifebuoy Buttress are some black walls.

1. **Bragg**   12m   VD   \
    Follow flakes and a corner in the centre.
    N.Williams, P.Williams 00.00.1978

Silent Fright Buttress

BOLT POLICY: No bolting.

This is located 90m south-west along the headland from Black Buttress. It has an impressive arete on the left, a lower square-cut subsidiary buttress in the centre and a prominent overhanging arete to its right (An Audience of Sheep).

1. **Silent Fright**   24m   E4,6a   *
    Climb the impressive arete at the left side of the wall, PR. Exit leftwards to a worrying finish.
    A.Sharp, P.Lewis 00.00.1985

2. **Summertime Blues**   15m   HVS,5a
    Climb the crack directly up the short steep wall on the right of Silent Fright.
    P.Lewis, A.Sharp 00.00.1985

3. **Playground Twist**   15m   E2,5c   *
    The crack just right of Summertime Blues.
    A.Sharp, P.Lewis 00.00.1985

4. **Executioner's Thrill**   15m   E4,6b   *
    A good testpiece up the bold, technical arete right of Playground Twist.
    A.Sharp, P.Lewis 00.00.1985

5. **The Mad Mad Mad Lundy Axeman**   12m   E3,5c
    Located on the wall 12m right of Executioner's Thrill. Start from a ledge at 2m, 5m left of faint parallel cracks in a black slabby wall. Follow the tricky slab above, with an awkward move to finish. Poor protection
    M.Crocker 02.08.1988

6. **Lundy Tilting**   15m   E2,5c
    Climb the left of two cracks 5m right of The Mad Mad Mad Lundy Axeman. Gain a ledge at 3m and follow the crack and arete to the top.
    M.Crocker 02.08.1987

7. **An Audience of Sheep**   15m   E5,6b
The flying arete bounding the buttress on its right. Gain a ledge down and left of the arete and then cross rightwards onto a projecting ledge, TR. Hard moves up the arete, PR, to a jug, BR, lead to amazing moves and a long reach for a jug at the apex.
M.Crocker, M.Ward 15.08.1987

60m further along is a short slabby wall, recognised by a square-cut window-like notch at the top of the slab.

8. **Wages of Sin**   12m   E4,6a
A good pitch, following the slight groove up the left side of the slab.
A.Sharp, P.Lewis 06.03.1988

Sea Level Crags

The easiest way to find the Sea Level crags on a first visit is to walk along the beach. For subsequent visits see the shortcuts listed in the access section. There are stakes in place at the top of some Sea Level crags.

Sheepbone Wall

BOLT POLICY: No bolting.
A gem of a crag located immediately below the seaward arete of Trial Wall. Scramble down to some ledges about 12m above the sea and abseil down one of the corners to a platform. The right-hand one (when facing seaward) is Chimney Crack, the left-hand one is Great Diedre. At the base of Chimney crack is an oval pool and a blunt arete to the left.

1. **First Diedre**   10m   D
Climb the groove to the left of the blunt arete.
J.Talbot 00.00.1968

2. **Mauk Wall**   10m   S,4a
Climb the steep wall right of the blunt arete and left of a prominent curving crack, passing a projecting block.
J.Talbot 00.00.1968

3. **Curving Crack**   10m   HS,4b
Climb the rightward-slanting crack.
J.Talbot 00.00.1968

4. **Chimney Crack**   10m   VD   *
The obvious corner and chimney crack right of Curving Crack.
J.Talbot 00.00.1968

5. **Skull**   10m   HS,4a
Climb the steep wall 1m right of Chimney Crack.
J.Talbot 00.00.1968

6. **Cross**   12m   D
Climb Skull for 4m to a sloping ledge. Step right from this to finish up a square-cut groove.
J.Talbot 00.00.1968

7. **Deep Cut**   18m   VD   *
Climb the wall 3m right of Cross to gain and finish up a steep crack.
J.Talbot 00.00.1968

8. **Great Diedre** 12m S,4a *
The obvious black corner 6m right of Deep Cut.
J.Talbot 00.00.1968

9. **Yellow Edge** 12m S *
Start just right of Great Diedre. Climb the right wall of the arete until a leftwards traverse to it can be made. Follow it to the top.
J.Talbot 00.00.1968

10. **Great Diedre II** 15m VS,4c
Climb the corner 3m right of Yellow Edge, with a tricky overhang at 8m. A slight variant climbs the crack in the left wall (HVS,5b).
C.Hird, G.Evans, G.Richardson 00.00.1975

11. **Pistas Canute** 15m VS,4b *
Climb the arete dividing Great Diedre II and Slanting Chimney, coming in from the left.
A.Beaton, C.Allen, M.Danford 00.00.1989

12. **Rhiannon's Route** 17m HVS,5a
Gain the Pistas Canute arete from the right.
A.Richardson, J.Beynon 00.00.1992

13. **Slanting Chimney** 14m VD
Ascend the obvious slanting crack.
M.Harber Pre-1978

14. **Gambolling Gareth's Arete** 17m E1,5a *
Gain the arete to the right from the right and climb it direct.
A.Richardson, R.Lloyd, J.Beynon 00.00.1992

15. **Recess Crack** 17m VS,4c
Climb the square-cut recess 6m right of Great Diedre II and then the crack splitting its back.
J.Talbot 00.00.1968

16. Gamble There's A Hold 16m E1,5b
The back arete forming the right edge of the recess.
M.Crocker solo 03.09.2003

17. **Barnacle Ramp** 17m D
The rightwards-rising crack and ramp right of Recess Crack.
J.Beynon solo 00.00.1992

18. Deep Water Go Slow 17m E3,5b * ⟍
The arete to the right.
M.Crocker solo 03.09.2003

At the right hand end of Sheepbone Wall is a cave. These two routes start from above the high water mark on a slabby ramp on the left

19. Error's Corner 9m E1,5b ⟍
Climb the corner, swinging right to finish.
M.Crocker, J.Harwood 07.09.2003

20. Error Flynn   12m   E4,6a   ⟍

Traverse fingerholds rightwards across the black wall above the cave to a crack. Follow the hairline crack and faint groove in the steepening wall to the top.
M.Crocker, J.Harwood 07.09.2003

Terrace Wall

BOLT POLICY: No bolting.
40m south of Trial Wall and Sheepbone Wall is an obvious terrace just above sea level, bounded on its right by a deep inlet. The route starts up the corner formed by the right (south) end of the terrace.

1. **Zig Zag**   15m   VD
Climb the corner to a ledge, then take a vague groove in the wall above on some wobbly jugs.
J.Talbot 00.00.1968

2. **Pillar Edge**   15m   HS,4a
Climb the left-hand arete of the inlet on its left side.
J.Talbot 00.00.1968

3. **Central Gully**   15m   D
The original line has been rationalised. Take the left-hand crack in the gully.
J.Talbot 00.00.1968

4. **Slab And Crack**   15m   D
Also rationalised. Climb the right-hand crack in the gully.
J.Talbot 00.00.1968

5. **Deception**   20m   S
Just right of the deep inlet is a crack and corner at half-height. Gain this by the pocketed slab below.
J.Talbot 00.00.1968

6. **Deceit**   20m   S
Gain and climb the less obvious corner to the right of Deception.
M.Harber 00.00.1982

7. **Fisherman's Bend**   15m   HS,4a
The centre of the wall 20m right of Deceit.
J.Talbot 00.00.1972

Sinister Sister Zawn

BOLT POLICY: No bolting.
40m further along the beach towards the Worms Head and below the white pole marking Lifebuoy Buttress, is a narrow zawn with a large jammed boulder at its back. Access is by scrambling down on the north side of the zawn..

1. My Favourite Colour   10m   E4,6a   ⟍
Start from a flat back ledge 12m above the zawn bed above the jammed boulder. Scramble up a mucky rift, then access the pink soaring crack. Exit right from this.
M.Crocker 04.09.2003

2. Spacetalk   10m   E2,5c   ⟍
From the top of the rift take the handrail rightwards to a commiting move onto a triangular hold gains the top.
M.Crocker, J.Harwood 07.09.2003

The next two routes stary from the jammed boulder.

3. Pop Idol   18m   E5,6b   ***   \
    Swing right into the right-hand of two cracks. Climb this until it closes then undercut left to and into overhangs.
    Pull up, PR into a pink groove and follow this to the top.
    M.Crocker 07.09.2003

4. Pop-Eyed   18m   E4,6a   **   \
    The crack and roofs right ot Pop Idol. The first ascensionist route description makes no sense, so good luck!
    M.Crocker 03.09.2003

5. Splash And Grab   18m   E6,6b   *   \
    The tapering wall to the right. Swing right from the boulder and move down the right hand crack to a horizontal
    break. Follow this right for 2m. Follow the black face above, trending slightly right to the left hand side of the arete
    (hex). Reach left to good holds and pockets in the thin upper wall. Gear is very specific.
    M.Crocker 07.09.2003

6. **Sinister Sister**   21m   E4,5c
    Follow the arete 5m right of the jammed boulder to the break. Arrange protection and continue up the arete and
    groove, TR.
    A.Sharp, P.Lewis 06.03.1988

7. **Wiggly Woo**   21m   HS,4b
    Climb the gully and obvious narrow pillar right of Sinister Sister. Some poor rock.
    J.Beynon, R.Lloyd, A.Richardson 00.00.1992

Evening Wall

BOLT POLICY: No bolting.
60m south of Sinister Sister Zawn is a yellow wall with a distinctive calcite patch and a large ledge at half-height to
the right. The first climb starts from the beach. Gain a small ledge 2m below a wide crack.

1. **Hey Mr Blue Sky**   18m   HVS,5b   *
    Cimb the wide crack to pass the ledge on the right. An awkward move gains the chockstone. Pull up onto the
    headwall and over the bulge, PR. Move left at the top to finish.
    L.Davies, P.Bruten, P.Thomas 09.06.1986

2. **Banana Split**   8m   E1,5b   \
    Start at the large ledge at half-height on the right. Ascend the groove on the left side of the ledge until a hard move
    gains the upper wall. Move right, missing PR, making thin moves to finish directly. Note that the route has
    suffered a recent rock fall. It is not known whether it has been climbed since. The grade and description are pre-
    rock fall.
    P.Bruten, L.Davies 00.00.1986

Yellow Zawn

BOLT POLICY: No bolting.
80m along the upper cliff path from the white pole or along the beach from Sinister Sister Zawn, is a deep zawn with
a cave at its back containing a 20m high, north-facing wall with a yellow arete. Descend by an easy scramble.

1. **Turning Japanese**   18m   E5,6a   *
    A route for Cyclone Rangers. Start at a large boulder. Climb a finger crack to a horizontal break then traverse right
    to a good slot on the yellow arete. Climb its left side.
    M.Crocker, M.Ward 15.08.1987

2. **Banzai!**   15m   E4,6a

Place bets now! A fine steep little route. Climb the arete easily to a sloping ledge. Make hard moves up a thin crack into a groove. Finish up a black wall heading slightly right.
M.Crocker, M.Ward 15.08.1987

60m right of Yellow Zawn and below An Audience Of Sheep are three pillars, seen when looking out to sea. The following route climbs the sheer south west wall on the middle pillar.

3. **The Secret**   17m   E5,6b   **

A direct line taking the centre of the smooth wall. Abseil to a good ledge at 3m, or scramble in at low water. Climb leftwards, then back right on white crystal rock, passing a poor PR with difficulty, to the horizontal break. Take the centre of the wall to finish.
M.Crocker, M.Ward 15.08.1987

The Platform Area

BOLT POLICY: No bolting.
These routes lie on a small rock promontory, directly below the prominent arete of An Audience of Sheep and north of and parallel to the very obvious large flat sea level platform. Approach is best made by following a path down to a good platform, on the south side of the promontory.

1. **Avoid Meeting The Portuguese Man Of War**   40m   VS,4a,4c,-   **

When deep water soloing the sea is normally used for protection. Here it is used as a hold. High tide is essential. Best soloed for obvious reasons.
1. 15m Drop down into the v-groove below the end of the path and traverse left at a low level under an obvious arete. Step up to belay in the through-cave.
2. 12m Crawl through the through cave, then traverse the left wall (looking out to sea) to a platform on the arete.
3. 13m Jump into the sea, at the lowest point of the buttress, swim across the zawn and finish easily up the wall on the far side of the zawn. (The leap can be made from the belay stance instead for added underwater time as The Leap Of Faith Finish).
L.Davies, P.Thomas 00.07.1989

2. **Stardust**   24m   HS,4a   **

A classic little pitch. Follow Avoid Meeting The Portuguese Man Of War until 5m before the arete visible from the start. Pull up over an overlap, then move left to gain cracks just right of the arete. Follow these to finish.
A.Sharp, J.Harwood 18.10.1981

3. **Year of The Snail**   24m   VS,4b   *

Start as for Stardust but continue up the centre of the wall.
M.Ward 16.08.1987

Poser Buttress

BOLT POLICY: No bolting.
A deep square-cut zawn 30m on, with a smooth south-facing wall containing four cracks. These are gained by abseil to a hanging stance. There is a big mooring ring can be used (just right of Splash Landing). Alternatively start from the floor of the zawn ¾ hour either side of low water. The routes on the greasy south wall will have to be done this way.

North Wall

1. **Normal Service**   20m   VS,4b

The most seaward crack.
A.Sharp, J.Harwood 05.12.1981

2. **Splash Landing**   20m   HVS,5a
   The next crack to the right (landwards).
   A.Sharp, J.Harwood 05.12.1981

3. **Dicky Five Stones**   20m   E3,5c   *
   Good. From the mooring ring, climb the wall between Splash Landing and The Poser.
   A.Sharp, P.Lewis 00.00.1990

4. **The Poser**   20m   E1,5b   **
   The third crack right from the sea. Good.
   T.Penning, A.Sharp, J.Harwood 23.05.1982

5. **Burning Rubber**   20m   E2,5b
   The fourth crack.
   T.Penning, A.Sharp, J.Harwood 23.05.1982

South Wall

6. **Chlorophyll Corner**   15m   VS,4c
   Climb a corner crack opposite Burning Rubber, near the back of the gully.
   T.Penning, A.Sharp, D.Hillier 27.06.1982

7. **Lobster Song**   15m   E2,5b
   Start directly up the arete right of Chlorophyll Corner, swing left and climb the slab, TR.
   L.Davies 00.00.1988

8. **Cincinatti Kid**   15m   VS,4c
   The crack just round the arete right of Chlorophyll Corner, in a narrow wall facing out of the gully.
   T.Penning, D.Hillier, A.Sharp 27.06.1981

Rhossili Bay

BOLT POLICY: No bolting.
About one third of the way along the beach from Poser Buttress to Kitchen Corner is a small cove with a wildly overhanging west wall. Two diagonal breaks trending left cut through the left side of this tidal wall.

.1. **Attrition**   35m   E5,6a   **   ʌ
   The lower of the two diagonal cracks. There is another 50m of unpleasant scrambling to top out after the climbing.
   P.Littlejohn, J.Mothersele 00.00.1997

Kitchen Corner

BOLT POLICY: No bolting.
Tthe deep inlet at the end of the mainland. Access is by continuing along the bottom of the upper cliff line to reach easy ledges. The routes have not been checked for this guide and require abseil escapes.

1. **Dove Crack**   12m   M   ʌ
   The wide chimney in the back of the cove.
   D.Jones, R.Owen, J.Edwards 00.00.1958

2. **Kitchen Slab**   12m   HS   ʌ
   The slab in the upper part of the cliff is gained and followed.
   D.Jones, R.Owen, J.Edwards 00.00.1958

FALL BAY TO MEWSLADE BAY

GR414874 to 421868
By Goi Ashmore, Adrian Berry, Pete Lewis, Andy Sharp & Chris Shorrock

TIDAL STATUS: ¾ hour either side of low water to non-tidal. See individual sections.

BOLTING POLICY: No bolting.

PREAMBLE

A beautiful and popular area, providing the greatest concentration of the best traditional routes on Gower and some of its most spectacular. It is possibly the best area for a first visit to Gower. The area lies between Fall Bay in the west and Mewslade Bayin the east. It contains a variety of gullies and buttresses, with climbing of all grades with both non-tidal and very tidal areas which are individually noted. If a little forethought is used, it is not too difficult to visit a couple of crags to prevent an overly tide-determined visit, for example by combining trips to Kings Wall and Lewes Castle, or Jacky's Tor and Catacomb Gully.

At low water it is possible to walk all the way round the lower cliffs for about an hour either side of low water, the critical cut off point being Jacky's Tor. It is possible to walk round the areas either side of Jacky's Tor for about 2 hours either side of low water. On a first visit it is best to follow the crag familarisation tour set out below. There are three very popular areas, King Wall and Lewes Castle, containing easy and middle grade routes respectively and the very impressive Yellow Wall.

The crags of Grey Wall, Upper Jacky's Tor and Rolly Bottom Buttress are described out of sequence with the lower crags at the end of the section, to aid the flow of the text.

ACCESS

There are two possible approaches depending on which end of the area one wishes to visit:

1. Fall Bay Approach

This is the best approach for cliffs to the west of Jacky's Tor (King Wall to Jacky's Tor). Drive to the end of the B4247 at Rhossili and use the (paying) car park in the farmer's field by the Worms Head Inn (GR415881). Walk down to the end of the first field, cross the fence and turn left. Continue across two fields to a track which leads to a lane, turn right into the lane and take the first opening on the left. Follow a track with a hedge on the left and at its end turn right into another field. Walk a short distance keeping a hedge to the right, cross a stile and turn left. Follow the edge of the field, cross the stile and descend an iron ladder. Lewes Castle is immediately in front on the left 10 minutes from the car park. Sea level crags can be gained by contouring round Lewes Castle at this level and walking down the platform above King Wall to reach Giant's Cave. King Wall is to the west (right when facing out to sea), the other crags to the east. Alternatively from the iron ladder, drop down to the beach and follow the coast round from the west (left) end of King Wall.

2. Mewslade Bay Approach

This is the best approach for the upper cliffs to the east of Jacky's Tor (as far as Grey Wall) and probably for the Tor itself. Turn left (south) off the B4247 at Pitton to Pitton Farm (GR 427877). Car parking is available (honesty box). Strike left from the entrance to the car park. Walk a short distance down a farm track then bear right past farm buildings to gain the path leading through a narrow valley to the East end of Mewslade Bay (7 mins walk).

DESCENTS: Described by crag.

CRAG FAMILIARISATION

The following tour may be useful. Looking east just before descending the iron ladder described in the Fall Bay approach, some prominent spikes of rock can be seen some distance away. This is on the opposite side of Upper Jacky's Tor from the recorded routes.

The main tour starts on Fall Bay Beach, no more than 1 hour before low water. Start heading eastwards (rightward if looking back to land from the sea). The first sea level crag is the long, 25m high King Wall, above which is the

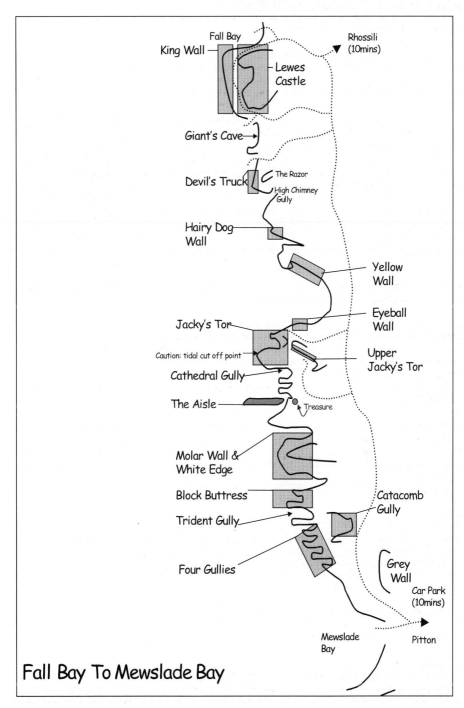

Fall Bay

King Wall

Lewes Castle

Rhossili (10mins)

Giant's Cave →

Devil's Truck

The Razor

High Chimney Gully

Hairy Dog Wall

Yellow Wall

Jacky's Tor

Eyeball Wall

Upper Jacky's Tor

Caution: tidal cut off point

Cathedral Gully

The Aisle

Treasure

Molar Wall & White Edge

Block Buttress

Catacomb Gully

Trident Gully

Four Gullies

Grey Wall

Car Park (10mins)

Mewslade Bay

Pitton

Fall Bay To Mewslade Bay

obvious non-tidal crag of Lewes Castle. Continuing east, where King Wall runs down into the sea, is a very obvious square-cut 25m high cave, Giant's Cave. To the east the crags become broken and a long spur runs out to sea. Running straight up from this spur is Devils' Truck.

Carefully traverse down and right across broken rock (behind which is High Chimney Gully) to gain a wide sandy beach, behind which is a cove full of huge boulders. This is Great Boulder Cove and the huge wall on its left (west side) is Yellow Wall. On the other side of this is Eyeball Wall. The small steeply overhung wall south (left) of Yellow Wall is Hairy Dog Wall and between this and Yellow Wall is Little Block Buttress.

On the other side of Great Boulder Cove is Jacky's Tor, a prominent narrow rectangular headland that blocks further vision. Beyond the toe of this is a steep incut gully, containing some steep cracks in its left (west) wall. This is Cathedral Wall, the next butress is The Pulpit.

Just to the east, the way appears to be blocked by a long low tongue of rock running out to sea. This is The Aisle. At the north (landward) end of The Aisle is a narrow chasm which passes behind. A roofless cave behind the chasm contains the route Treasure.

On the far (east) side of The Aisle the beach opens up again and after about 50m there is a high, narrow pillar leading up into the land. This is White Edge, below which is the unimpressive looking Molar Wall. The next headland east, which contains a deep gully on its east is Block Buttress, bounded on its east by Trident Gully.

Beyond Trident Gully the rock gradually decreases in height passing by Fourth, Third, Second and First Gully. The recess above these is Catacomb Gully. Mewslade Bay has now been reached and the rock tails off to the access path. The huge headland to the east is Thurba Head.

Walk up from the beach to the higher level crags and strike back west. The first unimpressive wall encountered is Grey Wall. After some time the pinnacles refered to at the start of the tour are encountered, to the east of which is Upper Jacky's Tor. On the far side of this the immediate way is barred by Great Boulder Cove, from where Yellow Wall can be seen over on the west. The path now skirts back above the crags to the iron ladder initially encountered. Now go and climb!

THE ROUTES

King Wall
GR414873

TIDAL STATUS: 2½ hours either side of low water.

DESCENTS: Descend down and right from the large platform above the crag to reach Giant's Cave, then double back.

This is the tier below The Great Terrace above which is Lewes Castle. It is the first sea level crag encountered when coming from Fall Bay. It provides a number of good lower grade routes. When the beach is exposed, descent is easiest by following the Great Terrace rightwards (east) into Giants Cave. Because the first 6m of the wall are easy, it is possible to traverse or abseil into many of the routes for some time after the tide has come back in. To aid route identification Great Cleft is in the middle of the wall.

1. **Niord**   24m   S
   Start 15m below and left of the left apex of King Wall, below a right-angled groove at 15m. Gain this groove and finish direct.
   J.Talbot 00.00.1970

2. **Skadi**   24m   S
   The vague ramp 2m right of Niord.
   J.Talbot 00.00.1970

3. **Llethrid**   26m   HS,4a
Climbs a vague right-trending ramp below the left-hand apex of the wall.
J.Talbot 00.00.1963

4. **Frigg**   26m   VS,4b
Start below the highest point of the wall (25m left of Great Cleft). Climb a shallow blackened groove leading towards the left end of the Great Terrace. Climb the groove, then trend left near the top where the groove peters out.
J.Talbot, D.Lewis 00.00.1963

5. **Bolder**   26m   VS,4b   *
A nice pitch up the slabby wall between Frigg and Beowulf.
J.Harwood, G.Evans 07.12.1980

6. **Beowulf**   29m   VS,4b
Climb a groove running rightward to a small overlap at 20m with a light brown stain below it. Traverse left above the overlap to a small pitted slab. Follow this via another overlap to the top.
J.Talbot, D.Lewis 00.00.1963

7. **Ragnarok**   29m   HS,4a   **
As for Beowulf but follow the groove to the top.
J.Talbot, D.Lewis 00.00.1963

8. **Trying Lines**   29m   VS,4c
Directly up the pillar right of Ragnarok.
G.Evans, J.Harwood 07.12.1980

9. **Sweyn**   29m   HS,4b
Follow thin calcite streaks on the broken wall right of Ragnarok, then directly up the wall above.
J.Talbot, D.Lewis 00.00.1963

10. **Gefion**   29m   HS,4b
The wall to the right of Sweyn, keeping left of the groove (Idun) bounding the left side of the obvious pillar in the centre of the wall.
J.Talbot, D.Lewis 00.00.1963

11. **Idun**   21m   S
The corner bounding the left-hand side of the pillar.
J.Talbot, D.Lewis 00.00.1964

12. **King Route**   21m   S
Start immediately right of Idun and climb the left-hand side of the pillar and the indefinite stepped groove slightly rightwards to the top.
D.Jones, J.Talbot 00.00.1959

13. **Freya**   21m   HS,4a
Climb a shallow groove in the centre of the pillar.
J.Talbot 00.00.1964

14. **Valkyrie**   21m   VS,5a
The cracked wall to the right of Freya, keeping left of an overlap at 15m.
J.Talbot 00.00.1964

15. **Vik**   21m   HS,4b
Climb a vague line right of Valkyrie and left of the arete of the wall.

J.Talbot 00.00.1963

16. **Cleft Corner**   21m   S
Take the subsidiary groove running up to Great Cleft from the left.
J.Talbot 00.00.1963

17. **Great Cleft**   21m   D
The obvious broken crack and groove left of a smooth recessed slab more or less halfway along the wall. Climb the wall to gain the crack at half-height.
J.Talbot, D.Jones 00.00.1959

To the right is a 20m wide wall, bounded on its right by a prominent arete.

18. **Wulst**   21m   S
Climb the wall just right of Great Cleft.
J.Talbot 00.00.1970

19. **Vanir**   21m   VS,4c
Start right of Wulst and climb up to a scoop and a tiny calcite knob in a hole. Move up to a shallow groove on the left to finish.
J.Talbot 00.00.1964

20. **Balder**   21m   VS,5a
The centre of the slab by a thin crack. Climb up leftward to gain a tiny ledge, move right and finish up the slab.
J.Talbot 00.00.1963

21. **Loki**   21m   HS
The slabs right of Balder and left of the more prominent cracks of Tyr to the right.
J.Talbot 00.00.1964

22. **Tyr**   21m   S,4a
The cracks to the right of Loki.
J.Talbot 00.00.1963

23. **Fafnir**   21m   HS,4b   **
A popular climb taking the corner at the right side of the recessed slab.
J.Talbot 00.00.1963

24. **Amble**   21m   VD
The prominent crack right of Fafnir.
J.Talbot 00.00.1961

25. **Pytt**   21m   S
The wall immediately right of Amble.
J.Talbot 00.00.1962

An indistinct line Fenris (J.Talbot 1962) seems to be covered by the lines of Pytt and Vorder.

26. **Vorder**   21m   S,4a
Climb the arete at the right side of the pitted wall.
J.Talbot 00.00.1963

27. **Ides**   30m   S
A rising traverse linking Vorder to Needle Crack.
J.Talbot 00.00.1963

28. **Thor**   21m   S,4a
The groove in the side wall to the right of Vorder, gained from Odin.
J.Talbot 00.00.1963

29. **Odin**   21m   VS,4b
A skinny man's route. Climb the obvious chimney and the crack above.
J.Talbot 00.00.1963

30. **Valhalla**   21m   HVS,4c
The wall right of Odin.
J.Talbot 00.00.1964
G.Evans, J.Bullock - Direct 00.00.1988

Nones (J.Talbot, B.Talbot 1965) has been superseded by the other routes hereabouts.

31. **Needle Crack**   21m   VS,4b   **
Climb the steep corner right of Odin to easier rock, then pleasantly up to the final steep section.
J.Talbot 00.00.1963

32. **Joe Says Its Cool**   24m   E2,5c
Supersedes the old routes Exodus (J.Talbot 1963) and Kluft (J.Talbot 1960). The overlaps right of Needle Crack.
A.Berry, H.Griffiths, J.Bottrill, J.Bullock, G.Evans 00.00.1993

33. **Nimbus**   24m   S,4c
Start just right of the arete of the corner of Needle Crack. Make an awkward move to gain the slab just right of the arete and take a diagonal line up right to a ledge. Continue directly to the top.
J.Talbot 00.00.1963

34. **Genesis**   18m   HD
The distinct rib 10m to the right of Nimbus.
Unknown Pre-1978

35. **Findel**   18m   M
The last deep fissure on the wall.
J.Talbot 00.00.1961

36. **Varus**   18m   M
Climbs the area of broken rock to the right of Findel.
J.Talbot 00.00.1961

37. **King Wall Girdle**   100m   VS,4c
A right to left girdle following any convenient line.
Traditional Pre-1978

Lewes Castle (Fall Bay Buttress)
GR414874

TIDAL STATUS: Non-Tidal.

DESCENTS: Either left (normally better) or right from the raised ground at the top, via well worn paths.

Lewes Castle West
This is the upper buttress overlooking Fall Bay and is justifiably popular. It provides excellent climbing, mostly at the VS and HVS, grades. It is non-tidal and the approach is via the path contouring round below the iron ladder on the Fall Bay approach, which leads to the Great Terrace. Towards the seaward (south) end is a prominent left-slanting groove leading up to the overhangs at their widest point (Osiris). Back left is a prominent vertical corner crack (Isis).

1. **Fall Bay Girdle**   85m   HVS,5a,4c,4b   **
   An excellent traverse line under the roofs. Omitting P1 makes the route VS.
   1. 24m Climb Ket to the break.
   2. 31m Traverse right via some awkward moves to gain the arete left of Isis. Cross the groove of Isis and belay in the cave where Isis crosses the overhang.
   3. 30m Traverse right until clear of the overhangs, then easily up to the top.
   R.Griffiths, M.Hogge 00.00.1967

The first prominent feature of the crag is a short corner above two holes halfway along the path (Ket).

2. **Bucket**   36m   HVS,5b   \
   Take the crack in the wall 2m left of the short corner. Climb past the crack, PR, to a ledge, go right to a corner (Ket), then carry on up the crack in the headwall.
   R.Wadey, M.Murray 00.09.1997

3. **Ket**   36m   HVS,5a
   Climb the short corner and then a subsequent shallow corner slightly left to a cave at two-thirds height. Finish up a broken groove on the left, taking care not to dislodge the monster block.
   E.Pardoe, R.Leigh 00.00.1967

4. **Mandrake**   36m   HVS,5b
   As for Ket, but finish directly up the crack rather than the broken groove.
   P.Christie, R.Evans, G.Morris 00.00.1986

5. **Eclipse**   36m   E1,5c   \
   Take the crack in the wall 2m to the right of the start of Ket. Climb the continuation wall steeply, PR, to gain a crack and follow his past overlaps above. Cross the overhang at twin cracks.
   R.Wadey, M.Murray 00.09.1997

6. **Seket**   36m   E1,5b
   Start 1m right of Eclipse at the foot of a groove, below a small triangular overhang at half-height, 4m left of the obvious corner crack of Isis. Climb a groove and slab to an overhang, over this past golos and climb a crack in the wall to the right. Follow broken grooves directly to the top.
   E.Pardoe, A.March 00.00.1968

7. **Monkey See And Monkey Do**   36m   E4,6a   *
   Start to the right of Seket below a faint groove with a PR at 5m. Climb this groove via a bold pull over an overlap (cruciai Friend 4). From the top of the groove, move up to a pancake, clip an inverted PR to the right, then pull through the overlap at a TR. Wander up and right to finish.
   A.Sharp, P.Lewis 17.02.2002

---

8. **Reptiles And Samurai**   36m   E4,6a   *

An excellent and direct line with some blind climbing. The gear is good, even at the start, given the patience to place it. Start right of Monkey See And Monkey Do. Climb straight up a white wall, good RPs. Pull over a bulge to a short groove. From the sloping shelf above, pull up direct or slightly right, lots of PRs. Overcome the roof, crux, poor PR, but good rock 3 in the lip. Continue up the short groove to a break. Move left to finish up the broken groove above.
M.Crocker, M.Ward 28.06.1987

9. **Welsh Witch**   36m   E3,6a

Climb the slabby groove immediately right of Reptiles And Samurai to the base of a slim square-cut groove right of Reptiles and just left of the main corner of Isis. Climb this easily, to gain a ledge, PR and some poor rock. Climb the crack to the right to gain the top of the Isis groove. Place a thread and finish direct.
A.Sharp, D.Morris, P.Lewis 24.03.2002

10. **Isis**   36m   HVS,5a   ***

Classic. Start below the obvious corner crack in the centre of the cliff. Climb a steep wall to gain the main corner crack, which is followed to the main overhangs. Traverse rightwards to a cave (possible belay), move right and climb the overhang at its narrowest point, then trend left to the top. A cheesy right-hand start is available up the left-hand of the cracks to the right.
R.Griffiths, E.Pardoe AL 00.02.1967

11. **Horus**   36m   HVS,5a   *

Start just right of Isis below two diverging cracks. Climb the right one, PR, to below a bulge. Step left to a small pinnacle and climb to a break. Cross the overhang as for Isis and finish direct.
P.Hinder, J.Talbot 00.00.1975

Lewes Castle

Photo: Adrian Berry

12. **Rhea**   36m   HVS,5a   **
Start below a short dark slab, 5m right of Isis, with a rightward-slanting groove/crack above. Climb to a recess and then the groove, PR. Move right onto a rib, follow this and the adjacent groove to a break. Pull through the overhang at the v-groove just left of its widest point.
R.Leigh, T.Smith 00.00.1967

13. **Lazy Sunday Afternoon**   36m   E2,5b   **
A poor and contrived start leads to the brilliant finish. It is much more sensible to gain the finish via Seth or Osiris. Start at the foot of a short steep wall midway between the starts of Rhea and Osiris, beneath the widest part of the overhangs above. Climb the wall and the rib above to belay on Osiris. Continue over the roof at its widest point, TR, PR and climb steeply up the wall above.
G.Evans, J.Bullock 00.00.1989
G.Lewis, S.Mundy - Final Roof 00.00.1982

14. **Frantic Sunday Morning**   36m   E2,5c
As for Seth, then step left and finish over the roof to the right of Lazy Sunday Afternooon. Contrived.
B. Heason, M.Heason 00.10.1997

15. **Osiris**   36m   VS,4c   ***
Splendid. Start at the prominent leftward-slanting groove system towards the right-hand end of the face. Follow the groove to the overhangs at their widest point (possible belay), PRs. Traverse right to pull over the overhang at its weakest point and so gain the top.
E.Pardoe, R.Griffiths AL 00.02.1967

16. **Seth**   36m   E1,5c   **
A good route, with a very tricky crux. Climb the lower groove of Osiris for 5m, then a steep crack in the right wall to a break. Finish as for Osiris, or move left for a three star outing by finishing up Lazy Sunday Afternoon and an E2 tick.
J.Talbot 00.00.1970

17. **Horsis**   36m   HVS,5a   *
Climb the lower part of the Osiris groove, then move diagonally right to another groove. Follow the left-hand cracks past a large block to the overhangs. Finish up the easy groove just right of the overhangs.
E.Pardoe, R.Griffiths 00.00.1968

18. **Ra**   36m   HVS,5a
Start to the right of the grooves of Osiris. Climb the wall to a groove/corner high on the face and swing left onto a rib near the top. Combines the better climbing of Nieblung (J.Talbot, P.Hinder 1973) and Father Christmas (J.Talbot, P.Hinder 1973).
G.Evans, P.Christie 00.00.1988

19. **Fallout**   36m   VS,4b   ●
Start at the lowest point of the front of the buttress and climb directly to the top.
J.Birch, J.Geeson 00.00.1967

20. **South East Diedre**   36m   HVS,5a
Start right of the base of the buttress, below an obvious south-east facing corner. Climb the corner until a bulge forces a move leftwards onto a pinnacle. From this gain and climb the final overhung corner to the top.
J.Talbot, P.Hinder 00.00.1972

21. **Continuity Corner**   36m   HVS,5a
The vague groove system 10m right of South East Diedre
J.Talbot 00.00.1973

22. **Gstelli**   15m   S
The gully dividing Lewes Castle West and East.
J.Talbot 00.00.1971

Lewes Castle East
To the east and separated from Fall Bay Buttress by Gstelli, is another large buttress overlooking the Great Terrace.
It has a cave at half-height and an obvious wide crack up on the right. The first route takes the wall right of the gully.

23. **Gethsemane**   31m   S,4a   **
Start below the right wall of the gully at a short wall with an open groove above. Tiptoe rightwards across the
wall to gain a ledge at the foot of the groove, follow it to a large ledge and move out right onto a rib which is
followed to the top.
SWMC 00.00.1966

24. **Eden**   31m   VS,4c
Start down and right of Gethsemane at two grooves. Climb the left-hand groove to below a triangular overhang,
hand traverse left and finish up the rib above the overhang.
J.Talbot 00.00.1971

25. **The Bottle**   31m   VS,4b   *
Start below the cave. Climb a crack and easy groove to the cave, move out left onto a pedestal and follow the
steep crack above to the top. A harder, more direct start gains the steep crack directly via an obvious groove/
corner (HVS,5b).
J.Talbot, P.Hinder 00.00.1974

26. **Cave Cracks**   31m   E2,4b,5c
1. 12m As for The Bottle to the cave.
2. 18m Climb to the roof, then swing in from the left to gain poor jams. Finish steeply up the obvious cracks.
P.Littlejohn, A.Davies 18.03.1980

27. **Cave Cracks Direct**   31m   E3,5c   *
Gain the jams above the lip from directly below.
A.Sharp, D.Morris, P.Lewis 24.03.2002

28. **Age Before Beauty**   31m   E1,5a
This takes the wall right of The Bottle and left of South West Diedre. Start at a small cave 3m right of the start of
The Bottle. Climb flakes rightward and move left into a shallow groove. Follow this and a shallow chimney to
a ledge. Finish up the wide crack, avoiding easier ground to the left.
G.Evans, P.Christie 00.00.1988

29. **South West Diedre**   33m   HVS,5a   **
Start 5m right of The Bottle. Climb a corner and groove to a ledge, step back left and up to a small overhang at
three-quarters height. Go over this and finish up the steep crack above.
SUMC 00.00.1967

30. **South West Diedre Variant**   33m   VS,4c   *
From the ledge below the overhang of the parent route, follow the corner crack to the right instead.
J.Kerry, C.Ryan 00.00.1968

31. **Instigator**   33m   HVS,5a
Start at a vertical crack 3m right of South West Diedre. Climb the crack to a definite widening, bridge up and then
climb a groove by its right wall to the recess below the corner crack. Step onto the rib or, better, follow a diagonal
line across the upper smooth wall.
J.Kerry, M.Hogge 00.00.1969

Fall Bay To Mewslade

The old route South East Pillar (HVS,5a C.Bonnington, J.Cleare 1964) has fallen down.

32. **The Revolution's Here**   36m   E4,6a   *   \
Climb the grooved rib right of Instigator to join that route at 25m. Follow flakes up the headwall to the top.
M.Crocker, J.Harwood 24.04.1999

33. **Combination**   45m   VS,4b
Start just left of the front of the buttress. Climb a blocky groove to the upper wall, hand traverse the curving crack
below the upper wall leftwards and continue round the arete to a recess below a corner crack. Finish up this.
J.Talbot, P.Hinder 00.00.1973

34. **South East Arete**   36m   E3,5c   *   \
Take the slim narrow left-facing corner just right of Combination into the easier-angled corner and climb onto the
headwall. Pull up to the wide crack of Combination left of the arete to a horizontal break. Using finger pockets
move up and right onto the arete to a large Friend placement and a juggy finish.
M.Crocker, J.Harwood 24.04.1999

35. **Rhydd**   36m   HVS,4c
Start just right of the pillar right of Combination. Climb the corner crack in its entirety past a hole near the top.
E.Pardoe, R.Griffiths 00.00.1968, G.Evans, K.Moran ALCH 00.00.1985

36. **Rash Prediction**   36m   E2,5b
Takes a direct line up to the small open corner at two-thirds height, 3m right of Rhydd. Care is needed at the top
due to loose rock. Start below the corner and move up to a small bulge. Climb over this and up to the corner.
Continue above until survival demands moving rightwards near the top.
C.Ryan, P.Greenwood 00.00.1970

37. **Every One's A Coconut**   36m   E2,5b   \
Start 1m right of Rash Prediction, climb the face carefully to a vertical crack line. Follow the crack and flake
above a bulge, then pull up a slight corner to the good horizontal break. Fix gear then walk right to the terrace to
escape the terminal moraine above.
M.Crocker, J.Harwood 24.04.1999

38. **Twilight**   36m   E1,5a   ●
Start 3m to the right of Every One's A Coconut. Follow grooves and corners direct to the top.
J.Talbot, P.Hinder 00.00.1972

Right of Twilight the crag becomes very broken. However at the far right, the upper portion of the cliff becomes more
solid and provides a small buttress.

39. **Till Rock Doth Us Part**   12m   E4,5c   *   \
Start 1m right of the groove with a crack on its left wall that bounds the impending buttress on its left. Climb straight
up via various thin cracks, move left beneath a vague rib, finishing up a thin crack to good holds.
E.Kellar, A.Wilson 00.00.1990
M.Crocker – Direct 24.04.1999

40. **Gerontology**   58m   VS,4b,4b,4b
A right to left girdle. Start as for Combination.
1. 28m Follow Combination to the recess below the upper wall. Traverse left along the horizontal crack to belay
below the wide corner crack.
2. 15m Step down leftwards into a groove (South West Diedre) then traverse left to the cave of The Bottle.
3. 15m Move left to a pedestal, step down and continue traversing across two grooves to ledges on Gethsemane.
Finish up this.
A.Beaton, M.Danford, G.Richardson 31.08.1986

The Pan
Down to the right of Lewes Castle is a recessed area of conglomerate, set above a hole. This is The Pan.

1. **JT Where Is He?**   8m   HVS,5a
   The shallow groove above the left end of a rightward-rising flake above The Pan.
   M.Crocker solo 24.04.1999

2. **Down The Pan**   9m   VS,4c
   The flake going rightward over The Pan.
   M.Crocker solo 24.04.1999

3. **That Cistern Feeling**   10m   E3,6a
   Reachy. Use the two big blocks on the conglomerate on the right and swing left onto a flake overhanging The Pan. Pull straight up the leaning brown wall to jugs and a bridge over the zawn. Finish up the easier face above.
   M.Crocker solo 24.04.1999

The rock now slopes down towards Giant's Cave.

Giant's Cave
GR415873

TIDAL STATUS: 2½ hours either side of low water.

DESCENTS: Descent is to the left (west) at the top, passing down the path running down and east of Lewes Castle to the Great Terrace.

The enormous square-cut cave east of Lewes Castle and round the (east) corner from King Wall. It contains a high concentration of Gower's harder testpieces, along with some of its most spectacular. The first climbs start right of the conglomerate of The Pan. The first feature is a pile of blocks, the remains of Flake Route (J.Talbot 1963).

1. **Flake Corner**   9m   VD
   The first corner right of the remains of Flake Route.
   J.Talbot 00.00.1963

2. **Wall Climb**   9m   VD
   The wall right of Flake Corner.
   J.Talbot 00.00.1963

3. **Slight**   9m   HVS,4c
   Just to the right is a shallow corner with a hairline crack.
   J.Talbot, D.Lewis 00.00.1963

4. **Killing Time**   10m   E2,6a   \
   To the right of Slight is a vague hanging arete.
   A.Berry. G.Morris 00.00.1997

5. **Red Admiral**   13m   E3,6a   *
   The more defined arete to the right.
   A.Sharp, P.Lewis 00.00.1984

6. **Wierdo**   12m   E5,6a   \
   The cracks in the slight wall right of Red Admiral and left of Errant.
   C.Savage, B.Heason 00.00.2000

7. **Errant**   14m   E2,5c   *

A good technical pitch up the clean corner just right. Scramble off left at the top.
J.Talbot, B.Talbot aid 00.00.1965
FFA Unknown Pre-1978

8. **Super Rock**   30m   E6,6b   **   ⟍

The line of old bolt holes up the wall between Errant and Masterpiece. A good nut at three-fifths height and a crucial Super-rock 5 in one of the pockets high up are required.
J.Talbot etc - Peter Smart's Route Pre-1977
FFA A.Berry 00.09.1997

9. **Masterpiece**   31m   E6,6b   ***

A fierce route based on the left arete of the cave. Start at the base of the arete and either swing in from the left, or more logically climb thin cracks on its right side to gain a thin, pocketed crack on the arete itself. Move up and use some pockets on the left to gain flat holds higher on the arete, above which more hard moves lead to the horizontal break. Climb the groove and continue straight up to finish.
P.Littlejohn, M.Campbell 13.05.1984

10. **Napalm In The Morning**   31m   E7,6c   ***   ⟍

An impressive route. Start up Masterpiece, but then follow the hairline cracks in the wall to its right on crimps and tinies, to join the traverse of Thriller, up which the route finishes. A Friend ½ may prove useful.
A.Berry 00.02.1998

11. **Thriller**   31m   E4,6a   **

An excellent adventure up the left side of the cave. Start at the wide crack at the seaward end of the left wall of the cave that leads to the roof. Climb the crack to the cave roof, traverse strenuously left to gain a hanging groove and follow this to the top.
J.Talbot, B.Talbot - Twm-Schon-Catti 00.00.1966
FFA P.Littlejohn, C.Hurley 02.05.1984

12. **A Rush Of Blood To The Head**   31m   E6,6b   **

As for Thriller to the roof then launch out along the roof, move 1m right to a crack and hole and finish up a groove.
M.Richards, A.Sharp 00.00.2001

13. **Can't Buy A Thrill**   31m   E5,6b   **

A strenuous exposed pitch requiring good footwork. As for Thriller to the roof then launch out along the roof, TR, on buckets and jams, pull over the lip and finish rightwards.
A.Sharp, P.Lewis 00.00.1986

14. **The Divine Guiding Light**   36m   E6,6b   ***

Follow thin cracks 5m right of Thriller and an overhanging flake, PR, to the horizontal break TR. Follow this, then pull up the crack to the roof, cross it on superb jams, TR, to a chimney. Squirm across into the blowhole and follow the light.
M.Crocker, M.Ward 16.08.1987

15. **Lost Souls**   60m   A2

An aid route. Start up the offwidth 12m right of The Divine Guiding Light, then move left to gain the traverse of that route. Finish as for Divine Guiding light.
M.Heason, S.Hodges 00.10.1997

16. **The Sistine Ceiling**   35m   E6,6c   ***   ⟍

Up the wall to the right of The Divine Guiding Light to the traverse. Continue straight up to the roof and work leftwards to gain the blowhole. 5BRs, subsequently removed and not repeated without.
P.Oxley 00.00.1993

Martyn Richards - Can't Buy a Thrill (E5,6b) Giant's Cave
(Page 64) Photo: Carl Ryan

Adrian Berry - Chasing the Dragon (1st Asc) (E8,6c) Yellow Wall
(Page 71) Photo: Carl Ryan

17. **Jesus Wept**   36m E6,6b   *** \
Gain the back right-hand corner of the cave and a good rest on conglomerate. Pull out rightwards, TR, to gain a jam crack. Follow the crack to a handrail leading out right to the blowhole.
P.Oxley 00.00.1989

18. **Charlie Don't Surf**   18m E4,6a   *
Low in the grade. Start below the hanging corner on the right side of the cave below where the roof ends. A boulder problem start leads to a corner and a steep exit leftwards.
A.Sharp, O.Jones 00.00.1986

19. **Toejam Football**   18m E4,6b   * \
The roof to the right of Charlie Don't Surf.
A.Sharp, P.Lewis 28.03.2002

20. **Madame Butterfly**   18m E5,6b   *
Climb an awkward narrow crack that widens to a large fissure. Climb the overhanging wall direct to a block overhang. Climb this at its centre and take the steep wall above, old PRs.
J.Talbot, R.Corbett - Tablette 00.00.1962, FFA A.Sharp, P.Lewis 00.00.1984

21. **Giant's Cave Traverse**   50m A3
Follow Madame Butterfly to the cave roof. Traverse the underside of the lip and finish as for Errant.
E.Pardoe, M.Hogge, F.Roberts 00.00.1968

22. **Nick'd**   50m E2,5b   *
A good, airy climb traversing right to left across the lip of the Giant's Cave. Start on the obvious ledges above the corner on the right side of the cave lip (Charlie Don't Surf). Climb down to the lip where easy climbing leftwards leads to a blank-looking section. Cross this and step down to a large foothold, continue leftwards past the final groove of Thriller to belay at the top of Errant.
A Wilson, E.Kellar 00.00.1990

On the buttress to the right of the cave are a number of easier routes.

23. **Shannara**   15m HS,4a
Start below and right of the arete. Climb steeply left to reach a groove in the arete. Gain the top via the left edge.
P.Hornsby, S.Hornsby 00.00.1978

24. **Betst**   15m D
Start right of Shannara to the right of the centre of the pillar, but step left and climb the wall.
J.Talbot, D.Lewis 00.00.1963

25. **Sham**   12m D   *
Start as for Betst, but climb the groove to the right.
J.Talbot 00.00.1960

26. **Ease**   12m M
The corner fissure to the right of Sham.
J.Talbot 00.00.1960

The Mushroom
Immediately east of Giant's Cave is a large spike block.

1. **Flake**   12m HS
On the east side of the block is an obvious traverse line. Follow it to the end, pull up and finish up the -scoops.
J.Talbot, B.Talbot 00.00.1965

Devil's Truck Area
GR415873

TIDAL STATUS: West (left) buttress non-tidal. Other facets 2½ hours either side of low water.

DESCENTS: Descent is by walking down the platform westwards towards Giant's Cave.

This is the headland east of Giants Cave and consists of four distinct areas. The western part of the crag rises up above a non-tidal platfrom. Beyond the arete of this wall is the east face, which continues back beyond the normal line of cliffs to give High Chimney Gully. East again is South Cracked Pillar.

South West Face

1. **Lytel**   8m   S
   The leftmost groove on the wall, above a low shelf.
   J.Talbot 00.00.1963

2. **Legge**   9m   S,4a
   The wall to the right of Lytel, gained from The Nose.
   J.Talbot 00.00.1963

3. **The Nose**   15m   HS,4a   *
   Climb the longer shallow groove to the right.
   J.Talbot 00.00.1963

4. **Nervus**   15m   VS,4c
   Climb the narrow recessed wall just right of The Nose, over an overlap with a red mark below it. Move right to finish up Transit.
   J.Talbot 00.00.1963

5. **Transit**   15m   HS,4b
   Climb the narrow wall to the overhanging nose. Traverse right and attain the deep-cut central diedre. Climb this using the right wall.
   J.Talbot 00.00.1963

6. **Aschen**   15m   HVS,4c   *
   Start in line with the central groove below an overhang at half-height. Climb up to the overhang, move left into the groove and follow it to the top.
   J.Talbot 00.00.1963

7. **Gull Corner**   15m   VS,4b
   Gain and follow the crack in the upper part of the right side of the wall.
   J.Talbot 00.00.1963

8. **White Lime**   15m   D
   Start below the crack of Gull Corner. Climb rightward and up a slab, just left of the arete of the buttress. Bear left to finish up the crest. It can be combined with The Razor.
   J.Talbot 00.00.1963

9. **The Razor**   19m   D   ●
   The ridge above White Lime.
   SUMC 00.00.1968

East Face

10. **Strogelen**   15m   VS,4c
    This takes the obvious groove at the left side of the east face, 4m right of the bounding arete.
    J.Talbot, B.Talbot Pre-1973

11. **Count Down**   15m   HVS,5a
    Hard for the grade. Climb the short groove capped by an overhang, just right of Strogelen. Step right and finish directly above the overhang.
    R.Corbett, J.Talbot 00.00.1964

12. **Endeavour**   15m   HVS,4c   *
    Climb the deep chimney 4m right of Count Down.
    R.Corbett, J.Talbot 00.00.1962

High Chimney Gully
Right of Endeavour, at sea level, a narrow cleft leads to the back of High Chimney Gully.

1. **High Chimney**   31m   S
   Climb the narrow chimney in the back left-hand corner of the gully.
   G.Evans, A.Tyas 00.00.1983

2. **Old Nic**   21m   E4,6a   *
   Start 3m right of High Chimney. Climb cracks to an innocuous looking overlap, which can sometimes be overcome. Finish up the groove above.
   A.Sharp, P.Lewis, J.Harwood 29.12.1985

3. **Top Of The Form**   21m   E4,6a   *
   Start 4m right of Old Nic below an overhanging groove. Climb the groove, moving out left at the roof to continue up the groove.
   A.Sharp, P.Lewis, J.Harwood 29.12.1985

4. **Saratoga**   18m   E4,6b
   Stroll up thin cracks on the left side of the east wall of High Chimney Gully until all hope of progress finishes. Continue for 4m without any holds to the top.
   A.Sharp, P.Lewis 00.00.1985

5. **Tom Cat**   15m   E3,5c
   The slim groove 5m right of Saratoga.
   A.Sharp, P.Lewis 00.00.1985

6. **Ledges**   21m   M
   Climb the right side of the east wall of the gully, just before the bounding arete.
   J.Talbot, B.Talbot 00.00.1965

South Cracked Pillar
This is the pillar just to the right of High Chimney Gully, with some deep slanting grooves on its east (right) side.

1. **Left South Wall**   18m   VD
   The face left of the obvious chimney (Divider).
   J.Talbot, B.Talbot 00.00.1965

2. **Divider**   18m   M
   The obvious central chimney crack.
   J.Talbot, B.Talbot 00.00.1965

3. **Right South Wall** 18m S
The face to the right of Divider.
J.Talbot, B.Talbot 00.00.1965

4. **West Corner** 15m D
The wall to the right of Divider, gaining the big corner groove out to the right.
J.Talbot, B.Talbot 00.00.1965

5. **South East Diedre** 15m VS,4c
The obvious rightwards slanting corner groove right of West Corner.
J.Talbot, B.Talbot 00.00.1965

Hairy Dog Wall
GR415874

TIDAL STATUS: 2½ hours either side of low water

DESCENTS: Either finish up P2 of Hairy Dog (not pleasant) and descend as for Great Boulder Cover, or scramble down and left, or reverse Pollux.

Just right of South Cracked Pillar is an acutely overhanging wall with a cave at its right end. This is Hairy Dog Wall. An obvious rightward-slanting groove breaks this wall near its right side. The first route takes the deep crack on the left side of the wall. Taped hands are advisable on the harder routes.

1. **Castor** 18m VS,4c
Climb the wide crack to an overhang, passed via the crack on the right.
J.Talbot, B.Talbot 00.00.1965

2. **Pollux** 18m S,4a
The overhanging crack right of Castor.
J.Talbot, B.Talbot 00.00.1965

To the right are a series of very steep cracks, the most prominent of which is Hairy Dog, with a jammed block at 3m.

3. **King Of Pain** 15m E6,6b *
Start 5m left of the start of Hairy Dog below a pocket at 3m. Climb the wall past the pocket to good holds and move right to finish up a desperate crack.
A.Sharp, P.Lewis 00.00.1985

4. **Pump Up The Gower** 15m E5,6a **
Start up Hairy Dog, then swing left to climb the flake-line between Hairy Dog and King Of Pain.
M.Richards, J.Brown 00.00.1996

5. **Hairy Dog** 33m E5,6a,4a **
1. 12m Climb onto the block at 3m and continue up the left-slanting crack to large ledges. Now lick your wounds.
2. 21m Continue easily to the top.
A.Sharp, J.Harwood AL 07.10.1984

6. **King Swing** 18m E5,6b **
As for Hairy Dog to the block, but take the right-slanting crack and the wall above.
A.Sharp, P.Lewis 00.00.1985

7. **Hound Of Hell** 15m E5,6a **
Climb the steep crack in the centre of the wall right of King Swing.
A.Sharp, P.Lewis 00.00.1985

8. **Sense Of Doubt**   36m   E3,6a   *
Start below the slanting groove, at the foot of the overhanging wall, well right of Hound Of Hell. Gain the groove and follow it to its end. Finish up the loose wall on the left.
J.Talbot, R.Corbett - Great Cave Corner 00.00.1962
FFA A.Sharp 00.10.1978

9. **Without A Doubt**   35m   E5,6c
The groove 3m right of Sense of Doubt. A boulder problem start leads to good holds at 4m (these can be lassoed for protection). Follow these holds to a break, traverse left and finish up Sense Of Doubt.
A.Sharp, P.Lewis 00.08.1987

10. **Cerberus**   30m   E5,6b   \
At the back of the zawn is a prominent hanging groove. Start at the offwidth and follow this past a thin crack to a roof. Climb leftwards to the base of the corner, then hand traverse leftwards on undercuts to gain easy ground. A Friend 2 is useful for the belay.
D.Thomas 08.05.1989

Great Boulder Cove
GR416873

TIDAL STATUS: Yellow Wall and crags to west 3 hours either side of low water (left) to non-tidal (right). Conglomerate, Eyeball Wall non-tidal.

DESCENTS: Descent from Little Block is by scrambling down the groove to the right. For 5 Minutes to Kill to Muppet Show a hanging rope to escape is very useful. Descent from Yellow Wall itself is best done by abseil from stakes above Yellow Regeneration (an extra rope might be useful). Alternatively, abseil from threads down the grassy banking opposite Yellow Wall and above Eyeball Wall. It is also possible to scramble down the grassy banking and ledges on the south east, but this is not recommended.

BIRD BAN: There is a ban on the Yellow Wall itself from 1st March to 15th August. However, the authorities have promised that this situation will now be reviewed yearly in May and the ban shortened if nesting is completed earlier. Contact the National Trust (Tel: 01792 391470) or the BMC Access Rep for details of any early lift.

This is the very impressive boulder-filled cove to the right of Hairy Dog Wall. It contains Gower's showpiece, Yellow Wall. If steep, spectacular and adventurous routes are your game then this is the place for you. It is seamed with grooves and overhangs and contains some of Gower's finest routes, rivalling the best in Britain. Yellow Wall and Transformer are the two classic routes of their grade in the area and are bound to cause problems for those used to the grading system in Pembroke.

Little Block

1. **West Edge**   12m   HS,4a
Climb the left arete of the south (seaward) face.
J.Talbot, D.Lewis 00.00.1964

2. **Centre Crack**   12m   D
The left side of the seaward face.
J.Talbot 00.00.1964

3. **South Wall**   12m   D
The centre of the seaward face, above a spike.
J.Talbot 00.00.1964

4. **Red Corner**   10m   D
   The red diedre to the right.
   J.Talbot 00.00.1964

5. **Centre Corner**   10m   D   *
   The prominent groove in the centre of the east face.
   J.Talbot 00.00.1964

6. **Wall Climb**   10m   HD
   The groove right again.
   J.Talbot 00.00.1964

7. **Overhang Crack**   10m   D
   A vague loose groove to the right of the arete.
   J.Talbot 00.00.1964

Yellow Wall

This is the rather obvious wall dominating the cove. The first easily identifiable feature is the square corner of Skylark.

1. **5 Minutes To Kill**   24m   E3,6a
   A vague line up the grooves left of Winter Warmer. Climb up and leftwards to a good ledge, step right and climb
   the arete and wall to gain a sloping ramp. Climb the right wall past a large flake then follow poor rock to the top.
   A.Sharp, R.Powles 26.10.1987

2. **Winter Warmer**   24m   E3,6a
   Takes the shallow groove systems just left of the corner of Skylark. Boulder out the bulge just left of Skylark, via
   a crack, to a ledge. Climb right into a groove then back left to gain a left sloping ramp. Join Muppet Show to finish.
   M.Learoyd, R.Thomas 00.00.1985

Yellow Wall   Photo: Carl Ryan

3. **Skylark**   39m   E2,5c   *   🏃
Start below an overhang above which is a clean-cut corner. Climb to the overhang at 4m, move to its left end,
then over it rightwards. Traverse rightwards into a clean-cut corner, climb it to a ledge, step up into a short
groove, then climb the wall above to finish up a crack in the steep wall just left of the arete.
C.King, S.Monks 00.10.1978

4. **Enigma**   39m   E4,6b   **   🏃
As for Muppet Show to the horizontal break at 4m, then follow a line of undercuts up leftwards to an overhang.
Climb through the small overhang via a thin crack, then move right into Muppet Show. Continue straight up the
bulging groove above until it blanks out. Traverse left to the arete on sloping holds and follow it delicately to the
top. It is possible gain the thin crack directly for a more sustained outing.
J.Talbot, R.Corbett - Red Slab 00.00.1962
FFA P.Littlejohn, S.Lewis, C.Curle 28.11.1982
A.American, A.Richardson – Direct 00.00.1985

5. **Enigma Variation**   39m   E5,6b   *   🏃
The final bulging groove of Enigma is taken directly, PR. A belay at the base of the groove is advisable.
M.Crocker, M.Ward 15.08.1987

6. **Muppet Show**   39m   E1,5a   *   🏃
A fine route. Climb a groove below a small jutting prow under the lowest line of overhangs, to the horizontal break
at 4m. Climb leftwards to below the bulging groove, then traverse left to reach easy ground at the top of the corner
of Skylark. Either abseil off old PRs and a block on the left, or finish up Skylark.
A.Sharp 00.00.1976
P.Littlejohn, C.King - Direct Finish 00.00.1977

Secret Combination (P.Littlejohn, S.Lewis 1982) used to take the wall to the right, but has been swept away.

7. **Heroin**   49m   E5,6a,6b,5b   *   🏃
1. 24m Follow Enigma to a large ledge in the groove just left of the arete.
2. 12m Move right onto the wall, PR, swing onto the arete and climb the wall left of the arete, PR, then move back
onto the arete which leads to a ledge, PB.
3. 12m Climb straight up the arete above. Exit left to finish.
M.Crocker, M.Ward 31.08.1986

8. **Chasing The Dragon**   45m   E8,6c   **   🏃 ↘
1. 15m As for Yellow Wall P1 to gain a belay in the cave halfway up, TB.
2. 30m Move up and right as for Yellow Wall, but at the base of the groove move left to the base of the wall and
make a very long reach up for a jug, PR. Hard powerful moves up the wall, PR, gain the arete and finish of
Heroin. Currently reckoned to be the hardest tradionally protected route in the guidebook.
A.Berry 02.09.1999

9. **Yellow Wall**   45m   E3,5c,5c   ***   🏃
Start beneath the most prominent groove in the centre-left of the wall beneath a triangular overhang.
1. 33m Climb the first groove to the overhang, move left to a possible belay in a cave. Move diagonally
rightwards, PR, to the obvious corner. Climb stylishly or fight your way to a large ledge.
2. 12m Climb the leftward-leaning groove on the left side of the ledge. A bold start leads to slightly more secure
climbing and the top.
J.Talbot, R.Corbett 00.00.1962
FFA P.Littlejohn, A.Houghton 00.02.1972

10. **Hard Liner**   45m   E6,6b,5b   **   ♂

A tiring and technical start leads to a wild excursion up the arete between Yellow Wall and Steam Train. Start as for Steam Train.

1. 33m Follow the groove of Steam Train to the roof. Continue direct up the overhanging grey groove, PR, and reach the main rising break (junction with Steam Train). Pull into the groove of Steam Train, then swing left into a bottomless groove. Climb the groove, PR, to gain a break above in the arete. Ignore the rightward escape and make two long moves up the final arete to the Yellow Wall belay ledge.

2. 12m Climb the cracks and flakes towards the right-hand side of the back wall to the top.

M.Crocker 05.10.1991

11. **Steam Train**   45m   E4,6a,5b   **   ♂

This takes the narrow groove and crack right of Yellow Wall. Start at a large boulder 1m right of Yellow Wall.

1. 33m Step right from the boulder and follow a shallow groove with a red left wall to the overhangs. Traverse right 3m and step up to another groove. Move up deviously to reach a horizontal break and a ledge.

2. 12m From the right end of the ledge, traverse rightwards around the arete to gain a red slab which is traversed to a groove (Transformer). Move up the groove 1m, then traverse left to another short groove that leads to the top. A direct finish climbs from the ledge up the middle of the wall above at 6a.

M.Fowler, M.Morrison 1pt 21.04.1977, FFA A.Sharp, P.Lewis 00.00.1985

P.Littlejohn, L. Foulkes – Direct 00.10.1985

12. **Transformer**   48m   E3,6a,5c   ***   ♂

The route takes the prominent slanting grooves in the centre-right of the wall. Start 6m right of Yellow Wall beneath a block overhang at the base of a corner.

1. 27m Climb round the hideous lower roof (crux), then follow the corner and rightward-slanting groove. At 20m, the groove curves back left to a platform and belay.

2. 21m Step right into a groove and follow this to the obvious deep crack on the right wall. Muscle up this to the top. A variation finish traverses left into a stepped groove system.

E.Pardoe, M.Hogge - Lap Of The Gods 00.00.1969

P.Littlejohn, A.McFarlane 00.00.1973

C.King, S.Monks – Direct 00.10.1978

Photo: Carl Ryan

13. **Yellow Regeneration** 51m E6,6b,6b *** 🕊

A magnificent route up the overhanging wall and arete between Transformer and Holy Grail. Start 6m right of Transformer. Some of the in-situ gear needs replacing.

1. 27m Climb a narrow groove to roofs, pull out left, TR, to gain a diagonal ramp, PR, then cross the overhung wall left to jugs, TR. Stand up and follow the diagonal crack left to move up onto an angular block.

2. 24m Climb up right to a narrow footledge below the arete, PR. Climb the arete, TR, then a long reach leads to easier ground.

M.Crocker, R.Thomas, M.Ward 30.08.1986

14. **Man Of The Earth** 40m E6,6b,6b *** 🕊

A thuggish route of the highest quality. Start at a slim groove between Transformer and Yellow Regeneration.

1. 20m Climb the groove, PR, to a break, then cross the overhanging right wall, PR, into a shallow groove, TR, leading to good holds. Swing up leftwards, PR, through overhanging rock to gain overhung ledges, PR. Power through a bulge, TR, to reach a break, TR. Climb past another break to a PB.

2. 20m Climb a shallow groove above, old BR, then swing left and climb a thin crack in the headwall, PR, TR, to good jugs. Finish awkwardly.

G.Gibson, R.Thomas 15.10.1989

15. **Skyhedral Wall** 45m E6,6b *** 🕊 ¹

A long pitch, albeit with three good shakeouts. Medium Friends and large wires are useful. Start at a small cave 3m right of Yellow Regeneration. Climb overhanging layback cracks, TR, PR, and swarm over a capping bulge on the left to reach a handrail leading rightward to a good rest. Climb diagonally left, PR, to a niche with plentiful jugs. Take a slim groove on the right to another niche, TR. Power over the bulge above, 2PRs and continue up a thin left-facing groove to a horizontal break. Hand-traverse left and from a thin short crack, crank over a bulge, PR, to a juggy rising break. Rockover into a shallow niche, reach a good break and bear left to finish at a small left-facing groove. Since the first ascent, the pitch has sometimes split by taking a stance out right, reducing the grade to E5.

M.Crocker 06.10.1991

16. **Holy Grail** 45m E2,5b ** 🕊

Not for those whose mothers smell of elderberries. More solid than it looks. This takes the broken corner formed where Yellow Wall meets the shattered face at the back of the cove, to reach the prominent acute corner high up on Yellow Wall. Start at a jutting block below an overhang at 21m. Climb deviously leftward to gain a small ledge. Move left to the corner and up to the overhang. Move left to gain the superb final corner and the top.

P.Littlejohn, J.Harwood 03.10.1980

17. **Gafaelwy** 45m E2,5b,5c * 🕊

Start right of Holy Grail, below a jutting block.

1. 27m Gain the jutting block, then up and left to the corner crack and overhang on Holy Grail. Go over this, then right to a stance below a wide chimney crack.

2. 21m Step left and climb a thin crack via overhangs to the top.

E.Pardoe, R.Griffiths - 00.11.1966

FFA S.Lewis, P.Littlejohn 00.00.1980

18. **Pilgrim** 42m E1,5b,5b ● 🕊

1. 27m As for Gafaelwy.

2. 15m Climb the obvious wide crack that trends right to the top.

E.Pardoe, L.Costello 00.00.1966

19. **Germany Calling** 50m E3,5c,5b,5a * 🕊

The obvious right to left break at one-third height. Start as for Man Of The Earth.

1. 20m Traverse to a belay on Yellow Wall.

2. 18m Traverse to Muppet Show.

3. 12m Finish up Muppet Show.

A.Sharp, P.Lewis 00.00.1985

20. **Transverse**   30m   E2,6a,5a

The traverse line below Germany Calling.

1. 21m Start as for Transformer. Climb to the first break and move left to gain the traverse line which is followed to Skylark. Belay.

2. 9m Finish up Skylark or continue traversing past Winter Warmer and down left to a ledge. Climb a thin crack to a sloping stance and the top.

G.Williams, J.Baylis, P.Kokelaar – Girdle 00.00.1969

FFA S.Lewis, G.Lewis 00.00.1985

Conglomerate Cliff

Opposite Yellow Wall and to the left of Eyeball Wall is a black slab. This must be one of the few cliffs in Britain to be threatened by a conglomerate cornice!

1. **Don't Look Up**   22m   E2,5c

Start just right of an earthy crack on the left side of the slab. Climb to a narrow ledge, move up a steep section, PR, and continue to an abseil point, PB, TB.

R.Thomas, J.Bullock 00.00.1990

2. **A Shadow Hanging Over Me**   22m   E1,5b

Start at the right-hand earthy crack. Climb up the crack then step out left onto the slab. Go up a short steep crack until moves over calcite encrustations, 2PR, lead to the steep upper section. Abseil off.

R.Thomas, J.Bullock 00.00.1990

Eyeball Wall

The smooth crack-seamed wall opposite Yellow Wall and right of Conglomerate Cliff provides a number of shorter routes. An abseil rope is recommended to avoid the epic scramble up from the finish of the rock.

1. **Contact 10.10**   12m   E4,6a

Climb the black scoop and thin crack on the left side of the face. Exit right from the crack to a shallow groove.

M.Crocker, M.Ward, R.Thomas 30.08.1986

2. **Fovea 40**   12m   E3,6a

Start down and right of Contact 10.10 under a scoop containing some conglomerate holds. Make tricky moves out of the scoop (in situ hex) and pull up on crozzles to a flat hold. Finish direct.

R.Thomas, M.Ward, M.Crocker 31.08.1986

3. **Eyeline**   12m   E3,5c

Climb the scoop and crack between Fovea 40 and Specky Four Eyes, with a prominent TR at 8m.

R.Thomas, M.Ward, M.Crocker 30.08.1986

4. **Specky Four Eyes**   12m   E2,5c

Start at the foot of a diagonal fault that runs rightward towards the headland. Climb a scoop moving right to a jug, then move up right and back left to a crack leading to a belay.

M.Crocker, M.Ward, R.Thomas 30.08.1986

5. **Eyeball to Eyeball**   12m   E2,5c

Start at the right side of the face. Climb to the left side of the diagonal fault line, poor TR. Move up to stand on another fault. Go over the bulge to a vertical slot, then up to a break above and a short wall to easier ground.

M.Ward, M.Crocker, R.Thomas 30.08.1986

Jacky's Tor
GR417872

TIDAL STATUS: Routes left (west) of V-Groove and right of Plot 13, 1½ hours either side of low water. Routes on the front of the buttress ¾ hour either side of low water. Routes in the cave of Shock And Awe are non-tidal.

DESCENTS: For Agamemnon and routes to the left (west) either scramble down the west side of the tor with extreme caution, or use the abseil descent above Eyeball Wall. For routes to the right, either abseil off the shaky spike above Plot 13, or walk off right (east) and descend down ridges to Cathedral Wall. Routes between Pluto and Slab And Wall have problematic descents – see the text.

Jacky's Tor is the prominent headland to the right (east) of Great Boulder Cove. It provides a number of good quality climbs. There is a deep cave left of the large front buttress and a lower subsidiary buttress left of the cave.

Subsidiary Buttress

There is a large sloping platform at the foot of the buttress. 2m above this and running along the left side of the buttress is a ledge. Rateau De Chevre starts below the left end of this – the old boulder problem of Lambert (J.Talbot 1969) takes the wall left again.

1. **Rateau De Chevre**   12m   M
    Climb to the left-hand end of the terrace, move up left and finish up a short corner.
    J.Talbot 00.00.1963

2. **Angel Flake**   12m   M
    The vague rib to the right of Rateau De Chevre.
    J.Talbot 00.00.1969

3. **Slanting Corner**   15m   D
    The first prominent diagonal groove to the right of Angel Flake.
    J.Talbot 00.00.1963

4. **Left Ramp**   15m   D
    To the right is the prominent red groove of Red Corner. Start up this, but step left and take the left-trending ramp above.
    J.Talbot 00.00.1963

5. **Red Corner**   21m   VD
    The prominent red groove. Gain the ledge and climb a groove above to a recess. Surmount the overhang and follow the slabby groove above to the top.
    J.Talbot, D.Lewis 00.00.1963

6. **Wall And Crest**   24m   VD
    Climb a very faint groove 2m right of Red Corner to gain and finish up Kinder.
    J.Talbot 00.00.1963

7. **Kinder**   24m   S
    Climb the centre of the front of the pillar to a large recess below the groove in the upper half of the buttress. Take the corner to the top.
    J.Talbot 00.00.1963

Kindergarten (J.Talbot 1970) is a rather pointless link-up of Kinder and Red Corner at half-height.

---

8. **Guardian** 24m S *

Start below the groove in the upper half of the buttress. Climb it to the large recess and traverse right to the arete. Follow this to the top.
J.Talbot, D.Lewis 00.00.1963

Cave Area

To the right is a gully containing a cave. An old route on the left wall is largely superseded by others (Wall and Crest, J.Talbot 1963). The following route can be used to access the floor of the cave.

9. **Cave Corner** 30m D

Scramble up from beach level to the cave then climb the easy left wall to finish up a groove.
Unknown Pre-1981

10. **Chantilly Lace** 21m HVS,5b **

A cracker, taking the steep corner left of the cave with good protection and good rock.
A.Sharp, J.Harwood 23.10.1982

11. **Shock And Awe** 21m E6,6c *** \\

Spectacular climbing up the central cave system to the right of Chantilly Lace, 3TRs.
M.Richards, A.Sharp, M.Jones, P.Lewis 27.03.2003

12. **Possessed** 22m E4,6a *

A sustained pitch, with plentiful but indifferent protection. Start right of the cave. Climb a flake crack to a small ledge, step left to gain a thin crack, PR, and climb this, PR, to easier ground.
J.Talbot, P.Perkins - Cave Overhang 00.00.1964
FFA A.Sharp, J.Harwood, D.Hillier 30.10.1982

13. **Repossessed** 22m E4,6a *

From the step left of Possessed continue up the groove between this and the Damned. Finish up Cave Traverse.
M.Richards, A.Sharp, M.Jones 27.03.2003

14. **The Damned** 22m E2,6a

A good, varied route. As for Possessed to the small ledge, move right and climb the crack to a small roof. Battle up the corner crack above and finish along the traverse line of Cave Traverse.
A.Sharp, D.Hillier 00.00.1982

15. **Cave Traverse** 39m HS,4a *

An exposed route. Climb into the cave and traverse rightwards to the first corner crack. Follow this to a recess, level with the top of the wall above the cave. Traverse left to ledges, 2PR.
R.Owen, C.Andrews, C.Edwards 00.00.1960

The following routes are on the wall to the right. The finishes are obviously lethal, so it is assumed that climbers will either abseil off, leaving some gear, or descend down and to the right. The descriptions are therefore terminated at the end of the solid rock.

16. **Pluto** 16m VS,4b

At sea level and below the cave of the tor, is a vague rib on the right wall, left of a narrow slab. Start up this, but swing left onto a knob at 5m and finish up grooves above to the ledge.
J.Talbot, R.Corbett 00.00.1961

17. **Narrow Slab** 15m VD

The narrow slab itself.
J.Talbot, R.Corbett 00.00.1961

18. **Seaward**   18m   D
The obvious corner 5m to the right of Narrow Slab, gaining a ledge off to the right.
J.Talbot, R.Corbett 00.00.1962

19. **Slab And Wall**   17m   VD
The wall right of Seaward.
J.Talbot, R.Corbett 00.00.1961

The routes Perambulatory Proliferation (M.O'Leary, C.Plantrose, P.Pilsbury 1971), Nestor (E.Pardoe, R.Griffiths 1969) and Menelaus (E.Pardoe, C.Knights 1969) have largely fallen down.

20. **Agamemnon**   27m   VS,4c   ●
Follow the steep broken groove just left of the front of the buttress taking care with the rock, to a traverse line leading rightwards at 25m. Belay. Either finish direct or traverse right to reach easier ground.
E.Pardoe, L.Costello 00.00.1969

Front Face
The following routes are on the superb rock of the front seaward face of the Tor. For V-Groove and Plot 13, keep a very close eye on the tide.

21. **V Groove**   27m   E3,5c   **
One of Gower's earliest classic hard routes. Delicate and technical at first, then more exposed and strenuous. Start below the rib left of the overhanging corner in the front of the buttress, climb it and the thin crack to gain the v-groove. Exit leftward from the notch and climb a shallow groove above to a ledge. Either traverse off rightwards or abseil from a shaky block.
E.Pardoe, D.Ellis 00.00.1966

22. **Plot 13**   27m   E4,6a   ***
A good addition, which is just shy of E5. Start at the overhanging chimney just right of V Groove. Bridge up the constricted chimney until it is possible to step down right below a sharp fin of rock. Climb the thin crack on its left side to the overhang. A hard move leads to a hidden hold above the overhang. Step right to the arete, PR, then move leftwards onto the face and make hard moves up and left. Continue up the face to the walk-off ledge.
R.Thomas, J.Bullock, L.Moran 31.05.1987

East Wall
Right (east) of the front face of Jacky's Tor is a bulging wall with a thin crack on its left side and a shallow groove at its right.

23. **Promise Of A Miracle**   25m   E5,6a
Start 5m right of Plot 13. Thin cracks lead to a large roof, which is passed on the right to reach an open corner. Move left into a shallow groove to finish.
M.Crocker, R.Thomas 24.10.1993

24. **Crank The Hummer**   24m   E3,6a   *
Take the thin crack right of Promise Of A Miracle. Climb to the start of the crack, PR, move over a small overhang and follow the crack to the top. The name is not a misprint.
A.Sharp, J.Harwood, P.Lewis 14.04.1984

25. **Stuntmaster**   18m   E5,6a
Start 3m right of Crank The Hummer. Climb just left of an arete, to enter a groove in the arete. Move left at the top.
M.Crocker, R.Thomas 24.10.1993

26. **Cut Across Shorty**   19m   E3,6a   *
The groove left of Red Diedre. Gain it by climbing the arete. The PR is on its last legs. The name is correct.
A.Sharp, J.Harwood 12.03.1983

27. **Red Diedre**   18m   HVS,5a   *
A steep corner skirts the overhanging area to the right of Cut Across Shorty. Climb easy rocks to gain the corner and climb it directly.
J.Talbot, D.Lewis 00.00.1963

28. **Mittel**   18m   VD
As for Red Diedre, but move right to finish up the arete.
J.Talbot, D.Lewis 00.00.1963

29. **Awry**   15m   S
The wall right of Mittel.
J.Talbot, R.Corbett 00.00.1962

Cathedral Wall Area
GR418872

TIDAL STATUS: 1½ hours either side of low water.

DESCENTS: Via ridges either side of the Cathedral Wall gully.

To the right (east) of Jacky's Tor are a number of prows and gullies. The most important of these is Cathedral Wall, the incut to the immediate east of the tor. To the right is the blunt ridge of The Pulpit with another gully just right. Right (east) again are the small promontory of The Prows and the area terminates at the obvious long low promontory of The Aisle which runs out to sea.

Cathedral Wall

1. **Prima**   15m   S
The corner at the left end of the steep left wall.
J.Talbot, R.Corbett 00.00.1961

2. **Hades**   15m   HS,4b
The crack 1m right of Prima.
J.Talbot, R.Corbett 00.00.1962

3. **Kalk**   18m   S
Start up the prominent crack in the wall 3m right of Prima, but move left as soon as possible and climb the centre of the wall.
J.Talbot 00.00.1962

4. **Owch**   15m   HS,4a
As for Kalk, but continue directly up the crack.
J.Talbot, R.Corbett 00.00.1961

5. **Dulfer**   18m   S,4a   *
The bulging groove and crack 3m right of Owch. Climb a steep wall on jugs to the groove, surmount a bulge, step left to a recess and follow the crack to the top.
J.Talbot, R.Corbett 00.00.1962

6. **Dolce Vita**   18m   HVS,4c
As for Dulfer to the bulge, then follow a steep and shallow groove up right. Climb the wall passing some spikes and finish slightly left.
R.Corbett, J.Talbot 00.00.1962

7. **Cyntaff**   18m   HVS,5a   **
A certain amount of determination is needed to climb the fine corner right of Dolce Vita.
P.Dyer, R.Corbett 00.00.1962

8. **Faint White Hope**   18m   E3,6a   *
The boldness of this route will depend on the level of the sand. Start at a short groove in the right wall of Cyntaff. Climb it to an overhang, make bold moves leftward and finish steeply up the wall above.
A.Sharp, J.Harwood 21.12.1980

At the back of the gully are two obvious grooves at a higher level, reached by easy scrambling.

9. **Adam**   12m   S,4a
The left-hand groove.
J.Talbot, R.Corbett 00.00.1962

10. **Kaos**   12m   VS,4c
From the foot of Eve, move out left and climb the central rib direct.
R.Corbett, J.Talbot 00.00.1962

11. **Eve**   12m   S,4a
The right-hand groove.
R.Corbett, J.Talbot 00.00.1962

12. **Eva**   12m   VS,4c
The crack in the wall right of Eve.
J.Talbot, R.Corbett 00.00.1962

Notre Dame (J.Talbot 1963), The End (J.Talbot 1963), Mitre (J.Talbot 1963), Five Cracks (R.Corbett, P.Dyer 1961), Left Crack (J.Talbot 1963), Left Corner (J.Talbot 1963) and Steps (J.Talbot 1963) cover much of the same ground as routes already described.

The Pulpit

Right (east) of Cathedral Gully is a protruding buttress, split left of centre by an easy descent chimney. Some 10m to the right is a more prominent chimney (Pulpit Fissure). There are two very easy scrambles, Magog (J.Talbot 1963) and Chink (J.Talbot 1963) which take indistinct lines up the south face of the buttress, but the only independent route is Gog.

1. **Gog**   12m   M
The seaward face of the buttress.
J.Talbot 00.00.1963

2. **Cleft**   12m   M
The cleft and groove right of the south face of the buttress.
J.Talbot 00.00.1963

3. **Indefinite**   10m   D
The left side-wall of the prominent chimney of Pulpit Fissure.
J.Talbot 00.00.1963

4. **Pulpit Fissure**   10m   D
The obvious chimney.
R.Corbett, J.Talbot 00.00.1962

5. **Schusselkar**   15m   VS,4c
Start up Pulpit Fissure, but move right as soon as possible to gain and finish up the wall to the right.
J.Talbot, R.Corbett 00.00.1962

To the right is another recessed inlet.

6. Yus Yus   15m   E2,5b   *   ↖
The arete left of smooth.
N.Taylor 02.08.1997

7. **Smoove**   15m   VS,4c
This climbs the smooth overhanging groove in the seaward end of the left wall of the recess. Climb the groove and pull out right on good holds to a ledge below another groove capped by an overhang. Take this and exit left.
R.Corbett, J.Talbot 00.00.1962

8. **Gold Kappel**   18m   VS,4c
As for Smoove, then move right over a smooth bulge to a ledge. Climb the right edge of the groove to the top.
J.Talbot, R.Corbett 00.00.1962

9. **Canalog**   15m   VS,4c
Climb the steep wall left of the prominent black hole right of Smoove.
R.Corbett, P.Perkins 00.00.1962

10. **The Beak**   18m   VD
Gain the black hole and traverse leftwards on tachyons to a ledge below the upper groove of Smoove, now climb the steep wall on the left.
J.Talbot, D.Jones 00.00.1961

11. **Checkmate**   13m   VS,4b
As for The Beak to the hole, then climb the corner above.
J.Talbot 00.00.1963

12. **Font**   13m   VS,4b
As for Checkmate to the upper corner, then move right and climb the narrow pillar.
J.Talbot 00.00.1963

There are two old routes Headstone (J.Talbot 1963) and Chalice (J.Talbot 1963) which cover similar ground to the routes described above.

The Prows

These are the rocky fins to the right (east) of The Pulpit.

1. **Back Chimney**   12m   M
The chimney separating the left-hand prow from the Pulpit.
J.Talbot, R.Corbett 00.00.1962

2. **South West Corner**   12m   S
Climbs the right side of the right wall of Back Chimney.
J.Talbot, R.Corbett 00.00.1962

3. **Flying Buttress**   16m M
Climbs the front (seaward) face of the left prow. A route that spawned at least two less famous imitations.
J.Talbot 00.00.1964

4. **Right Edge**   12m M
The wall to the right of Flying Buttress.
J.Talbot 00.00.1962

5. **Divide**   12m M
The chimney separating the two prows.
J.Talbot 00.00.1962

6. **Cheat**   13m VD
Start up Divide, but move out and climb the wall to the right.
J.Talbot 00.00.1962

7. **Central Crack**   12m S
The front of the right-hand prow.
J.Talbot 00.00.1962

8. **Right Curving Crack**   8m M
The crack to the right of Central Crack.
J.Talbot 00.00.1962

9. The Old Man   6m HS,4c
A few metres to the right is a finlike feature. Climb its seaward face.
J.Talbot 00.00.1962

The Aisle

This is the obvious low promontory running out to sea between the Cathedral Walls and Gullys areas. It is detached from the mainland and it is possible to pass behind it by a narrow gully. Descent is by scrambling down either side.

1. **North Edge**   12m VS,4c
The arete on the north (landward) end of the Aisle.
J.Talbot 00.00.1963

2. **Black Corner**   12m D
The groove 5m right of North Edge.
J.Talbot 00.00.1963

3. **Twin Corner Left**   12m D
The left-hand of two grooves, 5m to the right of Black Corner.
J.Talbot 00.00.1963

4. **Twin Corner Right**   12m VD
The right-hand groove.
J.Talbot 00.00.1963

Behind The Aisle is a hole. Go through this to reach the next routes. They can also be accessed by abseil.

5. **Sump It Up**   12m E1,5c
On the left (west) wall is a grey left-facing hanging corner. Gain it via easy flakes below and make a delicate move up into it to exit.
M.Crocker 05.12.1998

6. **Boom Boom Boris** 15m E4,6b

A hard and bold pitch. On the right wall, start 3m left of Treasure. Climb the wall on pockets to an overhang. Move out left and finish, crux.
A.Sharp, O.Jones 00.00.1986

7. **Treasure** 15m E3,5c *

The obvious thin crack in the east wall of the hole.
A.Sharp, J.Harwood 14.04.1984

8. **Zoom, Zoom, Doris** 12m E4,6a \

The wall right of Treasure. Pull right into a short right facing corner 3m right of Treasure. Move up over the roof and finish up the wall above.
M.Crocker 05.12.1998

Molar Wall and White Edge
GR419872

TIDAL STATUS: White Edge is non-tidal. Molar Wall 2½ hours either side of low water.

DESCENTS: Scramble down gullies (well) to the west or east.

This is the uninispiring area of rock 100m east of the Cathedral Wall Area. White Edge is the obvious white ridge set up above the sea and Molar Wall is the long, low, lower wall sticking out of the fishing boat bobbing sea. Which is not black. Unless there has been a serious accident in Swansea.

Molar Wall West
The small but clean west-facing facet.

Rampe (J.Talbot, B.Talbot 1966) and South West Corner (J.Talbot, B.Talbot 1966) could not be located for the guidebook.

1. **Don't Blow It** 10m E2,6a \

At the landward end of the inlet facing the Bochlwyd facet is a cave. Start from the non-tidal platform, immediately right of the cave. Boulder up to the obvious projecting flat hold. Proceed direct on pockets and then jugs to broken ground. Walk off right.
M.Crocker solo 05.12.1998

2. **Bochlwyd** 12m HVS,5a

Take the thin, narrow, leftward-trending crack on the left facet of the west-facing face.
J.Talbot 00.00.1964

3. **He Man** 12m E2,5c

Climb the crack-seamed wall via a straight line directly up the middle of the centre.
A.Richardson, S.Lewis 00.00.1987

4. **Muscle Man** 12m VS,4c

Climb the slab 3m right of He Man, then up the leaning overhanging wall and overlap via a long, tall reach.
A.Richardson, S.Lewis 00.00.1987

5. **Christa** 13m HS,4b

Start right at the right side of the wall where rocks project outwards protruding into the sandy sand. Climb left of a corner to below an overhang, cross it rightwards or, much harder, leftwards (5b).
J.Talbot, B.Talbot 00.00.0000

South Face

6. **Straight Crack**   9m   VD
Where the wall projects out south west, is a narrow recessed wall with a wide, deep, thin, narrow crack.
J.Talbot 00.00.1963

On the south face are two easy scrambling routes, Right and Left Buttress (J.Talbot, 1963).

7. **Recessed Wall**   15m   VD
The wall right of Straight Crack.
J.Talbot 00.00.1963

8. **Sharp Corner**   12m   D
The corner right again.
J.Talbot 00.00.1963

In the centre of the South facet is a recess with a cave at the back and a square-cut chimney groove to its right.

9. **Blocky Corner**   12m   VD
This takes left-corner of the Curving Corner feature.
J.Talbot 00.00.1963

10. **Curving Corner**   12m   HVS,5a
Fun. Climb the steep, smooth corner left of the cave until it is possible to gain the arete on the right.
D.Baines 00.00.1963

11. **Cavity Edge**   15m   D
The chimney to the right of Curving Corner.
J.Talbot 00.00.1963

12. **Cavity Crack**   15m   S
Tthe square-cut groove right of the cave, or move left at 7m up the left edge (Narrow Rib S, J.Talbot 1963)
J.Talbot 00.00.1963

13. **Deception Crack**   6m   S
Start at an easy recessed slab and climb a vertical narrow crack.
J.Talbot 00.00.1963

14. **Two Step Wall**   13m   HS,4b
Start on the right side of the wall and strenuously climb an overhang to a ledge. Climb the second overhanging section by a committing move right to a slippery ledge, then leftwards to the top.
J.Talbot 00.00.1963

Molar Wall East
The wall to the east.

15. **Thrutch**   7m   HS,4b
Based on a definite concavity 4m before Hairline. Climb to the overhang direct and then up to the upper ledges.
J.Talbot 00.00.1963

16. **Hairline**   7m   S
Follow the smooth wall to where a cleft is formed by a pinnacle. Climb a shallow blind Captain Cat on the left wall just before entering the cleft.
J.Talbot 00.00.1962

17. **First Corner** 7m S

The first corner in the upper wall left from Thrutch. Gain it by the smooth wall below.
J.Talbot 00.00.1963

18. **Second Corner** 9m S

The corner just left of First Corner.
J.Talbot 00.00.1963

19. **Twist** 12m HS,4a

Climb Second Corner to the bulge, then traverse left to reach another corner. Follow this to the top.
J.Talbot 00.00.1963

20. **Third Corner** 9m S

Climb 4m left of Second Corner, bearing left at the top.
J.Talbot 00.00.1963

White Edge

The obvious pillar of White Edge is above Molar Wall. The first two routes have not been checked and only the original descriptions are given.

1. **Herring Gull** 50m HS

This takes the first distinct diedre on the west side of White Edge, approaching from the cliff top. Start on easy broken rock, then go up the smooth steep wall just right of the corner. Move back left to the corner after a difficult move exit right to a small shallow recess. Move left to the natural continuation of the corner and finish by an awkward move.
J.Talbot 00.00.1970

2. **Yearling** 50m HS

Start as for Herring Gull, but climb the rounded wall direct to the recess, avoiding the lower corner. Now move up to the right and exit up the steep broken wall.
J.Talbot 00.00.1970

3. **Ha-He Verschneidung** 27m VS,4c

Takes the central groove in the upper half of the west flank of White Edge. Move right at the top.
J.Talbot 00.00.1970

4. **White Edge** 36m VD *

A good route, marred by some loose rock. It takes the knife-edged pillar with short excursions right or left. Bear left at the top.
J.Talbot, D.Lewis 00.00.1964

On the east flank are the following routes:

5. **Stretching Sargeant Ryan** 27m E4,6b *

Takes the narrow white pillar face right of the upper section of the arete. Start 8m left of White Elephant beneath a 4m groove. Climb to a ledge below the pillar face. Follow jugs up the centre of the face to a hand ledge. Pull up to a slanting line of shallow pockets. Make a hard move up to a superb flake, pull up, swing left, then climb directly up the pillar face.
M.Crocker, C.Ryan 27.11.1998

6. **White Whale** 21m E1,5b

Start 6m left of White Elephant. Start below three black streaks high on the buttress. Climb straight up via two ledges to reach a steep crack leading to the top.
J.Bullock, L.Moran 31.05.1987

7. **White Elephant** 21m E1,5b

At the extreme right side of the east flank is a prominent corner, bounded on the left by a clean wall. Start at the centre of the wall. Climb straight up past an old PR to a ledge, step right and climb the groove.
L.Moran, J.Bullock 31.05.1987

8. **Pigeon Crack** 21m VS,4c

The prominent corner on the right side of the east flank.
J.Talbot 00.00.1970

Block Buttress

GR419872

TIDAL STATUS: 2 hours either side of low water.

DESCENTS: Descend by scrambling down to the east.

The return of decent rock, routes and descriptions. This is the impressive, conspicuous buttress at the seaward end of the headland to the east of White Edge. Below and left of the highest point is a deep gully.

1. **South West Edge** 60m M

The easy rib and scramble on the left of the gully on the south side of the buttress.
J.Talbot, R.Corbett 00.00.1962

2. **Piz** 12m HS,4b

Climb the groove at the seaward end of the left (west) wall of the gully.
J.Talbot, R.Corbett 00.00.1962

3. **Kleine** 12m VS,4c

A poorly protected line up the wall right of Piz and left of Thing.
J.Talbot, R.Corbett 00.00.1962

4. **Thing** 21m HVS,5a

Follow the waterworn groove 7m right of Piz and just left of the seaweed covered rock. Take the easier corner above to finish.
J.Talbot 00.00.1964

5. Funny Fish In A Hole 21m E1,5c •

The steep crackline right of Thing.
N.Taylor 02.08.1997

6. **Cima** 36m E1,5b ∖

A large rockfall has removed the original upper part of this route. There used to be a massive overhang in place at the top! Start at the foot of the left of two cracks at the back of the gully. Climb the crack via a bulge to a recess (belay possible), step right and climb a rib to gain a corner. The old route used to finish direct, but it has only been done since the rockfall by finishing out left as for Thing.
J.Talbot, R.Corbett 00.00.1962

7. **Kaiser** 39m HVS,5a,4a **

1. 15m As for Cima to the recess.
2. 24m Step right onto a rib, then into the corner on the right. Follow this until it is possible to gain a traverse line on the right wall. Follow it to finish up the arete.
R.Corbett, D.Jones 00.00.1962

8. **The Limping Limpet**   31m   E5,6a   ⟍

A bold undertaking between Kaiser and Power Trap. From the niche of Power Trap, reach over the bulge to a good hold in the base of a faint runnel. Pull up and climb directly to the traverse of Kaiser. Finish up Power Trap.
M.Crocker, M.Ward 01.07.1987

9. **Power Trap**   36m   E3,5c   ***

Fierce, exposed climbing. A determined approach will work wonders at the start. Start at a steep crack system in the right wall of the gully. Climb the crack past a niche, then take a diagonal line leftwards, avoiding the arete, to finish just left of the arete.
E.Pardoe, R.Griffiths 2pt 00.00.1966
FFA P.Littlejohn, S.Jones 00.00.1970

10. **South Pillar Rib**   36m   HS,4a   **

This takes the narrow righthand pillar of the gully. Variations are possible. Climb the left-hand groove and gain the pillar front. Continue up the pillar until it narrows to an arete. Finish rightwards taking care with the rock.
J.Talbot, R.Corbett 00.00.1962

To the right of these routes is a cave at half-height.

11. **Burn The Boss**   24m   HVS,5a

Start in the cave. Move up the left rib of the cave and enter a crack. Follow it to the top as for South Buttress.
A.Sharp, J.Harwood 13.02.1983

12. **South Buttress**   50m   S

A poor route. Take a line right of a cave at half-height to a narrow rib, then trend leftwards to reach the centre of the wall above the cave. Finish direct.
SUMC 00.00.1969

13. **Deep Crack**   50m   HS

Climb the deep crack right of South Buttress to join it.
J.Talbot 00.00.1963

14. **Big Step**   50m   D

The fissure to the right of Deep Crack.
J.Talbot 00.00.1963

On the upper east face of Block Buttress, overlooking Trident Gully, is a pair of cracks near the seaward edge.

15. **Picket Line**   18m   E1,5b

Climb to the cracks and follow them to the top. This route is best gained via The Cloth Eared Brown Mullet.
G.Evans, J.Bullock 00.00.1984

Trident Gully and Ridge
GR419872

TIDAL STATUS: 1½ hours either side of low water.

DESCENTS: Scramble down easy ridges to the east.

This is is the deep inlet immediately east (right) of Block Buttress. Trident Ridge is just east again.

1. **Long Rib**   27m   M

The rib seperating Block Buttress and Trident Gully. A second pitch is available (Continuation VD R.Corbett, D.Thomas 1961).
J.Talbot 00.00.1961

Inside the gully are some good routes. Jsut before the guidebook went to press, however, the sand level had altered radically and unless it rises again, then the first two routes are probably several grades harder.

2. **The Cloth Eared Brown Mullet**	12m	E2,5c	*
Boldly gain the steep cracks on the left side of the west wall of the gully.
B.Disraeli, R.Cecil, A.Balfour 13.06.1878

3. **Ground Swell**	15m	E3,6a
This takes the centre of the white wall right of the previous route. Start at the foot of the ramp of West Pillar Corner. Climb sharp rock to twin undercuts at half-height. Tackle the wall above.
M.Ward, M.Crocker 11.07.1987

4. **Sharma**	15m	E3,5c
This takes a line of cracks in the right side of the wall. Start as for West Pillar Corner. Climb up to a spike, then climb awkwardly over a bulge onto a steep wall. Climb rightwards then straight up.
M.Crocker, M.Ward 11.07.1987

5. **West Pillar Corner**	24m	S,4a
This climbs the ramp running rightward up the left wall of the gully and finishes up the corner above.
J.Talbot, R.Corbett 00.00.1961

6. **Central Crack**	24m	VD
Just right of the ramp is a chimney. Climb the arete right of this and the broken crack in the wall above.
J.Talbot, R.Corbett 00.00.1961

7. **Meander**	24m	D
Start as for Central Crack, climb up and right to the arete overlooking the gully. Follow the arete to the top.
R.Corbett, J.Talbot 00.00.1961

8. Wriggler's Chimney	12m	HS,5a	**	\
Climb the back of the chimney itself.
N.Taylor solo 13.06.2003

9. **Kopf Out**	12m	HVS,5b
At the base of the arete where the gully gets very narrow is a short crack. Climb it and move rightwards to an obvious flake. Move right again and climb the centre of the steep wall. Using the back wall is cheating! Supersedes Pillar Kopf (J.Talbot 1964).
A.Richardson, S.Doerr 00.00.1989

At the back of the gully is a smooth pillar in a gloomy recess.

10. **Balm**	12m	VS,4c
The left edge of the pillar and the crack on the left.
G.Evans, J.Bullock 00.00.1980

11. **Malm**	12m	VS,4c
The right edge of the pillar to the roof, move right to a ledge, then take the wall above.
J.Talbot, B.Talbot 00.00.1966

12. **Trident Wall**	21m	E1,5b	*
Start at the centre of the concave right wall of the gully by a short water-worn groove. Climb up and left below the bulges before breaking out onto the upper wall and thence to the top. It is possible to cut straight through the bulges at the same grade.
J.Talbot, M.Hicks 00.00.1969

13. **South West Diedre**   21m   HS,4b

Climb the short groove on the seaward side of the right wall of the gully. Traverse easily along the flake to finish.
SUMC 00.00.1967

14. **Pillar Crest**   29m   M

An easy pleasant scramble up the crest of the buttress on the right (east) of the gully.
J.Talbot 00.00.1961

Trident Ridge Pillar

The following routes lie on the east side of the ridge housing Trident Wall. The left side of the wall is bounded by Pillar Crest. Just right of this is a groove line and the start of the wall proper.

15. **Pillar Groove**   9m   VD   \

Follow the groove or its right bounding side wall.
J.Harwood, M.Ismail 08.08.1998

16. **High And Mighty**   15m   E1,5b   \

Some 5m from the left (seaward) side of the east wall are two lines of weakness. Take the left one.
J.Harwood, R.High 16.11.1996

17. **Weak and Flabby**   15m   E3,5c   \

The right-hand weakness.
J.Harwood, R.High 16.11.1996

About 15m right of Pillar Crest, the wall enters a small narrow gully. A black bulge is obvious at about 6m.

18. **Questions**   14m   HVS,4c   \

Climb the wall to short cracks just left of the black bulge. Swing left and up the wall on painful rock to the top.
J.Harwood, M.Ismail 08.08.1998

19. **Answers**   14m   VS,4b   \

Start at the gully entrance and climb the east wall of Trident Pillar easily for 3m or so. Move left to below the black bulge. Swing across leftwards and pull up on enormous, painful holds to the top.
J.Harwood, M.Ismail 08.08.1998

The next crag to the east (right) at sea level is Fourth Gully. However above Trident Gully itself is Catacomb Gully.

Catacomb Gully

This lies above and behind Trident Gully. It is non-tidal and access is by scrambling down from the East or ascending Pillar Crest from the beach.

Left (west) Wall

1. **Celtic Uprising**   12m   E1,5b

Steep climbing 4m left of West Corner Crack. Climb to a line of leftward-trending finger flakes and follow them to their end. Pull up to an obvious pocket and finish as for Relics.
M.Crocker 01.08.1987

2. **Relics**   15m   E3,6a

A technical pitch 3m left of West Corner Crack. Climb past the remains of an old BR to twin vertical slots in the centre of a brown-streaked wall. Continue up and finish out leftwards.
M.Learoyd, H.Griffiths 00.00.1986

3. **Necropolis** 15m E4,5c
Start at an indefinite pillar just right of Relics and take a line straight up the wall past a crack and finger-ledge.
J.Bullock, D.McCarroll 15.09.2002

4. **West Corner Crack** 15m HS,4b
This takes the corner crack, widening to a chimney, midway into the gully on the left wall.
J.Talbot, R.Corbett 00.00.1961

5. **Ribbery** 15m Sev
Climb the rib right of West Corner Crack, just left of the arete.
J.Talbot, R.Corbett 00.00.1961

6. **Ribald** 15m HVS,5b
Climb the east-facing wall of Ribbery to join it at the top. Supersedes Wall And Crack (J.Talbot, B.Talbot 1965).
H.Griffiths, M.Learoyd 00.00.1986

7. **Rib And Crack** 15m HS,4a
A nice pitch taking the corner right of Ribbery.
J.Talbot, R.Corbett 00.00.1961

8. **The Jewel** 15m VS,4c *
A little gem following the shallow groove in the wall right of Rib and Crack. Move right at the top.
A.Sharp, J.Harwood 20.03.1982

9. **Sharp Eyed** 15m E5,6a *
A wall climb between The Jewel and Crypt. Start 3m right of the arete. Climb on spaced pockets, leftwards at first, to a vague break, thread on a spike. Move up right on better holds to the obvious flake. Finish left.
M.Crocker, M.Ward 11.07.1987

10. **My Wife and I** 15m E5,6a
Bold. Start right of the start of Sharp Eyed. Climb over a bulge in line with a hairline crack to good finger edges, make a long reach and continue straight up through bulges to the top.
M.Crocker 01.08.1987

11. **Crypt** 15m E2,5b
Dead good, but often wet. Climb the brown-stained corner crack and the overhangs above.
J.Bullock, G.Evans 09.12.1984

2. **The Dungeon** 15m E4,6a
Start as for Crypt then climb straight up the pillar on the right to a bulge. Pull into a thin crack and then gain a good break below a roof. Swing right and continue more easily.
M.Crocker 01.08.1987

Right (east) Wall

13. **Left Over** 15m D
Climb the left edge of the west-facing wall trending right at the top.
J.Talbot, R.Corbett 00.00.1961

14. **Gunpowder** 18m E3,6a
Start at the left end of the overhang which runs across the right wall of the gully. Pull through the overhang, old BRs, to a break. Continue directly to the top.
J.Talbot - Futility 00.00.1963
FFA A.Sharp 05.11.1987

15. **Franceschi**   15m   E2,5b   *
Surmount the overhang directly below a shallow groove in the upper wall and finish up the groove rightwards.
J.Talbot, B.Talbot 00.00.1965, FFA A.Sharp, J.Harwood 20.03.1982

16. **Franceschi Direct Finish**   14m   E2,5c
Finish directly up from the overhang of the parent route.
A.Sharp 05.11.1987

17. **Banana Man**   15m   E4,6a
Climb over the overhang 1m or so right of Franceshci, past a PR (missing) to finish as for Franceschi.
A.Forster, A.Sharp 18.09.1988

18. **Treason**   15m   E4,6b
Move through the roof at its right end and make a long reach to painful holds, PR. Finish up the groove.
A.Sharp 05.11.1987

19. **Nemesis**   12m   E3,6b
Climb the wall 2m right of Treason. PR (missing).
A.Sharp, A.Forster 18.09.1988

20. **Trubble**   11m   HVS,4c
Gain the finish of Gamma from the wall to the left.
R.Corbett, P.Perkins 00.00.1962

21. **Gamma**   11m   VS,4c
Follow the groove running up the right side of the overhang. Pull left above the overhang. Finish up the groove.
R.Corbett, P.Perkins 00.00.1982

22. **Beta**   11m   HS,4b
The crack to the right of Gamma.
R.Corbett, P.Perkins 00.00.1962

23. **Midel**   11m   VD
Climb the pillar between Beta and Alpha.
R.Corbett, P.Perkins 00.00.1962

24. **Alpha**   7m   D
The right-most crack.
J.Talbot, R.Corbett 00.00.1962

25. **Little Wall**   6m   D
A fine line up the short wall right of Alpha.
J.Talbot, R.Corbett 00.00.1962

The Pillar
This is the pillar at beach level just east of Trident Gully.

1. **Pillar Crest**   18m   M
The front of the pillar.
J.Talbot 00.00.1961

2. **Left Wall**   18m   M
The groove to to the right.
J.Talbot 00.00.1961

3. **Three Corners**   18m   VS,4c
    The fainter groove in the wall to the right.
    J.Talbot 00.00.1961

Four Gullies
GR419872

TIDAL STATUS: 2 hours either side of low water.

DESCENT: By scrambling down the obvious ridges.

Fourth Gully
This is the gully below and right of Catacomb Gully, with an obvious hanging block above a cave at the back.

1. **Narrow Cleft**   12m   M
    Easy scrambling up the pillar left of Fourth Gully.
    J.Talbot 00.00.1961

2. **Left Pillar Edge**   12m   M
    The front face of the left arm of the gully.
    J.Talbot 00.00.1961

3. **Ramp And Slab**   11m   D
    Climb a narrow ledge on the left wall of the gully, rising steeply to a short crack. Finish up this. It can also be
    climbed more directly at VS.
    J.Talbot, R.Corbett 00.00.1961

4. **Black Fissure**   11m   M
    At the back of the gully behind the overhang, climb the right crack leading up to Catacomb Gully.
    J.Talbot 00.00.1961

5. **Unnamed**   7m   HS,4a
    Follow a rising corner on the right side of the gully, which merges with a crack below the right side of the
    overhang. Exit up this.
    J.Talbot, D.Lewis 00.00.1962

Third Gully
This is situated right (east) of Fourth Gully. The centre of the gully is divided by a steep pillar rib and at half-height is
cut by a wide, flat, square ledge. To the right of the rib is a narrow deep cleft.

1. **West Side**   12m   M
    The left wall of the left arm of the gully.
    J.Talbot 00.00.1961

2. **West Pillar**   12m   M
    The front of the left arm of the gully.
    J.Talbot 00.00.1961

3. **KLAG (Rough!)**   11m   VS,5a
    Short, painful, but good. Climb the obvious crack to the right of West Pillar moving right at a small roof.
    K.Snook, L.Moran, A.Pedrick, G.Evans 00.00.1978

4. **Herzog Kamin**   18m   S
This takes the deep chimney crack at the back of the left-hand side of the central pillar rib.
J.Talbot 00.00.1963

5. **West Diedre**   15m   VD
A vague series of grooves in the right wall of the recess containing Herzog Kamin.
J.Talbot, R.Corbett 00.00.1961

6. **Main Diedre**   15m   D
The slightly more pronounced grooves to the right.
J.Talbot, R.Corbett 00.00.1961

7. **West Wall**   15m   HS
The black wall to the right, just left of the front face of the central dividing pillar.
J.Talbot 00.00.1964

8. **Central Rib**   15m   M
The front of the central pillar of the gully.
J.Talbot, R.Corbett 00.00.1961

9. **Buhl Riss**   12m   VS,4c
This route is located right in the back of the right-hand recess of the gully, gained by going underneath the rock arch. The route is the thin flake on the right side of the recess. Mislocated in previous guides.
J.Talbot 00.00.1969

10. **South West Corner**   6m   M
The scoop on the right wall of the gully, right of the recess containing Buhl Riss.
J.Talbot 00.00.1961

Second Gully
This is the narrow, deep-cut cleft right (east) of Third Gully.

1. **Botzong**   12m   S
This climbs the steep smooth chimney crack behind a large distinct jammed block at the back.
J.Talbot 00.00.1961

First Gully
This is the shallow gully to the right (east).

1. **Block Fissure**   6m   D
The fissure to the left of the block in the back of the gully.
J.Talbot 00.00.1961

2. **Block**   6m   S,4c
Climb the right-hand crack formed by the block on the right wall of the gully.
J.Talbot, D.Baines 00.00.1961

3. **Black Corner**   6m   S,4c
The left-hand corner on the right wall of the gully.
R.Corbett, J.Talbot 00.00.1961

4. **Small Corner**   6m   D
The right-hand corner on the right wall of the gully.
J.Talbot, R.Corbett 00.00.1961

UPPER CRAGS FALL BAY TO MEWSLADE

GR417873 to 419873

TIDAL STATUS: Non-Tidal.

BOLTING POLICY: No bolting.

ACCESS
Access is as for the lower crags (see start of Fall Bay to Mewslade section). If coming from the west (Fall Bay), strike leftwards (east) from the iron ladder to reach the obvious pinnacles on the west side of Upper Jacky's Tor. If coming from Mewslade, strike right (west) up the non-tidal path above the beach to reach the first substantial area (Grey Wall). The crags are reached from each other via the cliff top paths.

PREAMBLE
Apart from Upper Jacky's Tor, which has some good middle grade routes, this is a fairly mediocre area (especially Grey Wall). However, it is non-tidal and therefore useful when the tides are bad, although it is very much the poor relation of Lewes Castle. The crags are described from west to east (i.e. in the order Jacky's Tor, Rolly Bottom Buttress and Grey Wall).

DESCENTS: For all crags, by walking off west or east.

Upper Jacky's Tor
Above and behind Cathedral Wall is an extensive, non-tidal, upper tier of cliffs with a grass ramp at its foot. It provides a number of worthwhile climbs. At the foot of the cliff, towards the centre, is a detached pinnacle about 2m high, above and right of which, in the middle of the wall, is a large shield of rock bounded on the left by a crack. About 22m right of the pinnacle is a small cave. Right again is a distinct bulging buttress, Rolly Bottom Buttress. Access is best from the top of the cliff via a grassy slope to the east of the cliffs.

1. **Codpiece**   21m   HS,4a
   Start 11m right of the detached pinnacle. Climb a crack leading up and right to a ledge at half-height, traverse right to the detached shield and gain its top. Finish leftwards up the wall.
   A.Beaton, G.Richardson etc 00.00.1982

2. **Thanksgiving**   21m   HVS,5a   *
   Start at a groove 3m right of the detached pinnacle. Climb the groove leftwards to the overhangs, passing a ledge at half-height (Codpiece). Now take the continuation groove through the left side of the overhangs to finish.
   P.Littlejohn, A.N.Other 22.11.1982

3. **Praise Be**   20m   HVS,5a
   Start at the 2m detatched flake below a shield. Step right off the top of the flake and climb directly to a sloping break. Continue straight up the centre of the shield to a ledge on top. Finish up the wall and crack of Raindrops.
   M.Crocker 05.12.1998

4. **Raindrops**   21m   HVS,5a
   Start 2m right of Thanksgiving, directly below the shield. Climb cracks bearing rightwards for 3m, then continue direct to the right side of the shield. Surmount the shield and continue rightwards up the wall above. Finish up the wide crack in the left side of the bulges.
   G.Evans, G.Richardson 00.00.1981

5. **All There**   24m   VS,4c   *
   Start as for Raindrops. Climb cracks bearing rightwards to gain a shallow niche. Climb a crack leading to a bulge below the right side of the highest overhangs, traverse right and break through at the weakest point. Finish direct. It is possible to finish left from the bulge at a slightly harder standard.
   G.Evans, J.Bullock, R.Thomas 00.00.1982

6. **A Bit On The Side**   26m   VS,4b   *

Start 4m right of Thanksgiving, below a crack leading to a shallow recess at 6m. From the recess climb the broken cracks above to a small line of overhangs, traverse right and finish up a steep groove.

G.Richardson, M.Danford 00.00.1982

Rolly Bottom Buttress

This is the prominent buttress to the right (east) of Upper Jacky's Tor. It has an obvious black-stained wall in its centre.

1. **Rolly Poly Arete**   30m   E2,5c   \

The left arete of Rolly Bottom Buttress. Start as for that route and ascend ledges to pull onto a horizontal break below the arete (right of the groove). Take the arete on its right side to easy ground and finish up Rolly Bottom Buttress.

M.Crocker 05.12.1998

2. **Rolly Bottom Buttress**   30m   VS,4c

A little loose in places. Start at the left-hand side of the buttress, climb steep rock and gain a groove. At its top continue up a thinner crack in the same line to the top.

G.Evans, L.Moran 00.00.1990

3. **The Sandpiper**   30m   E3,5c   *

A sustained and worthwhile pitch. Climb straight up the black streak and the middle of the wall above, until a blind pull around a small roof leads to looser but easier climbing. Lots of small wires.

P.Boardman, G.Williams, W.Hurford 3pt - Rolly Bottom Buttress 00.00.1970

FFA A.Sharp, J.Harwood 12.03.1983

4. **Snidewhiner**   30m   E3,6a   \

The convex arete. Start as for Sandpiper, follow the enormous flake on the right and pull up into the horizontal break. Take the arete on its left side, via an undercut on the face, to a narrow incut hand ledge. Gain easier ground above and exit rightwards.

M.Crocker 05.12.1998

5. **Sidewinder**   30m   HVS,5a

Climb a short corner on the right side of the buttress and step left into a broken groove. Avoid it by taking the jamming crack on the right, to finish up a clean corner.

A.Sharp, J.Harwood 20.03.1982

Below and right of Rolly Bottom Buttress is a cave with a slab above it.

6. **Trivial Pursuit**   18m   HVD

Climb the right side of the cave to a ledge, step onto a block at the foot of the slab and continue to the path.

G.Evans, J.Bullock 00.00.1988

Grey Wall

The slightly loose and uninspiring crag above Mewslade Bay. It is rarely visited.

The old route Quergang (J.Talbot, B.Talbot 1966) has been superseded by more recent lines.

1. **Grey Day Plus**   15m   E2,5b   \

Start below the centre of the large roof at the left-hand end of the crag. Climb leftwards up the compact wall left of the obvious flake of The Queer Gang and exit round the left-hand side of the roof.

M.Crocker 07.11.1998

2. **The Queer Gang**   15m   E2,5b   \
    The obvious left-facing flake line and weakness in the roof. Follow the flake to the roof, extend for the big projecting block overhead, then finish up the groove above.
    M.Crocker 07.11.1998

3. **Direct**   30m   E3,5c
    A direct line just right of the overhang.
    R.Corbett - Direct 00.00.1962
    FFA P.James 00.00.1984

4. **Superdirect**   30m   E3,6a   \
    Start to the right of Direct. Climb to a bulge and take the grey streak above to good fingerholds and the horizontal break. Step left and finish easily.
    M.Crocker 07.11.1998

5. **Ermintrude**   13m   E1,5b
    Take a broken right of Superdirect to a niche before continuing direct to a horizontal crack and a small ledge, then the top.
    M.Jones, P.Murphy 00.00.1982

6. **Gurtrude**   15m   E2,5c   \
    The shallow groove right of Ermintrude.
    M.Crocker 07.11.1998

7. **PMC II**   13m   HVS,5b   *
    The groove right of Gurtrude and left of South East Chimney.
    S.Vince, J.Makin 00.00.0000

8. **Tipped To Be Massive**   15m   E3,5c   \
    From the foot of PMC II move right over the pillar and climb direct to a rightward slanting crack which leads to a horizontal break. Continue up the headwall via a series of flakes, slightly to the right.
    M.Crocker 07.11.1998

9. **South East Chimney**   15m   D
    Follow the obvious chimney to the top.
    J.Talbot, D.Thomas 00.00.1959

10. **Wall And Corner**   13m   VS,4b
    Start 2m right of South East Chimney. Climb rightwards to a ledge, then a corner on the right wall to the top.
    J.Talbot, D.Thomas 00.00.1959

THURBA HEAD

GR422872 to 422868
By Goi Ashmore

TIDAL STATUS: Thurba West is non-tidal. Thurba Head Front face is extremely tidal and is not recommended except at Spring Tides 1 hour either side of low water. The main area of Thurba Head is marginally tidal if the climber is prepared to traverse in as for Junior Jaws.

BOLT POLICY: No bolting. The old bolts on Thurba West and the BB above Thurba Head to remain.

PREAMBLE
Thurba Head itself contains some fine lines, which to the east of Right Crack (not inclusive) are generally on good rock. Although the south-facing front face is the most spectacular, it is a pain to get to. However, the routes to the east of Cool Britannia (inclusive) are very good and not as difficult to approach as you may have been led to believe. Thurba West contains a couple of reasonable routes, especially Museum Piece. There are a couple of recent minor routes in the rocks 150m east of Thurba Head itself, now called Thurba East.

ACCESS
From the main Rhossili road, turn left in Pitton (south) to Pitton Farm (GR427877), where car parking is available (honesty box). Strike left from the entrance to the car park. Walk a short distance down a farm track, then bear right past farm buildings to gain the path leading through a narrow valley. After about 5 minutes, where the sea starts to become visible, turn left (east) up the hill through an NT marked stile. A path wends gently up onto higher ground. For Thurba West, contour round towards the sea about 50m below the top of the hill to reach this small outcrop overlooking Mewslade Bay. For the main crag, continue to the top and walk out towards the headland until a path cuts down and left (east). Follow this for 100m, then strike out to sea, to reach a non-tidal platform below the shoulder of the head and at the east side of the area. The routes on the Front Face are normally approached by abseiling down from the non-tidal platform, leading to a highly tidal platform on the front face. This is only really practical on big tides. The routes on the east side are accessed by either abseil, or more commonly by traversing in from the platform above the high tide level. For Thurba East continue along the coastal path.

DESCENTS: For Thurba West, turn left at the top to reach the path. For Thurba Head front face, walk up to the top of the hill and contour back round to the non-tidal platform. For the main area, descent is by easy scramble down and right to the non-tidal platform.

BIRD BAN: There is a bird ban on Thurba Head itself (not Thurba West or East) from the 1st March to the 15th August. The ban may be lifted in the event of a shorter nesting season, so checking with the NT or BMC is recommended.

THE ROUTES

Thurba West
On the east side of Mewslade Bay, about 50m above the beach are some short buttresses. The central one of these, with a prominent convex upper half is Thurba West.

1. **Chimney Climb**   9m   D
   Climb the chimney situated at the left-hand end of the crag.
   J.Talbot, D.Thomas 00.00.1959

2. **Right Edge**   9m   VD
   Climb Chimney Climb to half-height, then move out right and climb the blunt arete.
   J.Talbot, D.Thomas 00.00.1959

3. **Cracked Wall**   9m   VD
   The blunt arete is gained directly.
   J.Talbot, D.Thomas 00.00.1959

Chris Savage - Man of the Earth - P1 (E6,6b) Yellow Wall
(Page 73) Photo: Carl Ryan

Chris Savage & Dave Pickford - Man of the Earth P2 (E6,6b) Yellow Wall
(Page 73) Photo: Carl Ryan

4. **South Corner**   12m   S
From 3m up Cracked Wall, traverse up and right to gain and finish up a corner.
J.Talbot, D.Thomas 00.00.1959

5. **Museum Piece**   10m   E4,6b   *
A tough little number with lots of old, but relatively good gear, free climbing the obvious line of BRs and PRs in
the centre of the crag. Very blind and quite powerful.
J.Talbot 00.00.1966 - South Wall
FFA A.Berry 00.00.1994
G.Ashmore ALCH 05.10.1997

6. **Nogolo**   13m   E3,6a   \
Through the roof about 7m right of Museum Piece.
M.Crocker 07.11.1998

7. **Amuseland**   10m   E1,5b   *
The prominent right-facing layback crack 5m to the right of Nogolo.
M.Crocker 07.11.1998

8. **Moneyeater**   10m   E3,6a   \
The wall and slots immediately right of Amuseland.
M.Crocker 07.11.1998

9. **Solo**   10m   E1,5b   *
About 12m right of where the overhang finally peters out, a groove and corner form the left end of a 10m wide
wall. Climb this groove and corner.
J.Talbot 00.00.1972

10. **Moneyspinner**   10m   HVS,5b
The wall to the right of Solo.
M.Crocker 07.11.1998

11. **Progression**   9m   VS,4b
The ivy-covered crack to the right of Solo.
J.Talbot 00.00.1972

Thurba Head

Front Face
The most obvious feature of the cliff is the steep pillar overlooking the sloping platform, bounded on the left by a gully
and chimney topped by large overhangs. On the right of the pillar is a large corner with a chimney at its foot. Off to
the left (west) are a number of highly overgrown gullies and ridges. The real routes start at Central Cleft. However,
the first couple of routes are mentioned for historical interest and have not been checked for this guide. They are
located to the west (left) of Central Cleft.

1. **Toad**   45m   S   ●   🕊
The first arete and groove on the left (west) side of the front face.
C.J.Lawrence, J.Brown 00.00.1968

2. **Pristine**   45m   S   ●   🕊
The gully between Toad and The Needle.
J.Talbot 00.00.1970

3. **Fountain**   45m   S   ●   ⚐
Climbs the wall right of Pristine.
J.Talbot 00.00.1970

4. **The Needle**   45m   M   ●   ⚐
Climb up to and past a Needle on the main face.
J.Talbot 00.00.1970

5. **Gully Climb**   45m   D   ●   ⚐
The first major gully to the right of the Needle.
J.Talbot 00.00.1970

6. **The Bastion**   45m   VD   ●   ⚐
The next arete to the east (right).
J.Talbot 00.00.1970

There is also a nonsensical east to west rising travese - Traverse Of The Gods (J.Talbot, 1970).

7. **Central Cleft**   42m   S   ⚐
A disgusting route after the nesting season, but a useful escape. Start below the gully and chimney left of the main pillar. Climb the chimney and groove bearing leftwards below overhangs to easy rocks, then climb the obvious deep groove above and left.
M.Hogge, E.Pardoe 00.00.1969

8. **Right Crack**   48m   E2,5b,-   *   ⚐
Perversely, this route takes the thin crack and groove in the left side of the central pillar. The first 25m are good, the rest is a bag. Start just right of the gully below a thin barnacled crack.
1. 39m Climb the crack and groove, then overcome an overhang directly. Continue to a bulge and tiny overlap of brown rock. Follow a diagonal line rightwards across the top of the pillar.
2. 9m Easy climbing remains to the top.
E.Pardoe, M.Hogge 00.00.1969
FFA P.Littlejohn, J.Harwood 03.10.1980

9. **The Thurba Pillar**   45m   E5,6b,4a   ***   ⚐
A superb pitch up the square-cut pillar between Right Crack and Earthly Powers. Start as for Right Crack.
1. 36m Climb steeply up the left arete of Earthly Powers. At 6m pull round left to the base of a crack on the face. At its end swing up left to a shallow niche below the slim section of the pillar. Climb the pillar using the right arete until better holds are gained slightly left. Continue up the leaning wall via a line of hairline cracks and a short angular groove to a belay.
2. 9m Climb the arete easily to the top.
M.Crocker 07.09.1985

10. **Earthly Powers**   45m   E5,5b,6a   ***   ⚐
Another superb route on good rock, attempting to climb the striking black groove line on the main pillar. Start beneath the groove an hour either side of low water.
1. 15m Climb steeply on good holds to a small stance beneath the black groove.
2. 30m Climb rightwards to the arete and move up to the band of overhangs. Traverse left beneath the overhang until above the blank section of the groove. Climb straight up steep ground to reach the broken crest of the buttress. Finish easily up this to block belays.
T.Penning - P1 06.07.1982
P.Littlejohn, T.Penning - P2 14.06.1983

11. **Unearthly Power** 35m E5,5b,6c ** 🐦
1. 15m As for Earthly Powers P1.
2. 20m Desperate bridging up the corner which Earthly Powers avoids to the right. Small wires are very useful. From the top of the corner, move right to finish up a short steep white headwall.
M.Crocker, J.Harwood 07.02.1999

East Section
The following routes are to the east of the main pillar of the crag and reached by traversing in from the tidal platform mentioned in the access section.

12. **Cool Britannia** 45m E6,6b ** 🐦 \
Takes the top half of the the spectacular arete to the right of Earthly Powers. From a belay in the chimney of Barnacle Bill, traverse out left and step up to place a large wire in the flake of Thin Ice. Step down and gain the arete, PR. Desperate moves up the arete past a crucial Rock 5 lead to a poor TR and PR, then an overlap. Pull over this strenuously to better holds and easy ground.
M.Crocker, J.Harwood 15.11.1998

13. **Thin Ice** 24m E4,6a ** 🐦
From the belay in chimney of Barnacle Bill, traverse left and climb the cracks in the wall right of Cool Britannia.
M.Crocker, G.Jenkin 07.09.1985

14. **Barnacle Bill** 24m E1,5b ** 🐦
A good climb taking the big corner right of the central pillar. Traverse in from the platform on the east to gain a large chimney (not visible from the start). A belay is wise. Climb the awkward chimney and the good crack up the subsequent groove.
R.Griffiths, P.Parker 1pt 09.05.1971, FFA J.Bullock, C.Lownds 28.07.1982

15. **Summer Wine** 24m E3,6a ** 🐦
A strenuous, well-protected pitch right at the top of the grade. Start beneath the thin groove right of Barnacle Bill at dead low water, or traverse in from the right (east). Climb to the overhang, move leftwards around this and follow the thin crack to a desperate move onto a sloping ledge. Finish more easily.
P.Littlejohn, T.Penning 14.06.1983

16. **The Thief That Never Was** 24m E3,6a 🐦 \
The arete between Summer Wine and Junior Jaws.
M.Crocker 01.11.1998

5m right of Barnacle Bill is a shallow corner easily visible from the non-tidal platform on the east.

17. **Junior Jaws** 21m E1,5b * 🐦
Start at high-tide level, below and slightly right of the upper section of the shallow corner. Climb up to the foot of the groove and pull in from the right. Climb the corner directly.
T.Penning, D.Hope 05.09.1982

18. **Laughing Gear** 18m E1,5a 🐦
The smaller groove right of Junior Jaws. Not well protected.
T.Penning, J.Harwood 12.09.1982

19. **Wimp** 18m S
Start below the open groove in the upper right part of the cliff, just left of a deep chimney crack which bounds the cliff on the right. Climb to the steep broken groove and the top.
G.Richardson, M.Danford 00.00.1982

20. **Delegation** 18m HVS,5a 🦋 \
The cracks and the mini groove right of Wimp, gained from the start of Wimp.
M.Richards, J.Harwood 28.08.1999

Thurba East

21. **Depression** 32m S \
About 150m east of the bay immediately east of Thurba Head is an easy angled crag above the path. Climb the left-hand rib of the crag on loose rock.
J.Harwood, E.Smith 08.05.1999

22. **Knight Games** 10m S \
Some distance on from Depression is a short crag above a short grey wall facing due south. Climb the centre of the wall, traversing off right to finish.
J.Harwood, E.Smith, M.Leask, M.Ismail 28.03.1999

23. **An Oxford Connection** 12m VD \
In the valley to the east of Knight Games with wooden fence in it is an east facing crag. Climb directly up about 3m right of the left-hand arete.
J.Harwood, M.Leask, E.Smith, M.Ismail 28.03.1999

RAMS GROVE CRAG AND SADDAM'S WALL

GR427867 to 431868
By Goi Ashmore

TIDAL STATUS: Non-tidal

BOLT POLICY: No bolting.

PREAMBLE
Saddam's Wall and the lower tier of Rams Grove Crag have considerable scope for further development. Saddam's Wall itself contains some good rock, although the brambles make it hard to get to. Rams Grove Crag is a fairly recent re-development. Sadly, it is not very good.

ACCESS
See Thurba Head Section. From the path at the end of the farm, strike left just before the gate leading to Mewslade and take the rightwards fork a short distance on. After about 15 minutes go through the gated stile to enter a wide valley leading down to the sea. Saddam's Wall is immediately to the left (east) when facing out to sea. Rams Grove is on the right (west) about 150m further on.

DESCENTS: For both crags descent is by walking down ridges to the right.

THE ROUTES

Saddam's Wall
The wall at the top of the valley on its east side. The rock is of the 'beautifully waterworn variety more often found underground.'

1. **Wam Bang Thank You Saddam** 15m E4,6a * \
Start in the centre of the crag just right of the ivy sheet. Climb a groove on big jugs to a hole at 12m. Move up and right to a bulge and pocket. Step up and extend for finger jugs slightly out left. Step right, reach a crack above the top bulge and cut loose for the top.
M.Crocker, J.Harwood 22.02.1998

2. **A Fragile Peace** 20m E3,5c ** \
Brilliant, on almost perfect rock. Start below a short crack up the right-hand side of the crag. Go up the crag to a fragile bulge. Stride left over a smooth slab then pull over a small overhang after a projecting foothold. Climb the waterworn face above to the top bulge and yard up on jugs out right to the exit.
M.Crocker, J.Harwood 22.02.1998

The Crag That Time Forgot

This crag, which could not be located for the guide, is somewhere in Ram Grove itself, probably one of the smaller crags west of Saddam's wall. It contains two routes, for which there were no real details at the time of writing. These are Jurassic Park E2,5c (J.Brown 1996) and The Land Before Time VS,4b (J.Brown, K.Misson 1996).

Rams Grove Crag

As the pebble beach of Rams Grove is approached, there are a number of small compact cliffs to the west. The first cliff contains a number of short climbs. It is characterised by two right-facing grooves that divide the cliff into thirds. The right-hand groove is Insatiable Appetite.

1. **Standing Guard** 21m HVS,5a
The groove/chimney which bounds the left side of the main part of the cliff.
N.Williams solo Pre-1991

2. **Windworn** 20m E5,6a
Committing. To the right of Standing Guard is a second rightward-facing groove (Sundrench). Climb the wall just left of the groove, but step left to the centre of a bulge. Use a good undercut to stretch for a jug and pull nervously up to a small grey slab. Take the crack leftwards to finish up poor rock.
M.Crocker, J.Harwood 09.02.1998

3. **Snowstorm** 18m E3,5c 1pt \
Start as for Windworn, but continue directly to a TR at 7m, then step left and surmount the bulge. Continue up the cracks and groove above.
P.Thomas, J.Harwood 1pt 12.02.1989

4. **Sundrench** 18m E4,6a
Follows the right-facing groove. As for Snowstorm to the steep grey wall barring entry to the groove, pull right into the groove and climb up the right wall to the top.
M.Crocker, J.Harwood 27.12.1997

5. **The Ram Of Radyr** 18m E4,6b
The brutish bulge right of the groove of Sundrench. Take poor rock to the widest part of the ledge beneath the concave stratum. Arrange gear, including a crucial Rock 5 in a pocket over the lip. Now move over onto the face. Step up right into a very slim groove and right again into a more obvious one, leading to the top.
M.Crocker, J.Harwood 27.12.1997

6. **Taste of Tradition** 18m E4,6a
Start 3m right of The Ram Of Radyr and climb to a bulge. Move left and then make a sustained series of moves up to a poor PR under the roof. Move over the roof and onto the slabby wall above then move left to gain a ledge. Continue up the cracked wall above to the top.
P.Thomas, J.Harwood 23.05.1989

7. **Beth** 16m E2,5b
As for Taste Of Tradition to the bulge, PR. Move slightly right over the bulge to a left-leaning groove. Continue on better holds to the top.
P.Thomas, J.Harwood 01.01.1989

8. **Where East Meets West**   20m   E4,6a
The arete to the right of Beth. Climb direct to small ledges beneath a bulge. Reach over to finger pockets, TR, then climb rightwards on undercuts to a hidden jug near the arete. Follow thin cracks in the arete above to finish.
M.Crocker 17.10.1998

9. **Malaysian Lust**   20m   E5,6b   *
The saving grace of the crag. Takes the leaning groove right of Where East Meets West and left of Insatiable Appetite. From the concave stratum pull up the rib, PR, into the groove, PR and reach the top passing a 'sexy hand spike'.
M.Crocker, J.Harwood 09.02.1998

10. **Insatiable Appetite**   13m   E1,5b
The obvious right-facing groove right of Malaysian Lust and about 20m from the right end of the crag. Climb up to a bulge and make an awkward move to enter the groove. Continue with less difficulty to the top.
N.Williams Pre-1991

11. **Don't Tell Anne**   13m   E3,6a
Climb the wall 3m right of Insatiable Appetite passing an overlap to reach small ledges. Take the easier groove above to the top. Committing and high in the grade.
M.Crocker, J.Harwood 27.12.1997

12. **Honey**   13m   E1,5b
Start 3m right of Don't Tell Anne below an obvious square-cut overhang at the top of the crag. Climb a wall until a move can be made leftward to a groove below the overhang. Continue up the groove at its right side.
A.Richardson, L.Moran 00.00.1988

13. **August Mank Holiday**   15m   E1,5b   \
The obvious diagonal line from the start of Honey to the groove of Insatiable Appetite.
M.Richards, J.Harwood 28.08.1999

14. **Sugar**   12m   E1,5b
Climb the vague grooves just right of Honey.
A.Richardson, L.Moran 00.00.1988

15. **50 Franc Menu**   12m   VS,4c
Start well to the right of Sugar, where the concave strata meets the ground. Climb the shallow yellow groove and then move rightwards into the groove above.
N.Williams solo Pre-1991

16. **Entre**   9m   VS,4c
Climb the cracked wall just right of 50 Franc Menu.
N.Williams solo Pre-1991

17. **Appetizer**   8m   S
The short broken groove on the far right of the crag.
N.Williams solo Pre-1991

Further seawards and due south of Rams Grove Crag proper is a lower tier.

18. **Soundstrip**   27m   E3,5c   \
About 25m from the right end of the lower tier is a 3m high pinnacle at the base of the cliff. The route starts just below it and takes the solid grey strip right of the left-leading crack left of the pinnacle. Climb the crack for 6m to superb gear, swing right onto the face and ascend direct to a slight break. Continue direct, then slightly leftwards to a slab beneath the left end of a small roof, TR. Move left, then back right to exit up an easy solid rib.
M.Crocker 09.02.1998

THREE SISTERS AND DEBORAH'S ZAWN

GR427867 to 434861
By Goi Ashmore

TIDAL STATUS: The Three Sisters are non-tidal. Deborah's zawn 4 hours either side of low water.

BOLTING POLICY: See individual crags.

PREAMBLE
This is a seldom frequented area of Gower, with some further potential for development - although this will require some dedicated trundling! The main crags of interest are the steep Third Sister and Deborah's Zawn, with the best quality rock and some very good E2-E5s. Of the other crags, there are a few easier routes that would be good if a little time was spent removing some (small but numerous) blocks. The crags are described from west to east, as they are approached from Rams Grove.

ACCESS
1. Pitton Approach
Approach from Pitton as for Rams Grove. At the seaward end of the valley of Rams Grove, turn left (west) to a good path that runs all the way along the cliff, scrambling up to each sister in turn. The path crosses a very rickety fence above a steep zawn below the Third Sister. The steep zawn is Deborah's Zawn, accessed by scrambling down its east (left when facing seaward) side.

2. Paviland Approach
As for Paviland (see below) to the dry valley where the sea becomes visible. From the stile at the landward end of the valley, cross a stile on the right (west) leading up to a higher level. Pass over two further stiles to reach a dry valley, with a rotten pinnacle visible on the far side (this leads down to the Deborah's Overhang Area). Instead of dropping down the valley with the pinnacle, continue up to the next spur. On the far side of this, a zig zag track leads down a faint gully and towards the sea. This leads to Third Sister in about 60m.

DESCENTS: Scramble down easily and obviously from the Three Sisters. For Deborah's Zawn, either abseil or lower off. For some routes this requires a hanging rope.

THE ROUTES

First Sister

BOLTING POLICY: Replacement of worn fixed gear on a point for point basis with bolts is permissible. No new sports routes allowed.

The First Sister is a compact cliff just east of the Rams Grove valley. It has an overhanging face with a snaking crack line in the centre (Sister of Mercy), whilst to the right is a Y-shaped depression.

1. **Mercy, Mercy, Mercy**   21m   E5,6a   *   \
    Start 4m left of the snaking crack at a tiny niche at 2m. Move up to place good wires in an incipient crackline, then make fingery moves right to a little black scoop. Swing left to a break, surmount the bulge above, PR and continue to a crack. Take the crack to the top, taking care with the exit move.
    M.Crocker 17.10.1998

2. **Sister of Mercy**   .   21m   E4,6a   *
    The clean, snaking crackline in the centre of the buttress. Climb steeply to the second of 2PRs. Climb the groove to an easier crack, which leads to the top on dubious rock.
    J.Bullock, G.Evans 1pt 21.06.1987
    FFA A.Price 00.09.1988

3. **Paparazzi Blues**   21m   E6,6b   *   \
A pump out taking the bulging rib overhanging the start of Sister Of Mercy. Follow Sister Of Mercy to a jug 1m above the first PR. Break out right with difficulty to vertical cracks in the rib. Climb the rib on its right side, exiting slightly right over a bulge.
M.Crocker, J.Harwood 22.02.1998

4. **The Angst Of Anti-Fashion**   21m   E5,6b   *
Climb the y-shaped depression at the right side of the cliff to reach a bulge forming the inverted crotch of the Y. Traverse left between overhangs to a hanging groove and pull up strenuously right, PR. Escape up a short flake.
M.Crocker, J.Harwood 22.02.1998

5. **South East Wall**   21m   E1,5b
As for The Angst of Anti-Fashion, but from the bulge take the right-hand arm.
J.Talbot, B.Talbot 00.00.1966
FFA J.Bullock, G.Evans 00.00.1984

6. **Solitary Brother**   21m   E3,6b   \
The rib to the right of South East Wall. Pull straight over the bulge and step immediately left to reach a thin flake crack. Climb the rib to the traverse of South East Wall and finish with difficulty.
M.Crocker 17.10.1998

7. **Brothers in Arms**   21m   HVS,5a
The obvious rightward-slanting corner/crack on the right of the crag.
G.Evans, J.Bullock 27.04.1986

Second Sister

BOLTING POLICY: Replacement of worn fixed gear on a point for point basis with bolts is permissible. No new sports routes allowed.

This is the buttress immediately east of the First Sister. It has an attractive slabby south wall, but is not quite as good as it appears when viewed from its east side. Some of the routes would be pretty good if anyone were prepared to do a little trundling. The most obvious feature is the prominent fin of Finnmark. The first two routes more or less end at a shoulder at 18m, where it is possible to scramble off left. The rest of the routes go to the top of the cliff.

1. **Barney Rubble**   18m   VD
Climb loose rock left of the fin of rock at the left side of the crag.
C.Allen, solo 00.00.1987

2. **Finnmark**   18m   E2,5b
From the ledge at the start of Barney Rubble, swing right round the arete to the obvious groove of South Wall. Move up and stretch left to the fin edge. Climb the right side to the top. An obvious, but disappointing route.
M.Crocker, J.Harwood 07.03.1998

3. **South Wall Variation**   28m   VS,4c   *
Gain the groove of South Wall as for Finnmark, but continue as for South Wall itself.
A.Richardson, J.Beynon 00.00.1989

4. **South Wall**   33m   VS,4c
Might be worth a star if it was trundled at the start. Start at the right edge of the ledge running across the start of the wall proper. Make a leftward-rising traverse to reach the corner crack and follow this to a ledge. Finish through the small overlap above the groove.
E.Pardoe, J.Talbot 00.00.1969

5. **Arrow**   33m   HVS,5a
Supersedes an earlier indirect route, Harrow (P.Kokelaar, G.Williams 1969). Climb the lower slabs just right of the start of South Wall, via a slanting crack line to gain the overhangs. Overcome these to gain the top.
G.Evans, P.Clay 18.10.1981

6. **Topless Admirers**   33m   HVS,5a
This takes a line of slabs and grooves 2m right of South Wall.
L.Davies, P.Thomas 00.04.1987

7. **Sister Sledge**   33m   E1,5a
Start as for Topless Admirers, then finish up the obvious grooves further right.
G.Lewis, P.Thomas, A.Richardson 00.00.1988

The crag has an eastern side wall.

8. **Sister Bliss**   13m   E5,6b   \
Start at the left end of the broken ledge running beneath the wall. Take the obvious leftward-rising overlap to gain a shallow hanging groove, TR. Finish directly on flakes up the leaning wall.
M.Crocker, J.Harwood 07.03.1998

9. **Bloodbond**   12m   E1,5b
Start as for Sister Bliss, then follow an intermittent crack on honeycombed rock right of a grey flake. Proceed directly on flakes up the unlikely wall above to the top, avoiding premature escapes into the groove on the right.
M.Crocker, J.Harwood 07.03.1998

10. **Sleuth**   12m   E3,5c
Take the concave slab (sic) above the middle of the ledge beneath the wall. Follow a very slight, overhanging flake a little leftwards onto the slab. Go directly up from an undercut onto the easier angled slab, keeping just left of the groove on the right. Exit with care.
M.Crocker, J.Harwood 07.03.1998

Sister 2½

BOLTING POLICY: Replacement of worn fixed gear on a point for point basis with bolts is permissible. No new sports routes allowed.

To the east (right) of the Second Sister is a compact wall at a high level. The routes peter out quite quickly and a pre-placed belay rope will help mitigate the full horrors of a top out.

1. **The Wettest April Since Records Began**   18m   E3,5c   \
Near the left-hand end of the cliff is a brown coloured crack. A few metres to the right is a slim groove in the grey wall leading up to the left of a jutting overhang. Climb the groove to a short flake crack below a bulge. Move right and through the bulge. Finish up an easier broken groove.
M.Crocker, J.Harwood 26.04.1998

The cliff now continues right, looking fairly blank and featureless in its lower half until an orange niche at 6m, some 9m from the right edge of the cliff. The next route takes the leaning wall left of the niche.

2. **Sisterly Luv**   15m   E5,6a   \
Follow the junction of the grey streak and white rock past Bristol PRs to a bulge. Overcome this to a crack leading rightwards to an overhang, a short groove on the right and a wobbly exit to the ledge.
M.Crocker, J.Harwood 26.04.1998

3. **The Beverly Sisters** 15m E3,5c \ •
    Start below and slightly to the right of the orange niche. Make committing moves into the niche and continue up the crack and wall to join Sisterly Luv at the overhang.
    M.Crocker, J.Harwood 26.04.1998

4. **In Between Sisters** 15m E4,6a \
    Start 4m left of a rubble zone at the right end of the wall. Move up to a small pocket on the smooth grey wall (crucial Rock 5 placement). Step right and move up on scoops to a bulge (TRs possible). Surmount the bulge direct. Abseil off at the top of the good rock.
    M.Crocker, J.Harwood 07.03.1998

Third Sister

BOLTING POLICY: Retro-bolting permissible with first ascensionist's permission. Replacement of worn fixed gear on a point for point basis with bolts is permissible. New sports routes allowed.

Situated 5 mins walk east of the Second Sister, this is a series of solid bulging and overhanging walls rising in a leftwards direction above the loose lower section. The starts of the left-hand routes involve exposure out of context with their length. Apart from Sexploration all the routes start from a grass terrace running up left at two-thirds height from just above a rickety fence. The most obvious feature is the shallow cave 4m up French Undressing, but beware, the nest is thought to belong to a Pterodactyl. The large two tiered crag below the Third Sister contains Sexploration.

1. **Sexploration** 30m E4,5c \
    Start 30m left of the wooden fence blow the Sister. Climb the broken wall to intersect an incipient crack in the white wall. Gain a good square-cut hold. Undercut over the bulge above and pull onto the hanging slab. Continue to good cracks and finish easily. Belay on the terrace, and scramble to the top of the cliff via a short chimney.
    M.Crocker 31.05.1998

The routes on the main crag are described from left to right, starting at the top of the terrace.

2. **Do Be Doo** 10m E3,6a *
    Take the bulging wall a few metres right of the boulder blocking the top of the terrace, below a vague arete, PR.
    M.Crocker, J.Harwood 26.04.1998

3. **Fire In Their Eyes** 10m E6,6b * \
    Start right of Do Be Doo and just left of Flaming Fingers. From a ragged pocket swing up the overhanging wall rightwards, PR. Pinch a rib (Friend 2), then move strenuously up to a leftwards pull PR, to the break. Continue to the top past a final PR.
    M.Crocker, J.Harwood 07.06.1998

4. **Flaming Fingers** 18m E5,6b *
    Start at a seat-like feature about 9m below the top of the terrace running up the crag, below a low PR. Power up this wall, 3PRs, to hit the chossy break. Step 3m left, and make a tricky move up into a thin flake crack to finish.
    M.Crocker 21.08.1988

5. **World In Action** 18m E5,6c *
    About halfway down the ramp follow a series of PRs and tats leading up the wall. Totally desperate.
    A.Sharp 00.00.1989

6. **Popped In, Souled Out** 21m E5,6b
    A tough route with deteriorating gear. Start just right of World In Action, below a PR. Pull up then make a long reach past a BR. Hard moves rightwards lead to a rest, PR. Continue directly gaining the headwall via some blind moves, poor PR. Finish past a TR.
    A.Sharp, P.Lewis, J.Harwood 06.02.1988

7. **Chilean Flame Flower**   15m   E6,6c
A desperate pitch up the leaning and reachy wall just right of Popped In, Souled Out, below a high PR. Climb the wall, with a very bold first clip and nightmare moves, second PR, to eventually gain the break at a worryingly loose block. Step a little right and pull easily up the headwall to finish.
M.Crocker 21.08.1988

8. **French Undressing**   18m   E3,6b   *
Start below the right side of the pterodactyl cave at 4m. Climb awkwardly up to this, PR and stand up, PR. Make the tricky crux move upwards and follow a vague crack to the top.
A.Sharp, P.Lewis 10.10.1987

9. **Twilight World**   18m   E3,6a   **
Start a little to the right of French Undressing below 2TRs. Climb a crack, PR, move left, TR, then straight up, TR, to an easy finish.
A.Sharp, P.Lewis, J.Harwood, A.Wilson, R.Powles, A.Hughes 10.10.1987

10. **South East Wall**   18m   E2,5b   **
A very good pitch following the rightward-slanting ramp/crackline marked by old PRs and BRs (no hangers) up the steep wall right of French Undressing. Start as for Twilight World, climb the crack, then move rightwards to gain the rightward-slanting crack and a steep finish.
J.Talbot, R.Corbett 00.00.1963
FFA A.Sharp, P.Lewis 00.00.1986

11. **Fiesta**   21m   E2,5c   *
A good, if slightly contrived pitch, on perfect rock. Start 3m right of South East Wall at a low PR. Climb up to the PR, then up to a crack, before contouring into a groove on the left to avoid South East Wall. From the pocket at the top of this groove, step left to join South East Wall at its penultimate PR.
A.Sharp, P.Lewis, J.Harwood 10.10.1987

12. **Bob's Your Uncle**   18m   E3,5c
Harder than it looks from the floor. Identify the rightward-slanting jam crack up and before the deep gash in the crag. Climb up to this on pockets and grooves, without much of a line, to hit the jam crack. Follow this and take the vague scoop at its end. Once the groove ends in poor rock, pull back left on good rock via a scallop, to gain the terrace.
A.Sharp, R.Powles 06.10.1987

13. **Ten Bears**   12m   HVS,4c
Climb the discontinuous crack system in the prow 6m right of Bob's Your Uncle. Finish with care. Rough As.
R.Powles, A.Hughes, A.Wilson 10.10.1987

Deborah's Zawn

BOLTING POLICY: Retro-bolting permissible with first ascensionist's permission. Replacement of worn fixed gear on a point for point basis with bolts is permissible. New sports routes not allowed.

This zawn is situated just below the path running beneath Third Sister. Easy scrambling down the east side leads to the bottom. The routes are accessible about 4 hours either side of low tide, but be warned, the tide does come in very quickly. The most obvious features are the rightward-rising traverse line of Silent Echo and the steep leftward-leaning crack of Resisting Arrest.

1. **Silent Echo**   19m   E1,5a   *
A strenuous pitch, for which a couple of small Friends are handy. From the left-hand end of the higher section of the zawn, climb steeply to the rightwards traverse line. Follow it across the face to a BB.
A.Sharp, P.Lewis 00.00.1985

2. **Debbie Reynolds**   15m   E5,6a   *
Start below the obvious flake in the leaning brown wall above and right of the start of Silent Echo. Climb straight up the back wall to a bulge. Gain the flake strenuously, PR. Finish up the leaning wall. PB back left.
M.Crocker 21.08.1988

3. **Silent Echo Direct Start**   16m   E2,5b   *
Start at a vague weakness, which bounds the left-hand side of the steeper right-hand section of the crag. Climb this awkwardly, to gain the traverse line at the base of the groove. Follow the groove to the BB.
R.Powles, A.Hughes 10.10.1987

4. **Can Anybody Hear?**   20m   E5,6b   \
A hanging rope is required for the top. As for Silent Echo Direct to the traverse line, but continue straight up the leaning pink wall to a hanging flake. Move up on a sloper (crucial rock 4), up to hand ledges and finish direct with difficulty, via a left-facing groove.
M.Crocker 31.05.1998

5. **Bolder Boulder**   18m   E4,6a   *
Start at a small arching overlap 2m right of the Silent Echo Direct Start. Climb through the overlap, PR, move up left on good holds and finish as for Silent Echo.
A.Sharp, P.Lewis, J.Harwood 11.10.1987

6. **Wide Eyed And Legless**   18m   E6,6c   \
The thin diagonal crack between Bolder Boulder and Resisting Arrest. A PR and in situ wire are currently missing.
A.Sharp, P.Lewis, J.Harwood 01.10.1987

7. **Resisting Arrest**   19m   E6,6b   **
Superbly powerful and totally off balance. About 7m right of the start of Silent Echo Direct Start is a prominent flake crack that curves leftwards into a prominent diagonal seam. Climb this system, passing good TRs to gain Silent Echo 2m below the lower off. Well protected.
A.Sharp, P.Lewis 00.00.1985

DEBORAH'S OVERHANG AREA

GR432862 to 434863
By Goi Ashmore

TIDAL STATUS: Deborah's Overhang and the The Tooth Fairy area are non-tidal. The Knave and Seaspit Small Cove are marginally tidal. TV Zawn 2 hours either side of low water.

BOLTING POLICY: Retro-bolting permissible with first ascensionist's permission. Replacement of worn fixed gear on a point for point basis with bolts is permissible. New sports routes allowed. No bolting allowed at Seaspit Small Cove.

PREAMBLE
An area with few routes but impressive rock in incredibly relaxed surroundings. Deborah's Overhang and TV Zawn are wildly overhanging sports crags but have serious seepage problems. The Knave and The Tooth Fairy Area are vertical traditionally protected crags of some interest. Seaspit Cove is perhaps the most worthless crag on Gower.

ACCESS
The crags can be approached from Rams Grove as for the Three Sisters. However the crags are best approached from Paviland (see below). As for Paviland to the dry valley where the sea becomes visible. From the stile at the landward end of the valley, cross a stile on the right (west) leading up to a higher level. Pass over two further stiles to reach a dry valley with a rotten pinnacle visible on the far side. Drop down this valley to reach an extensive broken, non-tidal area.

Deborah's Overhang is obvious on the right when facing out to sea and the Tooth Fairy Area is the continuation wall to the west running out to an arete, blocking further view. TV Zawn is directly below the Tooth Fairy Area.

The Tooth Fairy Area can be reached by a precarious and dangerous scramble from the main cliff. A safer approach is to take the gully as for the Paviland Approach mentioned (as for Three Sisters) and contour round to the left. The Knave can also be reached in this way. At low tides it is possible to walk along the exposed rocks from TV Zawn.

Seaspit Small Cove is reached by a 250m eastwards scramble rom the Overhang Area.

DESCENTS: Descent from the Knave is by walking down the slope on the landward side. Descents from the Tooth Fairy Area are by srambling up to the top of the ridge and then by walking down a terrace in either direction. Descents from TV Zawn are from lower offs as they are from some of the routes on Deborah's Overhang itself. Other routes at Deborah's Overhang and those at Seaspit Small Cove are by walking off right (east) from the top.

THE ROUTES

The Knave

This is the mini-Paviland, forming the headland between Deborah's Zawn and Deborah's Overhang. There are two routes on the seaward face, starting from a shallow niche at the horizontal break, 8m left of the upper left-hand end of the sloping platform that leads to the underside of the blowhole on the eastern flank.

1. **Beyond The Swell**   17m   E1,5b   \
    Climb the slab to the left side of an obvious pedestal below the line of roofs at 7m. Reach over the roof for a jug and continue with care to ledges at a break. Finish up a tricky little groove in the leaning headwall.
    M.Crocker 30.10.1998

2. **Between Two Storms**   17m   E1,5b   \
    Climb the pleasant initial slab to a brown scoop right of the pedestal. Pull up slight cracks in the bulging roof to better holds above. Swing left, move steeply up to rattling ledges then exit on the right.
    M.Crocker 30.10.1998

Above the upper left-hand (west) end of the sloping platform is a smooth grey slab, at which point the crag turns to an easterly orientation before the blowhole. The following routes start from the sloping platform.

3. **Not That Condor Moment**   10m   VS,4c   \
    From the base of the smooth grey slab, climb up to and over a bulge onto highly textured rock. Bear steeply rightwards to finish at the top of an unclimbed left-to-right gangway.
    M.Crocker 30.10.1998

4. **Knave's Slab**   10m   S   \
    The smooth grey slab running diagonally rightwards, exiting with caution.
    M.Crocker 30.10.1998

Round towards the landward side of the Knave, almost facing Deborah's Overhang itself, are two more routes.

5. **Nothing Is Forever**   15m   E3,5c   \
    The left side of the grey diamond-shaped wall. Start below a line of weakness 3m from its right edge. Climb the wall up a difficult left-facing groove, to reach a leftward-rising break. Swing right to climb the headwall.
    M.Crocker 30.10.1998

6. **Jack O'Diamonds**   15m   E3,5c   *   \
    Starting from the lowest part of the grey diamond shaped wall, pull boldly up onto the wall and continue to the left rising break. Stretch into the hanging groove to gain jugs and proceed steeply to the top.
    M.Crocker 30.10.1998

The Tooth Fairy Area
This is the white wall forming the west flank of the Deborah's Overhang area.

1. **Dentist's Chair**   18m   E3,5c
Climb the groove on the left (south) side of the tooth to a small overlap, step left into the main groove and follow this to the top.
A.Sharp, P.Lewis, J.Harwood 24.10.1987

2. **Open Wide Please**   18m   E5,6a
A bold and sustained pitch up the centre of the tooth, 4m right of Dentist's Chair. Trend left up the bulging wall into an open groove and follow this with difficulty until easier climbing leads to the top.
A.Sharp, P.Lewis 24.10.1987

3. **Gnasher**   17m   E5,6a   \
Start at the foot of the obvious left-facing flake crack in the centre of the tooth. Climb the crack to its close at a leftward-rising break. Finger traverse left along the break for 2m, then take the pockets and flakes straight up over a slight bulge, PR, to bigger holds and the narrow terrace.
M.Crocker 31.05.1998

4. **E By Gum**   15m   E5,6a   *
A new form of substance abuse for carrot crunchers and other southerners. Start 2m right of Gnasher at the base of the pink wall. Reach an obvious left-facing fin and continue slightly left to a bulge. Pass the bulge using a jug on the right and proceed up the incipient groove to a broken terrace and the top of the tooth on the left.
M.Crocker, J.Harwood 26.04.1998

5. **Scurvy**   10m   E3,5c
From a point 2½m right of the right end of the underlying ledge, climb up to the obvious pocket at 4m. Pull up and trend right to flakes and a loose exit onto the terrace.
M.Crocker 31.05.1998

Deborah's Overhang

1. **State of Grace**   45m   E4,5c,6a   *
The second pitch takes the large roof on the left of the crag and is characterised by two large holes.
1. 21m Climb a shallow groove below the left-hand (west) side of the roof to a big ledge. PB.
2. 24m Move left off the ledge and follow pockets past two holes to good belays well back, TRs.
A.Sharp, P.Lewis, J.Harwood 08.03.1986

2. **Debauching Deborah**   20m   E3,6a   Fr6c   *
In the centre of the crag, is a clean white groove leading to a platform below the roof. Start on the false beach immediately below the groove at vague ramp. Climb this to a slab and wander up to the cave. From the cave pull left into and go up the white scoop and arete to a BB just below the roof. Abseil.
R.Thomas 00.00.1997

3. **Deborah**   21m   E3,6b   Fr6c+
Start on the beach directly below a large hole and right of the start of Debauching Deborah. Climb the roof, 2BRs, harder than it looks, to a ledge, then easily to a roof. Traverse off right to finish.
A.Sharp, P.Lewis 00.00.1985

4. **Hydraulic Lunch**   15m   E7,6c   Fr8a   *
The old aid route through the right-hand side of the main roof proves painful and difficult! Ten mono cranks on old bolt holes lead to a jug and a pull on an evil sloper round the roof. A left hand little finger crank gains the chain.
J.Talbot, B.Talbot - Deborah's Overhang 00.00.1966
FFA G.Ashmore 03.05.1996

At east end of the overhang are two routes. The first one starts immediately right of the end of the roof.

5. **Three Minute Hero**   18m   E5,6b   Fr7a+   *
   Make dynamic moves up past a good Friend. If successful, clip some bolts, gain a hole and the easy upper
   section. A belay can be found on the rocks behind the terrace.
   A.Sharp, P.Lewis 00.00.1985

6. **Ground Control**   15m   E4,6b
   The crack and groove 3m right of Three Minute Hero.
   A.Sharp, P.Lewis 00.00.1985

TV Zawn
This is the zawn immediately underneath the main Deborah's roof. To reach it scramble down from the false beach
to the real beach and turn right. It is more extensive than it would appear from the outside, and contains a number of
routes and projects. The routes are described as approached, i.e. right to left. The last two lines are projects.

1. **Voyage Of The Zawn Treader**   8m   HVS,5b   Fr5
   The first bolt line through the roof. Once over the roof (crux) sidle leftwards to finish up New Zawn.
   G.Ashmore 15.11.1996

2. **New Zawn**   8m   E2,5c   Fr6a+
   The roof and subsequent slab to the left to a lower off.
   G.Ashmore 15.11.1996

3. **Going Down On Deborah**   10m   E3,6a   Fr6c
   The roof to the left and subsequent wall, prove an awkward and rewarding struggle.
   R.Thomas 07.11.1997

4. **Down Under Deborah**   12m   E4,6a   Fr7a   *
   The groove to the left.
   R.Thomas 17.07.1999

Seaspit Small Cove
250m east of Deborah's overhang, this 'crag' has a 12m wave of rubbishy orange rock. An uninspiring venue to say
the least, whose main function is to annoy the guidebook checker.

1. **Kithara**   12m   E3,6a
   Start 8m left of the prominent groove line, below an undercut at 2m. Pull up and move steeply rightward to reach
   a small spike above the bulge. Reach up to the left-rising break and finish up the easier upper groove.
   M.Crocker 30.10.1998

2. **Ne Pas Equipé**   12m   E4,6a
   Start 4m left of the crack and groove. Work through a bulge on undercuts to gain the left-sloping break. Move up
   into a grey groove with a pink patch overhead. Follow this to gain the top via a jug.
   M.Crocker 30.10.1998

3. **Staple Riot**   12m   E3,6a
   Traversing the left rising break from 2m left of the crack and groove, TRs. Finish direct after 6m. A bag.
   M.Crocker 30.10.1998

4. **Spit Grafitti**   12m   E2,5c
   The crack and groove.
   M.Crocker 30.10.1998

PAVILAND AND JUNIPER WALL

GR435859 to 438858
By Goi Ashmore

TIDAL STATUS: Paviland, Juniper Wall and Paviland Way Out West are non-tidal. The other crags vary from 1½ hours either side of low water to marginally tidal, see individual crags.

BOLTING POLICY: See individual crags.

PREAMBLE
Paviland and Juniper Wall are two of the most interesting crags on Gower for the middle grade climber. Juniper Wall has the excellent Assassin, the best route of its grade on Gower. Paviland has a much more extensive portfolio of routes in the HS to HVS range, many with two stars, as well as a small batch of well protected easier extremes. Juniper Wall faces east and gets the morning sun, whilst Paviland faces south to southwest, making a good double venue when the weather is an important factor. At first sight Paviland appears overgrown, but this is deceptive. Stallion Cove is a major new venue, with lots of potential for future sports routes on the massive leaning wall at the back, although all the current routes on the side walls are traditionally protected. There is a fine hotch-potch of interesting routes on the smaller crags too.

ACCESS
Follow the B4247 from Scurlage towards Rhossili to a sharp bend with a single white house on the left and Pilton Green Farm on the right (GR447872). Park on the grass leading to the farm. Take the path to the left of the white house, signposted to Paviland Cave, to reach a dry valley after about 15 minutes, at the landward end of which is a stile. The path continues down to the sea and Paviland Main Cliff is on the right (west). However, except for Liberty Zawn, there are better approaches to the Paviland Cliff mentioned below. For Juniper Wall and Eos Zawn, cross the stile, but strike immediately left (east) to follow a cliff top path through fields. Follow the path until a vague cwm leads down to the sea. Go down the cwm to get to the Wall just round the shoulder of the ridge. It is also possible to reach Juniper Wall by following the coastal path from Boiler Slab. This takes a lot longer, but makes for a good day out, especially if combined with some ridge climbing round Hollow Top or Horses Cliff.

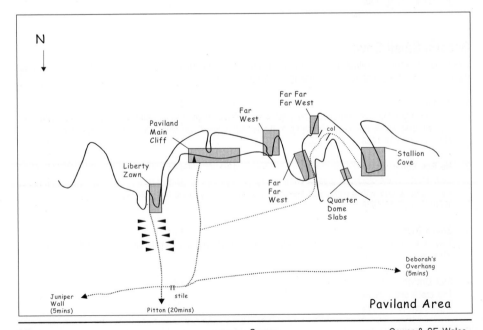

Paviland Main Cliff - From the stile at the top of the dry valley follow the wall down the valley and traverse around the back of the inlet to the seaward buttress on the right (west). An exciting but easy traverse past some blow holes leads to the front of the cliff. The most common approach for those familiar with the crag is to abseil off the large ring bolt and threads above the top of East Gully Groove. This can be found by taking the right-hand (west) path from the first stile, immediately crossing a second stile and walking towards the headland. Look for the yellow-topped bluff on the left-hand side of a small depression. The ring bolt is on the right-hand side of the depression (when facing the sea). There are back up threads in the cave 3m lower down.

Liberty Zawn – As for Paviland Main Cliff (non-abseil approach) to reach the toe of the buttress. Fix an abseil rope here and descend into the right-hand (west) gully.

Paviland Far Far West - Cross the stile at the top of the valley and bear right (west) up a slope to reach open cliff top. Head for the further of the two headlands to find a dry valley facing out to sea. Paviland Far Far West is the narrow tidal zawn below the bottom of the valley, reached either by abseil in from threads on the right (west) side, or by scrambling down the left (east) flank and doubling back round.

Paviland Far Far Far West – as for Paviland Far Far West but take the right-hand (west) side of the valley and continue seawards until a path runs up right (west) to a col. From the col, abseil in to the wall, which is left (east) of the apex of the headland.

Paviland Over and Out West (Quarterdome Slabs) – As for Paviland Far Far Far West, but go over the col and contour round to the vegetated slabs.

Stallion Cove (Paviland Wild West) – As for Paviland Far Far Far West, but from the col, follow a loose rake down towards the obvious sea cove.

Paviland Far West – As for Paviland Far Far West, taking the left (east) side of the valley. At the cliff line (the west flank of Paviland Main Cliff) is a narrow zawn directly below. Abseil in.

DESCENTS: See individual crags.

THE ROUTES

Stallion Cove (Paviland Wild West)

TIDAL STATUS: Routes on the west side can be approached 1 hour either side of low water. Machine Gun Kelly and Devolution 2 hours either side of low water, other routes on the east side are non-tidal. The tidal status of The Hole is unknown.

BOLTING POLICY: No bolting except on the back wall of the cove (i.e. the steeply overhanging wall left of Machine Gun Kelly).

DESCENTS: Descent on the west side is best done by reversing Ron The Common Man. Descent on the east side is either by abseiling off slings or by walking off to the right (east).

The leaning cave roof is one of the most impressive pieces of rock on Gower, whilst on either side, more amenable walls offer up a nice collection of routes. The routes on the west side of the cove are best reached by walking along the beach left of Machine Gun Kelly 1 hour either side of low water. The rake leading down from the Col forms a 10m high rift just before dropping down to the base of the cove and the routes on the east wall start in the rift.

The Hole
This lies somewhere to the west of Stallion Cove, but was not located at the time of writing.

1. **Le Sewage Pudding**   15m   E1,5a   \
   Start at the base of the hole. Step onto the slab and move up to a deep slot. Contine slightly left to reach the groove and overhang. Move right onto the subsidiary slab and climb direct to the top.
   M.Richards, J.Williams 00.05.1999

2. **Raspberry Nipple**   10m   VS,5a   \
   Atmospheric. Scramble down the western ridge of the hole until it is possible to traverse back right towards the cave and a belay ledge. From a short crack make a committing reach to jugs on the lip of the overhanging wall. Finish more easily in a direct line.
   M.Richards, J.Williams 00.05.1999

West Wall
There are two routes somewhere on the seaward face west of the main section of this wall, Outside Leg (VD) and Last Over Before Tea (VD), soloed by C.Evans. Descriptions were unavailable at the time of writing, but they are probably quite pleasant.

1. **Chill Air**   80m   S
   A long route with good positions but some alarmingly loose rock. Climb the bounding ridge of the west wall of Stallion Cove with a short detour right at 60m.
   R.High, J.Harwood 06.03.1999

The most obvious feature of the west wall is the huge chimney of Ron The Common Man. To the seaward side of this is a 20m high wall. The first route is on the left side of this wall. There is a spike belay at the base.

2. **Meg's Route**   24m   VS,4b
   At the seaward end of the west wall are two slanting grooves. Climb the left-hand groove to a rightward-trending diagonal crack. Continue left of this, to finish up the leaning wall past a matchbox-shaped hold.
   C.Evans, J.Williams 00.00.1999

3. **Rachel's Route**   24m   VS,4b
   The right-hand groove, finishing a metre or so to the right of Meg's Route.
   C.Evans, D.Morris 00.00.1999

4. **Line Of Totality**   24m   E3,5c   *
   To the right of Rachel's Route is a third route running up to a steep crack.
   M.Richards, T.Milner 00.07.1999

5. **Unnamed I**   24m   E3,5c
   A line up the wall to the right of Line Of Totality
   J.Williams 00.07.1999

6. **Parenting Orders And Bribery**   24m   VD
   The grooves left of Ron The Common Man, linked by a slab.
   C.Evans, J.Williams, D.Morris 00.00.1999

7. **Ron The Common Man**   24m   VD   **
   The huge chimney dominating the west wall.
   A.Sharp, P.Lewis 00.05.1999

8. **Unnamed II**   24m   E1,5b
   As for Ron The Common Man to two-thirds height. Pull out onto the right wall and climb a groove to finish.
   A.Sharp, P.Lewis 00.05.1999

East Wall

9. **Machine Gun Kelly**   31m   E5,6b,5b   *
P1 takes the vicious leaning crack above the base of the rift, P2 takes the centre of the headwall.
1. 16m From the base of the rift reach and follow jugs left to the arete at the foot of the crack (a sling flicked onto a spike protects the start). Power up the crack to massive holds over the lip. Scramble 6m to belay at the base of the inset headwall. Almost as hard as Undercut Crack at Bamford.
2. 15m Climb totally direct up the fawn coloured leaning wall to a ledge at 5m. Continue straight up, keeping about 2-3m right of a broken black crackline to easier ground and a belay in the niche. Traverse right and climb down the ledge to the usual descent.
M.Crocker – Pitch 2 10.10.1998, M.Crocker – Pitch 1 07.02.1999

10. **Devolution**   18m   E6,6b   **
The thin diagonal crack running through the roof right of Machine Gun Kelly to join the top of Colt 45 P1, 2PRs.
A.Sharp, M.Richards 00.00.1999

11. **Colt 45**   40m   E2,5c,4c   *
1. 25m From 2m further up the rift, transfer onto an obvious rightward sloping ramp. Follow the ramp over a bulge to reach a rounded grey jug. Move right and pull up to easier ground. Climb easily leftwards to belay on a good brown spike below a wide crack right of the headwall.
2. 15m Climb the wide crack for 4m then swing left onto a flake on the headwall. Continue up on pockets and sharp rock to a ledge. Fix gear, then traverse right to a belay on a large rock spike at a slightly lower level. Finishing direct from the headwall is Room 101 (4b, C.Evans, J.Williams 1999).
M.Crocker –Pitch 1 18.10.1998, M.Crocker, J.Harwood – Pitch 2 07.02.1998

12. **Marco Golo**   25m   E2,5b   *
Start halfway up the rift, at a low TR. Step across the rift into sharp cracks and follow these, stepping right at 5m to thinner cracks leading to the left-slanting break. Hand-traverse the break rightwards for 2m then climb straight up the bulge to a serrated sloping ledge and old golo. Continue directly up slabby grey rock to a belay ledge.
M.Crocker 18.10.1998

13. **Marco Golo Direct**   23m   E3,6b
Gain the rightmost cracks of Marco Golo just below the break, from directly below, avoiding holds in the start of the parent route. Contrived, but nice climbing on razors.
A.Sharp, P.Lewis 00.05.1999

14. **Moacs Are Extinct**   18m   HVS,5a   *
Start at the top of the rift. From a good flake on the wall climb to the base of a right-facing groove rising from a deep right-slanting break. Ascend the groove past an old in-situ Moac, to a ledge at the top of the wall.
M.Crocker 18.10.1998

15. **Dinosaurs Don't Clip**   18m   HS,4b
The wall and groove to the right of Moacs Are Extinct.
M.Richards, T.Milner 00.05.1999

Paviland Way Out West (Quarter Dome Slabs)

TIDAL STATUS: Non-tidal.

BOLTING POLICY: No bolting.

DESCENTS: From the top head right (east) to gain the gully initially used to approach the crag (i.e. that above Paviland Far Far West).

These are the fairly vegetated west-south-west facing slabs above and east of Stallion Cove.

1. **Flaming June!?** 20m E2,5b \
A delicious clean slab topped by nonsense. Start about 30m left (west) of the bounding ridge and col on the right. Take easy flake cracks onto the smoother grey slabs and climb direct on pockets, TR, to a bulge. Pull up onto the leaning wall and go up to the top.
M.Crocker, J.Harwood 07.06.1998

2. **Winter Looms So Soon** 25m E2,5b \
Start 10m left of Flaming June!? beneath the most prominent overhang at 15m. Climb a fairly obvious right-facing flake crack then transfer left onto another, old TR. Trend slightly right to a fawn coloured scoop in a bulge. Pull through the scoop to good incuts and move up to the overhang. Surmount the roof on the right and finish up the headwall, taking care with the exit.
M.Crocker 10.10.1998

Paviland Far Far Far West

TIDAL STATUS: Non-Tidal

BOLTING POLICY: No bolting.

DESCENTS: Descent is by abseil from the top. The finishes are loose and an abseil rope needs to be used to escape. The top is loose and requires care in placement of the abseil rope.

This is the south-facing slab at the front of the headland 250m west of Paviland Main Cliff, from which it is visible in profile. There are three slab climbs here at present, with considerable potential for further routes. The face containing the routes could be reached by an easy scramble from the west starting at the col to the north of the headland. Abseil approach is less stressful and is required for the top out anyway. The abseil is from a tat (back-up required) just 20m east of the high point of the headland.

At the left-hand side of the cliff is an obvious pink coloured niche at 20m. The three current routes take the smooth wide slab below the niche and end at the niche.

1. **The Time Directive** 20m VS,4c
Start below a break in the left-hand side of the overhang, beneath the white slab. Pull through the overhang to a break. Climb straight up the slab to slot slightly to the left. Take the crack and the rib above and step right into the niche.
M.Crocker, J.Harwood 07.06.1998

2. **On The Job** 20m HVS,4c *
Pull up and left through the right-hand end of the overhang, then climb straight up to the niche.
M.Crocker, J.Harwood 07.06.1998

3. **Spank Your Secretary** 20m VS,4c
Towards the right side of the slab are twin cracks. Climb easily to gain the blind left-hand crack. This leads to a flake crack, which is followed leftwards to the niche.
M.Crocker, J.Harwood 07.06.1998

Paviland Far Far West

TIDAL STATUS: The first couple of routes are affected at high water during spring tides, otherwise non-tidal.

DESCENTS: Abseil is most practical for reasons described below, else scramble down the east bank.

BOLTING POLICY: Bolts may be placed for lower offs only.

Paviland Far Far West, is less far out west than one might think! It has a steep western wall (left when looking landward) 15m high. It is advisable to lower off an abseil rope because of the chossy top and the poor state of the PBs. The routes start near a large jammed conglomerate chockstone at the base of the cliff.

1. **Hung Over**   15m   E1,5b
   Start 9m left of the chockstone, just left of a rock pedestal. Climb a short overhanging wall to reach large holds, TR, then up past a small overlap with a hole. Climb the wall above, TR, to a horizontal break.
   R.Thomas, J.Bullock 00.04.1988

2. **Threadbare**   15m   E1,5b   \
   Start 1m right of Hung Over. Step off the top of the rock pedestal past a hole and a small overhang, then trend leftwards to reach a depression with black streaks.
   J.Bullock, G.Evans 15.02.1987

3. **Nematode**   15m   E2,5b
   Start 1m right of the rock pedestal. Climb steeply, TR, past a hole containing another TR to reach a calcite area, TR. Finish straight up, TR.
   R.Thomas, J.Bullock, L.Moran 02.05.1988

4. **Rock Bottom**   15m   E1,5c   \
   Start just left of the chockstone. Step across and climb to a small scoop, TR, move left into a shallow groove, PR, then finish directly.
   J.Bullock, G.Evans 24.04.1988

5. **Chock A Block**   15m   E2,5b
   Start from the right-hand end of the chockstone. Pull up steeply, TR, then go up the steep wall, 2TR. Finish up the short wall above.
   J.Bullock, L.Moran, R.Thomas 00.05.1988

6. **Off The Peg**   15m   E2,5b
   Start 2m right of the chockstone at a TR above a small hole. Climb past the TR and up the wall to a small overhang, TR. Move over it, PR and up the wall above.
   J.Bullock, L.Moran, R.Thomas 00.05.1988

7. **Scarface**   15m   E1,5c
   Climb the wall 4m right of Off The Peg, TR, to reach a shattered groove. Follow this to the top.
   J.Bullock, L.Moran, R.Thomas 00.05.1988

8. **Stonewall**   15m   E1,5c
   Start 3m right of Scarface. Climb to a diagonal rightward-sloping ledge then up left, TR, to the top.
   J.Bullock, L.Moran, R.Thomas 00.05.1988

9. **Ledger**   15m   E2,5c
   From the base of the stone wall climb to a diagonal rightward-sloping ledge, then up and left past a TR to the top.
   R.Thomas, J.Bullock, L.Moran 00.05.1988

Paviland Far West

TIDAL STATUS: 2 hours either side of low water.

BOLTING POLICY: No bolting, except on the overhanging wall at the landward end of the zawn, where new sports routes are allowed.

DESCENTS: By abseil.

The cliff is characterised by a smooth overhanging white wall at its landward end and a large bowl-shaped cave in the back, containing an A2 Aid Route (A.Berry 1996) and the obvious corner of Smuts.

1. **Gunfire Hill**   21m   E1,5b   \
   Start at a left-slanting ramp, about 15m left of Smuts. Go up the ramp for 1m, then take a flake up and right. From the top of the flake continue straight to the top.
   M.Crocker, J.Harwood 07.06.1998

2. **Voortrekker**   21m   E5,6a   \
   Start below a black bulge 10m left of Smuts. Go up to the bulge and make hard moves left to pass the bulge. Continue slightly rightwards to a very slim groove that leads to the top.
   M.Crocker, J.Harwood 07.06.1998

3. **Rorke's Drift**   21m   E1,5b
   Climb the centre of the wall 4m left of Smuts, moving right to finish.
   A.Sharp, J.Harwood 23.02.1986

4. **Smuts**   21m   VS,4c
   The obvious corner in the wall at the west end of the cliff and climb the corner.
   A.Sharp, J.Harwood 23.02.1986

Paviland Main Cliff

TIDAL STATUS: Non-tidal.

BOLTING POLICY: No bolting.

DESCENTS: Either walk inland to gain the stile at the top of the dry valley or abseil from the huge ring bolt at the top of the cliff above East Gully Groove (see Access section). Routes below East Gully Groove end at the base of the main cliff, so the descent is as for the approach.

The routes are described from right to left since this is the direction of approach. The first feature to be seen is a large cave (Paviland Cave). High above and to the left is Shelob's Cave. Immediately left is an obvious groove/gully with numerous holes - East Gully Groove. Left again is a prominent calcite encrusted crack, taken by The Ring. There are many possible variations linking up routes, but only the major ones are described. The slabby buttress above Paviland Cave is loose and not recommended although routes have been recorded.

The first route described is situated on the east face (i..e overlooking the dry valley), above blow holes at the base of the cliff.

1. **Polly's Route**   45m   VD
   Take a vague line up the cleanest section of the slab, then trend up the crest of the ridge to finish at will.
   R.Cole, P.Cole 00.00.1976

The next route climbs through Shelob's Cave, high above Paviland Cave.

2. **Shelob**   36m   HS,4b   *
   'Don't do Shelob if you are fat or pregnant' (Jeremy Talbot 1997). An unusual route, with daft finishing moves in an exposed position. An optional stance is available in the cave. Climb easy vegetated slabs right of the obvious 'trench' of East Gully Groove, heading for the cave. Climb up the back of the cave and make a contorted sequence of moves, many old TRs, to exit through the hole. Short legs are an advantage.
   J.Talbot, C.Connick 00.00.1976

3. **East Gully Groove**   36m   HVS,5a   **
A good, well protected route. Climb the obvious gully in its entirety, passing Jeremy Talbot's workshop at half-height. Finish rightwards at the top. Some of the tats are getting a bit worse for wear.
J.Talbot, C.Connick 00.00.1976

The routes between East Gully Groove and The Ring are a little contrived and close together in places. Their descriptions may vary from the original lines due to rationalisation.

4. **Talons**   32m   E2,6a
A short fingery pitch up the right side of the steep smooth wall. Quite hard for the grade. Whilst originally climbed via the first pitch of Half Dome, with a belay in East Gully Groove, this is a bit pointless. Follow East Gully Groove to the first big hole, bridge up and lean out to a good hold on the left wall. Follow the pockets above with difficulty to finish, TRs, PRs.
A.Sharp, J.Harwood 01.01.1981

5. **The Cure**   33m   E3,6a   *
Essentially a direct on Half Dome. As for Half Dome, but continue more directly to the break, making a couple of hard pulls to rejoin Half Dome at the thread in its top crack.
J.Talbot, C.Connick – Cancer Pre-1979
FFA A.Sharp, J.Harwood 01.01.1985

6. **Half Dome**   36m   E2,5c   **
A good route. Start just to the right of the base of the slab on the left side of the gully and pull onto it. Head up the slab, moving slightly left to the good stance on Babylon (possible belay). Move right to the crack at the end of the ledge and move up into this, TR, finishing up and slightly left.
J.Talbot, C.Connick 1pt 00.00.1977
FFA A.Sharp, J.Harwood 01.01.1985

7. **Babylon**   42m   HVS,5a   *
This takes a line right of and parallel to The Ring. Start at a deep slot at the foot of East Gully Groove. Climb cracks in the wall 1m right of The Ring to reach the ledge (variations possible). Climb the cracks directly above and left of the more obvious Half Dome crack (good threads - not in situ).
J.Talbot, C.Connick 00.00.1977

8. **The Ring**   42m   HS,4b   **
The calcite-encrusted line rising from the foot of East Gully Groove. Climb to an obvious hole and follow the calcite line to the niche, possible belay. Climb the crack/groove above to the top.
J.Talbot, C.Connick 00.00.1976

The rest of the routes start across the gully at the base of The Ring. Standing about 20m left of the gully, two prominent cracks can be seen high up on the crag, about 20m apart. The right-hand one is the finish of Liang Shan Po, the left-hand one is the finish of Middle Earth. All these routes are as vegetated as they appear from the ground, but they are not too overgrown to climb, due to the bizarre Paviland plant-pot jugs.

9. **Liang Shan Po**   45m   E1,5b   *
Fine climbing. Start left The Ring. Climb the wall anywhere via a tiny overhang at half-height, past loads of TRs. Take the overhang direct via an obvious crack on the left of the arete, PR. Finish direct.
J.Talbot, C.Connick 00.00.1977

10. **Middle Earth**   45m   VS,4c   *
Another good route up the deep central groove and crack leading through the high central overhang left of Liang Shan Po, characterised by the steep and obvious jam crack. Start below the jam crack and climb the wall anywhere to gain a deep groove. Follow this to reach the jam crack. Either skirt round the crack to the left, or take it direct (HVS,5b). Follow the crack to the top.
J.Talbot, C.Connick 00.00.1977

11. **Black Widow**   45m   HVS,5a
Start midway between Middle Earth and Gimli. Climb the wall fairly directly to about mid-height then move up
and right to a shaky pillar, on Middle Earth. Go up left to below the roof and pull right on a good hold to the top.
J.Talbot, C.Connick - First Half 00.00.1977
G.Evans, D.Hopkins - Complete Route 00.00.1987

12. **Gimli**   42m   HVS,5a
This climbs the crack and groove up the right side of the high central overhang. Start in the recess containing a
hole, directly below the right side of the big roof. Climb cracks to the right end of the overhangs, move steeply
up the groove until below a final overhanging crack, move up left and back right to the top. Climbing direct from
the top of the crack is E1,5b and pretty tricky.
J.Talbot, C.Connick 00.00.1977

13. **Armageddon**   42m   HVS,5a   *
Gain the wide crack cutting the roof about 2m to the left of the upper crack of Gimli. The upper crack is hard for
a few moves, before easy ground is gained. Lots of TRs.
J.Talbot, C.Connick 00.00.1978

14. **Balrog**   42m   HVS,5a
Start below the left-hand side of the overhang. Saunter up a groove, onto an overhang and surmount this directly
via a crack to gain wobbly holds and a worryingly loose finishing groove. It is possible to skirt the roof on the
right, to gain a second groove and a further roof. Following this line, stepping left under the upper roof to gain the
same finish is about VS.
J.Talbot, C.Connick 00.00.1976

15. **West Arete**   45m   VD   ●
A bag situated at the far left-hand end of the face. Climb to an overlap and move right into a vague corner, then
left to the skyline arete. Finish up this.
J.Talbot, C.Connick 00.00.1977

A few loose routes have been recorded left of this but are held in place by beams from outer space and are not
recorded here.

16. **Fellowship Of The Ring**   39m   E1,5c,5a,4c   **
A fine high level girdle of the cliff.
1. 7m Follow the easy section of East Gully Groove to the base of the leftward-trending break cutting through Half
Dome etc. Make a very hard move left to start, TR. Continue across the break to belay in the obvious groove
line (The Ring).
2. 12m Step up and left from the Ring, then cross the slab on good crozzles, TR. Gain the deep groove with a
prominent jam crack above (Middle Earth). Either belay here, or on a shelf a few metres lower.
3. 20m From the base of the prominent jam crack, swing left onto a pedestal. Continue at this level, across
exposed territory, passing below a thin crack to gain a wide finishing groove.
J.Talbot, C.Connick 00.00.1977

17. **Red Lady**   48m   E1,5a,5b
A rather indefinite rising traverse.
1. 25m Start as for Half Dome. Climb onto the wall and make a leftward-rising ascent to the quartzy crack of The
Ring. Traverse left to Liang Shan Po and follow this for a short distance to the level of a small hole. Traverse left
to Middle Earth and belay in the crack below an obvious niche.
2. 23m Move leftwards to the crack of Gimli and swing left onto the wall above the large overhang. Swing left
and finish up Armageddon
J.Talbot, C.Connick 00.00.1977
FFA J.Bullock, G.Evans 00.00.1980

Below East Gully Groove

The line of weakness in the cliff taken by East Gully Groove also extends down into a zawn, the landward end of which is non-tidal. The zawn can be accessed down the eastern bank. A few poor routes of minor interest have been done. The most leftmost route starts at a slightly lower level than the other three and can identified by two old in-situ TRs.

1. **Mouse House**   9m   E2,5c
    The aforementioned route with 2TRs. The best route in the zawn.
    P.Donnithorne 00.00.1988

2. **Ferret**   7m   HVS,5a
    To the right of Mouse House is a rock step. Starting from near the left-hand end of the rock step, climb directly to the top, via a good spike runner.
    P.Donnithorne 00.00.1988

3. **Shrew**   7m   HVS,5a
    Climb the wall 2m right of Ferret, with a sling to protect the top out.
    P.Donnithorne 00.00.1988

4. **Rat**   9m   E3,6a
    To the right is a prominent flake crack, which looks from below like it tops out onto hideously loose blocks. Fortunately the blocks seem to be sound. Gain the flake crack from the left using pockets (good wires) and blast quickly up the crack to a bold, but easier finish.
    P.Donnithorne 00.00.1988

The following routes have proved very difficult to locate, even the first ascensionists having forgotten their whereabouts. They are in this zawn, probably at the tidal end.

5. **Ice Age**   15m   E3,5c
    The obvious layback crack in the left side of the zawn. Finish direct.
    A.Sharp, J.Harwood 23.02.1986

6. **Down Under**   21m   E5,6a   *
    A strenuous number. Start 6m right of Ice Age and climb an obvious line of leftward-trending flakes over a roof to the top.
    A.Sharp, P.Lewis, P.Thomas 00.00.1985

7. **Squeeze Please**   18m   VS,4c
    The chimney at the back of the zawn, finishing behind the chockstone
    P.Thomas, P.Lewis, A.Sharp 00.00.1985

Liberty Zawn

TIDAL STATUS: 1½ hours either side of low water.

BOLTING POLICY: No bolting.

DESCENTS: By abseil.
This is the zawn crossed at its narrow landward end when approaching the Main Cliff from the dry valley. It contains some good pitches, Liberty being worth a visit in its own right. The zawn to the east also contains some easy scrambling.

West Wall
The routes are described from right to left.

1. **Simple Minds**   20m   VS,4c
   The obvious ramp running up rightwards from the base of Liberty.
   P.Lewis, J.Harwood 09.02.1986

2. **Liberty**   12m   E2,5c   **
   A sustained pitch, with good wires, taking the obvious cracks in the centre of the wall on superb rock. A TR (not in situ) protects the start.
   A.Sharp, P.Lewis, J.Harwood 09.02.1986

3. **Mettel Fatigue**   12m   E3,6a   *
   From 3m up Liberty, place the good wires and make a tricky 'fall' leftwards onto a vague ramp and pocket, to gain a small hole. Pull round the overlap above the hole and finish up the easier wall above.
   A.Sharp, P.Lewis, J.Harwood 09.02.1986

East Wall
This is the west-facing wall of the gully.

4. **Yanks**   12m   E4,6c
   The obvious flake in the east wall of the gully has a very trying start, which, although theoretically 6b, is always so wet and barnacle encrusted that the 6c grade sticks - boots tend not to! Either lasso, or pre clip runners at the top of the flake and climb to its top. Step slightly left and finish direct.
   A.Sharp, J.Harwood 09.02.1986

Juniper Wall

TIDAL STATUS: The Main Cliff is non-tidal. Eos Zawn 1½ hours either side of low water.

BOLTING POLICY: No bolting.

DESCENTS: Descent from the main cliff is by following a path down the north (right) flank and doubling back round. Eos Zawn is best approached by abseil anyway.

Juniper Wall is triangular with prominent overhangs at its apex above the lower slabs/wall. A large overlap runs down from a corner beneath the centre of the main overhangs. In the centre of the crag below the overhangs is a slightly right-slanting groove and thin crack (Assassin). This is crossed at one and two-thirds height by two cracks rising leftwards across the crag, parallel with the right skyline. On the left side of the main overhangs is a prominent nest. This should be left alone, not for ornithological reasons, but because of the dire consequences of disturbing the resident, which is probably a Patrick Troughton era Dr. Who monster. Directly below the nest and about 4m below the overhangs is a clutch of pegs known as The Junction Stance. The lines, although good, tend to be a bit difficult to follow, so read the descriptions carefully. Belays on the top of the cliff are positioned well back.

1. **The Jackal Finish**   50m   E2,5c   *
   Climb any route to reach the Junction stance. Move up and left into an impending triangular corner (ancient bolts). Climb the corner to a huge PR and swing left onto a rib. Continue left for 3m, then pull up and right into a groove. Either traverse left up this groove to finish, or pull directly up to a ledge and finish up steep rock.
   M.Hogge 1pt 00.00.1968
   FFA J.Bullock, G.Evans 00.06.1982

2. **Overkill**   48m   HVS,4c,4c
   Good, slightly bold climbing on the P1, is a little spoiled by the P2, which is nothing more than a few metres of independent climbing used to reach the top of Assassin.
   1. 24m Start at the left side of the crag, below a crack in the slab 5m left of the prominent niche of Killer's Route. Climb the crack, then curve rightwards on discontinuous cracks below the overlap to gain the Junction Stance, 4m below the main overhangs, PB.

2. 24m Traverse right, bearing upwards, keeping about 2m below under the overlaps, to reach a more open area of rock. Finish diagonally right up these cracks (Assassin).
SUMC – P1 00.00.1968, M.Harber, D.Parsons – P2 00.00.1981

3. **Killer's Route**   42m   E2,4c,5b   *
Start below and left of the slightly rightward-slanting shallow central groove by a wide slanting crack and slab.
1. 20m Climb up left to a large triangular niche. Surmount the overhang above and continue up a crack to The Junction Stance, PB.
2. 22m Traverse rightwards for 3m and pull into a small overhung ledge in the corner. Pull over to another overhung ledge, quit it on its right and continue up steep but easy ground.
SUMC – P1 00.00.1968, G.Evans, J.Bullock – P2 00.06.1982

4. **Haaievinnesoep**   35m   E4,4b,6a   *   \
1. 20m As for Killer's Route to the Junction Stance.
2. 15m Clip the PR high up above the belay from the corner (The Jackal Finish) and step back down. Climb the headwall directly above the belay (crux) to gain an obvious scoop, 2PRs. Follow easy ground to finish up the corner above the Zygon nest.
G.Ashmore, J.Tracey 02.08.1997

5. **Barracuda**   38m   E5,6a,5c   *
A daring route following the obvious crozzly line left of Assassin.
1. 18m Climb directly up to a v formed by Assassin crossing Hair Raiser low down. The initial hard moves up to the start of the crozzly flakes are well protected by a good wire, but there then follows a 12m run out on tricky 5c moves to a jam crack. Place gear, breathe a sight of relief and amble easily up to an obvious leftward traverse leading to The Junction Stance.
2. 20m Gain P2 of Killer's Route, by pulling up right round the arete above the stance.
A.Sharp, J.Harwood 03.07.1982

6. **Assassin**   45m   HVS,5a   ***
Superb climbing up the rightward-slanting groove in the centre of the cliff. The best route on Gower at this grade. Climb the crack and slab that lead to a groove and a shallow niche at 21m. Continue using the twin cracks above, move right around the bulge and then left to a broken groove. Follow this with difficulty to a ledge, then move left to finish up a scoop.
E.Pardoe 00.00.1968
FFA J.Bullock, R.Thomas 22.06.1980

7. **Perch**   35m   E1,5b
Compared to Barracuda this is a sea cucumber. Climb to the overlap as for Hitman then continue up a pair of thin cracks to the break of Dry Riser. The wall above is climbed to the top finishing about 3m right of Assassin.
G.Evans, J.Bullock 08.10.1989

8. **Trevor, The Pint And The Pram**   33m   HVS,4c   *
Start below the obvious jammed block at 7m, to the right of the Assassin groove. Step onto the block from the left and continue up a vague rightward-sloping crack. From the upper diagonal crack (Dry Riser) move diagonally right across a steep wall, to gain a broken crack and follow this slightly left to the top. This route was referred to as Hitman in previous guides.
SUMC 00.00.1968

9. **Rattle And Hum**   35m   VS,4c
Start 2m right of Trevor, The Pint And The Pram and climb a rightwards slanting crack to the upper traverse line (Dry Riser) and a niche. Finish up the right-hand of the two shallow cracked grooves.
C.Allen, L.Cain 00.00.1986

10. **Task Force**   36m   VS,4c
Start at a small recess below a vague right-slanting groove 5m right of Hitman. Follow the groove rightwards to gain the upper traverse line (Dry Riser), then finish up the tricky groove above.
M.Harber, C.Horsfield 00.00.1982

11. **Ninja**   30m   VS,4b   *
Right of Task Force, just left of the start of the start of the diagonal crack of Hair Raiser, climb directly to a hanging block at 3m, then follow a zig zag crack to a shallow niche on the upper diagonal line (Dry Riser). Continue up left through a black bulge, to another shallow niche. Bear right to finish. Lacks definition and is slightly loose.
C.Allen, M.Danford, A.Beaton 00.00.1990

12. **Hair Raiser**   44m   HVS,5a,4c   *
This follows the lower of two leftward-slanting cracklines across the face. Start at the right end of the crack.
1. 24m Follow the crack to the apex of the easy angled slab below Assassin. Continue along the steepening crack and strenuously across a bulging wall to a niche (Killers Route). Continue for 4m to belays in a small recess.
2. 20m Move left to an overlap and follow it down for 4m. Pull up left at a slight break, to another overlap. Traverse left beneath this to finish at the gully.
M.Harber, S.Robinson 00.00.1982

13. **On The Horizon**   24m   VS,4b   *
Start at the bottom right-hand end of the lower diagonal crack (Hair Raiser), 5m left of the prominent black scoop (Socialist Worker). Follow parallel cracks rightward until they peter out, move right and up to a recess, taking care with the rock. Finish directly.
G.Richardson, J.Pratt, C.Lownds 00.00.1981

14. **On The Horizon Direct**   24m   VS,4c   *
Climb the crack between On The Horizon and Socialist Worker, to join the former at 10m.
A.Beaton, C.Allen, M.Danford 00.00.1990

15. **Socialist Worker**   27m   VS,4c   *
'It keeps going left'. Start at a shallow triangular black-stained scoop about halfway between the starts of the two diagonal traverse lines. Climb to the upper traverse line (Dry Riser), step left and climb the tricky groove as for Task Force. It is possible to climb 1m right at about the same grade.
L.Moran, K.Snook, G.Richardson 00.00.1977, J.Beynon, J.Clapham Variant 00.00.2001

16. **Dry Riser**   67m   HVS, 4c,4c**
A girdle taking the higher of the two diagonal cracks. Start at the right side of the cliff where the crack meets the ground.
1. 36m Climb the crack to below the main overhangs. Traverse 6m left to The Junction Stance.
2. 31m Traverse left for 7m and break through the overlap, just left of a tiny corner. Continue up and left to easy ground.
M.Harber, J.Mothersele 00.00.1977

Eos Zawn

BOLTING POLICY: No bolting.

The following routes lie in the tidal zawn directly underneath Juniper Wall. Access is possible by walking across the zawn from the east side, or by abseiling down from the start of Socialist Worker. There is a prominent gully in the zawn.

1. **Here**   12m   HS,4b

   Climb to below the roof of Erinyes, then move out left across the smooth wall above the overhanging bulge to reach an indefinite fault line running up left. This point can also be reached direct from the narrowing of the gully. Climb this fault for a short way. Then exit directly up the wall.
   J.Talbot 00.00.1972

2. **Erinyes**   12m   VD

   Climb to the back wall and move up left below an obvious roof. Bridge up to its lip, then move left to get onto the small sloping slab above it. Continue up the corner direct to finish.
   J.Talbot 00.00.1971

3. **Eos**   18m   D

   Climb into the gully by a ramp on its right side. Move to the foot of the overhanging wall at its back and climb the right corner.
   J.Talbot 00.00.1971

HOLLOW TOP TO PORT EYNON

GR442856 to 467844
By Goi Ashmore & Chris Shorrock

TIDAL STATUS: Varies from 1½ hours either side of low water to non-tidal. See individual sections.

BOLTING POLICY: No bolting.

DESCENTS: See individual crags.

PREAMBLE
A complex stretch of coastline offering much rock, but with the exception of the excellent Boiler Slab, few concentrations of routes. The area abounds in small isolated buttresses, White Edge being the best of these and the area is a pleasant place to walk and explore away from the hordes.

ACCESS
For crags west of and including Devil's Cwm, it is slightly quicker to approach as for Juniper Wall, in which case the crags are found in the order described. For other crags except Culver Hole and Port Eynon Cave, the Overton approach is quicker.

1. Juniper Wall Approach
As for Paviland and Juniper Wall to the stile at the landward end of the dry valley, then take the left-hand path (east) as for Juniper Wall. This leads across the cliff top path. After 250m a long, wide gully slopes gently down to the sea, with a broken slabby crag on its east side and Juniper Wall on its west. The broken slabby crag is Hollow Top. The more striking ridge Horses Cliff is seen to the east and is easily approached either from the crag running along the low line from Hollow Top, or by following the cliff top path to reach the same point.
Yellow Buttress - is on the far side of Horses Cliff.
Devils' Cwm - is in the next gully to the east of Horses Cliff. Crags further to the east (starting with White Edge) can be reached along the cliff top path.

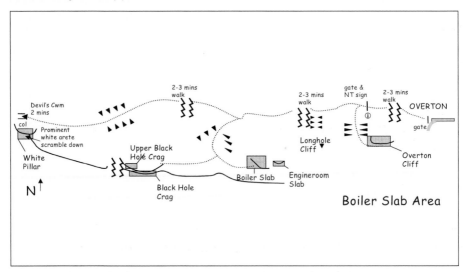

2. Overton Approach

Follow the A4118 to Port Eynon. Just before entering Port Eynon take the right turn signposted Overton. Drive through Overton to extremely limited parking in the village. Follow the road to the end where a lane continues (bearing slightly right). Follow the lane (GR455853) west along the cliff top to reach a gate at the head of the first prominent dry valley, with a National Trust sign marked Longhole Cliff. For Overton cliff, follow the dry valley downwards until the crag becomes visible on the left (east).

Longhole Cliff – Follow the cliff top path for 2 minutes until a vague dry valley is visible. Take this valley down to the crag.

Boiler Slab – Follow the cliff top path for 5 minutes to reach the third prominent dry valley. Turn down this to reach a lower path. At this point the crag is visible up on the left (east).

Black Hole Crag – As for Boiler Slab, but turn right (west) at the bottom of the dry valley. The crag is below the first dome-shaped headland.

White Pillar – As for Black Hole Crag, but follow the cliff top path up over the dome-shaped headland (behind it). From the far side of this headland, a clean white arete can be seen, marking the end of a system of dry valleys and blocking off the westward view. This is White Edge. The easiest way to reach it is to follow the path contouring round the field and drop down the second of the two dry valleys to hit a lower coastal path. Follow the lower coastal path until it starts to rise steeply up to a col. At this point contour around bearing left to reach the crag. The path over the col leads to Devil's Cwm.

3. Culver Hole and Port Eynon Cave Approach

Follow the A4118 to its end at Port Eynon (GR468852). Park in the beach car park and follow coastal paths west to the headland.

Port Eynon Cave - There are two caves one on either side of the point. The cave on the east side (encountered first) has no recorded routes at present. The second cave, 100m on and not visible from the top, can be accessed by scrambling down to its west.

Culver Hole – is 250m further along the coastal path in a zawn containing an in-situ dovecote.

THE ROUTES

Hollow Top
GR439858

TIDAL STATUS: Non-tidal.

DESCENTS: Walk down west or east.

1. **Hollow Top**   45m   M
    Hollow Top is the broken slabby crag overlooking Juniper Wall. The route takes any line up the slabby south western face.
    J.Talbot 00.00.1963

Horses Cliff
GR441857

TIDAL STATUS: Horses Cliff itself is non-tidal. The crag in the zawn below 3 hours either side of low water.

DESCENTS: Walk down west from Horses Cliff. The approach to the tidal zawn below is by abseil.

Horses Cliff is the second of the ridges east of Juniper Wall. It has a prominent tower at the seaward end.

1. **South West Wall**   45m   M
    Scramble up a diagonal line to reach South Ridge from the left.
    J.Talbot 00.00.1963

2. **The Corner**   45m   S
    Take the short corner on the west flank via a steep overhang, to reach and finish up South Ridge.
    J.Talbot 00.00.1969

3. **South Ridge**   45m   D
    A mountaineering route following the ridge of Horses Cliff.
    J.Talbot 00.00.1963

The zawn below the east side of Horses Cliff can be accessed by abseil. It contains two slabs.

4. **Faith**   15m   VD
    The left-hand slab.
    J.Talbot 00.00.1970

5. **Hope**   15m   D
    The right-hand slab.
    J.Talbot 00.00.1970

Yellow Buttress

GR442856

TIDAL STATUS: Non-tidal.

DESCENTS: Scramble off at the top and drop down east (left) well back from the top.

Yellow Buttress is more impressive than Horses Cliff, with a steep narrow ridge on the left and a series of grooves to the right. There is a prominent saddle at its base.

1. **South West Diedre**   18m   S
    A good line on the west (left) of the ridge. The rock requires careful handling.
    J.Talbot 00.00.1969

The steep bulging east face has two obvious groove lines.

2. **Left Groove**   15m   S
    The left-hand groove is gained by a traverse from the ribs on the left.
    Unknown Pre-1981

3. **Pink Pointless**   15m   E2,5b
    A poor route on crumbly rock. Climb the undercut slab between Left and Right Groove, to meet Right Groove at the base of the crack. Pull left into a scoop, which is followed to finish.
    M.Crocker 10.01.1999

4. **Right Groove**   25m   E2,5b   ●
    Perhaps the worst route on Gower. Loose in its upper section. The obvious 'jam' crack in the upper right wall of the tower is gained from the loose groove running up from the start of Pink Pointless and turns very crunchy at 20m.
    Unknown Pre-1981

Devil's Cwm

GR443856

TIDAL STATUS: The Freaks Come Out is Non-tidal. The other routes 2 hours either side of low water.

Gwyn Evans & Chris Wyatt - Chantilly Lace (HVS,5b) Jacky's Tor
(Page 76) Photo: Carl Ryan

Chris Wyatt & Gwyn Evans - Cave Traverse (HS,4a) Jacky's Tor
(Page 76) Photo: Carl Ryan

DESCENTS: Best done by abseil.

This is the rocky hollow falling for approximately 30m to the sea immediately east of Yellow Buttress.

1. **The Freaks Come Out**   20m   E4,6a   *   \
   The overhanging back wall of the cwm. Start from a slight ledge on the left (west) wall of the underlying cave-zawn, 3m left of the chimney line. From the first break move left to gain a handrail just over the lip of the second bulge. Swing left and pull up to a leftward-trending pocket line, which is followed to a second pocket line on the left TR. Launch up the leaning headwall, TR and swing left to the lip to exit leftwards. A pre-placed belay rope is strongly advised.
   M.Crocker, R.Thomas 11.01.1999

To the east of the Cwm are a series of slabs, which extend as far as White Edge, where the rock becomes well defined again. These routes are tidal.

2. **Devil's Groove**   20m   HD
   The slabs and grooves at the seaward end of Devil's Cwm.
   J.Talbot 00.00.1970

3. **The Shute**   20m   VD
   The corner to the east (right).
   J.Talbot 00.00.1970

4. **Cerberus**   20m   D
   A slabby route round the corner from The Shute.
   J.Talbot 00.00.1970

White Pillar
GR443854

TIDAL STATUS: 3 hours either side of low water.

DESCENTS: Descent is by scrambling down behind the east flank of the buttress.

This is a truly pleasant and relaxed spot. All the routes start from a tidal platform, reached by scrambling round from the east. It is roughly triangular shaped with a vague groove at its apex, which is the finish of West Kante. The face is of good quality rock lower down, but with a bit of loose rock towards the top and is split by a series of overlaps. The most prominent feature is the sentry box at 5m, which is taken by West Kante. There is a huge ring peg at the top!

1. **Crack And Slab**   25m   VD
   Climb cracks right of the left arete of the face to a ledge at 20m. Finish up the groove of West Kante.
   J.Talbot 00.00.1967

2. **West Kante**   25m   S,4a   **
   Climb to the obvious sentry box at 5m. Leave this via thin cracks to gain a broken groove. Follow this to a short slab below the headwall. Climb this direct to the prominent groove leading to the top.
   J.Talbot 00.00.1967

3. **Grey Slab**   27m   S
   Start at thin cracks just right of West Kante. Climb to just below the obvious lower band of overlaps. Traverse right just under these until they terminate and step up to climb a groove. Where it gets loose towards the top, step left to finish up another groove.
   J.Talbot 00.00.1967

4. **Sizzler**   25m   E1,5a
Start at the next thin cracks below the left-hand side of the lowest band of overlaps. Climb to and through these
with gear being awkward to place, then strike straight on up through the next bands to easier ground. Finish up
the headwall.
J.Harwood 16.08.1987

5. **Bermuda Shorts**   25m   HS,4a
Start right of Sizzler at a point below the groove bounding the right side of the middle overlap. Climb to the groove
and follow it to the top.
J.Harwood 16.08.1987

Black Hole Crag
GR446853

TIDAL STATUS: 2½ hours either side of low water.

DESCENTS: Toward the east of the crag, top out and scramble back down the gully at the east end of the crag.
Toward the west of the crag, either reverse one of the easy routes, or walk off left and scramble down easy rocks
at the west end of the crag.

Looking west from Boiler Slab, there is an obvious low rocky promontory running out to sea. Just west of this, at the
foot of a large dome-like headland, is a wall 90m long with a large pool at its east end. Approach is down either side
of the gully bounding its east side. Due to the direction of approach, the routes are described from right (east) to left
(west).

One route is found on the west (right when descending) wall of the descent gully.

1. **Water Monster**   7m   E4,6b
Start about 3m from the right edge of the wall. Climb up until it is possible to clip a PR and sling out to the right,
then move left and jump for the top.
G.Ashmore 29.08.2002

The east (right) side of the crag has a large pool at the bottom of a slabby wall, which has a red block overhang above
its centre.

2. **Right Wall**   12m   D   *
Gain the centre of the slab by traversing in from the left-hand side of the pool. Climb it directly, finishing right of
the block overhang.
J.Talbot 00.00.1963

3. **Left Pillar**   15m   M
At the left side of the pool is a vague rib. Climb this and the slab above to finish up a corner left of the left corner
of the block overhang.
J.Talbot 00.00.1963

4. **Rib And Slab**   15m   D
Climb the groove bounding the rib of Left Pillar on its left. Amble up the slab to join and finish as for Left Pillar.
J.Talbot 00.00.1963

Just to the left is another pool, with a prominent boulder in it. The next routes must be reached via stepping onto the
large boulder and leaning across then traversing in to their starts.

5. **Calcutta**   12m   D
Climb the rib directly behind the boulder on superb sharp blisters.
G.Ashmore 20.01.2001

6. **Shallow Corner**   12m   S,4a
   The very shallow corner, 2m left of the boulder, with a capping feature at 3m. Swing round this and finish direct. Good fun.
   J.Talbot 00.00.1963

7. **Right Rib**   12m   S
   Climb the corner crack to the left of Shallow Corner, with help from the rib bounding its left end.
   J.Talbot 00.00.1963

8. **Overhang Crack**   12m   S,4a
   The chimney groove in the centre of the wall, exiting by the left-hand crack at the blocks.
   J.Talot 00.00.1963

9. **Left Rib**   12m   S,4a
   Climb the rib left of the chimney and finish up the side of the flying fin.
   J.Talbot 00.00.1963

About 100m west (left), after two deep cuts in the terrace at the base of the crag, is another pool below a prominent narrowing cave crack. The major problem is accessing the base of the routes. Traversing in from the left is 5a and probably deserves a deep water solo grade. Climbing up the rib on the right and climbing down and left is easier.

10. **Cracked Wall**   12m   S
    Climb the most continuous of the three cracks in the right flanking wall of the cave crack.
    J.Talbot, B.Tabot 00.00.1965

11. **Deep Cleft**   12m   D   *
    The deep cleft. The route of the crag.
    J.Talbot, B.Talbot 00.00.1965

12. **Left Wall**   12m   M
    Climb the square wall left of Deep Cleft.
    J.Talbot 00.00.1963

Upper Black Hole Crag
GR446854

TIDAL STATUS: Non-tidal.

DESCENTS: Scramble down either side of the crag.

This crag lies well above Black Hole Crag and is immediately below the coastal path and beneath a large slabby cliff.

1. **Surfer's Arete**   25m   VD
   At a turn in the cliff is a prominent groove formed by a large block wall with an arete above. The climb goes up rock left of the groove line before stepping back to the arete and finishing up this.
   J.Harwood, E.Smith 16.05.1998

Boiler Slab and Engine Room Slab
GR451851

TIDAL STATUS: Non-tidal.

DESCENTS: The easiest descent is to drop down the back of the crag and walk down a gully to the right (south) between Boiler Slab and Engine Room Slab.

Boiler Slab

This is the best cliff in this section, containing some excellent easy and middle grade routes, making it quite a busy little spot. It is also worth a visit by mixed ability groups, with a couple of pleasant E1/2s. The crag has a broad slabby face with a broken buttress to the left and a large overhang at its centre top, with more overhangs below and right. The cliff is named after the wrecked ship's boiler which can be seen at low water.

The broken buttress to the left has been climbed on by many outdoor centre instructors for years, but no routes have been claimed.

1. **Scent Of Mutton**   19m   S,4a
   Find the most interesting line up the rock to the left of Classic. Better than it looks, but take care with some of the blocks in the central section.
   R.Thornton 00.00.1985

2. **Classic**   19m   HD   *
   Climb the obvious corner on the left side of the main slabby face, keeping to its right-hand slab.
   A.Osborne, B.Taylor 00.00.1949

3. **Column**   19m   S,4a   *
   Start 1m right of Classic. Climb directly up the right side of a shallow pillar just left of a groove, to a shallow depression with a patch of ivy. Climb over this and follow ledges to the top.
   J.Talbot 00.00.1967

4. **Dulfer**   19m   S,4a   *
   Continually interesting climbing. Follow the obvious corner right of Column untl it peters out. Step right and continue to the bulges above, step left and climb the break in the bulges, then climb directly to the top.
   A.Osborne, B.Taylor 00.00.1949

5. **Swirtler**   21m   HVS,5b
   Climb the right edge of the smooth slab 1m right of Dulfer to the bulges above. Go through these in a direct line between Dulfer and Direct. Feels a little contrived, but still pleasant enough.
   T.Moon, C.Maybury 00.00.1973

6. **Direct**   21m   VS,4c   *
   Start 4m right of Swirtler at a rib in a black-streaked slab. Climb the rib, then move left to surmount the arch at a good layoff flake. Follow the slab above to a small roof and pass it on the left. Finish direct through the bulges.
   J.Talbot 00.00.1968

7. **Termination**   21m   HVS,5a
   Start 3m right of Direct below a patch of ivy on the overhang above. Climb to it, over it and up the thin crack until it peters out. Traverse leftwards and exit over the bulging blocks left of the main overhang. Previously known as Hotplate.
   P.Hinder, V.Rees 00.00.1970

8. **Nuclear Arms**   21m   E2,5c   *
   A one move wonder. As for Termination to the traverse, but continue direct to the roof. Cross the roof directly near the poor PR (good back up wires under the roof).
   A.Sharp, J.Harwood 20.10.1985

9. **Middle Age Dread**   21m   E3,6a   *
   Start 4m right of Termination at a slight right-facing groove. Climb the groove boldly over the overlap and continue directly up the slabs to the main overhang at its widest point. Clip the PR on Nuclear Arms, then climb the roof to the right by a thin undercut in the roof and a slight flake above.
   A.Sharp, J.Harwood 20.10.1985

10. **Nemo**   18m   VS,4c

At the right-hand side of the main slab is an undercut recess. Climb out of the left-hand side of this via a groove containing a crack. Move right, then continue direct to a groove through the block overhangs above. Follow this groove taking the jutting overhang at the top directly.
P.Hinder 00.00.1970

11. **Tokyo**   21m   E1,5c   *

An enjoyable route with a technical move, or a long reach. Start just right of Nemo, below the widest part of the overlap and reach over from a good undercut to a good, if distant flake. Saunter up the slab with good gear, to take a finishing groove through the bulges.
A.Sharp, J.Harwood 20.10.1985

12. **Tokyo II**   21m   HVS,5b

Start at a vague crack in a slab 2m right of Tokyo. Gain an undercut in the overlap above. Pull over onto the slab, continuing directly to finish through the upper overlap using a rugby ball feature.
G.Evans, K.Snook 00.00.1988

13. **Ayesha**   21m   VS,4c   *

Start at the foot of a slab below the right end of the overlap, just under a series of thin undercut flakes. Follow these to finish up the left side of the left arete of the Pinnacle Crack groove.
J.Talbot 00.00.1971

14. **Pinnacle Crack**   24m   VD

This takes the obvious broken groove at the right of the main face.
J.Talbot 00.00.1969

15. **Girdle**   27m   VS,4c

Start up Classic and follow the obvious horizontal crack at half-height. Finish up Pinnacle Crack or Ayesha.
J.Talbot, M.Hicks, A.Barnie - Partial 00.00.1971
G.Evans, G.Richardson 28.12.1977

16. **Overhang Traverse**   36m   VS,4c

Climb Dulfer to the obvious horizontal crack, then go up to the next crack. Move rightwards to below a small roof then go up to the main roof. Follow the horizontal crack rightwards and exit up a deep cut to the right.
A.Bevan, R.Bowen, D.Jones - 00.00.1960
FFA C.Maybury, T.Moon 00.00.1973

Engine Room Slab

This is the small buttress around the corner to the east of Boiler Slab.

1. **Fly Tipping**   12m   S

On the western flank, climb through the bulges about 2m from their right end.
M.Jordan 00.00.1992

2. **Rib One**   12m   HD

Gain the square cut overhang right of the arete from the groove below, avoid it via the slab to the left.
J.Harwood, E.Smith 16.05.1998

3. **Rib Two**   12m   HD

As for Rib One, but climb the rubble to the right of the overhang. Poor.
J.Harwood, E.Smith 16.05.1998

Longhole Cliff
GR454869

TIDAL STATUS: Non-tidal.

DESCENTS: Descend down a gully to the west (left) of the crag.

A minor cliff just west of Overton Cliff.

1. **Guano Groove**   15m   D
    A wide groove near the west end of the cliff to its highest point.
    J.Robinson, solo 15.02.1997

2. **Crack 'N' Up**   15m   S,4b
    Cracked left wall of obvious corner at east end of cliff. Start and finish direct.
    J.Robinson, C.Shorrock 15.02.1997

Overton Cliff
GR455849

TIDAL STATUS: Non-tidal.

DESCENTS: Walk down the path on the east (right) side of the crag.

The cliff is to the east of the mouth of the valley and at first sight is impressive, but unfortunately the routes start from a grass ledge at the level of the cave on the south face, reducing the length to 14m.

1. **Bush Bay 'A'**   14m   D
    Start from the brambly bay on the west end of the crag. Climb up and left under the overhang to step across into a groove, with a choice of finishes, the easiest being on the left.
    C.Shorrock, J.Robinson 15.02.97

2. **Bush Baby**   14m   S
    Start in the brambly bay. Climb the arete on its right to the overhang, move right onto the face to a detached block and climb the shallow groove on the right of this on poor rock.
    J.Robinson, C.Shorrock 15.02.1997

3. **South West Corner**   14m   D
    This takes the corner left of the centre of the crag.
    A.Osborne, Brian Taylor 00.00.1952

4. **West Wall**   14m   S
    A vague line up the right wall of the corner.
    J.Talbot 00.00.1969

5. **Black Widow**   14m   HVS,5a   ●
    This climbs the lethal groove on the upper face, right of West Wall.
    T.Moon, C.Maybury 00.00.1973

6. **One Ton Plus**   13m   E3,5c   *   \
    Start 6m left of the cave. Climb a vague crack to finger pockets, TR and continue direct with a tricky move (large Friend). Trend right through the bulge to a huge hold over the lip and pull up easily to the top.
    M.Crocker 28.12.1998

7. **Featherweight**   13m   E4,6a   \
    Start 4m left of the cave. Reach a shallow rectangular recess and climb the face above (old BR stub on the right). Pull up to a thin flake (thin tape possible), then forcefully over the bulge to finish directly over a small roof.
    M.Crocker 28.12.1998

8. **South Wall**   14m   E1,5b   *
    This follows the line of old bolts and drilled pegs 5m left of the cave. It can be started directly to the bolt stub, or reached by traversing in from the base of the cave.
    J.Talbot 00.00.1968
    FFA G.Evans, G.Richardson 01.01.1978

9. **Air Jordan**   14m   E1,5b
    Climb straight up out of the cave and climb the wall directly above, with a good steep move.
    M.Jordan, G.Ashmore 18.02.2001

10. **Cave Crack**   14m   VS,4b
    This climbs the rib at the right of the cave, over a small overhang and up the groove to the top.
    T.Moon, C.Maybury 00.00.1973

Culver Hole
GR466845

TIDAL STATUS: 2½ hours either side of low water.

DESCENTS: Abseil or walk off to the left (west).

Culver Hole contains a dovecote (culver is an old word for dove). This is worth exploring which is more than can be said for the routes, which are pokey to say the least. A hanging rope is required for escape at the top.

1. **Thick Waist**   12m   E3,5c
    The grey groove in the left side of the face. Follow the rightward-slanting crack in the lower wall, then left to an in situ PR below the groove, which is loose and not recommended.
    M.Crocker, R.Thomas 23.10.1993

2. **New Body Buzz**   22m   E5,6a
    Intricate and strenuous climbing on pockets. Start below the shallow recess at the centre of the face. From the right side of the recess climb directly up to a projecting jug at 7m. Follow pockets up the wall above, TR to a good hold and a big rock placement. Move right and enter a round cave. Exit steeply leftwards TR, on pockets. Finish up a solid rib on the left.
    M.Crocker 10.10.1993

3. **Spinal (Con)Fusion**   22m   E4,6a
    Start left of the cave and climb into a pocketed recess TRs. Take the final bulge via a ragged pocket.
    M.Crocker, R.Thomas 23.10.1993

Port Eynon Cave
GR467844

TIDAL STATUS: 1½ hours either side of low water.

DESCENTS: Scramble in from the east of the crag.

1. **Port Eynon Cave Climb**   18m   S

    Start at the back of the cave and climb the right wall to a black hollow. Go up and out right then traverse delicately to a tiny ledge. Move up and across right to where the overhang eases. Climb the overhang directly to a good ledge and an easy wall.

    D.Lillicrap 00.00.1957

OXWICH

GR 506859 to 513850
By Goi Ashmore & Adrian Berry

TIDAL STATUS: The only tidal routes are those to the right of Kissing The Pink in the quarry (4 hours either side of low water), although routes as far as Written In Red may be inaccessible during extremely high seas. The boulder-hopping approach to the Quarry can be awkward at high tide and is not recommended on initial visits. The easy walk in along the beach is possible 2 ½ hours either side of low water. The rest of the area is non-tidal.

BOLTING POLICY: Retro-bolting permissible with first ascensionist's permission. Replacement of worn fixed gear on a point for point basis with bolts is permissible. New sports routes allowed. No bolting at Oxwich Point.

PREAMBLE
Oxwich Point contains a pleasant series of minor buttresses that are not often visited. They are exposed to the wind and are therefore cold in winter. By contrast Oxwich Quarry is the major sports climbing area of Gower, containing a large selection of fully equipped routes of most grades, especially E2-E5, but also including the hardest route in the guidebook. The red wall overlooking the sea is the best of the areas, with steep routes on good (some of them a little too good) holds. However, this wall does seep. Oxwich In The Woods dries much quicker and is very sheltered, but can be greasy and full of midges in hot weather. The routes of For Sportsmen of the Epoxy Clips, Red With Rage and Kissing The Pink are compulsory classics.

ACCESS
Follow the A4118 past Nicholaston to an obvious left turn signposted to the Oxwich Bay Hotel by the folly. Follow the minor road down to the Oxwich Bay complex and park on the beach (a pay booth is normally open). If the tide is out, it is easy to walk along the west flank of the beach for 300m until the obvious red wall at the start of the quarry (not visible from the parking area) comes into view (GR506859). If the tide is up, walk over to the Oxwich Bay Hotel and follow the small road south to a chapel. It is possible to scramble down and hop over boulders to reach the start of the main crag. However, be warned that the rock is very greasy and accidents are common. Also the descent down at the end may mean swimming at high tide. For Oxwich Point, follow the road to the chapel and take the footpaths through the woods and to the headland after about 25 minutes (GR513850). Oxwich Point can also be reached from Oxwich Green, going down the lane alongside the caravan site and following a ramp towards the crag. Limited parking is available.

DESCENTS: For Oxwich Point, walk off in either direction. The sports routes at Oxwich Quarry all have lower offs. Only one of the traditional routes in the quarry has no lower off, but it is possible to reach one with a little cunning.

Oxwich Point
There are two buttresses at Oxwich Point, West and East Buttress. The East Buttress is the first one encountered on the approach. The West Buttress is further on, just west of the headland.

The minor east buttress, easily recognised by its prominent overhanging nose, is passed en-route to the headland.

1. **Mortuary Crack**   9m   D
    This follows the obvious crack running up behind the blocky nose.
    B.Winterburn, C.Manison, J.Procter, J.Hobbs 00.00.1971

2. **Vampire Wall**   11m   VS,4c
    Start at the inner edge of the wall right of Mortuary Crack. Traverse to a small ledge in the middle. Move onto the nose and over it.
    J.Procter, B.Winterburn 00.00.1971

3. **Islay** 15m VS,4b

Start to the right of Vampire Wall below an ivy covered wall on the seaward side immediately below the overhanging nose. Climb a corner and up to sentry box on the right. Continue up to the overhang, then move onto the left wall and over the corner to finish.
J.Procter, T.Kitchen, B.Winterburn 00.00.1971

The West Buttress is more prominent. It is characterised by bulging walls split by a series of steep corners.

4. **Far South West Corner** 12m VS,4b

The prominent corner on the left of the buttress.
R.Owen, D.Jones 00.00.1959

5. **South Wall** 12m HS

Climb the wall right of Far South West Corner to half-height, then move left to finish as for Far South West Corner.
J.Talbot, D.Thomas 00.00.1959

Round to the right is a narrower chimney (South West Corner).

6. **Crowbar** 12m HVS,5a

The groove right of the left arete of the wall running across to South West Corner.
M.Murray, R.Wadey 00.06.1995

7. **Lichen Wall** 12m HVS,5a

Climb the centre of the wall which runs across to South West Corner.
J.Talbot, D.Thomas 00.00.1959
FFA E.Kellar, A.Richardson - Direct 00.00.1989

8. **South West Corner** 12m HS

Follow the shallow corner. Loose in its upper section.
R.Owen, D.Jones 00.00.1958

9. **South West Chimney** 12m HS

Further right is a much more prominent corner. Follow the wide chimney crack in the back.
R.Owen, D.Jones 00.00.1958

A route has been climbed up the wall to the right of South West Chimney (No Holds Barred, R.Wadey, P.Nicholas 1994) but no further details were available at the time of writing.

10. **Oxbow** 12m VS

The crackline just around the arete from South West Chimney.
J.Bullock, G.Evans Pre-1981

11. **Benbow** 12m VS

The steep crack line on the right side of the overhanging face.
J.Bullock, G.Evans Pre-1981

Oxwich Bay Quarry (Crag Ox)

The routes are described from right to left (i.e. as approached).

1. **Steel Yourself** 13m E2,5c Fr6a+ *

At the right side of the red wall is an undercut wall, with a vague arete bounding its right side. Crank up onto the wall from the right and climb up keeping left of the arete, to a finishing groove. A direct start is possible at Fr6c+.
R.Thomas 01.07.1995

2. **Settin' Stone**   13m   E5,6b   Fr7b

A hard move over the roof left of Steel Yourself, leads to a shallow groove. At the roof, pull left to a flake, then swing out onto the wall above the roof. A strange hold leads to the belay.
G.Gibson 25.08.1997

3. **Glue Year**   15m   E4,6a   Fr7a   **

Start left of Settin' Stone beneath a large block at 2m. Pull round this and climb the groove to reach a hard finish.
R.Thomas 00.00.1995

4. **Inspector Glueseau**   15m   E4,6a   Fr6c+   *

A good route to the left of Glue Year, following the groove in the angle of the wall. Start just left of Glue Year and climb up to a ledge. Follow a right-trending ramp, then pull out left to the BB.
R.Thomas 00.00.1995

5. **Foaming At The Gussett**   15m   E4,6b   Fr7a+

The wall left of Inspector Glueseau.
R.Thomas 00.00.1997

6. **Pissin' The Sink**   15m   E6,6b   Fr7b+

The short wall between Foaming At The Gussett and Kissin' The Pink has a desperate sloping finish.
G.Gibson 20.07.1997

7. **Kissin' The Pink**   20m   E3,6a   Fr6c   ***

A superb route up the flowstone forming the right arete of the prominent groove left of Pissin' The Sink.
E.Jones, G.Gibson, R.Thomas 09.10.1994

8. **Missin' The Drink**   20m   E5,6b   Fr7a+   ●

Rubbish. A short wall left of Kissin' The Pink leads to a ledge, then a long move up on filthy rock gains the groove and lower off of Kissin' The Pink.
G.Gibson 02.08.1997

To the left is a prominent prow high up on the crag. Left of this, above a rock step at the base of the crag are two routes.

9. **The Morgue The Merrier**   25m   E6,6c   Fr7c   **

This is the right-hand line, which sports two difficult moves.
G.Gibson 02.07.1997

10. **Bitchin'**   25m   E6,6b   Fr7b+   ***

The wall to the left of The Morgue The Merrier, has a desperate finale.
G.Gibson 26.08.1997

There are two bolted projects to the left. The left hand one is open.

11. **Red Snapper**   20m   E6,6b   Fr7b+   **

About 10m left of the prow of Bitchin' is an undercut section of the wall (three lines of bolts to the left). Climb this with a powerful move low down. Low in the grade.
G.Gibson 19.07.1999

The wall to the left has a solitary bolt but no route yet.. To the left a path leads up into the woods.

12. **Written In Red**   20m   E5,6b   Fr7b   *

The wall immediately above the start of the path, with a very tricky move at half-height. From a large hold move up and right onto a huge flake and a very blind finish.
G.Gibson 06.07.1997

13. **Red Letter Day**   20m   E6,6b   Fr7b+

As for Written In Red to the hard move, but instead of moving slightly right, continue straight up the arete above.
G.Gibson 19.07.1999

14. **Red With Rage**   22m   E5,6b   Fr7a+   ***

Superb. Start just above the step in the path at the left-hand side of the tidal platform. Amble up to a BR, then climb the fingery wall on good flakes to a horizontal slot out on the left. Make a long rockover to a big sloper well up and right. Pull up more easily, and finish up the left-trending groove.
G.Gibson, R.Thomas 01.07.1995

15. **Mars Attacks**   20m   E5,6b   Fr7a+   *

The wall left of Red With Rage. Instead of mantling directly up to the belay, climb the little arete on the left and move back right to finish.
G.Gibson 19.07.1997

16. **The Milkier Way**   15m   E6,6c   Fr7c

The vague scoop to the left of Mars Attacks, with some fingery climbing and a monstrous lurch at half-height.
G.Gibson 26.08.1997

17. **Red River Rock**   15m   E5,6b   Fr7b   **

The superb red wall to the left of The Milkier Way, moving left at the fourth BR to gain a flake and the belay of Two Of A Perfect Pair.
G.Gibson 16.08.1997

18. **Two Of A Perfect Pair**   15m   E6,6b   Fr7b+

Left of Red River Rock is a prominent left facing shallow groove with a rather obvious stuck-back-on hold. Gain this with interest! Move easily up the groove, until a hard undercut and stretch right gains jugs and a BB.
E.Travers-Jones 29.07.1996

19. **Resin D'Etre**   12m   E5,6b   Fr7a+   *

To the left of Two Of A Perfect Pair is an obvious circular hole at 3m. Climb up to this, and over the overlap to gain and finish up a groove.
R.Thomas 00.00.1995

20. **Beyond All Resin**   12m   E3,6a   *

A route with a hard start, which eases thereafter. Start at a couple of pockets under an arete and pull up and onto the arete. BR. Finish up the jam crack. Medium Friends useful.
R.Thomas, G.Gibson 28.05.1995

21. **Little Cracker**   14m   HVS,5a

Follow the obvious banana-shaped crack to the same lower off as Beyond All Resin. Friends and threads useful.
R.Thomas 00.00.1995

22. **Sika This**   12m   E3,6b   Fr7a

A route with a very frustrating start. Gain the good ledge at 2m left of Little Cracker, at a faint arete. Slap up a long, long way for thin edges, pull up and finish up the still tricky groove.
R.Thomas 00.00.1995

23. **Sniff That**   10m   E3,6a   Fr6c

A good route up the groove to the left of I'm Sika This.
R.Thomas 00.00.1995

The thin wall to the right is an open project. Send the cheque to Roy Thomas.

24. **Red October**   11m   E4,6a   Fr7a
The wall to the left again.
R.Thomas 00.10.1995

25. **Blight In August**   8m   E3,5c
The crack to the left of Red October is usually cheesy, TR.
R.Thomas 00.08.1995

The next 50m is covered in ivy and the trees are too close to the crag to allow routes. The next routes start well along the path at a 'tump' marking the right end of the first proper bay in the woods. It contains a very obvious layback flake (Extra Ordinary LIttle Cough).

26. **Tump Jumper**   8m   E3,6b   Fr7a   *
Not quite the one move wonder it looks. Jump from the tump onto the wall and climb the wall above.
R.Thomas, G.Gibson 01.07.1995

27. **Sweet September**   8m   E4,6a   Fr7a   *
The red wall right of the prominent layback flake in the bay. The start is a teaser.
R.Thomas 00.00.1995

28. **Extra Ordinary Little Cough/Nike**   10m   E1,5a   *
The well defined overhanging layback flake.
R.Thomas, G.Gibson 29.05.1995

29. **Ambrosia Mountain**   12m   E6,6b   Fr7b+
Fundamentally unpleasant. The corner groove left of Extra Ordinary Little Cough is climbed on vicious lay offs to a hard move onto a ledge. Fight up the corner to the last BR before the BB, realise that the chain is completely out of reach and fall off.
G.Gibson 29.05.1995

30. **Sansarete**   12m   E7,6c   8a   *
The arete bounding the left side of the bay. Its left-hand side has an awkward start and some technical moves through an overlap. Continue with difficulty to catch the shallow depression up and slightly right of the double bolts before clipping the BB to finish.
A.Berry 00.00.1996

31. **Plum Duff**   12m   E5,6b   Fr7b   *
About 20m left of Sansarete is another square-cut arete. Start on the left, but immediately swing round to climb its right side.
G.Gibson 28.05.1995

To the right of the arete of Plum Duff is a leaning red wall.

32. **Inferno**   20m   E7,6c   Fr8a+   *
The centre of the wall has a hard boulder problem at the top.
A.Berry 31.05.1999

The crag now turns through a right angle.

33. **Epoxy Clips Now**   25m   E4,6a   Fr7a
A mediocre route up the angle of the bay.
G.Gibson, R.Thomas 28.05.1995

34. Root Grabbing 25m E4,5b
The cracks to the left of Expoxy Clips Now.
A.Berry, P.Nicholas 00.00.1994

35. For Sportsmen Of The Epoxy Clips 25m E3,6a Fr6c+ ***
A classic. Start up the arete above the rock step. Climb this with difficulty, until it is possible to 'throw one and hold it'. Pull onto the slab and amble up to the top wall, which is climbed on good holds to a BB. Well protected.
R.Thomas, G.Gibson 28.05.1995

The quarry now drops down at a prominent rock step.

36. The Route Of All Evil 25m E8,7a Fr8b+ * \
The hardest route in the guidebook. The undercut groove in the centre of the wall running left from the rock step.
A.Berry 10.07.1999

The hanging face to the left of The Route Of All Evil is currently a project.

37. Big Cheese 20m E5,6a Fr7a **
To the left is a prominent flake high up. Gain this by some tricky moves, then follow the strenuous flake crack more easily to a final superb move up to the belay from a handjam.
R.Thomas 00.00.1997

38. Whey It Up 20m E6,6c Fr7c
A lot harder than it looks with a typically desperate Oxwich belay clip. Start in a faint groove in the wall to the left of Big Cheese. Climb the groove easily to what looks like a huge hold, which actually slopes at 40 degrees. Flail desperately about, until able to put the clip into the BB.
G.Gibson 21.04.1995

39. Say Cheese Please 20m E5,6b Fr7a+ *
A good route, with a hard one move crux. Just left of Whey It Up is an arete bounding a big red groove. Climb the arete direct.
G.Gibson, R.Thomas 28.08.1995

40. Red Leicester 20m E2,5b Fr6a
The big red groove.
R.Thomas, G.Gibson 21.04.1995

The big arete and the flake to the left are currently projects.

41. Resination 15m E4,6a Fr7a
The groove/wall just right of the big angled corner of Resin Hate. Better than it looks.
G.Gibson 20.07.1997

42. Resin Hate 15m E2,5b
The big angled corner. BB.
R.Thomas 00.00.1995

43. The Oxwich Blobby 15m E6,6b Fr7b+
The wall to the left of Resin Hate is often greasy.
G.Gibson 19.07.1997

44. The Oxwich Bobby 15m E4,6a Fr7a
The cheesy wall left of The Oxwich Blobby and right of a pillar formed by jam cracks.
G.Gibson 09.10.1995

45. No Resin, Why? 15m E2,5b

An interesting route. Grapple up the pillar, which is hard, to a jam crack that is also hard. BB. Friends and a large thread useful.
R. Thomas 09.10.1994

The crag now turns another corner.

46. Picking Berries 12m E4,6a Fr7a

Climb the cheesy groove just round the corner.
R. Thomas, G.Gibson 01.07.1995

47. Figura 12m E5,6b Fr7b \

The arete left of Picking Berries.
G.Gibson 00.00.1999

48. Stoned Dates 12m E4,6a Fr6c+ *

Left of the left arete of Picking Berries is a shelf at 2m. Awkwardly gain this, and climb the tufa pockets above.
R.Thomas 16.08.1998

The next routes are on the shorter buttress to the left.

49. Squeezing The Pips 6m VS,4c

The traditional crack left of the platform. BB.
R.Thomas 00.00.1997

50. Treading The Grapes 6m E2,5c Fr6b

A good technical problem up the wall to the left of Squeezing The Pips.
R.Thomas 00.00.1997

51. Pipsqueak 6m E2,6a Fr6b+

Left of Treading The Grapes is a vague crack and ramp leading to undercuts and a BB.
R.Thomas 00.00.1998

52. Teasing The Zits 6m E2,6a Fr6c

The slabby wall to a finishing crack left of Pipsqueak.
R.Thomas 00.00.1998

A little further on is the last buttress of any significance, The Secret Oxwich.

53. Jury's Out 10m E4,6b Fr7a *

The first feature on the buttress is a thin crack. Climb this, then make a tricky sequence into a groove out left. Hard moves on undercuts lead to a BB.
R.Thomas 00.00.1996

The wall to the left of Jury's Out, with a prominent boss of rock is a project.

54. Before The Beak 10m E5,6b Fr7a+ *

The sharp arete in the centre of the buttress.
R.Thomas 00.00.1997

55. Swift Justice 8m HVS,5a

The traditionally protected groove to the left of Before The Beak, BB.
R.Thomas 00.00.1996

56. **Open Verdict**   10m   E2,6a   Fr6b
The square cut groove/arete to the left of Swift Justice.
R.Thomas 00.00.1996

57. **The Last Arete**   6m   E2,6b   Fr6c
The short arete on the left side of the buttress, with a huge jump, BR. At the top swing to the BB of Open Verdict.
A.Berry 00.00.1996

CRAWLEY WOODS ROCKS

GR518879

The following information is from the 1970 Jeremy Talbot guide to Gower:

'Nicholaston Woods are known locally as Crawley Woods. This is a delightful little area of small crags situated about ½ mile west along the beach by Nicholaston Burrows. Once a popular training area, it has been fairly extensively climbed on by A.Osborn, B.Taylor and at a later date, by J.O.Talbot. Today it is out of fashion and profuse vegetation holds sway. No climbs are given in this area in the guide book. Access is easy from Tor Bay East or Oxwich.'

THE THREE TORS

GR525878 to 534878
By Chris Shorrock

TIDAL STATUS: 2 hours to non-tidal. See individual crags.

BOLTING POLICY: No bolting.

PREAMBLE

Lying between Oxwich and Three Cliffs Bay are a number of agreeable cliffs. Their surrounding golden beaches, sand dunes and tussocked gorse moorland, combined with an abundance of low grade single and multi-pitch routes makes the area ideal for families, novices and solo forays.

Great Tor is the very prominent feature at the end of the headland separating Oxwich Bay from Three Cliff Bay. Little Tor is a smaller headland set back a couple of hundred metres west across the beach and West Tor is a little further west and well above the beach.

ACCESS

A parking bay on the A4118 next to the Post Office and village shop in Penmaen, gives access via a wide gate on the left of the parking area, to a lane descending to a wooden gate. Directly after, a sandy path leads off right (west) across the plateau to the back of Tor Bay. Towards the end of the plateau one path bears left along the top of the cliff to the col at the top of Great Tor. Follow this path to access routes on the upper tier of Great Tor. For Great Tor East, take the left (east) gully down from the col to arrive at beach level.

From the plateau a second twisting path descends right to beach level, from where Great Tor lies to the east (left) and Little Tor to the west (right). West Tor lies beyond Little Tor. It is possible to access West Tor from the cliff top path when the tide is in. Follow the cliff top path west from the end of the plateau to a point about 100m before the first stile and follow a steep trail down and left with care to reach the upper tier.

DESCENTS: See individual crags.

THE ROUTES

West Tor

GR525878

TIDAL STATUS: The routes from Fartlek to End Crack are accessible 4 hours either side of low water. The rest of the crag is non-tidal.

DESCENTS: Descents from Fartlek to End Crack and Main Slab are down obvious paths. Descent from the Great Slab is by walking off right (east) at the top and descending the vague path to the east of the slab.

Lying 100m west of Little Tor, West Tor is comprised of three tiers of cliffs. The lowest is the Sea Level Slab. Directly above this lies the Main Slab, whilst up and right again, is the inappropriately named Great Slab. The Main Slab is best accessed from the beach (unless the tide is in), the Great Slab is best reached from the top by walking down its east flank as described in the access notes.

Sea Level Slab

Lies down at beach level, slightly west of the main slab. It is marginally tidal.

1. **Fartlek**   7m   E1,5c
   This diminutive route lies on a subsidiary buttress 10m left of Central Crack. It takes a thin crack up the centre.
   P.Lewis, A.Sharp 00.00.1985

2. **Central Crack**   7m   VD
The obvious wide crack is quite stern for the grade.
Unknown Pre-1973

3. **Right Crack**   7m   VD
Some 2 metres right of Central Crack are some drill holes at eye level, with a crack above. Climb up on the left side of this.
Unknown Pre-1973

To the right is a descent route, then an inset slab, at the left end of which is an arete.

4. **Accident At The Knave**   9m   E1,5b
Take the left side of the prominent arete diagonally down and right of the main slab and finish on its edge.
M.Crocker 13.03.1999

5. **End Crack**   8m   VD
The obvious right-slanting crack at the right end of the slab.
Unknown Pre-1973

Main Slab
Directly above the beach level slab is this compact face.

6. **Left Corner**   11m   VD
An indefinite route. Climb the left edge of the slab until it steepens. Move left into and up a short corner to the top.
J.Talbot, G.Jones 00.00.1959

7. **Curving Crack**   11m   HS,4b   *
Obvious from its name, this splendid climb is straightforward with a little thought.
J.Talbot, D.Corbett 00.00.1958

8. **Smooth Operator**   11m   E3,6a
A thin eliminate between Curving Crack and Innocent Savagery.
A.Sharp, P.Lewis 00.00.1985

9. **Innocent Savagery**   11m   HVS,5a
A tricky direct start attains the bunch of cracks right of Curving Crack.
J.Kerry - Central Route 00.00.1971
P.Lewis, A.Sharp 00.00.1985

10. **Diagonal (Popsi's Joy)**   11m   VS,4c
Climb the thin crack on the right side of the slab.
J.Kerry 00.00.1971

11. **Traverse**   12m   VD
Follows the footledge left across the slab.
J.Talbot, G.Jones 00.00.1959

Up and right through a great deal of scrub lies the Great Slab. The front face is vegetated.

12. **Uno**   18m   M
On the left (west) side of the slab is a short wall containing thin cracks, with a short chimney to the right. Gain the short chimney, then move left to a ledge. Finish up the ridge above. A poor route.
J.Talbot 00.00.1970

13. **Due**   21m   VD

Overgrown. Right of Uno is a wall with two cracks leading to an obvious rib. Follow these to finish direct.
J.Talbot 00.00.1970

14. **Tre**   21m   HS

The start is overgrown. Start 2m right of Due, below an overhanging flake. Move right round this to a ledge and follow an edge to the top of the rib on Due. Traverse right to a corner crack with a small overhang to finish.
J.Talbot 00.00.1970

15. **Nemesis**   21m   S

The start is overgrown. 12m right of Tre is a steep wall lined with cracks leading to a square ledge. A rib above leads to another ledge. Climb the wall above, which is bounded on the right by a smooth yellow pillar. Trend left to finish.
J.Talbot 00.00.1970

16. **Right Rib**   27m   D

Climb the right edge of the main face of the Great Slab, loose in its upper section.
R.Bradley 00.00.1998

The remaining routes lie to the right (east) of the main face, centred about a slab containing an inverted y-crack.

17. **West Diedre**   9m   S

A poor route up the corner left of Notched Rib. Scrambling leads to the top.
J.Talbot, G.Jones 00.00.1959

18. **Notched Rib**   15m   S   *

A hidden gem. Takes the rib on the left of the slab.
J.Talbot, D.homas 00.00.1959

19. **Electrico**   11m   E3,6b

A desperately technical little number taking the thin cracks in the centre of the slab. At this grade it is necessary to place wires in the thin crack from the corner on the left before starting, otherwise the route is much more serious (E5), with no gear until after the first crux.
J.Talbot, G.Jones - Direct A1 00.00.1959
FFA A.Sharp, P.Lewis 00.00.1985

20. **Right Edge (Cooking The Books)**   11m   E1,5a

The right arete of the slab, starting either direct up the arete, or from the pedestal of Central Route, via the solution pocket. Originally utilised peg protection.
J.Talbot, G.Jones 00.00.1959

Little Tor
GR526877

TIDAL STATUS: 4 hours either side of low water.

DESCENTS: Descend down either flank of the Tor.

This pleasant crag consists of two buttresses rising from the beach. The western buttress is much the shorter, whilst its fellow leads to the top of the Little Tor headland.

1. **Wall Climb II**   7m   HS,4c

The ragged cracks left of the first proper crack encountered.
J.Talbot 00.00.1960

2. **Central Crack**   7m   VD
    The first crack.
    J.Talbot, G.Jones 00.00.1959

3. **Wall Climb I**   7m   HVS,5b
    With blinkes and some pain, climb the wall between Central and Thin Crack.
    J.Talbot 00.00.1960

4. **Thin Crack**   9m   S,4b
    The narrow crack right of Central Crack.
    J.Talbot, G.Jones 00.00.1959

5. **Right Crack**   9m   VD
    The wider chimney/crack right again.
    J.Talbot, G.Jones 00.00.1959

The section of the crag to the right, is set back a little. It previously contained Left Slab VS (J.Talbot, G.Jones 1959) and Quartz S (J.Talbot, G.Jones 1959) which were demolished by a rock fall. Left White replaces these.

6. **Left White**   12m   HVS,5a
    Takes the smooth quartz coated slab, keeping 2½m left of the corner (Right Corner).
    C.Wyatt, G.Evans 00.05.2000

The next routes are on the main crag, where the height starts to increase. The obvious proud pillar, Central Flake, is the most obvious feature.

7. **Right Corner**   15m   S
    The steep corner on the left side of the buttress.
    J.Talbot, G.Jones 00.00.1959

8. **Left Edge (Tri Cornel)**   18m   D
    Start at the left edge of the slab and follow cracks then tiny corners to ledges and the top.
    J.Brailsford, St.AMRT 1954/55

9. **Centre Route**   18m   VD
    Climb the narrow face between Left Edge and Left Flake Corner, stepping left to avoid the bulge at the top.
    J.Talbot, G.Jones 00.00.1959

10. **Left Flake Corner**   18m   VD
    Follow the corner bounding the left edge of Central Flake.
    J.Brailsford, St.AMRT 1954/5

11. **Central Flake**   18m   S,4a   *
    Climb the middle of the raised central slab.
    J.Brailsford, St.AMRT 1954/55

12. **Flake Corner**   18m   VD
    Climb the corner and wall right of Central Flake.
    J.Brailsford, St.AMRT 1954/55

13. **Direct Centre**   18m   S
    Ascend directly up the wall right of Flake Corner.
    J.Brailsford, St.AMRT 1954/55

---

14. **Right Edge**   18m   VD   *
Climb the right edge of the Tor.
J.Brailsford, St.AMRT 1954/55

A number of vague lines of (M) to (S) take the series of walls and ribs leading inland from Little Tor.

Little Star Wall
Set back from and east (right) of Little Tor lies this quality venue, consisting of a short steep wall. The first obvious feature is the wide crack on the left of the wall (Scout Crack).

15. **Blankety Blank**   10m   E2,5c
The wall 3m left of Scout Crack.
B.Franklin 09.04.1980

16. **Scout Crack**   12m   S,4a   **
An excellent route providing good crackline fare. Even touching the adjacent ledge induces disgrace.
J.Brailsford, St.AMRT 1954/55

17. **Superdirect**   10m   E1,5c   *
A popular problem up the wall 3m right of Scout Crack.
SUMC 1pt 00.00.1965
FFA J.Perrin, C.Tringham 00.00.1970

18. **Twinkle**   12m   S   *
Follow the prominent break running up and right across the wall to a finish in Twin Crack Left. A direct variant from the calcite mark goes at 4c.
J.Brailsford, St.AMRT1954/55

19. **Stella**   10m   VS,4c
This takes the wall between Twinkle and Twin Crack Left.
J.Brailsford, St.AMRT 1954/55

20. **Twin Crack Left**   9m   VD
The left of two cracks with a peapod recess en route 1m right of Stella.
J.Brailsford, St.AMRT 1954/55

21. **Twin Crack Right**   7m   D
The shorter right-hand crack.
J.Brailsford, StAMRT 1954/55

Great Tor Proper
GR529877 to 531876

TIDAL STATUS: The upper tier is non-tidal. Climbs on the lower tier are accessible 1½ - 2 hours either side of low water.

DESCENTS: Routes on the upper tier terminate at the approach col, so refer to the notes below. Descent from routes on the lower tier are made by following the path leading to the beach from the non-tidal platform on the west side of the tor, or by scrambling back to beach level on the east.

Great Tor is the prominent headland situated east of Little Tor. Climbs on the lower tier are best accessed from Tor Bay beach as described in the access for Little Tor. Climbs on the Upper Tier are best accessed from the path running to the headland, which reaches the second of two cols just before Great Tor proper. The eastern (left) branch is followed to reach the Col routes and the start of East Ridge. Great Tor East is also accessible from this path. The western (right) branch leads down past the Northern Upper Tier and can be followed all the way down to the beach, consequently reaching the Lower Tier. It is possible to scramble round the entire Tor from the base of either gully at an easy standard, at well above high tide level.

Great Tor Upper Tier
The front face of the upper tier is heavily vegetated, and there are no routes at present. The routes that do exist are clustered around the east and west flanks. Moving down the east branch of the col, to get to East Ridge, the Col routes are visible on the landward side of the gully.

North Facing Wall containing routes westwards from the col (Southern Freeze (11) etc)

East Ridge

Upper Tier

Lower Tier

Curving Corner (23)

West Chimney (14)

Routes behind the Great Flake

Great Tor

Photo: Adrian Berry

The Col Routes

The Great Flake

East Ridge

Great Tor

Photo:Adrian Berry

Eastwards from the Col

The Col Routes
At the top of the inland side of the east descent gully from the neck of the tor, lie a series of grooves and ribs. Although these appear vegetated, the routes are clean and are on good juggy rock.

1. **Shag**   15m   VD
   Climb the left most arete on jugs after a tricky start.
   D.Irving, C.Shorrock 00.00.1999

2. **Kestrel**   15m   S
   The narrow wall between Shag and the cave leads to a bulge. Either skirt this on the left before returning to the corner, or climb the corner direct at the same grade.
   J.Talbot 00.00.1971

3. **Cormorant**   18m   VD
   The groove right of the cave contains an arete. Climb this with occasional help from the left edge of the groove.
   J.Talbot 00.00.1971

4. **Magpie**   21m   S   *
   The groove to the right of Comorant, containing two bulges.
   J.Talbot 00.00.1971

5. **Chough**   21m   VD
   The bulbous arete and grooved arete above and to the right of Magpie.
   D.Irving 00.00.1999

6. **Wandl**   12m   HS,4c
Up and right a steep crack leaves a grassy bay. Climb this.
J.Talbot 00.00.1971

East Ridge Area
At the base of the east gully is a non tidal platform. Scramble round southward (out to sea and above the high tide level) to a good ledge, just before the east arete proper. Here is a prominent clean finger crack, marking the start of East Ridge.

7. **Ginger Groover**   18m   VD
Follow the vague grooves just right of the arete and 2m left of East Ridge, via two bulges. Amble off or continue as for East Ridge.
B.Merrifield 00.00.1998

8. **East Ridge**   73m   S,-,-,-,-   ***
Excellent positions, splendid climbing and good gear, weaving around the East Ridge of the Tor.
1. 18m Climb the crack in the wall and either step right, or follow the groove above to exit at a wide ledge.
2. 18m From the west end of the terrace climb a groove in the seaward face of the ridge before continuing up the arete to a stance by a flake.
3. 13m Follow the splendidly exposed arete to a grassy stance.
4. 24m Wander up the rest of the arete and the slabs above to belay on the summit, with superb views.
A.Osborn, S.Osborn 00.00.1952

9. **East Ridge Variations**   73m   HS,4b,4b   ***
Good variations on the first two pitches of the parent route. Start 2m right of East Ridge beneath twin cracks.
1. 17m Follow the twin cracks steeply to an easing before a wide ledge.
2. 17m The crack in the centre of the back wall leads to the ridge and the tradtional finish of East Ridge.
Unknown Pre-1970

Further left, the shelves lead to the ledge at the top of the Great Flake area of the Lower Tier.

Westwards from the Col
There is a north-facing leaning wall about 50m down the banking.

10. **Gower Kut**   18m   E6,6b
Pain! The thin cracks in the pillar of rock, PRs.
J.Talbot, D. Thomas - North Face A1 00.00.1959, FFA G.Ashmore 31.05.1998

11. **Southern Freeze**   18m   E1,5b
The cracks right of Gower Kut starting from a grassy scoop. Good to start, but deteriorates after the ledge.
J.Harwood, A.Sharp 24.01.1980

12. **Mistral**   25m   E4,6a   **
Amenable for the grade. Start as for Southern Freeze. Balance up the groove in the arete and reach a sloping ledge at 4m. Step right onto the arete PR and climb it with technical moves, PR, to bigger holds slightly right. Pull onto the capping slab and walk off onto the summit.
M.Crocker, J.Harwood 21.03.1999

The next route starts at a much lower level, at the base of a slab.

13. **North Corner**   39m   HVS,5a
The stepped corner. Climb the quartz-flecked slab until it is possible to move left to the foot of the corner. Finish up the final slab. The route is vegetated and the grade may no longer be accurate.
R.Owen, C.Andrews 00.00.1959

The next two routes are on the narrow west facing edge of the Tor, seaward from North Corner and facing back towards Little Tor.

14. **Direct**   42m   E1,5a
Start below the narrow west face at an easy-angled calcite-flecked slab some way up the beach. Follow a direct line up the centre of the west face with poor protection.
R.Owen, C.Andrews 00.00.1959

15. **South Edge**   42m   HS,4a
Start as for Direct. Climb the right edge of the slab to its top. The rock needs care in the upper reaches.
J.Talbot, D.Thomas 00.00.1959

Great Tor Lower Tier
Routes on the lower tier are described from west to east (left to right facing inland), as approached from Tor Beach.

The first area of rock encountered is a small twin slab lying midway along the west side of the headland. The left twin is lower, the right twin contains a deep crack running to three-quarters height.

There is a 4m boulder problem up the left-hand slab (Bulge, 4b, C.Andrews 1959).

1. **Two Cracks**   7m   HS,4b
Follow the crack stepping right into a second where it ends.
J.Talbot, D.Thomas 00.00.1959

2. **Piton Climb**   7m   VS,5a
Climb the wall just right of Two Cracks. Step left into the crack at its top and move up and left to finish.
J.Talbot, D.Thomas 00.00.1959

A little to the right of Piton Climb is a sheer south-facing slab.

3. **Dimpletown**   10m   E3,6a   *
A little gem. From the lowest part of the slab climb direct on small holds. A Bristol blade PR at half-height protects.
M.Crocker, J.Harwood 23.03.1999

The wall now turns to face west. The prominent features of the wall are a left-slanting crack with a narrow black corner 5m to the right and a sharp arete 5m right again. Beyond this is an obvious chimney (West Chimney).

4. **Only The Hardy**   10m   E1,5a
Climb the wall and shallow groove 2m left of a prominent left-slanting crack.
M.Crocker, J.Harwood 23.03.1999

5. **The Grunting Professor**   9m   E1,5c
The left-slanting crack.
M.Crocker, J.Harwood 23.03.1999

6. **Blow Monica**   9m   E1,5c
Start 2m left of the crack leading into the narrow black corner. Work up to a brown flake groove and take pockets to the top.
M.Crocker, J.Harwood 23.03.1999

7. **The Cramps In The Cold**   10m   E2,5c
Good climbing. Follow good, widely spaced holds 2m left of the arete of the black corner, finishing immediately left of a wide crystalline crack.
M.Crocker, J.Harwood 23.03.1999

8. **Mighty Mouse**   10m   HVS,5b

Start to the right, about 2m left of the black corner of Third Time Lucky. Climb the wall direct via a thin crack and shallow groove to the top.

J.Harwood, M.Ismail 01.05.1999

9. **Third Time Lucky**   12m   VS,4c

Climb the narrow black corner.

T.Hulff, L.Ashton 00.00.1999

10. **The Ramp With No Holds**   10m   E3,6a

Gain and climb the shallow ramp right of the narrow black corner to a jug. Finish direct past the stuck on jug.

M.Crocker, J.Harwood 23.03.1999

11. **Term Of Office**   12m   E1,5b

Climb the crack on the left side of the arete to the right.

T.Hulff, L.Ashton 00.00.1999

Moving seaward from the cracked slab is a series of steep low walls, terminating in an obvious arete, beyond which lies an obvious chimney.

12. **Another Quiet Night At Adrian's**   12m   VS,4b

Reach the arete from a ledge on its right and climb it.

L.Ashton, J.Robinson 00.00.1999

13. **South Wall**   HVS,5a

The thin crack in the wall between Another Quiet Night At Adrian's and West Chimney.

J.Talbot, D.Thomas 00.00.1959

14. **West Chimney**   15m   S,4b   *

The obvious chimney is highly intriguing.

D.Jones, R.Owen 1954/55

15. **Training For Ogmore**   14m   E1,5a

The centre of the unstable wall to the right of West Chimney.

J.Brown, E.Mair-Thomas 00.00.1996

16. **South Crack**   10m   S

The seaward-facing slab just right of Training For Ogmore is climbed by a crack and delicate finish.

J.Talbot, D.Thomas 00.00.1959

The lower tier now turns to face south at the line of Left Edge.

17. **Broken Wall**   12m   D

Takes the centre of the narrow stepped wall left of Left Edge.

J.Talbot 00.00.1959

18. **Left Edge**   18m   S

This follows the left edge of the bubbly wall. Start at the left end of a small ledge, climb the crack to a shallow groove in the arete. Finish up the crack above.

J.Talbot 00.00.1960

19. **Bubbly Wall**   18m   VS,4b   *

Start as for West Corner but step left onto the wall and follow a thin crack to the top.

J.Talbot, D.Thomas 00.00.1960

20. **West Corner**   12m   D
Climbs the corner behind the left edge of the Great Flake (the area of rock shielding this wall from the sea).
A.Osborn, S.Osborn 00.00.1952

21. **Barnacle**   13m   VS,4c
Start 3m right of West Corner below a distinct hole in the rock. Climb past the hole and continue to a good ledge.
Finish up the yellow wall above.
J.Talbot 00.00.1960

22. **Preuss Crack**   13m   HS,4b   *
Start at a distinct short crack in the lower wall, 3m right of Barnacle. From the end of the crack, bear left, climbing
a conglomerate crack above to finish.
J.Talbot 00.00.1960

23. **Curving Corner**   13m   VS,4c
A bold route that climbs a crack beneath the left end of an obvious ledge. Follow the thin crack above the left end
of the ledge.
J.Talbot 00.00.1960

24. **Direct II**   18m   HVS,4c
From the ledge of Curving Corner, climb the thin wall directly. Bold.
J.Talbot 00.00.1960

25. **Right Curving Corner**   21m   S,4c
As for Curving Corner to the ledge, traverse right to below a corner and follow it to the top.
J.Talbot 00.00.1960

26. **Brown Slab**   21m   VD
This takes the wall right of the corner of Right Curving Corner on big holds, after a difficult start.
J.Talbot 00.00.1960

27. **Holey Wall**   24m   VD
Gain and climb the short crack right of Brown Slab.
J.Talbot 00.00.1960

Next is a slightly recessed wall containing a crack on its right (Right Corner).

28. **Left Corner**   15m   VD
Start as for Right Corner but exit the crack immediately, moving left and up to finish.
J.Talbot, D.Thomas 00.00.1958

29. **Direct I**   15m   HS,4b
The slab between the Corner Routes.
J.Talbot 00.00.1959

30. **Right Corner**   15m   D
Climb the crack following it rightwards to the top via a corner.
J.Talbot, D.Thomas 00.00.1959

31. **Block Wall**   16m   VD
Begin as for Right Corner, then traverse right above the pool to finish direct on good holds.
J.Talbot 00.00.1959

32. **Central Crack I**   16m   D   *
Start at the right side of the pool and climb a crack to the top.
J.Talbot, D.Thomas 00.00.1959

33. **Right Crack I**   16m   VD
Start at the smaller block, then climb a wide crack, which narrows to the top.
J.Talbot 00.00.1959

34. **Right Side**   6m   D
Start at the top of the largest block, to climb delicately and directly to the top.
J.Talbot 00.00.1959

The last climbing in the south frontal section, to the right (east) of the other climbs is on a recessed yellow face, crossed by two right to left rising ramps.

35. **Left Pillar**   10m   HS
Climb the left pillar directly, passing the ramp en route.
J.Talbot, D.Thomas 00.00.1959

36. **Central Crack II**   12m   S
The crack above the centre of the lower ramp.
J.Talbot, D.Thomas 00.00.1959

37. **Right Pillar**   12m   HVS,5a
The steep slab right again, bold.
Traditional 00.00.0000

To the right lie two cracks, both start from the right end of the lower ramp.

38. **Left Crack I**   10m   VD
The thinner left-hand crack.
J.Talbot, D.Thomas 00.00.1959

39. **Right Crack II**   10m   D
The ledgey corner and wider right-hand crack.
J.Talbot, D.Thomas 00.00.1959

40. **Cracked Up**   10m   VD
Climb the first weakness in the upper ramp. Step left to a crack, then climb the curving crack above the ledge.
Unknown Pre-1998

41. **Cracked It**   8m   D
From the first weakness of Cracked Up, take the wider crack passing ledges en route.
Unknown Pre-1998

42. **Central Route**   8m   S
A disjointed crack, often filled with barnacles, splits the centre of the wall right again.
J.Talbot 00.00.1960

43. **Left Crack II**   6m   D
The left slanting cracks just before the end of the seaward face.
J.Talbot, D.Thomas 00.00.1959

Great Tor East
GR531876 to 531876

TIDAL STATUS: Obscenities is Non-tidal. The other routes 1½ to 3 hours either side of low water, increasing towards the end of the section.

DESCENTS: Descents are by scrambling down various grooves in the area.

Another pleasant area with many easy routes. Worthy of description, if only to help take some pressure off Three Cliffs and Little Tor. The cliffs are described moving landwards (left to right facing away from the sea) along the eastern coastline of the Great Tor headland, which forms the west side of Three Cliffs Bay. Although the area is liberally covered with rock a series of inlets and bays provide the main interest, the first encountered being Shallow Cut.

Shallow Cut
About 25m right of the starting platform of East Ridge is a shallow recess with a chimney in the back.

1. **Stefan Hermann And The Mothers Of Invention** 10m HS,4a
   Climb the chimney and subsequent corner forming the left side of the recess.
   D.Dilligence Pre-2003

2. **Careless McGee** 10m HVD
   Scramble up to the ledge half-way up the right corner of the recess and finish up the corner crack.
   D.Dilligence Pre-2003

3. **Another Brixius In The Wall** 10m M
   The right-hand arete of the recess.
   D.Dilligence Pre-2003

Deep Cut
This distinctive gash lies below a prominent subsidiary ridge to the east of East Ridge. Climbing is only possible around low water.

4. **Left Edge** 15m VD
   The left edge of Deep Cut contains two corners. Follow the first over a bulge to a slabby finish.
   J.Talbot 00.00.1960

5. **The Camille Wester Fan Club** 15m VS,4c
   The right-hand corner.
   D.Dilligence Pre-2003

6. **Chasm** 18m HVD
   The right wall of Deep Cut contains a leftward rising ledge. Gain and follow this from the right of a bulge. Chimney up the back wall, to gain a ledge on the right. Finish up the crack above.
   J.Talbot 00.00.1960

7. **Left Crack** 15m S *
   Follow Chasm to the ledge, then take a short corner to a ledge. Choose from a cluster of cracks to finish.
   J.Talbot 00.00.1960

8. **Right Edge** 18m M
   The right edge of Deep Cut.
   J.Talbot 00.00.1960

9. **Arcelor Bandit**   18m   VD
   The arete 3m right of Right Edge.
   D.Dilligence Pre-2003

10. **LEG And Jakob's Triple Trigger ABS Restructuring**   18m   D
    The shallow corner immediately right of Arcelor Bandit.
    G.Ashmore 15.03.2003

The next route lies above the beach level line of outcrops, in a conspicuous recess.

11. **Obscenities**   12m   E4 6b   \
    Tthe right wall and rib of the cave. Climb the rib, TR, 2PRs, to the roof. Pull through into the groove via very thin
    moves until a 'thank God' hold can be reached. Continue direct to the top (a pre-placed rope belay is advisable).
    E.Kellar, A.Wilson 00.00.1990

Odin's Wall

The most attractive of the crags lying on the west side of Three Cliffs Bay, Odin's Wall, is composed of the best Gower
Limestone and provides a variety of well protected quality lines. It is the wall at right angles to the last few routes
described, some 70m back from the headland.

12. **Left Corner And Crack**   18m   HVS,5a
    The left end of the wall forms a corner. Climb this to a big ledge and follow the crack above.
    J.Talbot 00.00.1961

13. **Cave Crack Direct**   20m   VS,4b   *
    Follow Left Corner And Crack to the ledge. Traverse delicately right into a hollow and finish up the crack above.
    J.Talbot 00.00.1959

14. **Cave Crack**   18m   HS,4b
    Follow Cave Crack Direct to the hollow, but finish up the diagonal crack on the right.
    R.Owen, D.Jones, A.Bevan 00.00.1959

15. **Direct**   21m   VS,5a
    Start at a recess to the right of a cave. Step over the pool to use the recess to gain the cracks above. Climb these
    with conviction, to a rest and an easier finish.
    J.Talbot, D.Thomas 00.00.1959

16. **Fiechtl**   18m   S
    A niche forms the start of the next pronounced crack to the right. Follow this until a horizontal break leads to a
    series of cracks forming the right side of the main wall.
    J.Talbot, D.Thomas 00.00.1959

17. **Wide Crack**   18m   D
    Start as for Fiechtl. Climb the tricky wide crack, chimney and corner to the top.
    R.Owen, D.Jones 00.00.1959

18. **Pillar Crack**   15m   D
    The chimney right of Wide Crack often has a pool at its barnacle-ridden base. A preferable start lies 1m left, before
    joining the chimney at a ledge.
    R.Owen, D.Jones 00.00.1959

19. **Girdle Traverse**   18m   VS,4c
    Start as for Fiechtl and continue leftwards at mid height to finish on the ledge of Left Corner and Crack.
    Unknown Pre-1991

Odin's Wall East Facet
Slightly right and up from Odin's Wall lie a series of pillars and corners. The first pillar of note is called the Second Pillar.

Second Pillar
The first route here follows the obvious South East facing cracked corner at the top left of the bay.

20. **Left Corner**   12m   D
    Follow the crack, with good jams past a bulge.
    J.Talbot 00.00.1959

21. **South Wall**   12m   D
    From the base of the crack Left Corner, step right and climb the narrow wall.
    J.Talbot 00.00.1959

22. **East Edge**   15m   D
    Follow the arete to the right of South Wall, taking care with the rock near the top.
    J.Talbot 00.00.1959

23. **Wall And Corner**   15m   VD
    The wall just before Left Crack.
    J.Talbot 00.00.1960

24. **Left Crack**   15m   D
    Set back from the last route is a gashed feature. Climb this.
    J.Talbot 00.00.1960

First Pillar
Is nothing more than a continuation of the rock.

25. **South Face**   15m   D
    The steep juggy face just to the right of Left Crack.
    J.Talbot 00.00.1960

26. **Left Edge**   15m   S
    Take the arete with little in the way of protection.
    J.Talbot 00.00.1960

27. **Left Pillar Direct**   15m   VD
    Takes the narrow east face of the First Pillar.
    J.Talbot 00.00.1960

28. **East Corner Crack**   16m   D
    A good line up the cracked corner, bounding the right side of the pillar.
    J.Talbot, D.Thomas 00.00.1959

The rest of this recessed bay can be climbed anywhere at less than Moderatestandard. The cliff now becomes more broken. The next bay, 150m on is known as Third Corner, Which may house a route up some grooves on the left wall (Living Wall HVS,5a, L.Cole, M.Condick 09.04.2002). The next area to be encountered, 100m past Third Bay houses a number of good lines.

Second Corner
The left wall of the Second Corner is marked by a v-shaped nose at its centre. Left of this nose lie two corners.

29. **Left Corner**   8m   D
    The left of the two corners.
    J.Talbot 1959

30. **Buttress**   8m   M
The rock between Left Corner and Sharp Edge.
J.Talbot 1959)

31. **Sharp Edge**   10m   VD
Takes the short slab followed by the corner above, which provides good laybacking.
J.Talbot 00.00.1959

32. **The Nose**   10m   HS,4a
Start in a hollow just right of the slab of Sharp Edge. Climb up left to a ledge on that route, before swinging right
onto the nose which is taken to the top.
J.Talbot 00.00.1959

33. **Quartz Slab**   10m   VD
Attain the quartz flecked slab just right of The Nose. Follow this with help from the crack to the right, to a bulge.
Surmount this to follow the edge above.
J.Talbot 00.00.1959

34. **Right Block Buttress**   8m   S
The wall right of Quartz Slab, is climbed by moving firstly a little right and then back into the centre of the wall
to finish.
J.Talbot 00.00.1959

The South Wall
This buttress forms the right face of the Second Corner. It is notable for the chimney that splits it.

35. **Dr. Focke's Pension Fund**   7m   HVS,5b
A problem up a vague groove in the left arete of the chimney recess.
G.Ashmore 15.03.2003

36. **South Chimney And Slab**   15m   VD   *
From the back of the chimney, back and footing gains a ledge, from where a crack leads to a steepening. Step
up and left over this, to finish up the slab above. Entertaining.
J.Talbot 00.00.1959

37. **Left Arete**   7m   S,4c
Climb the slabby right face of the arete to the right. Delicate.
J.Kerry, A. Randall 00.00.1970

38. RIP Norman   7m   D   \
Off to the right is a hole. Crawl in through this and climb the chimney above.
L.Cole 16.03.2003

39. Taste Of Spring Chicken   7m   S   \
Off to the right is a platform. Follow the corner up from this and the crack above.
L.Cole 07.03.2002

40. Scary Cow Don't Jump   7m   E1,5c   \
Climb the arete from a small boulder.
L.Cole 07.03.2002

Dave Goodman - V Groove (E3,5c) Jacky's Tor
(Page 77) Photo: Carl Ryan

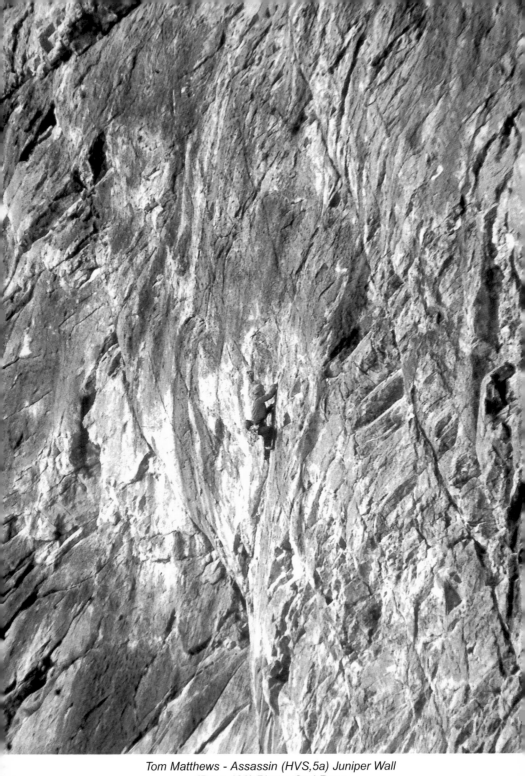

Tom Matthews - Assassin (HVS,5a) Juniper Wall
(Page 123) Photo: Carl Ryan

First Corner

100 metres along the coast lies another bay of cliffs. The left wall leans gently and is full of cracks, the right wall being composed of an hectic arrangement of pillars. Just before the East Wall is reached a small slabby zawn has Monty's Slab HS,5a (J.Kerry, A.March 1971) following a vague crack diagonally left after a hard start. Climbing the slab a few metres left is Master Bates Smear HVS,5b(LM.Condick, L.Cole 2002).

The gently leaning east wall contains a number of routes.

41. Onion Crack (Weeping Crack)   9m   VS,5a   *
The last crack on the right end of the wall is the most obvious.
J.Talbot 00.00.1962

Block Corner D (J.Talbot 1959) bounds the right end of the leaning wall. Right of this is a pillar and a cave entrance.

42. Left Corner Block Wall   12m   D
Ascend the groove on the left of the cave. At half-height, move right around a flake, then step back up left to a narrow corner and a conglomerate top out.
J.Talbot 00.00.1959

South Wall

A cave at its left-hand end is followed rightwards by a series of pillars of varying height, to another through cave and a holed slab.

43. Block Wall   12m   S,4a
Bridge the cave just right of Left Corner Block Wall. Pull up into the crack above. From the crack an obvious foothold is used to cross the wall leftwards to a crack. Follow this to a small conglomerate overhang, then move right and up to the top.
J.Talbot 00.00.1959

44. Central Pillar   13m   HS,4b
A corner just right of the cave leads to a ledge beneath an arete. Swing left onto the face along a horizontal crack, to join Block Wall.
J.Talbot 00.00.1959

The corner right of Central Pillar is Stalactite HD (J.Talbot 1959), whose right arete is Commitment 4b (J.Talbot 1959). Stepping down and right is a through cave with a slab to its right.

45. Hole Slab   8m   D
Begin at a shallow corner at the right side of the slab (the corner itself is Right Corner M (J.Talbot 1959). Step left as soon as possible onto the slab. Move up to the distinct hole, exiting up the slab above.
J.Talbot 00.00.1959

46. Proud Slab   7m   D
The proud slab right of Right Corner.
Unknown Pre-1978

Ramp Zawn

A narrow zawn whose left wall lies at about 40 degrees and whose right wall is composed of boulders. It is due north from the Rock Island and has a steep slab at its back.

47. Cracked Slab   12m   VD
Follow the crack in the slab.
S.Jacques 00.00.1998

48. Lucy Slab   12m   VD
   On the tidal island itself, climb the centre of the main face.
   L.Cole 07.03.2002

49. Look-out Lucy   12m   D
   Climb the crack to the right of Lucy Slab.
   L.Cole 07.03.2002

THREE CLIFFS AND POBBLES BAYS

GR537877 to 543875
By Chris Shorrock

TIDAL STATUS: Three Cliffs 3 hours, Pobbles West 4 hours, Pobbles East 1½ hours, Scoop Corner 1 hour either side of low water.

BOLTING POLICY: **NO BOLTING.**

PREAMBLE

Protruding into the centre of a deep sandy bay to the South East of Penmaen, Three Cliffs provides Gower with its most picturesque venue. Add to this its number of quality easy to mid-grade routes and its lack of seriousness and it is easy to see why the crag is extremely popular. Pobbles Bay West lying only 100m to the east provides a useful overspill, or somewhere to retreat to when the tides threaten. Pobbles Bay East is considerably more tidal but offers some easier routes, which are far better than the over-popular venue of King Wall and on better rock. Scoop Corner is a recent rediscovery, perhaps worth a quick solo if in the area.

ACCESS

1. Penmaen Access

On the A4118 before Penmaen, when approaching from Swansea turn right (north) at a telephone kiosk and bench (GR532887), into a National Trust car park. Cross back over the road to an obvious track (at North Hill Farm) and follow signposts for the beach. Cross the river via obvious stepping stones. The rear of the Three Cliffs is visible ahead. At low to mid tides, Pobbles Bay can be reached by walking eastwards round the front of the arch.

2. Southgate Access

Take the offshoot of the B4436 leading into Southgate, then a right-hand lane (Bendrick Drive) just after the Golf Club (it will be necessary to park a little further on and walk back). Follow a path through fields and round a wood to gain a path leading down through dunes to Pobbles after about 15 minutes. It is also possible to follow the cliff top road and path as described in the Shire Combe area approach.

DESCENTS: Three Cliffs descents are by easy scrambling left (west) down the ridge and Pobbles West by easy scrambling at several places along the crag. Pobbles East and Scoop corner, by scrambling down and left in both cases.

THE ROUTES

Three Cliffs

This is the prominent cliff on the east side of Three Cliff Bay. It consists of three pinnacles and a large through-cave that lies between the highest pinnacles. It is very popular and often crowded in summer. All but one of the routes (Back Beat) are on the south (seaward) face.

1. **Left Crack**   15m   M
    At the left (west) end of the cliff, climb broken rock to a short slab, over this to a ledge, then up a crack to finish.
    J.Brailsford, St.AMRT 1954/55

2. **Right Crack I**   16m   M
    Follow Left Crack to the ledge, then take the crack bearing up and right.
    J.Brailsford, St.AMRT 1954/55

3. **Wall Climb I**   9m   D
    Climb the slab right of the lower section of Right Crack.
    J.Brailsford, St.AMRT 1954/55

Three Cliffs

Photo: Carl Ryan

4. **Cleft I**   10m   D
   This is the first of the two obvious clefts right of Wall Climb I.
   J.Brailsford, St.AMRT 1954/55

5. **Wall Climb II**   10m   D
   The slab to the right.
   J.Brailsford, St.AMRT 1954/55

6. **Cleft II**   11m   VD
   Climb the right-hand of two clefts and the slab above, keeping left of a small block overhang.
   J.Brailsford, St.AMRT 1954/55

7. **Wall Climb**   11m   D
   The narrow slab right of Cleft II and just left of a shallow corner, finishing by the right side of the block overhang.
   J.Brailsford, St.AMRT 1954/55

8. **Left Corner I**   11m   M
   Climb the shallow corner bounding the left edge of a raised slab.
   J.Brailsford, St.AMRT 1954/55

9. **Initiation Flake**   12m   S   *
   Climb the raised slab in its centre.
   J.Brailsford, St.AMRT 1954/55

10. **Right Corner I**   12m   D
    Takes the corner bounding the right edge of the raised slab.
    J.Brailsford, St.AMRT 1954/55

11. **Meander**   12m   D
Climb the slab right of the corner to finish on a ridge.
J.Brailsford, St.AMRT 1954/55

In a recess between the first and second pinnacles lies a smooth slab topped by an overhang.

12. **Bulge**   15m   VD
Climb the slabby wall left of a corner.
J.Brailsford, St.AMRT 1954/55

13. **Left Corner II**   16m   D
This follows the corner bounding the slab on the left.
J.Brailsford, St.AMRT 1954/55

14. **Inverted V**   16m   HVS,4c   *
Boldly climb the centre of the slab to the apex of the overhang. Pull through this to finish.
J.Brailsford, St.AMRT 1pt 1954/55
R.Owens, C.Edwards 00.00.1959

15. **Spouse Crack**   16m   S
Climb the thin crack on the right side of the slab to an overhang at the top of the corner. Pull over this to gain an easy groove. Follow this or move left to the crack above the overhang.
J.Brailsford, St.AMRT 1954/55

16. **Right Crack II**   15m   S
Follow Spouse Crack above the bulge, then move left by the overhang and follow the definite crack system running up above it.
J.Talbot, R.Corbett 00.00.1959

17. **Quartz Corner**   16m   HS,4b
This follows the narrow slabby corner right of the recessed slab. Climb this to a calcite slab, then move right over an overhang and go up a crack to the top.
J.Brailsford, St.AMRT 1954/55

18. **Joggled Wall**   18m   VD   *
Climb the rough brown slab right of Quartz Corner, beginning just right of centre. Step left to avoid the overhang and enter a shallow corner. The left edge of the slab can be climbed at the same grade.
J.Brailsford, St.AMRT 1954/55

19. **Joggled Wall Direct**   18m   HS,4a   *
Takes the overhang Joggled Wall avoids.
C.Edwards, R.Owens, C.Andrews 00.00.1959

20. **Left Edge**   17m   HS,4b
This takes the left raised edge of the shiny slab right of Joggled Wall. Finish as for Joggled Wall Direct.
C.Edwards, R.Owen, C. Andrews 00.00.1959

21. **Perseverance**   18m   HS,4b   *
Climb the centre of the shiny slab by some thin, well protected moves.
J.Brailsford, St.AMRT 1954/55

A series of grooves and ridges to the right provide a variety of descents, centred around Right Corner.

22. **Right Corner II**   18m   M
The smooth right-angled groove.
J.Brailsford, St.AMRT 1954/55

23. **Arch Slab**   24m   VS,4c   **
Start on the left wall outside the large cave, below a groove. Climb the groove until just above the lip of the cave.
From a diagonal quartz break traverse right to the apex of the cave. Finish directly up the slab above.
R.Owen, C.Edwards, C.Andrews 00.00.1959

24. **Under Milk Wood**   21m   VS,4a   *
An entertaining struggle up the slab within the left side of the cave. Follow the slab diagonally to a subsidiary
cave and thread. Enter the cave and wriggle towards the light. Alternatively move the route to Pembroke, up the
grade two or three notches, give it ten stars for quality and write tedious adventure stories about it. The larger-
framed will have to abseil off a tat before the top.
R.McElliot, R.Hoare 00.00.1984

25. **The Steal**   24m   E4,6a   *
Often greasy. On the right side of the cave is a subsidiary slab running down from the apex of the cave. Start
below the slab and gain it with difficulty, PR. Move up the slab to the apex, PR, then finish directly.
S.Lewis, A.Richardson, C.Curle 00.00.1987

26. **Scavenger**   26m   VS,4c   ***
A classic line following the corner right of the cave. Make a tricky move up from a platform, to gain the corner,
which is followed by a mixture of slab and crack manoeuvres. Finish at a ledge and PB.
J.Brailsford, St.AMRT 1954/55

Three Cliffs

Photo: Carl Ryan

27. **Scavenger Variations**   26m   VS,4c   *

Climb in from the right wall of the cave to a spike on the left edge of the Scavenger slab and join the parent route. From a point where the route is level with the cave apex, struggle rightwards up a steep wall to easier ground.
J.Kerry - Start 00.00.1970
P.Greenwood, C.Ryan – Finish 00.00.1970

28. **Hangel**   27m   VS,4c

Climb Scavenger until level with the start of a small recessed slab to the left. Swing right along an overhanging ramp to reach a slab above. Follow its left edge to belay near the PB of Scavenger.
R.Owen, C.Edwards, C.Andrews 1954/55

29. **October**   30m   S

A poor route that starts at the foot of Scavenger. Move up right to a ledge at 3m. Now follow a blocky gangway left, to swing onto the face above and to the right. Follow a series of vegetated grooves on the right to the top.
G.Blake, J.Blundell 00.00.1972

30. **Plumb Line**   45m   D

Start at a slabby buttress at the foot of the third pinnacle. Climb the buttress and then the narrow raised slab to more broken slabs near the crest, which are followed to the top.
J.Brailsford, St.AMRT 1954/55

31. **Disappointment**   45m   D

An obvious groove lies just right of the crest of Plumb Line. Climb this stepping right at two-thirds height into the narrower continuation groove.
J.Brailsford, St.AMRT 1954/55

32. **Consolation**   31m   VD

This artificial but worthwhile line takes the slabs right of Disappointment.
J.Brailsford, St.AMRT 1954/55

33. **Traverse Of The Three Pinnacles**   76m   M   *

A good scramble from left (west) to right (east) keeping to the crest and taking in all the summits.
Unknown Pre-1970

34. **The Battle Of Midway**   150m   VS,5b

Traverse the crag from the left end, above the high water level, to gain Arch Slab. As for Arch Slab then step down into Scavenger, which is reversed to gain Scavenger Variations. Finish up Disapointment.
A.Berry solo 26.12.2000

35. **Back Beat**   25m   E3,5c   *

A route taking the crack on the left side of the arch on the north (landward) side of the Three Cliffs Arch. Lower off rope advised.
M.Crocker, J.Harwood 01.05.1994

Pobbles Bay West

A series of inlets and gullies lined with slabs provide a number of short easy routes at the far west end of Pobbles Bay (100m east of Three Cliffs). It is ideal for a visit with novices or when the tide is closing in on Three Cliffs. The first feature, lying some 75m right of Disappointment is a cave. To the right of the cave is a small slab with overhangs above its left side and a slabby pillar on the right.

1. **Main Wall**   11m   S

Climb a frequently wet corner at the left end of the cliff. Step left at half-height to finish up the wall.
J.Talbot, R.Corbett 1954/55

2. **Gwyn's Route**   11m   VS,5a   *
From a pedestal at the base of main wall, climb through the three overhangs directly.
SUMC Pre-1973

3. **Left Corner**   11m   VD
Climb the shallow corner right of Gwyn's Route.
J.Brailsford, St.AMRT 1954/55

4. **Left Pillar**   11m   VD
Takes the left side of the raised slab right of Left Corner.
J.Brailsford, St.AMRT 1954/55

5. **Pillar Route**   11m   D
Climb the right side of the same slab.
J.Brailsford, St.AMRT 1954/55

6. **Right Edge I**   10m   M
Follow the edge to the top.
J.Brailsford, St.AMRT 1954/55

To the right (east) is a small gully. The first route is on the left arete.

7. **Brant Minor**   11m   VS,5a
Climb the arete on its left. Swing left onto a ledge and finish up the wall above.
J.Brailsford, St.AMRT 1954/55

8. **Brant Direct Minor**   11m   VS,4c
Climb the slim groove immediately right and finish up the crack above.
J.Brailsford, St.AMRT 1954/55

9. **Barry Slapper**   11m   E2,6a
The slim groove to the right gives a difficult problem with a bad landing.
G.Ashmore solo 21.05.2001

10. **East Fissure Wall**   11m   VD
Climb the steep back wall of the gully.
J.Talbot, R.Corbett1954/55

11. **Shy Slab**   10m   S
The steep narrow bubbly slab to the right of the gully is bold.
J.Brailsford, St.AMRT 1954/55

12. **Square Cut**   9m   D
The next narrow slab to the right.
J.Brailsford, St.AMRT 1954/55

13. **Right Edge II**   9m   D
The next arete to the right.
J.Brailsford, St.AMRT 1954/55

14. **Two Tier Slab**   9m   D
This is obvious by its name and can be climbed by many variations at about the same grade.
Unknown Pre-1973

Right again is another deeper gully, with a slabby back wall.

15. **Little Corner**   6m   VD
Climb the slab between the left end of the gully and Fissure Direct. Variations are possible at the same grade.
J.Brailsford, St.AMRT 1954/55

16. **Fissure Direct**   10m   VD
Climbs the obvious polished fissure and the slab above.
J.Brailsford, St.AMRT 1954/55

17. **Fissure Route**   9m   D
Follow Fissure Direct until a step right gains the upper crack.
J.Brailsford, St.AMRT 1954/55

18. **Soap Gut**   10m   VD
The slab right of Fissure Direct.
J.Brailsford, St.AMRT 1954/55

19. **Scoop**   9m   D
From the scoop follow the cracks above.
J.Brailsford, St.AMRT 1954/55

20. **Girdle**   9m   VD
The obvious line from right to left, starting at Scoop.
J.Brailsford, St.AMRT 1954/55

21. **Blind Crack**   8m   D
The slab and blind crack just right of Scoop.
J.Brailsford, St.AMRT 1954/55

22. **First Slab**   9m   M
Just right again lies the final route of the gully wall.
J.Brailsford, St.AMRT 1954/55

23. **Recessed Wall**   9m   VD
This climbs the recessed wall just to the right.
Unknown Pre-1971

Pobbles East

This crag is on the far east side of Pobbles Bay and not immediately obvious. It is about halfway between where the path from the Southgate approach leads out onto the beach and the eastern headland (Shire Combe), just to the east (right when facing inland) of where a long rock platform 10m above the beach finishes, tucked into a cylindrical cove.

Cave Section
To the west (left) of the opening of the cylindrical cove is an obvious smooth slab.

1. **The Groove**   12m   M   *
The groove left of the corner bounding the smooth slab.
J.Brailsford, St.AMRT 1954/55

2. **Slab Route**   12m   S
Start up the corner bounding the left side of the slab, to gain a prominent slot out right. Swing right on this and finish directly up the slab.
J.Brailsford, St.AMRT 1954/55

3. **Limpet Route** 12m HVS,5b *
Gain the vague groove in the centre of the slab from directly below. Hard to start and not well protected.
J.Brailsford, St.AMRT 1954/55

4. **Barnacle Bulge** 12m VS,4c *
Gain the right arete of the slab via the small capped groove on its left. Tricky!
J.Brailsford, St.AMRT 1954/55

5. **Insanity** 14m HVS,5b
A stiff boulder problem up the bulge 2m right of the arete gives access to an indefinite crack.
J.Brailsford, St.AMRT 1954/55

6. **Smalt** 15m VS,4c **
To the right is an obvious diagonal crack. Gain this with interest and follow it with superb moves.
G.Ashmore solo 20.02.1999

7. **Blue Glass** 15m VS,5b *
To the right is an innocuous looking scoop. Somehow rock into it, and climb it more easily. Poorly protected.
G.Ashmore solo 20.02.1999

8. **Corner Groove** 15m D *
The corner groove to the right.
J.Brailsford, St.AMRT 1954/55

9. **Twin Crack Slab** 15m M *
The cracked slab to the right.
J.Brailsford, St.AMRT 1954/55

10. **Jagged Edge** 15m HVD
The right arete of the slab.
J.Brailsford, St.AMRT 1954/55

11. **Blue Lights Crack** 15m VS,5a
The steep bulging wall right of Jagged Edge.
J.Brailsford, St.AMRT 1954/55

12. **The Poseidon Enigma** 15m E3,6b
Scurry into the cave at the back left side of the cove. Just before the back of the cave make a technical mantle and rock up to a tenuous position on the slab. Work along the lip of the slab rightwards with help from the back wall, to gain a crack leading to the top.
A.Berry solo 26.12.2000

The back wall of the gully contains a through hole and slab, whilst the east wall has a prominent conglomerate overhang and is bounded on its south by a small zawn.

East Wall

13. **Fourth Buttress** 12m VS,4c
The buttress just to the right of the conglomerate overhang, has a v-cleft with a crack above. Follow this, then step right where it steepens to finish up a shallow corner.
J.Talbot, D.Thomas 00.00.1959

14. **Third Buttress**   12m   D   *
The corner 4m to the right of Fourth Buttress.
J.Talbot, D.Thomas 00.00.1959

15. **Second Buttress**   12m   VD
The next corner/scoop to the right of Third Buttress.
J.Talbot, D.Thomas 00.00.1959

16. **Cracked Arete**   11m   M
The arete with a cleft 5m to the right of Second Buttress.
Unknown Pre-1970

17. **First Buttress**   10m   M
The slab containing a flared crack to the right of Cracked Arete.
J.Talbot, D.Thomas 00.00.1959

18. **Gully Slab**   9m   D
Climb the landward wall of the small zawn bounding the right side of the area.
Unknown Pre-1970

19. **Quergang**   45m   HS,4b
Start at the back of the small gully on the east wall. Climb to a point level with the middle of the slab. Traverse the slab leftwards and then cross a series of corners and slabs until below the conglomerate overhang. Step left onto the middle of the slab to a vague crack, which is followed past a prominent hole to finish.
J.Talbot, D.Thomas 00.00.1959

Scoop Corner
About 100m on from Pobbles East, towards Shire Combe, is a recessed scoop like bay. At the back, facing west, a definite crack runs up and right, with two distinct corner slabs at different levels rising up and left from it.

1. **Corners Edge**   10m   VD
Start at the foot of the crack and step left onto the slab. Move left to the arete and follow this to finish.
Unknown Pre-1970

2. **Lower Corner**   10m   D
Starts as for Corners Edge, but swing through a bulge to gain and finish up the corner.
J.Talbot, D.Thomas 00.00.1959

3. **Upper Corner**   10m   VD
Climb the lower crack on the right.
J.Talbot, D.Thomas 00.00.1959

SHIRE COMBE TO WATCH HOUSE EAST

GR544874 to 549873
By Goi Ashmore

TIDAL STATUS: 1 hour either side of low water to non-tidal. See individual crags.

BOLTING POLICY: No bolting except for Watch House East. At Watch House East - Retro-bolting permissible with first ascensionist's permission. Replacement of worn fixed gear on a point for point basis with bolts is permissible. New sports routes allowed.

PREAMBLE

This is a complex stretch of coastline running from Shire Combe at the south-east tip of Pobbles Bay to West Cliff Beach. Shire Combe is the large tidal feature easily visible from Three Cliffs and contains a good selection of routes on slabby rock. To the east of Shire Combe are a series of small, mostly tidal crags, containing some good routes for those in search of some solitude. Access and orientation is not easy. For the first time visitor, walking along the non-tidal path contouring eastwards from Shire Combe and past Anemone Wall, eventually dropping down onto the beach just before Watch House East is recommended. The area is dominated by the prominent fin of White Edge. If White Edge can be located successfully from the top (not easy), it is worth noting that Ravenscliff Gully and Watch House East are most easily reached by following the path running down the east flank of the edge.

ACCESS

From the B4436 follow the offshoot into Southgate and continue to the National Trust Car Park by a roundabout at the end of the village (GR554873). Park here and follow the private road along the cliff top westward (right when looking out to sea) until a wide path breaks off left, just before its end at Number 18 (The Watch House). Follow this path for 200m until an iron stake is seen on the left (and opposite a water tower well over to the right). Continue along the cliff top for 70m until a rocky ridge runs down and left, where the aspect of the underlying slopes changes from south to south-west. Scramble down here to reach a wave-cut platform. Shire Combe is the crag resting against the headland, Anemone wall is the smooth cracked slab 100m to the east. The other crags in this area can be reached by following the path back eastwards. Watch House East itself can be more efficiently reached by walking onto the beach (2 hours either side of low water) from Fox Hole (see Fox Hole) and this is an easy way back out to the car park for those who have made the full crag trip.

DESCENTS: All the crags other than White Edge and Watch House Crag are reached by scrambling down from the lower level coastal path, rendering descent information superfluous. White Edge can be descended to its east (right), whilst routes at Watch House require a lower off rope to be preplaced anyway.

THE ROUTES

Shire Combe Buttress And West Slab

GR544874

TIDAL STATUS: 1½ hours either side of low water.

Routes on Shire Combe Buttress are accessed from the east side (left when looking out to sea). Routes on the west side can be accessed by the cave formed by the slab resting against the headland, or by climbing round the seaward face. A vegetated expedition - Shire Combe West Face (Unknown 1965) climbs somewhere up the broad slabby area to the west of Shire Combe proper, but the first routes are on the west side (left side of the crag facing back inland).

1. **Main Slab**   12m   HD
    Start about 12m left (west) of the cleft between the buttress and the rear slab at a large, square, sloping ledge. Climb a short recessed area of easy rock, then go directly up over the upper slab to the top and a good ledge.
    J.Talbot, D.Thomas 00.00.1959

2. **Vice Squad** 25m HVS,5a
    Climbs the chimney to the right forming the west side of the main buttress.
    A.Berry, J.Preece 00.00.1990

There are a couple of easy scambles up the loose front face of the buttress, Recessed Slab and Fossil Slab (J.Talbot, D.Thomas 1959). The next routes are on the east (right) face of the buttress.

3. **East Face** 36m D
    This climbs the seaward arete of the right (east) wall of the main buttress. Continue up right via short walls from the ledge at one-third height.
    J.Talbot, D.Thomas 1954/55

4. **The Jackal** 27m HVS,5a
    Start at the foot of the overhanging corner on the east wall. Climb the corner until able to move left across the overhanging wall to gain a ledge on the arete. Continue easily up the wall trending left to the top or, harder, finish up the twin cracks on Eastern Promise.
    N.Williams, P.Williams 00.00.1980

5. **Eastern Promise** 27m E2,5c *
    A fine pitch. Start as for The Jackal but continue to the overhang. Go over this leftwards and finish up twin cracks.
    E.Pardoe, P.Kokelaar – Gullimot A1 00.00.1965
    FFA A.Sharp, J.Harwood 03.12.1983

6. **Cwyrt-Y-Bella** 27m E4,6b
    Take the flake and thin crack to the right of Eastern Promise to gain the roof right of Eastern Promise. Finish over the roof. 2PRs.
    M.Crocker, J.Harwood 31.01.1993

The next routes start inside the cleft formed by the buttress and the headland.

7. **Il Bel Camino** 27m HVS,5a **
    A superb route, excellent rock and a unique atmosphere. The route is approached by scrambling through the cleft. Start directly below a boulder choke formed where the slab rests against the headland. Climb the cleft to the choke then move right around the choke to a groove which is followed to the top.
    A.Sharp, J.Harwood 03.12.1983

8. **Painter's Paradise** 27m VS,4c
    This climbs the slab right of Il Bel Camino to join it at its top groove. Approach by scrambling in from the chimney to the east.
    C.Hebbelthwaite, J.Beynon 00.00.1988

9. **Great Slab Climb** 60m HS
    Follow Painter's Paradise to the junction with the top groove of Il Bel Camino (possible stance). Drop down and traverse under the arch to come out at the west side of the main buttress. Climb up the slab above to finish.
    P.Hinder, V.Rees 00.00.1972

Anemone Wall Area
GR545873

TIDAL STATUS: At dead low water there is a through-cave which provides a start for the routes as far as Anemone Wall. At all but spring tides or rough seas, it is possible to gain the routes a few metres up them, without any change in grades.

This is the slab 100m to the east of the headland. Access is down the easy slab to the east.

1. **Great Chimney**   23m   VS,4b
   Start at the left end of the ledge at the foot of the slab. Gain the chimney from the rib bounding the slab on the left and climb it, taking care with blocks at the top.
   R.Owens, D.Jones 00.00.1959

2. **Honesty**   18m   HVS,4c
   Start as for Great Chimney then step onto the slab at a good hold. Climb the slab just to the right of the right edge of the chimney, with some unnerving moves.
   J.Kerry, A.Randall 00.00.1970

3. **Pickpocket**   21m   HVS,5b
   An artificial route directly up the slab between Great Chimney and Anemone Wall. Using the crack is forbidden.
   J.Kerry, A.T.Randall 00.00.1970

4. **Anemone Wall**   21m   VS,4c   **
   Start where the crevasse closes and traverse left to the obvious diagonal crack. When it peters out at a pocket, climb direct.
   J.Brailsford, St.AMRT 1954/55

5. **Alternate**   18m   S
   Follow discontinuous cracks and water-worn grooves right of Anemone Wall directly to the top.
   J.Brailsford, St.AMRT 1954/55

The more broken slab to the right of Alternate gives a number of easier climbs.

6. **Respite**   18m   VD
   Start 1m right of Alternate and climb the slab direct.
   J.Brailsford, St.AMRT 1954/55

7. **Wide Crack**   13m   D
   The wide crack to the right of Respite.
   J.Brailsford, St.AMRT 1954/55

8. **Girdle Traverse**   22m   HS,4c
   Traverse the slab from left to right along the obvious thin break.
   J.Brailsford, St.AMRT 1954/55

From Shire Combe and Anemone wall, a series of rocky platforms run eastward above the high tide level towards the prominent ridge of White Edge. Below the rocky platforms are a series of tidal zawns, which possess a number of good easy routes. Although it may be more efficient to approach these via the descent for White Edge, they are described as approached from Shire Combe, to aid identification on the first visit.

White Cove
GR546873

TIDAL STATUS: 1½ hours either side of low water

Continuing eastward (right) from Anemone wall for 100m is a prominent inlet, characterised by an undercut pillar at the landward end. (If coming from the White Edge approach, this is the inlet just beyond the second gully to the left of Ravenscliff). The crag provides some of the better easy climbing on Gower. Those planning to protect their routes should carry a good selection of slings for spike runners.

On the west (left looking landward) wall is a rock scar, the remains of White Slab D (J.Talbot 1962). Just to the right is a mustard-coloured patch of lichen.

1. **Centre**   12m   D
    The centre of the left wall of the zawn, passing the mustard coloured lichen just to its left.
    J.Talbot 00.00.1962

2. **Right Wall**   12m   M
    The wall 5m left of the pillar, passing the prominent overlap on its left.
    J.Talbot 00.00.1962

3. **Abraham's Route**   12m   VS,4c
    From the base of the crag, climb directly up to and through the centre of the overhang.
    J.White 14.04.1982

4. **Ramp**   14m   D
    Ramble anywhere up the wall left of the pillar to gain a ramp, then follow the vague right-trending groove that
    bounds the right-hand side of the overlap.
    J.Talbot 00.00.1962

5. **Left Pillar Crack**   12m   S,4c
    As for Pillar Direct to start, then step left to climb the obvious wide groove.
    J.Talbot 00.00.1962

6. **Pillar Direct**   12m   S,4c   *
    May be easier if the level of the beach is higher. The front of the pillar, gained by a superb boulder problem start.
    J.Talbot 00.00.1962

7. **Right Pillar Crack**   12m   M
    The right-hand crack, gained by wandering in up easy slabs out right. There is a boulder problem direct start,
    Jam Today, Jam Tommorrow 4b (G.Ashmore 09.01.1999)
    J.Talbot 00.00.1962

8. **Eve**   14m   D   *
    The narrow runnel right of the corner gives pleasant climbing. Where the runnel runs out, trend left to finish.
    J.Talbot 00.00.1962

9. **Zig Zag**   15m   M
    A slight variant, connecting Wall And Groove to the top of Eve, traversing under the overhang.
    J.Talbot 00.00.1962

10. **Wall And Groove**   15m   M
    As for Groove and Corner, until a slab opens out on the left wall. Step left to finish up the centre of the slab. The
    arete of the slab can be gained from directly below and followed on its left – Jones Route S,4a (J.White
    14.04.1982).
    J.Talbot 00.00.1962

11. **Groove And Corner**   15m   M   *
    The obvious crack and angled groove in the right wall of the inlet.
    J.Talbot 00.00.1962

12. **White Slab**   15m   D   *
    The centre of the white slab right of Groove And Corner.
    J.Talbot 00.00.1962

Ravenscliff Gully

GR547873

TIDAL STATUS: 1½ hours either side of low water

This is a small zawn below a prominent cave, which lies about 100m east of White Cove and 150m west of White Edge. The base of the zawn can be reached by an easy scramble down its western flank, or via the waterworn chute in its centre. The west wall is a slabby pillar near the back of the zawn, the east wall consists of a seaward and a landward pillar, split by a chimney (easy descent).

West Wall

1. **South Edge**   12m   M
   The left arete of the wall.
   J.Talbot 00.00.1962

2. **South West Kante**   12m   S   *
   To the right of South Edge is a punchbowl like hollow. Enter and climb this, then break through the capping overlap on a superb flake.
   J.Talbot 00.00.1962

3. **Direct**   12m   VD
   Climb the prominent runnels to the right of South West Kante, bearing right over the overlaps above.
   J.Talbot 00.00.1962

4. **North Corner**   9m   D
   The shallow corner groove to the right of Direct.
   J.Talbot 00.00.1962

East Wall

There are two routes on the landward pillar.

5. **Andere**   10m   M
   A vague line, starting in the centre of the wall and trending up left on flakes.
   J.Talbot 00.00.1962

6. **Nure**   8m   HS,4c
   Climb the centre of the leaning wall directly.
   J.Talbot 00.00.1962

The scar to the right is the remains of Alte D (J.Talbot 1962). The seaward pillar is split by a smooth recess.

7. **Ribs**   12m   M
   Start up the left side of the recess, but quickly move out left, then climb the slab diagonally leftwards.
   J.Talbot 00.00.1962

8. **Fault**   10m   HD
   The prominent crack at the right-hand side of the smooth recess.
   J.Talbot 00.00.1962

9. **Slab**   10m   D
   Good. Climb the overlap and slab to the right of Ribs.
   J.Talbot 00.00.1962

White Edge (Pennard Edge)
GR547873

TIDAL STATUS: Non-Tidal

150m to the east of Ravenscliff Gully, the obvious feature of White Edge can be seen well above sea level.

1. **South East Ridge**   30m   S   *
    Good positions. Mostly easier than Severe, there are a couple of rickety sections that would scare beginners.
    It can be started down by sea leve but, the bottom is nothing more than scrambling, so start at the base of the
    obvious upper ridge. Keep left of the arete when it is not possible to climb direct.
    Unknown 00.00.1965

Watch House Crag
GR548873

TIDAL STATUS: Non-tidal.

A very minor crag for the suicidally jaded. Watch House Crag is located in the prominent gully about 40m above sea
level seen from the beach, 100m on from White Edge. The routes are all on the right wall. There is a tidal zawn below
the crag, currently undeveloped. A lower off rope is strongly recommended.

1. **Mr Angry**   15m   VS,4b   ●
    Loose. Start at a leftwards slanting groove, with some sandy rock at its base. Climb the groove for 6m then
    move rightwards to finish straight up over a tiny overlap.
    E.Alsford, P.Donnithorne 16.09.1988

2. **Fob**   15m   E1,5c
    Start 3m right of Mr Angry. Make awkward moves up a thin crack, then continue directly, taking care with loose
    undercuts on the overlap.
    G.Evans, N.Lewis 18.09.1986

3. **Mainspring**   18m   E1,6a
    Start 3m down the slope from Fob. Mantleshelf with difficulty over the initial bulge and continue directly, PR, to
    a grassy ledge. Finish diagonally up the final wall. Belay well back.
    G.Evans, N.Lewis, J.Bullock 23.07.1986

4. **Chronometer**   18m   E1,5a
    Start at a slot below the left side of the bulges in the middle of the cliff. Climb to them and follow them leftwards.
    J.Bullock, L.Moran 09.07.1986

5. **Escapement**   18m   E2,5b
    A strenuous line through bulges just left of a calcite streak.
    J.Bullock, L.Moran 09.07.1986

6. **Alarm Clock**   18m   E1,5a
    This takes the rib and slight bulge right of the calcite streak.
    L.Moran, J.Bullock 14.07.1986

West Promontory Corner
GR548873

TIDAL STATUS: 2 hours either side of low water.

In the centre of the bay containing Watch House Crag is a promontory of rock jutting out in the sea. There are some routes located in a short corner where the promontary hits the shoreline, on its west (left when facing inland).

1. **V Crack** 12m S,4a *
   An awkard yet enjoyable little number, well worth seeking out. The obvious corner crack, with a shelf at 2m. Stay in the corner!
   J.Talbot, B.Talbot 00.00.1965

2. **Broken Wall** 12m M
   The vague groove right of V Crack and the subsequent slab.
   J.Talbot, B.Talbot 00.00.1965

Watch House East
GR549873

TIDAL STATUS: Virtually non-tidal.

This is the steep buttress well to the east of Watch House Crag, just round the corner from Foxhole. The cliff is barrel-shaped and has an obvious depression in its upper section, with a wide corner crack leading up right. To the right, the crag is severely undercut and a groove line running up to the left gives the line of Clip Joint. It is best to lower off the routes and a PR in a small rock outcrop and a sling around a stout gorse bush just below the clearing are provided. The path up the side of the crag leads back up to the minor coastal road and the car park. It is also possible to scramble eastwards round the headland to Foxhole, on a vague path just above the high tide level.

1. **Straining Pitch** 18m E3,6a
   Start just left of a small flying buttress at the left end of the crag. Climb steeply, TR, to reach a ledge, TR. Step right to a layback crack and climb this, 2PR, to a ledge. Climb straight over the overhang above to a PB.
   J.Bullock, G.Evans 00.00.1989

2. **Jump To Conclusion** 18m E3,6a
   Start 6m right of Straining Pitch below a brownish overhang at 16m. Climb to the base of the overhang and lurch/jump/dyno for a jug up left. Pull over and continue straight up to reach a ledge at the foot of a left slanting groove. Climb the right arete of the groove to reach large holds.
   J.Bullock, M.Kydd, G.Evans 02.09.1989

3. **Pump Action** 21m E4,6a
   Start 3m right of Jump To Conclusions at a prominent red and white stratified niche. Climb this to ledge, step right and continue steeply, 2 PR, to a large pocket below the final problem! Over this to reach good finishing holds and a further niche, PR. Step right and climb a groove and corner crack to reach belays in a small rock outcrop.
   J.Bullock, R.Thomas 00.00.1989

4. **Clip Joint** 21m E3,6a
   Start where a red-tipped rock meets the cliff. Climb an overhanging crack, TR, with increasing difficulty to reach a good incut, PR. Move right to reach a chockstone and bridge up the groove onto a slab, TR. Continue up a rounded arete to the right of a corner crack.
   J.Bullock, G.Evans 16.05.1989

5. **No Rest For The Wicked**   21m   E5,6a
   A line right of Clip Joint without touching the boulder.
   A.Berry 00.00.1995

6. **The Road To Nowhere**   21m   E2,5b
   The obvious lower right to left traverse line. Not as innocuous as it appears. Start at the niche of Pump Action. Climb to an undercut area of white rock and follow the traverse line by horizontal techniques until it is possible to become vertical again. Teeter up to the second TR on Straining Pitch, before continuing up the hollow flakes to reach a rounded spike, where a grass cornice abuts the crag. Abseil off a sling around this.
   G.Evans, J.Bullock 16.05.1989

7. **Hue And Cry**   21m   E2,5c
   A half-height traverse. Above the rounded spike at the end of The Road To Nowhere is a TR. Start from this thread, reached by abseil. Move right to the layback crack of Straining Pitch and follow this to good holds. Descend rightwards to the ledge of Jump To Conclusions and continue steeply right to the slab of Clip Joint. Finish up this.
   G.Evans, J.Bullock 23.05.1989
   D.Butler, C.Davies 00.00.1975

FOXHOLE COVE

GR551872
By Goi Ashmore

TIDAL STATUS: Foxhole Crag itself is non-tidal. The lower crags 2½ hours either side of low water.

BOLTING POLICY: No bolting except at Foxhole itself. At Foxhole - Retro-bolting permissible with first ascensionist's permission. Replacement of worn fixed gear on a point for point basis with bolts is permissible. New sports routes allowed.

PREAMBLE

Foxhole Cove is the small bay between Watch House East and Heatherslade Bay itself. Foxhole itself is a superbly steep crag, basically the roof of a large cave, tucked back well back and above the sea at the back of the cove. It contains some of the best sport routes on Gower. The crag does seep after prolonged rain, but otherwise it performs good umbrella service. It is always possible to climb in or out of the sun by selecting the correct wall. There are a number of smaller areas and the easy routes on Wrinkle and Grey Slab, well worth seeking out.

ACCESS

Note that this is not the Fox Hole marked on the OS map. From the B4436 follow the offshoot into Southgate and continue to the National Trust Car Park by a roundabout at the end of the village (GR554873). Park here and follow the private road along the cliff top westward (right when looking out to sea) until opposite Number 9. Go down and left to the top of a gully. Scramble carefully down this taking care not to miss the path leading left across the top of the cave otherwise you will arrive at the base of the crag rather too quickly. Follow a poor path down for 50m, which comes to the cave entrance of Foxhole itself. The lower crags are reached by scrambling down in front of the cave. Deep Cut is to the west (right looking out to sea), Wrinkle Slab and Grey Wall to the east.

DESCENTS: Most routes at Foxhole itself have lower offs. However, a hanging rope is required for some of the older routes and there are stakes at the top of the crag. Descents for the other crags are by easy scrambling.

THE ROUTES

1. **Unholy Alliance**   12m   E5,6a
    On the left wall of the crag, outside the cave proper, is a steep tower. Take a vague flake line up this. Bold.
    M.Crocker, J.Harwood 01.05.1994

2. **Connard Canard**   12m   E6,6b   Fr7b
    The wall to the right of Unholy Alliance proves harder than it looks and is tricky to on-sight.
    G.Gibson 01.09.1998

3. **Goose In Lucy**   12m   E3,6a   Fr6c   **
    Down to the right of Connard Cannard, just inside the cave, are a couple of finger pockets. Gain and use these to work up to a bounce to get the conglomerate ledge. Climb the steep wall above on superb undercuts and jugs.
    R.Thomas, S.Coles 11.05.1996

4. **Pioneers Of The Hypnotic Groove**   25m   E6,6a   Fr7b   ***
    A stunning route climbing the angle of the cave at 45 degrees all the way up. Looks improbable, but the holds are massive! At the lip continue up the groove above to TB and abseil off. One of the BRs is currently missing, but a Friend 1½ can be used instead.
    R.Thomas 6pt 00.00.1994, FFA G.Ashmore, S.Coles, J.Tracey 19.04.1996

5. **Palace Of Swords Reversed**   15m   E7,6c   Fr8a   **
    Start below the hanging arete right of the groove of Pioneers Of The Hypnotic Groove and follow the BRs to where the lines diverge. Take the right-hand line with some very powerful moves to eventually gain good conglomerate holds and the slab. Lower off, or move right to finish up Foxy Lady. The left-hand line of bolts is a project.
    G.Ashmore 08.09.1996

Foxhole

Photo: Adrian Berry

6. **Chicken Licken**   10m   E4,6a   Fr6c+
    Climb the overhanging wall just left of the arete marking the right end of the lower cave roof.
    R.Thomas 19.07.1996

To the right is small left trending wall at right angles to the cave and left of a prominent groove.

7. **No Epoxy Au Oxley**   35m   E3,5c   *
    A partial girdle of the crag. Start up the cracks in the left side of the left-trending wall, to gain a slab running
    leftwards across to the final groove of Pioneers Of The Hypnotic Groove. Traverse easily across the slab to gain
    the Pioneers etc. groove which is followed to a TB. Abseil.
    FA R.Thomas 00.00.1994

8. **Little Miss Lover**   25m   E4,6a
    As for No Epoxy Au Oxley but when halfway across the traverse, 2m after the conglomerate holds, pull up the
    impending wall to good holds and a hidden PR. Follow a steep crack to the top. A lower off rope is required.
    M.Crocker 01.05.1994

The following two routes have had their starts swapped round for convienience. The grades are not really affected.

9. **Foxy Lady**   25m   E4,6a   Fr6c+   **
    As for No Epoxy Au Oxley to a conglomerate jug 3½m along the traverse below a thin layback flake, PRs. Pull
    up to this and layback furiously to the BB.
    J.Bullock, R.Thomas 00.05.1990

10. **The Hooker**   21m   E4,6a   Fr6c+   **
Start up the prominent groove right of No Epoxy Au Oxley and climb this, PR, to gain the traverse slab. Move 2m left and up to a PR and fight up the difficult impending headwall.
J.Bullock, R.Thomas 00.06.1990

11. **Joy De Viva**   18m   E5,6a   Fr7a   ***
Start up the Hooker as described, but at the top of the initial groove move out right to conglomerate on the right wall and finish direct up a vague groove. Excellent sustained climbing.
G.Gibson 05.07.1997

12. **Turkey Lurking**   30m   E6,6b   Fr7c   *
Hard to follow. As for Power Struggle to a point 3m below the top. Blast leftwards, all very difficult to read, to eventually finish at the top of Foxy Lady.
E.Travers-Jones 10.08.1996

13. **Power Struggle**   15m   E5,6c   Fr7b+   *
On the right wall of the crag is another big hole/flake at 4m. Gain this via the handrail on the right, move powerfully up and left to finish direct.
M.Crocker, J.Harwood 01.05.1994

14. **Ducky Lucky**   12m   E4,6b   Fr7a+   *
A sharp but worthwhile route to the right of Power Struggle.
R.Thomas 10.08.1996

15. **The Day The Sky Fell In**   10m   E3,6a   Fr6b+
The last groove on the right-hand wall of the cave.
R.Thomas 18.05.1996

Deep Cut (Dark Side of the Moon Zawn)

This is the narrow east-facing zawn at sea level, below and west of Fox Hole proper. It has an overhanging north-facing wall, which takes time to dry out and a low angled slab. Some of the first few routes have almost certainly been done before.

1. **Talbot's Peugeot**   10m   VS,5a
Start at the extreme left side of the overhanging wall. Layback up the arete to finish above a prominent roof.
G.Ashmore solo 19.08.1996

2. **Mind Of A Talbot**   7m   VS,5b
The vague diagonal scoops to the right of Talbot's Peugeot.
G.Ashmore solo 19.08.1996

3. **Antipodean Hero**   8m   HVS,5a
The first real line. Climb to the prominent roof right of Mind Of A Talbot. Reach over this, move right to a sharp flake and finish direct. Awkward!
R.Thomas 19.08.1996

4. **Malice Down Under**   8m   HVS,5a
A worthwhile route up a line of square jugs to the right of Antipodean Hero.
R.Thomas 19.08.1996

5. **Maurice In Undies Land**   8m   E1,5c
The wall to the right of Malice Down Under, PR.
R.Thomas 19.08.1996

6. **The Illywhacker**   8m   E4,6a   *

Climb the centre of the north wall directly on small holds past twin PRs. The crux is at the top on the crozzly rib and a fall could be interesting, depending on the level of the pebbles.
A.Long 00.00.1991

7. **Roygoi**   8m   E5,6a   \

Bridge up the cleft at the right-hand side of the wall for 2m, then move onto the wall and rock up for a finger flake. Follow a thin crack, to finish just right of The Illywhacker.
M.Crocker, J.Harwood 28.02.1998

8. **Requin**   8m   HS

Climbs the leftmost groove at the back of the zawn.
J.Talbot 00.00.1962

9. **Deep Cut Slab**   12m   HVD

Worthwhile. On the slabby side of the zawn is a diagonal runnel. Start where this touches the ground and balance up it to gain a sloping indentation. Get established on this, then climb directly up the slab above to finish.
J.Talbot 00.00.1962

Wrinkle Slab
This brown slab is below and east of Fox Hole proper, where the rocks start to open out.

1. **Direct**   12m   D

Climb the centre of the slab.
J.Talbot, D.Thomas 00.00.1959

2. **East Corner**   12m   M

Climb the corner bounding the slab to below an overhang which is turned on the left.
J.Talbot, D.Thomas 00.00.1959

Grey Wall
This is the eastwards continuation of Wrinkle Slab, starting with an arete.

1. **West Edge**   12m   D

The left arete of the slab.
J.Talbot, D.Thomas 00.00.1959

2. **West Side**   12m   D

Takes the slab to the right of West Edge. Many variations are possible.
J.Talbot, D.Thomas 00.00.1959

3. **Cleft**   12m   VD   *

In the middle of the slab is an obvious "4" shaped sentry box. Climb this and the delicate slab above.
J.Talbot, D.Thomas 00.00.1959

4. **Ramp**   12m   HVD

An artificial climb squeezed in between Cleft and East Corner.
J.Talbot, D.Thomas 00.00.1959

5. **East Corner**   12m   M   *

The obvious corner bounding the slab on its right-hand side.
J.Talbot, D.Thomas 00.00.1959

Some 100m to the east (right) is Great Corner, described under the Heatherslade Section.

HEATHERSLADE BAY

GR552872 to 553872
By Goi Ashmore

TIDAL STATUS: Heatherslade Buttress and Little Corner are non-tidal. Other crags 3 hours either side of low water.

BOLTING POLICY: No bolting.

PREAMBLE

This is a small climbing venue, consisting of a few easy tidal routes scattered around the west side of Heatherslade bay and the non-tidal Heatherslade Buttress above the east side of the bay. The rock at sea level is good, and Heatherslade is a well known beach for family picnics. The climbing may provide an hour or so of entertainment for family climbers, beginners, or those wanting to finish the day with some pleasant soloing.

ACCESS

Park in the National Trust Car Park at Southgate (see Foxhole Cove for details). For the crags at sea level, follow the path straight down from car park, to meet a path running westward above high tide level. Follow this path, dropping down just before the sandy conglomerate corner at the back west end of the beach. A prominent narrow zawn lies below this conglomerate corner. Headland Slabs are the two-tiered grey white slabs to the west of the zawn. Little Corner is slightly further on to the west and Great Corner 75m west again. Note that 100m on from Great Corner is Grey Slab, which gives routes of grades more in keeping with the Heatherslade area. For convenience, however, it is described under the Fox Hole Cove section.

For Heatherslade Buttress, take the second gully eastwards from the NT car park at Southgate. The crag forms the east wall of the gully, and is obvious from the cliff top path.

DESCENTS: Are by easy scrambling at various points hereabouts.

THE ROUTES

These are described from left to right, i.e. in the opposite direction to the approach.

Great Corner

This is the prominent wide angled corner on the west headland of Heatherslade Bay about 75m west of Headland Slab. It is easily recognised by a prominent corner crack and a strip of pink rock above the left-hand slab, where the roof originally taken by some of the climbs once was. The rock is clean and good throughout. The climbs described do not exactly correspond to the original lines, due to the loss of the roof.

1. **West Rib**   15m   M
    Climb the rib that stands proud of two easy grooves towards the left-hand end of the slab.
    J.Talbot 00.00.1959

2. **Square Cut**   15m   D
    Climb the groove halfway between Central Corner Crack and West Rib. Follow the prominent crack bounding the left-hand end of the pink patch.
    J.Talbot 00.00.1959

The cracks at either side of West Rib provide some good fun, but do not merit a grade.

3. **Direct**   15m   S
    Pull onto the slab directly below the centre of the upper pink patch and move directly up to it. Pull onto the pink section and follow a thin crack up its centre. Not well protected.
    J.Talbot 00.00.1959

The old route Twin Slab (J.Talbot, G. Jones 1958), has now fallen down.

4. **Central Corner Crack**   15m   M
The obvious corner crack.
J.Talbot 00.00.1959

5. **Black Slab**   15m   HVD
Climb the corner passing the initial bulge, move right onto the sidewall, then follow vague overlaps to the top.
J.Talbot 00.00.1959

Little Corner
West of the Headland Slab and well above the high tide level is a prominent corner.

1. **Block**   12m   HS,4b
Direct over an obvious overhang.
J.Talbot, G. Jones 00.00.1958

Headland Slab

1. **Route One**   7m   VD
The front face of the slab, passing through an overlap.
J.Talbot 00.00.1959

2. **Route Two**   7m   HD
Follows a vague groove up the white slab right of Route One.
J.Talbot 00.00.1959

3. **Route Three**   9m   D
Starting in the base of the gully, climb the groove left of the prominent white quartz ramp.
J.Talbot 00.00.1959

Heatherslade Buttress
This prominent buttress situated above the eastern side of Heatherslade bay is not particularly inspiring.

1. **GBH**   13m   HVS,4c
Start below a grassy ledge on the left side of the cliff. Gain a ledge and pull into a depression on its right side. Continue leftward then rightward to the overhang. Take this on the right, then move rightwards to the top.
R.Small, P.Carling 00.00.1974

2. **Felony**   13m   HVS,5a
Start below and right of the grassy ledge. Climb to a bulge and gain a small ledge below an overhang. Traverse right to a loose groove, climb it and bear left over the next overhang.
D.Butler, C.Davies 00.00.1975

3. **Indecent Exposure**   11m   HVS,4c
Start 6m left of an indefinite corner bounding the buttress on the left. Climb to small ledges at the foot of a corner capped by a block overhang. Gain the overhang, traverse left for 1½m and finish direct.
R.Small, P.Carling 00.00.1974

4. **Petty Larceny**   11m   S
Climb the indefinite corner on the right and the loose groove above.
P.Carling, R.Small 00.00.1974

5. **Bandolier**   24m   VS,4c
A left to right girdle at half-height.
R.Small, P.Carling 00.00.1974

MINCHEN HOLE TO HUNTS BAY

GR556868 to 562867
By Roy Thomas & Goi Ashmore

TIDAL STATUS: 1 hour to non-tidal. See individual crags.

BOLTING POLICY: See individual crags.

PREAMBLE
From Heatherslade, tidal rocks run all the way round to Hunts Bay. As well as the sea level crags, there are a number of non-tidal caves. Two of these caves would be of national climbing significance. Bacon Hole with its 50m roof, which would provide one of Europe's most impressive sports venues, but climbing is currently banned. Minchen Hole, which contained several superb sports routes is also banned and much of the gear has gone missing. However, the routes have been noted in case this situation ever changes. There are also a couple of smaller caves, where climbing is permitted and Bosco's Den provides a fair number of good routes in a venue that comes into its own on a hot summer day.

ACCESS

1. Minchen Hole to Spring Zawn Approach
Park in the NT car park at Southgate (see Fox Hole Cove for details). On foot, follow the cliff top road running east from the car park. Follow this road, then strike out southwards towards the highest mound in the local area at the top of the third gully along. Follow a footpath down the west side of the mound, to meet the path running along the cliffs above high tide level. Follow this path eastwards (left) for 200m, to arrive at the (very) obvious entrance to Minchen Hole. Scramble across the gully (do not enter the cave) and scramble out to the far side to reach Marble Arch after 100m and Bowen's Corner and Spring Zawn further on.

2. Bosco's Den Area
As for the Minchen approach, but continue along the cliff top path to reach a minor road on the left (Bosco's Drive GR558870). Strike seaward to a bench and follow a path diagonally down left towards sea level. Two promontaries can be seen heading out to sea. The left (east) promontary has a quarry at its landward end (Golden Wall). Head towards this promontary to find a short pinnacle. Either abseil in from this pinnacle or follow a path down the west side (right when facing seaward) and scramble east round the headland (only possible 2½ hours either side of low water). This gives access to Bosco's Wall, Gulch and Cave. To get to Bucketland, cross the beach eastwards 1½ hours either side of low water. Note that most routes have lower offs and so either leave the abseil rope in, or make sure that you do not get cut off by the tide when leaving the crag.

3. White Quartz Wall
As for the Minchen Hole approach, but walk down the cliff top road to Hunt's Farm on the left after about 15 minutes (GR564873). Turn down the valley bellow Hunt's Farm until at the level of the path near the edge of the coastal turf. Turn right (facing seawards) down this and follow the path until it starts to rise up. Skirt down and left and descend easy rocks to gain a plaform below the crag. Bacon Hole is 100m further round to the west.

DESCENTS: See individual crags.

CLIMBING BAN: Minchen Hole, Bosco's Den (although not the much more extensive Bosco's wall, Gulch and Cave) are currently banned for climbing. Please avoid them in order not to jeopardise access to other crags.

THE ROUTES

Minchen (Mitchin) Hole
GR556868

TIDAL STATUS: Non-Tidal.

BOLTING POLICY: No bolting.

DESCENTS: Was by lower off.

CLIMBING BAN: No climbing is allowed at Minchen Hole. The routes are recorded for historical purposes.

This huge non-tidal zawn and cave resembles a roofless gothic cathedral.

The following routes were on the west wall of Minchen Hole, well above the floor of the cave, and used to start from a grassy terrace.

1. **Fringe Benefits**   10m E2,5c Fr6b   ☹
    Used to take the leftmost line on the wall.
    R.Thomas 04.05.1998

2. **Beyond The Fringe**   10m E2,5c Fr6b * ☹
    Used to take the wall to the right of Fringe Benefits, passing the huge conglomerate hold at the start.
    R.Thomas 04.05.1998

3. **Triple Sigh**   10m E3,6a Fr6b+   ☹
    Used to take the rib to the right of Beyond The Fringe.
    R.Thomas 14.05.1998

4. **Swim With The Sharks**   15m E3,6a Fr6c ** ☹
    Used to take the wall to the right of the rib.
    R.Thomas 10.05.1998

5. **Jump The Sun**   15m E5,6a Fr7a+ *** ☹
    Used to be stunning. Used to start lower down than the previous routes below a series of overlapping roofs. Climb to these, pull over the roof to a good hold and finish with difficulty.
    R.Thomas 01.09.1998

6. **Crawling King Snake**   25m E5,6b Fr7b * ☹
    Used to take the large arete to the right of Jump The Sun on on glued holds direct to an awkward finish.
    G.Gibson 00.00.1999

To the right of the arete is a big slab.

7. **The Dove From Above**   28m E2,5c Fr6a+ * ☹
    Used to take the left-hand line on the slab.
    R.Thomas 09.07.1998

8. **Blight At The End Of The Funnel** 28m E1,5b Fr5+   ☹
    Used to take the right-hand line on the slab, passing a conglomerate 'Bees Nest'.
    R.Thomas 08.06.1998

On the east wall, working from left to right used to be the next routes.

9. **The Raven**   28m   E4,6a   Fr7a   ***   ⊗

Used to be a totally blinding route, based on the prominent square-cut groove, high up in the centre of the main section of the right wall.
G.Gibson 25.05.1998

10. **Voice From The Pulpit**   25m   E5,6b   Fr7a+   *   ⊗

Used to be another good route, unfortunately marred by the huge ledge at half-height. Used to start right of a left-facing corner, at a smooth wall below some conglomerate overhangs. Make desperate moves up the lower wall, and through the unnerving conglomerate band to land on the ledge, TR. Follow the sustained headwall directly behind to a BB.
G.Gibson 00.05.1998

11. **Stuck On You**   15m   E4,6a   ⊗

A poor route that used to follow the wall to the right of Voice Of The Pulpit and pull through the loose conglomerate on greasy hidden jugs with a growing sense of panic, to pull out onto a ledge. Scramble up poor conglomerate behind to a BB hidden in a gully.
G.Gibson 00.05.1998

12. **The Minchkins**   17m   E3,6a   Fr6c   ⊗

Used to be marginally better (but still not particularly nice) up to and through the conglomerate band.
G.Gibson 00.05.1998

13. **Gary's Talking Climbs**   25m   E2,5c   Fr6b   *   ⊗

Used to be pleasant route following the pillar of rock, right of the conglomerate overhangs. At the top of the pillar, it used to wander carefully up on conglomerate jugs to the lower off.
G.Gibson 00.05.1998

14. **Pinch A Minch**   15m   HVS,5a   Fr5   ⊗

Used to go up the right-hand side of the pillar.
G.Gibson 00.05.1998

Marble Arch
GR556868

TIDAL STATUS: 1 hour either side of low water.

BOLTING POLICY: No bolting.

DESCENTS: Descend down the rib to the east of the cove.

About 100m east of Minchen Hole is a strange cove containing a rock arch, beneath which is a permanent 1m pool with a seaweed floor. There is an easy slab on the east side, which provides scope for some easy new routes. There is only one recorded route here at present.

1. **Deep Water Polo**   12m   E1,6a

This route traverses in at a low level from the west side of the seaward end of the rock pool, to gain a jam below the arch. Pull up the arch to finish up obvious pockets. The route has only been done so far as a deep water solo but there is never more than 12 inches of water below it, &c, &c.
G.Ashmore 22.07.2000

Bowen's Parlour
GR557868

BOLTING POLICY: New sports routes allowed.

TIDAL STATUS: Non-tidal.

This is the next cove east of Marble Arch which contains a prominent cave out of reach of the tide. The cave has a false conglomerate ceiling which should not be touched. There are no routes here as yet, but there is potential. Access has negotiated for sports climbing and as it was agreed that in situ lower offs should be used to prevent damage to the cliff top, rather than the use of hanging ropes.

Spring Zawn
GR557869

TIDAL STATUS: 1½ hours either side of low water.

BOLTING POLICY: No bolting.

DESCENTS: Descend down the west rib of the zawn.

This is the tidal zawn containing a fresh water spring at the base, about 100m east of Bowen's Parlour. The spring is on the east wall.

1. **Young's Modulus**   15m   E2,5c
   The wall 4m left of the spring.
   R.Thomas, P.Hadley 00.08.1999

2. **Fountain Of Eternal Uncouth**   20m   E3,6a   *
   The wall to the right of Young's Modulus and just left of the spring, TR.
   R.Thomas, P.Hadley 00.08.1999

3. **Youth Springs Eternal**   20m   E1,5b
   The crack at the seaward end of the wall.
   P.Hadley, R.Thomas 00.08.1999

Bosco's Den Area
GR558869

TIDAL STATUS: Bosco's Wall 2 hours either side of low water. Bosco's Gulch and Bosco's Cave are non-tidal, but note that access out without jumaring is only 2½ hours either side of low water.

BOLTING POLICY: Bosco's Wall – bolt lower offs only. Bosco's Gulch and Bosco's Cave - Retro-bolting permissible with first ascensionist's permission. Replacement of worn fixed gear on a point for point basis with bolts is permissible. New sports routes allowed.

DESCENTS: Descent to the crags as in the access notes. All routes should have lower offs, providing the Clampetts have not returned.

CLIMBING BAN: Bosco's Den itself (i.e. the deep rift further back than Bosco's Gulch) is banned for climbing purposes. The Cave up and right is not affected.

Bosco's Den is the rift on the east side of this promontary. Bosco's Wall forms the east side of the promontary itself and is connected to Bosco's Den by Bosco's Gulch. Bosco's Cave is situated up and right (east) at a higher level, well to the right of Bosco's Den itself.

Bosco's Wall

1. **Swansea Hillbillies**   20m   E1,5b
Towards the seaward end of the wall are two routes containing red tats. This is the left-hand one, which finishes at a lower off at 20m.
R.Thomas 20.06.1999

2. **Geoff's A Spanner**   20m   E1,5b
The the right-hand route, which moves up to a flake above a bulge. From the flake wander up and left to the belay of the previous route.
R.Thomas 20.06.1999

3. **Simple Simon**   20m   E2,5c   *
Right again is a PR at 5m. Climb to the PR and move slightly left, then back right to a TR. Climb up to and past the TR to some thin moves to gain an overlap at its right end, TR. Pull up on suspect rock, PR, TR to a BB.
R.Thomas 29.05.1999

4. **Clapham Injunction**   20m   E3,5c
As for Simple Simon to gain the first TR. Move right and up to poor wires and a good PR. Climb the wall direct to step left at the top to the belay of the previous route. A direct start past the long TR is awaited.
R.Thomas 29.05.1999

5. **Gold Teeth In Them There Hills**   20m   E2,5c   *
Start 2m left of a prominent boulder towards the landward end of the crag. Climb up a set of flakes to a PR and TRs. Finish up and slightly left, TR to a lower off.
R.Thomas 29.05.1999

6. **Hanger Them High**   20m   E2,5c
Start immediately left of the prominent boulder. Climb flakes to TR and pull slightly rightward round the overlap. Finish direct past cracks and a TR to a lower off.
R.Thomas 29.05.1999

7. **Y'All Come Back Now**   20m   E2,5c   **
Start from the prominent boulder and climb the wall direct with a tricky start, TR, to a lower off.
R.Thomas 06.06.1999

Bosco's Gulch

This is the continuation of Bosco's Wall.

1. **The Clampetts**   20m   E3,6a   Fr6c   *
To the right of the boulder climb the wall trending slightly left to the lower off of Y'All Come Back Now.
G.Gibson 00.06.1999

2. **Jump Over My Shadow**   25m   E4,6a   Fr7a   *
Start to the right of The Clampetts and climb an undercut layback crack to gain a slab. Pull through an overlap and gain the ledge and a tricky finish on the headwall.
G.Gibson 00.06.1999

3. **Conglomeration**   25m   E4,6a   Fr7a   *
Way up to the right, is a huge square lump of conglomerate. Gain and pass this to gain the ledge and blind headwall above.
G.Gibson 00.06.1999

4. **Standing On A Beach**   25m   E3,6a   Fr6c
Scramble up the corner to gain a ledge, then step back onto the wall and follow the left-hand bolt line past various huge conglomerate deposits.
G.Gibson 00.06.1999

5. **Reign Of The Deer**   25m   E4,6a   Fr7a   *
As for Standing On A Beach, but take the right-hand finish.
G.Gibson 00.03.2000

The cave at the back of the Gulch is forbidden territory to climbers. Up to the right is another cave. It is easily reached by scrambling up from the beach. There are two projects on the left wall.

6. **Squeal Like A Hog**   25m   E3,6a   Fr6c   *
The main section of the cave is blessed with a diagonal line up cracks and cursed with some heavy metal. Climb it with extreme awkwardness and poorly spaced bolts.
J.Bullock, G.Morris 00.00.2000

7. **The Millennium Thug**   25m   E4,6b   Fr7a
Powerful climbing up the east wall of the cave and cutting through Squeal Like A Hog.
G.Gibson 03.03.2000

Bucketland
GR560868

TIDAL STATUS: 1 hour either side of low water. However, note that the escape require enough time to get back to and out of Bosco's Den Area.

BOLTING POLICY: New sports routes allowed.

DESCENTS: By abseil.

1.**The Strategy Of Sea Power**   10m   A2
The bolted line through the roof.
R.Bacon 31.05.2000

Bacon Hole
GR562867

TIDAL STATUS: Non-tidal but only accessible from Quartz Wall 2 hours either side of low water.

DESCENTS: Not applicable.

CLIMBING BAN: Climbing is banned at this massive cave crag.

In the centre of this monster cave is a seam running right from the back to the front. This has been aided to at least mid way as Gogs 30m A3/4 (P.Hadley, R.Scheer, F.Hipper, J.Jellicoe, D.Beatty 31.05.1999)

Quartz Corner
GR562867

TIDAL STATUS: The crag is not really tidal, but it would be very wet during high seas.

BOLTING POLICY: No bolting.

DESCENT: Is by scrambling careful down the east side of the crag.

A small crag in a forlorn position, with some reasonable routes. Nearby Bacon Hole is subject to a bird ban from 1st March to 1st August, so please avoid walking round west from Quartz Corner during this period. The gear is often sparse. The area is divided by an obvious corner.

1. **West Edge**   15m   S
    The left arete of the left (west) wall.
    J.Talbot 00.00.1960

2. **Quartz Wall**   15m   HS
    The wall 5m left of the central corner of the crag.
    J.Talbot 00.00.1960

3. **Groove And Wall**   15m   S
    This is the distinct groove 2m right of Quartz Wall, finishing direct.
    J.Talbot 00.00.1960

4. **Right Pillar**   15m   S
    Follow Groove And Wall to the hole, then climb the crack right to an overhang. Finish slightly right.
    J.Talbot 00.00.1960

5. **Nose And Slab**   15m   M
    To the right of Right Pillar is a flying rib. Climb the left side of this to finish up an easy slab.
    J.Talbot 00.00.1960

6. **Great Corner**   15m   M
    Climb the large angled corner in the centre of the crag.
    J.Talbot 00.00.1960

7. **West Wall**   15m   HS,4a
    Climb the left side of the wall right of Great Corner.
    J.Talbot 00.00.1960

8. **Direct**   15m   HS,4a
    Climb the wall right of West Wall via a faint groove.
    J.Talbot 00.00.1960

9. **South Edge**   12m   HVD
    Climb the right-hand side of the wall right of Direct.
    J.Talbot 00.00.1960

Ben Merryfield - Scavenger (VS,4c) Three Cliffs
(Page 166) Photo: Chris Shorrock

Goi Ashmore - Palace of Swords (1st Asc) (Fr8a) Foxhole
(Page 180) Photo: Malcolm Terry

PENNARD AND GRAVES END

GR567866 to 573865
By Adrian Berry, Goi Ashmore & Chris Shorrock

TIDAL STATUS: Lower Sea Cliffs 2½ hours either side of low water. All other crags are non-tidal

BOLTING POLICY: No bolting.

PREAMBLE
Pennard is the sweep of white rocks that dominate the far east skyline on the eastern Gower. The rock is generally very good, but there are still some loose blocks on the less compact buttresses such as High Pennard and sections of Graves End. There is a very good collection in the E1 to E3 range in the Pennard Buttress to High Pennard section as well as some very good easier routes on the right-hand section of Pennard Buttress and Graves End. In contrast to most other areas on Gower the easier routes are quite steep, but with reassuringly large holds. The aspect is quite good (South to South West facing), but the crags are exposed and can catch the wind. Some of the threads on the harder routes may need replacing.

ACCESS
Follow the offshoot of the B4436 to its end at the roundabout in Southgate. Park in the National Trust car park. Follow the narrow road east for about 1 mile to a valley running to the sea from Hunts Farm (GR564873) just before the road becomes a private road – there is a prominent wide shallow valley running down to the sea at this point. There are twopossible approaches from here.

1.Pennard
The first follows a path down the valley (past a prominent horse worn circle) to the coastal footpath and heads east (left) along to the base of the cliffs.

2. Pennard and High Pennard
A better, but not so obvious, approach is to follow the cliff top path past two huts on the left. Just past these a prominent rocky headland is seen (there is a pond on the left). Go just past this headland and descend towards the sea. High Pennard is to your left (east) and Pennard Buttress is to your right (west).

Pennard Cliffs
Photo Gwyn Evans

The Great Pillar – as for either Pennard approach, but follow the path below the High Pennard cliffs for 100m.

Lower Sea Cliffs – as for Pennard and Great Pillar, then continue 100m further east along the coastal path, after passing in front of the great detached Tower to a smaller buttress, blocking off the profile of the coastline. Under this is a smooth waterworn gully. Descend this to find the Sea Cliffs on the west (right when facing out to sea).

Graves End – as for Pennard and Great Pillar, but just east of Great Pillar scramble up a gully to the west end of the higher buttress. Graves End East is the natural extension to the east of Graves End itself. It can also be approached by walking along the cliff top above High Pennard. Graves End Sea Cliff is a very small buttress at sea level about 150m east of the end of Graves End East, reached by scrambling down from the path at the end of the turf.

DESCENTS: See individual crags.

THE ROUTES

Pennard Buttress
GR567866

DESCENTS: Descent is by walking back from the top of the crag and following a path down the east side.

This is the steep, high pillar at the left-hand end of the main Pennard Section, with a prominent bulge and tats on its left-hand side. Further to the right, the crag becomes two-tiered. The upper wall is very compact with excellent rock and contains the majority of the E2-E3 climbing. The smaller lower crag that continues rightwards from the base of the main pillar is very solid, with some excellent short routes of various grades, particularly good in the HS-HVS, range. The obvious wall at the right-hand side of the valley is High Pennard.

The top part of the main pillar is quite loose and for some routes (like The Throb or 5 Years To Live), it is best to either arrange a hanging rope from the top of the crag, or take a disposible sling to ab off the spike at the end of the first pitches.

1. **The Throb**   30m   E4,6a   *
    Probably E5 at the moment, given the state of the second TR, which is in dire need of replacement. It is normal to clip the first TR on Five Years To Live before embarking on the route. Start below a line of thin crozzly cracks below and left of a groove through the roofs. Follow these, TR, to a hard move to gain the base of the groove. Follow the slightly rickety groove to hit vegetation and wade up a further 15m to gain a spike belay (TR). Abseil off. It is also possible to step right from the top of the groove to finish up Arosfa.
    A.Sharp, J.Harwood 25.03.1984

2. **Five Years To Live**   30m   E5,6b   *
    A near-sports route, with some interesting and complicated moves on steep ground. It used to sport a BR, but a good TR has been substituted, albeit one that could do with replacing. Start under the obvious bulge and move up to a TR in a line of pockets. Cross the bulge rightwards,TR to a PR on the arete. Climb the arete to a break, stand up, and shuffle up to the top of the groove. Scramble up to a rock spike belay. Scramble off left, with protection from the rock spike, or leave a sling on the spike (back up advised). Abseil.
    M.Crocker 04.09.1988

3. **Arosfa**   45m   E4,6b,5a   *
    The first PR on P1 has recently been glued back in. As a result it is no longer possible to use the good pocket, making the route considerably harder.
    1. 30m Start right of Five Years To Live at a groove, with an obvious capping overhang at 15m. Climb easily up to the groove, then make a thoroughly desperate series of moves before continuing easily up to the roof, very poor PR. Turn the roof on the right. Follow a crack up 'rocking' ground to reach a ledge. Belay in the corner, TR.
    2. 12m Turn the large overhangs above on the left and continue up the wall, PR, to join and finish up Alpha.
    E.Pardoe, R.Griffiths – Tin Tack 00.00.1968
    FFA A.Sharp, J.Harwood 03.12.1983

Pennard Buttress

Photo: Gwyn Evans

4. **Alpha**   36m   HVS,4c,5a
Start at the foot of the buttress just right of Arosfa, below an overhang-capped corner. Attempting this route whilst birds are nesting is highly inadvisable. Watch out for snakes as well!
1. 18m Climb a rib to the corner, turn the overhang on the right and follow a rib to the upper of two ledges. It is also possible to turn the overhang on its left.
2. 18m Traverse right for 5m and climb the wall steeply to a groove, which leads to the impressive square-cut corner and the top. It is recommended that the location of the finishing corner is worked out before embarking on the route – it is the prominent square groove left of Tom Tom.
Harold Insley etc. 1958/9

The crag is now much shorter.

5. **Beta**   16m   VD
Start at the foot of the wide crack right of Alpha, which separates the main buttress from the lower wall. Climb it to a niche below a bulge, move right and continue to ledges.
Harold Insley,etc 1958/9

6. **Unnamed**   14m   E1,5a
The wall between Beta and Beta Plus can be climbed, but is rather loose and poorly protected.
Unknown Pre-1998

7. **Beta Plus**   14m   HS,4b
The corner 4m right of Beta, past a new PR. Turn the overhang on its left or right.
R.Griffiths, E.Pardoe 00.06.1966

8. **Hun**   14m   VS,4b
Climb the arete right of Beta Plus, joining that route at the top. Contrived.
D.Thomas 00.00.1996

9. **Knucklefluster**   11m   E2,5c   *
A technical pitch up the wall just right of Beta Plus. Climb the wall until a move rightwards gains a good hold, TR, then move steeply to the break. Step left and finish up Beta Plus or over the roof.
A.Sharp, P.Lewis 00.00.1984

10. **Knuckleduster**   11m   E3,6a
A bold but poor eliminate squeezed in between Knucklefluster and Gamma Minus. Climb the wall and overhang directly, PR. A side runner is used at this grade.
A.Long 00.00.1989

11. **Gamma Minus**   12m   E1,5b
This climbs the prominent corner right of Knucklefluster to the black bulge. Make an interesting move onto the right arete. Follow this and the crack left of the overhang to the top.
E.Pardoe, R.Griffiths 00.00.1967

12. **Kiwis Can't Climb**   12m   E1,5c
A contrived route taking the left arete of Gamma. Where Gamma moves left, step right and pull over the roof.
Unknown 00.00.1984

13. **Gamma**   12m   HVS,5b   *
A well protected and exciting little pitch. Start up the next corner, then as soon as possible, traverse left below the groove until good holds can be followed up to the roof. Move right and finish in a fine position.
E.Pardoe, R.Griffiths 00.06.1966

14. **Trundleweed**   12m   E1,5b
Climb the rib and short groove 1m right of Gamma.
P.Donnithorne, T.Meen 31.05.1987

15. **Delta**   13m   S,4b
The steep and delicate groove right of Gamma.
M.Hogge, J.Birch 00.00.1967

16. **Delta Minus**   12m   D
Takes the next obvious leftward-slanting break.
SUMC 00.00.1966

17. **Flaked Ivy Chimney**   12m   VD   \
The steep chimney just right of Delta Minus.
C.Shorrock solo 21.09.1996

18. **Vandal**   9m   S
A direct line up the short steep wall just right again.
J.Brailsford et al Pre-1960

19. **Girdle Traverse**   53m   HVS, 5a,4c,4b   *
A right to left girdle of the lower wall.
1. 18m Start as for Delta Minus. Climb into the overhung corner of Gamma and make delicate moves to the arete. Enter the corner to the left and traverse below the overhang to a ledge on Beta Plus.
2. 14m Descend leftwards to below a bulge, then move up to the foot of the corner of Alpha.
3. 21m Traverse 3m under overhangs before pulling onto the wall above. Continue left across two grooves before stepping down onto a grass ledge and belay in the gully.
J.Williams, P.Kokelaar 00.00.1967

Directly above the lower wall is an impressive sheet of white rock which forms the right flank of Pennard Buttress.

Pennard Buttress

Photo: Adrian Berry

20. **Tom Tom**   24m   E2,5c
Start below the prominent square-cut corner, high on the left side of the buttress (Alpha P2). Climb up to the corner, TR, then climb its right wall and arete.
P.Donnithorne, E.Alsford 00.00.1988

21. **Dan Dare**   21m   E2,5c   **
Enjoyable, sustained and well protected - the route of the buttress. Start from the small bush below the centre of the blank sheet of rock right of Tom Tom. Gain the vague hollow and move right to the foot of a scoop, follow this with superb small wires to a sharp rock spike (thin tape runner) and the break. Traverse left to an open groove and follow this to the top.
J.Bullock, G.Evans 06.05.1982

22. **Desperate Dan**   26m   E3,5c   **
A good sustained extension to Dan Dare. As for Dan Dare to the break. Move right to below an obvious undercut flake. Gain this with difficulty and move up the groove to finish. Hard work.
J.Bullock, G.Royle 07.08.1984

23. **White Feather**   21m   E4,6a
A strenuous but contrived start with a slightly better finishing groove. Just left of Timorous Tarzan is a steep crack. Follow this, with feet on Timorous Tarzan, TR, to the break and a small roof just before the final groove. The final groove is protected by 2PRs. The first is situated 1m above the break, and to the right of the groove. The second is hidden in the groove itself. An Alternative finish (E3) joins Desperate Dan at the break.
A.Sharp, O.Jones 00.00.1986

24. **Timorous Tarzan**   36m   E1,5a
This climbs the calcite-encrusted layback crack on the right side of the wall. Climb the crack to its finish, then traverse right on loose-looking holds to an obvious groove. Climb this to the top.
P.Littlejohn, J.Harwood 03.10.1980

25. **Timorous Tarzan True Finish**   32m   E2,5c
Climb the wall above the layback crack and clip the second PR on White Feather.
J.Harwood 1pt 28.05.1986
FFA A.Sharp, O.Jones 00.00.1986

26. **Bald Eagle**   24m   E4,6a
Climb the rib right of Timorous Tarzan, then step left and climb the groove of White Feather.
A.Sharp, J.Harwood 15.04.1984

27. **Gull Way**   24m   VS,4b
Takes the obvious steep corner, finishing as for Timorous Tarzan.
G.Evans, G.Richardson 00.00.1981

In the right side of the steep wall, right of the wide central groove, are two holes in a broken crackline.

28. **Digby**   22m   E2,5b   ●
Start below the holes and follow the crack to a ledge. From the right-hand end of this climb straight up, 2TRs, to the top.
J.Bullock, G.Evans 06.05.1982, J.Bullock, G.Evans – Direct 00.08.1987

The broken crack containing the holes provides a poor climb at VS,4b (Unknown Pre-1991).

High Pennard
GR568866

DESCENTS: Descent is by scrambling down a gully on the west of the crag.

This is the obvious gently bulging buttress at the other side of the valley from Pennard buttress. It does still contain some wobbly blocks, so caution is advised. There are some excellent routes in the E1 to E3 range, making it a good companion to the upper right-hand section of Pennard Buttress. Skive is a must.

1. **Left Edge**   24m   E1,5b
A slightly loose route up the pillar that bounds the cliff on the left side. Climb the left side of the pillar for 3m, then traverse right to a hole. Move up left past a PR and move right to a corner leading to the top
E.Pardoe, D.Barker 00.00.1968

2. **Blood First**   24m   E3,5c
Climb direct to the hole on Left Edge, then climb past it trending slightly right, PR, until it is possible to step right into the corner groove of Loony Left
E.Kellar, P.Nicholas 00.00.1989

3. **Loony Left**   24m   E2,5c   *
Start between Blood First and Sudan. Climb direct to the right side of the overlap right of Left Edge, poor TR, good Friend 1.5. Move over the roof by technical moves and a long stretch, then amble up the corner to the top.
J.Bullock, L.Cain 07.06.1987

4. **Sudan**   24m   E2,5c   *
Start at the base of the pillar which forms the vague arete of the crag. Climb up and right to the overhang under the nose of the front of the pillar. Take the thin crack left of the nose, hard but reasonably well protected crux, then move right onto the pillar. Continue directly and boldly to the top.
R.Leigh, T.Smith A0 00.00.1966
FFA P.Littlejohn, J.Harwood 03.10.1980

High Pennard

Photo: Adrien Berry

5. **Wandering Star**   24m   E1,5c   ●   \
An indefinite line attempting to climb the shallow hanging groove right of Sudan. Start just right of Sudan and climb to the break, move right and attempt to gain the groove with a brief excursion into Skive. Finish over the roof between Skive and its direct finish.
A.Richardson, N.Gyerke 00.00.1987

6. **Skive**   24m   HVS,5a   ***
A great route. Start 3m right of Sudan at the base of the obvious groove which splits the crag. Climb the obvious crack through two roofs. At the third, traverse left for 3m and climb deteriorating rock to the top.
R.Griffiths, E.Pardoe 00.11.1966

7. **Skive Direct**   24m   E1,5b   ***
A more logical finish. At the third roof finish directly up the final groove of Shogun.
R.Griffiths, J.Bayliss 00.06.1967

8. **Shogun**   24m   E3,6a   **
A route requiring a certain amount of inner self to surmount the roof. Climb direct to the obvious weakness in the overlap just right of Skive and surmount it. Move left and climb a vague arete to reach Skive at the horizontal break. Finish up the groove above, taking care with the rock. The grade assumes that the low PR is not in situ (as on the first ascent).
J.Bullock, G.Evans 15.09.1982

9. **King Rat**   24m   E3,6a   *
A directissima giving good climbing. Follow Shogun over its roof to a horizontal slot in a small overlap, climb the wall direct, TR, to the horizontal break. Continue directly by a hidden layback flake, finish directly, PR.
A.Richardson, A.Long 00.00.1987

---

10. **Samurai** 24m E3,6a ***

The best route at Pennard. Follow Shogun over the roof to the horizontal slot as for King Rat, then step right to a shallow groove. Climb this past a small overhang, PR. Continue directly to the top.
J.Bullock, L.Moran 02.07.1986

11. **Kensai** 27m E3,5c

Start directly below the upper groove of Phreatic Line. The initial groove is very serious. Climb to an obvious rightward-curving overhang and follow it to a junction with Phreatic Line, below the layback groove. Pull straight over via a finger crack then step right into Seepage, finish leftwards via a curving crack.
J.Bullock, L.Moran, G.Evans 30.08.1986

12. **Kensai/Phraetic Line Combination** 24m E3,5c **

Climb Kensai to join Phreatic line.
J.Bullock 00.08.1986

13. **Phreatic Line** 24m E3,5c *

Takes the layback groove in the upper wall right of Samurai. Start at the right side of the crag below a pillar. Climb the groove bounding the left side of the pillar to a big square ledge. Move up to the overlap and the TR of Seepage. Traverse left for 5m and pull up to gain the base of the layback flake which is followed to the top.
E.Pardoe 1pt 00.00.1968
FFA P.Littlejohn, J.Harwood 03.10.1980, G.Ashmore, I.Fisher ALCH 24.04.1999

14. **Seepage** 24m E1,5b

From the square ledge on Phreatic Line, climb the wall direct to the overlap, TR. Swing left for 2m and pull over the bulge at a thin crack. Move right into a groove which is followed to finish.
E.Pardoe, C.Knight 00.00.1969

15. **Noble House** 24m E1,5b

Climbs the loose groove and upper wall right of Seepage. From the square ledge on Phreatic Line, go diagonally right to cross and gain the top of a shattered groove. Move onto a wall above the overhang, step left and climb to the top.
J.Bullock, G.Evans 07.11.1982

16. **The Amazing Bugblatter Beast Of Zarg** 36m E3,6a *

A good right to left traverse. The route originally finished up Left Edge after a belay in Skive, but the finish described makes for a better route. Follow Seepage to the overlap and climb left along the obvious break, via a devious crux to finish up the groove of Skive.
A.Richardson, N.Gyerke 00.00.1987
G.Ashmore, I.Fisher ALCH 24.04.1999

To the right the cliffs deteriorate and although lines have been recorded in the past, they have now collapsed.

The Great Tower

GR569866

DESCENTS: Scramble down the gully to the east of the tower.

This is the obvious pillar right of High Pennard. Take care with the rock.

1. **South East Chimney** 15m D ●

An unpleasant climb. Climb a short wall, then move up right into a deep gully. Climb this, very unpleasant and vegetated, then left to the top.
Harold Insley, etc.1958/9

2. **Triattsdyffi**   18m   E1,5b   ●
A well-positioned but friable route up the left side of the face. Start below and slightly right of the obvious crack at 6m. Climb the wall and crack. From the top of the crack make a hard move up and left onto the edge. Follow the wide crack above to the top.
E.Pardoe, R.Leigh 00.00.1967

3. **South East Edge**   18m   E1,5b
High on the right side of the tower is a clean crack. Climb the right edge of the wall, just left of the ivy, to a corner level with the bottom of the crack. Traverse left onto the face and up to a good ledge. Follow the crack and groove to the top.
Harold Insley etc. 1958/59
J.Talbot - Direct A0 00.00.1968
FFA J.Bullock, G.Evans 00.00.1981

4. **Don's Quiet Corner**   24m   E4,6a   \
Climbs the east pillar. Climb the centre of the steepening lower slab to an incipient break. Keeping between the crack on the left and the groove on the right, climb straight up the rib to a poor break. Pull onto a ledge and finish direct, taking care not to disturb Mr.Whitelock's remains.
M.Crocker, G.Lynch 15.04.2000

PENNARD Lower Sea Cliffs
GR569864

DESCENTS: Scramble down the east of the crag.

These routes take various lines on the short recessed wall above a platform, which is exposed except at high tide. The left-hand reddish diedre is taken by Red Corner.

1. **Red Wall**   8m   HVS,5a
The wall left of Red Corner.
J.Talbot 00.00.1967

2. **Red Corner**   8m   VS,4b
The red diedre on the left of the crag.
J.Talbot 00.00.1967

3. **Tor Wall**   8m   VS,4c
The upper wall right of Red Corner, gained from Deep Crack.
J.Talbot 00.00.1967

4. **Deep Crack**   8m   S
The corner crack right of Red Corner.
J.Talbot, B.Talbot 00.00.1967

5. **Cave And Wall**   8m   HVS,4c
The centre of the recessed wall right of Deep Crack is poorly protected.
J.Talbot, B.Talbot 00.00.1967

6. **Scoop**   8m   S,4b
The scoop bounding the recessed wall on the right.
J.Talbot 00.00.1967

7. **Great Block**   8m   VS,5a   *
The block bounding the buttress on its right has a tough problem start.
J.Talbot, B.Talbot 00.00.1967

Graves End Wall
GR570864

To the east of The Great Tower, looking up the grassy gully, is a short wall with a larger wall on the terrace above. It has an obvious horizontal break at about 4m, with the upper wall bulging gently. The climbs are described relative to a small cave at the bottom left-hand side of the main face.

1. **Over Easy** 13m S,4a *
   The wall and groove 3m right of the small cave.
   M.Danford, G.Richardson 00.00.1978

2. **Too Late** 13m S
   The wall and broken crack 3m right of Over Easy.
   G.Richardson, M.Danford 17.02.1983

3. **Marguerite** 13m VD
   The obvious broken crack 9m right of the small cave.
   G.Evans, J.Bullock 00.00.1981

4. **Vertical Smile** 13m VS,4c *
   A popular route. Start just right of Marguerite. Climb the wall to a ledge, traverse right and follow a groove to the top. There is a direct start gaining the groove/crack from directly below E1,5b.
   G.Evans, J.Bullock 00.00.1981
   N.Low, M.Low - Direct 00.00.1987

5. **Helter Skelter** 13m E2,5b
   Climb the wall below the top crack of Vertical Smile, to a small ledge. Climb onto the wall above via a flake and continue up a crack above.
   H.Jones A.Healy 24.04.1984

6. **Sun Fix** 15m E3,6a
   A nice pitch up the cracks in the wall 5m right of Helter Skelter. Climb through the roofs, step right at the break and climb directly up the wall.
   A.Sharp, J.Harwood 10.09.1985

7. **Toetector** 15m HVS,5a
   Start 2m right of Sun Fix, where there is a thin crack with block overhangs at 4m. Climb to and through the overhangs and move right onto a flake. Finish with an awkward move left from the top of the flake.
   J.Bullock, G.Evans 00.00.1978

8. **Laissez Faire** 15m E3,6a
   The strenuous curving crack 6m right of Toetector. A slight left-hand start (Thickhead E2,5c A.Richardson, A.Giles, etc 1986) starts up the left-hand crack.
   A.Sharp, J.Harwood 10.09.1985

9. **Fever Pitch** 15m E3,5c
   Climb the wall and bulge between Laissez-Faire and TR1 to a break, then climb the bulging wall above to join TR1 at the recess.Contrived.
   A.Long, A.Richardson 00.00.1991

10. **TR1** 15m E2,5c *
    Start 3m right of Laissez Faire at a corner capped by a triangular block overhang. Climb the corner and overhang onto the obvious break, step left and up into a small recess and then direct to the top.
    J.Bullock, G.Evans, G.Richardson 26.05.1982

11. **Drakensburg**   50m   E2,5b

A girdle starting up TR1 and finishing up Vertical Smile. Stances can be taken en route.
J.Brown, D.Nolan 00.00.1995

12. **Mental Floss**   15m   E4,6a   *

Climb the steep wall 2m right of TR1 to the break, move right and finish directly up the wall.
A.Sharp, J.Harwood 10.09.1985

13. **Solar**   15m   E4,6a   *

Climb the shallow corner 4m right of TR1, then the pocketed wall and scoop above.
A.Sharp, J.Harwood 10.09.1985

2m right of Solar the wall is recessed with an obvious flake up on the left and a jammed block high on the right.

14. **Left Corner**   13m   VS,4c

The initial steep wall leads to a wide crack defining the flake.
J.Talbot, G.Jones 00.00.1959

15. **Brave Face**   13m   E5,6a

The wall between Left and Right Corner.
A.Berry 00.00.1992

16. **Right Corner**   13m   HS,4b

The steep corner right of the recess leads to a half-height ledge. Follow the crack in the wall above.
J.Talbot, G.Jones 00.00.1959

17. **Thorium**   13m   HVS,5b

A right-hand start to Right Corner.
J.Kerry 00.00.1971

18. **Sunflower**   13m   E4,6a

The wall between Right Corner and Left Pillar, with a slightly unstable lower section. RPs in the crack above the ledge prevent a ground fall, but a fall before the TR will result in sore ankles!
J.Brown, A.Berry 00.00.1995

19. **Left Pillar**   16m   VS,4b

Climb the pillar left of the cave via the steep groove. Finish rightwards above the cave.
J.Talbot, G.Jones 00.00.1959

20. **Kamin**   13m   VS,5a   *

A popular problem. Climb out of the back of the cave. Finish direct from the ledge.
J.Talbot, G.Jones 00.00.1958

21. **Friendly**   13m   HVS,5a

The wall right of Kamin.
C.Squires 00.00.1995

22. **Neatfeet**   12m   E4,5c   \

The arete above and right of Kamin.
M.Crocker, J.Harwood 25.03.2000

23. **Chasm**   13m   D

A useful descent route just right of the cave.
Harold Insley etc. 1958/9

24. **Gower Gully Joke**　　　　　　　　7m　　　E5,6a　　　　　　　\
Climb the overhanging crack in the right wall of the Chasm gully.
M.Crocker, J.Harwood 25.03.2000

25. **Crevice**　　　　　　　　　　　9m　　　S,4b
Climb the smooth crack right of Gower Gully Joke.
H.Insley etc. 1958/9

The short wall to the right of Crevice has a crack and two wide corner cracks.

26. **Ivy Saviour**　　　　　　　　　8m　　　VS,5a
The first crack.
K.Wood, G.Evans 00.00.1974

27. **Cycle Track**　　　　　　　　　8m　　　VS,4c
The wide corner crack.
G.Evans, K.Wood 00.00.1974

28. **Monkey**　　　　　　　　　　8m　　　HS,4b
The next corner.
N.Williams 00.00.1980

Further to the right is an easy descent, followed by a long smooth wall, which boasts excellent pocketed limestone.

29. **Miguel**　　　　　　　　　　9m　　　E3,6b　　　　　　　\
Fight up the thin cracks 6m right of Monkey, taking care with the protection.
M.Crocker, R.Thomas 05.03.1989

About one-third of the way along the wall is an obvious shallow groove (Sunny Surprise).

30. **All Too Distant**　　　　　　　9m　　　HVS,5a
Start about 5m left of the groove above a small rock step and directly below the end of the small grass ledge near
the top of the crag. Climb the wall on incuts and pockets, TR.
P.Donnithorne solo 30.12.1988

31. **Commit**　　　　　　　　　　12m　　　E1,5c
The smooth groove immediately right of All To Distant, keeping left of the crack at 5m.
P.Donnithorne, N.Ashcroft 30.12.1988

32. **Sunny Surprise**　　　　　　　12m　　　E2,5c
As for Commit, but take the crack up right at 5m.
P.Donnithorne, N.Ashcroft 29.12.1988

33. **Eduoardo**　　　　　　　　　12m　　　E3,6b
Start below the obvious tiny overlap at half-height below a short step in the path about 2m right of Sunny Surprise.
Climb to the overlap and good pockets. Move right and finish direct.
M.Crocker, R.Thomas 05.03.1989

About 2m right of Eduoardo is an obvious capped groove (Slow Worm).

34. **The Hideaway**　　　　　　　12m　　　E3,6a
Climb the wall just left of the groove, PR missing.
P.Donnithorne, N.Ashcroft 30.12.1988

35. **Slow Worm**   12m   VS,4c
Climb the groove to the capping overlap. Pull over this on its right and finish direct.
N.Ashcroft, P.Donnithorne 30.12.1988

36. **Sweet, Sweet, Sweet**   12m   E3,5c
Right of Slow Worm is a small cave at the base of the cliff. Climb the flake-like feature just left of the cave, TR.
P.Donnithorne, N.Ashcroft 29.12.1988

The ivy covered groove to the right marks the start of Graves End East.

Graves End East
GR572864

DESCENTS: Down gullies at various points.

This area is the natural extension to Graves End Wall and can be approached either by following the top or the base of Graves End wall eastwards. The top path drops down at the descent gully. Bear westwards to gain the left end of the crag, or east for routes right of Little 'Un. Nettlebed buttress has some good bouldering (5b-6b) and is also surprisingly sheltered. At the far left end is a vague arete.

1. **Baboon Traverse**   27m   VS,4c
An entertaining traverse following the obvious break line from the foot of Cornel to the end of the buttress.
N.Williams 00.00.1980

2. **Cornel**   15m   VS,4b
This takes the first corner 5m right of the left end of the crag.
J.Bullock, G.Evans 00.00.1977

To the right are two obvious flake cracks. The right-hand one contains a PR (Restful) the left-hand one is Nettlebed.

3. **Clapham Common**   18m   E4,6a
The wall left of the flake of Nettlebed.
M.Crocker, J.Clapham 19.03.2000

4. **Nettlebed**   15m   E1,5b
The leftmost of the two flake cracks is gained via a problem start and some very loose jugs.
K.Wood, G.Evans 00.00.1974

5. **Restful**   15m   E3,5c
To the right of Nettlebed is an obvious curving flake. This is gained via an infamous problem using a corner to reach the break. Make steep moves into the flake and follow it to the top. The PR at 5m is missing.
G.Evans, J.Bullock 1pt 00.00.1984
FFA M.Learoyd, R.Thomas 1986

6. **Ass Over Tit**   18m   E4,6a
The wall immediately right of Restful, TRs.
M.Crocker, J.Clapham 19.03.2000

7. **The Toboganning Incident**   18m   E4,6b   *
The left curling crack immediately left of the arete right of Ass Over Tit. Bounce up a short hanging crack to reach a break. Pockets above lead into the crack which is followed to an exit right at the top.
M.Crocker, J.Harwood 02.01.2000

8. **Little 'Un**   15m   VS,4c
The last corner groove on the buttress.
G.Evans 00.00.1980

To the east of the descent gully are some definite pillars.

9. **Where Will It All End?**   12m   E3,5c
The arete of the left pillar, finishing just left of the capping blocks.
M.Crocker solo 19.03.2000

The old route Buttress (J.Talbot, G.Jones 1959) has been superseded by other routes hereabouts.

10. **Marmite**   15m   VS,4c   *
Supersedes Slab Corner (J.Talbot, G.Jones 1959). Take the obvious groove and bulging flake on the left face of the second pillar.
G.Evans, J.Bullock 29.06.1977

11. **Taipan**   15m   E1,5b
A very contrived eliminate up thin cracks right of Marmite, constantly struggling to avoid using holds in that route.
G.Evans, J.Bullock 15.09.1982

12. **Graves End Arete**   15m   E4,6a
An exciting, if fragile pitch up the leaning arete of the second buttress. Gain the cracks in the arete directly through the bulges at the start. Follow them with difficulty. Mean and not adequately protected before the upper crack.
M.Crocker, R.Thomas 05.03.1989

13. **Coffin Crack**   15m   VS,5a   *
This takes the wide crack/groove on the east side of the buttress.
J.Bullock, G.Evans 29.06.1977

14. **Cleansing Agent**   12m   VS,4c
The thin crack left of the jammed boulder cave. Gain and follow the crack steeply to a ledge, then continue up the groove above.
G.Evans, J.Bullock 00.00.1978

15. **Marmolata**   13m   VS,4c
Start right of the jammed boulder cave. Turn the jammed boulder to the right and finish up the crack above.
J.Talbot, G.Jones 00.00.1959

16. **Breakout**   13m   HVS,5b   *
The obvious crack on the front face of the buttress east of Marmolata puts the hard into (Yorkshire) Hard VS. Depending on your strengths it is either a classic test of jamming technique, or the hardest layback on Gower. Either way it proves more difficult than it looks.
N.Williams, P.Williams 00.00.1979

17. **A Grave End**   15m   E5,6a   *
The blunt white arete immediately right of Breakout. Clamber up onto a ledge on the right. Grope left round the arete, swing left onto it and finish more easily up cracks in the arete. Watch out for the block in the evemt of a fall.
M.Crocker 19.03.2000

18. **White Wall**   12m   VD
Scramble up the front of the final pillar of the crag.
J.Talbot, G.Jones 00.00.1959

19. **Overlapping Wall**   12m   VS

Right of White Wall, climb a thin overhanging crack in a wall, gain a right slanting crack, up this to a crack splitting a block and over the block to finish.

J.White 16.04.1983

Graves End Sea Cliff

Below and 150m east of Graves End East is a small sea level promontory with a recess on its east side. It is easily identified by the arete of Greystone, which has a thin flake on its landward side.

20. **Greystone**   7m   E2,5c

The east facing arete of the promontory.

M.Crocker, J.Harwoood 25.03.2000

21. **Unnamed I**   7m   D

The corner crack to the right.

Unknown Pre-2000

22. **Unnamed II**   7m   VD

The arete to to the right.

Unknown Pre-2000

23. **Unnamed III**   7m   VS,4b

The arete right again.

Unknown Pre-2000

BANTAM BAY

GR574865
By Adrian Berry

TIDAL STATUS: Non-tidal, although the approach is sometimes cut off at spring tides.

BOLTING POLICY: No bolting.

PREAMBLE
This is the sort of crag that only a local or seasoned Gower visitor would be interested in finding. It does tend to become dirty from under-use and the finishes are atrocious, but the climbing is good.

ACCESS
The walk in is either by following the path round from Graves End or Pwll Du for ½ mile (refer to these sections for details) to reach the first obvious cove, which is Bantam Bay itself.

DESCENTS: A lower off rope is essential for the routes here.

THE ROUTES
The routes start at a small crag just round to the left of Bantam Bay proper.

1. **The Rugby Club**   15m   VS,4c
   At the left side is a small pinnacle with an overhanging crack at its left-hand side.
   P.Christie, G.Morris Pre-1991

2. **Big Crack**   15m   VS,4c
   The distinctive crack on the far left end of the craglet proper.
   J.Bullock, L.Moran Pre-1991

3. **Phil Lynott**   15m   HVS,5a
   To the right of the crack is a shallow overhanging corner.
   P.Christie, G.Morris Pre-1991

4. **Stepped Corner**   15m   E1,5b
   At the right-hand side of the bay is a stepped corner.
   J.Bullock, L.Moran Pre-1991

Further right, the crag becomes slabby and overgrown until the rock breaks through with a roof and corner.

5. **Egged On**   18m   E2,5c
   Follow cracks to the middle of the roof, which is taken at its centre. Move right to finish.
   M.Learoyd, R.Thomas 00.11.1985

6. **Rampant Cockerel**   18m   E2,5c
   The corner to the obvious roof. Move right and pull over it strenuously. Continue up the wall above.
   C.Parkin, P.Blackburn 00.00.1985

7. **Don't Count Your Chickens**   18m   E2,5c
   Start just right of the arete at an overhang. Boulder to gain a crack, which leads to hard moves left onto a ledge.
   Move back right and to the top.
   P.Blackburn, J.Kitching 00.00.1985

8. **Ruffled Feathers**   18m   E2,6b   *
   A good route taking the perfect splitting crack in the centre of the wall. The start is a heinous boulder problem taken from the left.
   M.Learoyd, R.Thomas, G.Royle 07.11.1985

9. **Gift Horse**   18m   E1,5b
   The obvious corner crack.
   G.Royle, R.Thomas, M.Learoyd 07.11.1985

10. **Wide Eyed And Legless**   18m   E1,5b
    The thin crack in the short wall to the right. Step back left and follow the groove above. This route has been completely overgrown by ivy.
    P.Blackburn, J.Kitching 00.00.1985

There is also a 12m quarried wall further back, undercut by a cave left of centre. There is an obvious rusty stain.

11. **Fought Shitening Crack**   12m   E4,5c   \
    The wide crack on the left, to a bold swing right to the finish of Alarm Race.
    M.Crocker, J.Harwood 22.07.2001

12. **Alarm Race**   12m   E4,5c   *   \
    The overhanging finger jam cracks just left of the chimney and the obvious continuation.
    M.Crocker, J.Harwood 22.07.2001

13. **Roast Dinner Man's Rift**   12m   E3,5c   \
    The obvious chimney.
    M.Crocker 22.07.2001

14. **Hip 'Op**   12m   E6,6b   ***   \
    Start 2m right of the chimney, pull up flake cracks into a groove and gain good lay offs above, TR. Stretch right onto the headwall, PR and make a long move for pockets and the top.
    M.Crocker, J.Harwood 22.07.2001

15. **Piss Off**   12m   E6,6b   \
    To the right, hard moves up the rust streak by a boss of rock past microwires lead to an exit through conglomerate. Sounds great.
    M.Crocker, J.Harwood 25.03.2000

16. **Lift Off**   11m   E1,5b   \
    Gain the slim corner moving right at the top to join Blast Off.
    M.Crocker, J.Harwood 25.03.2000

17. **Blast Off**   11m   E2,5b   \
    The overhanging cracks right of the slim corner.
    M.Crocker, J.Harwood 25.03.2000

41. **Right Edge**   12m   S
    Gain Direct from the diagonal crack down and right. Finish up Direct, or up the arete.
    Unknown 00.00.1958

PWLL DU BAY

GR574870 to 575871
By Adrian Berry & Goi Ashmore

TIDAL STATUS: Non-tidal.

BOLTING POLICY: Retro-bolting permissible with first ascensionist's permission. Replacement of worn fixed gear on a point for point basis with bolts is permissible. New sports routes allowed.

PREAMBLE
The main climbing is the sports climbing in the quarry situated on the west side of Pwll Du Bay. The quarry is in the sun until noon, making it a good cold or hot weather venue depending on the time of the visit, although seepage can be a problem as it washes fine sand down over the top of the crag. The two other buttresses are of passing interest, except for Fin, which will take most people several visits. Pwll Du itself is a lovely bay with a big shingle beach and freshwater stream. It contains, without doubt, one of the best hard routes in South Wales.

ACCESS
It is possible to take the coastal path east from Graves End, but the best approach is from Bishopston. It used to be possible to park at the headland, but it became a target for car thieves so parking is no longer allowed. Park at Pyle Corner in Bishopston (GR581876). This is the only corner in Bishopston and is characterised by a few shops.

From Pyle Corner walk to the coast down Pwll Du Lane until it ends at the coast. Note that Pwll Du Lane swings left at a thatched cottage. Avoid going straight on unless you want to wish to take in Bishopston Valley too. At the headland, turn right (west) and descend into the bay along a rough track. Pwll Du Quarry rapidly comes into view on the far side. Either turn left after a while and walk across the beach, or when the tide is in, continue along the rough track and access the west side of the bay past a few houses.

For Pwll Du Buttress and Goonland, the buttresses over to the right of the quarry, scramble up through irritatingly dense brambles and assorted vegetation. There are no real paths.

DESCENTS: Sports routes in the Quarry have lower offs. The older tradtional routes generally require hanging ropes, which need to be placed by scrambling up from well to the left of the crag. Take great care traversing along the cliff top if doing so. The descent for Pwll Du buttress is down a gully to the left.

THE ROUTES

Pwll Du Quarry
GR574870

The first line on the left of the quarry is utterly filthy and is a long abandoned project. Its PR should not be confused with that of Ashes To Ashes.

1. **Ashes To Ashes**   21m   E3,6a
   This takes the prominent groove up the left side of the crag. A problem move leads to a PR, then move right to the base of a groove, PR. Climb this, then cross left to the arete and climb the hanging crack, PR, to just below the top. A jammed nut marks the end of the route, but a back up rope is advised for the abseil.
   R.Thomas, J.Bullock, L.Moran 00.10.1986

The next routes are bolt protected sport routes which all end by lowering off from double bolts.

2. **Forty For Three**   11m   E5,6b   Fr7b   *
   A route with some awkwardly spaced bolts and long reaches, down and left of the central prow of the quarry. Finish at the double bolts. It is possible to finish up the top part of Senser (Eighty For Six E6,6b, Fr7c+ \ ).
   M.Crocker 10.07.1994

3. **Senser Part I**   11m   E6,6b   Fr7b+   **
Senser, as far as the first double BB.
M.Crocker 24.07.1994

4. **Senser**   22m   E6,6b   Fr7c+   ***
One of the best hard routes in South Wales. A good one to try, with no desperate moves. Start at a faint arete left of the central twisting groove of the crag and under the central prow. Move up and left and keep rocking up to a big jump for a hold by twin BRs. Undercut painfully up passing a BR which is impossible to clip en-route. Make a hard jump right for a square block just after the clip! Finish up and slightly right to the BB of Jezebel.
M.Crocker 24.07.1994

5. **Jezebel**   20m   E5,6a   Fr7a+   *
The central twisting groove line of the crag.
M.Crocker 09.07.1994

6. **Crock Block**   12m   E3,6a   Fr6c   *
A good warm up. Start under the obvious rectangular block and bridge up onto this. Make hard moves up onto the slab to a BB.
R.Thomas 00.07.1994

7. **Old Slapper**   10m   E4,6b   Fr7a
One very hard and frustrating move, which has taken the scalps of a couple of big cheeses who thought it would be a breeze after Senser. The short groove and rib right of Crock Block succumbs to either a large number of slap attempts, or a stylish egyptian. Pull onto the slab to finish.
R.Thomas 00.00.1994

8. **Skedaddle**   12m   E4,6a   Fr7a
A poor route up the groove and wall round the right of Old slapper. Spaced BRs are a problem for the short - classic Crocker stuff! BB as for Old Slapper.
M.Crocker 24.07.1994

9. **Dust To Dust**   21m   E4,5c
Just to the right of Skeddadle is a line of shallow grooves. Climb the first groove, PR, to a jug. Move up the slabby wall to the next groove and roof, swing left into a crack and the top.
M.Crocker, R.Thomas 20.07.1986

10. **The Flight Of Icarus**   21m   E3,5c   1pt
A dirty route taking the layback crack just right of Dust to Dust. Climb the crack past an overhang. Finish via large ledges and a mossy pull over. There is a stake at the top.
A.Berry, J.Bullock 1pt 00.00.1990

Goonland
Above and to the right of Pwll Du Quarry, is an interesting collection of rocks with a route.

1. **Cross The Rubicon**   9m   E6,6b   Fr7b+   *   \
The centre of the wall past the BRs.
M.Crocker 22.07.2001

Pwll Du Buttress
GR575871

Situated to the right of Pwll Du Quarry and originally called Lower Goonland Rocks, is a clean buttress with a slanting crack on its right and a wide chimney on its left.

1. **Fin**   12m   E6,6c   Fr7c+   **   \
   The prominent arete on the left end of the buttress provides a series of aesthetic powerful moves and escapes the seepage problems of other Gower sport routes. Might just be Fr8a.
   A.Berry 00.00.1994

2. **DT's**   15m   E1,5b
   Climb a thin crack to reach the wide chimney, which is followed to the top.
   G.Evans, G.Richardson 00.00.1983

3. **Star Trek**   15m   E1,5a
   Start right of DT's and 4m down the slope. Climb the wall to a bulging crack, move right to a ledge below two cracks, climb the left crack and boldly layback over a bulge to the top.
   J.Bullock, G.Evans 26.04.1984

4. **Llareggub**   21m   E1,5b
   From the lowest point of the buttress gain a rib and then a groove. From its top move right to the crack and layback to the top. Climbed on the 30th anniversary of Dylan Thomas' death.
   G.Evans, J.Bullock 00.00.1983

5. **Where Eagles Dare**   18m   HVS,5a
   This takes the obvious hanging flake on the right side of the buttress. Start right of Llareggub and climb the steep crack to a ledge at half-height. Layback the flake before moving left at the top.
   J.Kerry, A.Marsh 00.00.1970

CASWELL BAY

GR587874 to 590874
By Adrian Berry, Chris Shorrock, Myles Jordan & Goi Ashmore

TIDAL STATUS: 2½ hours either side of low water.

BOLTING POLICY: No bolting.

PREAMBLE
A pleasant slabby series of cliffs with some fine climbing for the lower grade climber. Situated within easy reach of Swansea and only 5 mins from the road, it is Gower's most populated beach in summer and is not the crag for the self conscious climber.

ACCESS
From Swansea go towards Mumbles, at the mini-roundabout in Mumbles (White Rose pub on the corner) turn right and head up the hill. At the top of the hill turn left at signs for Caswell Bay and follow the twisting road (B4593) to the Bay. Park in an obvious "pay or be fined" car park opposite the beach. The climbing is on a series of slabs on the west side of the bay. The most prominent of these is Great Slab, with an obvious through cave at the base. About 50m West is Yellow Flecked Slab and 50m further on is Far South Slab, bounded by a tapering triangular fissure at its West end.

DESCENTS: For the Far South Slab, scramble down either side. For other routes descent is via a path west for a short distance then down easy slabs and corners, or east if the tide is high.

THE ROUTES

Far South Slab
This is the most westerly of the slabs at Caswell and the most seaward. It consists of a slabby wall of fine quality rock, with generally good gear. It is therefore ideal for new leaders or for a pleasant half hour of soloing. The west (left) end is bounded by an obvious triangular fissure, called rather logically, Fissure.

1. **West Slab**   15m   D
   Gain and climb the slab left of Fissure, with an awkard start.
   Unknown 00.00.1958

2. **Fissure**   14m   D
   The obvious triangular Fissure, starting on its left wall.
   Unknown 00.00.1958

3. **White Slab**   14m   D
   Start at the base of the first proper crack (Curve) right of Fissure, but climb the slab directly.
   Unknown 00.00.1958

4. **Curve**   14m   D
   The first of the diagonal cracks running to the top of the crag.
   Unknown 00.00.1958

5. **Central Flake**   13m   D
   The second of the diagonal cracks running to the top of the crag.
   Unknown 00.00.1958

6. **Direct**   13m   HD
   Follow a thinner diagonal crack right of Central Flake, to join Central Crack at 5m.
   Unknown 00.00.1958

7. **Central Crack** 12m M
    Climb the central crack of the slab. A contrived variant up the slab to the right is possible (Black Slab VS,4c).
    Unknown 00.00.1958

8. **Right Corner** 12m HVD
    Easy, but poorly protected. The very faint left facing groove to the right of Central Crack.
    Unknown 00.00.1958

9. **Smooth Slab** 12m VS,4c
    The smooth black slab to the right of Right Corner.
    Unknown 00.00.1958

10. **Left Y Crack** 13m D
    Climb the left arm of the y-crack, right of Smooth Slab.
    Unknown 00.00.1958

11. **Y Wall** 10m D
    Climb the right arm of the y-crack, right of Smooth Slab.
    Unknown 00.00.1958

Yellow Flecked Slab
To the east of Far South Slab and west of a prominent inlet leading to the base of the Great Slab, is a yellow stained slab about 20m high. It is bounded on its west (left) side by a diagonal chimney and a loose corner.

12. **West Fissure** 20m VD ● ∖
    The diagonal chimney on the left side of the wall is vegetated and probably quite lethal.
    Unknown 00.00.1958

13. **Coloured Slab** 20m S *
    Climb the slab about 5m right of West Fissure.
    Unknown 00.00.1958

14. **Direct** 21m VD *
    At the base of the slab is a rock step. Start from this and climb the slab about 5m right of Coloured Slab, finishing up a shallow scoop.
    Unknown 00.00.1958

15. **Grooved Slab** 18m HD
    To the right of Direct is an area of honeycombed rock at the base of the slab. Climb the left side of these combs to gain the left end of a horizontal crack. Finish direct.
    Unknown 00.00.1958

16. **Curving Crack** 21m D
    Start right of Grooved Slab at a weakness in the honeycombes. Finish slightly left.
    Unknown 00.00.1958

17. **Loch** 15m D
    The arete to the right of Curving Crack and before a series of shallow corners.
    Unknown 00.00.1958

18. **First Corner** 21m VD
    Climb the corner to the right of Loch and finish up the slab above.
    Unknown 00.00.1958

Caswell Great Slab

Photo: Adrian Berry

19. **Second Corner**   21m   VD
Climb the shallow groove to the right of First Corner.
Unknown 00.00.1958

20. **Third Corner**   21m   VD
The corner right of Second Corner.
Unknown 00.00.1958

21. **East Edge**   21m   VD
The arete to the right of Third Corner.
Unknown 00.00.1958

The rock now drops back into a vague zawn, at the back of which is the obvious Central Slab. The more continuous west (left) side of the zawn has two narrow slabs running up it.

22. **Purple Haze**   21m   VS,4b
Start up the first of the two narrow slabs, but break leftwards onto ledges and finish via a short slab.
P.Thomas, R.Bennett 00.00.1983

23. **Sibling Arete**   27m   E2,5b
Climb the right arete of the first narrow slab in its entirety. No protection.
S.Lewis, G.Lewis 00.00.1982

24. **Once In A Blue Moon**   27m   HVS,5a
Gain the second narrow slab from the corner on its left. Take the subsequent corner to finish up the earthy crack.
D.Butler, C.Davies 00.00.1976

Great Slab
This is the most obvious and highest slab at Caswell, containing the through-cave at its base.

25. **What Not**   22m   S
Start below the Great Slab at a narrow slab leading up to an earthy gully on its left. Climb the narrow slab to its top, then traverse right on obvious pockets to the left edge of the central slab. Follow the edge to the top. This point can also be reached by traversing in from Nat Not at a harder grade (Left Edge VS,4b J.Brown, A.Kyffin 1996).
G.Evans, etc. 26.04.1977

26. **Pleistocene Dinosaur**   22m   E1,5b
Reach the cave apex via the huge block overhang and obvious large hole. Climb the slab to the overlap. Finish up the slab above.
D.Butler, C.Davies 00.00.1976
A.Berry, J.Preece, D.Naylor - ALCH 00.00.1990

27. **Nat Not**   22m   VS,4c   **
The best route at Caswell. Start on the rock neck below the Central Slab. Traverse deviously into and climb the right wall of the through-cave to its apex. Pull over this onto the slab above and continue directly.
G.Evans, M.Danford, G.Richardson 26.04.1977

28. **Bridge Over Troubled Waters**   22m   E3,6a   \
The roof of the through-cave in its entirety, starting at its depth and bridging until a finish as for Nat Not is possible.
A.Berry, D.Thomas 00.00.1997

29. **Great Slab**   21m   HS,4b   *
Climb the centre of the Great Slab linking up the two obvious holes. Not well protected.
Unknown 00.00.1958

30. **Right Edge**   21m   VS,4b
Follow the right side of the slab. Poorly protected.
Unknown 00.00.1958

31. **Mac The Knife**   22m   E5,6b   *
Painfully attack the overhanging crack in the right wall of the central slab, to finish up the central groove to the top.
P.Littlejohn, C.Hurley 02.05.1984

32. **Frantic Corner**   25m   E4,6a   \
Start on the block below the lower shelf of Antic Corner, step up onto the slab and using the right edge, move gingerly into the corner and up into the block overhang. Follow a line of flakes left into Mac The Knife at a large 'handle' hold. From here attack the upper wall left of the finish of Mac The Knife.
A.Berry 00.00.1992

33. **Antic Corner**   20m   E1,5b
Start in the east (right) entrance to the through-cave. Chimney up and pull onto the slab at the foot of the corner. Follow this via an overhang, to the foot of a grass tongue. Climb the rib on the right to the top.
D.Butler, C.Davies 00.00.1976

34. **El Condor Pasa**   21m   E3,6b   •
Provides a logical continuation to the direct start of Antic Corner. Start as for Shufflebottom Crack, then pull over an overlap to gain the pod of Antic Corner. Continue up to the block overhang, which is taken at its right-hand side, then the arete above.
A.Berry 19.04.1992

35. **Shufflebottom Crack**   22m   HVS,5a
A fun route requiring unique contortions. Start at the foot of a wide smooth crack right of Antic Corner. Climb the crack to the overhang and shuffle up it to the slab. Move up and over to the right edge and finish up this. Belay well back across the path.
G.Evans, P.Clay 08.08.1981

36. **Great Gully**   24m   M
To the right of the Great Slab routes is a square-cut gap before a prominent yellow raised slab is reached. Gain this gap via the offwidth below and continue up the slabs above.
Unknown 00.00.1958

The next routes are on the yellow raised slab to the east (right) of The Great Slab proper.

37. **Flake Variation**   16m   HD
Start left of the slab and climb up a groove to gain a ledge on the arete. Swing right to finish up a wide crack.
Unknown 00.00.1958

38. **Main Crack**   16m   D
The left crack on the front face of the slab, finishing up the wide upper crack of Flake Variation.
Unknown 00.00.1958

39. **Scoop**   15m   S
Some 4m up the east (right) arete of the slab is a ledge. Gain this either by the right-hand crack on the front face, or from a scoop round to the right of the arete. Finish up thin cracks.
Unknown 00.00.1958

40. **Direct**   12m   HS,4a
Climb jumbled rock to gain a corner right of an arete over to the right.
Unknown 00.00.1958

41. **Right Edge**   12m   S
Gain Direct from the diagonal crack down and right. Finish up Direct, or up the arete.
Unknown 00.00.1958

42. **Colorado**   5m   E4,5c   \
An exciting micro route that takes the south east arete of the enormous boulder situated right of the main climbing
area on small flakes with a tricky finish. No kit.
A.Berry 13.04.1992

WHITESHELL POINT

GR598869
By Adrian Berry

TIDAL STATUS: 2½ hours either side of low water.

BOLTING POLICY: No bolting.

PREAMBLE
A short leaning wall situated on the east side of the headland on the east side of Caswell bay. There are some hollow
holds at the top that are worth respecting.

ACCESS
Park at the Caswell Bay car park (see Caswell for more details). Approach by following the cliff path east (left when
looking out to sea) past steps that climb up to the headland. From just past the top of the steps, follow an obvious path
that leads down past the top of the crag. Belays are set well back.

THE ROUTES

1. **Shiver**   10m   HVS,5a
Start off prominent boulder at a faint crack 2m left of East Of Eden. Make a hard pull to gain the break, then follow
the pocketed wall above.
D.Thomas, A.Berry 23.10.1997

2. **East Of Eden**   10m   E2,5c
Start at the base of an obvious diagonal crack that runs rightwards from a pointed boulder. Make a sharp pull to
gain the break, then launch directly up the wall, with surprisingly good protection. Finish just left of prominent
block at the top.
A.Berry 23.10.1997

3. **The Getaway**   12m   E1,5c
As for East Of Eden to the break, then follow the break all the way left above the cave.
A.Berry 23.10.1997

RAMS TOR BAYS

GR615870
By Ren Hoek

TIDAL STATUS: About 2½ hours either side of low water.

BOLTING POLICY: No bolting.

PREAMBLE
A number of new routes by various combinations of H.Jones, D.Bowman and A.Wilson which were mentioned but without details in High Magazine in September 1985. Many of these were later claimed by C.Squires and J.Brown, but again no proper details are available. The routes have been climbed on by various groups over the years and the 1985 names and grades seem to fit appropriately.

ACCESS
From Rotherslade follow the cliff path east towards Limeslade for about 500m. At a break in the fence, there are two isolated fenceposts. The crag lies just below these posts.

DESCENTS: Descents is to the left (facing out) down an earthy slope, or right across the top of the back wall, passing two metal stakes.

THE ROUTES
The crag is formed by an undercut west-facing wall and a back wall set at a right angle. There is a prominent corner at the junction and a wide crack towards the left of the wall. The routes are described from left to right.

1. **Dream Of Tormented Ejaculation**   25m   HVS,4c
   Follow the hideous chimney, then the more open wall leftwards at the left end of the back wall.
   H.Jones, D.Bowman, A.Wilson 00.00.1985

2. **Crystal Eye**   25m   E1,5b
   An obvious layback crack just left of the cave leads across into the corner on the right. From the half-height ledge go diagonally left across the steep slab and pull into the bottomless finishhing groove. Take care at the top.
   C.Wyatt 00.00.2001

3. **Suicide Groove**   21m   HVS,4c
   The obvious angle corner. As for Crystal Eye to the ledge, then up the corner finishing out right below the roof.
   H.Jones, D.Bowman, A.Wilson 00.00.1985

The next six routes are undercut and start with a long step from the large boulder midway along the wall.

4. **Fat Crack**   18m   VS,4b
   The obvious wide crack.
   H.Jones, D.Bowman, A.Wilson 00.00.1985

5. **Something's On The Wall**   18m   VS,4b
   The wall right of Fat Crack.
   H.Jones, D.Bowman, A.Wilson 00.00.1985

6. **Romey**   15m   HS,4a
   Move slightly left from the step across. Finish direct.
   H.Jones, D.Bowman, A.Wilson 00.00.1985

7. **Something's On The Move**   15m   S
   From the step, move directly up to the niche and finish direct.
   H.Jones, D.Bowman, A.Wilson 00.00.1985

8. **Lizetta's Route**   15m   HS,4a
Climb the wall right of the niche.
H.Jones, D.Bowman, A.Wilson 00.00.1985

9. **Stormwatch**   12m   HS,4b
Start below a small cave. Gain this, then finish up cracks.
H.Jones, D.Bowman, A.Wilson 00.00.1985

11. **Where Did You Get That Girly Voice?**   9m   VS,4c
The left arete of the last right-angled corner.
M.Richards 00.00.1994

12. **Oyster Bubble**   9m   VS,4b
The last right-angled corner.
H.Jones, D.Bowman, A.Wilson 00.00.1985

13. **Space Oddity**   19m   HVS,5b
The obvious rising line across the face, finishing near Suicide Groove.
H.Jones, D.Bowman, A.Wilson 00.00.1985

14. **Muttley**   9m   VS,5a
The crack in the wall right of Oyster Bubble.
H.Jones, D.Bowman, A.Wilson 00.00.1985

15. **Dastardly**   9m   E1,5b
The crack in the bulge to the right of Muttley.
H.Jones, D.Bowman, A.Wilson 00.00.1985

RAMS TOR

GR617868
By Adrian Berry

TIDAL STATUS: Routes left of Nostradamus are Non-tidal. Routes to the right 2-3 hours either side of low water.

BOLTING POLICY: Retro-bolting permissible with first ascensionist's permission. Replacement of worn fixed gear on a point for point basis with bolts is permissible. New sports routes allowed.

PREAMBLE
The crag consists of an upper slab above a steeply undercut base. There is a roof along much of the crag at half-height. The northern end of the crag is currently undeveloped. At the time of writing, few of the routes are properly equipped. They could do with rebolting, as much of the gear is critically rotten and a lot of the lower offs are missing. There are stakes at the top and a back up lower off rope is strongly advised. The routes would be good if re-equipped.

ACCESS
A quicker approach for locals is from the clifftop path from Rotherslade. Visitors should follow the B4433 through Mumbles to park at the Limeslade bay. This is just west of the Mumbles headland (GR627872), it has a small ice cream parlour/cafe above it. Walk west along the coastal path for about 500m until it starts to climb up some steps. The top of the steps is are directly above the crag. Descent to the crag is either down the west (right when facing seaward) side of the bay on a steep path, or by abseiling down on from stakes above the east side.

THE ROUTES

1. **Unseconded**   30m   E5,6b   *   \
A traverse of the upper slab. Start as for The Cool Crux Clan and move across and slightly up into Rain Dance. From Rain Dance, step down, across and back up to another BR, then continue at about the same level to a final slight rise to reach Captain Hook. Finish as for Captain Hook. BRs.
A.Berry 00.00.1996

2. **Girdle Traverse**   45m   E2,5b
As for The Cool Crux Clan to the one-third height break, then follow this to the end of the crag.
M.Furniss, A.Wilson 03.03.1985

3. **The Cool Crux Clan**   14m   E4,6a   Fr7a   *
Start 5m left of the north (left) end of the main roof, below a faint groove at the top. Gain the groove directly. BRs.
A.Berry, G.Morris 00.00.1993

4. **Ride The Funky Wave, Babe**   17m   E4,6a   Fr6c+
As for The Cool Crux Clan to the break at one-third height. Traverse right for 3m and finish direct. BRs, PR.
N.Thomas etc. 00.00.1992

5. **Ride The Funky Wave, Babe Direct**   14m   E4,6a   Fr6c+
A direct start to the parent route.
A.Berry 00.00.1992

6. **Rain Dance Dance**   14m   E5,6b   Fr7b   *
Start about 1m right of where the obvious roof starts. Gain this fairly directly and cross it with a hard move at the lip, 3BRs.
A.Berry, P.Christie 00.00.1993

7. **Hypocritical Mass**   14m   E5,6c   Fr7b+   *
Start just left of the left-hand boulder jammed at the base of the crag. Make a desperate move to start, then gain the roof easily. Cross the roof on crystals to a thin pull round the lip and finish easily up the slab, BRs.
A.Berry 00.00.1993

8. **Captain Hook**   14m   E5,6b   *   \
Gain the vague groove in the upper slab from below and climb it on marginal gear.
A.Berry 00.00.0000

9. **Nostradamus**   14m   E5,6b   ***
Start just to the right of the right-hand jammed block and climb direct past a BR.
A.Berry 00.00.1993

10. **The Loneliness Of The Long Distance Runner**   14m   E6,6b   \
Start just to the right of Nostradamus at a TR in the lowest break and take a bold and fairly direct line to the top past a BR.
A.Berry, N. Thomas 00.00.1993

11. **One Small Step**   13m   E3,5c   *
Right at the far end of the crag, either leap to a jug in space, or make a 6a move. Traverse right, then up to finish.
A.Berry, J.Brown 00.00.1993

MUMBLES LIGHT HOUSE CAVE

GR635871
By Adrian Berry

TIDAL STATUS: Extremely Tidal. ¾ hour either side of low water.

BOLTING POLICY: No bolting.

PREAMBLE
These are some fine new routes in unusual surroundings. The rock and the lines are good. Only the extremely tidal nature is a nuisance.

ACCESS
As parking is a problem, the most sensible approach is to follow the B4433 and park at Bracelet Bay (see Rams Tor for more details). Walk back to the Mumbles Point Headland and walk into the beach to the islet of the lighthouse. The routes are in the cave below the lighthouse.

DESCENTS: Scramble down at various points.

THE ROUTES

1. **Magra Thea** 20m E6,6b **
   From the left side of the cave, follow the crack and cross a roof to easy climbing. Very strenuous, with good gear, which is difficult to place.
   A.Berry, G.Morris 25.05.1997

2. **The Resteruant At The End Of The Universe** 20m HVS,5b
   On the right-hand side of the cave is an overhang with a pocket in it. Climb direct to the overhang, take it slightly to the right, then follow the groove line to the top.
   A.Berry, S.Davies 02.03.1997

3. **The Big Bang Burger Bar** 20m HS,4b
   The groove a few metres to the right of The Resteraunt At The End Of The Universe.
   A.Berry, S.Davies 02.03.1997

CONSERVATIVE CLUB CRAG

GR620877
This cliff was a sheet of limestone on the hill behind the Mumbles Conservative Club. Unfortunately it has been netted over and turned into a construction site. The following routes are recorded for historical purposes only.

Cortez The Killer (E3,5c A.Richardson, S.Lewis1984), Out of The Blue (E2,5c C.Pound, P.Saunders 1981), Hurricane (E4,6a S.Lewis, A.Richardson 1984), Blood On The Tracks (E2,5c C.Pound, P.Saunders 1981), Energy Crisis HVS,5a P.Saunders 1981), Antelope Special (HVS,5a C.Pound, G.Lewis 1982), Floating Voter (E3,5c A.Long, C.Hebblethwaite 1989, A.Richardson - Variation 1991)

BARLAND QUARRY

GR575895
By Goi Ashmore

TIDAL STATUS: Non-tidal (if it is tidal then global warming has really got out of hand).

BOLTING POLICY: Retro-bolting permissible with first ascensionist's permission. Replacement of worn fixed gear on a point for point basis with bolts is permissible. New sports routes allowed.

PREAMBLE
From the road and the quarry gates, the quarry appears scrappy, broken and loose, but there is a very impressive 60m high sweep of slab that is not visible until the quarry is entered. The routes consist of technical slab climbing on thin holds and are well bolted. The slab gets the morning and early afternoon sun. Don't Jis On My Sofa is worth a visit in its own right for those who would otherwise be put off by the profusion of E4 climbing. It has been described out of west-east sequence due to its inland status.

ACCESS
This is the quarry on the right (north) hand side of the big bend coming out of Bishopston on the B4436, immediately past the turn off to Pwll Du. Due to a number of break-ins from the nearby lay bay, it is better to park in full view of the houses in Kittle Village, just up the hill, before walking back down to the quarry gates. The access situation is currently unclear. Enter the quarry and follow the gravel track round to the left to reach the very obvious main slab.

DESCENTS: All routes descend by lowering off or abseil. The two long routes require more than one abseil even with a 60m rope.

THE ROUTES

After a short initial slab, a superb low angled 60m slab dominates the quarry. Some bolt hangers on a couple of routes are missing at present, but the bolts and nuts are in.

1. **Jap's Eye**   12m   E1,5c   Fr6a
   The first short route up the slab has a tricky finish.
   R.Thomas 00.01.1998

2. **Cheesy Flaps**   13m   HVS,5a   Fr5
   The line to the right of Jap's Eye is somewhat broken.
   R.Thomas 20.03.1999

3. **Double Dutch**   15m   E3,6b   Fr6c+
   The slab to the right of Cheesy Flaps has a very hard start, but is considerably easier above.
   G.Gibson 00.01.1998

4. **Miss You**   17m   E2,6a   Fr6b+
   The start of the quality climbing on the slab, with a tricky finish.
   G.Gibson 00.00.1998

5. **Rotbeest**   17m   E5,6c   Fr7b+
   The first route on the continuous area of slab has a hideous move at two-thirds height.
   G.Ashmore 25.08.1997

6. **Wandelanden Tak**   17m   E4,6a   Fr7a   *
   The next line on the slab, starting above a pile of stones and a big stick. A technical start leads to a tricky section to gain the fifth BR, then step right from the good edge to join Geef Onze Fietsen Terug. Lower off the twin BB.
   G.Ashmore 17.08.1997

7. **Geef Onze Fietsen Terug!**   50m   E4,6a   Fr6c+   **
The first long long route that swaggers up the biggest section of unbroken slabs. Take a lot of quickdraws. Start where a pile of bicycles used to be at the base of the crag (about 4m right of Wandelanden Tak) and make technical moves up to a BB (possible belay). Easier but enjoyable climbing leads up to the big overlap. Surmount this and continue up to the BB by the long hole at 50m. Abseil off.
G.Ashmore, J.Tracey 16.08.1997

8. **Stoeipoesje**   18m   E4,6a   Fr6c+   *
Marginally more run out than the other routes - the slab right of Geef Onze Fietsen Terug to a BB at18m.
G.Ashmore 25.08.1997

9. **Wij Zitten Nog In Een Sneeuwstorm**   18m   E3,6a   Fr6b+
The slab to the right of Stoeipoesje and left of the groove, to a scoop at 18m. Step right to the belay of the next route.
G.Ashmore 13.04.1998

10. **Stinking Of Fish**   18m   E2,5c   Fr6a
The crack in the slab right of Wij Zitten Nog In Een Sneeuwstorm to join and finish up Telefunken U47. A Rock 8 protects the entry to the groove.
R.Thomas 07.06.1998

11. **Telefunken U47**   18m   VS,4c   Fr4+
The obvious groove to a BB at 18m.
R.Thomas 07.06.1998

12. **Don't Jis On My Sofa**   50m   E2,5c   Fr6a+   *
As for Telefunken U47 to the BB, then continue up to a vague corner in the roof. Swing left to a good jug and finish up the slightly tricky slab above BB. Abseil off.
R.Thomas 00.08.1998

13. **Ik Kan Mijn Ei Niet Kwijt**   18m   E5,6b   Fr7a+   \
Totally hideous. The slab to the right of Don't Jis On My Sofa has a hard start. If successful, continue more easily, to a totally vile series of huge rock ups on smears, stepping left to reach the BB.
G.Ashmore 14.09.1998

By the way many requests have been made for the English translations of the Dutch names. I don't see why if French names don't have to be and they are pretty idiomatic, but, in order of appearance: Horrid Creature (ruder in Dutch), Walking Stick (Stick Insect really), Give Us Our Bicycles Back (normally something shouted in abuse at German tourists), Play Cat (Sex Kitten really), We Are In A Snowstorm and finally I Can't Get My Egg Out (more properly Horribly Frustrating). Haaivinnesoep by the way is Shark's Fin Soup and if anyone notices I'm half Chilean not half Dutch. Adios!

Martin Crocker - A Grave End (1st Asc) (E5,6a) Graves End
(Page 206) Photo: Carl Ryan

Dave Mills - Pluto (VS,4c) Ogmore
(Page 243) Photo: Carl Ryan

Bridgend Area

BOX BAY

GR804775 to 810768
By Ed Rees

TIDAL STATUS: 3 hours either side of low water.

BOLTING POLICY: No bolting.

PREAMBLE

This is a newly rediscovered crag of very good quality sea-washed and chemically weathered limestone in a pleasant situation. The routes are mostly in the S-VS range with good gear and good lines. There is also the most extensive and worthwhile bouldering in the guidebook area, concentrated in the zawns and on the walls about 300m west of the crag, as well on as the frozen wave of rock some 200m to the east. Many of the routes on the Main Face have been previously climbed by Mick Reynolds (the BBC cameraman on Everest) and Dave Hillman, but details are not available, so ascents are credited to the first to record them.

ACCESS

Leave the M4 at J37 for Porthcawl and follow the A4229 towards the town. At the third roundabout follow the signs to Nottage and Rest Bay. Follow the road for about a mile to a minor road junction overlooking the sea. Bear left, then turn left up a minor road 100m further on. Park on the grass to the left. The crag is more or less due south of this parking spot, although on the first visit it is best to approach from the west. To get to this point, cross the main road and follow the minor road beyond it towards the very obvious golf club building, passing a bluff on the seaward side. About 100m after the bluff, drop down to the sea and then strike back westwards (away from the direction of approach). About 200m on, after some low cliffs with some excellent bouldering, is the long incut of China Zawn, also called The Long Geo, the first area where the rocks are 10m high. Some 25m right from this is Death Zawn and round the corner is the largest (17m) of the walls, the square-cut Main Face.

DESCENTS: Descents are by obvious scrambles down gullies at various points.

THE ROUTES

The rock is sound on both the overhanging left wall (Mao Wall) and the longer slabby right-hand face.

Mao Wall

1. **Chairman Mao**   10m   HS,4a
   The corner at the left end of the wall.
   E.Rees, The Old Harrovians 00.00.1999

2. **Roy Sauce**   10m   E1,5b
   From the base of the wall, climb flake cracks in the arete directly to the top.
   M.Crocker, J.Harwood 26.05.2002

3. **Harrowed Ground**   12m   HVS,5a
   From the base of the wall climb the right trending crack to good jugs and the top.
   P.Smith, The Old Harrovians 00.00.1999

4. **No Spring Chicken**   12m   E3,6a
   Start 2m right of Harrowed Ground. Rock over onto the ledge, make a long reach,then storm directly up the wall, 2PRs.
   R.Thomas, P.Smith 00.00.1999

5. **Porthcawl Beach Party**   12m   E5,6a   *   \
   Right of No Spring Chicken is an overhanging groove. Climb this for 4m, then swing left and climb up via small holds either side of the thin crack in the left wall. Gain the wider crack and finish spectacularly.
   M.Crocker, J.Harwood 21.07.2002

6. **A Quest For The Truth Of The Origin Of.....**   12m   E3,5c   *
   The Innards Of A Pancake Roll
   Start at the back of the zawn and follow a rightward-trending ramp for 4m. Move onto the steep face on the left and gain a pancake. Finish direct. Good on the rare occaisions that it dries out.
   M.Crocker, J.Harwood 26.05.2002

The Right Wall

7. **Witches And Bitches**   20m   HS,4a
   Traverse the obvious break from the highest boulder at the back of the zawn to finish over the central overlap.
   N.O'Neill, The Old Harrovians 00.00.1999

8. **Limpet Slot**   12m   E1,6a   \
   Start opposite Quest etc. Pull up to a slot and finish direct.
   M.Crocker, J.Harwood 22.06.2002

9. **Barnacles Have No Soles**   12m   E2,6a
   Start 2m right of Limpet Slot. Stick clip the PR and make difficult moves upto the break. Finish Direct.
   G.Ashmore 16.08.2002

10. **Pre-Placing Barnacles**   12m   E6,6b
    Short and nasty. Start below the central of three runnels at the top of the cliff. Pull desperately up on a chicken head above a terrible landing and make a hard move up to the break. Finish easily.
    M.Crocker solo 21.07.2002

11. **Lemon Grass**   12m   E1,5c
    Start opposite Spring Chicken at a polished right-facing layaway. Make thin moves up and finish via the v-cleft.
    R.Thomas 00.00.1999

12. **Sir Psychosexy**   12m   HVS,5b   *
    Start 1m right of Lemon Grass below a chicken head chert knobble in the blank wall. Use it to gain a break and better holds, then follow solution cavities to the top.
    J.Crocker, D.Jones 02.07.1993

13. **Wide Eyed And Glueless**   12m   E1,5b
    Start 1m right of Sir Psychosexy at a runnel and make thin moves up. Finish direct from the ledge.
    R.Thomas 00.00.1999

14. **Pie Eyed And Clueless**   12m   HVS,5a
    To the right a shelf at 3m peters out. Climb to the shelf, then move left from a layaway. Finish direct.
    R.Thomas 00.00.1999

15. **Wide Legged And Crotchless**   12m   E1,5a
    Climb the bold, blank wall 2m to the right of Pie Eyed And Glueless.
    R.Thomas 00.00.1999

16. **Lemon Chicken**   12m   VS,4c
    Start 3m right of Wide Eyed etc. below a spike of rock. Climb to this and continue direct.
    P.Smith, The Old Harrovians 00.00.1999

17. **Johnny And His Chinese Eye**   12m   HS,4b
    Climb the wall 1m right of Lemon Chicken, through the left-hand quartzite sheet.
    E.Rees, The Old Harrovians 00.00.1999

Box Bay

18. **Soy Sauce** 12m HS,4b
Climb the wall 1m right of Lemon Chicken.
N.O'Neill, K.O'Neill 00.00.1999

19. **Orange Duck** 12m HS,4b
Climb just left of the arete of the easy descent staircase.
R.Thomas 00.00.1999

20. **Palm Pain** 8m VS,4c
To the right of the staircase is a rectangular recess. Climb up to the left-hand side of the recess and finish direct.
J.Harwood 23.06.2002

21. **Cato And The Hunchback Disguise** 8m VS,4c *
Climb straight through the centre of the rectangular recess on spectacularly good holds.
N.O'Neill, The Old Harrovians 00.00.1999

22. **Sunday Outing** 8m VS,4c
Start below the right-hand end of the recess. Climb to it, then swing right and continue up on big jugs.
J.Harwood 23.06.2002

23. **Prowl In The Evening Sun's Rays** 8m HVS,5a
Start 3m right of the recess and make a bold move up to gain jugs and some good moves.
G.Ashmore 16.07.2002

24. **Bitches And Witches** 20m HS,4a *
Start from the ledge 7m to the right of the staircase descent. Climb across left with feet at the level of the bottom of the recess and continue roughly at the same level, to finish just left of Lemon Grass.
E.Rees, The Old Harrovians 00.00.1999

Death Zawn
This is the square-cut zawn about 25m east of Chinese Wall (The Long Geo). It has a steep left-hand wall. The following two routes replace Do It In 517s (J.Crocker, D.Jones 1993).

25. **Sunbleached** 12m HS,4b
Start just left of the base of the arete and climb a groove to finish through a big cleft.
C.Shorrock, A.Glawe 13.04.1995

26. **SanctiMoanious** 12m HVS,5b
Climb the arete, starting on the right and moving to the left at half-height.
G.Ashmore, R.Thomas 21.07.2002

27. **Brittle Bone Syndrome** 12m E1,5a
Climb off a boulder on the right of the arete. Follow a crack trending right until it opens out into a giant orifice. Reach strenuously back left and finish up the headwall.
P.Smith, The Old Harrovians 00.00.1999

28. **Chee Tor Girdle Traverse** 12m E2,5c *
Climb the vague crack to the right of Brittle Bone Syndrome, moan about the TRs and finish up the tower.
G.Ashmore, R.Thomas, M.Jordan 18.07.2002

29. **Stone Washed** 12m E1,5b *
Start 4m right of Brittle Bone Syndrome and climb the obvious crack.
M.Jordan, C.Shorrock 14.12.1997

30. **Sustentaculum Tali** 12m E1,5c *
The thin wall to the right, PR.
R.Thomas 00.00.1999

31. **Herpisimplex 10** 12m E1,5b
Just next to a large chimney climb the thin crack without touching the far wall.
N.O'Neill, The Old Harrovians 00.00.1999

32. **In Sickness And In Health** 12m HS,4a
Bridge up the chimney, with protection placed in Herpisimplex 10.
E.Rees and The Old Harrovians 00.00.1999

There is a short route (The Geo Graduate 4b, C.Shorrock 1995).

The Main Face
Round to the right (east) is the obvious main face, a 17m high rectangular wall with various prominent cracks. To its west (left) is a narrow zawn containing a pool and a boulder. Left of the zawn is an area with a raised pavement at its base.

33. **The Gas Filled Dolphin Carcass** 8m VD
Climb the wall above the pavement.
C.Shorrock, A.Glawe 07.04.1995

34. **Where's Me Spinach?** 8m VS,4c
From the toe block above the pool at the right end of the pavement, reach out and thug strenuously onto the arete. Climb this directly to the top.
J.Crocker solo 02.05.1993

35. **Howard's Way** 15m HVS,5a
A fine and surprisingly exposed traverse around the arete onto the steep wall above the pool. Start at the right end of the pavement and climb the left ramp of the block. From here traverse deviously around Spinach arete on good holds to the ledge of Don't Snog etc. Finish directly up the crack or continue right to the end of the wall.
M.Jordan, C.Shorrock 14.12.1997

36. **Bikinis Are Yum** 9m E3,6b
From the boulder in the pool, make desperate moves up using the evil vertical slot. Use holds on the left to gain the break. Continue to the ledge. The route remained unrepeated for nearly ten years and there is some local scepticism about the first ascent.
J.Crocker 18.05.1993

37. **Plutonic Plankton** 10m E2,5c
From the boulder in the pool, lean accross and pull into the smooth crack. Follow this to easier ground.
J.Crocker 14.05.1993

38. **Don't Snog The Labrador** 9m HS,4c
Gain the prominent right-hand crack in the left wall of the zawn, by traversing in from the back of the zawn.
J.Crocker, T.Pearce 02.05.1993

The next three routes are on the right-hand wall of the zawn.

39. **Junk** 9m VD
Climb the wall towards the back of the zawn following a crack line and a small overlap.
J.Crocker solo 02.05.1993

40. **Rise Above the Water**   8m   HS,4b   *
From the boulder in the pool, step rightward into a smooth corner and gain a ledge at 4m. Step left and follow the arete to the top.
M.O'Neill, The Old Harrovians 00.00.1999

41. **Cow Eyed Arete**   8m   HS,4b
To the right of the pool and bounding the left-hand end of the main wall is a square-cut recess. The left wall of the recess is formed by a pillar. This route takes the left arete of the pillar.
P.Smith, The Old Harrovians 00.00.1999

42. **My Friend Shep**   8m   HVS,5a
Climb the groove in the left arete of the square-cut recess left of the gully bounding the left side of the main wall.
E.Rees, The Old Harrovians 00.00.1999

43. **Left Corner**   12m   VD
The obvious corner at the left side of the main cliff.
Unknown Pre-1995

44. **Aah-ck-ak-ak-ak**   14m   VD
The first crack right of Left Corner.
T.Pearce, J.Crocker 11.05.1993

45. **Jellyfish Tickler**   14m   HS,4b
The wall just to the right, starting by an obvious pocket.
G.Ashmore 01.04.1995

46. **Peaceful Easy Feeling**   14m   S   *
To the right is an obvious crack, which forks at 5m. Climb this taking the left-hand fork.
T.Pearce, J.Crocker 11.05.1993

47. **Jack's Noisy Squealing**   14m   S
As for Peaceful Easy Feeling, but climb the right-hand fork.
C.Shorrock, A.Glawe, D.Herbert 07.04.1995

48. **Valley Girls**   14m   S
The wall right of Jack's Noisy Squealing finishing up the right edge of Up And Down.
A.Glawe, C.Shorrock 13.04.1995

49. **Up And Down**   14m   D
The obvious groove toward the centre of the crag.
T.Pearce, J.Crocker 11.05.1993

To the right is an obvious rectangular cut-out at 4m.

50. **Olive Oyle**   14m   S
The wall to the left of the left crack rising out of the letterbox.
J.Crocker solo 02.05.1993

51. **Popeye**   14m   S
The left-hand crack rising from the letterbox.
J.Crocker solo 02.05.1993

52. **Sweet Pea Souper**   14m   VS,4c   *
Climb the wall between the two cracks rising from the letterbox.
C.Shorrock, A.Glawe 13.04.1995

53. **Bluto**   14m   S
The right-hand crack rising from the letterbox.
J.Crocker solo 02.05.1993

54. **Estuary Scum On The Welsh Riviera**   14m   HVS,5b
Climb the tricky wall down and right of Bluto, finishing more easily.
G.Ashmore solo 02.07.2002

55. **Slingshot**   14m   VD
The groove about 5m right.
J.Crocker, T.Pearce 00.00.1993

56. **Mill Pond**   20m   S   *
Traverse the face at two-thirds height from the ledge right of Slingshot, finish up the crack of Aah-ck-ak-ak-ak.
Best done at the end of a summer day at high tide, with the sun setting over the sea and a beer waiting at the top.
E.Rees, The Old Harrovians 00.00.1999

Right of Slingshot is a black buttress.

57. **Black Buttress**   10m   S
The front of the buttress.
C.Shorrock, A.Glawe 13.04.1995

58. **Prickly Bulge**   10m   S,4b
The gully wall of the buttress.
C.Shorrock solo 13.04.1995

59. **Injector Chimney**   10m   D
The chimney to the right of Prickly Bulge.
C.Shorrock solo 13.04.1995

Tto the right is a series of blocky overlaps.

60. **Strapadictome**   8m   E1,5b
Pull straight up the juggy blocks.
E.Rees, The Old Harrovians 00.00.1999

61. **The Overhangs**   7m   E2,5c   *
At the east end of the main face, set further back is a cave. Climb up a groove in the cave to the roof, then pull
through the roof, using the cracks to the left.
R.Mogridge, R.O'Brien 00.00.1999

Little Zawn
This is the square-cut rift just to the east of the main face, which provides a convenient descent. The left wall can be
climbed at about Moderate (The Slab, C.Shorrock solo 1995). The routes described are on the steeper right-hand
wall.

62. **Belayers Folly**   7m   VS,4c
Climb the central jam crack, taking care with the finishing holds.
C.Shorrock, A.Glawe, D.Herbert 07.04.1995

63. **Dead In The Water**   7m   VS,5a
The thin crack right of Jacob's Ladder.
E.Rees, The Old Harrovians 00.00.1999

Box Bay

64. **The Electrician**   7m   E1,5b
    Climb the wall between Dead In The Water and the arete on its right.
    E.Rees, The Old Harrovians 00.00.1999

65. **The Drowning Man**   8m   D
    The arete itself.
    Unknown Pre-1998

CASTLE UPON ALUN QUARRY

GR 906757
By Goi Ashmore

TIDAL STATUS: Non-tidal.

BOLTING POLICY: Retro-bolting permissible with first ascensionist's permission. Replacement of worn fixed gear on a point for point basis with bolts is permissible. New sports routes allowed.

PREAMBLE
Although quite large, only the left-hand wall of the quarry has so far been developed. It is a steep 70-85 degree slab of good quality, but one that only really dries out in late spring and summer. It may take a 'peeling' to remove the moss carpets on routes on the right hand side of the crag. There are a couple of trad routes, but most of the climbing consists of thin, but well protected sports routes in the E2 to E4 range. Worth a visit.

ACCESS
From Junction 35 of the M4 follow the A473 to Bridgend. Several stretches of dual carriageway lead to a roundabout, just after a petrol station on the right, with a left turn signposted to Ogmore By Sea. Take this left turn and continue until Corntown is signposted off to the left. Follow this road until after ¼ mile there is a shop on the right, where a narrow road forks off up the hill on the right. Take this road over the crest of a slight hill. The road goes straight down for about 1 mile, where there is a solitary stone wall ringed house on the right. Take the narrow road on the right immediately after the house, and follow this to a ford. Cross the ford and contiue for about half a mile, passing under a bridge to reach a small parking space next to the river. A footpath through the trees on the right is followed to reach the quarry after about 10 minutes walk. The direct approach from the ford, going through the gate behind, crossing the railway and walking left for about 100m is, of course, strictly forbidden.

DESCENTS: Most routes have lower offs, else abseil from trees.

THE ROUTES
The routes are described from left to right as approached.

1. **Eugene Genie**   12m   E4,6b   Fr7a   *
   The first line on the slab proves quite thin.
   E.Travers-Jones 00.00.1995

2. **Cordoba Express**   15m   E4,6a   Fr6c+   *
   Start as for Eugene Genie to the first BR, step up, then move right to a good bucket. Finish directly with interest.
   R.Thomas 00.00.1995

3. **Barry Freight**   15m   E3,5c   Fr6b+
   The next bolt line to the right. BB on the left.
   R.Thomas 00.00.1997

4. **A Freem Of White Horses**   15m   E3,5c
    To the right is a slot at 6m. Gain this (good Friends) and make some thin moves slightly left, to finish up the wall on slots. A hanging rope is advisable for the top.
    A.Freem Pre-1991

5. **California Freeming**   15m   E2,5c
    Climb to the Friend slot move slightly right and finish up a good crack. A hanging rope is needed for the top.
    A.Freem Pre-1991

6. **Pubic Enema**   15m   E2,5c   Fr6b
    To the right at the top of the crag is a square-cut groove. Gain this with some thin moves and climb it with care at the very top.
    R.Thomas 00.00.1995

7. **Freeming Of Jeannie**   17m   HVS,5a
    A diagonal pocketed crack slants up and right to a slot at 15m. Make a committing stretch up to the BB of Branch Line to finish.
    A.Freem Pre-1991

8. **Branch Line**   15m   E1,5c
    The slab to the right to step left into the previous route just after the top BR. Follow it to a BB.
    R.Thomas 00.00.1995

There are three unrealized projects to the right.

9. **Anal Retention**   14m   E3,6a   Fr6c   **
    The route of the crag. Up and right of the alcove at the base of the crag is a white section of rock. Climb this by technical moves.
    R.Thomas 12.09.1996

10. **Banal Pretention**   12m   E3,6a   Fr6c
    Up to the right is a slot at 3m. Gain this by a technical sequence and continue with difficulty.
    R.Thomas 00.00.1996

11. **The Trainspotter**   11m   E2,6a   Fr6b
    At the top of the banking are two shorter lines. This is the left-hand one, with a tricky start.
    R.Thomas, J.Bullock 00.00.1995

12. **Weak Lemon Drink**   9m   E2,6a   Fr6b+
    The line to the right has a hard start followed by a dyno for the big triangular pocket. Finish direct.
    R.Thomas, John Bullock 00.00.1995

OGMORE

GR873740 to 884732
By Roy Thomas

TIDAL STATUS: Highly variable, but never more than 3½ hours either side of low water at the east end of the cliff and never more than 3 hours either side of low water at the west. Normally about 2 hours average either side of low water along the cliff. Recessed areas like the Biscuit slightly longer. Some routes, especially those on Elephant Wall, Scutch Wall and Fire Wall have platforms which extend accessibility.

BOLTING POLICY: No bolting.

PREAMBLE

With no shadow of a doubt, Ogmore is one of the most important sea cliffs in Britain. Unsurprisingly it contains the greatest concentration of South East Wales' best traditionally protected routes. It is wild, steep, exciting and seriously underrated. You will either love it or hate it but whichever it is you must encounter "the Ogmore experience". Climbers used to Pembroke will probably find it a little intimidating, but with petrol at the price it is, perhaps fiscal prudence will overcome fear.

Ogmore is a limestone sea cliff situated between Ogmore by Sea and Southerndown. It offers climbing of a strenuous nature; steep, overhanging, but generally well supplied with holds. The rock is mostly good but some of the finishes may require care. It can suffer from seepage and is extremely tidal, with the tide rising 6m to 9m up the cliff, so beware of in-situ gear and use tide tables. It is a great crag for those who value adventure and excitement in their climbing, but is no place for the incompetent

Ogmore has recently been touted as a deep-water soloing venue. Whilst it is true that there are some routes with good depths of water below them at high tide, it is important to remember that the tidal range is staggering and staggeringly variable. More importantly, the soloist should be aware that there are very strong currents hereabouts and a lot of low-level sea caves. Being swept into one of these and drowned is a serious possibility. Aspirants should always check the fall out zones at low water, before conisdering a deep water solo. The impressive deep-water solos that have been made at this crag are not listed separately unless they cover genuinely new ground, although some are mentioned in the history section. The lunatic solos of some routes at low water are not listed separately either.

ACCESS

The layout of Ogmore is difficult to get to grips with and abseil in is the most practical way of approach. However, due to the tides, escape can be difficult, without a little forethought. It is therefore strongly recommended that climbers unfamiliar with the cliff take the familiarisation tour described below. There are two approaches from the road. The western approach is the most useful, for anything to the west of Mother Earth. For the eastern end of the crag, the Southerndown Approach is more useful, but a parking fee is due at some times of the year. Most climbers who are familiar with the crag will tend to abseil in from various points. These are noted in the Crag Familiarisation tour, but be warned that the stakes are of unknown origin or age; always find a way to back them up.

1. Western Access
Follow the B4524 from Ogmore by Sea towards Southerndown (Dunraven Bay) until it reaches a sharp bend passing West Farm (just after the sign marking the boundary of Southerndown). Park above the cliffs in a grassy area bounded by concrete posts. The Old Stable Tea Shop was ideally situated here for those who have cocked the tides up or require a 'pick me up' after their route, but is currently not trading. Descend a grassy gully towards the sea to reach a narrow path running westwards. When facing out to sea, a pinnacle is visible to the east (left). This marks the start of Exposure Explosion and is more or less directly above the line of Jumping Jack Flash.

2. Southerndown Access
Follow the B4524 a little further to a sharp left-hand bend at the Three Golden Cups pub, but go straight on down the smaller road sign-posted 'Beach'. Park in the car park at the base of the hill (parking fee in spring and summer) and walk out to the concrete slipway. Turn back west (right if facing out to sea) to walk into the crag. Note that it is only possible to walk all the way along the base of the cliff at dead low water on spring tides, due to the cut off points round Davy Jones' Locker and Scutch.

CRAG FAMILIARISATION
This section has been compiled to help climbers on their first visit check out the crag from the top. It is not a intended as a substitute for walking along the base of the crag, guidebook in hand and is only provided to help orientation.

In the Crag Familiarisation section, left means left when facing out to sea unless otherwsie stated. Common abseil areas are numbered for ease of reference denoted as A(n). P(n) denotes a photograph.

1. From the Western Access, walk down the descent gully to the pinnacle on the left. This is the starting point for Exposure Explosion and climbers often use this as an abseil point (A4).

2. Walk about 50m right, passing stakes (A3) on the way to a second cluster of stakes (A2). Directly below (A2) is the line of Pluto. Looking back to the left gives you the view (P1) of Elephant Wall. Note the line of Exposure Explosion, which is the narrower half-height break, not the wider upper break. Also take note of the line of Jumping Jack Flash, a useful escape route. Above Elephant Wall is (A5).

3. Walk about 50m right, passing a rift in the top of the cliff (move up a level to avoid this). Directly in front is a short protruding buttress. This is taken by Route 1, a useful escape. Above Route 1 is a common abseil point used to access the western end of the crag.

P1: Elephant Wall   Photo: Roy Thomas

4. Walk back to the initial gully, then up and over the shoulder of the hill, taking care not to get too close to the edge. Some abseil stakes will be seen at a slightly lower level. With care, descend to these (A5) and look back along the crag (P2). This gives you a good view of the Elephant Wall Bay area – the 'Popular End' of the crag. Route 1 buttress (A1) is clearly visible as is the corner of Abbey Road.

5. Walk leftwards along the crag, dropping down several tiers with care, to locate some stakes and a jutting flat topped ledge (A6) after about 70m. This is the top of Scutch. The corner to the right is taken by Yorkshire Pud. On the left side of the ledge, is the corner of Siren, with the top wall of The Uncanny being clearly visible. Further on, Fire Wall (P3) is clearly visible as is the line of The Bishop, the only real escape route from the Sorcery/Fire area. Above Fire Wall is (A8).

P2: Popular End

Photo: Roy Thomas

P3: Fire Wall *Photo: Carl Ryan*

6. Walk back up a couple of levels and continue past (A6), which itself is above Sorcery. A further stake is above the finish of Spellbinder (A7). After 70m, the top section of Fire Wall is clearly visible. Note the lines of Fire, Fury and Burn 'Em Up, all of which are classics of the crag at their respective grades. The abseil stakes are clearly visible (A8). Walk over to these.

7. From the top of Fire Wall, looking back, Sorcery Wall is visible (P4). Note the position of the buttress of Scutch (A6) and the chimney of Siren, a possible escape route. The toe of the buttress of Scutch is normally sea-washed, except at very low tides when escape can be made to the Elephant Wall area. The only easily distinguishable lines are Spellbinder and Warlock.

P4: Sorcery Wall

Photo: Carl Ryan

P5: Quimble Area

Photo: Roy Thomas

8. Continue left, at a higher level, to reach a bay. On the far side of the bay are two prominent caves (P5). The easternmost one (right) is Davy Jones' Locker. Except at low tides this is also a cut off point. The prominent flake crack is Quimble. This is not recommended as an escape route, as it is of questionable stability. Near the cliff edge are some stakes (A9), which could be used to access the Biscuit Routes around Cream Crackers. Continue round the top of the cliff carefully heading for a vista above the aforementioned line of Quimble.

9. From the top of Quimble (about 100m away) The Biscuit is clearly visible. Note the spectacular arete of Cream Crackers. Above is (A9). The only way to escape The Biscuit routes other than jumaring is by walking underneath the arete of Cream Crackers, passing a 100m long wall (Dracula area) to get to Fire Wall and The Bishop.

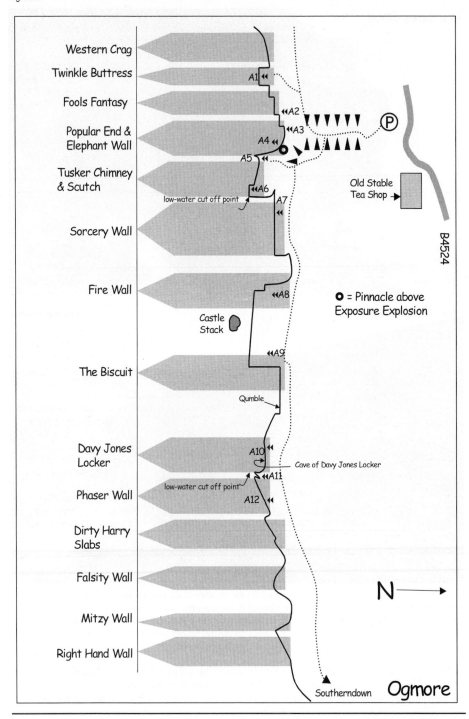

Western Crag

Twinkle Buttress

A1 ◀◀

Fools Fantasy

◀◀A2

Popular End &
Elephant Wall

◀◀A3

A4 ◀◀

A5 ◀◀

Tusker Chimney
& Scutch

◀◀A6

low-water cut off point

A7

Sorcery Wall

◀◀

Old Stable
Tea Shop →

B4524

Fire Wall

◀◀A8

Castle
Stack

O = Pinnacle above
Exposure Explosion

◀◀A9

The Biscuit

Qumble

Davy Jones
Locker

A10 ◀◀

Cave of Davy Jones Locker

◀◀A11

low-water cut off point

Phaser Wall

A12 ◀◀

Dirty Harry
Slabs

Falsity Wall

Mitzy Wall

N →

Right Hand Wall

Southerndown

Ogmore

10. Walk on for another 100m to find a faint rise and possibly some abseil stakes (A10). These are above Twenty-First Century. About another 50m on are more stakes (A11). These are at the top of The Hatch, the escape route for the entire eastern end of the crag. There is another abseil stake about 20m on. This is above Phaser (A12).

The crag is now totally featureless at the top and the eastern end of the crag is not as tidal or inaccessible as the western end. The crag familiarisation tour therefore ends. Getting familiar with the eastern end is best achieved by walking in from the Southerndown access, referring to the normal text. For anyone persevering, the tops of Falsity Area and the Falls Road Slabs will be obvious as the only two features that can be made out from the top of the crag. Here ends the geography lesson, go and climb on the crag for the geology and physics lessons and avoid the marine biology lessons by using tide tables.

NORMAL APPROACHES

Approach Points	From	To	Mean Tide Access
A1	Spangle Texture	Fool's Fantasy	2 hours either side of low
A2	Wipeout	Abbey Road	2 hours either side of low Wipeout a bit less
A3	Abbey Road	Pinocchio	2 hours either side of low
A4	Questimodo	Pinnochio	2 hours either side of low
A5	Easy Livin'	Yorkshire Pud	For routes on Elephant Wall 3 hours either side of low when belaying on higher ledges, else 2 hours.
A6	Yorkshire Pud	Warlock	1½ hours either side of low for routes on Sorcery Wall. Best to go for a spring tide for these routes. 2 ½ hours either side for Scutch Buttress if a slightly higher stance is taken.
A7	Mantra	Warlock	As above
A8	Tiger Sanction	Cream Crackers	1½ hours either side of low for Fire Wall, although a higher belay gives 2 hours. 2 hours for Dracula area.
A9	Cream Crackers	Quimble	Up to 3 hours either side of low, but retreat not possible after 2.
A10	Quimble	Davy Jones' Locker	1 hour either side of low
A11	The Hatch	Any point to the east	3 hours either side of low
A12	Phaser	Any point to the east	3 hours either side of low

Routes further on are approached by walking in from the Southerndown Approach.

DESCENTS: See above and by abseil.

THE ROUTES
Routes are described relative to each other looking back in at the crag from below.

The Western Crag
At the far left (west) end of the crag is a large square cave with a prominent rock scar to its right. The following three routes are on the wall left of the cave. They lead to a large ledge with stake belays that are also useful for abseiling. These routes are 100m to the left (west) of Route 1.

---

1. **Spangle Texture**   18m   VS,4b
    Start 4m left of the cave. Gain the first horizontal crack, traverse left and go directly up to a belay on the large ledge.
    S.Blackman, M.Eden 00.00.1984

2. **In Dispute With Nappy Rash**   18m   HVS,5a
    Start 3m left of the cave. Climb easily onto a ledge, continue to the upper horizontal break and traverse slightly left until a line of holds lead to the large ledge.
    G.Lewis, S.Lewis 00.00.1983

3. **Raw Energy**   18m   E2,5c   *
    Start just left of the cave. Climb via an undercut ledge and flake crack to the roof. Pull up left onto the obvious nose, move left up the wall, PR and continue over the small roof to the large ledge.
    M.Learoyd, R.Thomas, G.Royle 00.00.1984

The right side of the prominent white buttress forming the right side of the square cave houses the remains of The Pursuit Of Happiness (S.Bartlett, S.Kennedy 2pt 1980, FFA A.Sharp, Owen Jones 1986). Two new routes occupy the area of the cave.

4. **Lipstick**   27m   E3,6a   \
    Start at the left edge of the cave, at a ragged undercut ledge at head height as for Raw Energy. Pull onto the ledge and climb rightwards into a white corner. Make a hard move over the bulge to gain good holds up and right on the wall. Traverse right for 6m along the lip of the roof, until a line of weakness leads over a small overhang to the terrace.
    M.Crocker, D.Sergeant 18.07.1999

5. **Winchfactor Five**   20m   E2 5c   \
    The smooth groove right of the cave. Move up to a slot place a crucial Friend 2½, then traverse right to a sloping ledge at the foot of the groove. Follow the groove to the right-hand limit of the cave roof. Swing right and finish up a well-protected pocketed crack through the bulge.
    M.Crocker, D. Sergeant 18.07.1999

The long wall to the right of the square cave has few notable features and contains two routes.

6. **Chill Factor**   18m   HVS,5a
    A route that has been affected by storms. Start right of the cave, just left of a grey arete. Climb up for 1½m before moving right onto the arete and up to an overhang. Step left to a ledge, back right and climb the roof to the top.
    P.Littlejohn, S.Lewis 11.01.1981

7. **Side Step**   24m   VS,4b
    Start just right of a shallow cave at the featureless wall. Climb diagonally left for 15m to follow a weakness in the upper wall.
    J.Harwood, C.Horsfield 10.05.1978

The obvious buttress to the right (east) is Twinkle Buttress. Some 18m left is a line of overhangs high up.

8. **Kite**   18m   E1,5b
    Climb to the lower overhangs 4m from their left end. Follow a crack round the first overhang, then move left over the top overhang to finish.
    S.Lewis, J.Harwood 04.10.1978

9. **Swing Wing**   18m   E3,5c
    Start as for Kite. Climb to the first overhang and pull over this. Move right to a short corner, then leftwards and back right, to finish over the final overhang.
    P.Littlejohn, T.Penning 18.01.1983

10. **Mighty Steel**   18m   E5,6c   \
Start from a recessed ledge right of Kite. Climb to the first roof, PR, undercut through the break in the roof, to better holds, then direct, PR, through the roofs to a recess and an exit leftwards.
M.Crocker, M.Ward 26.04.1987

11. **Storm Damage**   18m   E2,5b
Start below a slabby white rib. Climb to the right side of the roofs then directly over to the top.
M.Crocker, R.Thomas 29.03.1987

12. **Christmas Cracker**   18m   HVS,4c   *
Start 9m right of Kite, below the right side of the overhangs at a shallow groove. Climb the right rib of the groove for 9m then move up right to a bulge. Climb back left above the bulge, surmount the overhang and finish up the obvious groove to the left.
P.Thomas, J.Mothersele 00.00.1972

13. **Christmas Hangover**   18m   HS,4b
Climbs the groove just right of Christmas Cracker. Climb the nose to a ledge, then follow the line of least resistance up right to finish.
J.Mothersele 00.00.1972

14. **Slippery Jim**   18m   HVS,4c
Start just right of Christmas Hangover. Aim for the corner at the left side of the overhang. From this climb slightly left, moving up rightwards to finish up the groove.
J.Harwood, C.Horsfield 01.12.1974

15. **Strategic Zap Attack**   18m   E3,6b   *
Start just left of Twinkle Buttress and surmount the large roof at 12m. Powerful moves are needed to get over the roof at its widest point, PR.
M.Crocker, M.Ward, R.Thomas 26.04.1987

16. **Wazzock**   18m   HVS,5a   *
Start below the right hand side of the Strategic Zap Attack roof, below a groove. Gain the groove and climb it direct on good holds. Finish directly over the overlap.
J.Kerry 00.00.1971

Twinkle Buttress
The small prominent buttress standing out from the general line of the cliff. Descent is possible by Route 1 or by abseil (A1).

17. **Pillock**   15m   VS,4c
The overhanging chimney and shallow groove just left of Twinkle.
P.Thomas 00.00.1972

18. **Twinkle**   12m   D
Takes the easiest line on the left edge of the buttress.
J.Mothersele 00.00.1972

19. **Route 1**   12m   D
The obvious corner to the right of the buttress.
J.Mothersele 00.00.1972

20. **Canute Left Hand**   12m   HVS,5b
Take the middle of the face between Route 1 and Canute directly, to finish just left of Canute.
J.Harwood, M.Ismail 20.09.1998

21. Canute   12m   VD
To the right of Route 1 is a wall with a shallow corner on its right. Climb the crack on the right and move round left onto the wall. Follow a shallow groove up to the left.
C.Horsfield 00.00.1972

22. Canute Right Hand   12m   HVS,5a
Climb Canute to step right under a bulge to the foot of a shallow corner. Finish up this.
P.Thomas 00.00.1972

The next feature is the obvious corner and roof of Leprechaun.

23. Leprechaun   18m   E2,5c   *
A claasic piece of awkward climbing. Start 9m right of Route 1 at an obvious corner capped by a large overhang. Gain the overhang then move right to a bottomless corner. Go up to a flake crack then move left across blocks to the top.
J.Kerry 1pt 00.00.1973
FFA P.Littlejohn, J.Harwood, J.Mothersele 22.06.1977

The line of Oedipus Variation E3,6b (M.Learoyd, G.Royle 1984) has fallen down.

Fools Fantasy Area
To the right of Leprechaun, after a featureless undercut wall is a cave recess, with a large roof running over its back wall. The first route is based around the left arete of the recess.

24. Oedipus   18m   E3,6b
Gymnastic. Climb the left side of the blunt arete right of Leprechaun to bulges, then move up right and back left to gain a ledge above the roof. Move onto the face above and finish.
P.Littlejohn, A.Sharp 25.05.1978

25. Astrobrain   18m   E6,6b   *   \
Start just right of Oedipus. Climb steeply up right to a crack and into a pod. Traverse right to a block then up right again until a few moves lead to a PR. Bold moves up and left lead to an exit.
P.Littlejohn, R.Thomas 00.07.1986

26. Fools Fantasy   33m   E5,6a   **
A spectacularly awkward pitch which follows the lip of the cave. Climb a groove left of the cave to the first roof. Traverse rightwards around this and continue to beneath the main overhangs. Traverse right to pull round the right end of the roof finishing up a groove. The pegs are little more than rust, but good gear can still be placed. Hint: three ropes to start might relieve the drag, if one is dropped above the first lip.
P.Thomas, C.Horsfield 00.00.1974
FFA P.Littlejohn 06.07.1977

7. Wipeout   27m   E4,5c
A strenuous and greasy route. Climb the left-hand of the two overhanging grooves right of Fool's Fantasy, past a bulge, until it is possible to swing right and finish up a short wall. Gear is good but exceedingly awkward to place.
P.Thomas, C.Horsfield 00.00.1974
FFA P.Littlejohn, J.Mothersele 07.05.1977

28. Right Little Raver   27m   E5,6a   *
Good wall climbing between Wipeout and Nyth. Climb on good holds to a nut where the face is smoother and steeper. Continue to a flat greasy hold, then move up left to good nuts in a thin flake. Make a hard move up to gain the obvious crack out right, then traverse left into Wipeout to finish.
P.Littlejohn, M.Moran 29.04.1984

Fool's Fantasy Area

29. **Nyth**   27m   E3,6a   *
   The right-hand of the overhanging grooves right of Fools Fantasy. Climb the wall, keeping left of the crack, until level with the base of the groove. Climb the groove to the top.
   P.Thomas, J.Harwood 1pt 18.06.1975
   FFA P.Littlejohn, J.Mothersele 19.05.1977

30. **Disneyworld**   27m   E6,6c
   Climb the wall underneath the roof stack left of Pluto. At the roof, swing right onto the wall of Pluto, TRs. Step round left and make problematic moves over the roof, then continue up the wall above, 2 PRs.
   M.Crocker, R.Thomas 00.00.1990

31. **Pluto**   27m   VS,4c   ***
   A good line through some spectacular terrain, a must for any aspiring Ogmore leader. Climb the v-chimney 2m right of Nyth. Swing left near the top, to finish up the arete. It is also possible to finish direct at a slightly harder grade.
   C.Horsfield, P.Thomas 00.00.1972

Ogmore Popular End
Pluto marks the left side of a shallow bay 95 metres across.

32. **Open Invitation**   27m   E5,6b
   The smooth wall between Pluto and Finger Print gives a technical, reachy climb, with gear that is spaced and difficult to place. Might be E6 to on-sight. Ascend the easy crack just left of Finger Print and continue direct up the steep wall to a horizontal crack (good wires out left). Move right up to the next horizontal break, (crucial rock 3 or friend 0) then make a hard move to a small overlap and climb the thin crack in the leaning wall to the top.
   M.Crocker, M.Ward 01.06.1985

33. **Finger Print**   27m   E4,6a   **

A classy roof problem. Start under an overhang on the wall right of Pluto. Climb to the overhang, place wires above the roof where the PR used to be, then move over it and continue steeply up the crack to finish.
A.Sharp, S.Lewis 00.00.1977

34. **Thumbs Up**   27m   E4,6a   *

A fine pitch, which is slightly run out. Follow Fingerprint over the overhang, then traverse right above the lip to a small ledge. Climb the awkward wall above to the top.
P.Littlejohn, J.Mothersele 27.04.1984

To the right is a series of right facing and trending corners, with overhangs at their base. (Abbey Road to Megalopolis).

35. **Brothers In Arms**   27m   E6,6b   *

Amenable for the grade. The obvious crack in the impending left wall of the corner of Abbey Road. Climb to a small roof and good wires. Move over this into the thin crack above and a crafty no hands knee bar. Continue, 2PRs, up and into the crack, which splits a larger roof above. Continue through the roof and the crack above to the top.
M.Learoyd, R.Thomas 1pt 00.00.1985
FFA A.Sharp, P.Lewis 00.00.1986

36. **Abbey Road**   27m   HVS,5a   ***

Airy climbing up the first of the right-facing corners. Bridge up the cave for 4m then traverse right onto the wall. Climb to the overhang and follow the awkward right-hand groove to the next overhang. Step left and up to finish.
P.Thomas, C.Horsfield 00.00.1972

Ogmore Popular End   Photo: Roy Thomas

37. Roof Of The World   24m   E5,6b   **
A technical route with a complicated roof section and good protection. Follow The Gremlin to the roof at 12m, PR, step left and climb through the roof using a concealed pocket on the lip, PR. Finish up the wall just left of the arete to the top.
M.Crocker, M.Ward, R.Thomas 26.04.1987

38. The Gremlin   27m   E1,5a   *
Right of Abbey Road are two shallow grooves which meet at a more obvious v-groove. Climb the left, cracked groove and continue rightwards round the overhangs to a niche. Traverse right under the bulging wall to a groove and the top.
J.Kerry 00.00.1972

39. The Arrow   27m   E2,5c   **
A good pitch cutting through The Gremlin, with a taxing move to gain the smooth groove. Climb to a small roof 2m right of Gremlin. Move left onto the wall. Gain the smooth groove/corner, then pull out left at the roof and continue round the overhanging blocks on the left to finish up a short corner on the right.
J.Kerry 00.00.1972
FFA A.Sharp, J.Harwood 20.08.1977

40. Titanic   27m   E4,6a
Climb the capped groove and arete right of The Arrow. Swing left with difficulty to gain a bottomless and unfriendly crack and the finishing groove of Gremlin.
J.Kerry 00.00.1972
FFA A.Sharp 17.04.1979

41. Mauritania   27m   E5,6b   \
Climb to the roof as for Titanic. Struggle out right over the roofs until it is possible to swing back left to the top, TR.
M.Crocker, R.Thomas 30.10.1988

42. Megalopolis   33m   E1,5a   *
A little left of centre of the left part of the bay 12m right of Abbey Road is a clean wall bounded on its left by a continuous overhang and a roof at the top. Bridge the cave to gain a corner crack leading to the roof. Traverse right to the second overhang. Overcome this to finish right. Hexes give more secure protection than friends.
J.Kerry 00.00.1972

43. Rat Fink   27m   HVS,4c   *
Bold. Climb the centre of the wall right of Megalopolis and move right to gain a thin crack. Climb it to a horizontal break 3m below the overhang and step right, away from the end of the Megalopolis traverse. Climb up the wall and finish slightly rightwards.It is also possibe to come in from the arete at E1.
P.Thomas, C.Horsfield 00.00.1974

44. Rat Fink Direct Start   24m   E1,5b   *
Start 3m right of Rat Fink. Climb steeply and pull over the roof using a large hold to gain the upper wall of Rat Fink.
P.Thomas, J.Harwood 17.05.1987

Many of the routes in the next section have been affected by storms. Questimodo (P.Littlejohn, A.Sharp 1977), A Sugar Free Diet (M.Crocker, R.Thomas 1989) and Drill For Glory (M.Crocker, M.Ward, R.Thomas 1988) are no longer viable.

45. Questimodo Direct   22m   E5,6a
This has survived the waves. Boldly layback the blank groove rising above the shallow cave right of Ratfink.
M.Crocker, R.Thomas 00.00.1988

The next section is characterised by three obvious flat roofs at 22m, just before the angle of the bay.

46. **Loaded Question**   27m   E3,5c   **

Interesting. Start below and to the left of the three large roofs. Climb the wall to a ledge at 9m and traverse left on undercuts to gain a thin finishing crack.

P.Littlejohn, J.Mothersele 20.06.1977

47. **Implausible Suggestion**   27m   E5,6a   **

Climb the wall just right of Loaded Question to gain the same ledge at 9m. Head up and right to the widest point of the roof, PR, small wires, then cut wildly out through it to an easy finish.

R.Thomas 00.08.1999

48. **Jumping Jack Flash**   33m   E1,5c   *

This takes the chimney between the two left-hand roofs. Climb a groove 5m left of a round cave to a niche below an overhang. Pull onto the left wall and continue to a recess below the overhang. Move right to blocks then left to a chimney. Climb the chimney and the crack on the left to finish.

P.Thomas, C.Horsfield 00.00.1974

FFA A.Sharp, J.Harwood 20.08.1977

49. **Griffin**   32m   E3,6a   **

Start just right of Jumping Jack Flash at a round cave. Climb the vague corner left of the round cave until it becomes a vertical cave at 7m. Place good runners in the back right hand wall of the cave, then swing across its left wall to a hanging groove. Up this to easier ground and a stance in the corner below the main overhang and finish up either corner.

C.Heard, R.Heard A1 00.00.1976

FFA A.Sharp, J.Harwood 14.09.1977

50. **Pinocchio**   36m   HVS,4c   ***

This should be on every climber's tick list. The climb finishes up a short chimney on the right side of the three overhangs. Climb a leftward rising crack/corner line below and right of the overhangs to a ledge beneath a steep wall. Traverse left past a crack above and climb the bulging wall to a chimney. Climb the chimney, step left along the lip of the overhang, with your stomach in your mouth. Continue up left to a crack which is followed to a pinnacle, sit down and consider those who were at their limit when it was graded VS!

J.Kerry, C.Horsfield 00.00.1972

51. **The Flasher**   84m   HVS,4a,4b,4c,5a,4c

A poor right to left girdle, starting at the pinnacle as for Exposure Explosion. The only good pitch is above Fingerprint at 5a.

1. 7m Move round the outside of the pinnacle, descend a crack/chimney to belay under an overhang.

2. 21m Follow the break out left to a corner, (Megalopolis).

3. 22m Continue along the break into a corner (Abbey Road) via a steep hand traverse.

4. 16m Traverse around the arete and descend slightly before reaching the top of a crack, (Fingerprint). Continue into a corner then move out left onto the arete.

5. 18m Traverse left to a swing across a bottomless corner. Cross a grassy groove and climb a crack on the left to finish.

S.Robinson F.Lunnon AL 18.04.1979 - 10.08.1980

52. **Exposure Explosion**   84m   HVS,4a,4b,4c,4c,4a,4a,5a***

A brilliant left to right girdle that has seen its fair share of epics with people being lowered into the sea, complete with expensive cameras and watches, due to poor rope work and an inability to communicate. The route is best climbed when "the waves are crashing below slobbering and sucking like some disgusting animal". It starts from the pinnacle described in the Western Approach (A4).

1. 7m From the right (east) side of the pinnacle descend a crack and chimney to belay in a confined area at the start of the traverse.

2. 20m Follow the break out right to a stance on the arete prior to entering Wet Look cave (This is the top of Elephant Wall P1).

3. 8m Traverse round the arete to the cave of Wet Look.

4. 11m Climb rightwards out of the cave to belay on good ledges outside the cave.

5. 26m Continue right to belay on a small stance on a prominent buttress (this is part of Scutch).

6. 7m Traverse right around the arete to a belay in a corner/chimney (Siren).

7. 8m Traverse right for 5m then make hard moves up to gain the top.

L.Ainsworth, etc. - P2-P7 00.00.1974

P.Thomas, C.Horsfield - All 00.00.1974

Elephant Wall Area

This is the rather featureless pale wall forming the right side of the 'Popular End' bay. Pinocchio takes the left side of it. The following routes from Easy Livin' to Elephant Wall may be climbed when the tide is quite high, by abseiling to a small ledge below a fine wall split by two horizontal breaks. There is an abseil point at the top (A5). Large Friends are useful and above the second break the rock should be treated with some care. The wall is sunny in the evenings and usually free of seepage.

53. **Easy Livin'**   36m   E3,5c   **

A fine climb with a bold start and a tricky middle section. Start in the middle of the ledge and climb up a groove. Step left and move left into a groove leading to the first horizontal break. Pull around the left side of an overlap and climb the steep wall to the second, more friable, break. Finish direct.

P.Littlejohn, J.Mothersele 23.06.1977

54. **Wave Band**   36m   E2,5b   *

Start below the faint cracks in the smooth steep rock right of Easy Livin'. Climb easily to the ledges below the smooth steep rock. From their right side climb directly up the smooth wall crossing two breaks to reach a short crack leading to the top.

P.Littlejohn, J.Harwood 26.10.1977

Ogmore- Elephant Wall Area

Elephant Wall

Photo: Roy Thomas

55. Slime Crime   36m   HVS,5a

As for Wave Band to the ledges. Follow a short corner on the right side of the face to a horizontal break, pull into the hanging corner and continue directly to the top.

J.Harwood, M.Rhodes 17.02.1980

56. Elephant Wall   35m   VS,4b   *

Start as for Wave Band to the ledges. Step right and climb the knobbly wall to the horizontal break and a possible stance. Step up and right at the break and climb a short groove and steep wall above.

P.Watkin 00.00.1972

Tusker Chimney Area

The next routes are round the right arete of Elephant Wall, in a recessed bay.

57. Mind Probe   33m   E2,5b   *

Strenuous and bold at the start. Climb the chimney 8m right of Elephant Wall and just left of an arete for 5m. Move left to a diagonal crack in the arete. Climb the crack then traverse left into a groove on the front of Elephant Wall and continue to the horizontal break. Finish up the groove in the arete.

A.Sharp, P.Thomas 00.00.1972

58. Wet Probe   33m   E3,5c   *

As for Mind Probe, but continue straight up from the diagonal crack.

B.Brewer, A.McCarthy 08.07.1999

59. Wet Look   33m   HVS,4c,4c   *

This gains the wet cave high up on the crag.

1. 15m Climb the bulging wall below the left side of the cave to gain the cave.
2. 18m Traverse left on small holds to reach good horizontal cracks, used to gain and climb a chimney.

P.Thomas, C.Horsfield 00.00.1971

2m right is a square-cut chimney taken by Tusker Chimney and a prominent black prow taken by Domestic Bliss.

60. Tusker Chimney   33m   HVS,5a,5b   **

A route of character, with two contrasting pitches. Start below the square-cut chimney in the right part of the bay.

1. 22m Climb the leftward-slanting crack and square-cut chimney to a roof. Step left onto a small slab and traverse right under the roof, then move up to a belay ledge.
2. 11m Climb easily up and right, then take a steep wall to a crescent shaped overhang. Make a hard traverse right, then finish up a groove.

C.Horsfield, P.Thomas 00.00.1972

61. Flyover   36m   E3,5c,5b   **

Fine positions on the exposed top pitch. Start 2m right of Tusker Chimney.

1. 18m Climb a capped groove until a traverse left can be made, passing the remains of a PR, to a good hold. Take the edge above then move right to belay as for Tusker Chimney.
2. 18m Pull up the wall to reach a leftwards traverse above the lip of the cave and beneath a small roof. Follow this to a crack splitting the roof, leading to a ledge and easier ground.

R.Thomas, G.Royle 00.05.1986

62. Domestic Bliss   30m   E1,5b,5a

1. 18m Up the groove as for Flyover, but swing right onto a prow. Climb up a rib to the Tusker Chimney belay.
2. 12m Climb the steep wall left of Tusker Chimney. Trend back right after overcoming the bulge.

M.Learoyd, R.Thomas, G.Royle 00.00.1984

63. **Domestic Responsibility**   30m   E2,5a,5c   *
1. 18m Start on the right side of the black prow right of Flyover. Step onto a crinkly wall and move up left to good holds on an arete. Pull round left at a horizontal crack and move up to belay as for Tusker Chimney.
2. 12m Move up and right below the finish of Tusker Chimney. Make a long reach for a hidden jug and finish steeply up the wall above.
G.Lewis, C.Hurley 00.00.1983

64. **Tusker Right Hand**   33m   HVS,5b
Climb the chimney and crack 6m right of Tusker Chimney to the horizontal break, then climb directly up the wall 1m left of an obvious crack (Flash Harry).
C.Horsfield 00.00.1972

65. **Flash Harry**   24m   HS,4a   **
The best route of its grade at Ogmore, taking a proud buttress 13m right of Tusker Chimney. Climb via a groove to an obvious crack 1½m right of Tusker Right Hand, thence to the top.
P.Thomas 00.00.1972

66. **Yorkshire Pud**   24m   S
A slight variant on Tim's Route. Follow the easiest line up the cracked arete right of Flash Harry.
M.Rhodes, J.Harwood 20.01.1980

67. **Tim's Route**   24m   VD
Start just left of the obvious corner on the right side of the bay and follow the easiest line up the right-hand side of the grooved arete.
J.Mothersele 00.00.1972

68. **Mordred**   24m   HVS,4c
The obvious corner right of Tim's Route and 9m right of Flash Harry on the left side of a seaward-facing buttress.
B.Davies 00.00.1972

Scutch Buttress
This is the pillar just right of Mordred. The toe of the buttress is difficult to pass except at very low tides.

69. **The Dribbling Douh What**   24m   HVS,4c
Climb the arete right of Mordred. Poorly protected.
P.Thomas, A.Sharp 00.00.1975

70. **Scutch**   27m   HVS,5b
Climb front of the buttress to a steep crinkly wall. Move left to its centre and gain the horizontal break with difficulty. Continue carefully to the top.
P.Thomas, J.Harwood 12.06.1974

71. **Cold Front**   27m   HVS,5b
As for Scutch, but keep to the right side of the face. Step onto the arete 3m below the horizontal break and climb a groove above the break to finish.
M.Learoyd, R.Thomas, H.Griffiths 00.00.1984

Tiger Bay
Right of Scutch Buttress is the start of the huge Tiger Bay area. The prominent chimney bounding the left side wall is Siren Direct. To the right of the large cave of Siren is a wall of steep compact rock, Sorcery Wall. The crag makes a long sweep into a recessed bay, before moving out seaward as Fire Wall. Running between Scutch Butress and Siren direct is the left retaining wall of the bay, which is split by an obvious diagonal chimney ramp, Siren Direct.

Left Wall

72. **Quick Draw**   27m   E4,6a   **
Start at the toe of the arete right of Cold Front on its right-hand side. Climb to a deep crack and follow the curving line rightwards, TR, to join the sloping ramp/chimney of Siren. Hard moves up and left, PR, gain a small ledge. From here climb a groove to a PR, move out left onto the main open face, TR, pull over a small overhang and continue to the top.
R.Thomas, J.Bullock 04.05.1987

73. **Hired Gun**   27m   E4,6a   *
A sustained pitch. Start at the ramp of Siren and climb a green crack to broken blocks below the overhang (directly up from where Quick Draw swings left). Swing left over an overhang and continue to the top.
M.Learoyd, G.Royle 00.00.1984

74. **Siren**   33m   HVS,5a   *
This follows a rampline in a chimney running up towards the top of the Siren Direct chimney. Gain the ramp from the left and follow it until it narrows (or from below at dead low tide). Make blind moves right and climb the chimney/corner to finish. Intimidating for the grade.
Unknown Pre-1975

75. **Fair Exchange**   30m   E3,6a
An obvious horizontal crack runs from Siren to the flake crack in the left side wall of the chimney of Siren Direct. Gain this crack from Siren and follow it to the jagged flake crack. Climb it, TRs, to join the chimney of Siren Direct.
R.Thomas, John Bullock 1pt 00.00.1984
FFA A.Sharp, O.Jones 00.00.1986

76. **Siren Direct**   21m   VS,4c
Start on the right of the cave and climb the overhanging, narrowing chimney to join Siren.
M.Learoyd, H.Griffiths Pre-1983

Traverses Of Tiger Bay

77. **Total Eclipse Of The Sun**   200m   E8 6b   ***   \
A momentous traverse of Tiger Bay, graded from the deep water solo. The grade for a conventional ascent is unknown. Soloing applicants will need to study the drop-out zones at low tide and reserve any serious attempts to times when sea, weather, and tidal conditions come together in an optimal state. This is a spring tide, but one low enough to allow the crossing to Sorcery to be made. The climbing is very sustained, and involves three contrasting crux sections, 8-12m above the sea, with as little as 3m of water below. Elsewhere, sea depth rarely exceeds 5m. Despite the lack of water, chalk bag protection is required, which has allegedly been supplied by a pair of £4.99 water wings. The route is described in sections for convenience although it was soloed right through on the only ascent to date. These would be possible belays for a conventional ascent.
1. Reverse Siren to ledges near the bottom of the scoop. Cut loose rightwards across the hand-traverse of Fair Exchange to get into the chimney. Step right onto Mantra and make a 6a traverse right and down slightly to the projecting ledge on Sorcery.
2. Move up and swing right onto the ramp of Spellbinder. Follow this to the wide slot after 7m. Move right along the lip of the large roof passing a 6b crux to easier ground on Zardoz. Move up and continue right beneath a roof (as for Daughter of Regals P2), until good holds lead over the bulge and rightwards to a rest on a slight rib (escape onto A Bigger Splash possible).
3. Drop down 2m to the start of a spectacular undercut hand traverse moving across a corner above Warlock. Make increasingly difficult moves to swing around onto a sit-down ledge on the arete past a second 6b crux and gain the stance of Warlock.
4. Reverse a slab diagonally rightwards for 10m to a corner that bounds the left side of the back wall of the cave. Traverse the back-wall at half-height, then use a projecting plate to gain good ledges on the right arete of the back wall (5c). Traverse right to the top of a cleft at the back of the cave.

5. Traverse right beneath the roof to a blank-out. Summon up finger-power and make a hard, greasy 6b move to jugs and a shake-out on the edge of a descending ramp. Reverse the ramp, shedding height reassuringly quickly and gain a rest on a projecting ledge just above the high water mark. Work rightwards, pleasantly low, across Fury, to the line of holds on Fire.

6. Climb Fire to a good hand-ledge above its crux (5c). Make a short hand-traverse right into the broken crack of Brimstone, and follow it carefully to the top.

7. Reverse steeply up the grass banking, turn right and go to the pub.
M.Crocker solo 10.8.1999

| 78. **A Bigger Splash** | 73m | E3,5c,5b | *** |

An excellent, sustained girdle from left to right. Start from the chimney of Siren and finish above the huge sea cave above Tiger Sanction. Muscles are needed on the P1 and a cool head on P2. Start 9m down the chimney of Siren Direct.

1. 45m Traversing right along a line of weakness 2m lower than the final pitch of Exposure Explosion. Move right around the arete and climb strenuously until the angle eases (possible belay and escape). Climb up and right and continue the traverse to a projecting ledge on the arete.

2. 27m Traverse into a corner formed by the back of the zawn. Climb up and traverse right along the lip of the huge roof until it is possible to climb up for 3m to a line of flat holds. Step right to a crack and climb this and the break above to finish. Stake belay well back.
P.Littlejohn solo - P1 04.07.1977
P.Littlejohn, A.Sharp, S.Lewis 01.10.1977

Sorcery Wall

This is the wall running across the back of Tiger Bay, bounded on its right by Fire Wall. The first obvious feature is the groove above a prominent shelf, Sorcery itself. The first route is just right of the chimney of Siren Direct.

| 79. **Mantra** | 36m | E5,6a | ** |

Takes a strenuous and intimidating line up the left of the wall immediately right of Siren Direct. Climb the right hand side of a rib on the right edge of the cave to a small slot. Pull right round the bulge to some small ledges, then climb boldly diagonally rightwards to good holds in a horizontal break. Continue direct to the Bigger Splash break, then follow a thin continuation crack to the top.
M.Crocker, M.Ward 01.06.1985

| 80. **The Enchanted** | 36m | E5,6a | * ᨖ |

Currently done as a deep water solo since it has no gear. Traverse 2m right from the small foot-ledges on Mantra and power up a small green corner. Finish direct to gain the break of A Bigger Splash.
M.Crocker solo 10.08.99

| 81. **The Uncanny Direct** | 36m | E6,6c | *** |

Start below an initial leaning wall 4m right of Mantra, down and left of the projecting shelf of Sorcery. Climb easily to a recess at 3m, possible belay, then cross bulges, PR, TR, to a ledge then an overlap on the arete, PR. Pull over the overlap and static up right to a good hold. Another hard move gains The Bigger Splash break, from where a direct line up the thin crack, left of a shallow scoop in the headwall, leads to the top.
P.Oxley 14.05.1988

| 82. **The Uncanny** | 36m | E6,6c | ** |

The orignal line, gaining the overlap from the shelf of Sorcery. Bolder than the direct version.
M.Crocker, M.Ward 16.06.1985

| 83. **Buzzarena** | 40m | E6,6c | ** • |

From the projecting ledge of Sorcery, make one move up, then span left for a finger hold. Up the arete on improving holds to the the break of A Bigger Splash. Graded for a deep water solo, gaining the Sorcery shelf by traversing in along the footledges from Mantra. The grade for a conventional ascent is unknown.
M.Crocker solo 10.08.1999

Siren Area

Photo: Carl Ryan

84. **Sorcery**   36m   E6,6b   **

A committing climb taking a shallow overhanging groove 9m right of Siren, possibly the first E6 of this type in Britain. Gain the projecting ledge at 7m via an akward flake groove. Climb up right to the bold groove. Move up this until it is possible to move right and up to gain a horizontal break (A Bigger Splash). Traverse left for 3m then go directly through the overhangs via a groove to the top.
P.Littlejohn, S.Robinson 25.07.1979

85. **Spellbinder**   45m   E4,6a   ***

A superbly sustained climb through spectacular territory, giving one of the best E4s in Brtiain. The boldness of the start can be reduced with small wires and patience. Start right of Sorcery at a vague corner beneath the rightward-rising ramp line. Climb to a big slot and good thread, then traverse up and right, crux, to gain a smaller slot. From the right end of the slot, climb straight up to reach the horizontal break of Bigger Splash. Continue directly over the overhang and steep wall above to a groove by a detached block. From ledges finish up the arete of the large corner on the right, or walk off left.
P.Littlejohn, A.Sharp 29.09.1977

86. **Flying Wizard**   42m   E5,6a   **

As for Spellbinder to below the widest part of the roofs. Break out left over the roofs and climb steeply to the top.
P.Littlejohn, T.Penning 15.07.1983

87. **Worn Out Superman**   30m   E6,6b   ***

Staggering. Start 4m right of Spellbinder, under an overhanging scoop. Go up the scoop, swing rightwards along a break and over a small roof, 2TRs, to gain the Spellbinder ramp. Step right and from a short crack go through the bulge above, PR, to reach Bigger Splash. Break through the ceiling above via a notch, PR. Trend leftwards then rightwards up the committing headwall to the top. At the time of writing (2003) the threads are missing.
M.Crocker, R.Thomas 20.10.1990

88. **Zardoz**   45m   E5,6b,5c   **

Bold. Start beneath the broad white wall to the right of Spellbinder, just to the right of a roof.

1. 24m Climb to ledges beneath the roof. Move right to gain a small sloping ledge then make devious moves leftwards over a bulge to gain a shallow groove, leading to good holds beneath the next set of overhangs. Break left, then go straight up to a small hanging stance where the angle eases (on A Bigger Splash).

2. 21m Climb rightwards to a line of overhangs and traverse right to stand on the obvious projecting strata. Climb straight up the compact upper wall for 4m before bearing slightly right to the top.

P.Littlejohn, A.Richardson 14.04.1982

89. **Daughter of Regals**   45m   E5,6b,6a   ***

1. 27m As for Zardoz until after the groove below the second roof, then traverse right for 3m to a narrowing and pull over to a ledge and a hanging stance.

2. 18m Climb the 2m roof above the stance slightly right of the belay, to a good break. Trend right to an arete and finish via a thin crack on its left side.

M.Crocker, M.Ward 30.06.1985

90. **Totality**   25m   E6 6b   *** \

Totally inspiring climbing up the line of cracks and the roofed corner right of Daughter Of Regals and left of Warlock. Strenuous with protection hard to get and place. Start on the right-hand side of an inlet in the wave-cut platform immediately left of Warlock. Swing left above the inlet and gain and stand up on a finger-jug up to the left, bold. Pull up to a rest in a corner at the foot of the crack system. Pass the roof and off-width above with difficulty to power up bulging rock to jugs in a niche below another roof. Extend past a TR to a final roof, PR. A final strenuous move gains a jug-line above. Swing left and follow easier rock for 5m to a good belay ledge. Escape up Warlock P2 to the right.

M.Crocker, E.Travers-Jones 14·08.1999

91. **Warlock**   51m   E6,6b,5b   ***

Magnificent, although the gear is totally rotten and badly in need of replacement. Start 6m right of Zardoz from a narrow platform, just left of the huge cave and on the right side of a narrow rift.

1. 24m Climb the bulging wall TR, and groove, PRs, to below the roof. Traverse right along a narrow wall until a series of hard moves up right gains a jug on the hanging arete, PRs. Climb a short corner to a good stance.

2. 27m Traverse spectacularly left to a thin crack and follow this and an easy groove to a projecting ledge on the right. Finish up a wide crack.

R.Thomas, C.Parkin 06.01.1985

FFA M.Crocker, M.Ward 31.08.1985

The final manifestation of the back wall of Tiger Bay is a huge cave with a steeply undercut base. Tereus and The Tiger Sanction gain this wall by coming in from the right.

92. **Tereus**   51m   E6,6a,6b,5b   ** \

Start just outside the mouth of the cave at its right-hand side.

1. 21m Climb easily leftwards to a bay. Continue left to a break below bulging rock and swing left into a bottomless groove on small holds. Climb the groove for 2m and traverse left to a crack leading to the Total Eclipse break. Traverse left to belay on a small stance on the arete.

2. 18m Move up to the base of the hanging back wall. Trend left to pass a roof and gain a wide break. Mantle awkwardly onto a projecting block in another break, PR and gain a hanging groove on the right. Follow the groove to the right-hand end of the balanced block on Tiger Sanction. Tiptoe left along this and pull left to a belay on the foot ledge at the base of the headwall.

3. 12m Finish as for A Bigger Splash P2.

D.Pickford, M.Crocker AL 20.05.2001

93. **The Tiger Sanction**   57m   E5,6a,5c   * \

The original daunting expedition into the cave at the back of Tiger Bay. Start on its right side 6m left of the corner of Fury

1. 33m Climb up to a leftwards pointing block ledge, step right then climb the wall to a TR below the roofs. Move

left, pull over the roof and swing left round a rib. Traverse left, low at first, PR, then at a slightly higher level to a projecting shattered rib just right of the huge crack line, PB. Place a high runner to protect the second.

2. 30m Pull up left then traverse left on biscuits to a short bottomless groove. Up the groove, then step left onto a balanced block and pull over the roof onto the headwall. Climb the headwall stepping left to exit at a short crack.
M.Crocker, G.Gibson 25.08.1985

Fire Wall
The obvious right-hand wall of Tiger Bay.

94. **Fury**   30m   E3,5c   *

In the centre of Fire wall is an obvious arched recess. Climb the left corner of the recess then move up and pull leftwards round an overlap to a ledge. Climb the compact wall and continue carefully up the cheese band to a small ledge. Step right then climb straight up on good holds.
P.Littlejohn, C.Heard 00.00.1983

95. **Burn 'Em Up**   33m   E5,6b   ***

A brilliant pitch up the centre of Fire Wall, good rock and protection. Follow Fury to ledges below the first roof, swing right onto the wall and climb a thin crack, then move right to and through the second roof. Climb directly up the centre of a convex overlap (crux), to gain a PR and the cheese band. Finish direct.
M.Crocker, R.Thomas 21.07.1985

96. **Fire**   30m   E3,5c   **

RPs at the start and friends in the middle section have removed much of the bite of this fine pitch. Climb a vague crack 6m from the right edge of Fire Wall to a roof, over this then up the wall above to smooth rock and a rest. Climb conglomerate holds to regain good rock, a thin crack and the top.
P.Littlejohn, J.Mothersele 18.05.1977

Fire Wall   *Photo: Carl Ryan*

97. Deep Fry   36m   E5,6b   \
A direct start to Brimstone. Unrepeated since the loss of the crucial PR. Start 2m right of Fire. Climb a groove to where it starts to overhang. More difficult climbing past the remains of a PR, leads to good holds enabling the crack of Brimstone to be gained. Finish up Brimstone.
M.Crocker, M.Ward 26.04.1986

98. Brimstone   30m   E1,5a   *
This climb gains the shattered crack on the right edge of Fire Wall via a traverse from the corner round to the right. Climb the left wall of the corner to a crack 2m right of the arete, move up to good holds and traverse strenuously left around the arete to the base of the crack. Climb it.
P.Littlejohn, J.Mothersele 00.03.1977

The route The Kickenside (E1,5b S.Lewis, J.Harwood 1978) has been superceded by others. It linked up the start of the Knave with the finish of Well Blessed.

99. The Knave   27m   E3,5c
Climb the arete between Brimstone and the Bishop to meet the hand traverse of Brimstone. Hard moves up right lead to a groove. Up this, then left to large holds right of Brimstone. Finish direct.
M.Learoyd, R.Thomas 00.00.1985

100.Well Blessed   27m   E2,5b
Climb the easier lower section of The Bishop, until it is possible to move left to horizontal holds below a small pod. Move past the pod and climb the right-hand groove up to the overhangs. Move through these carefully to the top.
R.Thomas, G.Royle 00.00.1984

101.The Bishop   27m   HVS,4c,4b   *
On the right side of the bay is a large, protruding buttress. The climb takes the chimney and cave on its left.
1. 13m Climb easily to the cave, bridge up this, pull over the roof to gain a small, square chimney and belay.
2. 14m Traverse right to the arete and continue up a groove taking care near the top.
C.Horsfield, P.Thomas A0 00.00.1972
FFA P.Thomas, A.Sharp 00.00.1975

102.Cone Country   27m   HVS,5a   *
Climb the middle of the wall right of The Bishop to the overhang, traverse 1m right and pull over just left of the arete. Continue up the groove as for The Bishop.
P.Lewis, J.Harwood 03.07.1980

103.Bute Street   30m   E3,5b
The left side of the seaward face of the buttress to an overhang. Step right to the centre of the face, over the overhang on friable holds and up for 3m. Traverse left to join the groove of The Bishop.
P.Watkin, P.Thomas 00.00.1971
FFA P.Littlejohn, J.Harwood 11.12.1977

The buttress now returns in a high wall to the obvious corner crack of Poseidon.

104.Spring Tide   27m   E2,5b   **
Climb just right of the left edge of the wall until a band of high horizontal cracks is reached. Pull over these until a final smoother wall leads to the top.
R.Thomas, G.Davies 00.00.1984

Spring Tide and Low Ebb can be joined up by a hand traverse - Beyond Poseidon (E2,5b R.Thomas, G.Royle 1984).

105. Low Ebb   30m   E3,5c   **

Excellent, sustained climbing with the crux at the top. Climb the finger crack a metre or two left of Poseidon, then move onto steep horizontal strata. Follow these directly up the centre of the face to the bottom of a smooth steep headwall. Up this to finish.
R.Thomas, J.Bullock 00.00.1984

106. Poseidon   27m   HVS,5a   *

Follows the obvious corner crack. Climb the initial groove and step left into the corner. Follow this gingerly over a small overhang to a larger one. Traverse right to a ledge and continue to the top.
P.Thomas, J.Mothersele 00.00.1972

107. Poseidon Direct Finish   12m   E1,5a

From the overhang on Poseidon continue straight up the corner and exit with great care.
R.Thomas, R.Haslum 00.00.1983

The Castle Area

There is now a broad sweep of crag continuing to a small sea stack (The Castle). The bottom part of the crag is mostly good rock but care should be taken with all the exits, which are on rubble. A generally disappointing area.

108. Scorcher   30m   E3,6a

Start 3m right of Poseidon at a crack. Climb direct for 6m, move right to a runner slot, step up right and climb to the overhangs. Pass these via a thin crack. Continue for 3m, then move right and up to a corner at an overhang. Turn it on the left to a final crack and the top.
P.Littlejohn, C.Heard 09.07.1983

109. Dracula   42m   E2,5c,5b,4b   *

A good route, but ensure that P3 is your mate's lead. Start below a pod like recess right of the large cave.
1. 9m Climb to the recess, then out of it, before making a hard traverse left to reach a stance above the roof.
2. 21m Move left and reach a hanging groove/crack, which cuts through the roof. Up this strenuously to better holds. Continue until able to move right to the middle of a long ledge.
3. 12m Traverse left and pull into the obvious groove/chimney leading to the top.
P.Thomas, C.Horsfield 00.00.1974
FFA P.Littlejohn, Ward-Tetley 05.04.1977

110. Son of Dracula   35m   E4,6a,5a   *

1. 21m Climb into the recess as for Dracula. Move out right onto the face and climb the wall and shallow overhanging grooves leading through the overhang on the left to a ledge. Belay just above.
2. 14m Traverse right for 3m then climb up left above an overhang, finishing up the slab.
P.Littlejohn, J.Mothersele 18.05.1977

111. Blood Lust   36m   E4,6b,4c   *   \

1. 24m Climb the wall just right of Dracula, trending left at the top, to a break. Move up and right into a groove, PR. Follow this and the wall above the roofs, moving left to ledges and a belay.
2. 12m Climb a crack and groove to the top.
M.Crocker, R.Thomas 21.07.1985

112. Dog Day Afternoon   39m   E1,5b,4b

A fine first pitch, steep and interesting. Start 4m right of Dracula and 13m right of the corner of Poseidon below a rightward-slanting line.
1. 27m Climb to a horizontal crack at the base of some smoother rock. Move up rightwards to a white niche, follow the groove above and finish rightwards taking care with some holds.
2. 12m Climb the corner crack on the left to the top.
P.Littlejohn, J.Mothersele AL 06.03.1977

Gav Williams - Waveband (E2,5c) Ogmore
(Page 247) Photo: Carl Ryan

Alison Pesticco - Flash Harry (HS,4a) Ogmore
(Page 249) Photo: Carl Ryan

113.   **Flying Fortress**   39m   E1,5b,4c
1. 24m As for Dog Day Afternoon to the white niche. Climb up rightwards to a corner, then right onto the arete. Continue up a loose groove to belay on the left of a large ledge.
2. 15m Climb the slab just right of the arete for 6m, move left and climb a groove to the final overhang, which is turned on the left.
S.Massey, S.Bartlett 06.04.1979

114. **Keep Smiling**   39m   E2,4b,5b,5c
This crosses Dog Day Afternoon on a counter diagonal line. Start beneath a large cave at 7m.
1. 7m Climb to the cave.
2. 21m Traverse to the arete and move up to a small cave. Traverse left for 6m past a groove (Dog Day Afternoon) to reach a crack leading to a huge detached flake overhang. Climb diagonally leftwards from the flake overhang to a stance, TR.
3. 11m Climb to the final large roof and surmount it via the widest and most central crack.
D.Cuthbertson, P.Littlejohn 15.02.1981

115. **Wounded Knee**   42m   E3,5b,4c
Strenuous and committing climbing weaving through the overhangs left of Stronghold. Start 3m left of the overhung cave, 12m left of the arete opposite The Castle stack.
1. 27m Climb the wall on good holds, then traverse right below the overhangs to the crack rising from the cave. From its top gain the arete and climb direct through the overhangs to reach a crack leading to ledges. Belay as for Stronghold, on the largest ledge to the left.
2. 15m As for Flying Fortress.
P.Littlejohn, J.Mothersele 24.04.1977

116. **Stronghold**   42m   HVS,5a,4c
Start 4m left of the arete opposite The Castle stack at a leaning wall of conglomerate rock that gives surprisingly solid climbing.
1. 27m Climb up and left to some conspicuous slots. Continue up for 3m then go diagonally left to reach an area of ledges.
2. 15m As for Flying Fortress.
P.Littlejohn, J.Mothersele AL 13.03.1977

117. **The Castle**   44m   VS,4b,4b
Start opposite The Castle stack, at a boulder below obvious grooves in the upper wall.
1. 22m Climb to a flat ledge, continue up right, then left to another ledge. Take care with the rock.
2. 21m Climb a groove and pull over a bulge to a ledge. Follow another groove for 3m to a chockstone, then traverse left to another groove. Climb this to an earthy groove and finish up the crack on the left.
J.Kerry, C.Horsfield 00.00.1972

118. **Western Shout Out**   39m   HVS,4c,5a
Loose and poor. It takes the lower arete and left-hand crack high on the wall.
1. 16m Climb the arete on the left to an overhanging cleft. Take this on the right to a flat ledge.
2. 22m From the ledge move left following a broken crack and smaller ledges to a larger one (escape possible leftwards). Move up a thin crack in a short steep wall, making an awkward mantleshelf on the right. Follow the dirty crack in the wall to a large niche, to exit carefully past the overhang.
S.Robinson, F.Lunnon 24.03.1979

119. **Weakhold**   45m   HVS,5a
A wandering right to left girdle. Climb the arete opposite the Castle for 10m, traverse left into a bay and finish up The Castle.
G.Lewis, etc 00.00.1984

Ogmore

The Biscuit
The next bay is composed of horizontal strata of brittle yellow rock, the Ogmore biscuit variety. The climbing is exposed, frightening and topping out generally leaves people shaking. Well worthwhile and more deserving of the accolade of adventure climbing than anything at Linney Head. The area is bounded on the left by the spectacularly obvious arete of Cream Crackers. Routes can be reached by abseil (A9).

120.**Wafer Thin**   39m   E2,5b
    1. 21m Climb the lower left-hand arete of the area to a ledge, PB.
    2. 18m Move up left onto a rocking block and pull over to a small ledge, PR. Continue up the crack.
    R.Thomas, J.Bullock 00.00.1988

121.**Cream Crackers**   42m   E5,5a,5c   **
    This takes the left side of the upper arete of the Biscuit. Totally 'out-there'.
    1. 21m As for Wafer Thin P1.
    2. 21m Pull directly over the prow at the start of the arete, PR, then move left onto the left side of the arete. Continue up this, 2PRs, to finish as for Information Received.
    R.Thomas, G.Royle, J.Bullock 00.00.1988

122.**Short Dread**   42m   E5,5a,5c   **
    1. 21m Climb the crack on the right side of the arete to a belay ledge.
    2. 21m Continue up P2 of Cream Crackers.
    R.Thomas, E.Travers-Jones 15.08.2000

123.**Information Received**   42m   E4,5a,5c
    A true biscuit route.
    1. 21m As for Wafer Thin or Short Dread P1.
    2. 21m Climb easily to a ledge. Swing up horizontal bands, TR, to pull around to the right side of an arete. Climb a short wall to beneath a small overhang, PR, up the crack on the right, PR, then back left, PR, to a scab of rock, PR. Climb just right of the arete, PR, then up the actual arete to the top.
    R.Thomas, G.Royle, M.Learoyd, J.Bullock 00.00.1986

124.**Takes The Biscuit**   45m   E4,5c   *   \
    A strenuous and demanding route right of Information Received. Start 3m right of the arete by a large boulder with a chimney above. Climb the chimney until it is possible to move left onto the wall, TR. Continue up the wall, PR, to gain the horizontal break, PRs, possible belay. Move left to gain a steep crack, follow this, PR, TR, to more horizontal bands. Move right, PR, to reach a continuation crack which is followed past 3TRs, to the top.
    R.Thomas, J.Bullock - lower section 06.09.1988
    R.Thomas, M.Crocker 30.10.1988

125.**Here Today**   45m   E3,5b,5b   \
    The chimney, yellow slab and steep headwall right of Takes The Biscuit. Start at a green cave.
    1. 15m Climb out of the cave and go up the steep chimney, PR, to exit left to a ledge. PB.
    2. 30m Climb the slabby yellow wall, PR, to finish up a steep crack.
    R.Thomas, G.Royle, J.Bullock 00.00.1988

126.**Mother Earth**   45m   E2,5a   *   \
    At the back of the bay is an earthy chimney providing the longest, most entertaining chimney pitch in South East Wales. Start left of the chimney and climb conglomerate rock until it is possible to step right into the chimney. Follow it past numerous threaded chockstones until an escape can be made rightwards just below the top to avoid the final mud slopes.
    R.Thomas, J.Bullock 00.00.1989

The next routes are on the large concave wall right of the earthy chimney. Several stakes are in position above the yellow wall and Quimble (A10).

127.Sleepless Nights   39m   E4,5c   *   \

A route of character approached easily by abseil at all but the highest tides. Friends are useful in the upper section. Start 10m right of Mother Earth. Climb the conglomerate pile then traverse left onto the wall above, PR. Climb this to easier angled rock, 3PRs, TR. Follow the upper wall just left of a shallow niche, PR, then continue up a disjointed crack, poor TR, over several bulges. Belay below the top on the abseil rope.
R.Thomas, G.Royle 28.10.1987

128.Best Of Friends   39m   E2,5a   \

Technically easy but serious. Large Friends are useful. Start 3m right of Sleepless Nights at a pile of conglomerate rock. Climb the rubble to a large jammed boulder, then over a small roof and follow a faint crack to the easy angled section, PR. Move rightwards then climb the steep upper wall over several bulges to gain a crack just below the top, exit rightwards.
R.Thomas, G.Royle, G.Davies 27.09.1987

129.Floozie   42m   XS,4b,4b

Looser than it looks! This takes the upper arete of the concave wall.
1. 21m Climb the rubble as for Best Of Friends and follow a rightward-rising traverse and a sharp broken corner, then move carefully rightwards to belay on the arete.
2. 21m Move right around the arete, following steep corners to the top.
G.Lewis, S.Robinson, F.Lunnon 06.07.1980

Further right is a high yellow wall with a block-strewn ledge at half-height. The finish to some routes is a steep earth bank and it is advisable to leave a rope in place. Brushing of the holds will be needed. The routes start from the large ledge which is best approached by abseil (A10).

130.Suspended Sentence   22m   E4,5c   \

The left-hand crack in the wall. Start at the left side of the ledge. Climb a shattered crack to a smaller ledge, step right to the main crack 2TRs and up it to a small overhang, PR. Pull out right to finish.
R.Thomas, G.Royle 00.05.1986

131.No Reprieve   22m   E3,5c   \

Start at the ledge, left of the right-hand crack. Climb a short wall to a ledge, move up left and follow a line of ledges to a leftward-rising flake traverse leading to a crack. Climb the final wall and crack, PR, TR. Belay on the rope.
R.Thomas, J.Bullock, M.Learoyd 00.05.1986

132.Have Mercy   21m   E4,6a   \

Climb the thin crack in the right side of the wall exiting to the right.
M.Crocker, G.Gibson, M.Ward 25.08.1985

133.Quimble   30m   VS,4b

Harrowment! The obvious line at the right side of this dubious section of cliff. Start below the prominent left-facing corner on the right side of the yellow wall. Climb to a niche, step left, move up to a ledge and climb the corner with little protection.
R.Crockett, M.Harber 30.03.1980

On the right side of the bay are the remains of several large sea caves. Huge rockfalls have destroyed the routes described in previous publications. The following remained at the time of writing (2003).

134.Towaway Zone   13m   HVS,5a

Only P1 remains! It is possible to combine this with P2 of Motor Torpedo. Start on the left side of the first, smaller, cave. Climb a shallow groove and crack to a small roof then traverse right to a ledge.
L.Foulkes, P.Lewis 00.00.1980

135.Motor Torpedo 48m E4,6a,5b \

A wild route breaking through the left side of the roofs of the largest cave. Start at the left side of the cave.
1. 27m Climb a short, sea washed wall, then a steeper compact wall rightwards to a small ledge in its centre. Move back left to some small ledges, PR. Traverse left along the lip of the roof to good jams, PR, up to a horizontal break, then move left to a good stance on a ledge.
2. 21m Traverse back right, avoiding the blocks, to a crack in the headwall. Climb it on good holds over a small roof. Trend left up the wall exiting directly.
M.Crocker, R.Thomas AL 08.06.1986

136.Goodnight Cowboy 30m E2,5b \

A line that has had three first ascents but only the last has stayed in place. Start at the sea-washed rocks between the caves or abseil into the cave. Climb smooth rock to gain a crack leading to the cave. Traverse left onto a very small ledge below a faint groove. Follow the groove to ledges then up a steep wall on incuts, PR, to gain a larger ledge. Take the groove above, 2PRs, until it is possible to escape with care up earthy ledges.
J.Mothersele, J.Kerry 00.00.1974
A.Dance, A.Richardson 00.00.1984
R.Thomas, J.Bullock 00.00.1989

Right of the rock fall is the cave from which the now defunct route, AIDS (E3,5c, some rests, R.Thomas, G.Lewis 1984) existed. On the buttress that remains are the next routes.

137.Sub Sonar 27m E4,6a \

Supersedes AIDS. Start at the shallow cave 5m left of Ultra Virus. Step onto a prow, and go through the roof on jugs, finishing as for Ultra Virus.
M.Crocker, R.Thomas 14.11.1994

138.Ultra Virus 30m E4,6a **

Great climbing through the roofs. Climb easily to a ledge below the widest part of the roof. Overcome the roof on the right 2PRs, then climb direct up the overhanging wall, PR, to a ledge at its top. Step right and climb the final wall leftwards.
M.Crocker, R.Thomas 11.05.1986

139.Last Buck 24m E1,5b

This takes a faint groove in the left side of the steep smooth white face to the right of Ultra Virus. Gain the groove easily and follow it strenuously to ledges. Finish direct.
C.Heard, R.Thomas 05.07.1980

140.Harmony 27m E1,5a * \

Follow Last Buck to the base of the white face, then continue up the face a couple of metres right of Last Buck to a wide break. Continue up the steepening headwall to exit up a slight flake/groove.
M.Crocker, J. Harwood 23.09.2001

141.Fast Buck 24m HVS,5a

Start on the left of the face almost below Last Buck. Climb easily rightwards until the wall steepens, continue right again to reach a detached block. Climb carefully to the top.
P.Littlejohn 03.07.1977

142.The Rock Block 25m E4,6a \

The blunt arete left of Trusty Blade. From Trusty Blade, gain a groove in the arete move left and exit via the chimney of Trusty Blade.
M.Crocker, R.Thomas 14.11.1993

143.A Foot In The Face   18m   E3,5c   \
As for The Rock Block to the short overhanging groove. Using holds to the right pull up then left above the overhang to good holds. Finish up and right to gain the safer right-hand exit of Trusty Blade.
M.Crocker 23.09.2001

144.Trusty Blade   27m   E2,5b
Start from the left edge of the cave on the right end of the wall. Climb up and onto the black prow, move steeply up to the base of a groove, PR. Follow the groove until it is possible to exit onto a ledge. Climb the loose chimney on the left.
R.Thomas, J.Bullock 00.00.1984

145.Trust To Luck   25m   E2,5b   \
A direct line up the right side of Fast Buck Wall. Start from the large rounded ledge, move up to a large overhang. Move round leftwards round this then take the brown streak to join the finish of Trusty Blade.
M.Crocker, R.Thomas 14.11.1993

?   Rainbow For Rory   20m   E6,6b   *** \
Climb easily up the right edge of the cave for 3m. Traverse left to a bottomless corner right of the roof stack at the back of the cave. Swing left across the lowest roof, overcome the next one then the third to grasp the highest handrail. Traverse left until a trick move at the end gains the finish of Trusty Blade. The route was done as a deep water solo and the grade for a conventional ascent is not known.
M.Crocker solo 12.08.2003

The routes from Trust The Grade to Happyrash have been done as deep water solos, so the grade at low water is unknown. They are described separately to the main text for this reason. Approach is by a bouncing abseil from two spikes (one very long) to arrive 2m left of the left-facing corner of Fast Luck. At high spring tide there should be about 6m of water below the base of the routes. Be careful with some of the blocky top outs and remember that there are strong undercurrents and sea caves at this crag.

146.Trust The Grade   15m   E3,5b   \
Jump south in the event of a fall. Climb the right edge of the cave, swing right and over a bulge and zig-zag up the wall above.
M.Crocker solo 06.05.2001

147.Mindfuck   15m   E5,5c   *** \
Traverse right from the ledge for 5m. Pull through a small overhang to a rest and follow left-facing flakes above. Swing right up bulging ground above.
M.Crocker solo 06.05.2001

148.Happyrash   15m   E5,6a   **
As for Mindfuck, but continue right for 2m to move up to the base of a small groove. Swing left, move up 2m, then span back right to gain positive flat holds through bulging ground to the top.
M.Crocker solo 06.05.2001

Davy Jones' Locker
To the right is the huge, atmospheric, sandy-floored cave of Davy Jones Locker. At all but the lowest tides the point to the right (east) of this cave is impassable.

149.Fast Luck   27m   E2,5b   *
Start at the buttress 15m left of Davy Jones' Locker, below an obvious corner high up. Climb up easily at first then move boldly over to gain the corner and follow this to the top.
R.Thomas, G.Royle 00.00.1984

150. Delirious 30m E6,4b,6b \

A gruelling route still one of the most serious undertakings at Ogmore. Start on the left side of the cave housing Davy Jones' Locker, left of a chimney.

1. 9m Climb the groove and rib to a good ledge.

2. 21m Pull into a short right groove and follow it strenuously to good spikes, then diagonally right to a large roof. A long reach, TR, leads to heel hooks along the lip and over it to a bulging wall. Finish straight up this.

M.Crocker, M.Ward 16.03.1986

? No Fakin' It 25m E7,6b ** \

Another last minute deep water solo addition, with an ambiguous description. Traverse right from an unspecified point into a right facinf corner. Above and right is a ceiling. Use a fingerjam in the corner to extend for a pocket way out right on the lip. Swing right to the ledge of Twenty First Century. Immediately left of a short overhung scoop and left of the end of the ledge use a finger pocket to get through the overhang and climb the overhanging wall to gain ledges about 2m left of Skullthuggery.

M.Crocker solo 16.06.2003

151. Twenty First Century 45m E5,5c,6a **

A tremendous route. Start just right of Delirious and left of a slanting chimney in the left retaining wall of the cave. An extra rope left at the top to back up the belay stakes would be wise.

1. 24m Climb a groove left of the chimney, swing left to a ledge at a break, climb steeply to a slot below a roof and pull over on jugs. Move up right, PR, and rightwards along a traverse line to a good stance on the edge of the cave.

2. 21m Traverse left at a higher level and climb a short groove, PR, over a roof on jugs and straight up the wall. Move out and out, passing a lot of very rusty PRs, until it is possible to pull over to easier ground and the top.

M.Crocker, R.Thomas 19.10.1986

152. Skullthuggery 45m E6,6a,6b ** \

Start as for Davy Jones' Locker at low tide or abseil down Twenty First Century and clip its gear.

1. 24m Follow Davy Jones' Locker to the top of the corner, swing up left and walk to the stance of Twenty First

Davy Jones Locker

Photo: Roy Thomas

Century.

2. 21m Cross the ceiling above the belay rightwards PR, to gain a ledge. Climb direct passing 2PRs, then when the good holds run out make fearsome moves to overcome the final roof, PR. Move leftwards, taking care with the loose rock on the easier finish.

M.Crocker, R.Thomas 00.00.1989

153. Davy Jones' Locker   51m   E7,6a,6b   ***   \

Those who are widely travelled enough to have walked into the bowels of the great sea cave of Davy Jones' Locker will agree that the cave roof represents one of the most spectacular challenges in Britain, taking one of its biggest free roofs. Start from the rear left of the cave at low tide. Retreat is cut off within 3 hours, so timing is important to ensure that the second climber is battling his way across the final roof as the sea thunders into the back of the cave.

1. 27m Climb fairly steadily up the face right of a rightward-trending crack line to a deep break. Pull up a short groove to good holds on a beak of rock. Make committing moves into the roof capped groove above and traverse rightwards, on the lip of the first low level ceiling, to the 'keyhole'. Spare a thought for the late Charlie Heard who was benighted here on his own during the first ascent.

2. 24m Cross the first 2m ceiling, PR on the lip, and grapple greasily around to jugs, TR. Above is an aven where a no hands rest may be gained. Drop out and with deft handwork extend around the 2m ceiling to move awkwardly up to another aven, The Aven Haven, for another no hands rest. When and if recovered, fight across the 11m stepped roof on jugs. Keep enough strength for the final stretch, many PRs. From the lip scramble up to the top.

G.Andrew, C.Heard 25-26.03.1978

FFA M.Crocker, R.Thomas 00.00.1989

From the small sandy shelf that forms the floor of the cave it is possible to scramble up a short wall on the right to reach ledges and a rock platform. There are large stakes in place above The Hatch for a convenient abseil approach (A11). The first three routes have so far been done as deep water solos and the grade for a conventional ascent is unknown.

?   Superstitious   21m   HXS,6a   ***   \

Climbed on Friday the 13th. Possibly the largest free roof ever soloed, 18m of pumping arm work from right to left across DJL's cave. Be warned there is a boulder below the last few metres. From the small rectangular blosk in the arete climb up and left to the roof proper. There is a hanging flake on the lip to the left. Gain this then move left for a few metres before taking a higher set of holds left to a yellow scar in a wilderness of overhangs. Keep lowat the scar and immediately left gain the horizontal above. Continue left, then on finger jams make a final grope to the penultimate roof. Swing left for another metre or so, then enter the hanging corner on the lip of the cave. Climb the corner to top out on ledges on the right. Pre-placed rope handy to avoid rubble on the top out.

M.Crocker solo 13.06.2003

154. A.F.A.!   20m   E6,6a   ***   \

Approach as for Terrorism. From the left-most of the foot-ledges on the nose, reach over a roof to the right-hand end of a handrail on a hanging flake. Follow these leftwards above the main roof for 3m, then pull up to a slight niche. Make a long move up to flat holds and keep locking up to a prominent leftwards pointing spike. Exit diagonally right.

M.Crocker solo 21.07.2002

155. Terrorism   20m   E6,6a   ***   \

From the Hatch traverse easily left for 6m onto the arete at the right hand side of the Davy Jones' cave. From a small rectangular block in the arete, climb up and slight leftwards through small roofs and bulging rock to easier ground at a left facing block hold at 10m. Finish carefully up a broken groove.

M.Crocker solo 16.09.2001

156. These Dangerous Seas   20m   E5,6a   *   \

From 1m right of the initial block on Terrorism, climb slightly rightwards to a series of small, spaced jugs leading to poorer holds below a black slab. Take a central line up this slab and finish on the right with care.

M.Crocker solo 16.09.2001

157. Automatic 24m E4,6a *

A fine strenuous route. Start 3m left of the overhanging crack of Fast Reactions at the right edge of the cave. Pull over the first roof to an obvious jug, pull over the next roof, missing PR, and trend leftwards over the bulges above to a slight niche. Continue more easily up the wall.
M.Crocker, R.Thomas 27.12.1985

158. Fast Reactions 26m E2,5b *

Start from the ledge at the bottom of the corner crack of The Hatch. Climb a strenuous leftward-slanting overhanging crack splitting a series of small stepped roofs.
A.Sharp, P.Lewis 00.00.1977

159. The Hatch 24m HS,4a *

Gain the obvious corner and climb it direct.
P.Littlejohn solo 00.05.1975

160. Here Comes The Rain 24m VS,4c

As for The Hatch to a ledge, traverse right along the lip of the overhang, then climb the arete.
M.Ward, M.Crocker 16.03.1986

161. One Cool Vibe 24m E3,5c

This attacks the same arete as Here Comes The Rain, but from the right-hand side. Start 6m right of The Hatch. Climb rightwards on ledges then back left to the arete, continue straight up keeping just right of the arete to exit slightly leftwards.
M.Crocker, R.Thomas 27.12.1985

Phaser Wall

162. Crushproof   21m   HVS,5a
Start 7m right of The Hatch, just left of a jutting prow. Climb the wall over an obvious flat block and continue direct to easier ground. Belay well back.
A.Sharp, J.Harwood 20.08.1977

163. Cold Steel   21m   E2,5b
Start below the overhanging prow right of Crushproof, left of an overhanging crack. Climb to a ledge and pull past the first overhang. Move right to a bottomless groove. Climb direct until the angle eases and the top is reached.
P.Littlejohn, A.Davies 16.03.1980

Phaser Wall
To the right of the prow is a bay of overhanging rock. This area can be approached by abseiling down The Hatch (A11) or from above Phaser itself (A12).

164. Glycogen   24m   E1,5a   ***
Brilliant, energy sapping climbing that is low in the grade. It is possible to lie down in the horizontal strata to rest, but be sure to photograph the antics as the climber tries to get out again! Climb the overhanging crack on the left side of the bay over two roofs and finish up the chimney crack above.
A.Sharp, J.Harwood 17.08.1977

The routes from Overboard Man to Drain Wave are currently filthy.

165. Overboard Man   27m   E4,5c
Strenuous and not easy to protect. Start 1m right of Glycogen at a vague crack line. Climb to small overhung ledges, then left for 1m and up to a small overhang. Move right then finish direct.
P.Littlejohn, P.Boardman 24.11.1977

166. Brawn Drain   27m   E4,5c   \
Start between Glycogen and Phaser at a vague weakness. Climb up to and past the first overhangs, moving slightly left to a horizontal break at 9m. Traverse right to a ledge above the main overhang. Climb diagonally left and break through the roofs to a steep wall. Climb direct for 3m before moving left to easier ground.
P.Littlejohn 18.04.1979

167. Drain Wave   36m   E3,5b
A wandering line. Climb Brawn Drain until it is possible to traverse right to a large ledge (Phaser). Continue diagonally right to a crack then up to a large ledge on the right. Finish diagonally rightwards.
S.Lewis, C.Curle 00.00.1981

168. Phaser   30m   E3,5c   ***
A wild pitch, typifying the Ogmore experience and certainly one of the best routes at the crag. This takes the second and more pronounced crack right of Glycogen. Climb rightwards through the roof to gain a ledge below the crack and power up it.
P.Littlejohn, J.Harwood 26.05.1977

169. Flipside Genocide   30m   E5,6a   \
A direct line in two pitches through the green roof right of Phaser. No further details.
D.Musgrove, S.Coles, D.Irving 00.08.1995

170. Whatever Next?   30m   E5,5c   \
Start 1m left of the green chimney/cave of Butch Cassidy. Committing and strenuous. Climb up a deep crack, and traverse left and move up left, PR. Pull over the roofs and climb the very steep wall using a series of horizontal holds to gain a large ledge. Finish direct and belay well back.
P.Littlejohn, R.Thomas 00.00.1986

171.Butch Cassidy   36m   VS,4b   *
Start below the large roof with a vertical cave. Gain the roof and continue up the right side of the chimney to a ledge. Go behind a large chockstone to the arete on the right and continue to the top.
J.Harwood, C.Elliot 27.07.1977

172.Stray Dog   33m   HVS,4c
As for Fashoda Chimney to the top of the main overhang and traverse left along the lip. Move up on steep rock to a doubtful block, then left to a niche. Continue up the left-slanting crack to the top.
F.Lunnon, S.Robinson 18.05.1980

173.Fashoda Chimney   35m   VD   *
A pleasant climb, taking the obvious corner/chimney right of Butch Cassidy, bounding the right side of Phaser Wall. Climb a slab, then a corner to a large ledge and up the wide chimney to an overhang. Traverse right to the arete and final corner, taking care with the rock.
C.Heard, R.Heard 00.00.1975

Ogmore - Phaser Wall

Dirty Harry Walls
To the right the crag forms three long slabs divided by corner cracks. The routes make up in length and adventure what they lack in rock quality and reasonable/sensible protection. In other words they are serious.

First Slab

174.General Gordon   35m   VS
This follows the friable left edge of the slab right of Fashoda Chimney. Climb a crack to an overhang, traverse left to a ledge and finish up the corner.
J.Mothersele, G.Jones 00.00.1971

175.Khartoum   42m   E2,5a
Start at the featureless slab to the right of General Gordon. Climb the centre of the slab marked by a vague crack line, until it steepens below the headwall, PR. Follow horizontal bands to finish up a steep crack.
C.Heard, C.Pound, R.Thomas 00.00.1981

176.Never Again   42m   HVS,4b   ●
Poor and loose. Climb the lower slab 12m left of Lady Jane to a crack in the steeper upper half.
G.Royle, R.Thomas 00.07.1986

177.Lady Jane   45m   HVS,4a,4c
Star below a corner crack on the right of the left slab. Serious in its upper section. Climb the slab past the first overhang to a ledge (possible belay). Climb up to a second roof, taking care with the rock. Step left to finish up a corner.
J.Kerry, C.Horsfield 00.00.1972

178.No Shadow of Doubt   45m   E3,5c,5c 2pt   \
A spectacular outing. Start as for Lady Jane.
1. 21m Climb the slab of Lady Jane, hand traverse right above the first roof and move up the bulging wall above, PR, to the arete. Climb this to a ledge. Large Friends are useful.
2. 24m Move 3m left up to a roof then use 2PA to gain the wall above and the top, PR, TR.
R.Thomas, J.Bullock, M.Learoyd 2pt 00.08.1985

Second Slab

179.Camptrail   39m   HVS,5a   ●
This takes the left edge of the slab, loose. Climb 3m right of the arete to a ledge on the left. Continue in the same

line to finish.
P.Littlejohn, J.Mothersele 13.12.1977

180. **Jermyn Street**   44m   E1,5a   ●

This route climbs the middle slab 6m left of Falls Road. Start at a ledge 4m up the corner crack of Falls Road. Climb up leftwards for 6m to a slight ridge, continue up for 18m then trend left to reach a faint crack leading to the top.
P.Littlejohn, J.Harwood 11.12.1977

181. **Marooned**   42m   HVS,4c,4c   ●

A climb without a finish. Continuously loose. Start in the centre of the slab left of Falls Road.
1. 22m Climb through the lower overhangs, then up and left to belay at the halfway ledge on the arete.
2. 20m Traverse left round the arete into Lady Jane and finish up that climb.
S.Lewis, J.Harwood 18.10.1978

182. **Red Light**   42m   E1,5a   ●

Serious. Start 4m left of Falls Road and climb until 6m from the top. Traverse right and finish up a crack line.
P.Littlejohn, M.Price 16.03.1980

183. **Falls Road**   45m   HVS,4c   ●

The obvious corner/crack on the right of the slab. Climb the corner for 21m then move onto an earthy ledge. Follow a groove to exit right above an overhang. The upper section is filthy and has poor protection.
C.Horsfield, P.Thomas 00.00.1974

Falsity Wall

The crag now faces west again.

184. **Norwegian Wood**   45m   E2,5b

Climb a shallow groove 1m right of Falls Road to the ledge on Falls Road. Follow a rightward-trending calcite line over a small roof, using friable horizontal bands. Gain a ledge in the middle of the wall, PR, possible belay. Follow a calcite line rightwards to finish up the arete.
A.Sharp, J.Harwood, P.Lewis 14.09.1977

185. **Yesterday's Hero**   42m   E2,5b

A more direct and solid line gaining the ledge of Norwegian Wood. Start at a thin crack between Norwegian Wood and the initial corner of Falsity. Climb the crack to a break, step left, then through the roof and up to ledges, PB possible. Continue as for Norwegian Wood.
L.Foulkes, P.Lewis 00.00.1980

The upper reaches of this wall contain two black streaks.

186. **Black Looks**   42m   E4,5b,5c

A frighteningly serious pitch. Leaving a rope for the final grass section is advisable.
1. 24m As for Falsity to the ledge, PB.
2. 18m Climb up then left to the larger black streak and horizontal break. Move up and left to a sick looking PR, then move right and up to widely spaced horizontal breaks, escaping left at the top. Large Friends are useful.
R.Thomas, M.Learoyd, G.Royle 00.00.1984

187. **Spring Fever**   42m   E3,5b,5c   *

This takes the right-hand of the black streaks.
1. 24m As for Black Looks.
2. 18m Climb up and slightly right from the belay ledge, to the base of the streak. Up the wall steeply, PR, to exit slightly right.
R.Thomas, G.Royle 00.00.1987

188. Falsity   42m   E2,5b   *

Good steep climbing. Start at the obvious short corner-crack on the right side of the wall. Climb the groove, then the wall rightwards to two flowstone bands and a break. Move left through an overhang to a ledge, PB possible. Finish as for Norwegian Wood.
P.Littlejohn, J.Mothersele 20.06.1977

189. Far City   42m   E2,5b,5c

A serious route wandering up the right side of the Norwegian Wood wall.
1. 27m Climb Falsity for 4m and traverse right 6m. Up steep friable rock for 15m to a large ledge.
2. 15m Walk rightwards until beneath a hanging corner. Climb it exiting left to finish up a wall and diagonal ramp.
L.Foulkes, D.Renshaw 00.00.1983

Third Slab
To the right is the third, largest and loosest slab.

190. Easy Action   42m   VS,4b   ●

Start 6m left of the prominent central crack 5m from the left side of the slab, below a crack 5m up. Climb to the latter crack from the left and climb it to its top, finishing up the wall above.
T.Penning, P.Cresswell 18.10.1981

191. Sense Of Adventure   45m   VS,4a,4a   ●

Climb the crack in the centre of the slab to its top. Continue up a line of weakness and left to finish.
J.Harwood, P.Lewis 03.07.1980

192. Wimaway   45m   HVS,4a,4b   ●

This climbs the corner between Sense Of Adventure and the right-hand side of the slab.
1. 30m Climb to a corner and follow this to a stance on the left.
2. 15m Finish directly.
A.Sharp, J.Harwood 15.05.1981

It is advisable to leave a rope in place down the finishing grassy gully for the next routes.

193. Surprise Package   36m   VS,4a   ●

Start just right of Wimaway at a boulder. Step off the boulder, move right to a groove, climb this and the wall above for 24m then move right to a grassy gully (poor belay) to finish carefully.
A.Sharp, J.Harwood 15.05.1981

194. Gepe   30m   VS,4b

Climb the deep chimney-cleft on the right side of the third slab to a corner. Finish up the gully.
J.Harwood solo 17.05.1981

The next routes do not finish on the top of the cliff. It is sensible to leave an abseil rope in place.

195. Pontoon   24m   VS,4b

Climb the groove in the rib just right of the deep cleft of Gepe. Abseil at 24m.
C.Horsfield, J.Harwood 25.05.1977

196. Simple Twist   24m   E2,5c

Start 4m right of Gepe, left of a short corner below the left side of a square-cut roof. Climb the wall into the corner, then move right and around the arete to a crack. Climb it to its top. Abseil.
P.Littlejohn 26.05.1977

197. Twist   21m   HVS,5a

Start beneath a square cut roof 6m right of Gepe. Climb rightwards to the ledge on Sandstorm, then move up and traverse left above the roof to finish up a crack. Abseil.
J.Harwood 00.00.1977

198. Sandstorm   27m   VS,4b

This climbs the wide, dirty groove right of Twist to a shallow cave, before traversing left to the belay of Twist.
J.Harwood 00.00.1977

Mitzy Wall

The cliff now turns through a right angle and provides better rock and routes. At the left side of this section is a set of huge overhangs split by two vertical breaks. Storms have virtually destroyed The Hunchback (E1,5a P.Littlejohn, C.King 1978) and The Bills, The Bills (E3,5b P.Littlejohn, C.Brooks 1984).

199. Mitzy   15m   E3,6b   \

Start beneath an obvious split in the roof to the right of the overhangs. This has lost yet more of its roof in recent storms, so the grade is highly speculative. Climb to the roof and struggle over it to a second roof. Abseil.
A.Sharp, P.Lewis 28.10.1978

To the right is a deep depression starting from a small, flat platform. On its right side is an obvious arete. It is possible to traverse right along a large ledge to descend from these routes. A preplaced abseil rope would be the thinking man's option.

200. Night Games   21m   E3,5c

Start from the platform and climb an undercut wall to gain a thin crack in the wall left of the arete. Climb this to a belay ledge. Abseil.
M.Learoyd, R.Thomas 00.07.1985

201. To Mitzy a Pup   30m   E3,6a   *

This takes the arete. Climb the wall to a ledge, step left and climb the arete to its top (Hex 10 belay). Traverse right or abseil.
A.Sharp, P.Lewis 22.07.1979

202. The Pod   27m   VS,4b   *

Climb the obvious pod-shaped chimney until a traverse right leads to the arete. Belay on the right.
J.Harwood, C.Horsfield 00.00.1977

203. Two Peas   25m   E1 5a

Gain the arete by a rightward hand traverse and finish direct.
R.Thomas, S.Coles 00.05.1994

204. Philosan   21m   VS,4b

Climb a crack, swing right to the arete and continue to a fault, which is followed to ledges. Move right to descend.
C.Horsfield, J.Harwood 23.03.1977

205. Fly Power   21m   VS,4b

Start just left of Duff. Climb a leftward-leaning crack to a ledge. Continue to another leftward-leaning crack, then the belay. Traverse right to descend.
J.Harwood, C.Horsfield 23.03.1977

206. Duff   21m   S,4a

Start 3m left of the right edge of the next wall. Climb the wall via a crack to a ledge. Continue rightwards to a ledge and traverse right to descend.
J.Harwood 20.07.1977

Right-Hand Wall
The cliff now turns to face the sea once more and contains some short routes that are useful when the tide is unfavourable.

207.**Against The Grain**   18m   E3,5c
   Now slightly more difficult to start the overhang. The large overhang where the cliff turns to face the sea. Climb a short problem wall on the left to gain a ledge then swing right over the roof, TR on the lip.
   R.Thomas, G.Royle 00.00.1985

208.**Via Normale**   21m   D
   Climb the crack line just right of the large overhang. A useful descent.
   J.Harwood 10.09.1974

209.**Moonlight Flit**   14m   E1,5b
   Start 3m left of the second crack line at a green, bulging wall. Make hard moves to start and gain a ledge. Finish up the overhangs above.
   R.Thomas, G.Royle, R.Haslum 00.00.1983

210.**L'Escargot**   14m   VS,4b
   The second crack line. Climb to a ledge and then a corner to more ledges. Traverse left to descend Via Normale.
   J.Harwood, C.Horsfield 24.09.1976

211.**Tri-Via**   14m   VS,5a
   Climb the faint crack between the second and third cracks until bigger holds lead to a ledge. Finish up the overhangs above. Descent as above.
   R.Thomas, G.Davies 00.00.1981

212.**Overdue**   14m   VS,4b
   Climb the third crack line to ledges, then over bulges to another ledge. Descent as above.
   J.Harwood, C.Horsfield 24.09.1976

213.**Overpaid**   14m   E1,5c
   Start in the centre of the wall right of Overdue. Make a hard move to reach small holds and a ledge. Continue up overhanging rock on large holds.
   R.Thomas, G.Davies 00.00.1980

214.**Arkle**   14m   HVS,5b
   Climb the crack line above the edge of the rock pool of Becher's Brook.
   A.Sharp, J.Harwood 20.08.1977

215.**Red Rum**   14m   VS,4c   *
   The right-hand crack line above the pool. Traverse right over the water to reach the crack.
   P.Littlejohn, J.Harwood, C.Horsfield 25.05.1977

216.**Becher's Brook**   27m   VS,4b
   The narrow cleft at the back of the rock pool reached by an entertaining traverse or swim! Climb the crack, widening to a chimney, to ledges. Traverse right to the top of the seaward ridge. Descend easily to the right.
   P.Thomas, J.Harwood 10.09.1974

217.**Foinaven**   22m   HVS,5a
   Climb Becher's Brook for 4m then traverse right to a crack. Finish direct. Descend rightwards.
   C.Heard, A.March 00.00.1977

PANT QUARRY

GR895760
By Windsor Davies

TIDAL STATUS: Non-tidal.

BOLTING POLICY: Retro-bolting permissible with first ascensionist's permission. Replacement of worn fixed gear on a point for point basis with bolts is permissible. New sports routes allowed.

ACCESS
From the A48 near Bridgend, take the B4625 through Ewenny and continue past a working quarry on the right. Pass through some woods either side of the road and then about $^1/_3$ mile after the woods finish and ½ mile before St. Brides Major is this large quarry on the right. Sadly there are access problems.

PREAMBLE
Unfortunately at the time of writing the quarry is being re-used for various industrial purposes. This is a shame because the right-hand main wall is one of the most impressive vertical sheets of limestone in the country. It is mostly a natural face of strange scalloped rock, which was revealed when the quarry exposed the natural joint that created it. Most of the routes are sports routes, many of which are 40m long. There is loads of scope for development if access is ever secured in the future.

DESCENTS: All routes have BBs so lower off or abseil. Be very careful as a 60m rope will not always get you down. It is not recommended to use the method of descent utilized by one of the guidebook team for the last 20m, which is normally fatal.

THE ROUTES
These are described as approached, i.e. from right to left, starting with the right wall of the crag.

The League Of Gentlemen Wall
This is the short wall on the right hand side of the right wall of the crag, starting from a terrace at 8m. Somehow attain the terrace to end up at a BB.

1.	**Special Stuff**	12m	E2,5c	Fr6b	☺
	The right-hand crack system on the wall.				
	S.James 00.00.2000				
2.	**Precious Things**	12m	E2,5c	Fr6b	☺
	The featureless slab to the left.				
	S.James 00.00.2000				
3.	**Welcome to Royston Vasey**	12m	E3,6b	Fr6c+	☺
	The next crack system, directly above the BB.				
	R.Phillipps 00.00.2000				
4.	**Gentlemen's Relish**	12m	E2,5b	Fr6a	☺
	The crack system on the left side of the wall.				
	J.Richards 00.00.2000				

Pantyhose Wall
Is the short wall to the left of and a slightly lower level than The League Of Gentlemen Wall.

5.	**Ladder Of Desire**	14m	E3,5c	Fr6b+	☺
	The right-hand line on the wall.				
	R.Thomas 15.06.2000				

6. **Bask Seperatist**   14m   E5,6b   Fr7a+   ☹
A thin sharp line in the centre of the wall.
G.Ashmore 12.05.2001

7. **Pantyhose**   14m   HVS,5b   Fr5+   ☹
The cheesy groove system on the left side of the wall.
R.Thomas 19.06.2000

Domino Wall
To the left again is a rectangular wall, housing two routes.

8. **Pantyliner**   15m   E1,5c   Fr6a+   ☹
The right-hand route.
R.Thomas 00.00.2000

9. **Drip Free**   15m   E2,5c   Fr6b   ☹
The left-hand route.
R.Thomas 00.00.2000

Terrace
At the right-hand side of the main face of the crag, is a continuation, located above a terrace. The terrace can be gained at its left-hand side by scrambling up a loose groove below a tree. Starting from a platform at a much higher level than the rest of the terrace is the line of I Can I Can't.

10. **I Can I Can't**   16m   E2,6a   Fr6b+   *   ☹
Jolly climbing with an interesting crux move at two-thirds height.
S.James 12.06.2000

11. **Totally Invalid**   27m   E3,6a   Fr6c   **   ☹
The face just left of the gully marking the right-hand end of the terrace proper.
G.Gibson 22.10.2000

12. **Angela's Ashes**   25m   E3,6a   Fr6c   **   ☹
The line immediately left of Totally Invalid.
S.James 10.06.2000

13. **Ponty Pandy**   27m   E3,6a   Fr6c   *   ☹
Hard for the grade. The line left of Angela's Ashes, starting below an arch shaped overlap. From the end of the groove at 18m, traverse right for 3m then make a tricky move up left to a thin flake and the finish.
G.Ashmore, M.Jordan 06.04.2000

14. **Llandfill-A-Gogoch**   25m   E5,6b   Fr7b   **   ☹
To the left of Ponty Pandy is a blocky groove, pull up this and make awkward moves to gain a blank headwall. Continue direct to a tenuous finish.
G.Ashmore, I.Fisher 27.04.2000

15. **Project (Knot Tonight)**   27m   E6,6c   (Fr7c+)   ☹
The undercut wall left of Llandfill-A-Gogoch has been done with one fall (actually two, but the second one was a deck out to the quarry floor). It awaits the re-activation of the crag to be completed (Hands Off!).
G.Ashmore 1pt 13.06.2001

The wall just left is still a project.

16. **Time To Dai** 27m E6,6b Fr7b+ ** ☹

A line with an awkward crux, starting just right of the tree at the left end of the terrace.
G.Gibson 00.00.2000

Main Wall Proper

This huge expanse of rock runs from the left hand end of the terrace to the obvious bounding corner (Clampitt Corner) on the left. Be careful when lowering off as a 50m rope will NOT get you down from ANY of the routes right of Welsh Fargo (inclusive) and 2 lowers are required on some routes even with a 60m rope. This is one of the most impressive limestone sheets anywhere in the UK, with strange climbing on water-worn scallops, requiring a certain amount of forearm stamina! The routes are described from right to left. The first route starts down and left of the left hand end of the terrace, below a prominent overlap at 25m.

17. **Dai Laffin** 37m E7,6c Fr8a ** ☹

Much harder than first appearances suggest with a depressingly hard crux sequence at the top. Start below and left of the left-hand end of the terrace at a slight corner, below small overlap at 10m. Make razor moves up to the overlap, then follow the bolts out right to easier climbing. Follow the crescent shaped line with increasing difficulty to eventually gain the overlap, which is surmounted at its centre. A good semi-rest and easier climbing gains the increasingly difficult headwall and eventually a lower off.
G.Ashmore 27.06.2000

18. **Maesteg-A-Saurus** 37m E7,6c Fr8a ** ☹

As for Dai Laffin to the overlap at 10m, but pull out left and climb the fingery wall to a good shakeout. A series of big holds leads to a shakeout on undercuts at 20m. Swing right and move up with extreme difficulty to gain the big overlap just right of Dai Laffin. Finish as for Dai Laffin.
G.Ashmore 08.07.2000

The wall to the left of Maesteg-A-Saurus is still a project.

19. **Total Pants** 30m E5,6a Fr7a+ ** ☹

To the left is a prominent banana-shaped groove starting at 15m. Just right of this and at a higher level is a prominent corner. Start down and right of the corner and follow a line of flakes to a ledge at 15m. Take the right -hand line of bolts directly up the wall on pockets.
G.Gibson 00.00.2000

20. **Panteon Shot** 30m E4,6b Fr7a * ☹

As for Totally Pants, but continue up the left-hand line of bolts to gain the obvious corner groove high up.
R.Thomas 00.00.2000

21. **Matt's Groove** 30m E5,6a Fr7a+ *** ☹

A superb route with interesting moves and a pumpy crux. Follow Totally Pants to the ledge at 15m. Hand traverse the ledge to gain the bottom of the banana shaped groove. Climb this for 6m, until it is possible to move out onto the left wall and make hard moves up to the double bolt lower off. The direct finish is still a project.
Matt Hirst 00.00.2000

22. **Three Turd Slab** 14m E7,6c Fr8a * ☹

A searing route up the blank wall below Matt's Route, finishing just below the base of the groove.
T.Starke 00.00.2000

23. **Welsh Fargo** 37m E6,6b Fr7c+ *** ☹

A swaggering route up the centre of the most exposed area of the main wall. Start from a gravel heap about 4m right of a prominent line of holes at 27m. Make a hard move to start and pleasant slab climbing to gain a semi-rest at 15m. Blast up to the pockets to a shakeout, then move up and right to a sustained sequence to finish.
G.Ashmore 29.05.2000

24. **Thieving Little Scrote**   38m   Fr7c   E6,6c   ***   ⊗
A superb route which gains the corner high up on the crag via some very thin moves. Start up Caught Mid Shot, but then work right along the ledge to gain the start of the difficulties. Climb direct to the corner past an unbelievable crux and finish up the corner.
I.Fisher 1pt 00.08.2000
FFA C.Savage 00.05.2001

25. **Caught Mid-Shot**   14m   E4,6a   Fr7a   *   ⊗
Climb the short groove which gains the right-hand end of a vague terrace to the left of Welsh Fargo to a lower off.
M.Hirst, I.Fisher 10.06.2000

26. **For Whom The Siren Goes**   18m   E6,6b   Fr7b+   **   ⊗
From the lower off of Caught Mid Shot, amble up left then climb the desperate wall to a lower off in the middle of nowhere.
M.Hirst 13.06.2001

27. **Shot Yer Load**   17m   E5,6b   Fr7b   *   ⊗
The wall to the left has a very hard and reachy crux at half-height.
M.Hirst 09.07.2000

28. **Her Helmut Schmutt**   10m   E2,5c   Fr6b   ⊗
The short wall to the left. Lower off the visually stunning equipment.
R.Thomas 15.07.2000

29. **Helmut Cheese**   32m   E4,6a   Fr7a   **   ⊗
A sustained route to the left again, swinging in from the base of Pinch The Helmet.
R.Thomas 29.07.2000

30. **Pinch The Helmet**   21m   E3,5c   Fr6b   *   ⊗
To the left is a prominent groove. Climb this to an optional lower off at the top of the initial groove (Fr6a). From the lower off, move diagonally out right to gain a ledge and a lower off.
R.Thomas 13.07.2000

31. **Radical Re-Entry**   24m   E4,6a   Fr7a   **   ⊗
A hard, sequency route up the centre of the faint pillar. From a sloping shelf at the top of the pillar, climb the diagonal crack above to a small shelf and a lower off.
R.Thomas 01.07.2000

32. **Twisted To Fit**   27m   E5,6a   Fr7a+   **   ⊗
Start up a faint groove below and left of Pinch The Helmet. Continue up the wall to the left to reach a diagonally sloping ramp, leading left to the base of a prominent pillar of rock.
G.Gibson 00.00.2000

33. **Flick The Frenulum**   15m   E4,6a   Fr7a   ⊗
The digonal curving crack on the lower wall of the crag. Harder than it looks.
R.Thomas 00.00.2000

The rest of the routes on the wall to the left are currently unrealised projects.

34. **Clampitt Corner**   40m   HVS,5a   ⊗
Somehow gain the ledge below the impressive corner bounding the left-hand side of the main wall. Belay and climb it to a BB, then abseil off. The only trad route on the crag. Shame on it!
S.James, R.Philipps 00.00.2000

35. **Opening Shot**   17m   E2,5c   Fr6b   *   ☹
Some 100m the left of the main wall is a slab. Climb it with some interesting technical moves.
M.Hirst 05.06.2000

Rusty Walls
On the left side of the crag are a number of lesser walls. These are gained by following the gravel track up from near the quarry entrance. At the second bend the track splits to give access to a lower and an upper tier. About 200m along the lower tier are a clutch of routes on a buttress which is bounded on its right-hand side by an area of red earth. These routes are described from left to right as approached.

36. **Red With Age**   18m   E1,5b   Fr6a   ☹
The left-hand route, rising from a fin.
R.Thomas 00.00.1999

37. **Runnel Vision**   18m   E5,6b   Fr7a+   ☹
Up the faint depression in the centre of the wall, to gain easier climbing above. The small have to make some really nasty moves on slopers, in which case the technical grade is more like 6c.
E.Travers-Jones 13.06.2000

38. **Rusty Roy**   18m   E2,5b   Fr6a   ☹
The right-hand line on the wall.
R.Thomas 00.00.1999

100m right is a black wall, containing the routes below:

39. **Young And Tender**   12m   E1,5b   Fr6a   ☹
The corner groove.
R.Thomas, N.O'Neill, M.Hirst, R.Jones 00.08.2000

40. **Tough Old Meat**   12m   E3,6a   Fr6c   ☹
The wall to the right.
R.Thomas, N.O'Neill, M.Hirst, R.Jones 00.08.2000

The wall to the right is still a project.

41. **Chew On This**   12m   E2,5c   Fr6b   ☹
The arete at the end of the wall.
R.Thomas, N.O'Neill, M.Hirst, R.Jones 00.08.2000

The Cheesy Tower
Going back to the split in the track and not far up the upper tier, is a grey tower with an undercut start.

42. **Top Cheese**   20m   E2,5c   Fr6b   ☹
The left-hand line
R.Thomas 00.00.2000

43. **Bottom Cheese**   20m   E1,5b   Fr6a   ☹
The right-hand line is quite good.
R.Thomas 00.00.2000

WITCHES POINT

GR885726 to 886726
By Goi Ashmore

TIDAL STATUS: Apart from White Witch Crag, the crag is not really tidal. Only on high spring tides are routes from Staple Diet leftward and the belay platforms From Hanging By A Thread rightward tidal. The direct approach across the beach is tidal and cut off 1½ hours or so either side of high tide. Even then it is possible to abseil in or scramble out via Tufa Terrace, or scramble out to the Gantry. White Witch Crag, 2 hours either side of low water.

BOLTING POLICY: Retro-bolting permissible with first ascensionist's permission. Replacement of worn fixed gear on a point for point basis with bolts is permissible. New sports routes allowed.

PREAMBLE

This is one of the showpiece sports crags of the area. Seepage is only a problem from October to March and outside this period, the crag dries surprisingly quickly. The Dunraven Cliff section has superb quality compact limestone very much reminiscent of Lower Pen Trwyn. This is the ideal summer venue - shade at the crag, sun 100m away on the Beach - wine, barbecues, a private section of Southerdown beach when the tide cuts off the maddening hordes. Any time else, bring a down jacket, as an unfavourable wind across the beach can be chilling. The generally non-tidal nature means a day can easily be split between Ogmore and Witches Point.

ACCESS

As for the Southerdown approach to Ogmore to the car park. The crag is in the far left corner of the beach when looking out to sea. White Witch Crag is the obvious square buttress 150m to the right. The easiest approach when the tide is good is to cut straight across the beach to either crag. If the tide is in, follow a path up the shoulder of the hill on the far side of the car park and then walk down towards the point itself. About 100m down from the crest is a hollow on the right, with a vague path. This leads (carefully) down to Tufa Terrace. Abseil into the main crag from here. About 150m further on a vaguer path cuts down right and doubles back along the cliff to reach the Gantry Area. White Witch crag is reached 150m further on, below some abseil stakes about 75m back from the tip of the point.

DESCENTS: All routes on Witches Point itself have lower offs. For White Witch, abseil as above.

THE ROUTES

Stone Wings Cliff

Stone Wings Cliff is the very steep left-hand section of the crag, extending rightwards to the descent gully running down from Tufa Terrace. The rock at the left-hand end can be a little snappy compared to that on Dunraven cliff, but the quality of the routes is superb. In general, the rock improves from left to right, and the easier routes are on the right -hand vertical section. The right-hand section gets the sun from 5 pm onwards in summer, but the left-hand side only catches the sun in the late evening. The crag can be a bit greasy after high tides. A useful warning: some of the Liassic beds at the base of the crag are sharp, so watch out for standing on your rope. This is the ideal crag for upper middle grade sports climbers with This God Is Mine and Staple Diet being outstanding. Stone Wings, by contrast is hideous. All the routes are clip ups except The Uninvited Guest, where a Friend 3 or medium sized Hexes prove useful and Stone Wings, which is completely trad.

1. **In Search Of Bedrock**   24m   E5,6a   Fr7a+
    Scary, despite being a clip up. As for Liassic Lark, but then move out left above the bulge, to pumpy, powerful climbing on wobbly holds to the BB. A true anti-classic!
    R.Thomas, G.Gibson 16.07.1994

2. **Liassic Lark**   14m   E4,6a   Fr7a   *
    The all too obvious overhanging jam crack through the bulge. Above the bulge step right to a BB.
    R.Thomas 00.08.1994

3. **Help, Help Me Rhondda**   12m   E6,6c   Fr7c   *
    The wall to the right is quite straightforward to the undercuts at the base of the bulge. The next 2m provides a very powerful, but mercifully short sequence.
    E.Travers-Jones 00.08.1993

4. **This God Is Mine**   17m   E6,6b   Fr7b+   **
    Super climbing at the bottom end of the grade. The obvious bulge containing twin cracks in the upper wall to the right is gained with difficulty, but climbed on superb holds.
    G.Gibson, R.Thomas 06.08.1994

5. **Masada**   17m   E7,6c   Fr8a+   ***
    A classic of the '90s, upgraded by popular demand. The undercut wall to the right is hard, sustained and has a powerful crux at the end of an exhausting series of locks and lurches.
    E.Travers-Jones 00.00.1995

6. **Stone Wings**   17m   E5,6a
    The big, bad, trad crack to the right is now free of its rest point. It is still utterly hideous. Tape up. Hexes are essential, Friends have ripped on many ascents and attempts and legs have been broken.
    P.Littlejohn, S.Robinson 1pt 27.07.1979
    FFA G.Gibson, R.Thomas 19.06.1994

7. **The Uninvited Guest**   17m   E5,6c   Fr7b+
    The wall to the right of Stone Wings, with a hard crux to reach the square-cut groove. From the top of the groove finish up the (easy) top section of Stone Wings. A Friend 3 is required for the top.
    G.Gibson, R.Thomas 02.07.1994

8. **Staple Diet**   17m   E6,6a   Fr7b   **
    The impressive hanging groove at the right-hand side of the steep overhanging section is climbed with no hard moves, to final powerful moves up and out of a crack.
    P.Thomas – The Snark A1 00.00.1973
    FFA G.Gibson, R.Thomas 01.06.1993

9. **Tragic Moustache**   15m   E4,6a   Fr7a   *
    Just to the right is a small boulder, above which are two bolt lines. Climb the left-hand one with difficulty to the ramp. Step up and climb the wall to finish blindly over the roof to a monster bucket, which can be wet.
    G.Gibson, R.Thomas 05.06.1993

10. **Five O'Clock Shadow**   15m   E4,6a   Fr6c+   **
    From the boulder, climb the right-hand boulder problem to a big flake and a ramp. Continue up the awkward wall and faint rib to the obvious v-groove in the roof. Finish up this with difficulty.
    R.Thomas, G.Gibson 30.05.1996

11. **Pelagic Mush**   14m   E1,5c   Fr6a
    The overlapping wall to the right is followed to ledges and a finish up the groove.
    R.Thomas, G.Gibson 30.05.1993

12. **Sideburn**   11m   E2,6a   Fr6b+
    A short hard boulder problem type route up the blind flake to the right.
    R.Thomas 04.06.1993

13. **Spear The Bearded Clam**   11m   E1,5b   Fr5+
    A filler in to the right.
    R.Thomas 00.00.1998

---

14. **Slurp The Savoury Oyster**　　　　　　　　11m　　　E1,5b　　Fr5+
A filler in to the right again.
R.Thomas 00.00.1998

15. **Magic Touch**　　　　　　　　　　　20m　　　E2,5c　　Fr6b　　*
A rising diagonal line. From the start of Pelagic Mush, traverse out left onto the shelf, and follow a rising traverse line leftwards to a belay above the top of Staple Diet. Quite a naughty piece of retro-bolting.
P.Littlejohn 05.06.1979

There is a short break in the crag here, the escape route at high water. It is advisable, if you plan to use this to exit, to abseil in and leave the rope, as the ramp is often slippery. There are belays at the base of Its Tufa At The Top.

Tufa Gully
This can be reached by scrambling down a grassy scoop by a gorse bush from the top (the usual high water escape route) or by scrambling up the ramp that divides Stone Wings Cliff from Dunraven cliff. The routes are short and some are a little cheesy, but all are worthwhile, especially Its Tufa At The Top. The crag is accessible at all tides, but it can be greasy after high tides/sea mist and seeps in winter. It never really gets the sun. All the routes are clip ups.

The obvious tufas in the centre are the start of Its Tufa At The Top. The first route is just left of these.

16. **Tufa Joy**　　　　　　　　　　　　11m　　　E4,6a　　Fr6c+
Better than it appears. Make a tricky move up on dirty rock to a shakeout, then pull round the roof on hidden jugs. Slope off right at the top to the BB on Its Tufa At The Top.
G.Gibson, R.Thomas 05.07.1993

17. **Its Tufa At The Top**　　　　　　　　12m　　　E4,6a　　Fr7a　　**
The obvious superb tufa above the slings is followed to the roof. Negotiation of this is the crux.
R.Thomas, G.Gibson 06.06.1993

18. **Its Tufa At The Bottom**　　　　　　　12m　　　E5,6c　　Fr7b
The difficulty of this route is heavily dependent on reach (6a if tall). The fainter tufa to the right of Its Tufa At The Top, with a desperate start.
G.Gibson, R.Thomas 03.07.1993

19. **Tufa Tennis**　　　　　　　　　　　12m　　　E4,6a　　Fr6c+　　*
An oddball route with a blind jump, making it very hard to on-sight. Start right of Its Tufa At The Bottom below a prominent leaf of rock. Climb to the roof, then guess where the hidden bucket is.
R.Thomas 03.07.1993

Duraven Cliff
The rock on this section of the crag is excellent, the lines are good and the positions really good, especially from Hanging By A Thread on. The crag gets the evening sun and is very rarely greasy. All the routes except for Hanging By A Thread, can be done irrespective of the tide. Left of Hanging By A Thread by standing on the boulders, to the right by using the belays on the non-tidal platform. Routes right of Hanging By A Thread are best reached by abseiling down from the Gantry if the tide is high, otherwise scramble up from the base. This is the first section of the crag to dry out after the winter - if there are no black streaks evident, it is dry.

20. **Croeso-I-Gymru**　　　　　　　　　14m　　　E3,6a　　Fr6b+
To the right of the gully leading up to Tufa Terrace is a groove before the ground drops away rightward. Climb this, BRs, medium wires to an awkward pull out onto the slab. Step underneath and climb the arete, PR, BB.
M.Crocker, R.Thomas 23.08.1986

21. **The World vs Gibson**   15m   E4,6a   Fr7a   **
Difficult to on-sight. Follow the left edge of the short wall right of the starting groove of Croeso-I-Gymru. Rock right to a hidden finger pocket. Move up to the break and traverse right into an obvious shallow, soaring groove. Climb this with a final tricky move for the belay.
M.Crocker, R.Thomas 23.08.1986

22. **Straining At The Leash**   14m   E5,6c   Fr7b   **
To the right is a series of overlapping bulges. Climb these blindly and powerfully to a baffling move to gain the lip of the slab. If successful pull onto the slab and sidle up leftwards to the belay.
G.Gibson 15.05.1993

23. **Leave It To The Dogs**   17m   E5,6b   Fr7a+   **
To the right is an obvious hanging groove. Gain this with difficulty, via large slopers down and left. Enter the groove to a good shakeout and swing up the arete to finish.
G.Gibson, R.Thomas 04.07.1993

24. **There's Life In The Old Dog Yet**   17m   E3,6a   Fr6c+   *
Start right of Leave It To The Dogs underneath and left of the prominent flake on Plus Ca Change. Work easily up until a ramp leads left through a small roof. Climb the wall above more easily, on excellent pockets.
R.Thomas, G.Gibson 16.05.1993

25. **Plus Ca Change**   20m   E5,6b   Fr7b   *
Up and right is an obvious 'stuck on' flake next to a ring bolt. Saunter up to this and make a couple of very difficult moves up and slightly left to get a good hold. Pull onto the upper wall and climb this awkwardly, moving right to a BB.
G.Gibson, E.Travers-Jones 30.05.1993

26. **Hanging By A Thread**   21m   E3,6a   Fr6c   ***
The best sports route of its grade in the area. Check out the old plough blade gear in the break! Climb the lower wall from the big boulder platform down and right of Plus Ca Change, heading for a prominent v-groove. Pull straight through this groove and shakeout. The next 8m is devious and continually difficult. BB over on the right.
R.Thomas, M.Learoyd 00.08.1986

27. **Edge-More**   15m   E6,6b   Fr7b+   ⟍
Quite a good route, but uses a bolt on hold, which needs removing. A crucial hold has come off further up, and the route has not been climbed since. Climb the groove right of Edge-Hog to horizontal flakes. Pull up the impending wall via the bolt on, make a horrible jump for a flake out right, thus enabling the BB to be clipped.
G.Gibson, R.Thomas 03.07.1994

28. **Edge-Hog**   23m   E6,6b   Fr7b+   ***
Low in the grade, with a superbly positioned crux high above the water and well out from the belayer. Start at the BB by a very sharp arete. Climb the arete to the roof and pull out onto the upper wall. Lean right back off a heelhook and enjoy the position, then make three swift and difficult pulls up to reach the top slab. The belay is a little further up.
G.Gibson 11.07.1993

29. **Grow Up!**   21m   E6,6b   Fr7c   *
A surprising line through very steep territory, that proves remarkably thuggish. Those without a long reach will have problems. Start round to the right of the next arete after Edge-Hog, BB. Climb to the roof, undercut over and space walk out left, with increasing difficulty to somehow gain the finishing groove. Sadly this can be a little greasy, but the positions more than compensate. Lowering off can be exciting, especially at high tide!
M.Crocker 14.05.1994

The Gantry

This is the short vertical wall above and right of the big roof at the right-hand section of Dunraven crag. It is best accessed by walking down from the top of the crag, then doubling back round. Be careful of wet grass. The crag gets the afternoon sun so is rarely greasy. It is the only part of the Beach that is pleasant in winter.

30. **The Overlook**   14m   E6,6b   Fr7b+   *
The right side of the huge cave roof at the right side of the crag. From the Gantry ledge, gain a good jam and improvise out to a bucket. Gain the lip easily, but then make a tricky move to finish on the easy upper wall.
G.Gibson 15.05.1994

31. **Anchors Away**   9m   E3,5c   Fr6b+   *
Start at a BB where the ground drops away from the left end of the Gantry. Climb the exposed wall to a BB.
R.Thomas 15.05.1994

32. **Cast Adrift**   9m   E3,6a   Fr6b+
The wall to the right of Anchors Away.
R.Thomas, G.Gibson 11.07.1994

33. **Broken On The Rocks**   9m   E2,5c   Fr6b
The wall to the right of Broken On The Rocks.
R.Thomas, G.Gibson 11.07.1994

34. **Marooned**   9m   E2,6a   Fr6b
The wall to the right of Broken On The Rocks, traversing left to the BB of the last route to finish.
R.Thomas, G.Gibson 11.07.1994

White Witch Crag

This is the very obvious square, white crag about halfway between Dunraven Cliff and the tip of the point. Being so far out along the tip it can be a bit greasy below the roof and exposed to the wind. However, it does get more sun than the main crag and all the routes (except one) are on superbly compact rock.

35. **Pthegthorga Phlem**   12m   E2,5a   ●
Bridgend Steve's route up the chossy groove left of the main section of the crag. Loose.
S.James, E.Travers-Jones 00.00.1996

36. **Evil Ways**   15m   E5,6b   *
A superbly technical proposition. Start below the left-hand end of the main crag roof. Climb easily to the lip and using a footlock, reach over the roof (PR), crux. Stand up, more PRs, and teeter up the ever so slightly slabby upper wall to a baffling final move, PR.
M.Crocker 19.07.1986

37. **Evil K'nee Full**   18m   E5,6b   ***
Awesome, with a hilarious no hands rest for the short, involving a one leg knee bar at the lip. Start right of Evil Ways, below a prominent jugs on the lip of the roof. Climb up to the roof (bomber wires) and stretch to the jug, PR. Turn the lip and stand up to a possible no hands head jam rest below the overlap. Move up a faint rib, PRs, to a tricky crux move up for a sharp edge and finish through the v-groove in the roof, PR.
R.Thomas 02.09.1996

38. **Thin Lizzy**   18m   E4,6a   *
Protection is hard to arrange. Start below a corner at the right hand end of the roof. Flick a tape over the rock knob before pulling off the ground, crux. Once established, move up the tricky crack to the roof, TRs. Step slightly down and move left to a good jug, then up to gain a v-groove and a PR. Finish with interest, taking care with some of the flakes.
R.Thomas, M.Crocker 19.07.1986

39. **White Witch** 31m E5,6b * ⸝

Probably still unrepeated due to the corroded gear. Pull over the roof as for Thin Lizzy, then traverse out above the lip, 2 PRs. Step up and continue traversing to finish up Evil Ways.
M.Crocker, R.Thomas 19.07.1986

WITCHES TIP

GR 884726
By Roy Thomas

TIDAL STATUS: 1½ hours either side of low water.

BOLTING POLICY: No bolting.

PREAMBLE
On the very tip of Witches Point, facing out to sea and not visible from Southerdown Beach, are a series of short solid walls. These have a very favourable sunny aspect, but are very tidal.

ACCESS
As for Witches Point and take the non-tidal approach over the hill. Walk down the fisherman's path to its end, and then doubling back left away from Southerndown beach. There is virtually no loose rock, except at the very top of a few routes.

DESCENTS: By scrambling down the west (beach) side of the cliff.

THE ROUTES

1. **Betty Swallocks** 5m HVS,6a ⸝

The obvious bulging arete at the left end of the crag has a terrible landing.
E.Travers-Jones solo 00.00.1996

5m right is a platform.

2. **Paternoster** 9m E2,5c

Swing up left from the platform and take the overhang left of Fisherman's Friend.
R.Thomas, G.Royle 00.06.1987

3. **Fisherman's Friend** 11m E2,5b

Climb up left to swing through the obvious crack over the overhang.
D.Meek, S.Robinson 21.09.1986

4. **Jilter's Wall** 11m E2,5c *

Start just right of Fisherman's Friend and climb the white wall past a PR above the platform.
R.Thomas, G.Royle 00.07.1987

5. **Wanker's Crack** 11m VS,4b

Climb the crack 2m right past the stump of an old PR.
J.Harwood 00.00.1975

6. **Leg Over** 7m E2,6a

Swing left from another platform, TR. Pull over the small overhang, PR.
R.Thomas, G.Royle 00.07.1987

7. **Pull Over** 7m E1,6a
Climb directly past a large blue TR to the right of Leg Over.
G.Royle, R.Thomas 00.07.1987

8. **Hand Over** 6m HVS,5a
Take the faint rounded corner 1m right, starting from a slightly higher level.
J.Harwood 00.00.1975

Right again is a higher level and an obvious thin undercut black corner.

9. **Undercut** 9m E1,5c
Gain the crack and climb it.
S.Robinson, D.Meek 21.09.1986

10. **Step Aside** 9m E1,5c
Right of Undercut climb the obvious painful sloping crack.
R.Thomas, M.Learoyd 21.09.1986

11. **Cold Shoulder** 9m HVS,5b
Gain a ramp on the right, move up to a black spike and continue up the wall above.
J.Harwood 00.00.1975

12. **Breakout** 12m HVS,5a
Gain the ramp from the right, then move back right and up crozzly cracks.
J.Harwood 00.00.1975

13. **Fast Flow** 11m E1,5b
Start 4m right of Breakout at a shallow scoop. Climb direct to and past a TR in the brown flowstone.
J.Harwood 00.00.1975

14. **Surprise, Surprise** 13m E1,5b
Gain the faint flake 9m right again, by moving up and left, then back right.
M.Learoyd, R.Thomas 21.09.1986

15. **Waiting Game** 13m HVS,5a
From a dip in the platform prior to the corner, layback the obvious crack and climb the wall above.
R.Thomas, M.Learoyd 21.09.1986

16. **Fools Rush In** 15m E3,6a
The arete right again, poor TR. Gymnastic to start.
R.Thomas, G.Royle 00.10.1986

17. **Lasting Impression** 15m E3,5c
The rightward trending corner line. Move right at the roof, and exit right.
M.Learoyd, R.Thomas, D.Meek, S.Robinson 21.09.1986

18. **Life And Soul** 15m HVS,5a
The cracks 4m to the right.
D.Meek, S.Robinson 21.09.1986

19. **Relics** 14m HVS,4c
Climb the wall 3m left of the end of the crack, past an ancient PR.
M.Learoyd solo 21.09.1986

Inland Limestone

BALTIC QUARRY

GR063116
By Ren Hoek

BOLTING POLICY: Retro-bolting permissible with first ascensionist's permission. Replacement of worn fixed gear on a point for point basis with bolts is permissible. New sports routes allowed.

PREAMBLE
Baltic Quarry lies high on the hillside, facing west and overlooking Ponsticill. Although part of the North Bay reaches 30m and sports an interesting route, the main interest lies in the extensive short cliffs. The rock quality is excellent and although many of the routes are more safely led, the main value of the quarry lies in the fine soloing to be had.

ACCESS

1. Taf Fechan Approach
Park in the lay-by as for Taf Fechan (see Taf Fechan Access) and follow the Brecon Mountain Railway north for ½ mile before striking up the hillside to the Southern Bay.

2. Ponsticill Approach
Park at Pontsticill reservoir dam (GR062119). Cross the Brecon Mountain railway and strike diagonally southeast up the hillside to the Northern bay.

DESCENTS: Scrambling at various points.

THE ROUTES

Northern Bay

1. **Minuscule**   6m   VS,5b
   The short arete started from the left.
   M.Crocker solo 28.02.1987

2. **Taff's Not Well**   12m   VS,4b
   The left-hand of two prominent aretes.
   M.Crocker solo 28.02.1987

3. **Rediscovery**   10m   VS,5a
   The right-hand arete.
   M.Crocker solo 28.02.1987

4. **Andy Borehole**   6m   VS,5a
   The long borehole in the smooth wall right of Rediscovery.
   M.Crocker solo 28.02.1987

5. **Holiday Fever**   9m   E1,5b
   Start 9m right of Andy Borehole. Climb a thin crackline, under a sapling.
   A.Gostick solo 05.06.1988

Over to the right is a prominent rock arch.

6. **Exam Blues**   9m   HVS,5b
   Start 4m left of the rock arch and climb a wall and crack.
   A.Gostick solo 05.06.1988

7. **Temptress** 9m VS,5a
The thin crack 2m right of Exam Blues.
A.Gostick solo 05.06.1988

8. **The Arch** 9m E1,6b
Pull through the rock arch with difficulty, then trend rightwards to finish.
M.Crocker solo 15.03. 1987

9. **Slagged Off** 9m E1,6b
Climb the steep wall and short square-cut groove right of The Arch and below a tree.
M.Crocker solo 15.03.1987

10. **Lonesome Pine** 9m E3,6a
To the right of Slagged Off is a steep wall terminating at an arete. Climb the wall.
M.Crocker solo 15.03.1987

11. **Slight Alterations** 9m E3,6a *
The calcite cracks in the arete overlooking the south edge of the spoil heap has a dynamic finish.
M.Crocker, R.Thomas, G.Royle 15.03.1987

12. **Not So Plain Jane** 9m E2,5b
The groove to the right of Slight Alterations.
A.Gostick solo 05.06.1988

13. **Health Inspector '87** 9m E5,6a
The right side of the blunt arete between the grooves right of Not So Plain Jane.
M.Crocker, R.Thomas, G.Royle 15.03.1987

14. **Sanitize** 12m E2,6a
The calcitic wall right of Health Inspector '87, with a hard move to start and a long reach for the upper break. Bear right to lower off a small hawthorn.
M.Crocker, M.Ward 10.03.1987

15. **Sterilise** 12m E2,6b
The grooved arete right of Sanitize provides a difficult problem. Finish up the left side.
M.Crocker solo 22.04.1987

Over to the right is a smooth wall.

16. **Unknown** 10m E1,5c
Climb the line on slots at the left side of the smooth wall.
Unknown 00.00.1988

17. **Light Speed** 9m E2,6c
Climb directly up the smooth wall, BR.
M.Crocker 22.04.1987

18. **Why Wimp Out?** 6m HVS,5c
Nice climbing up the centre of the short leaning wall towards the south end of the quarry.

Baltic Quarry

M.Crocker solo 22.04.1987

Southern Bay

19. **Iron Awe**   9m   HVS,5b
Climb the centre of the rust coloured wall in the left-hand side of the bay, exiting rightwards.
M.Crocker solo 22.04.1987

20. **Metal Mistake**   9m   E3,6b
A direct line up the left side of the steep block wall via a projecting handhold at 3m. Replacing a bolt hanger
reduces the grade to E1.
M.Crocker solo 22.04.1987

21. **Harmony Of The Skies**   9m   E3,6b
The thin crack to the right of Metal Mistake.
M.Ward, M.Crocker 15.03.1987

22. **Smile**   9m   VS,5a
The smooth grey wall right of Harmony Of The Skies.
M.Crocker solo 10.03. 1987

23. **Appear, Smear, Disappear Then Reappear**   12m   E2,6a   *
Climb directly up the faint line of weakness in the calcite slab right of Smile. Finish direct or traverse off right.
M.Crocker solo 10.03.1987

24. **Bumbling About In Bhutan**   12m   E4,6b
Enter the pod right of Appear etc. and pull straight over the bulge to finish rightwards.
M.Crocker, M.Ward 10.03.1987

25. **Tortured**   9m   VS,4c
The fine left-hand crack.
M.Crocker solo 10.03.1987

26. **Traction**   9m   VS,5a
The right-hand crack.
M.Crocker solo 10.03.1987

27. **Curb All Intransigence**   9m   E1,5c
The fine square-cut arete on its right-hand side.
M.Crocker solo 10.03.1987

CEFN COED

GR034080 to 038085
By Chris Shorrock

BOLTING POLICY: Bridge Cliff - Retro-bolting permissible with first ascensionist's permission. Replacement of worn fixed gear on a point for point basis with bolts is permissible. New sports routes allowed. Rest of Crag – no bolting.

PREAMBLE
The Crag is carboniferous limestone that has been extensively quarried. Over recent times the cliff has started to become very vegetated. This has meant that many routes from previous generations are currently underground. Some should stay that way, but others would benefit from a clean. Occasionally, dedicated local climbers clean up a batch of routes and routes such as Bifid - although not currently clean - are surprisingly good.

ACCESS
The cliff lies just off the A465 'Heads of the Valleys Road' at Cefn Coed-Y-Cymmer, which is 1½ miles north of Merthyr Tydfil. Park in the lay-by on the left (driving downhill) side of the road, just before the Cefn Coed turn-off. From the lay-by cross the road, step over a crash barrier and follow the fence rightward for 50m to a gap at a trench and an obvious descent path (Central Descent).

DESCENTS: Either by the approach gullies or by abseil.

THE ROUTES

Far East Wall
This is situated about 200m left (facing in) of the Central Descent. It is heavily vegetated. At the far left is a wall split by two chimneys.

1. **Rosie**   33m   VS4b   ●
   Climb a broken corner left of the left-hand chimney to a tree. Follow a scoop and groove, then finish up left.
   J.Kerry, A.Randall 00.00.1970

2. **Happiness is Clog Shaped**   33m   HVS,5a
   As for Rosie, but move right into a finishing chimney.
   W.Hughes, I.Jones 00.00.1970

3. **Jelly Baby Lay By**   33m   VS   ●
   The right-hand chimney gained from the right.
   W.Hughes, I.Jones 00.00.1970

East Amphitheatre
The next climb starts about 50m left of the Central Descent and 50m right of a grassy slope.

4. **Styx**   11m   HVS   ●
   An indefinite groove/crack on the left-hand buttress.
   Unknown Pre-1973

5. **Groper**   12m   VS   ●
   The prominent crack/chimney to the right of Styx.
   Unknown Pre-1973

6. **Trundle**   15m   S   ●
   The prominent grooves on the nose of the buttress right of Groper.
   Unknown Pre-1973

7. **Girdle Of East Amphitheatre**   61m   VS   ●
    A left to right traverse starting up Trundle and finishing somewhere round the remains of Lumberjack.
    Unknown Pre-1973

The crag now starts to turn into an amphitheatre. Ben Hur might like it, but you won't.

8. **Arthur Castle**   19m   HVS
    The overhanging crack at the left end of the amphitheatre.
    Unknown Pre-1973

9. **Viking**   27m   VS   ●
    The cracks 1m right of Arthur Castle.
    P.Watkin, P.Thomas 00.00.1969

10. **Odin**   32m   HS   ●
    To the right of Odin is a prominent corner. Climb the left arete.
    P.Watkin, P.Thomas 00.00.1969

Right of Odin is a cave at ground level.

11. **The Blue Tailed Fly**   33m   HVS,4c   ●
    Climb a groove 3m left of the cave. Keep moving up and left to finish up second groove.
    J.Kerry, P.Watkin 00.00.1969

12. **The Owl**   33m   VS,4c   ●
    Climb the overlap just left of the cave and finish up grooves above.
    C.Horsfield, J.Kerry, P.Thomas 00.00.1970

13. **Gold Block**   35m   HVS,5a   ●
    Start right of the cave at a corner and climb to a detached block in the overhang. Once over the overhang wander
    up to a v-chimney. Finish rightwards from the chimney.
    P.Watkin, C.Horsfield 00.00.1970
    FFA S.Lewis, J.Harwood 13.05.1980

To the right, the two routes Gold Block (P.Watkins, C.Jones 1970) and Lumberjack (Unkown 1970) have sensibly
fallen down. At the right side of the amphitheatre is a corner crack.

14. **Sweet Briar**   35m   HS   ●
    Climb the corner crack, passing overhangs on their right. Wander vaguely up the walls above to finish.
    Unknown Pre-1973

15. **Lumberjack**   35m   VS   ●
    The original route has collapsed. It is not known if the line has been re-climbed. Climb the remains of the right-
    hand of three corner grooves right of Sweet Briar. Wander up grooves to eventually reach a large grassy bay,
    then finish up the rib on the right.
    Unknown Pre-1970

Main Wall East
To the right of the East Amphitheatre is Main Wall East. This runs from a prominent hole to the Central Way Down.

16. **Manikin**   35m   VS   ●
    Climb a mossy corner right of the hole to a ledge, up a groove to overhangs, then left to a tree. Climb a smooth
    groove and gain a crack to finish.
    Unknown Pre-1973

Martin Crocker - Total Eclipse of the Sun (1st Asc) (E8,6b) Ogmore
(Page 250) Photo: Carl Ryan

John Woods & friend - Spellbinder (E4,6a) Ogmore
(Page 252) Photo: Carl Ryan

17. **Squirrel**   35m   VS   ●
The groove 5m right of Manikin.
Unknown Pre-1973

18. **Unter Den Linden**   35m   VS   ●
A line joining the first tree of Squirrel to Champs Elysees.
Unknown Pre-1973

19. **Champs Elysees**   30m   HVS,5a
A series of walls and grooves 8m right of the prominent hole.
J.Kerry, W.Hughes 00.00.1970

20. **Hari Kiri**   30m   VS   ●
7m right of Champs Elysees is a shallow groove and chimney. Climb this until it is possible to walk off.
Unknown Pre-1973

21. **Square Cut**   35m   VS   ●
Climb the prominent right-facing corner 3m right of Hari Kari, exiting left. Move right and follow an overhanging crack and groove to finish.
P.Watkin, P.Thomas 00.00.1970

22. **Godiva Groove**   35m   HS   ●
Start 3m right of Square Cut at a groove which is overhung at its base and climb up to a tree. Escape diagonally right across grass to a corner and chimney.
P.Thomas, P.Watkin 1970

23. **Spade**   36m   VS   ●
Start at an obvious corner 5m right of Godiva Groove. Climb a series of aretes and grooves to a chimney and the top.
Unknown Pre-1973

To the right of Spade is an obvious pond, fed by the waterfall of Washing Machine Wall.

24. **J.C.B**   33m   VS   ●
The shallow corner left of the waterfall.
Unknown Pre-1973

25. **Washing Machine Wall**   30m   HS,4b   ●
The obvious waterfall above the pond is climbed to overhangs. Avoid these on the left.
W.Hughes, G.Stainforth 00.00.1970

26. **Beginners Rib**   30m   M
The easy angled buttress right of Washing Machine Wall.
Unknown Pre-1973

27. **Cleavage**   24m   S
The obvious chimney 15m right of the pond, gained from the left.
UWIST MC 00.00.1970

28. **Gethsemane**   30m   D   ●
The monsterous groove just right of Cleavage.
Unknown Pre-1973

29. **Excavation**   27m   S   ●
The slab right of Cleavage.
W.Hughes, D.Ellis 00.00.1970

30. **Saes**   27m   VS   ●
Gain and climb the v-chimney right of Excavation.
Unknown Pre-1973

31. **Sir Mortimer Wheeler**   29m   S   ●
Climb a groove and crack 3m right of Saes.
D.Elias, etc. 00.00.1970

32. **Draught Porridge**   30m   VD   ●
The indefinite buttress, groove and corner 3m right of Sir Mortimer Wheeler.
Unknown Pre-1973

33. **The Flea**   30m   HS   ●
An indefinite buttress, groove and overhang right of Draught Porridge.
Unknown Pre-1973

34. **The Fly**   30m   HVS,5a
Start about 18m left of the Central Descent. Gain a crack in the overhanging wall down and left of a square-cut chimney and follow it to a grass terrace. Finish up the wall above.
P.Watkin, C.Horsfield 00.00.1970

35. **The Flue**   30m   E1,5b
Climb the wall right of The Fly, moving right to a cave. Move left to a chimney, corner and overhang. Step out left and finish directly.
C.Horsfield, P.Watkin 00.00.1970
FFA S.Lewis, J.Harwood 17.08.1978

36. **Lily The Pink**   30m   VS,5a
Start right of The Flue and gain a grassy groove and crack. Exit right onto a wall which is followed to the top.
C.Horsfield, W.Hughes 00.00.1970

37. **Llen**   30m   HVS,5a   ●
Follow an obvious crack in the buttress right of Lily The Pink. Wander up and climb the wall between trees to a small ledge. Swing left to gain the crack and follow it to the top. Supersedes Ground Hog (S Unknown 1970).
J.Harwood 23.04.1980

38. **M.M.**   27m   S   ●
The wall right of Llen.
Unknown Pre-1973

39. **Root**   15m   VD   ●
The first corner left of the Central Descent.
Unknown Pre-1973

Main Wall West
To the right of Root the Central Descent is flanked by two prominent buttresses separated by a steep grass gully. To the right of this is the start of Main Wall West. Further right is a fence and a prominent pine tree overhanging the top of the cliff, below which is the obvious line of Bifid.

40. Diane 21m VS,4c ●
Climb a steep crack in the right-hand buttress and wander off up and left to finish.
M.Yoyce 00.00.1971

41. Aphrodite 21m HVS,5a ●
The wall right of Diane.
J.Kerry, W.Hughes 00.00.1970

42. Icarus Pillar 15m VS,4c ●
Start right of Aphrodite. Climb up to a large bay, then move rightward up the overhanging crack to the top.
J.Kerry, W.Hughes 00.00.1970

43. Finale 33m VS,4b ●
Start right of Icarus Pillar at an indefinite groove. Climb up to a cave, a large ledge and slabs, then step right onto the wall and finish over the overhang.
C.Horsfield, E.Tebbert 00.00.1971

44. Mr.Noah 30m S ●
Start right of Finale and cut straight through it to a corner crack.
Unknown Pre-1973

45. Strand 27m VD ●
Climb a short v-groove to the right of Mr. Noah to gain a grass ledge. Climb the obvious corner/crack on the right to the top of a pinnacle.
Unknown Pre-1973

46. Embassy 30m VS
A wandering wall to the right of Strand.
Unknown Pre-1973

47. Hamlet 30m VS ●
Start right of Embassy and follow two corners. Finish up a groove and steep wall past a spur of rock on the left.
Unknown Pre-1973

48. Condor 30m VS 1pt ●
The corner systems right of Hamlet, PA, exiting at will.
Unknown Pre-1973

49. Venus 30m VS,4c
Climb a prominent open corner right of Condor and beneath a massive overhanging block. Avoid this on its left, then climb a further corner and finish up further blocks.
J.Kerry, C.Horsfield 00.00.1971

50. Lyre 30m HVS,5a
As for Venus but avoid the block on its right and finish up and right.
C.Horsfield, J.Kerry 00.00.1970

51. Queen Bee 30m HVS,5a ●
Right of Lyre is a large triangular overhang. Gain this from a crack, then wander up the walls above.
J.Kerry, C.Horsfield 00.00.1970

52. Lute 30m D
From the start of Queen Bee follow a line of easy ledges up right to a wide crack. Step right onto a ledge then left onto a chockstone and finish up a crack.
D.Ellis, P.Watkin 00.00.1969

53. Land Waster 36m VS,4b
A right to left traverse linking up the top of Lute to the top of Finale.
T.Penning, P.Cresswell 29.09.1980

54. Fred Carno 24m HVS,5a
Start 4m right of Lute. Climb short walls and short grooves to the final overhang. Move right then escape left.
J.Harwood, J.Williams, C.Horsfield 28.06.1978

To the right of Fred Carno is a cave.

55. Hells Teeth 24m HVS,5a
Climb a short corner just left of the cave, then step left to ledges. Follow a shallow corner for 2m, then step left onto an overhung slab. Climb the subsequent overhang on its right.
J.Kerry, P.Thomas 00.00.1970

56. Knuckleduster 24m HVS,5b
Climb to the first ledge on Hells Teeth then diagonally right past a tree to a cave. Climb an overhanging crack and chimney above to a roof, then move back into the crack and over a roof. Finish up and left.
C.Horsfield, J.Harwood, J.Williams 05.07.1978

57. The Fang 26m E2,5b
Start below and right of the cave. Climb a wall to the cave, traverse right and move onto the wall just right of a downward pointing spike. Climb a thin crack then a small corner to another horizontal crack. Traverse right to the arete and finish via a sloping ledge.
J.Kerry 00.00.1970
P.Littlejohn - Direct 00.00.1978

58. Spelaean 30m VS,4b *
To the right of The Fang is a prominent bottomless corner. Gain this from the left, climb it to the overhang and exit leftward to a steep wall and the top.
J.Kerry, C.Horsfield 00.00.1978

59. What A Waste 30m HVS,5b
Climb the wall 3m right of Spelaean to an overhang. Gain a small corner up and left. Follow this until it is possible to move right to a ledge. Continue up a shallow corner and wall to the top.
S.Lewis, J.Harwood 17.08.1978

60. Soup Dragon 29m VS,4b
Climb the wall 8m right of Spelaean, then move up right into a crack/chimney. Finish up a short wall.
J.Kerry, C.Horsfield 00.00.1970

61. The Music Tree 27m VS,4b
The short wall, corner and chimney just right of Soup Dragon.
J.Kerry, C.Horsfield 00.00.1970

62. The Iron Chicken 29m HVS,4c *
The obvious vegetated crack right of Music Tree. Finish leftward.
C.Horsfield, J.Kerry 00.00.1970
J.Harwood, C.Horsfield - Direct 13.08.1975

63. The Throwback 24m E2,5c *
Start just right of The Iron Chicken at an obvious corner capped by a roof. Climb direct to the roof, over it on the left, then step right to finish.
P.Stott, R.Thomas 00.00.1980

64. **The Sharp Alternative** 24m E3,5c \
The crackline right of The Throwback.
M.Learoyd, P.Ingram 00.00.1985

To the right, just by the fence, is the obvious groove of Bifid. The buttresses here are cleaner and well defined. Towards the left end of the buttress is a prominent crack.

65. **Walter Mitty** 32m HS,4a *
Gain the prominent crack from the right. Climb it, then step left then up and right to gain a ledge. Finish up the steep wall to a tree.
C.Horsfield, J.Kerry 00.00.1970

66. **Linda's Wall** 33m E4,6a *
Start as for Walter Mitty. Traverse right onto the wall to a ledge then climb up to the long shallow scoop, TR. Move up right to gain the horizontal break and traverse left to a PR below the overhang. Now sprint for the ledge 3m above the overhang and then the top. Well done.
T.Penning, P.Cresswell 24.08.1980
FFA A.Sharp, P.Lewis 06.06.1982

67. **Alex In Wonderland** 30m E4,6a *
A difficult route taking the grooves in the right side of Linda's Wall. Climb Bifid until halfway up the chimney. Traverse left to the grooves and climb them, PR, to the break, shake out, rev up and pull over the roof via a thin crack to finish up the wider crack above.
T.Penning, C.Court 07.06.1984

68. **Bifid** 32m E1,5b **
A classic taking the big chimney just by the fence. Climb the chimney to its top and climb the shallow groove, PR, above to a small tree. Traverse left to a crack and up this leftward to a ledge. Traverse right to the top.
C.Horsfield, P.Thomas A0 00.00.1970
FFA Unknown Pre-1973

69. **The Great Arete** 30m E4,5c *
Climb Bifid for 3m, then move rightwards to the right-hand arete of Bifid's chimney. Continue to the break, have a shake, and move left to finish up the buttress.
T.Penning, C.Court 05.06.1984

70. **The Art Of Motorcycle Maintenance** 33m HVS,5b
Climb Bifid for 3m then move right onto the left edge of The Great Wall. Move up rightward to reach a crack which is climbed to an overhang. Finish as for The Great Wall.
T.Penning, P.Cresswell 04.11.1979

71. **The Great Wall** 32m HVS,5b *
A good route. Start at the right side of the wall beneath and right of a crackline. Climb the wall and step left to the crack, which is followed to the overhang. Traverse left for 4m to an overhanging crack and climb to a ledge. Continue over the overhang on the right and finish rightward.
J.Kerry, C.Horsfield 00.00.1970

72. **Age of Reason** 24m E1,5b
Start as for The Great Wall. Climb the narrow slab right of the crack of The Great Wall using the arete. Pull over the small overhang and climb the wall above, TRs. Move left around the bulge to exit right at the second overhang. Side runners protect.
R.Davies, O.Jones 13.06.1988

Cefn Coed

73. **The Fugitive**   24m   VS,4b
This takes the crack and chimney above and right of The Great Wall.
P.Thomas, J.Kerry 00.00.1970

74. **Sword of Damocles**   24m   HVS,5a   *
The sword is long gone! Start at a shallow corner just right of The Fugitive. Climb to a small overhang, then move up and right into a niche and roof. Move left and finish up right.
C.Jones, D.Parsons 00.00.1970
J.Harwood, C.Horsfield ALCH 04.05.1977

The West Amphitheatre
This is the amphitheatre immediately right of Great Wall.

75. **Upidee**   27m   HVS,5a
Start beneath a huge detached block at 15m. Climb up, then traverse left to a shallow overgrown groove, PR. Move onto a small ledge and up to the detached block, which is climbed via a v-chimney to a flat ledge. Climb up, then traverse left across the overhanging wall to finish direct.
C.Horsfield, J.Kerry 00.00.1970

76. **Apollo 13**   26m   HVS,5a   *
Climb a shattered flake 2m right of Upidee, then move right into the corner at the prominent ledge, PR. Climb the corner for 2m then step left to climb cracks in the wall to reach the top of the block on Upidee. Move right and climb the grooves to the top.
C.Horsfield, J.Kerry 00.00.1970

77. **Agricola**   24m   E1,5c   *
As for Apollo 13 to the PR. Move up to another PR, then traverse right under the overhang to the arete and a sloping ledge. Climb a crack, then go up diagonally right to a ledge and a small tree. Move slightly left and climb the overhang directly to the top.
J.Kerry, W.Hughes 00.00.1970
FFA J.Harwood, J.Matthews 19.05.1976

78. **Three Nuns**   21m   VS,4c
The shallow corner 5m right of Agricola is climbed using the right wall. At the overlap traverse right and swing up the wall to a stance.
C.Jones, D.Parsons 00.00.1970

79. **Peanut Butter**   19m   VS,4b
The s-shaped crack 3m right of Three Nuns.
W.Hughes, C.Horsfield 00.00.1970

80. **The Pratter**   19m   VS,4b   ●
The groove near some blocks about 15m right of Peanut Butter.
Unknown Pre-1973

There are two girdles of the main cliff.

81. **Knacker's Yard**   59m   HVS,4c,4b,5a,4a
1. 18m Follow Queen Bee to the top of the prow, step down and hand traverse right past a bush and a borehole to the gully of Lute. Step right to a belay.
2. 7m Step right to a sloping ledge leading to short overhanging corners. Climb these to belay above the overhang on Hells Teeth.

3. 24m Step down and traverse right on undercuts to a crack in the centre of the shattered buttress. Descend for 2m and move right across large blocks to reach the hand traverse of Spelaean. Continue rightward to a belay on Soup Dragon.
4. 10m Step right and finish up Music Tree.
C.Horsfield, J.Williams AL, J.Harwood 05.07.1978

82. **The Great Boer Trek**   77m   E3,4b,5b,5b,4c
A full expedition requiring a strong and competent party.
1. 6m Climb Three Nuns to a ledge and belay.
2. 22m Traverse left across the wall to a crack, move down under the overhang and traverse to the block on Upidee. Continue this traverse to a stance in a chimney.
3. 18m Hand traverse The Great Wall and move around the corner to the top of the chimney on Bifid. Follow the traverse line to the top of Walter Mitty.
4. 30m Step down and left to follow grass ledges to the foot of the final corner of Spelaean and finish up this.
J.Kerry, W.Hughes 00.00.1970

The Bridge Cliff
At the right-hand side of the amphitheatre is a prominent rectangular pillar. From the right arete of this, a long low wall runs under the bridge, providing some all-weather climbing. Unfortunately the routes do get dirty, so a brush up is advisable.

83. **Parsons Pleasure**   12m   D
The obvious corner left of the left arete of the rectangular buttress.
D.Parsons Pre-1973

84. **Here And There**   9m   E1,5b
The centre of the wall right of Parsons Pleasure, starting from the right. A direct start is 6a.
G.Gibson solo 17.05.1985

85. **Arris**   9m   E4,6a
The left arete of the rectangular buttress.
A.Sharp 00.00.1982

86. **John Henry**   12m   A2
The thin crack in the centre of the buttress.
P.Thomas, D.Davies 00.00.1970

87. **'Ere Lies Henry**   12m   E5,6c   *
Partially frees John Henry. Make a couple of moves up the thin crack, then move right to climb the wall right of the crack with some help from the arete. Step left near the top to gain the easy finishing crack of John Henry.
P.Littlejohn, A.Sharp, J.Harwood 30.04.1985

88. **Belly Ache**   11m   E4,5c   \
The right arete of 'Ere Lies Henry is climbed in its entirity.
G.Gibson solo 17.05.1985

89. **Tough Of The Track**   12m   E4,6a   *
Climb the wall immediately right of Belly Ache (missing PR), to finish just left of an overlap.
A.Sharp, P.Lewis 00.00.1984

90. **Grains From The Veins**   12m   E4,6c
Climb the wall 2m right of Tough Of The Track, finishing just right of the overlap.
A.Sharp 00.00.1984

91. **Death Of A Salesman**   12m   E3,5c   *
Start at a short groove just right of Grains From The Veins. A thought provoking start, PR, gives way to thin moves up and left to a good hold. Move right to gain a dusty finish.
T.Penning, J.Harwood 24.04.1984

92. **Pride and Prejudice**   12m   E3,6a   *
Start as for Death Of A Salesman. Climb up for 3m then move right to good holds. Move up to an overlap, then finish up the steep wall.
A.Sharp, P.Lewis 00.00.1985

93. **Trimmet**   12m   E3,6a   *
Start 4m right of Pride And Prejudice, just right of a tree stump and climb the disjointed cracks with difficulty.
D.Parsons, P.Wood A100.00.1969
FFA A.Sharp, P.Lewis 22.07.1978

94. **Daniel Baboon**   12m   E3,6b
Somehow gain and climb the short groove right of Trimmet. Follow it into Trimmet to finish.
M.Danford, D.Parsons - Ping A1 00.00.1970
FFA A.Sharp, T.Penning 03.06.1984

95. **Laughing Carrot**   12m   E3,6b
Gain the bottomless groove/flake right of Daniel Baboon. Climb the flake and finish up the difficult wall.
A.Sharp, R.Smith 00.00.1984

96. **Mad Dogs**   12m   E4,6b
Desperate climbing up the crack line right of Daniel Baboon, then a sprint up the wall to the top.
A.Sharp, J.Harwood 12.07.1983

97. **Santa Anna**   12m   E1,5b
Start just right of Mad Dogs. Climb the groove and wall above two iron spikes.
T.James, W.Williamson, M.Danford A1 00.00.1970
FFA C.Court, T.Penning 07.06.1984

98. **Bewitched (Davy Pocket)**   12m   E2,5c
Climb up the wall just right of Santa Anna.
A.Sharp, P.Lewis 00.00.1984

99. **Rock Lobster**   12m   E4,6a
Start just right of Bewitched. Climb direct to a large pocket at 7m, pull over the bulge, PR and finish up Gold Monkey.
O.Jones, R.Davies 15.05.1987

100. **Gold Monkey**   12m   E2,5b
This climbs the obvious square groove above two more iron spikes.
T.Penning, A.Sharp 07.06.1984

101. **Singapore Girl**   12m   E5,6c
A finger stretcher. Start just right of Gold Monkey beneath a small overhang. Climb over it PR (missing), then follow some thin layaways to the left of two spikes.
A.Sharp, P.Lewis 00.00.1984

102. **The Brood**   12m   E3,6b 1pt
Start below the right-hand spike. Climb to a PA (mssing) and continue to the two spike runners.
C.Heald, G.Stainforth - Gunagimi A100.00.1970
A.Sharp, P.Lewis 1pt 00.00.1984

103. **Goblin Groove**   9m   HVS,5a
Climb the clean corner just right of The Brood.
J.Kerry, C.Horsfield 00.00.1970

104. **Sup 13**   9m   VD
The wide crack just right of Goblin Groove.
Unknown 00.00.0000

105. **S'wet**   9m   S
The cracked corner just right of Sup 13.
Unknown 00.00.0000

106. **Pong**   7m   VS,4b
The thin continuous crack 2m right of S'wet.
Unknown 1973-1978

107. **Tree Route**   12m   VD
From 2m right of Pong, make an ascending traverse rightwards, then finish directly up from a tree.
Unknown Pre-1973

108. **Fat**   9m   S
Gain the shelf above the tree on Tree Route from down and to the right. Finish as for Tree Route.
Unknown Pre-1973

109. **Celia**   9m   A1
Peg straight up the steep wall 3m right of Fat.
Unknown Pre-1973

110. **Nameless Groove**   12m   S
The groove directly behind a tree, 5m right of Celia.
Unknown Pre-1973

111. **Puff**   9m   HS,4b
The thin crack just right of Nameless Groove.
Unknown Pre-1973

112. **Eliminate**   11m   HVS,5a
The thin cracks 2m right of Puff.
Unknown Pre-1973

113. **X-Ray**   11m   S
The cracks 2m right of Eliminate.
Unknown Pre-1973

114. **Elm Tree Groove**   6m   D
About 5m right of X-Ray is an obvious corner crack. Climb this to exit through tree roots.
Unknown Pre-1973

115. **Jug Wall**   6m   M
Climb the wall just right of Elm Tree Groove on big holds.
Unknown Pre-1973

116. **Duck**   7m   VD
The crack just to the right of Jug Wall.
Unknown Pre-1973

117. **Duckling**   7m   VS,4b
The crack to the right of Duck. Finish up the slanting corner.
Unknown Pre-1973

118. **Plip**   6m   HS,4a
5m right of Duckling is a tree. Climb up by this and step right to finish up a flake.
Unknown Pre-1973

119. **Plop**   6m   HS,4a
Try to avoid the tree and climb the wall 2m right of Plip.
Unknown Pre-1973

120. **Gog**   8m   HS
The overgrown, messy groove 8m right of Plop.
Unknown Pre-1973

121. **Unfinished Symphony**   7m   VS,4c
The crack and dirty scoop 6m right of Gog.
Unknown Pre-1973

122. **Wee Willie Winkie**   24m   E2,5c,5c
A right to left traverse, superseding Jumbo The Elephant (Unknown Pre-1973).
1. 12m Climb Gold Monkey to the obvious traverse line, move left and belay on the last set of iron spikes.
2. 12m Continue along the finger traverse to Death Of A Salesman and continue around the arete to finish.
T.Penning, C.Court 07.06.1984

CLOGAU MAWR

GR725192
By Ren Hoek

BOLTING POLICY: Retro-bolting permissible with first ascensionist's permission. Replacement of worn fixed gear on a point for point basis with bolts is permissible. New sports routes allowed.

PREAMBLE
Some short limestone walls visible from and very close to the A4609. In the centre of the bay is a 12m wall, with four cracklines.

ACCESS
From Brynamman follow the A4069 Llangadog road for 3 miles until a car park is reached just below the crest of the hill as for Herbert's Quarry. Clogau Maur is about 1km WNW of Herbert's Quarry.

DESCENTS: Walk off.

THE ROUTES

1. **Crack One**   12m   E4,6b   *   \
The left-most crack.
M.Crocker 19.06.1994

2. **Crack Two**   12m   E2,5b   \
The second crack from the left with an obvious pod.
M.Crocker 19.06.1994

3. **Crack Three**   12m   E1,5b   \
The third crack from the left gained via the overlap.
M.Crocker 19.06.1994

4. **Crack Four**   10m   E2,5c   \
The rightmost crack, mantling onto the grassy ledge at the top.
M.Crocker 19.06.1994

5. **Think Of A Name**   12m   E2,5b   *   \
The obvious thin righward-slanting groove in the grey wall towards the left side of the crag. Mantle onto the ledge below the groove, from the left, past a spike runner. Ascend the groove (runners in a shot hole), to reach a small tree and shuffle right at the top.
M.Crocker 19.06.1994

DARREN FACH

GR019104 to 021102
By Ren Hoek

BOLTING POLICY: No bolting.

PREAMBLE

A fairly minor crag. The crag is on private land and no access could be gained during guidebook work. It is assumed that the crag is banned. The routes therefore appear primarily for historical record and in case access ever changes.

ACCESS

2 miles up the A470 from the A465 junction is a wooded area up and right. The crag is above and behind the wood.

DESCENTS: UNKNOWN

THE ROUTES

At the left end of the outcrop are several small buttresses. The first of these has a deep recess running up its left side.

1. **Sleight**   7m   M   ☹
The left-hand corner crack of the recess, with some dubious blocks.
Unknown Pre-1973

2. **Infirmary**   9m   S   ☹
Climb the rib just left of Sleight to a ledge and finish up a crack. Loose.
Unknown Pre-1973

3. **Far From The Maddening Crowd**   9m   VD   ☹
The groove in the centre of the buttress just right of Sleight, finishing straight over an overlap on good holds.
Unknown Pre-1973

4. **Beer Gut**   9m   HVD   ☹
Start just right of Far From The Maddening Crowd and climb rightward over crumbling rock to the top of a short flake. Step left above the bulge then go straight up to the top.
Unknown Pre-1973

About 6m to the right of Beer Gut is a small buttress.

5. **Rattler**   7m   HVD   ☹
Climb the overhang on the left side of the buttress to a slab. Step left to the arete which leads to the top.
Unknown Pre-1973

Darren Fach

Past much vegetation is a clean 6m wall giving several good problems, bounded on its right by a chockstone-filled groove (which can be climbed at about Mod). About 20m beyond this is a prominent buttress of good rock.

6. **Krakatoa**   7m   M   ☹
   The little corner crack on the left side of the buttress.
   Unknown Pre-1973

7. **Paracutin**   9m   VD   ☹
   Start at the corner of the buttress and move left to gain the crack in the wall just right of Krakatoa. Move right from the hawthorn and finish direct.
   Unknown Pre-1973

8. **Doom**   11m   VD   ☹
   From the start of Paracutin move up right to a tree below a v-groove. Climb this to finish up a short wall.
   Unknown Pre-1973

9. **Doomwatch**   11m   S   ☹
   Start at a large 'cup handle' below the groove of Doom. Climb the bulging wall to the tree, then move right onto a steep rib. Follow this directly to the top.
   Unknown Pre-1973

About 5m to the right is a steep wall capped by a convex overhang. About 50m further on is a sombre corner with a large tombstone-like flake at its foot.

10. **Graveyard Groove**   11m   VD   ☹
    Climb the sombre corner past trees to a grass ledge. Finish up a short wall.
    Unknown Pre-1973

11. **Undertaker**   11m   S   ☹
    The obvious capped groove just right of Graveyard Groove. An apparently unsupported block beneath the overhang is used to exit out right.
    Unknown Pre-1973

12. **Orang**   12m   VD   ☹
    Further on from Undertaker is an obvious steep leftward-facing corner crack, with an undercut start.
    Unknown Pre-1973

13. **Grappler**   12m   VS   ☹
    Climb the curving corner right of Orang over an overlap onto a slab below the overhangs. Move right, then straight up and over the blocks to finishing jugs. Go up right to a dirty ledge and short wall to the top.
    Unknown Pre-1973

14. **Lightflight**   9m   VD   ☹
    The groove about 50m left of the southern boundary fence, is climbed by a crack in its left wall.
    Unknown Pre-1973

15. **Chockstone Chimney**   9m   M   ☹
    The chimney about 30m further right of Lightflight.
    Unknown Pre-1973

DARREN FAWR

GR022098 to 023096
By Ren Hoek

BOLTING POLICY: No bolting.

PREAMBLE
A long escarpment above the A470 3 miles north of Merthyr. There are some older routes of dubious quality and considerable scope for new routing. Extreme care should be taken when removing loose rock, due to the road below.

ACCESS
Follow the A470 past the A470/A465 interchange for about 1½ miles. The crag is the clearly visible escarpment up on the right. Park appropriately and scramble up to the base of the crag.

DESCENTS: It is possible to walk off well to the right of the crag.

THE ROUTES

1. **Wuthering Heights**   23m   S
    At the left end of the cliff is a long wall. Follow the central flake crack. Avoid an overlap at 14m by a short traverse left to a grassy ledge, then follow a short rake easily up right to the top. Good thread belays some distance back.
    Unknown Pre-1973

2. **Avalanche**   24m   E3,5c   *   \
    In the centre of the crag is a TR at 4m. Pass this and a PR. Continue, passing the left side of an overhang, PR. Continue past another PR to the top and belay well back.
    P.Donnithorne, E.Alsford 19.09.1988

3. **Landslide**   24m   E4,6a   *   \
    Start 6m right of Avalanche below a PR at 3m. Pass this and a TR by a shallow cave. Move up right past a TR over an overlap, TR to a small ledge. Continue up the wall, PR and finish leftwards. Belay well back.
    P.Donnithorne, E.Alsford 19.09.1988

4. **Darenot**   20m   VD
    The right-hand of two cracks left of the gully at the right end of the crag. Start 3m right of a ledge, tree belay. Step off a pedestal and climb the crack to a ledge. A short wall and scrambling leads to the top. Block belay far back.
    Unknown Pre-1973

The next three routes are on the tower on the right of the gully. There is a thread belay about 6m back.

5. **Rock And Roll**   18m   VD
    A short wall leads leftward to a shallow groove just left of the front of the tower. Climb the groove to gain Thunderguts. Finish up the wall above.
    Unknown Pre-1973

6. **Thunderguts**   20m   VS
    The front of the tower is split by a crack. Climb the crack to a grassy stance, PB. Take the wall directly above the belay, keeping left of some loose blocks.
    Unknown Pre-1973

7. **Scalar**   23m   S
    A steep and exposed climb on the face 3m right of Thunderguts. Start just left of two trees, at a recess. Climb straight up for 10m and move left to a sapling below a steep groove. Climb the groove and pull over some doubtful looking blocks onto a ledge. Finish directly up the headwall.
    Unknown Pre-1973

DINAS ROCK

GR912080 to 916082
By Goi Ashmore

BOLTING POLICY: For The Main Slab and Cats Wall, no bolting. All other parts of the crag - Retro-bolting permissible with first ascensionist's permission. Replacement of worn fixed gear on a point for point basis with bolts is permissible. New sports routes allowed.

PREAMBLE

One of the best crags in the country. The selection of long and technical Fr7a-Fr7b+ sports routes on the main cliff is superb, whilst the cave and roadside slabs areas gives more of the same but at a slabby angle in the 6b+ - 7a range. There are also some monster trad routes and the finger-wrecking Kennelgarth wall. Finally there is the Main Slabs area, which despite being of much lesser stature, still seems to attract more visitors than the rest of the crag.

Access to the crag is sensitive and the place is becoming a bit trashed due to far too many visiting groups and far too much rubbish being left. Please take a bag with you when you visit and do not leave until its full (sadly even the biggest bags seem to fill up all too quickly). The area is a major natural treasure, with slow worms and ivy curtains. Hopefully the wardens will realise that it is groups that are trashing the place and not small parties of visiting climbers.

Despite heavy curtains of vegetation above and around the crag, it dries out very quickly and few routes seep. Subversive Body Pumping and Spore Wars are useful ever-dry routes. There is quite a lot of lichen and dust on the main crag and so it may not always be possible to on-sight routes, as they require a good wire-brushing after the winter. This is best done by bolt-to-bolting the routes rather than abbing in so as to protect the upper vegetation sanctuary (although its essential to ab in for routes around Sai Finish). Some of the upper sections on routes can have the odd loose hold, so be careful on the main crag and get your second to stand under the overlap at the base of the crag if necessary.

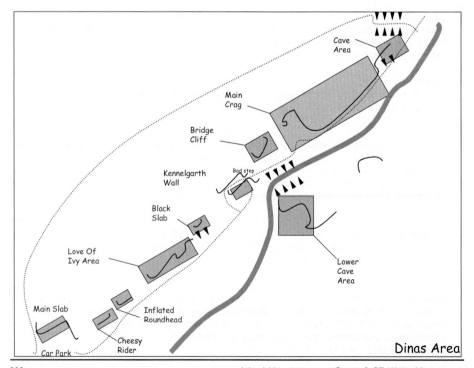

Dinas Area

On fine days, the crag is in the sun through to about 4pm in spring and autumn (6pm in summer) but despite its sheltered position, the valley is a wind-funnel and so it can be cold once in the shade. Summer visits are not usually a good idea unless the weather is cool enough to climb during the day, as the evening midges are shocking.

ACCESS

From the A465 'Heads of The Valleys Road' turn off at the eastern Glynneath exit (the first if coming from Merthyr, the second if coming from Neath) and follow the slip road to a set of traffic lights at a crossroads. Turn right at the lights, then about ¼ mile down the road turn left (signposted to Pont Nedd Fechan). This is the B4242 road. Follow this road for about 2 miles to the Dinas Rock Inn and carry straight on here where the main road bends leftwards up a steep hill. Drive to the end of the estate and take a right turn over a bridge to the main car park. The gates of the park are usually locked at 6pm so if you plan a later stay, then park in the parking area at the end of the estate before the bridge turning. The Main Slab is soon visible on the left. For routes as far as Kennelgarh Wall follow the footpath running out of the car park alongside the easy-angled slab on the right. Routes further on can be accessed by scrambling up the waterfall, as long as the flow is not too high. The approach to the main section of the cliff is by taking the path running up to the left of the car park to a plateau. Walk right along the plateau for 5 minutes until a valley runs down and right to the stream. Turn back right to arrive at the far end of the Main Crag.

DESCENTS: Lowering off or abseil is the most practical for almost all the routes at the crag. For the Main Slab, it is also possible to walk off and right at the top to get back to the path leading to the car park.

THE ROUTES

The routes are described from left to right as approached, with the exception of the Lower Cave Area, which is described next to Kennelgarth Wall.

The Main Slab
The main slab is flanked on the right by loose slabs that are best avoided. The first route starts from the track above the car park on a short wall on the left side of the face. The wall has a good abseil tree which is handy for cleaning the routes prior to an ascent.

1. **Evening Wall**   l6m   VD   ●
    Climb a crack in the left-hand side of a short wall.
    Unknown Pre-1973

2. **Flake Wall**   39m   HS,4a   ●
    Loose. Climb a short wall left of the arete to a tree. Continue up via a flake to the top.
    Unknown Pre-1973

3. **Slickenside**   41m   E2,5c   *
    Start on the left side of the main face just right of the arete at thin cracks. Climb the cracks to a ledge at 18m. Continue more easily until it steepens, then follow a crack, PR, to the arete and the top.
    P.Leyshon, D.Parsons – Slowcoach Pre-1973
    FFA P.Littlejohn, D.Renshaw. 14.06.1979

4. **Churchill**   38m   E4,6b   *
    Start at the first groove right of Slickenside. Climb the groove past several PRs to a small hole at 13m, step right and finish up a crack and open groove above. It is also possible to finish up Slickenside.
    P.Leyshon, D.Parsons Pre-1973
    FFA P.Littlejohn, S.Lewis 31.03.1982

5. **Frizzy Bits**   38m   E3,5c   *
    Start at cracks just right of Churchill. Climb the cracks to a shallow groove/pod and continue up the finger crack. Finish up the dirty groove or step left to join Slickenside. An altenative start comes in from the right.
    D.Parsons, P.Leyshon - Helen Pre-1973
    FFA A.Sharp, P.Lewis.14.04.1979
    A.Sharp, J.Harwood – Alternative Start 29.03.1981

6. **Angus Anglepoise**   38m   E3,6a
Takes a thin crack between Frizzy Bits and Jeepers Creepers in its entirety. Start 3m right of Frizzy Bits.
P.Donnithorne, T.Meen 26.11.1987.

7. **Jeepers Creepers**   38m   HVS,5a
Climb the obvious groove in the centre of the face.
P.Watkin, C.Jones 00.00.1970

8. **Sense of Humour**   38m   E2,5c   *
Start at thin cracks 2m right of Jeepers Creepers. Climb the cracks until a difficult traverse left about 2m below
a tree can be made into Jeepers Creepers. Finish up Jeepers Creepers or abseil from the tree.
P.Josty – Josty Pre-1973
A.Sharp, P.Lewis 16.04.1979

9. **Sense**   38m   E2,5c   *
A more committing direct version of Sense of Humour. Follow Sense of Humour to its traverse, then continue
directly up the cracks to the arete passing a tree to the top.
S.Lewis, G.Lewis. 00.00.1982

10. **Frisky**   45m   E2,5c   *
A diagonal right to left traverse. Follow Sense of Humour to its junction with Jeepers Creepers. Continue left
finishing up Slickenside.
A.Sharp.11.04.1980

11. **The Coffin**   30m   VS,4a   ●
'Advisable to have a priest and undertaker present'. Climb the wide groove on the right of the face with poor rock
and protection.
C.Jones, D.Parsons 00.00.1967

12. **Porth Crawl**   33m   E2,5b
Start just right of The Coffin. Climb the wall for 6m then the groove for 6m. Traverse right onto a sloping ledge,
then gain a crack which is followed to the top.
A.Sharp, J.Harwood 06.05.1980

The Roadside Crags

This is the area alongside the path leading up the river from the car park to Kennelgarth Wall. It consists of a number
of short walls and slabs, with quite a bit to tempt the sub-Fr7a climber. It should be noted that the wardens have
expressed concern about the vegetation in this area. Under no circumstances should any more trees be pruned, and
the ivy curtains should not be interfered with under any circumstances. The first area encountered is the Cheesy
Rider Wall, set back behind the trees. The next area along is The Inflated Roundhead Wall. After this comes the
obvious continuous section of For Love Of Ivy. Just before the Kennelgarth area is a short black slab containing Moth.

Cheesy Rider Area

13. **Fromage Frais**   12m   E1,5b   Fr5+
The left-hand line, following the handrail rightwards to the lower off of Rob Roy.
R.Thomas 01.02.1998

14. **Rob Roy**   12m   E4,6b   Fr7a
This is the next line on the wall, that was stolen twice from the equipper!
S.Doerr 00.00.1995

15. **Cheesy Rider**   12m   E2,6a   Fr6b
The wall right of Rob Roy is cleaning up nicely and is now quite popular. It may soon be worth a star.
R.Thomas 08.06.1995

16. **Scraping The Barrel**   8m   HVS,5b   Fr5+
This is the left-hand line on the short lower wall to the right of Cheesy Rider.
R.Thomas 00.00.1997

17. **Tapping The Keg**   8m   E2,5c   Fr6a+
The right-hand line.
R.Thomas 00.00.1997

The Inflated Roundhead Area

18. **Pinheads**   11m   E3,6a   Fr6b+
Start from the banking at the left-hand side of the wall and climb the thin wall. Poor and bold.
G.Gibson, R.Thomas 31.01.1998

19. **Skin 'Ed**   15m   E6,6b   Fr7b+
The fingery wall behind the tree to the right.
G.Gibson 30.03.1997

20. **The Inflated Roundhead**   15m   E5,6b   Fr7a+   *
Now considerably harder since holds came off and the route was straightened out, but less bold. Climb the wall below the flake feature at 9m. From this move up to a jug and finish direct via a hard move and a major stretch.
M.Crocker, R.Thomas 14.04.1988

21. **Charlie's Rusks**   15m   E3,6a   Fr6c
The wall to the right of The Inflated Roundhead has blind and awkward climbing.
G.Gibson 05.01.1997

22. **The Deflated Dickhead**   15m   E2,6a   Fr6b   *
The wall to the right of Charlie's Rusks, cutting through the diagonal ramp. Harder than it looks.
R.Thomas 00.00.1997

23. **The Dented Cavalier**   20m   E2,5b   ●   \
A bag. Start to the right of The Deflated Dickhead at a waterworn scoop. Climb this, then take a wandering line past overlaps to reach trees at the top. Abseil off.
T.Penning, J.Harwood 05.10.1982

24. **The Dumbfounded Dunderhead**   11m   E2,6a   Fr6b
The short arete at the right-hand side of this section.
R.Thomas 00.00.1997

For Love Of Ivy Area

This is the extensive area of undercut slabs and walls 50m on from The Inflated Roundhead Area.

25. **Connect One**   15m   E1,5b   Fr6a
The first bolt line of this section. From the last BR go diagonally up and right to the BB of South West Guru. Supersedes Bulgy Bear (P.Donnithorne, N.Thomas 1988).
G.Gibson, R.Thomas 03.02.1997

26. **South West Guru**   14m   E1,6a   Fr6b
The next line on the two tiered slab, finishing up a seam.
A.Sharp, P.Lewis 26.04.1988

27. **Deadly Nightshade**   14m   E3,6a   Fr6c
Climb the centre of the tiered slab via a hard rock-over. From the lip continue up a rib to a BB at the apex.
A.Price solo 00.10.1988

28. **Screaming Lampshades**   12m   E3,6b   Fr6c+
Start right of Deadly Nightshade and just left of the cave. Make a hard move up over the overlap, then easily up to the last BR. Sidle up and left to the BB of Deadly Nightshade.
G.Gibson, R.Thomas 03.02.1997

29. **Big Ears Takes Flight**   11m   E3,6a   Fr6c
Overcome the roof of the cave 2m right of its left-hand end. Continue more easily up the slab, TB.
R.Thomas 03.03.1997

30. **The Wake**   11m   E2,6a   Fr6b
Start at the right-hand side of the cave and pull up onto a big flake to clip the first BR. Step down, then climb up 1m to the right of the BR. Step left onto the big jug under the BR. Make a tricky move left, then continue up on superb conglomerate micro-holds to finish.
R.Thomas 03.03.1997

31. **Bob's Birthday Party**   14m   E2,5c   Fr6b
Start down and left of the sapling. Climb to it, then move left. Make puzzling moves up the slab to a thin flake. Move up then gain the BB of The Wake.
R.Powles, A.Sharp, P.Lewis 01.10.1988

32. **Cujo**   15m   E3,6a   Fr6c   *
Good climbing with a desperate stretch to finish. As for Bob's Birthday Party to the sapling, but move straight up to the top of the flake. Rock up the slab on a thin conglomerate strip, then make increasingly difficult moves up the steepening wall to a big hidden jug over the top.
G.Gibson 03.02.1997

33. **Thinner**   20m   E4,6a   Fr6c+   *
Start at a clearing 8m to the right of Cujo, and down and left of the obvious layback corner crack. Climb the left-hand bolt line to gain the slab right of Cujo, then take a thin and fairly desperate line up the wall above on some conglomerate holds to another stretching finish.
G.Gibson, R.Thomas 29.03.1997

34. **The Running Man**   20m   E4,6b   Fr7a   *
Typical Sharpy stuff, with two very thin moves. Start at the thin layback crack right of Cujo and climb this easily to the slab. Move up the steepening slab to the thin moves and make a slightly unnerving mantle up to finish. Step left to the lower off of Thinner.
A.Sharp 01.10.1988

35. **Miss Alto**   18m   E2,5c   Fr6a+   *
A line that cuts up to and through For Love of Ivy. Friend 3 useful. BB.
G.Gibson, R.Thomas, H.Gibson 28.03.1997

36. **For Love Of Ivy**   27m   HVS,5a
The big layback corner crack where the slab becomes a wall.
C.Connick, C.Smith 00.05.1979

37. **The Regulators**   23m   E6,6b   Fr7c   \
A hard line directly up the steep arete to the right of For Love Of Ivy.
G.Gibson 25.05.1997

38. **The De-Regulators**   21m   E5,6b   Fr7a+
The wall to the right of The Regulators.
G.Gibson 01.02.1998

39. **Beware of Poachers**   23m   E5,6b   Fr7a+   ●
A dreadful route on appalling rock up the cheese right of The De-Regulators, BB.
P.Donnithorne 04.10.1988
A. Price, A.Long - Direct 00.00.1988

40. **Open Roads**   20m   E3,6a   Fr6b+
A marginally better route up the wall to the right of Beware Of Poachers.
G.Gibson 05.01.1997

41. **Squash The Squaddie**   20m   E2,5c   Fr6b
The wall right of Open Roads, via a thin crack.
A.Price, S.Elias 00.09.1988

42. **Unnamed Route I**   31m   E1,5b
A defunct route since the development of the Adam's Family routes. Start from the base of Sqaush The Squaddie
and follow the diagonal rampline up and right. Arc back left through an overlap to finish at a tree.
L.Francombe, A.Reed 00.00.1981

To the right of Unnamed Route I is a prominent diagonal overlap.

43. **Thousand Yard Stare**   12m   E3,6a   Fr6c+   *
Take the left-hand line through the overlap.
A.Price, S.Thomas 00.10.1988

44. **Pugsley**   12m   E5,6a   Fr7a   *
The harder and blinder right-hand line.
G.Gibson, R.Thomas 21.04.1995

45. **Munsterosity**   12m   E5,6a   Fr7b   *
A little monster. Take the faint rib forming the arete of the wall on huge, unhelpful slopers. Almost replaces Herman
Munster (A.Sharp, T.Benjamin, A.Brown 1983), that pulled up the wall to the right and now has a dangerously
loose block.
G.Gibson 27.05.1995

46. **Morticia**   14m   E4,6a   ●
Dangerously loose. If it does not give you a wobbler, then the 6m long ledges must have fallen down. Not a
sports routes despite the bolts. It takes the gross mustard-coloured wall right of Munsterosity. Apparently there
was some power left in the drill. The worst route at the crag and not even worthy of 'anti-classic' status.
G.Gibson, R.Thomas 27.05.1995

Black Slab
To the right of the Adam's Family routes, the rock gives way to a series of grassy bankings. Upon turning the corner,
the Cave Area is visible ahead and to the right and Kennelgarth Wall to the left. Before reaching this section, there is
a small black slab set high up on the left.

47. **Gypsy**   12m   HVS,4c
Climb the middle of the slab,
T.Penning, J.Harwood 07.05.1985

48. **Moth**   12m   E1,5c
The slab to the right of Gypsy.
P.Donnithorne, T.Meen 00.00.1986

Kennelgarth Wall

100m up the path on the left bank is the obvious Kennelgarth wall, leaning quite steeply at its right-hand end. By and large the routes are short and very sharp, with fingery climbing dominating. The undercut base of the wall is good for bouldering on steep rounded jugs, but please try to avoid bouldering up the start of the routes as they have become very polished in a short space of time. It is sometimes necessary to jump back down onto the final bolt from the top to lower off.

49. **Technitis**   8m   E2,6b   Fr6c
The short left-hand line on the wall, with one very technical move.
P.Donnithorne, T.Meen 00.00.1988

50. **By Proxy**   9m   E4,6a   Fr7a
The wall to the right of Technitis.
G.Gibson, R.Thomas 30.03.1997

51. **Out Come The Freaks**   9m   E4,6b   Fr7a+
A hop, skip and a jump in rapid succession that starts below the arched overlap to the right.
A.Sharp 23.05.1988

52. **Fings Ain't What They Used To Be**   11m   E5,6b   Fr7b   **
A desperate route that would have been more aptly named Fingers Ain't What They Used To Be. Follow the hairline crack to the right of Out Come The Freaks on good pockets to a left-slanting crack, PR. Make a very trying sequence up and left onto the upper wall, with difficult pulls on slots to finish, 2PRs.
A.Sharp, P.Thomas, P.Lewis 15.05.1988

53. **Kennelgarth**   12m   E6,6a   Fr7b   *
A blind route that is flashed with ease if the hard-to-spot two-finger hold at the top is found. Jump up to the triangular sentry box and climb this to a slot out left. Make a long reach up for a two-finger edge, then fall back right for a jug from whence the BB can be clipped.
A.Sharp, P.Lewis 1pt 00.00.1984
G.Ashmore 23.07.1994

The wall to the right of Kennelgarth remains a project and there is another on the wall above Kennelgarth.

The Lower Cave Area

This is the big cave on the opposite bank to Kennelgarth Wall, best reached by hopping across the stream. This section of the crag is very environmentally sensitive, so climbing should be low-profile, especially to the right of the cave.

An old route In Like Peter (VS,4a T.Penning, P.Cresswell 1980) climbed a crack up the slab above the left-hand side of the cave. It is now possible to climb the route without leaving the ground. The first surviving route takes the striking steep jam crack above the left side of the cave.

54. **Imperial Girl**   20m   E4,5c   *
The obvious jam crack is reached from the left and followed with an excessive expenditure of effort past 2TRs to easier ground. Abseil.
T.Penning, J.Harwood 24.07.1984

55. **Smeagol**   24m   A2
Climb the roof crack 1m right of the left edge of the cave.
P.Thomas Pre-1973

56. **Rat On A Hot Tin Roof**   21m   E5,6a 1pt
Start as for Smeagol. Climb up to the hand traverse crack (good thread) in the back of the cave. Follow this to good holds on the lip. Using a nut for aid pull into the scoop. Abseil.
A.Sharp, P.Lewis 1pt 00.00.1984

57. **Apathy**   24m   A2
Climb the roof crack to the right of Rat On A Hot Tin Roof and finish up the wall above.
P.Thomas, C.Elliot 00.00.1975

58. **Strider**   39m   HVS,4c   *
A good climb taking the obvious chimney and arete to the right of the cave. Climb the chimney, the slab and a shallow groove to the left of a niche. Step down and right, then move up and right across a steep slab to the arete. Traverse right to finish up a groove.
P.Thomas, C.Horsfield 00.00.1970

59. **Strider Direct**   35m   HVS,5a
Start at a crack just right of the chimney. Climb this moving left, then right onto the face of the buttress. Continue past small trees to a steep slab, then move right at the arete, which is followed past some loose rock to the top.
Unknown Pre-1978

Cats Wall
The routes start from a vegetated ledge above and to the right of the cave.

60. **Cats**   15m   E2,5b
Worthwhile. Start from the left end of the ledge. Tiptoe left to reach a TR and good holds. Swing left and climb more easily to the top.
T.Penning, M.Learoyd, A.Sharp 12.05.1985

61. **Evita**   13m   E3,6a
Technical climbing on good rock. Start below a small corner on the left of the ledge. Climb past a PR at 4m and continue to a ledge. Finish up and right.
T.Penning, M.Learoyd, A.Sharp, P.Lewis 12.05.1985

62. **Picnic at Hanging Rock**   13m   HVS,5a
Start from the middle of the ledge and climb the obvious corner.
M.Learoyd, A.Sharp, P.Lewis, T.Penning 12.05.1985

63. **The Horror Show**   9m   E3,6a
Start from the right end of the ledge. Climb the bulging wall to a good rest below a thin crack, climb the crack, TR, TB. Abseil.
A.Sharp, P.Lewis, T.Penning, M.Learoyd 12.05.1985

The sections beyond Kennelgarth and the Lower Cave Area can be approached by scrambling up the waterfall in normal conditions. Otherwise use the alternative approach in the access section. The Main Crag is reached at the top of the waterfalls, and the Bridge Cliff is reached by following a path back left.

The Bridge Cliff.
This is the cliff above the waterfall.

64. **Kick The Dog Next Door**   24m   E2,5c
A serious route. Start 3m left of the chimney of Continental Touch at a cleaned face. Gain a small tree and ledge, then climb more steeply up the centre of the wall above.
R.Thomas, M.Crocker 30.04.1988

65. **Continental Touch**   27m   E1,5b
Climb the chimney/groove on the left side of the main buttress to the top, PR.
A.Sharp, J.Harwood 06.08.1985

66. **Torrents Of Spring**   26m   E3,5c 2pt
Start left of Torrid Nights beneath the large cave, reached by scrambling up vegetated slabs. Climb leftwards out of the cave, then up a short, shattered wall to a horizontal crack, TR. Continue more steeply into a groove below an overhang. Traverse right beneath the overhang, to finish left of the finish of Torrid Nights, or use 2PA and climb the roof.
R.Thomas, J.Bullock, G.Royle 2pt 00.04.1988

67. **Torrid Nights**   30m   E3,5c   *
Climb easily for 9m then step up right and back left to a sapling. Move into a corner, then right again to an arete. Pull over a bulge and up left to a small corner. Finish up and left.
T.Penning, J.Harwood 31.07.1984

68. **Bitterstrain**   13m   E1,5c
Scramble up to a belay area right of Torrid Nights and 6m left of an enormous wedged boulder. Move boldly up on sloping holds to a crack, then move up and left to large blocks. From here a difficult move gains a PB. Abseil.
P.Donnithorne, N.Ashcroft 17.04.1988

69. **Obscuritree**   15m   E1,5c
Start on some blocks above the large wedged boulder. Make a difficult move over an overhang, PR, step up left to a small tree, then past a TR to another small tree. Step up and right, PR, to yet another small tree. Finish direct.
P.Donnithorne, E.Alsford 16.09.1988

70. **New Human**   42m   VS,4b
Start just left of the lowest overhang at the centre of the face. Climb across the overhung slab moving left under the roof to a cave. Trend right to another cave and follow the groove above to the top.
C.Connick, D.Hughes 00.09.1979

71. **Black Fox**   33m   E4,5c,6b
Start at a small slab 6m right of Torrid Nights.
1. 18m Climb the slab and groove above, moving left to a TB.
2. 15m Climb the overhang above. Continue up the slab above 2 PRs, to a holly tree. Abseil.
A.Sharp, J.Harwood, P.Lewis 06.08.1985

72. **Cool Hand Fluke**   21m   E3,5c
Start 4.5m right of Black Fox. Climb the slab/wall and go through the left side of a roof with difficulty. Abseil.
A.Sharp, J.Harwood 05.10.1985

73. **Running Blind**   21m   E4,6b
Climb the slab and groove 3m right of Cool Hand Fluke to a roof. Up over this to a tree. Abseil off.
A.Sharp, P.Lewis 00.00.1985

74. **Tree Bee**   15m   HVS,5a
The right side of the wall right of Running Blind. Hanging rope belay recommended. There is a slightly harder alternative up the arete to the right.
J.Harwood 02.08.1988

Main Crag
The main crag is round the corner from the Bridge Cliff. It is impossible to miss this crag and indeed it should not be missed. It is one of the most impressive in South East Wales. The left-hand section of the crag is dominated by the enormous roof, but there is some climbing in the recess up and left of where the roof starts. Only a few routes tackle the challenge of the main roof and the majority of the climbing is on the impressive section right of where the roof peters out, taking the steep, overlapping grooves.

For people who like long sports routes, with short technical sections between good rests, this is probably the best crag in Britain. Further on, the lower overhangs merge into a brambly bank, but there is an extremely good section starting from the top of the bank, offering some brilliant E3's and a couple of mean thuggy leaning walls.

The Tower
This is the prominent tower set up and left from the recess at the left side of the Main Crag.

75. **Pis En Lit**   18m   E2,5c   Fr6b
The line just left of the arete of the tower, starting directly over the overlap. Stepping in from the right reduces the grade to Fr6a+.
R.Thomas, G.Gibson 15.02.1998

76. **Illegal Congress**   18m   E2,5c   Fr6b
Climbs the wall right of the arete of the buttress.
R.Thomas, G.Gibson 15.02.1998

77. **Family Values**   18m   E2,5c   Fr6a+
The wall right of Illegal Congress.
R.Thomas 00.00.1998

The Recess

78. **Descent Route**   45m
Not the best of descents. Start at a large jammed block reached by scrambling up left from the main overhang. Climb the right side of the block and a short crack, then move right into a gully leading to the top.
Unknown Pre-1973

79. **Ivy Nest**   24m   VD
Climb the deep cleft 4m right of Descent Route.
Unknown Pre-1973

80. **Stray Cats**   24m   E4,6a
Good, steep climbing. Start just right of Ivy Nest. Pull over a small overhang with difficulty to good holds. Move right, BR, to a groove, and follow this to the top.
P.Tilson M.Danford Sisyphus A2 00.00.1972
FFA A.Sharp, J.Harwood 09.08.1983

81. **Puss Off**   20m   E4,6a   Fr7a
The roof right of Stray Cats to a BB.
G.Gibson 22.03.1998

Dinas

The following routes start below a platform running across to the arete of the main crag.

82. **Each Way Nudger**   15m   E3,6a   Fr6c
Start where the platform starts on the left. Climb up for 4m then continue via a shallow thin crack to gain the bulge.
Pull over this leftwards, BB.
G.Gibson, M.Ward, T.Penning, C.Court, P.Creswell 19.05.1985

The following two routes climb direct lines through the now defunct Gentle Push E4,6a (P.Littlejohn, C.Court 1985).

83. **When Push Comes To Shove**   20m   E4,6b   Fr7a+
To the right of Each Way Nudger at half-height is prominent roof. Gain this directly, pull through it desperately to
below some overlaps. Climb right of the BR out on the left, then swing left for 3m to the BB of Each Way Nudger.
G.Gibson 15.02.1998

84. **Call a Spade a Spade**   20m   E3,6a   Fr6c
The right-hand line through the half-height overlap, swimming right at the top through exploding cheese, BB.
G.Gibson, R.Thomas 15.02.1998

85. **Unnamed Route 2**   18m   HVS,5a
Start as For Call A Spade A Spade. Climb up right to a small overhang. Pull over this and move right to a big
flake. Climb this and the groove above, on the left, to the top.
L.Francombe, A.Reed 00.00.1981

86. **Totally Radish**   24m   E3,6a   Fr6b+   *
Start just below the prominent arete bounding the left side of the main crag. Move up left to a small cave, then pull
up onto the roof. Panic at the lack of holds until a hidden borehole is found. Once established, climb the left side
of the arete above. The route to the right is Durbin 2, Watson Nil, described below.
G.Gibson, R.Thomas 22.03.1998

The Left-hand Section
This area starts where the banking drops away from the recess and the roof proper starts.

87. **Finger Pinch**   24m   E3,5c
Largely superseded since the arrival of Durbin Two, Watson Nil, but still an easy way through some impressive
terrain. The bolts on D2,W0 replace the PR and TR, but the last bolt is a bit naughty, although for the purist, there
is a good rock slot round to the left. Walk along the ledge leading from the recess area to the arete, pull onto the
arete (excellent TR here - not in situ), and climb this via grooves and a small overlap to the top. BB.
P.Donnithorne, T.Meen 00.00.1986

88. **Wild Magic**   31m   E3,6a   *
As for Finger Pinch, but cross below the bottom of a groove, then move up and right to a horizontal break. Follow
this to gain a layback crack leading up the wide groove, PR. Abseil from trees at the top.
T.Penning, A. Sharp, P.Creswell 11.07.1982

89. **Lip Trick**   42m   E3,6a,5c   *
1. 21m A wild trip on the very lip of the overhang. Follow Wild Magic to the PR. Continue traversing (crux) PR,
to a PB.
2. 21m Climb up then right to a groove. Climb this for 3m until it is possible to move right to a crack (Gastro).
Follow this passing old PRs to the top.
T.Penning, P.Littlejohn 05.07.1983

90. **Cautious Lip**   48m   E6,6a,6b,6a   ***   \
A brilliant left to right girdle of the lip of the main overhang, with outrageous positions.
1. 18m As for Wild Magic.
2. 12m Move right into the crack of Gastro, NR and climb down this for 4m. Traverse right with difficulty into Bangkok and belay.
3. 18m Traverse right and Finish up Caution To The Wind.
A.Sharp, P.Lewis 00.00.1985

The next batch of routes start to the right of the left arete of the crag. They take lines directly through the roof and await big brothers and sisters.

91. **Durbin Two, Watson Nil**   24m   E6,6b   Fr7c   **
Start below and left of the jam crack at the left-hand side of the roof, below what looks like a good pocket in the roof. Climb easily to the roof and explode powerfully through to the lip. It is essential to avoid autocorrelation when turning the lip and the sequence required is rather bizarre, but a sneaky hint is tape up your ankles. An unsubtle hint is use a series of overhead footlocks. Finish up the right side of the arete.
G.Ashmore 23.03.1997

92. **Giant Killer**   35m   E6,6a,6a   **
Formerly the most fearsome route at Dinas and one that retains considerable status. Most of the gear is in situ, but a thorough cleaning is required to return it to classic status. The second pitch is rarely done and most abseil off after the lip to avoid the vegetation. Gain the hanging corner right of Durbin Two, Watson Nil from the right and follow it to the roof, PR. Traverse right to gain a crack leading out to the lip. Gain this, PR, and in situ nuts to make a long move to gain the lip (good Friend). Turn the lip, BR and pull up easily to a slight niche and belay or ab off. The second pitch takes the groove above past several PRs.
P.Littlejohn, T.Penning 1pt 26.06.1983, FFA M.Crocker, R.Thomas 14.04.1988

Dinas Main Crag

Photo: Carl Ryan

Dinas

93. **Gastro**   25m   A2
To the right of Giant Killer, a row of rather large bolts leads through the roof to the lip.
C.Mortlock Pre-1973

The following routes are located above the roof, towards the right-hand end of the roof.

94. **Bangkok**   21m   E5,6b
Abseil in to a TB on the lip of the roofs, 5m left of Caution To The Wind. Follow a line of pockets up the arete above, moving right to finish, 2TRs, PR.
A.Sharp, J.Harwood, P.Lewis 27.07.1985

95. **Caution To The Wind**   21m   E4,6a   *
Abseil in to a groove about 5m left of Springboard. Climb the groove TR, to a PB.
A.Sharp, P.Lewis 00.00.1985

96. **Sai Finish**   21m   E5,6b   *
From 3m above the belay on Caution To The Wind, move left to finish up a slim groove.
A.Sharp, J.Harwood 05.10.1985

97. **Springboard**   42m   A2,E3,6a,5a
Start below a crack splitting the roof on the right-hand end of the Main Overhang. It is also possible to reach pitch 2 via an abseil to the lip of the overhang.
1. 24m Use aid to gain the lip of the overhang. Free climb to gain the groove above and follow this to a tree stump and belay.
2. 18m Step left and climb up to exit left on to vegetation.
P.Watkin, C.Jones - Pre-1973, FFA P. Littlejohn, M Harber 16.06.1979

Right-hand Section
This is the huge sheet of limestone right of where the monster roof peters out. It contains some of the best sports routes known to mankind. The first real feature is the bottomless and holdless groove of Subversive Body Pumping, but just left of this are twin bolts in the roof and a line of jugs leading left above it - this is Spore/Sport Wars.

98. **Sport Wars**   25m   E6,6b 1pt   Fr7b+   *
Start left of the prominent Subversive groove and pull to the roof. Cross this using a BA. Pull round the lip, and make a complex sequence leftwards (crux) to eventually bridge out across a groove. Follow the left wall/arete of the groove on wobbly blocks to a BB some 11m above.
G.Gibson 1pt 27.08.1995

99. **Spore Wars**   29m   E6,6b 1pt   Fr7b+   **
As for Sport Wars to the bridging rest. Pull right into the groove (where a belay used to be). Move right and finish up Subversive Body Pumping. Not properly equipped at present.
M.Crocker, R.Thomas 1pt 17.04.1988

100. **Bloody Sport Climbers!**   27m   E7,6c   Fr8a   **
Spore/Sport Wars free. Powerful, but easier (Fr7c+) for the tall.
G.Ashmore 20.05.1997

101. **Subversive Body Pumping**   26m   E5,6c   Fr7b+   *
The aforementioned bottomless, holdless, groove is entered with extreme difficulty. Bridge up until a good hold allows access to the arete. Climb this - a bit run out - to a ledge, then swing right above the bottomless groove, with a final awkward move up to the chain.
M.Crocker, R.Thomas 06.03.1988

102.**Powers That Be**   45m   E6,6c   Fr7c+   **

A total mauler which partially traverses the crag. Pull into the groove as for Subversive Body Pumping and climb it for 4m. Step out to gain a conglomerate hold and a prominent wedged block above. Move desperately up and improvise rightwards to eventually gain a good no-hands rest on Berlin. Follow Berlin for a couple of moves, but step right to a vague flake and gain the top roof of Still Life. Cut through the roof as for Still Life to finish.
M.Crocker, R.Thomas 30.04.1988

103.**Berlin**   23m   E5,6b   Fr7a+   ***

A definitive classic of its grade. About 11m right of the Subversive groove is a prominent rectangular hold at about 3m Gain this with difficulty and pull up to the break. Pull over the first roof (crux), then amble up the slab to a groove. Pull round this, over an overlap and into the upper groove. Make a baffling move out right, then continue to the next BR. Swing blindly left into a short finishing groove and finish easily. BB.
G.Gibson, M.Ward, M.Crocker 18.05.1985

104.**Still Life**   27m   E6,6b   Fr7b+   ***

More stunning climbing. As for Berlin to the ring bolt, but then traverse right on thin edges and undercuts to a dyno for a suspicious looking hole. Step up on this, and follow the complex and tiring groove above it to gain a good rest and flake leading to below the final roof. Use undercuts to reach a monster bucket on the lip, cut loose and soak up the exposure as you dangle above the river. Finish easily, BB.

G.Gibson, R.Thomas 30.04.1994

105.**Chives Of Freedom**   27m   E6,6c   Fr7c   **

Direct! Start below the obvious square groove dominating the centre of the crag (The Big Time). Climb easily up to a shakeout below the roof, then thug through this with little if any technique required, to a big jug and no-hands rest at the base of The Big Time groove. Pull up into the Still Life groove and keeping on blasting up Still Life to the top.

A.Sharp, P.Lewis 1pt - Angel Heart 24.04.1988

FFA G.Ashmore 05.06.1994

106.**The Big Time**   27m   E6,6c   **   \

As for Chives Of Freedom to the BR just below the groove. Climb up the groove past poor PRs and a substantial run out, RPs to a BR at the break. The original route traversed off right here. Pull through the roof with difficulty, BRs and continue up the headwall to a BB.

P.Littlejohn, T.Penning, J.Harwood 1pt 07.05.1985

FFA G.Gibson, R.Thomas 08.04.1995

107.**Crock Of Gold**   26m   E6,6c   Fr7c   *

A difficult route taking the centre of the big wall right of The Big Time, with two contrasting sections. Start just to the right of a tufa pillar and sapling growing from the roof. Monkey leftward and climb the tufa pillar to a baffling sequence through the roof. From the no-hands rest above the roof, continue fairly directly to a real stopper rock-up (crux). Continue thinly to a hairline crack and gain the break via a final tenuous move.

M.Crocker, R.Thomas 17.04.1988

108.**The Sharp Cereal Professor**   26m   E5,6b   Fr7b   **

An excellent line. Start right of Crock Of Gold and climb the groove to the right of the tufa on good holds to the roof. A blind, hard reach or a lurch gains a good hold above the lip. Pull through, move up and then trend out rightwards on the slabby wall. A hard move through a small arched overlap gains access to the finishing slab.

G.Gibson 01.05.1994

An older route (Salem's Lot A.Sharp, P. Lewis 1985) took the start of Crock Of Gold to the sapling and the finish of The Sharp Cereal Professor. Impressive for its time, it could still be climbed at about Fr7b+.

109.**Harlem**   27m   E6,6b   Fr7b+   ***

A superb route at the bottom of the grade. Just right of The Sharp Cereal Professor is the first of two prominent and large holes in the roof. Climb up a slightly cheesy arete to gain the hole and pull through the roof on big buckets. Make an improbable, but quite easy, rock-out right using a sharp mono, to a rest before the next roof. Pull leftwards through this, then quickly move out left to a groove. Climb the groove and finish up the slab above.

A.Sharp, P.Lewis 2pt 00.00.1985

FFA M.Crocker, R.Thomas 15.04.1988

110.**Hawaiian Chance**   24m   E6,6c   Fr7c   *

Start just just right of Harlem. Climb to the roof and a tree stump, then make oddball moves through the roof, TR and BR, to a slippery arete, BR. Gain Spain at the TRs, good rest. Pull into the groove of Spain, then swing left round the arete (crux) level with a ring bolt. If successful gain good holds and a BR. It may be advisable to lower off the last BR rather than climb the unstable (but easy) upper section to the TB.

G.Gibson, R.Thomas 12.05.1991

111. **Spain**   24m   E4,6a   ***

Good climbing in exciting positions. Start beneath a rock tube at 9m. Climb to a small tree. Pull over the bulge into a scoop, step up and move left to the arete and climb steeply past 2TRs to gain a rest in the hanging groove above. Reluctantly step right onto the lip of the overhang and traverse right to a groove on the arete, TRs. Step up and swing left PR, then pull over the roof to gain the crack above, TR. Finish up the crack to tree belays. Unfortunately this route interferes with the proper bolt placements on adjacent sports routes, thus demonstrating another problem with traditionally protected routes.
G.Gibson 23.03.1985

112. **Groovy Tube Day**   24m   E1,5b   *

A unique route, which explores the obvious tube. Follow Spain into the scoop, step up and move right into the tube (possible belay). Exit from the top of the tube and climb the corner above to the trees. Abseil.
C.Connick, D.Hughes 00.00.1978

113. **On The Broadwalk**   65m   E1,5a,5b,5c   **

Nice climbing and good positions. Start as for Spain.
1. 13m Follow Spain to belay in the tube.
2. 18m Traverse right from the top of the tube and move up onto the slab at a crack. Follow the crack, then move right to a small foothold at the lip of the overhang. A long low step to a mantleshelf leads to good holds. Move right to a small tree and PB.
3. 18m Traverse right, then up and right again to a small tree and TR out right. Swing right onto a large block and continue to a large tree. Abseil.
C.Connick, D.Hughes 16.06.1979
FFA A.Sharp, R.Powles 00.00.1981

114. **Dr. Van Steiner**   24m   E5,6b   Fr7b

A bag. Start right of the Spain scoop and climb desperately over an overlap to the roof. Head up towards the tube, but pull up the arete to join Spain at the upper TRs.
G.Gibson 26.05.1991, G.Ashmore - ALCH 08.08.1999

115. **Venice**   12m   E4,6b   \

The short roof crack to the right, yet to be re-equipped.
A.Sharp, J.Harwood, P.Lewis, M.Waters, G.Barker 18.08.1985

116. **Day Screamer**   22m   E3,5c

A dirty start leads to good climbing above. Start 5m right of Venice. Climb the overhang and crack above to a ledge. Step left, then up the slab and overlap above to a tree belay. Abseil.
A.Sharp, J.Harwood, P.Lewis 18.08.1985

The Cave Area

This is a good, steep section of the crag, set up above the river just right of the main crag. It is accessed by scrambling up the path to a tree below the obvious cave. BBs are in place. Only a few of the routes seep and it stays mostly dry in light rain. One word of caution, there is some blocky material on the top roofs and there has been at least one near fatal accident in the past, although this was lowering from the tree. If in doubt, lower off whatever staples are available before the capping roof. This approach does not detract from most of the routes.

117. **Academy Awards**   29m   E3,6a   Fr6c   **

Starting from the path, below the left-hand end of the terrace, move easily up to the obvious roof at 6m. Move through this via a painful slot and continue up the easy wall to a prominent long v-groove. Negotiation of this often proves difficult. Pull out of the slot to good holds on the upper slab and finish direct to a BB.
R.Thomas 00.00.1995

118. **Dream Academy**   18m   E3,6a   Fr6b+   *

From the BB on the terrace, trend up and right up a ramp gaining the roof at a groove. Pull into this. Finish direct.
T.Penning, J.Harwood 14.05.1985

119. **El Camino Del Roy**   18m   E3,6a   Fr6c   ***
   A classic. To the right is a prominent sharp-cut square groove at 11m. Gain this directly and climb it with difficulty to make an awkward move onto the upper slab. Finish directly over the upper slab.
   R.Thomas, G.Gibson 14.05.1994

120. **Danny La Rue**   18m   E5,6b   Fr7b
   A poor route up the wall to the right of El Camino.
   G.Gibson, R.Thomas 08.04.1995

121. **Incidentally X**   18m   E5,6c   Fr7b+   *
   A bouldery little number to the right of Danny La Rue, climbed by means of an improbable heel-hook and a pinch.
   G.Gibson 23.03.1985, G.Gibson - ALCH 00.00.1995

122. **Tortilla Flats**   18m   E5,6b   Fr7b   *
   A horribly dirty start up the arete to the right, leads to the base of a slanting groove. This is full of cheese, but the hidden monos in the back of the groove are good - if you can guess where they are! The crux is at the top of the groove - a jump for a large pocket. Finish easily.
   G.Gibson 09.04.1995

123. **Pour Marcel**   17m   E5,6b   Fr7b   *
   Climb up the right-hand side of the cave, then make difficult moves up on small pockets. From these reach a sloper either statically or 'by the best jump you'll get all year'. Finish direct with some interest.
   G.Gibson 14.05.1994

The next two routes supersede Let's Tango In Paris E3,6b (G.Gibson 1991), that came in from Brazilian Blend.

124. **Brazilian Blend**   21m   E4,6a   Fr6c+   **
   Start up the corner to the right and pull round the roof to the right. Pull blindly up left and finish up the slab above.
   G.Gibson 19.05.1985

125. **Sverige**   20m   E3,6b   Fr7a
   Start up the sloping corner right of Brazilian Blend then pull left to the centre of the wall at 9m. Surmount the overlap and make some tricky moves up to the final roof. Only for those who have ticked the rest of the wall.
   G.Gibson, T.Penning, M.Ward 19.05.1985

126. **Ma's Strict**   17m   E5,6b   Fr7a+   *
   As for Sverige, but pull over rightwards at a tree stump. Climb the extremely sequency wall above on small pockets to a baffling move through a roof.
   G.Gibson, R.Thomas 25.03.1995

127. **Breakout**   15m   E3,6a   Fr6c   **
   Nothing too difficult. Basically follow the natural line up from where Sverige and Ma's Strict go left.
   A.Sharp, J.Harwood 01.09.1983

128. **Vitamin Z**   21m   E4,6b
   Start at a corner to the right of the caves, climb the corner, step right and make a hard pull over the bulge, poor PR. Pull past this with difficulty and continue to an abseil tree
   A.Sharp, P.Lewis 00.00.1985

129. **Under The Boardwalk**   27m   E3,6a
   Start as for Vitamin Z. Climb the corner to some large blocks on the right. Move up left over the bulge to the horizontal break. Climb left to an obvious groove, and follow this to a tree belay. Abseil off.
   L.Francombe, A. Reed 00.00.1981

There is a small, strange-looking crag across the river from the main crag. It has no known routes at present.

FERNLEA SLABS

GR237916
By Myles Jordan & Goi Ashmore

BOLTING POLICY: Retro-bolting permissible with first ascensionist's permission. Replacement of worn fixed gear on a point for point basis with bolts is permissible. New sports routes allowed.

PREAMBLE
Some slabs in a disused quarry of poor quality shattered limestone, set at a very low angle. Protection is spaced. It is currently about 60m high, but it is being slowly filled in. Hopefully this process will accelerate in the near future!

ACCESS
Leave the M4 at junction 27 and take the A467 towards Risca. Turn right towards Risca, then left at the next roundabout. Go through the town heading towards Cross Keys. Take a right turn immediately before the Esso Petrol Station, go up a short steep hill and over a level crossing. Follow the road up round a short bend to the main gate of the quarry on your left. Park here. On second thoughts go home. This crag is worthless.

DESCENTS: By abseil.

THE ROUTES

1. **Predator**   18m   HS,4b
   On the far left of the slabs, scramble up to two trees at the left side of a blocky ledge. Climb direct.
   A.McCarthy solo 00.03.1993

2. **Terminator**   18m   HS,4b
   Climb the slab from a start on the right of the ledge, about 3m right of Predator by two large blocks.
   P.Shea solo 00.03.1993

3. **Running Man**   23m   VS
   As for Terminator, but diagonally rightwards for 6m past a horizontal crack. Climb directly up to the large ledge.
   A.McCarthy solo 00.03.1993

4. **New Neighbours**   50m   VD
   Start under the left end of the shattered rock/scree ledge at two fine cracks. Up these then up the scree to belay on large blocks. Follow the brown crack to the large ledge, possible belay. Climb the good crack to the top.
   P.Shea solo 00.03.1993

5. **Temptress**   34m   VS,4c
   Start 8m right of New Neighbours at the top of a mound at the clean, uninterrupted sweep of slab. Climb straight up, 2BRs, PR.
   A.McCarthy, R.Day 00.03.1993

6. **Tormented Ejaculation**   34m   HVS,4c
   Start 3m right of Temptress below two broken scoops. Climb up between the scoops and climb diagonally rightwards to a good tree belay on the large ledge.
   A.McCarthy, P.Shea 00.03.1993

7. **The Rats And The Flies**   25m   VS,4c
   Start at the bottom of the earth mound under a broken scoop with a sapling growing in it. Climb to the scoop, then straight up passing 2BRs.
   P.Shea 00.03.1993

Fernlea Slabs

8. **Enjoy The Bounce And Swing**   25m   HVS,4c
Start 3m right of two oil barrels. Climb to the scoop, with a good crack above and then to the obvious tree.
Unknown 00.00.1993

9. **Quick Slippers**   19m   HVS,4c
Start 6m right of The Rats And The Flies at a righ-slanting crack. Up this to a ledge, then up to the larger ledge.
A.McCarthy solo 00.03.1993

10. **Golden Gear**   25m   HVS,4c
Start by patches of pink quartz. Climb up past these on the continuous strip of slab between the broken scoops
and follow a thin crack leftwards to the large ledge.
A.McCarthy, P.Shea, A.Williams 00.03.1993

11. **Smells Fishy**   19m   HVS,4c
A line to the right of Golden Gear.
G.Lewis, C.Stort 17.04.1993

12. **Fishy Smell**   19m   HVS,4c
Start right of Smells Fishy next to small bushess by the clean slab. Climb up to tree belays.
A.McCarthy solo 00.03.1993

13. **With Johnny Custard On Night Manoeuvres**   60m   HVS,4c,4c,4b
Starts in the centre of the slabs below the left side of a broken area 30m up.
1. 30m Climb up past a flake and small bush to tree belays.
2. 30m Move up and left to a diagonal crack. Move up left to a bush, then up and left again. Belay at a good tree.
3. The final 20m pitch takes the highest part of the slab. Take care with the rock in the upper sections.
G.Lewis, J.Custance 24.03.1993

14. **Feather Found**   35m   VS,4c,4a
1. Start 3m right of With Johnny Custard etc. Climb up the blank slab to a thin crack and scramble up loose blocks
to a tree belay.
2. Climb easily up the slab above to twin grey trees.
P.Shea, G.Lewis 00.03.1993

15. **Thea**   35m   HVS,4c
Climb a line right of Feather Found, joining that route just below the twin trees.
G.Lewis, C.Stort 14.04.1993

16. **Pussy Willow**   30m   HVS,4c,4a
1. Right of Thea is a large scoop at ground level by some small trees. Start 3m left of this and climb straight up
the slab passing a sapling, then rightwards to a tree belay.
2. Climb directly above the belay to more trees.
G.Lewis, P.Shea 00.03.1993

17. **Walk Like An Egyptian**   120m   HVS,4b,4c,4c
A leftward-rising traverse line. Start right of a large scoop on top of a pile of large blocks.
1. 34m Follow an obvious leftward-slanting crack past a break, to traverse left to belay on top of Fishy Smell.
2. 26m Climb up leftwards to good tree belays on the end of the large ledge, bold.
3. 60m Climb up and leftwards, then traverse for about 30m at this level until it is possible to climb good clean
rock to the top.
A. McCarthy, P.Shea 00.03.1993

Some climbs have been made out of the large scoop next to Walk Like An Egyptian at about S but the rock is very
poor. A low level girdle takes the full length of the main sweep of the slabs starting from Temptress and finishing down
the crack of Walk Like An Egyptian P1, staying just below the broken scoops. It is sustained at about 4c.

*Stefan Doerr & Paul Christie - Burn 'Em Up (E5.6b) Ogmore
(Page 254) Photo: Carl Ryan*

Martyn Richards - This God is Mine (Fr7b+) Witches Point
(Page 277) Photo: Carl Ryan

HERBERT'S QUARRY

GR733188
By Ren Hoek

BOLTING POLICY: Retro-bolting permissible with first ascensionist's permission. Replacement of worn fixed gear on a point for point basis with bolts is permissible. New sports routes allowed.

PREAMBLE
Situated in the Carmarthen Fans (Black Mountains) north of Swansea is an esoteric series of walls ideal for those climbers wanting to go where few have gone before. There is plenty of scope for new routing.

ACCESS
From Brynamman follow the A4069 Llangadog road for 3 miles until a car park is reached just below the crest of the hill. A track on the right leads to the quarry.

DESCENTS: Are by abseil.

THE ROUTES

West Wall
Towards the right-hand side of the cliff is a pinkish groove.

1. **Woolly Bully**   15m   HVS,5a
   Climb the pink groove, 3PRs.
   P.Donnithorne, E.Alsford 00.00.1988

2. **Doochie Coochie**   12m   E4,6b
   Start 4m left of a muddy corner. Climb a wall, 2PRs, difficult moves lead up and left to finish.
   P.Donnithorne, E.Alsford 00.00.1988

East Wall
This is the large quarry, furthest from the road. A 24m wall is topped with blocks.

3. **Nine Below Zero**   24m   E4,6a   *
   Start just left of Can't Do My Homework. Climb up, PR, then move left and up, TR, 2PRs, BR. Continue to a horizontal break, then go leftwards over blocks to a BB. Abseil.
   P.Donnithorne, E.Alsford 00.00.1988

4. **Can't Do My Homework**   12m   E1,5b   *
   The line just left of Mojo, 2BRs.
   P.Donnithorne, E.Alsford 00.00.1988

5. **Mojo**   12m   VS,4c   *
   Climb a crack on the right-hand side of the vertical wall, TR, to a bay at half height, PB. Abseil.
   E.Alsford, P.Donnithorne 00.00.1988

THE LLANGATTOCK ESCARPMENT

GR215147 to 173167
By John Harwood

BOLTING POLICY: No bolting.

PREAMBLE

The Llangattock escarpment extends for 3 miles on the South side of the Usk valley overlooking Crickhowell. Most of the routes are in old limestone quarries of a generally solid nature. It is an exposed cliff that faces north and so it can be cold when windy. However, it offers superb views across the valley to the hills beyond and houses a wide variety of fine routes including some of the most serious in the area. It tends to be regarded as a semi-detached outpost of the South East Wales area, more often frequented by the Wye Valley scene, but although it is not a true rival for Ogmore, it does offer a large number of 'big leads' and deserves more attention.

Three points should be noted to ensure a safe and productive visit. First, because it faces north, seepage can be a problem. Paradoxically, cold, windy conditions often give the driest rock and the best opportunities. Second, the steep, boulder-strewn slopes at the top of the crag often have to be safeguarded with a rope. Dust and/or mud may also affect the tops of climbs, which, if they are difficult, may have to be brushed. Finally, a hostile local farmer keeps removing belay stakes (particularly in the Chwar Pant Y Rhiw area) so, again, check before embarking on that big lead!

It has been said that Llangattock is an acquired taste, or that it is esoteric. That may be. To the author of this section it has provided some of the most memorable climbing days in South Wales. The challenge of the climbs, the wonderful setting and the peace and tranquility of nature away from the maddening crowds have given memories to treasure. Give it a serious try and sample the 'Llangattock Experience'.

ACCESS

In April 1998 after years of work by Brecon Beacons National Park Authority and the BMC an access agreement was finally reached to allow climbing on Llangattock hillside. A group booking system has been established and group leaders intending to visit the crag should contact Crickhowell Adventure Gear (Tel: 01873 810149) to make bookings.

Bookings can be made up to 8 weeks in advance and there is a limit of 3 groups of up to 15 people (total per group) per day. A small charge is payable to help cover wardening costs and the BMC Access Fund also makes an annual contribution towards costs. There will be no bookings when stock gathering is taking place.

Indidividual climbers access is not affected.

1. Main Approach

NOTE: The Llangattock Escarpment passes through Craig-Y-Cilau National Nature Reserve. Climbing on Chwar Mawr and Craig Agen Allewdd is by permit only.

For the Eastern Edge (GR215147 to GR205154) to Chwar Pant-Y-Rhiw (GR203155 to GR195157) there are several access possibilities. The easiest is via Gilwern, (just off the A465 'Heads of The Valleys Road'). Take a lane (Church Road) opposite the Corn Exchange Inn, which leads after a mile or so to Llanelly church. Go around the church yard to the left (north) and take the second turning left (opposite a telephone box). Follow this single track lane, praying that you do not meet an on-coming Land Rover, for about a mile. Just after the cattle grid, the lane goes up to meet a road contouring the hillside. Turn sharply right onto this and follow it for another mile to the NT car park on the left. Do not park anywhere else if you value your car (see note about local farmer above!) but, like all NT car parks in the hills, beware of thieves and leave nothing of value. The contouring road can also be gained from Brynmawr, if approaching from the west along the A465.

The Eastern Edge is directly above the car park, Chwar Pant-Y-Rhiw is to the right and is reached by following the main track to some old ruins, from where the right-hand fork leads to the Pinnacle Bay.

2. Craig-Y-Castell Approach

For Craig-Y-Castell continue through Gilwern on the A4077 to Llangattock, then follow the Beaufort road uphill towards the B4560 and park just beyond a cattle grid (at about GR177168). The cliff can be seen above the bracken slope on the left.

DESCENTS: Descents are generally down obvious paths.

THE ROUTES

The Far Eastern Edge

This is the small cliff at the extreme left-hand end of the escarpment. From the west side of the car park a small track leads straight through bracken to the Eastern Edge. Follow this to the edge and then walk about 300m east to reach the Far Eastern Edge.

The edge here is formed around a main central bay. There is a slabby area on the left below a skyline level tree. The central part has an overhang at 6m and a central groove below, which is often wet. The right-hand part features a small cave below an arete.

Although less imposing than many other parts of Llangattock, the Far Eastern Edge has a number of interesting routes and is well worth a visit.

1. **Mirror**   25m   VS,4c
    Start right of grass ledges on the left side of the bay. Climb up a corner in the lower slabs and avoid a prickly bush to reach ledges. Move right and climb cracks on the left to finish.
    J.Harwood, ANO 31.00.1983

2. **Waiting For Those Summer Evenings**   25m   HVS,5a
    Start immediately right of Mirror at a thin crack leading to the small overhang. Surmount this, then a move right, PR gains the right-hand side of the slab. Finish easily.
    P.Bruten, L.Davies, P.Thomas 16.04.1989

3. **Barndoorer**   25m   VS,4c
    Start as for Waiting For Those Summer Evenings, but strike immediately right towards the right end of the overhang. Using the arete, quickly make an awkward move, then ascend the right edge of the slab.
    L.Davies 06.04.1991

4. **Only The Lonely**   25m   HVS,5a
    A variation on Barndoorer. Gain the right-hand side of the overhang and using the arete, making a barn-door move to gain the upper wall. Finish easily.
    L.Davies 00.00.1991

5. **Reunion**   22m   E1,5b   *
    This finishes up the left side of the clean wall below the prominent skyline tree. Start as for Only The Lonely and climb the corner and a second corner to round the overhang and reaches ledges. Follow finger cracks up the left side of the clean wall.
    J.Harwood 27.05.1986

6. **Class Of 66**   22m   E2,5c
    Start 3m right of Reunion below the skyline tree. Climb up slabs to just left of centre of the clean top wall. Climb this via a very shallow depression in the grey wall.
    J.Harwood 27.05.1986

7. **Rock In A Slot**   22m   E3,5c   *
    Follow the water marks on the right side of the clean wall, immediately below the rowan tree at the cliff top. 2PRs.
    T.Penning, J.Boosey, K.Mumford, J.Harwood 05.09.1999

8. **Invert** 22m HVS,5a
    Climb slabs below the prominent skyline tree to the top wall. Move right and climb the wall, just right of the
    smoothest part to a small ledge. Move up and left to finish at the tree.
    J.Harwood, ANO 31.05.1983

The central part of the bay is distinguished by a long overhang, at about 6m. A crack on the left side leads to a break
level with the overhang.

9. **Whoops Brian** 12m HS,4a
    Climb the crack to the break at 6m. Move left to reach easy ground and then go up to a tree. It is also possible
    to climb the strepped crack directly above the break. This is 5a and a bit loose.
    A.Bidwell, D.Jury 18.10.1998

10. **Alien Summer** 18m E3,5c
    The best line on the central wall. Climb the corner in the centre of the central wall to the roof. Move left and follow
    the finger cracks in the wall above to exit left.
    J.Boosey, T.Penning, K.Mumford, J.Harwood 05.09.1999

11. **Schools Out Forever** 30m E4,6a * \
    An improbable line taking the short, hanging groove above the overhang 7m right of Alien Summer. Climb the
    wall to the break and a gap in the overhang, PR, jammed nut. Pull over and left into the hanging groove and climb
    to the overhang, PR. Traverse left to ledges, then climb up past two small trees to a ledge. Finish up the groove
    on the right past a borehole thread.
    T.Penning, N.Mullin 24.09.2002

The right-hand part of the bay houses a cliff divided into two by an arete. At the bottom of the arete is a small cave.

12. **Sound Barrier** 20m E3,6a *
    A good pitch up the left side of the steep wall, which is the left flank of the righthand cliff. Climb easily up to reach
    the steep wall and follow a thin crack on its left side, 4PRs. Trend right at the top to a bushy tree belay.
    T.Penning, J.Boosey, K.Mumford, J.Harwood 05.09.1999

13. **Edge Of Silence** 22m E4,6b *
    An interesting pitch taking the thin crack in the steep wall to the left of the arete of Cotton Wood Café. Start 6m left
    of the small cave. Climb up with interest to reach the crack. Follow this with even more interest, 3PRs.
    T.Penning, J.Harwood, B.Sparrow 18.08.1998

14. **Cotton Wood Café** 22m E2,5b *
    Start at a small cave below the arete on the right-hand side of the bay. Climb a rounded groove above the cave
    to ledges at 10m, trend left to the arete and finish up this.
    J.James,S.Thompson 00.00.1986

15. **Wowaiuh** 12m VS,4b
    Start as for Cotton Wood Café but follow the obvious rightward-rising traverse line to a ledge (the BB has gone,
    so improvise an escape)!
    L.Davies, P.Thomas 00.00.1990

16. **Wrestling The Polar Bear** 20m E3,5c *
    The overhanging crackline just right of Cottonwood Café. Finish as for the latter or as for Hesitation.
    P.Thomas, L.Davies 00.00.1990

17. **Hesitation** 20m HVS,4c *
    Takes the crack and groove just right of Wrestling The Polar Bear and then two walls to finish at the obvious tree.
    Pleasant.
    T.Penning, J.Harwood, D.Jury, B.Sparrow, D.Parker 18.10.1998

18. **Bid The Return**   10m   E3,6a   \
It is not known whether this route has been repeated since the BR was removed. Start 4m right of Wrestling The Polar Bear, below an obvious shothole at 2m. Move up and right to the shot hole, then up and left to gain the groove, (BR, removed). Climb the groove with difficulty to exit right.
L.Davies, P.Thomas 00.04.1993

The Eastern Edge
This part of the Llangattock Escarpment lies immediately above the car park and can be approached in less than 10 minutes by a track which leads up through bracken from the west side of the car park.

The Eastern Edge can be divided into three sections. The main central section is a rather featureless wall which has two horizontal faults, just above and just below half-height respectively, which are often greasy and run across most of its width. At the left (east) end, around the corner past an easy descent ridge, is a smaller section containing an obvious bottomless chimney - the line of Grenoble. At the right side of the Eastern Edge, around a slight corner is Fighting Cock Buttress, after which the long, steep, smooth Winning Wall forms the next section of the crag.

Grenoble Buttress
Just before Grenoble buttress is a short area of cliff, with an arete.

19. **Lost In Time**   14m   HVS,5a   \
Climb just left of the arete.
N.Mullin, T.Penning 24.09.2002

20. **Nic Of Time**   14m   HVS,5b   \
The central line on the arete.
N.Mullin, T.Penning 24.09.2002

21. **Bite Size**   25m   VS,4a
To the left of the chimney of Grenoble is a slab. This loose climb takes the groove in the slab.
T.Penning, J.Harwood 18.05.1982

22. **Little Jerk**   25m   HVS,5a
Another loose climb which takes the cracked groove to the right of Bite Size.
T.Penning, J.Harwood 18.05.1982

23. **Heart Bypass**   30m   E2,5c   *   \
As for Heart Route below to the giant thread. Move left past a PR to gain a crack and finish up this.
T.Penning, J.Harwood, T.Forsyth 25.08.2002

24. **Heart Route**   30m   E3,5c   **   \
Start at the obvious crack up and left from the lowest part of the face. From the crack go up to a short, shallow chimney to the start of the upper wall, PR, thread. Pull up and move left to a giant thread. Continue direct past 2PRs to finish up a final groove. One of the best routes here, superseding Mistral (E2,5b, J.Harwood 1986).
T.Penning, N.Mullin 03.09.2002

25. **Grenoble**   30m   VS,4c
Takes the very obvious chimney. Climb a crack and move left to gain the chimney which is followed to the top and a stake belay. Currently vegetated.
T.Penning, J.Harwood 18.05.1982

26. **Poison Ivy**   30m   E2,5b   \
Start below the middle of the wall to the right of Grenoble. Climb to a short corner in the overhang and pull over on large creaky holds, PRs. Make a tricky move up and finish more easily.
T.Penning, C.Day, G.Bartram 15.09.2002

Llangattock

At the back right-hand side of the Grenoble bay are two caves with a hanging slab to the right.

27. **Old Shep**   7m   E1,5a
Delightful but short. Meander up the slab, PR.
L.Davies, P.Thomas 00.00.1989

28. **Wicked Lauren**   6m   E2,5b
Very, very short. Ascend the waterworn groove to the right of Old Shep.
P.Thomas, L.Davies 00.00.1989

Main Area
The main part of the Eastern Edge comes next. It is bounded on the left by an easy descent ridge. Although there are a few stakes in place (particularly in the Azolla area), some forward planning is advised before embarking on a lead!

At the right side of this section of the cliff, a small tree grows from the grass ledge about 5m up and just left of the arete. In the centre there is a blocky overhang at half-height, beneath which is a cave entrance at ground level. Penwood Special takes the crack towards the right side of the overhang. In the middle of the wall to the left a small semi-circular chimney (ZX) can be seen in the upper part.

About 15m left of the Rowan tree is the first route.

29. **Gavin Cytlau Likes Putty**   8m   HVS,5a   \
Start about 5m left of a groove (Em Won) and climb the wall to finish by the obvious crack. Walk off left.
N.Mullin, T.Forsyth 25.08.2002

30. **Em Won**   18m   E2,5b   \
The obvious groove 6m left of the tree.
N.Mullin, T.Forsyth, J.Harwood, T.Penning 25.08.2002

31. **Company Flow**   14m   VS,4c   \
The crack 5m right of Em Won. At the grassy break traverse right to the Rowan.
N.Mullin, T.Forsyth 25.08.2002

32. **Flik On The Rope**   12m   E1,5b   \
Start just right of Company Flow, below a bottomless crack. At the top of the crack, trend right to finish at the tree.
T.Forsyth, N.Mullin, J.Harwood, T. Penning 25.08.2002

33. **20,000 Leagues Under The Sea**   10m   E3,6a   \
The line right of Flik.
T.Penning 00.10.1998

34. **The Mile High Club**   10m   E3,6a   \
The thin crack to the right, PR.
T.Penning, J.Harwood, T.Forsyth 25.08.2002

35. **Bitter Bark**   33m   E2,5b
Start beneath a groove, just left of a wall with a semi-circular chimney in its upper half. Climb the wall to the ledge, move right, then left to a hollow. Pull into the obvious groove and follow it, PR, to the top.
T.Penning, J.Harwood 08.06.1982

36. **Z.X.**   33m   E1,5b   *
Start under the semi-circular chimney in the upper wall. Climb a groove and wall, then the chimney to exit right.
T.Penning, J.Harwood 08.09.1981

37. **Space Between My Ears**   33m   E2,5b

How did it get that name? Start as for Z.X. Climb, trending rightwards to a tree. Continue on poor rock and climb a short corner to a hawthorn. Step left and climb to the top.
T.Penning, J.Harwood 11.05.1982

38. **Penwood Special**   23m   E2,5b   *

Right of Z.X. is a line of overhangs at 12m. Climb a crack in a left facing corner to the right-hand end of the overhangs. Traverse left for a metre and pull into a wide groove, which is followed more easily to the top.
T.Penning, J.Harwood 20.07.1982

To the right of the overhangs of Penwood Special is a long rather featureless wall with two horizontal grassy bands, the upper one at half-height.

39. **Wall Of Glass**   30m   HVS,5a

Start on the left side of the wall. Climb the crack to a grassy ledge and very thin tree, then move up and left to climb a short corner at 20m height. Traverse right for 3m, then gain the top.
T.Penning, J.Harwood 25.08.1981

40. **No Ref**   30m   HVS,5a

Climb a thin crack right of Wall Of Glass to a grass ledge, move right, then left to join Wall Of Glass. Finish leftwards up the slabby corner.
J.Harwood solo 26.08.1983

41. **The Gambler**   30m   E2,5b   *

Originally given HVS! Start beneath a slanting crack in the centre of the long wall, at three short cracks at ground level. Climb the cracks to a grass ledge, step left and climb up to the slanting crack and then to the top.
T.Penning, J.Harwood 25.08.1981

42. **Bruten Lee**   26m   HVS,5a

Start 3m right. Climb a thin crack and a brown groove in the upper wall.
P.Thomas, L.Davies, P.Bruten 00.00.1984

43. **Azolla**   26m   VS,4b

A good introduction to the wall and the most obvious line. Start at a pair of obvious cracks below a shallow groove in the upper cliff and at the left side of the highest part of the grass underneath. Climb the left crack, step left and then continue straight to the top via a groove.
T.Penning, J.Harwood 25.08.1981

44. **The Backsliding B**   26m   HVS,5a

Climb the crack just right of Azolla, joining the latter near the top.
J.Harwood 26.08.1983

There is an obvious flowstone wall to the right of Azolla.

45. **Parson's Pleasure**   27m   E2,5b

Climbs the left side of the stalactite wall to the right of Azolla. Start midway between the starts of Azolla and Wonderful Life. Go up to the first break, PR and continue straight up the wall past a second break on slightly friable rock to the top. Continually interesting.
T.Penning, I.Parsons, J.Harwood 13.04.1997

46. **Boozey's First Climb**   27m   E3,5c   *

Climbs the centre of the flowstone wall, left of Wonderful Life. The best pitch on the 'featureless wall'. Start at the right side of the cliff, just before the grass landing drops away. Climb the thin crack passing a PR at 3m, then move up to the first horizontal break. Continue to the second break and on to the top.
T.Penning, J.Boosey, J.Harwood, I.Hattam 11.10.1998

47. Wonderful Life   30m   HVS,5a
At the right edge of the 'featureless wall' there is a tree on a ledge at 5m, above some overhangs. Start 5m left of the tree. Go diagonally up to the ledge left of the tree and then gain the shallow groove above the tree, which is followed to the top.
T.Penning, J.Harwood 25.08.1981

48. Animal Lunch Box   27m   E5,6a
A powerful pitch giving varied climbing of a serious nature. If you like that sort of thing, the pitch may be worth a star! To the right of Wonderful Life the cliff is dominated by a large roof. About 6m from the right end of the roof is a slim crack/groove. Climb the crack/groove to the roof and move right to a PR. Using a Friend for aid, reach over the roof to an obvious flake crack. Surmount the roof and get established above. Continue cautiously up a band of obviously loose rock to better climbing on the upper grey wall. 2TRs indicate the interesting finish. An impressive climb.
T.Penning 04.10.1998

Fighting Cock Buttress
Around the corner from the 'featureless wall' is the right-hand section of the Eastern Edge. It is topped by loose bands and contains some exciting looking rock! It is bounded on the right by the long, smooth wall – Winning Wall. At its right side is an area of grey rock, with a prominent right-facing groove which is taking by Fighting Cock.

49. Vendetta   33m   E3,6a   *
Climb the groove left of the start of Fighting Cock, TR, then a rib to a sloping ledge. Pull over a roof and pull up right into a short groove. Move up leftwards then pull round a bulge and up a steep wall. Climb a slim groove exiting right at its end.
M.Crocker, M.Ward 15.06.1985

50. Fighting Cock   26m   E3,5c   *
A good climb with a bold finish. Climb a short crack below and right of an obvious groove, then move across left to gain the groove. Climb it to the top. Belay well back.
T.Penning, G.Gibson, P.Cresswell, C.Court 02.09.1984

51. Race Against Time   14m   E1,5b
Start 3m right of Fighting Cock. Climb to an overhang from the right, PR, pull over and finish via the crack above.
L.Davies, P.Thomas 24.05.1986

Winning Wall
This long steep wall contains some of the hardest routes at Llangattock. It is approached by walking right from the Eastern Edge. The smooth part of the wall has a very shallow groove line in its centre (Winning) and is bounded on its right by the crack-line of Cold Snatch. Further right still is an area of overhangs, with a big roof near the base.

52. Wonderlands   27m   E6,6b   *
Extremely thin and sustained. The in-situ gear is old and fragile. Climb a shallow groove at the left-hand end of the wall. Move left across an unstable ledge and climb directly up the grey flowstone wall, PR, 2BRs. A long reach from a projecting hold gains a long, dirty, grassy ledge. Continue easily to a good tree. Needs cleaning.
M.Crocker 08.08.1987

53. Mad Hatter   20m   E5,6a
A much easier proposition than Wonderlands, but still serious. Start below an obvious grey streak in the wall left of Stay Sharp. Climb to a nose (missing TR), to a further TR, and continue with difficulty, PR. Stretch for a small hold and then finish rightwards.
G.Gibson, H.Gibson 31.08.1984

54. Stay Sharp   27m   E4,6a

Start below an obvious leftward-curving water-worn groove. Climb up and trend right to a grassy ledge, then move left to beneath the slanting groove, poor PR. Climb straight up, PR, to good holds and continue up the corner to the top. Stake belay above.

A.Sharp, T.Penning 25.07.1982

55. Winning   27m   E3,5c   **

One of the best routes at Llangattock, taking an improbable line up the wall about 10m right of the curving groove of Stay Sharp. Climb cracks in the centre of the wall to a loose band, step up and go left into a very shallow groove line, 2PRs. Climb the groove to a small pocket, move up, PR, and trend rightwards to finish.

T.Penning, J.Harwood, C.Court 12.06.1984

56. Hitman   27m   E4,6b   *

Start 6m right of Winning at crack lines leading to the top of an easy ledge system. Climb to the top of the ledges and move straight up, TR. Step left, BR, then climb direct by a series of extending moves to the top, PR.

G.Gibson 03.07.1987

57. Culmination Crack   27m   E3,6a

A tough finish. Start as for Hitman, with easy climbing below and left of a crack high up on the cliff. Climb straight up over ledges, then traverse right to the crack, PR. Finish directly.

G.Gibson, T.Penning, P.Cresswell, C.Court 02.09.1984

58. Cold Snatch   33m   E1,5b   *

Climbs the crackline that bounds the right side of the smooth part of Winning Wall. Start 6m left of a large overhang at the base of the cliff, below and left of a grassy ledge. Climb thin cracks, move right and up to the grass ledge and a band of shattered rock. Step back left to a thin crack and follow this to the top.

P.Littlejohn, D.Renshaw 29.06.1979

59. The Big Bright Green Pleasure Machine   40m   E2,5c   *

Climb Cold Snatch to the band of shattered rock, traverse right to a ledge, PR, below a short corner capped by a small overhang. Pull into the corner, 2PRs, then move rightwards and up to a ledge. Traverse left and finish up cracks. There is an alternative finish from the short corner on the right, which goes back left to gain a diagonal left trending crack which finishes at the top of Cold Snatch.

T.Penning, J.Harwood 23.08.1982

60. Mean Green   40m   E4,6a

A short, direct start to the previous two routes. Climb a short groove right of Cold Snatch, PR (missing). Finish as for The Big Bright Green Pleasure Machine.

A.Sharp, P.Lewis 00.00.1983

61. Liberator   40m   E4,6a   **

Start 2m right of Mean Green. Climb a thin crack, PR, until forced right into a shallow corner, PR. This leads to an overhang. Swing left to a good ledge, move up right into the short corner of The Big Bright etc, 2PRs and climb the crack above taking its left-hand branch to finish.

C.Court, L.Davies 12.06.1986

62. The Roaring Eighties   43m   E5,6a

A magnificent challenge through the roofs between Pleasure Machine and West Wind, which has recently suffered a major rock-fall. The original description is included for optimists! Start 7m right of Liberator. Up a shallow groove past a roof to a break at 8m, traverse right to steep rock. Up to a good hold and pull over a roof and the next roof using a tree, which is no longer in situ! Traverse right until difficult moves gain a good flat hold up and right. Climb a shallow groove above and finish up a thin curving crack on the right. Many PRs.

M.Crocker, R.Thomas 26.07.1985

63. **West Wind**   36m   E1,5a   *

Start 3m right of the large overhang. Climb the wall bearing slightly left to a break. Move left and up to a narrow ledge. Climb the wall via a flake, before moving right to a groove, which is climbed to the top. Belay well back.
P.Littlejohn, D.Renshaw 29.06.1979

64. **Tramp**   8m   HVS,4c

The small groove, flowstone and scoop right of West Wind.
L.Davies solo 00.03.1986

Right-hand Area

Right of Winning Wall, the cliff is broken until a large area of flowstone/cave at ground level. Left of the cave is a corner and left again another corner with flowstone above. Approach is via the main diagonal track from the car park.

65. **Domino Theory**   38m   HVS,4c

Climb the shallow corner, step right then continue up the deep cracks to the top.
T.Penning, J.Harwood 27.04.1982

66. **Sister Sledge**   33m   E1,5b

Climb the shallow corner with the crack in the back, some 3m left of the cave at ground level, to reach a curving corner crack. Follow the corner crack to the top. Loose.
C.Court, T.Penning, J.Harwood 12.06.1984

67. **Angel In My Pocket**   33m   E3,5c   *

Serious but satisfying. Start 5m right of the cave. Climb a left-trending ramp leading to an overhang. Pull over it and continue, TRs (some missing), to the top.
T.Penning, A.Sharp, J.Harwood 29.05.1984

68. **The Dark Ages**   30m   E2,5b   *

Start on a block below a scoop at 7m and directly below the slanting chimney of Sir Hammer. Climb leftwards to a break, move up right into the scoop and step back left onto a ledge. Climb the sheet above via a crack, TR. Move left and up to finish.
M.Crocker, M.Ward 29.06.1985

A recent rock-fall has rendered the following two climbs very dangerous, with much unstable rock to negotiate.

69. **Sir Hammer**   33m   E1,5b   \

Start beneath a chimney-crack line on the right-hand side of the wall. Climb a thin crack and a small overhang on its right, then up the chimney to exit rightwards.
T.Penning, J.Harwood 20.07.1982

70. **Second Generation**   33m   E2,5b   \

Start just right of Sir Hammer. Climb a corner onto the wall above, then a shallow corner to the top.
T.Penning, P.Cresswell, C.Court 08.05.1984

At the far right-hand end of the Eastern Edge is a square slab (Nerve Test Slab) above a small ruin on the main diagonal track from the car park.

71. **Nerve Test**   22m   E2,5c

Start by scrambling up to the left side of a slab. Traverse right, with feet on poor rock to a ledge, then climb sloping ledges and a thin crack to the top of the slab. Scramble off rightwards.
T.Penning, J.Harwood 27.04.1982

72. **Shock Dose** 30m E2,5b

The slab right of Nerve Test. Climb the right-hand of twin cracks in the initial wall and step left to a ledge. Move up, then leftwards to gain twin cracks and the top.
M.Crocker, M.Ward 15.06.1985

73. **Aegina** 20m E1,5a

As for Shock Dose to the ledge, step right and continue up the wall, TR, moving right to finish up a corner.
L.Davies, D.Leitch 19.07.1986

Chwar Pant Y Rhiw

This is the most popular section of Llangattock and is approached easily in about 10 minutes by following the main track which leaves the west side of the car park. At the small ruin, take the right-hand fork in the track to reach the Pinnacle Bay Area.

Chwar Pant Y Rhiw is broadly split into two sections. The left (Eastern) side contains a mixture of grades including some suitable beginners routes. For that reason it has been popular with Outdoor Centres. The cliff is divided into halves at a ridge (Corner Buttrees Arete), beyond which things become distinctly more impressive. Indeed, an area of formidable overhangs gives the right-hand side of Chwar Pant Y Rhiw some of the hardest and most serious routes at Llangattock.

Pinnacle Bay

At the extreme left-hand end of the bay, high up on the grass slope, is a small buttress of natural limestone. Below and right of this the cliff starts in earnest.

74. **The Pinnacle** 10m S

Climb anywhere up the centre of the small natural buttress on the left-hand end of the bay.
Unknown Pre-1973

At the left-hand end of the main cliff is a broad shallow recess between two noses, normally with a muddy pool to its right.

75. **Scoop** 16m VD

Start at the shallow recess between the noses. Climb on the right for 3m, then traverse left to gain a ledge above the left-hand nose. Finish left or right.
Unknown Pre-1978

76. **Spirogyra Corner** 20m HS,4a

In all but the driest weather there is a muddy pool at the foot of the wall right of Scoop. Start 3m left of the pool. Climb a groove with a small overhang at 5m to gain a nose, then to a ledge and silver birch tree. Move up to a rock tower and take this on the right.
Unknown Pre-1978

77. **White Wall Direct** 20m VS,4b *

The White Wall is obvious, being lighter coloured than its surroundings, due to drainage. Start just right of the pool at three grassy ledges. Scramble to the second ledge, then climb to a nose, which is taken on the right. Move left then climb a rib on its right to finish.
Unknown Pre-1978

78. **Little Red Rooster** 20m HVS,5b

Climb the shallow corner 6m right of White Wall Direct and continue directly to the top.
C.Court solo 00.00.1983

79. Excalibur   20m   E1,5b
A difficult start. Climb the steep wall, PR, right of Little Red Rooster to finish on easier ground.
C.Court solo 00.00.1983

80. Switchblade   20m   HVS,5a
Climb the obvious short corner right of Excalibur to a small overhang. Pull over this and climb the short wall above. Finish as for Straighter.
C.Court solo 00.00.1983

81. Straighter   20m   S   *
Start 9m right of the pool to the left of some grey rubble. Climb a blunt pillar and short wall to a ledge. Finish up the rib.
Unknown Pre-1973

82. Diagonal   22m   S
Start 4m right of Straighter at a corner/crack beneath a nose. Gain a slabby scoop, then traverse left and up to a very short rust-coloured corner. Continue to a tiny overhang and finish leftwards.
Unknown Pre-1973

83. Ornithology   22m   S
Climb to the slabby scoop as for Diagonal, then move right to another scoop. Exit right and follow ledges up left to finish up a corner above a small cave.
Unknown Pre-1973

84. Apollo XI   22m   VS,4c
Climb a short steep crack right of the corner crack of Diagonal to a ledge. Continue over small ledges to a short chimney leading to a good ledge below a bulging nose. Finish up the corner right of the nose.
Unknown Pre-1973

85. Bespoke   22m   VD
Start at a steep wall right of a short open chimney and left of an overhang. Climb a crack system and steep wall before moving right to a scoop. Finish direct, via a cracked wall.
Unknown Pre-1973

86. Spiral Stairs   23m   D
Start as for Bespoke. Climb right over short steps to a blank wall and continue right to easy ground. Scramble back left and finish via mossy blocks and a cracked wall.
Unknown Pre-1973

87. Straight Stairs   23m   VS,4b
Climb a corner to the left of the blank wall, over an overhang and finish easily.
J.Harwood, M.Ismail 18.07.1998

88. Original Route   23m   D
Right of Bespoke the cliff projects to form a blunt toe. Climb over easy steps and a short wall, then trend right to various finishes.
Unknown Pre-1973

89. Pant-Ing   23m   VS,4b
Start in a slight depression right of Original Route and climb straight over slabby walls, trending left with difficulty, to reach a deep crack on the right side of the headwall. Climb this to the top.
J.Harwood, M.Ismail 18.07.1998

90. **Piton Traverse**   21m   VD
Start 6m right of Original Route, 12m left of a large shallow chimney below and just left of a bushy tree at half-height. Traverse left to ledges then back right to a recess below the final wall. Cross a nose to a ledge and finish by a corner/crack.
Unknown Pre-1973

91. **Raven Route**   21m   VD   *
Climb the shallow groove 4m right of Piton Traverse and step right onto a steep wall. Move up right then left to a large ledge. Climb the black wall on its right and finish up the corner/crack.
Unknown Pre-1973

92. **Crusty Wall**   21m   S
Climb a grey wall just left of a large chimney to a ledge. Finish straight up.
Unknown Pre-1973

93. **Sad Groove**   21m   S
Climb the large shallow chimney, which is below and just left of a bushy hawthorn tree at half-height, finishing up loose cracks.
Unknown Pre-1973

To the right of Sad Groove the lower part of the cliff is smoother.

94. **John's Jaunt**   19m   HVS,4c
Climb a thin crack 4m right of the large chimney, then a short wall to a ledge right of the hawthorn. Finish straight up. Getting onto the ledge is awful!
J.Harwood 11.08.1977

95. **Dus**   19m   VS,4b
Start at shallow groove 9m right of a large chimney. Climb up and left to a ledge at 6m, move right and up to a grass ledge. Finish straight up.
J.Harwood 11.08.1977

96. **The Pedestal**   19m   VS,4b
Start at the right edge of a blank wall. Climb a shallow corner leading to a shale ledge, with a small pedestal. Gain the shale band above and finish via a mantleshelf and a short crack.
Unknown Pre-1973

Right of the blank part, the wall is more broken and obviously loose. Then there is a break in the cliff. To its right the wall is marked by a line of overhangs.

97. **Man About The House**   9m   HVS,5c
Start below and left of the overhangs at a steep slab 2m right of an obvious crack. Climb just right of the nose to pass a small overhang.
L.Davies solo Pre-28.06.1984
C.Court direct 00.00.1985

98. **Jailbird**   19m   HVS,5a
Climb the crackline in the centre of the slab, passing a small overhang. Finish as for The Creaking Flakes.
C.Court solo 00.00.1983

99. **The Creaking Flakes**   20m   E1,5b
Start 3m right of Jailbird. Climb a steep rib and trend left to flakes, move left and up to a hawthorn. Climb the corner behind and finish by either of two cracks.
Unknown Pre-1973

---

100. Entertainer   19m   E2,5b

Start 2m right of The Creaking Flakes. Climb an inverted v, pass a small overhang, PR and finish up an arete.
P.Bruten, L.Davies 07.09.1985

101. Wildest Dreams   20m   E2,5c   *

Climb a crack in a shallow corner right of Entertainer. Step right and pull over two bulges, PR, to a hawthorn. Finish up the corner left of a nose.
D.Hillier, S.Edwards 00.00.1982

102. Visions In Blue   9m   E4,6a

Climb the wall and bulging crack right of Wildest Dreams past a poor PR.
L.Davies, P.Bruten 20.07.1985

To the right of the area of overhangs is an obvious cone of grass (!) The following climb starts from the top of this cone.

103. Ramblin' Sid   19m   S

The first break in the overhangs, above a cone of grass. Climb a corner and short wall to a tree, then follow a sloping corner to a choice of cracks to finish.
Unknown Pre-1973

To the right of Ramblin' Sid, the wall bends outwards and is split by a number of grooves. Its bounding right edge is taken by Break Of Day.

104. Hideaway   18m   S

Start right of the overhangs above the grass cone. Climb an overhanging corner, moving right at a yellow block, to finish up the wall above.
Unknown Pre-1973

Right of Hideaway the wall projects and passes a cave at ground level.

105. Hidden Rib   18m   VD

Climb a grey groove and broken slab on the left to a yellow block. Climb over this and finish up the wall above.
Unknown Pre-1973

106. Nice One   19m   HS 4b

The groove between Hidden Rib and Fingernail Crack.
L.Davies solo 00.08.1986

107. Fingernail Crack   19m   S

Start 3m right of Hidden Rib. Climb a thin jagged crack in a corner and go left via steps to a grass ledge. Finish up the wall above.
Unknown Pre-1973

108. Break Of Day   19m   HS,4a   \

The wall immediately right of Fingernail Crack, to gain the obvious break. Climb the arete to the ledge and finish up cracks in the wall.
L.Davies solo 00.00.1986

Around the corner from Break Of Day is a cave.

109. Cuticle   19m   VS,4a

Right of Fingernail Crack and left of a cave entrance is a smooth 4m wall. There are many ways up it.
Unknown Pre-1973

110. **Hymns And Arias**   7m   E1,5c
A boulder problem with a good landing. Climb a steep wall, right of Cuticle, with a small overhang at 4m. This is just left of the obvious crack of Purple Putty.
L.Davies 00.00.1985

111. **Purple Putty**   19m   VS,4c
Start at an obvious crack 2m left of a cave entrance. Climb up over a loose bulge at 4m to a shale band, traverse right to a crack and finish up this. Needs cleaning.
D.Hillier solo 00.00.1982

112. **High Frequency**   19m   E2,5b
Committing. Start at the left side of the cave. Climb up slightly right, over the loose band to finish just left of a shallow corner. Take care with the rock.
C.Court, M.Davey 00.00.1983

113. **Heat Of The Moment**   19m   E2,5b
Start 2m right of the cave. Climb up and step left over the cave to a block at the shale band. Finish via cracks and a flared corner. Friable.
D.Hillier, P.Jones 00.00.1982

114. **Strawberry Flare**   23m   HVS,5a   \
Start 6m right of the cave entrance at an obvious crack. Climb the crack past a block to the shale band and finish up the corner above.
Unknown 1978-1983

115. **Little Overhang**   19m   HVS,5a
Start 12m right of the cave at a crack in a corner with a small block overhang at 4m. Climb above the overhang to a resting ledge on the right. Move left to reach a shale band and finish up left via steps and the final wall.
Unknown Pre-1973

116. **Puraka**   18m   HVS,4c   *
Start as for Little Overhang. Climb to the resting ledge, then go up right to reach the shale band. Finish up a short corner.
Unknown Pre-1973

117. **Gold Rush**   18m   E1,5b   *
A good climb. Start 12m right of Puraka in a cracked corner under a roof. Climb the corner and then at 7m an overhang on its left. Continue up the wall above and finish through the break in the top overhang.
C.Court, L.Davies 00.00.1984

118. **Apache**   18m   HVS,5a
Start 15m right of Puraka. Climb an obvious arete with a triangular block at 4m, then the corner above.
C.Court, M.Shepherd 00.00.1983

119. **Cowboy**   14m   VS,4b
Towards the right-hand end of this section of cliff, 2m right of Apache, before a small buttress where the cliff turns, there is a sharp projecting rib. Climb a corner on its left to gain the top of the rib, then follow steps to the upper wall which is climbed via some thin cracks.
Unknown Pre-1973

The shale band crossed by the next two routes, is currently in a dreadful state (probably as a result of the cone of grass by Ramblin Sid).

120. Passage to Andrea 18m E3,6a *

An alternative start to Julie Andrea. Start 2m right of Cowboy and just right of the rib. Climb a shallow groove and crack line, PR, then move up and right to the tree. Finish as for Julie Andrea or abseil.
I.Waddington, Gwent M.C. 00.00.1986

121. Julie Andrea 18m E3,6a

Sustained and technical. Start 3m right of Passage to Andrea. Climb a bulging crack to the tree at half-height, then step up and right to a small ledge. Trend left to a shallow corner, PR, and straight up to finish.
C.Court, T.Penning 08.05.1984

122. White Tiger 17m E3,5c *

Bold climbing. Start at a large corner 9m right of Julie Andrea. Climb the cracked corner to its top, then move right over the bulge and easily up to a ledge at half-height. Climb the wall above, trending right, poor PR - but good Friend above, to a small ledge. Move back left and finish directly.
C.Court 00.00.1983

The next thirteen climbs start from a ledge halfway up the cliff, which is easily reached from the right. At the back of the ledge is a loose looking corner (Brer Rabbit, VDiff, Pre-1973) above a spiny bush. The first climb starts 15m left of Brer Rabbit, at the far left end of the ledge, below a very thin crack in the wall above and about 3m left of the obvious crack of Don't Walk Over My Head.

123. Wild Life 8m E2,6a

Start below the thin crack. Climb a ramp then trend right to a narrow ledge below the thin crack, PR. Finish straight up the crack.
C.Court, L.Davies, P.Thomas 25.06.1986

124. Don't Walk Over My Head 8m VS,4b *

This takes the obvious crack line in the wall left of Brere Rabbit and 3m right of Wild Life.
Unknown Pre-1978

125. No Shit 8m VS,4b

Start 3m left of Brere Rabbit below a rib. Climb the wall to take the rib on its right.
C.Court, N.Haines 00.00.1982

126. Brere Rabbit 8m VD

The loose-looking corner.
Unknown 1973-1978

127. Rotten Wall 8m S

Climb the obvious crack right of Brere Rabbit.
Unknown Pre-1973

128. Night Shift 8m HVS,5b

Right of Rotten Wall is a crack, and right again of this is a line up the wall. Climb this to the top with protection from side runners.
L.Davies, P.Thomas 00.00.1986

To the right are three corners.

129. Limbo 9m S

Climb the left-hand corner.
Unknown Pre-1973

130.**Misty Haze**   9m   HS,4a
The arete right of Limbo.
P.Thomas solo Pre-14.05.1984

131.**Missing Link**   9m   S
The second corner.
Unknown Pre-1973

132.**Dunno**   9m   HS,4a
The third corner, finishing left or direct at VS,4b.
P.Thomas solo Pre-00.05.1984

133.**Middle Corner**   9m   HS,4a
A right-hand finish to Dunno.
Unknown Pre-1973

134.**Corner Buttress**   12m   D
A useful descent. From the toe of the buttress where the cliff turns, scramble up toand climb the right-hand corner.
Unknown Pre-1973

135.**Corner Buttress Arete**   12m   VS,4b
Climb the buttress, where the cliff turns and faces northwest.
Unknown Pre-1973

After turning the corner, the cliff is dominated by a steep wall, covered in flowstone. It is bounded on its right by the obvious right facing corner of Hangman.

Flowstone Wall
The following seven routes offer pleasant climbing on what is usually good rock.

136.**I Can See Clearly**   17m   VS,4c
Start as for Corner Buttress Direct. Traverse the flowstone wall from left to right at 12m. Finish up Perk.
L.Davies, P. Bruten 10.06.1986

137.**Man of Mystery**   12m   VS,4b
Start 3m right of Corner Buttress Arete. Climb cracks just right of the arete to the top.
C.Court, N.Haines 00.00.1982

138.**Suddenly Last Summer**   14m   VS,4c
Start on the slope leading down from Corner Buttress Arete, under the steep flowstone wall at a small recess. Climb cracks above the recess, traverse 1m right and finish straight up past a diagonal web of flowstone.
T.Penning solo 29.09.1981

139.**Christmas Spirit**   15m   VS,4b
Start at a crack just right of Suddenly Last Summer. Climb the crack to finish up Suddenly Last Summer.
L.Davies, P.Thomas 00.00.1983

140.**Perk**   18m   VS,4b   *
Pleasant climbing on good rock. Start on a block at the lowest point of the flowstone wall and follow the line of least resistance to the steep headwall. Traverse right into the large crack to finish, or move left to finish direct.
J.Harwood 11.08.1977
L.Davies, P. Bruten, P. Thomas - Direct 00.00.1984

141. Knight Flyer   18m   VS,4b
Start 4m right of Perk. Climb a crack and wall above, then trend left to finish as for Perk.
C. Court, N. Haines 00.00.1982

142. Free Runner   18m   VS,4c
Start 3m right of Knight Flyer. Climb flowstone right of a small tree, to finish up a faint crackline.
P.Thomas, L.Davies Pre 26.06.1984

143. Bridlevale Wall   21m   E2,5b   *
A good introduction to the harder flowstone climbing. Start at a short crack above a grass cone and slightly right of the centre of the wall. Climb the crack to the flowstone and follow this directly to the top.
T.Penning, J.Harwood, M. Learoyd 15.05.1984

144. Wild Touch   24m   E3,6a   *
The hardest route on the flowstone wall. Start about 4m left of the crackline of Passage of Time, which is at the right side of the flowstone wall. Climb the flowstone directly, to a faint crackline and finish up this.
C. Parker, ANO 05.10.1983

145. Cry Havoc   24m   E2,5c   **
Excellent climbing with good protection. Start just left of Passage of Time. Climb to a disjointed crackline and follow it to a small hole. Then either traverse right to join Passage of Time or continue directly (more strenuous, but about the same grade) to the top.
T.Penning, P. Cresswell 30.11.1980
Direct: T.Penning, J.Harwood, C. Court 01.05.1984

146. Passage of Time   24m   E1,5b   **
An excellent climb marred only by its exit. Start on the right side of the flowstone wall at a block with a fine crack above it. Climb the crack and finish up and left.
P.Littlejohn, D.Renshaw 12.06.1979

147. Edge of Time   33m   E1,5b   *
This climb takes the arete right of Passage of Time. Climb Passage of Time until level with a small overhang. Traverse right to the arete and climb it easily, but in a fine position, to the top. A spectacular and easy alternative is to abseil down the arete to belay on the lip of the overhang. Climbing back is VS,4b and offers a very exposed pitch for the grade.
T.Penning, J.Harwood 15.05.1984

Main Area

To the right of Flowstone Wall, the cliff is dominated by a series of daunting overhangs, where only the bold dare to venture! Most of the climbs follow powerful lines and offer the true 'Llangattock Experience'. Some cleaning may be needed to remove the debris swept down from the winter rains. Care should always be taken to safeguard exits and if necessary the state of the in-situ gear.

148. Hangman   30m   E4,6a   *   \
A difficult climb. Start on the right of the flowstone wall below and right of a big corner, right of a huge boulder. Climb a groove to the overhang, then traverse left to beneath the corner. Move up left over the overhang into the corner and climb this to exit right. Belay well back. A small rockfall near the bottom of the corner may mean the climb is now more difficult.
The Hanging Corner A2 Unknown Pre-1973
P. Littlejohn, D. Renshaw 29.06.1979

149. **More Fool You**   30m   E5,6a   *
Start as for Hangman. Climb the groove to the overhang, then traverse right to a ledge. Pull over the roof and move right to a resting place, PRs, BRs. Step back left and climb the wall, PR, to the top. Belay well back, or leave a rope in place. The in situ gear is in a bad way.
Unknown Butterfly Wall A2 Pre-1973
A.Sharp, P.Lewis 05.07.1979

150. **Fool's Executioner**   33m   E3,6a   *
This climb takes the diagonal crack leading out right from More Fool You. Follow More Fool You to beneath the overhang (possible belay). Pull over the overhang and then move across right to the crack. Climb the crack to the top and belay well back.
T.Penning, P.Cresswell 19.06.1983

151. **Johnny Cum Lately**   33m   E3,6a   *
An impressive route, with some dubious rock. Start at a crack below the red overhang to the right of the corner of Hangman. Climb the crack to its top. Swing right, PR, to a ledge beneath the centre of the overhang. Climb up to the overhang and traverse left on undercuts to a good resting place. Continue up the crack above to exit left. Belay well back.
T.Penning, A.Sharp 31.08.1982

152. **Acid Rain**   30m   E5,6b
The start is desperate. Start right of Johnny Cum Lately, at a shallow corner crack. Climb the crack to the overhang. Pull round this into the short v-groove (crux), which is followed to a ledge beneath the main groove. Climb this groove to exit left. Belay well back.
Unknown Cavemen's Route A2 Pre-1973
A.Sharp, J.Harwood 1pt. 11.09.1982
FFA C.Parker 00.00.1983

The smooth wall right of the groove of Acid Rain, ends at a rounded arete with blocky overhangs beneath. Right of this is a deep-set groove, the line of IQ Test.

153. **I.Q. Test**   42m   E5,5c 5pts   *
A powerful and serious pitch taking the awe-inspiring groove line at the left end of the central overhangs. Climb the groove past a small tree to a PR at 7m. Move left using PA, F 1-1/2, and nut, until the wall can be climbed to the main overhang. Two PAs are used to cross the roof to the foot of the groove, PR, TR. Climb into the main groove using a large flake on the right and continue past the yellow rock band, PR. Traverse left at the top of the yellow band for 3m. Climb easier ground to the top. More rewarding for those who like adventurous climbing!
T.Penning, J.Harwood 5pts 16.08.1988

154. **Heaven Can Wait**   21m   E4,5c 2pts   *
An impressive pitch, which climbs the centre of the large central overhangs to reach the shallow basin above. Start at a groove below the central overhangs. Climb the groove to a break (Friend 4) and traverse right until a ledge can be gained. Climb the grey wall, 2PRs, move left and up to below the roof. 2PA lead to spectacular moves via two large flakes to the end of the roof, PR. Move up and left to the belay on Children Of The Moon. Finish up this or abseil.
T.Penning, J.Harwood 2pts 09.08.1988

155. **Maggie's Gate**   20m   E4,6a   \
Climb Heaven can wait to the ledge. Climb the thin crack above with difficulty, PR to a ledge. Pull up and out left to another ledge. Continue past a sapling on suspect rock and belay well back. Spectacular.
T.Penning, G.Cytlau 08.10.2002

156. The Hundred Years War   30m   E3,5c   *

Fine climbing above the overhang. To the right of Heaven Can Wait there is a break in the large overhangs at 10m. Start below and right of two slanting grooves, at a capped corner. Climb the corner to exit left at a shale ledge, beneath the overhang. Pull over the overhang, step left, then climb straight up, PR, via twin cracks to exit right. Belay well back.
T.Penning, J.Harwood 07.09.1982

157. Obsession   30m   E4,5c   **

An alternative finish to the Hundred Years War. Offering excellent climbing on rock which is solid apart from the shale band. Follow The Hundred Years War to just above the overhang, then continue up the shallow corner to the right of the twin cracks, 2PRs.
T.Penning, J.Harwood 23.08.1988

158. Children of the Moon   75m   E3,6a,5b   *

A sensational right to left traverse above the main overhangs.
1. 36m Climb The Hundred Years War to just above the overhang, and level with the lip of the big overhangs. Traverse left, 2PRs, (crux) to easier ground. Climb up left to a good ledge and belay in the huge shallow bowl. There is a logbook here for fellow lunatics to sign and make comments.
2. 39m. Continue left over detached flakes into the big v-groove of IQ Test. Step across left on to the wall and move up, PR. Continue left around the arete and on to a steep wall. Make your way to the top and belay well back.
T.Penning, P. Cresswell 20.05.1984

159. American Mi Mi   33m   E4,6a   *

Start beneath a large detached block at 6m up and to the right of The Hundred Years War. Climb carefully onto the block from the left. Pull over the overhang and climb to another overhang with a groove on its left. Climb the groove to the top.
T.Penning, J.Harwood, C.Court 1pt 27.07.1983
FFA A.Sharp, P.Lewis 00.00.1983

160. Split Second Rhyming   30m   E3,6a

A difficult climb. Start below an obvious curving crack, 6m up and to the right of American Mi Mi. Climb a wall to blocks, make hard moves into a groove and layback out left. Continue up the groove above to the top.
A.Sharp, P.Lewis 00.00.1983

The central overhangs now peter out and the next feature is a pair of grooves.

161. Average Hand   30m   E2,5c   *

Start below the left-hand groove. Climb a crack, move slightly left and pull over a bulge into the groove which is followed to the top.
T.Penning, J.Harwood 25.07.1982

162. 5 Miles Out   30m   E2,5b   *

Start at a shallow left-facing corner, below the right-hand groove. Climb the corner into the groove and follow this with interest to the top.
T.Penning, P. Cresswell, A. Sharp 18.07.1982

163. Animal Eric   30m   E2,6a   *

A hard start. Start just right of 5 Miles Out. Climb a short wall (crux), PR, to the left-hand of two cracks. Follow this crack to exit right then left.
A. Sharp, J.Harwood (start only) 11.09.1982
T.Penning, J.Harwood 14.09.1982

164. Singapore Sling   30m   HVS,5a   *
Start at a shallow corner leading to the right-hand of two cracks. Climb the corner to a small ledge at 4m. Climb the steep wall on the right and the crack above to exit leftwards.
T.Penning, J.Harwood 07.09.1982

165. Belshazzar's Dream   23m   VS,4b
Start at a shallow corner just left of a grassy cone. Climb the corner to a deep groove with a sapling. Move right to a small ledge 3m above the sapling. Finish up the wall.
Unknown Pre-1973

166. Thread Bear   21m   HS,4b
This climb takes the left side of the flowstone wall right of the grassy cone.
T.Penning, J.Harwood 29.09.1981

167. Hairy Bear   18m   HVS,4c
This climb takes a line up the white flowstone just right of Thread Bear.
T.Penning solo 10.06.1984

Black Wall
This is the steep black wall of flowstone at the right end of the Main Area, with a large corner at its right-hand end.

168. Funky Flowstone Route   18m   E3,6b   *
Start on the left side of Black Wall. Climb into a niche and up on to a ledge above. Climb straight up to some pockets, TR, then move up right on to a rounded ledge. Step back left and finish direct.
M.Crocker, G.Jenkin 09.06.1985

169. The Black Adder   18m   E3,5c   *
Serious with a hard move high up. Climb the line of black flowstone on the right-hand end of the wall.
T.Penning, P.Cresswell, C.Court 10.06.1984

170. Skin Tight   21m   E4,5c
Serious. The arete right of The Black Adder. Climb straight up and continue just left of the arete to easier ground. Belay well back.
M.Crocker, R.Thomas 26.07.1985

171. Spindrift   18m   HVS,5a
To the right of Skin Tight is a large corner. This climb takes the obvious crack in the right-hand wall.
C.Court, T.Penning 10.06.1984

172. Crack Down   18m   E2,5c
Around the corner from Spindrift are two prominent cracks. This strenuous climb takes the one on the left.
C.Court, L.Davies 00.00.1984

Chwar Mawr
GR195157 to 185158

This crag is within the Craig-y-Cilau National Nature Reserve with whom negotiations for a permit to climb must be made. The following routes have been recorded in the past, prior to 1973, but no-one is known to have received permission since then.

Unknown Wall (S), Mur Ddu (S), Shoot Route (HS), Insley's Groove HVS (presumably Harold Insley Pre-1973), Weeping Wall (S), Black Brow (VS), The Harrow (HS), Banana Skin (VS), Pothole Route (D), Rabbit Hole Route (S), Eglwys Faen Buttress (S) all Unknown Pre-1973.

Llangattock

Craig Agen Allwedd
GR185158 to 183165
This crag is within the Craig-y-Cilau National Nature Reserve with whom negotiations for a permit to climb must be made. The following routes have been recorded in the past, prior to 1973, but no-one is known to have received permission since then.

Munchmeadow (M), Gnat's Dinner (VS), Alan's Arete (VS), Al Fresco (S) all Unknown Pre-1973.

Craig Y Castell
GR173167
From the lay-by, just beyond the cattle grid, cross the road and follow the obvious track up to the left end of the cliff.

At the left-hand end of the cliff is a small buttress where the woods begin. At the left side of the buttress is an easy descent marked by a silver birch at its top. Right of the small buttress, the cliff sticks out in a small prow and 10m right is a small bay above a hawthorn tree. 10m right of the hawthorn is another small bay with another hawthorn tree at the cliff top. 20m right is a small brown wall, below abseil bars on the clifftop, then the cliff leads past a small cave (Catacomb) to a bay with a vegetated right corner (God's Teeth). The cliff then becomes overhanging. Right of the overhangs is a polished buttress (Rowan Route). The cliff continues to a grassy rise at its base with a vegetated corner (Green Corner) to its right. Further right is an ivy covered overhang, and 50m right of this is an obvious corner (Stupid Sapling). Some 20m right of this corner is a large overhang at 10m and 30m further right is a short chimney which marks the end of the routes described. To the right of this chimney are some small walls which may be climbed from D to VS.

The first route described is just before the woods at the left most end of the cliff.

173. **Mudfall Wall**   10m   VS   \
    A mud-streaked face at the far left of the crag, just before it disappears into the jungle of the reserve. Start left of centre then traverse right, then back left to finish.
    Unknown Pre-1973

174. **Crackin Wall**   12m   E1,5b
    The obvious crack on the left side of the prow near the left-hand end of the cliff.
    C.Court, M.Bishop 00.00.1984

175. **The Left Twin**   15m   VD
    Start 6m right of Crackin Wall and follow twin cracks on the right side of the prow.
    Unknown Pre-1973

176. **The Right Twin**   15m   VD
    Start 3m right of The Left Twin. Climb cracks to a ledge, then the groove and cracks above.
    Unknown Pre-1973

177. **The Rock Garden**   15m   VD   \
    Loose. The sloping ramp 3m right.
    Unknown 1973-1978

178. **Stromboli**   23m   HS,4a
    Gain and climb the corner 10m right of the hawthorn tree at the base of the crag.
    Unknown Pre-1973

179. **Rebecca**   24m   VS,4b
    The thin crack right of Stromboli. Finish right of the hawthorn bush.
    Unknown Pre-1973

180.**Storm**   24m   E2,5b   **
Start 6m right of Rebecca, below a gap in the block overhang at 8m. Climb to and over the worrying feature to a ledge. Step right and follow a crack to finish.
P.Littlejohn, S.Lewis 30.06.1979

181.**Tempest**   17m   E1,5b
Just right of Storm. Climb a crack and the overhang via an obvious block. Finish direct.
C.Court, M.Bishop 00.00.1984

182.**The Ascent of Rum Doodle**   18m   VS,4b
Start right of Tempest and left of the small brown wall, below an obvious clean corner on the upper wall. Climb cracks, step left to a crack in the corner and follow this to the top.
Unknown Pre-1978

183.**Abseil Wall**   18m   VD
The easiest line on the wall below the abseil bars. Climb a groove on the right side of the brown wall. Climb the groove to exit onto the right arete below bulges (junction with Daedalus). Move left and up the wall until the left edge can be gained and then the top. Solid rock, albeit polished by countless feet (moving in the wrong direction).
J.Harwood 21.08.1999

184.**Daedalus**   17m   VD
Start right of the brown wall. Climb a crack curving beneath an overhang, then pass it on the left. Finish easily.
Unknown Pre-1973

185.**Daedalus Direct**   17m   Sev   \
The left arete of the original start on good holds to a junction with that route at 6m.
L.Davies solo 00.08.1993

186.**Heaven's Gate**   17m   HVS,5b
Follow Daedalus to beneath the overhang, then pull over this to gain a thin crack.
L.Davies, P.Thomas 17.05.1985

187.**Cool Touch**   17m   E2,5b
A faint line just right of Daedalus. Climb to an overhang (loose), then finish via the ledge above.
L.Davies, P.Thomas, M.Henry 31.05.1985

188.**Fleet Feet**   17m   E1,5c
Climb the centre of the wall between Cool Touch and Catacomb. A difficult start leads to easier ground above.
C.Court, M.Bishop 00.00.1984

Next the cliff leads past a small cave.

189.**Catacomb**   17m   VS,4b
Climb out of the small cave. Finish left of an overhang.
Unknown Pre-1973

190.**Accidentally Right**   17m   VS,4b
Climb Catacomb to an overhang, traverse right along a ledge to finish up the corner of Orang Utang.
J.Hamill-Keays, J.Hamill-Keays 00.00.1989

191.**OrangUtang**   17m   VD
Start between the cave and a large tree growing out of the rock at a slight rib. Climb a crack and corner above to the top.
Unknown Pre-1973

192. Sheisskopf   17m   S
Climb up behind the large tree to a hawthorn. Climb the wall and overhang above to finish.
N.Grant, N.Kingsford 00.00.1978

193. Jackorner   17m   VS,4b
Climb cracks to the right of the large tree and continue over ledges to a hawthorn stump. Climb flowstone to finish up the corner above.
N.Grant, N.Kingsford 00.00.1980

194. Beware of Crocodiles In The Trees   17m   E1,5a   *
Follow the deep crack right of Jackorner to an overhang. Surmount this to gain the niche and small hawthorn. Move up and left to cracks and the obvious tree to finish.
L.Davies, P.Thomas 00.05.1993

195. Tales Of The Unexpected   17m   E2,5c   *
Start beneath the overhang 4m right of Jackorner. A poorly protected start leads to the overhang, poor PR, but good wires above. Pull over this to finish straight up.
L.Davies, P.Bruten 18.05.1985

196. The Rain Man   17m   E2,5b   *   \
Start 2m right of Tales Of The Unexpected and climb directly to the right-hand side of the overhang. Move leftwards through the overhang, poor PR. Step up right to finish as for Gods' Teeth.
L.Davies, G.Christmas 00.08.1993

About 18m right from the tree growing out of the rock is a vegetated corner.

197. God's Teeth   17m   VS,4c
A poor climb keeping just left of a vegetated corner.
Unknown Pre-1973

198. Rockfall Climb   20m   VS,4b
The original description does not match the rock, so the following is the probable line. Start just right of a cave at the base of the right side of the vegetated corner. Climb a shallow groove then trend right to finish up the shallow corner of Duty Free.
N.Grant, N.Kingsford 00.00.1979

199. Duty Free   21m   VS,4c   *
Start 4m right of Rockfall Climb, below an obvious corner and right of block overhangs at the top of the cliff. Climb a shallow corner crack to ledges below a roof with a large corner on its right. Move right and finish up a corner.
C.Court, M.Bishop 00.00.1984

200. The Descendant   17m   HVS,4c
An alternative start to Duty Free which gains that route at 9m by climbing up the arete.
L.Davies solo 00.08.1993

There now follows a bowl capped by overhangs. The next climb breaks through the roofs via cracks at their left side.

201. How To Stuff A Wild Bikini   20m   E2,5c   *
Start to the right of Duty Free, at a thin crack. Climb easily to a band of overhangs and pull over these, past a detached flake.
C.Court, P.Bruten 00.00.1984

Right of the overhangs is a short, mud-streaked, polished buttress.

202. Trading Places   15m   HS,4b

Start to the right of the overhangs, but left of a grassy mound. Climb a steep crack in a short polished buttress until it merges with Rowan Route.
L.Davies, J.Smith 00.00.1986

203. The Route To Rowan   17m   VS,4b

An alternative start to Rowan Route, which ascends the prow/arete of the polished buttress, directly right of Trading Places to a junction with Rowan Route at 6m.
L.Davies solo 00.08.1993

204. Rowan Route   20m   VD

Start from the grass on the right. Climb direct, past small rowan trees on the left, to the top.
Unknown Pre-1973

205. Tarzan Boy   15m   E1,5b

Start at a groove 2m right of Rowan Route at the high part of the grass, below a small weakness in an overhang at 5m. Climb up and over the overhang, trend left to a flake crack and finish up the steep wall.
P.Bruten, L.Davies 03.08.1986

206. Split Indifferences   18m   VS,4c

Start at a shallow crack line 3m right of Tarzan Boy. Follow the crack to reach grassy ledges. Trend up and left to the centre of a small wall. Climb straight up via a thin crack, PR.
L.Davies, J.Smith 15.05.1986

207. Canyouhandlit   17m   VS

Start 6m right of Rowan Route. Climb the wall leftwards to grassy ledges. Continue leftwards to finish up a corner past trees.
N.Grant, N.Kingsford 00.00.1979

208. Irrelevant Grope   17m   VS,4c

Climb a crack in a groove as for Typhoid, move right at an overhang and finish up flowstone.
D.Hope 00.00.1980

209. Typhoid   15m   VS

Start 7m right of Rowan Route, at a shallow groove. Go almost directly up the wall and left past the overhang. Move back right to finish up a curving crack in a groove.
Unknown Pre-1973

210. Lime Juice   17m   E1,5c

Start right of Irrelevant Grope. Climb a smooth wall, then an obvious crack up the headwall.
C.Court, P. Bruten 00.00.1984

211. Fresh   17m   E1,5b

A variation start to Lime Juice taking a thin line to its right. Finish up the crack in the headwall.
L.Davies solo 00.00.1985

212. Castell Main XXXX   15m   E2,5b

Climb the obvious corner right of Fresh to its top and exit via some holds on the right-hand side. Step left then up and right onto the flowstone wall above. Finish straight up.
C.Court solo 00.00.1986

213. No Peg Route   17m   HS

Start just right of Castell Main XXXX. Climb flowstone to a ledge, then the wall above.
N.Grant, N.Kinsford 00.00.1978

109.Cuticle   19m   VS,4a

Right of Fingernail Crack and left of a cave entrance is a smooth 4m wall. There are many ways up it.
Unknown Pre-1973Kingsford 00.00.1978

214.Once Shy   17m   S

Start at an overhanging crack, right of No Peg Route and just left of a flake on the ground. Climb the crack, step
right and finish up the wall or, after 4m, traverse right to a sandy groove and follow this.
N.Grant, N.Kinsford 00.00.1978

215.Lucky Nut   15m   VS,4b

Start right of a flake in the ground and about 10m left of a green corner. Climb through a break in a small overhang,
past a hawthorn, and finish direct.
N.Grant, N.Kingsford 00.00.1978

216.Green Corner   15m   VD   ●

Climb the obvious vegetated corner.
Unknown Pre-1973

To the right is an ivy-covered overhang and 40m right again is the prominent corner of Stupid Sapling. Several routes
have been reported in the area from ancient times (pre-1973) but their descriptions completely bamboozled the
previous guidebook writer who omitted them. Only three of them have been successfully re-identified by the intrepid
Professor Harwood.

217.Once Bitten   17m   VD

Start 6m right of an ivy covered overhang. Climb a broken corner, move right, and finish up the rightwards
leaning groove. This may be a line previously referred to as Poor Tom (pre-1973).
Unknown Pre-1973

218.Valhalla   17m   VS,4b

Climb the broken corner of Once Bitten until it is possible to take the crack on the left.
Unknown Pre-1973

219.Central Slab Direct   15m   VD

Start just right of Once Bitten. Climb the centre of three slabs (Possibly the old line of Arctic Wall Unknown Pre-
1973).
N.Grant, N.Kingsford 00.00.1980

On the next wall to the right (just right of a large tree growing at 3m) there is a tottering flake on the halfway ledge.

220.The Needle   15m   VD

Start below the tottering flake. Climb a crack and corner to the flake. Then up to a small cave. Finish out left.
Unknown Pre-1973

221.Mountain Hash   15m   S

Start below and right of the tottering flake of The Needle. Climb broken rock to a ledge, then the cracks above,
to finish between two rowan trees.
Unknown Pre-1973

222.Fisher's Folly   20m   VS,4c

Start at a v-groove about 6m left of Stupid Sapling. Climb to a break, traverse right and move up to a large ledge.
Trend right to a grassy ledge, then finish up the broken crack.
Unknown Pre-1973

223. **Stupid Sapling**   15m   VD
Climb the prominent corner.
Unknown Pre-1973

224. **The Hobbit**   15m   VS,4b
Climb the obvious crack 2m right of Stupid Sapling. Step right to finish.
Unknown Pre-1973

225. **Castell Craig**   15m   E1,5b   *
Follow cracks in the wall 2m right of Flash. 2 PRs.
C.Court, M.Rosser 00.00.1986

226. **S Route**   15m   S
Start 4m right of Stupid Sapling. Climb a corner to a flake crack, then climb this to finish up flowstone.
Unknown Pre-1973

227. **Chicken**   17m   VS,4c
Start at a tree 10m right of Stupid Sapling. Climb up behind the tree, then traverse right to a bush and finish direct. Rather pointless.
N.Grant, N.Kingsford 00.00.1979

10m right of the tree of Chicken is a large overhang at 10m with rather unstable looking rock all around. Just right and at a lower level is another overhang at 6m.

228. **Red Mike**   17m   VS,4c
Start below the right end of the overhang at 6m and below a finishing groove. Gain the groove from the left.
T.Penning, P. Cresswell 18.04.1982

229. **I Should Smile**   17m   E3,5c
Climb the weakness in the wall right of Red Mike, finishing up the very thin cracks in the headwall above.
P.Thomas, L.Davies 03.07.1985

To the right of the overhangs are three cracks, the left one leading to a groove with a large tree at its top.

230. **Diarrhoea Crack**   17m   VS,4c
Climb the left-hand crack and finish up the wide groove above.
N.Grant, N.Kingsford 1pt. 00.00.1979
FFA T.Penning solo 18.04.1982

231. **Road to Nowhere**   17m   E1,5c
Climb the thin central crack.
L.Davies, P.Bruten, P.Thomas 00.00.1985

232. **Crack of Gwent**   17m   E1,5b   *
Climb the right-hand crack.
Gwent M.C. 00.00.1985

233. Developing World   18m   E2,6a
An eliminate. Follow a shallow groove (between Crack of Gwent and Quiet Hero) for 6m BR, to join Crack of Gwent. The BR has been removed and it is not known if the route has yet been ascended without it.
L.Davies, P.Thomas 00.00.1988

234. **Quiet Hero**   17m   E2,5b

Start 2m right of Crack of Gwent just right of some iron sticking out of the ground. Climb an arete to a flake crack above, then move up to finish more easily.

P.Thomas, L.Davies 14.06.1986

235. **Peaches And Cream**   18m   E2,5c   *

Start at a short blocky groove 6m right of the cave. Climb the wall PR, to the overhang. Pull over this and into a right-facing corner on good jams. Finish leftwards.

C.Court, L.Davies 00.00.1985

236. **Slurry**   17m   S

Start 4m left of Briar Crack, where the overhangs end. Climb a groove to a bramble, move up right and climb a corner to finish rightwards.

N.Grant, N.Kingsford 00.00.1980

237. **Only Yesterday**   15m   VS,4b

Climb the grooves above the start of Slurry, i.e. a direct finish.

L.Davies, D. Leitch 14.00.1986

238. **Briar Crack**   6m   VD

The short chimney, just before the cliff becomes very scrappy.

Unknonw Pre-1978

239. **Jug Thug**   8m   E2,5b

Start 6m right of Briar Crack. Climb the broken crack line through a series of overhangs.

C.Court solo 00.00.1986

240. **Redstart**   8m   HVS

Start 3m right of Jug Thug at a hawthorn. Climb to a ledge left of the hawthorn. Move out left at the same level to beneath the corner of the overhang. Move up and left to a crack, then finish up the steep headwall.

Unknown Pre-1973

MORLAIS QUARRY

GR047098
By Chris Shorrock

BOLTING POLICY: No Bolting.

PREAMBLE

A series of four limestone quarries situated on the west and north slopes of Morlais Hill about 1¾ miles north of Merthyr Tydfil. Each of the quarries has its own atmosphere; the Lower Tier with its grassy base and extensive ledges has a pleasant, sheltered feel, the Middle Tier is very open and popular with groups. It has plenty of routes at all grades and provides good views north to the Brecon Beacons. The Upper Tier has a secluded feel despite being the closest to the road, whilst the East Tier is situated in an industrial moonscape.

Generally the climbs are clean and free of debris, although they can be a little polished on the Middle Tier. The quarries get plenty of sun but are hideous places to climb if at all wet.

Note that car theives are extremely active in this area, so leave no valuables in your vehicles.

ACCESS

1.Lower, Middle and Upper Tiers
Approach from the roundabout at the junction between the A465 Heads of the Valleys road and the A470 Cardiff to Brecon road. Follow the A465 east and take the first exit after ¼ mile. This leads to an offset crossroads. Head almost straight across the junction sign-posted Pontsticill - Torpantau - Talybont. Follow the road through Trefechan to eventually reach a junction just before a pub (Aberclais Inn).

For the Lower and Middle Tiers stay on the main road until a second pub (Pontsarn Inn) is reached. Park here (a small fee is requested by the owners). From the north side of the carpark a path descends to a disused railway viaduct. Cross the viaduct then turn right onto the Morlais Heritage Trail. Almost immediately turn left to ascend steeply up a path to the centre of the Middle Tier.

For the Upper Tier and alternative approach to the middle tiers turn right (signposted Dowlais) over a bridge and up a hill. Before the top of the hill (GR 049092) a minor junction is reached with a disused tramway leading off to the left. Park around here (considerately). A fence with an access point 100m right of the tramway provides access to the Upper Tier, whilst the tramway itself is followed pleasantly to the Windy Wall section of the Middle Tier.

2.East Tier
Approach from the Lower or Middle Tier by walking up and southeast to GR 056096 – an obvious north-facing buttress with two vertical cracks bounded to the left by a corner.

Alternmatively approach from the Brecon Mountain Railway Station GR 059098 by walking along the base of the quarried escarpment westwards to the crag.

DESCENTS: Walk off at various points.

THE ROUTES

The Lower Tier
The right-hand end of the cliff is reached by a path descending from the left end of the Middle Tier beneath the Great Wall. The left end of the cliff is bounded by an earth mound, whilst the centre has a descent path running from left to right.

1. **Terminal Arete**   15m   VD
    A broken slab above the top of the earth mound at the left end of the quarry.
    C.Shorrock 00.08.2001

2. **More Lice**   15m   VS,4c

At the base of the earth mound is a buttress, climb a depression in the centre of this to a ledge and saplings. Finish either up the groove or the wall to its right (better, but bold).
M.Salter, C.Shorrock 00.10.2001

3. **Maul Ice**   15m   S

On the right side of the buttress is a borehole, climb just right of this to a small grassy ledge. Finish up the corner.
C.Shorrock, M.Salter 00.10.2001

25m right again are some bushes on a grassy ledge 2m above the quarry floor.

4. **Noviciate**   24m   S

Just left of the bushes is a cracked groove. Climb this to a grass ledge, step right and continue up the wall and short groove to finish straight up the wall.
C.Mortlock Pre-1973

5. **Hawthorn Wall**   27m   S

Behind the bushes is another groove, climb this to a grass ledge, then continue up the wall trending right to a ledge. Finish up the groove on the left.
C.Mortlock Pre-1973

6. **Comici Special**   27m   HVS,5a

Climb a short left facing corner 5m right of Hawthorn Special to a ledge, then walls via another grass ledge. Finish via a groove and crack.
J.Harwood, P.Thomas 00.00.1975

5m right again is a hawthorn bush with a short blocky arete above it.

7. **Delivery**   27m   HVS,5a   *

Ascend the wall 1m left of the bush to a ledge, move left and up ledges to a groove, then right to the top.
J.Harwood, S.Lewis 00.00.1976

8. **Manibus Abort**   30m   VS,4b

Climb the groove above the bush to a grass ledge, then up to a frail tree. Traverse left to the groove of Delivery and then step right and climb a steep wall and short walls above.
Unknown Pre-1991

9. **R.I.P.**   24m   VS,4b

Right again is a left-facing corner, just left of an arete. Climb the corner to a grass ledge, traverse left to a steep, loose, groove which is followed to the top.
A.Sharp, S.Evans 00.00.1974

10. **The Sickle**   24m   VS,4c   *

Climb the left-hand of a trio of grooves just right of the arete to a grassy terrace. Continue up for 3m, move right and then follow a groove to the top.
Unknown Pre-1978

11. **Central Groove**   7m   S

The central groove.
C.Shorrock, M.Salter 00.10.2001

12. **The Grunt**   7m   HVS,5b

Layback strenuously up the right-hand groove.
P.Thomas solo Pre-1991

13. **Raspberries**   25m   HVS,4c
Climb the shattered crack between The Grunt and Greenmantle, then follow the discontinuous walls above.
P.Bruten, L.Davies 00.08.1984

14. **Greenmantle**   27m   HVS,5a   *
Climb the borehole 3m right of The Grunt to a grassy terrace then mantleshelf on to a small ledge 3m left of the arete. Follow discontinuous walls above, keeping just left of the arete.
Unknown 00.00.1973

A wide ledge (descent route) now crosses the face at half-height. The next routes start from this.

15. **Wall Street**   7m   E1,5a
An unprotected route climbing the wall just left of centre and above a bush.
T.Penning, G.Horler 00.00.1983

16. **Bahama Crisis**   7m   HVS,5b
The vague crack midway between Wall Street and Cerebellum.
T.Penning, K.Barrat 00.00.1983

Right again is a tufaceous scoop with cracks on either side of it.

17. **Cerebellum**   7m   HVS,5b   *
Climb the left-hand crack. There is an alternative version, which gains the scoop from the crack.
J.Harwood, C.Horsfield 00.00.1976

18. **Khamil Rhouge**   12m   E2,6a   *
Start as for the scoop version of Cerebellum, but finish up the right-hand side of the nose of the scoop.
L.Davies, P.Thomas 00.06.1986

19. **Compact**   7m   VS,4b
Climb the right-hand crack past a small tree.
J.Harwood solo Pre-1985

20. **Corset**   36m   VS,4c
This pleasant traverse requires a good knowledge of the next few routes. Either start up Corset, or begin at the right end of the ledge of Exile. Climb up and move right, go round the corner to a ledge and continue to a small groove (PR on The Go Between). Traverse across grass ledges around an arete and step down to a grassy ledge beneath the summit overhang. Step right and finish as for Narcotic.
J.Harwood, J.Matthews 00.00.1976

To the right the wall is crossed by a rightward-sloping ramp.

21. **Crisis, What Crisis?**   12m   E4,6b
Climb the vague aretes between Compact and Exile with a hard start.
A.Sharp, L.Sharp 00.00.1981

22. **Exile**   12m   E3,5c
Committing with no protection. Start left of the ramp and then follow it to a red groove. Leave the groove by moving left to reach good holds near the top.
A. Sharp, L.Sharp 00.00.1981

23. **Dead Red**   12m   E3,5c
As for Exile to the red groove but continue rightwards to gain a second groove.
A. Sharp, L.Sharp 00.00.1981

Morlais

24. **Morlais Eliminate**   12m   E3,5c
The wall immediately right of Dead Red is poorly protected. Climb it to a poor PR at a thin overlap and continue via a short crack to a move left at the top.
T.Penning 00.00.1984

25. **Triple Cross**   17m   E3,5c   *
Climb the shallow groove between Dead Red and The Go Between, exit right to a small toe ledge then up left to the top.
T.Penning, P.Cresswell 00.00.1983

26. **The Go Between**   27m   E2,5b   *
Start 3m right of a tree. Climb easily to a short groove leading to the top, PR.
J.Harwood, I.Carey 00.00.1976
FFA A.Sharp, J.Harwood 00.08.1980

27. **Whispering Grass**   33m   HVS,5a
Start at a corner at the back of a small bay, 6m right of the tree. Climb the corner past two ledges to finish up and right above a bush on grassy ledges.
J.Harwood, P.Thomas 00.00.1975

28. **Busy Bee**   33m   HS,4a
Climb the buttress 3m right of the small bay, then follow the shallow arete until it merges into a corner and a finishing crack.
J.Harwood, S.Lewis 00.00.1976

29. **Gallery**   30m   VS,4b   *
Bold in the middle. Climb a corner above a grass ledge 4m right of Busy Bee and 6m left of a prominent borehole. From its top follow a further groove until a grass ledge can be reached on the right. Move leftwards and follow a corner on the left side of the summit overhang.
J.Harwood, P.Thomas 00.00.1973

30. **Narcotic**   30m   VS,4b
Ascend the groove 2m right of Gallery to a ledge. Move slightly right and climb water-stained rock to the right side of the summit overhang and the top.
S.Lewis, J.Harwood 00.00.1976

31. **Bore**   12m   HVS,5a
Climb the borehole 4m right of Narcotic to a ledge. Follow water-worn grooves up to an easy rightward-traverse just below the top.
Unknown Pre-1991

32. **Green Corner**   12m   S
The obvious corner is climbed to a big ledge. Walk right to a groove which is followed to the top.
N.Grant, N.Kingsford 00.00.1976

33. **Flake Crack**   12m   VD
The crack on the right wall of the corner. Walk right along the ledge to gain the finishing groove.
Unknown Pre-1991

34. **Double Constraint**   12m   S
Right of Green Corner is a small bay with a shallow groove in its left wall. Climb this to a ledge and then a tree. Move right to finish up the groove.
D. Ellis Pre-1974

Martin Crocker - Edge Hog (Fr7b+) Witches Point
(Page 279) Photo: Gary Gibson

Goi Ashmore - Bloody Sport Climbers (1st Asc) (Fr8a) Dinas
(Page 314) Photo: Carl Ryan

35. **T.A.P.** 6m VD

10m right of Double Constraint is a small tree at the base of a groove, gain and climb the groove.
Unknown Pre-1991

The Middle Tier

At the left-hand end is a bay whose right-hand side is formed by the obvious Great Wall. Right of this is easier angled terrain, terminating in the vertical Castle Bay. After some more broken ground (The Ramparts) the crag regains its composure with Windy Wall which lies above a platform of rock and has overhangs at the top.

36. **Old Friends** 13m VD

The arete of the left wall of Great Wall Bay.
D.Webb, C.Shorrock 00.00.2001

The Great Wall

37. **To The Batmobile** 15m HVS,5b *

Start on a ledge a third of the way up the left-hand side of The Great Wall. Climb a crack past a sapling with a hard move left near the top.
D.Hillier, A.Cummings 00.00.1982

38. **Grace Under Pressure** 15m E1,5b

The wall right of To The Batmobile.
A.Cummings 00.00.1980

39. **Phobia** 18m E1,5b *

Climb the obvious water-worn groove, to the overlap. Traverse right along a sloping ramp then finish direct.
P.Watkin A1 Pre-1973
FFA P.Thomas, J.Harwood 00.00.1975

40. **The Rattling Finish** 17m E2,5c *

As for Phobia, but climb the overhang direct.
T.Penning, A.Sharp 00.00.1982

41. **Blade Runner** 18m E3,5c **

Good technical climbing. Climb Phobia for 3m, then move right to a narrow ledge. Climb straight up then right to another ledge, PR. Follow the crack leftwards to finish as for Phobia.
T.Penning, A.Sharp etc. 00.00.1982

42. **Rogues Gallery** 18m E5,6b *

Start just right of Phobia at a shallow groove. Climb the groove to a thin ledge on the left. Move up right, BR (missing) and continue boldly to a ledge at two-thirds height. Move left to a thin finishing crack.
G.Gibson 00.09.1984

43. **No Mercy** 21m E6,6c *

The wall between Rogues Gallery and Partners in Crime. A faint thin crack leads to a ledge. Move up rightwards via ripples to pass a BR (missing). Finish with less difficulty.
G.Gibson 00.05.1985

44. **Partners in Crime** 18m E5,6c **

Start below a line of thin cracks on the right side of the wall. Climb the crack to where it fades, then make hard moves to pass a PR. Continue, PR, to reach a ledge at two-thirds height. Traverse left to finish up a thin crack.
C.Jones - Partners A1 00.00.1970
FFA A.Sharp, J.Harwood 00.08.1983

45. **Fly Arete**   18m   HS

Start 2m left of the right arete of The Great Wall. Climb the wall to swing right onto a ledge on the arete. Follow the arete to the top.

Unknown Pre-1978

46. **Massascent Groove**   18m   VD   *

The groove and crack starting to the right of the arete of The Great Wall.

Unknown Pre-1978

47. **Ledge Way**   18m   VD

Right again is an open left-facing corner. Climb the corner or its left wall, then either move left to a ledge or continue direct up the corner. Finish straight up the groove or step right to ledges.

Unknown Pre-1978

48. **Eliminate Slab**   18m   HVS,4b

The smooth face just right of the corner is bold.

Unknown Pre-1978

49. **Tiptoe**   15m   S   *

Right of Eliminate Slab is a ledge at 1m. Climb the shallow right-facing corner above the ledge.

Unknown Pre-1978

50. **Spectacle**   15m   VD   *

About 2m right of Tiptoe is a borehole. Climb the shallow indefinite groove above it.

Unknown Pre-1978

51. **Serpent**   15m   VD

Start just left of an overhanging block. Climb over the small overlap and finish up easy slabs above.

Unknown Pre-1978

52. **Lost Groove**   15m   D

The left-hand groove between the overhanging block and a narrow prow. Scrambling remains.

Unknown Pre-1978

53. **Two Corners**   15m   VD   *

The right-hand groove between the overhanging block and a narrow prow. Climb the groove and corner above.

Unknown Pre-1978

54. **S.T.E.P.**   15m   S

Climb the groove right of the prow to ledges. Finish via the corner up and to the right.

M.Danford, P.Wood 00.00.1973

Castle Bay

Castle Bay is the steeply walled bay 12m right of the narrow prow. In the back wall of the bay are some obvious polished grooves – the line of Top Cat.

55. **Gold Medal**   13m   VS,4b

This takes the blank-looking wall left of the grooves of Top Cat.

A.Sharp, P.Hamer 00.00.1984

56. **Top Cat**   13m   S

The obvious polished grooves in the back wall of the bay.

Unknown Pre-1978

57. **Name Game**   13m   HS,4a
Interesting climbing up the wall right of Top Cat.
P.Hamer, A.Sharp 00.00.1984

58. **Great Corner**   13m   S   *
The back corner of the bay is good, but can be wet.
Unknown Pre-1978

59. **Castle Wall**   11m   VS,4b   *
The first obvious crack on the right wall of Castle Bay.
Unknown Pre-1978

60. **Arisk**   9m   VS,4b
Climb a thin crack in the centre of the wall right of Castle wall. Climb diagonally right (4b) or directly up (4c) from the ledge to finish.
Unknown Pre-1978

61. **Squeeze It In**   9m   E1,5a
Contrived. Climb the wall right of Arisk to a ledge. Move left into Arisk and finish direct.
G.Horler, N.Ward, M.Rose, M.Broomfield, S.Rack, D.Barton 00.00.1984

62. **Wall Cracks**   6m   HVS,5a   *
The thin cracks at the right end of the wall, PRs.
J.Harwood 00.00.1975

The Ramparts
Castle Bay ends at a short arete. About 5m right of the arete is a ledge and corner at two-thirds height.

63. **Dirty Corner**   9m   D
Reach the ledge at 6m via a groove on the left (D), or more enjoyably by the steep buttress beneath (5a) or the wall to the right (4b).
Unknown Pre-1978

64. **Sixties Groove**   9m   VD
The pleasant, shallow, left-facing groove/corner right of Dirty Corner.
Unknown Pre-1970

65. **Easy Route**   12m   M
About 3m right of Sixties Route is a gently-angled, polished groove.
Unknown Pre-1973

There now follows a 50m section of broken cliff before a more continuous section rises from a rock platform some 5m above the quarry floor. About 8m left of a tree at the left end of the platform is a low-angled buttress.

66. **Rocks Like The Rockies**   18m   S
Climb the groove in the gently angled buttress to the overlap. Traverse left beneath the overlap to finish up another groove.
C.Shorrock, D.Webb 00.00.2001

Windy Wall
This crag lies above the rock platform at the right end of the Middle Tier. Above the left end of the platform is a ledge.

67. **Griptight**   6m   HS,4b
Climb the corner to the left of an obvious horizontal scaffolding bar.
Unknown Pre-1978

68. **Gripfix**   7m   HS,4b
Climb the centre of the wall right of Griptight starting at the scaffolding bar.
Unknown Pre-1978

69. **Parting Company**   18m   S
From the left end of the main face of Windy Wall climb a shallow groove to a ledge. Finish up another groove formed by the left side of two detached blocks.
Unknown Pre-1978

70. **Windy**   18m   HVS,5b
Start beneath the right of the detached blocks. Climb the serious lower wall, then the crack splitting the blocks.
J.Harwood 00.00.1976

71. **Pullover**   18m   HVS,5a
A serious climb starting just right of a borehole. Climb up left to a shallow recess then over the overhang and up the wall above.
K.Hughes, D.Hillman 00.00.1970

72. **Breezing**   18m   HVS,5b
Climb the wall 2m right of Pullover, PR. Finish past the left end of the overhang.
C.Court, K.Anderson, A.Jones 00.00.1984

73. **Overdrive**   18m   E1,5a
Climb the wall 2m right of Pullover to the overhang, which is climbed on its right side.
Unknown Pre-1978

74. **Oxo**   18m   VS,4b
Climb to the steep corner on the right of the overhangs, then traverse left to beneath blocks. Pass the blocks on either side.
Unknown Pre-1978

75. **Philanderer**   13m   VS,4c   *
Start as for Oxo but continue up the corner.
Unknown Pre-1978

76. **Blue Buska**   13m   E3,5c   *
Climb up to a bulge just right of Philanderer, gain the hanging groove via a gymnastic move (2 old BRs) and follow it to the top.
T.Penning, A.Sharp 00.00.1982

77. **Grease Monkey**   12m   VD
Climb the open left-facing groove 2m right of Philanderer.
Unknown Pre-1978

78. **Groovy**   12m   S
This takes the obvious clean cut groove just right of Grease Monkey.
Unknown Pre-1978

79. **Pull Through**   12m   S
Climb the worn slab just right of Groovy, to finish through a gap in the blocky overhang.
Unknown Pre-1978

80. **Blockhead**   12m   S
Climb the right side of the narrow slab to pass right of the overhangs via a short groove.
Unknown Pre-1978

81. **Tree Corner**   12m   S   *
Climb the obvious tree-less groove in the centre of the buttress.
Unknown Pre-1978

82. **Split Buttress**   12m   VD
Climb the shallow groove in the front of the small prow, then the left side of the wall above.
M.Danford, P.Wood 00.00.1971

83. **Fork Left**   9m   VS,4c
Right of the small prow is a groove that splits at half-height. Climb the left fork.
Unknown Pre-1978

84. **Fork Right**   9m   S,4a
Follow Fork Left but finish by the right fork.
M.Danford, P.Wood 00.00.1971

85. **Sting**   8m   VD
Climb the groove 2m right of the Fork routes.
Unknown Pre-1978

The Upper Tier
Some 100m right of the left-hand end of the quarry is hawthorn tree at the top of the crag. Below are a grey wall and a left to right slanting ramp.

86. **Bypass**   13m   D
Begin beneath an arete (Elastic) 4m left of the hawthorn at the top. Climb the rightward-slanting ramp.
Unknown Pre-1991

87. **Elastic**   10m   VS,4b
The left arete of the wall above Bypass, avoiding easy ground on the left.
J.Harwood solo 00.08.1980

88. **Guts**   10m   VS,4b
Follow Bypass to a small arete. From the arete, climb the wall above.
Unknown Pre-1991

89. **After Dinner Crack**   10m   VS,4b
Follow Bypass, then a thin crack 1m right of Guts.
Unknown Pre-1991

90. **Extension**   9m   HVS 5a
About 1m right of the finish of Bypass is a short wall leading to some cracks. Climb these to pull through a steep area onto the arete. Finish next to Bypass.
A.Sharp, J.Harwood 00.08.1980

91. **Left Hand Trinity**   9m   E1,5b
The first of three cracks that start above ledge-ridden ground. Bold and with some very loose rock at the top. Poor.
Unknown Pre-1991

92. Central Trinity 9m VS,4b
The second crack is steep and sustained but with slightly better rock than its harder neighbour.
M.Salter, C.Shorrock 00.10.2001

93. Right Hand Trinity 9m S
The third crack has plenty of protection but still retains worrying finishing holds.
C.Shorrock, M.Salter 00.10.2001

94. Ledge and Corner 9m VD
The corner that starts above the ledges just right of Right Hand Trinity.
Unknown Pre-1991

95. Intermission 16m VS,4c
The wall is now higher. Climb the slight left-facing groove, avoiding the worst rock by moving out onto the arete.
Unknown Pre-1991

96. The Writer 16m VS,4b
Right of Intermission is a shallow right-facing corner. Gain this, then climb it, taking care with the rock.
Unknown Pre-1991

A diagonal descent rake leads down to the next section. About 15m right of the base of the descent is a hawthorn tree some 3m up, above a trio of ledges below a white wall.

97. Hiccup 15m HVS,4c
About 4m left of the hawthorn is a flake crack. Climb the wall right of the flake crack until it is possible to swing left above it. Climb the wall above.
J.Harwood solo 00.00.1975

98. Morning Star 15m E3,6a *
The wall 3m right of Hiccup.
T.Penning, J.Harwood 00.00.1985

99. Clive's Crack 21m HVS,5a
Start 3m right of the tree. Reach a borehole and follow this to reach a grassy ledge on the right.
J. Harwood 00.00.1975

100. Fairy Steps 27m VD
This climbs the obvious diagonal line from right to left, starting 10m right of Clive's Crack.
Unknown Pre-1978

101. Evening Gem 18m E4,6a *
The line of the quarry. Climb the shallow, rounded groove above the start of Fairy Steps and 3m left of a brown stain. Exit left or directly and climb the short wall to a tree.
P.Littlejohn, J.Mothersele 00.00.1977
P.George, A.N.Other - Direct 00.00.1989

102. Autonomy 18m E2,5b
Climb the series of grooves between Evening Gem and the brown stain, to a final wide crack.
J.Harwood, W.Gray 00.00.1977

103. Stretch 18m VS,4b
Climb the brown-stained wall moving left to a groove just above half-height.
Unknown Pre-1991

104.**Zig Zag**   27m   HS,4a
This climbs the right to left ramp 5m right of Stretch.
P.Watkin 00.00.1970

105.**Hair Of The Dog**   12m   E3,6a   *
Start just right of Zig Zag and climb between two flakes to follow a borehole, PR.
T.Penning, C.Court 00.00.1985

106.**Afternoon Delight**   9m   E2,5c   *
Start at a tree 9m right of Hair Of The Dog. Climb the wall PR, then mantleshelf left to a faint corner at the top.
C.Court, T.Penning 00.00.1985

107.**High Noon**   9m   E2,6a   *
The crack and short corner 2m right of Afternoon Delight, PR.
C.Court, T.Penning 00.00.1985

A broken section of crag runs across to a protruding wall.

108.**Snuff Stuff**   9m   VS,4b
The slanting groove in the left side of the wall. Unprotected.
T.Penning solo 00.00.1985

109.**Compact Slab**   10m   VD
The compact slab 12m right of Snuff Stuff is gained from its left edge and exited on its left. A direct start is 6a.
M.Salter 00.10.2001

Midway between the Upper Tier and the tramline to the Middle Tier is another quarry with a good section of rock at its centre. This has produced a number of climbs up to 15m in height at various grades. No documentation of these climbs has come to light, so the faces remain for your unconstrained pleasure.

The East Tier

See Approach 2 for access to this north-facing buttress. It has two vertical cracks and is bounded on the left by a corner.

110. **Little Owl**   15m   S
Climb the corner.
A.Giles, R.Davies 00.00.1988

111. **One Between The Eyes**   15m   HVS,5a
The left-hand crack.
A.Giles, R.Davies 00.00.1988

112. **Terminator**   15m   E2,5c
The fainter right-hand crack.
R.Powles, A.Hughes 00.00.1988

TAF FECHAN

GR062105
By Ren Hoek

BOLTING POLICY: No bolting.

PREAMBLE

Taf Fechan is one of several quarries situated to the South and East of Taf Fechan reservoir, 2½ miles north of Merthyr Tydfil. The rock is carboniferous limestone that has been quarried, the upper part is weathered and there is a lot of loose rock on the ledges.

ACCESS

From A4060/A465 roundabout at Dowlais Top take the minor exit (A4102) to Dowlais (westward). Follow the road to a roundabout, turning right and then take the right fork where the road splits under the A465 flyover. Follow this for 1 mile passing the Pant railway station (Brecon Mountain Railway). About ½ mile further on is a pull in on the left opposite a charred telegraph pole. Climb the steep bank behind the telegraph pole to cross over the railway line and find the quarry.

DESCENTS: By abseil.

THE ROUTES

1. **Metalworks**   18m   HVS,5a
    The second thin crack of the wall. Climb over overhangs and follow a thin crack above to a ledge and a tree.
    A.Williams, P.Leyshon 2pt 00.00.1968
    FFA Unknown Pre-1991

2. **Take Off**   18m   D
    Start 6m right of a water spout. Climb to a ledge, traverse left on loose rock past a tree to belay.
    D.Ellis, C.Taylor 00.00.1967

3. **Monument To Insanitary**   21m   VD
    Climb a short wall to a chimney, follow this to a ledge, then climb up right and scramble to a tree belay.
    D.Ellis, J.Parry 00.00.1967

4. **Anthrax**   30m   VD
    Start 2m right of the chimney. Climb the wall left of a small overhang, then step right to a groove. Climb this and the steep groove above on the right, finish up loose rock to a tree belay.
    D.Ellis, P.Leyshon 00.00.1967

5. **Thunder Crack**   30m   VS,4b
    Start in the corner right of the chimney. Climb right to the foot of two cracks which join at the bottom. Follow the left-hand crack to a grass ledge, then scramble to a tree belay.
    D.Ellis, P.Leyshon, P.Minett 00.00.1967

6. **Lightning Crack**   30m   VS,4b
    Start right of Thunder Crack and climb the right-hand crack. Move left and scramble to a tree belay.
    P.Watkin, D.Parsons 00.00.1967

7. **The Godforsaken Gash**   15m   E2,5c
    Start right of Lightning Crack. Climb a ramp to a ledge, follow a thin crack and pull up left to a rightward slanting crack, PR. Climb to a ledge and abseil off a tree.
    M.Crocker, R.Thomas, M.Ward 31.12.1986

Next are four corners.

8. **Thorny Problem**   19m   S
   The left-hand corner. Exit leftward.
   P.Leyshon, D.Ellis, M.Berry 00.00.1967

9. **Renaissance**   18m   E2,5b
   This takes the left arete of Trilogy. Climb the awkward arete to a ledge, then move up the right side of the arete to a horizontal crack. Continue up the left side of the arete. Belay at a tree on the left.
   M.Crocker, M.Ward 27.12.1986

10. **Trilogy**   20m   HVS,4c
    The second of the four corners. Climb to an overhang and traverse left to a tree belay.
    C.Jones, D.Parsons 1pt 00.00.1967
    FFA Unknown Pre-1991

11. **Get A Load Of This**   21m   E4,6a
    The right arete of Trilogy. Start below Trilogy, scramble up to a ledge and climb the smooth arete, PR, to a small ledge, then another ledge to exit left above the final step of the arete.
    M.Crocker, M.Ward 27.12.1986

12. **Eulogy**   36m   VS,4b
    The third corner.
    C.Jones, D.Parsons 00.00.1967

13. **Biology**   36m   S
    The fourth corner.
    C.Jones, D.Parsons 00.00.1967

14. **Diogenes**   23m   VS,4b
    Start left of an arete with a small overhang near its base. Climb to a tree, follow the crack to a downward growing tree. Continue to a grass ledge and a short wall to a tree belay.
    D.Ellis, C.Taylor 00.00.1967

15. **Point Five Arete**   23m   VS,4b
    Start at a short corner under a small overhang on the arete. Climb the corner, go left round the overhang then back right onto the arete. Move to one ledge then another and climb the wall on the left to a ledge. Finish up the arete.
    D.Parsons, C.Jones, P.Leyshon 2pt 00.00.1968
    FFA Unknown Pre-1979

16. **Father To Be**   23m   E1,5b
    Climb a crack 3m right of the arete to a grassy ledge, traverse right and climb a short corner to a ledge and tree belay.
    C.Jones, D.Parsons 4pt 00.00.1968
    FFA T.Penning, A.Sharp 15.07.1982

17. **The Rambler**   35m   S
    Start at a large rectangular block (The Coffin). Climb to an overhang, step right and climb a corner to a ledge. Climb up right to a corner, follow this to grass ledges. Finish up the right wall of the corner and scramble off to a belay. A variation start, The Coffin (VS 4b), climbs to the overhang, moves left and climbs a smooth corner to a ledge. Traverse right to join the main route.
    P.Leyshon, W.Evans, M.Shaw, A.Foss 00.00.1967
    C.Jones, D.Parsons - Variation Start 00.00.1967

18. **Hiatus** 36m HS,4a
Start 4m right of a large rectangular block. Climb a groove to a small triangular slab and follow it to a grassy ledge. Move left and climb a corner to exit rightward on poor rock.
C.Taylor, D.Ellis 00.00.1967

19. **Detergent** 36m HS,4a
Start 6m right of the large block. Climb a vegetated corner to ledges then left to a crack. Finish up poor rock.
D.Ellis, P.Leyshon 00.00.1967

20. **Prince Of Wales** 36m VS,4c
This takes the left-hand crack in the wall right of Detergent.
P.Leyshon, S.Lawton 00.00.1968

21. **Nose Picker** 36m S
The right-hand crack.
P.Leyshon, D.Ellis 00.00.1967

22. **Grooved Arete** 12m S
Start right of the arete. Climb a groove to a tree.
C.Jones, C.Taylor 00.00.1967

23. **What's The Mara Boo Boo** 12m E1,5b
Start just right of Grooved Arete. Ascend a groove, move through a small overhang to a ledge and step right to climb a crack. Move left to finish. There is a direct start at 6a taking a small groove to the main line, PR.
P.Bruten, L.Davies 00.00.1988

24. **That Was Then, This Is Now** 15m E4,6a
Start 3m right of Grooved Arete. From a ledge climb a thin crack to a narrow ledge system, TR. Move up right and climb the steep wall, PR. Finish rightward, BB.
M.Ward, M.Crocker 27.12.1986

25. **Spitting Distance** 15m E2,5c
Climb a thin crack system 3m right of That Was Then etc. to a ledge, step right and climb a thin crack to finish rightward, BB.
M.Ward, M.Crocker 31.12.1986

26. **A.N.D.** 15m VS,4c
Climb the prominent clean corner in the centre of the cliff, right of a steep wall.
D.Parsons, C.Jones 00.00.1967

27. **Sneak Preview** 14m S
Start 3m right of A.N.D. at a borehole. Climb a shallow corner to an overhang, step left and up the short ramp to a ledge on the right. Step left and climb a groove then left again and up to a tree.
D.Ellis, I.Lazlo 00.00.1967

The next four routes are mentioned in the 1973 guide and omitted in the 1991 guide. They may or may not have fallen down (the guidebook writer could not tell).

28. **Picardy** 36m HS \
The short corner 11m of A.N.D. below an overhanging block. 'A horrifying route on massive detached blocks.' Up the corner then left onto the overhanging block. Move up and right to belay left of a rose bush at 11m. The wide crack to the right leads to grass ledges after 17m. The final steep wall leads to a tree at the top.
Unknown Pre-1973

29. **Legerdemain** 19m VD ⟍

5m right of Picardy at a broken groove. Take this, then slightly right to a chimney. Walk up and across grass past a tree and a large pedestal. Belay. Take the easiest groove, which is a little to the right above a small prow of rock.
Unknown Pre-1973

30. **Climate** 36m S ⟍

A poor climb 7m right of Picardy. Climb the shallow groove to a grass ledge at 7m. Belay. Continue up the groove and niche, then scramble past massive blocks on the right. Follow a line just left of the poised blocks in the grooved wall.
Unknown Pre-1973

31. **Shambles** 36m VD ⟍

The first ascent line is a little unclear. Follow Climate for 3m, step right and move into a corner which is climbed past an overhanging block on at the top. Tree belay over on the right. Follow the short wall behind the tree, then onto the large blocks with care, scrambling up to finish.
Unknown Pre-1973

32. **Thales** 21m HS,4a

Supersedes Racal. The obvious corner in the right centre of the cliff, 30m right of A.N.D.
P.Nulington, D.Ellis, P.Leyshon 00.00.1967

33. **Andromeda** 21m VS,4b

The wide crack to the right of Thales.
P.Leyshon, D.Ellis 00.00.1967

34. **Decades Roll On** 15m E3,5c ⟍

Start 4m right of Andromeda. Climb up and move left round a bulge. Climb the arete directly, PR, to a horizontal break and twin cracks. Move right onto the tip of the upper arete and then to a big ledge and trees.
M.Crocker, R.Thomas 31.12.1986

The cliff now becomes very broken and the routes are not recommended.

35. **Curates Egg** 21m D ●

Twin cracks right of Andromeda.
P.Leyshon, W.Evans 00.00.1967

36. **Rockfall** 21m S ●

The steep, crack-seamed wall left of the scree.
P.Leyshon, D.Ellis, P.Minett, W.Evans 00.00.1967

37. **Post Script** 21m VS ●

Climb the steep stepped groove in the corner of the scree.
D.Ellis, M.O'Byrne 1pt 00.00.1967
FFA P.Leyshon, W.Evans 00.00.1967

38. **Severn Bridge** 21m HS ●

Climb a cracked slab at the left end of the debris covered platform.
P.Leyshon, D.Ellis 00.00.1967

39. **Gardener** 18m VD ●

Start at a borehole on the right of a pinnacle. Climb the groove to a grassy terrace, climb the niche and step right to a ledge and belay.
H.Ball, P.Leyshon 00.00.1967

40. **Cringe**   12m   VD   •
Start 6m right of Gardener. Climb to a ledge, step right and climb to a tree.
P.Leyshon, P.Minett 00.00.1967

41. **Nameless Crack**   15m   S   •
The crack in the centre of the long wall, starting at a tree.
Unknown Pre-1978

42. **Nitwit**   15m   M   •
The break right of Nameless Crack.
P.Leyshon 00.00.1967

43. **Thomas The Tank**   9m   HVS,5b   \
Thewall right of Nitwit. Gain the PR on the left, move right, then up to the belay ledge. Scramble off up and right.
L.Davies, P.Bruten 00.00.1990

44. **Abandonment**   12m   D   •
The grooved arete at the right-hand end of the long wall.
Unknown Pre-1973

The following climbs are found at the southern end of the quarry opposite a small railway bridge. The small cliff is obvious, a square-cut buttress starting at half-height above a corner/pillar.

45. **Locomotion**   11m   E2,5b   \
Ascend the pillar to a ledge. Step left and a series of committing moves will gain the top.
P.Thomas, L.Davies 00.00.1989

46. **Unknown**   10m   HVS,5b   \
Around left from Man Monkey is a smooth upper wall with a PR on its left side above the obvious traverse lines.
Unknown Pre-1991

47. **Man Monkey**   11m   E1,5a   \
Gain the ledge as for Locomotion and climb directly to the top via the tree.
L.Davies, P.Thomas 00.00.1989

There are two girdles of the cliff, The Big Dipper and Playtex.

48. **The Big Dipper**   116m   VS
A meandering left to right girdle of the left-hand section of the crag. Start in a bay at the far left of the quarry, at blocks left of a big roof.
1. 14m Climb loose blocks left of the roof and walk along a ledge to a tree.
2. 21m Go diagonally right and cross right above an isolated wall and down to a tree on the right.
3. 21m Move right, down then right and climb a chimney. Move up and right to a wooded ledge.
4. 15m Drop down and traverse right to a second groove, climb it then move down under a roof. Exit on the right wall to a ledge.
5. 24m Traverse right above a wall and up to a big ledge on the right. Continue right and climb down the upper part of a corner. Step right around an edge and traverse rightward then step down to a ledge.
6. Finish as for Eulogy.
D.Ellis, L.Ainsworth 00.00.1967

49. **Playtex**   111m   HVS,5a 1pt
A left to right girdle. Start up Lightning Crack to an arete, step right onto a wall, traverse to a breakline at 15m. Belay as convenient. Finish as for Sneak Preview.
C.Jones, D.Parsons, P.Leyshon 1pt 00.00.1968

TAFFS WELL MAIN

GR127828 to 129826
By Goi Ashmore

BOLTING POLICY: Retro-bolting permissible with first ascensionist's permission. Replacement of worn fixed gear on a point for point basis with bolts is permissible. New sports routes allowed.

PREAMBLE

Taffs Well is a large west-facing quarried crag easily accessible from the M4 and therefore deserves more traffic (sorry). The right-hand bay is currently in the process of being regeared and all the routes are clean and in good condition. However, further traffic would be particularly useful for keeping the routes in the central section clean and keeping the undergrowth subdued.

ACCESS

The crag is approximately 5 miles north of Cardiff overlooking the A470 between Tongwynlais and Taff's Well. From junction 32 of the M4 follow the A470 towards Merthyr and take the first exit. Turn immediately right to come to the roundabout at the base of the crag and parking in the laybay at the base of the cliff, where it meets the roundabout. Immediately behind the crag is the landmark of Castell Coch, clearly visible from the motorway. Go through the gate and head left for the Shield and the Central Section. For routes between The Rib and Ghengis Khan, follow the path immediately above the gate and walk right along the base of the crag. For The Red Bay Proper, follow the gravel track for 50m until a path heads leftwards up into the woods to the base of the corner of Gladiator.

To aid familiarisation, the most obvious feature of the Central and Shield sections is the central arete of Pine Tree. This is about 75m left of the entrance gate. For The Red Bay, the most obvious feature is the huge red corner of Gladiator.

DESCENTS: The traditional method of descent is to walk rightwards from the top of the cliff to meet a path leading back down to the right-hand end of the crag. However, some climbers prefer to make multiple abseils down off trees, but be careful to ensure that there are trees for the intermediate abseil points. The sports routes in The Red Bay have lower offs, but be aware that a 60m rope will NOT get you to the base of the crag if lowering off most of the routes above Western Traverse.

THE ROUTES

The Shield
On the far left of the crag is a huge slab - The Shield, with some of the bestr routes, although most are poorly protected. The routes are reached by scrambling along a very poorly defined path from just above the start of Pine Tree.

1. **Changes**   30m   E3,5c   *
    A left to right girdle. Start by scrambling up to a grassy ledge on the left, 3m to the left of Crimes of Fashion. Climb to the prow for 2m then step right onto the face, PR. Climb across right to the hollow flake on Promises and step down to a small ledge. Traverse right more easily past a hole until a difficult move is made to reach easier ground, beneath Thin Air. Continue across to the vegetated ledge on Nero. Finish by any route.
    A.Sharp, P.Lewis 10.10.1979

2. **Crimes Of Fashion**   24m   E4,6b   *
    Reasonably protected. Start 2m right of the left edge of the slab. Make difficult moves past a BR and climb direct, BR, PR, to another BR. Climb diagonally rightward, PR, then more easily to abseil off a tree.
    A.Sharp, P.Lewis, J.Harwood 00.03.1988

3. **Promises**   24m   E5,6b   *
    A serious and unforgiving pitch. Start 3m right of Crimes of Fashion, below a brown streak. Climb up with difficulty on pockets to a ledge, continue to a hollow flake and follow it, moving right on pockets near the top.
    A.Sharp, P.Lewis 14.10.1979

4. **Spuriously Yours**   24m   E5,6c   *   \
Start 3m right of Promises behind a small hawthorn. Pull onto the wall on widely spaced pockets, then swing boldly right, BR. Trend desperately up right to better holds and a small ledge, then climb directly up the slab, TR, on good pockets, to join Promises. Move up and traverse right to lower off a tree at the left end of Catwalk ledge.
M.Crocker, R.Thomas 28.03.1987

5. **Diamonds**   36m   E5,6a   *
Very serious. Start at the base of The Shield at two small trees, right of Spuriously Yours. Follow the groove to a sloping shelf, TR, the only runner. Continue direct to a large crystal lined pocket, move 2m left then straight up the slab on spaced holds to another crystal scoop. Climb up slightly right to ledges near the top. Exit left.
P.Littlejohn, S.Lewis 17.07.1979

6. **The Hitachi Job**   35m   E5,6b   *   \
Start as for Diamonds/Skywalker. Climb with difficulty up the wall just right of the first part of Skywalker, 2BRs. Join Skywalker at the end of its diagonal section. Gain a ledge on the left and climb the middle of the wall between Diamonds and Skywalker, 2BRs. Finish up Diamonds from the tree covered ledge.
M.Crocker, J.Harwood 12.07.1992

7. **Skywalker**   36m   E5,6a   *
Serious. As for Diamonds to the sloping shelf at 12m, TR. Traverse right and move up to a projecting ledge and continue right to a PR. Climb to a PR, then traverse right and continue diagonally to a smooth white slab which is climbed to a tree. Up for 3m then break right on good pockets to a PR, move up left, PR, to a shattered scoop which is followed to the top.
P.Littlejohn 21.06.1979

8. **Sir Clive Dangerous**   36m   E5,6a   \
Start 12m right of Skywalker, below a shallow groove (Nero). Climb a bulging wall on sometimes friable holds, step left onto a slab at 12m and follow Skywalker to the top.
A.Sharp, C.Richards 00.00.1988

9. **Nero**   61m   VS,4b,4a
Start at the highest tree, directly below a groove 12m left of the right edge of The Shield.
1. 30m Climb the groove to a ledge on the right, then climb a short wall to an earthy ledge, possible BB. Traverse right to two small trees, then right again to the arete of Pine Tree. Continue up to a tree belay.
2. 31m Climb up and right to the final short wall, traverse right onto the nose and finish straight up.
K.Hughes 00.00.1960

10. **When In Rome**   39m   E2,5b
Start as for Nero. Climb the wall right of the groove of Nero to the BB. Continue as for Cowpoke or Thin Air.
A.Sharp, W.Jewell 00.00.1985

Cowpoke Area (Central Section)

Just to the right of The Shield is a slabby buttress. The routes frequently cross each other and some future rationalisation of lines may be sensible.

11. **Cowpoke**   45m   E1,5a,5a   *
Start at the lowest point of the slabby buttress.
1. 15m Climb the slabby buttress to its top. Move over left to belay at a tree near a small iron spike.
2. 30m Climb the short shallow corner above, old BR, then move up and left to an earthy ledge, possible belay. Climb up to a break just left of a small bush. Traverse left to a ledge, then climb the wall above to the top.
J.Harwood, J.Richards 11.05.1975, FFA A.Sharp, S.Lewis 00.00.1975

12. **The Hobbit**   68m   HVS,5a,4c,-
1. 15m As for Cowpoke P1.

2. 24m Climb over a small bulge just right of a short, shallow groove and continue up the slab, passing twin trees on their right to a corner. Climb this to a tree belay on the right.
3. 30m Move up and right to the short final wall, traverse right onto the nose and finish straight up.
C.Hurley 00.00.1980

13. Cowchaps   45m   E2,5c
1. 15m As for Cowpoke P1.
2. 30m Climb over a small bulge just right of the shallow groove of The Hobbit and continue leftwards to reach the left-hand tree on Nero. Make difficult moves up the slab above the two trees and then climb the wall first up and then leftwards to reach the PR on Flying Fresian. Finish as for that route.
J.Harwood 20.12.1986

The next two routes are alternative finishes to Nero, Cowpoke and Cowchaps.

14. Thin Air   24m   HVS,5a   *
Start at the earthy ledge on P2 of Nero. Traverse left until it is possible to climb straight up, 2PRs, to the vegetated ledge on Cowpoke. Finish as for Cowpoke.
C.Hurley, P.Hurley 12.11.1977

15. Flying Friesian   21m   E3,5b
From Thin Air, climb up to reach the break and small bush as for Cowpoke, move right and climb straight up. Move up and right on loose rock to reach easier ground which is followed to the top.
S.Bartlett, H.Nicholls 26.09.1978

The centre of the pillar is a useful landmark.

16. Pine Tree   73m   HVD   **
A popular climb, making a good long outing. Start at the lowest point of the buttress/pillar.
1. 39m Climb the slabby pillar to its top, traverse right then up a groove to a large pine tree belay.
2. 34m Climb the wall behind the belay. Follow slabs slightly right, then diagonally right to the final short wall - The Nose. Traverse round the corner to the right onto The Nose and up in a fine and exposed position to the top.
B.Powell 00.00.1961

17. Catwalk   36m   S
A right to left girdle. Start from the third tree of Pine Tree P2. Step left around the obvious block to foot ledges and follow these down left. Continue the traverse along the moustache of ledges to the vegetated ledge of Cowpoke and finish up the wall above.
College of Advanced Technology 00.00.1960

Sub Wall Gully Area (Central Section)

18. Sub Wall Gully   57m   S
Start in the trees 18m up right from the slabby buttress below and to the right of Pine Tree, beneath a small tree. Up to a small tree, then follow the rising traverse line for 8m. Climb over the small bulge above and follow a groove and short wall to a broken ledge. Continue up the slabs to join P2 of Pine Tree.
Unknown 00.00.1960

19. Rainy Day Arete   73m   VS,4c,-
Start as for Sub Wall Gully.
1. 36m Follow Sub Wall Gully to the rising traverse, move over the bulge, step left and climb up for 8m to a short corner. From a borehole above, move right and up to a large bulge, which is turned on the left. Follow the arete until it is possible to reach a grassy ledge and PB.
2. 36m Traverse left for 6m then climb straight up to finish as for Pine Tree.
P.Thomas, J.Harwood AL 04.09.1979

20. **Sub Wall**   70m   HS,-,-,   *
A good route despite a scrappy first pitch. Start at an obvious corner 15m up to the right of Sub Wall Gully.
1. 33m Climb the corner until it steepens and step left to ledges. Climb up passing a huge block on its left to reach the grassy ledge of Rainy Day Arete, PB.
2. 36m Climb straight up to the impending head wall, then traverse left to join Pine Tree.
B.Powell 00.00.1961

21. **Noel Way**   69m   VS,-,-   ●
1. 33m As for Sub Wall.
2. 36m Serious, with poor rock. Reverse the previous pitch for 13m until it is possible to reach the left-hand end of a gangway crossing the wall on the right, follow this to a final wall and pull over to ledges and a scramble to belays.
J.Noel 00.00.1960

22. **All Those Years Ago**   12m   E4,6a
Climb a blunt rib in a short steep wall right of the start of Sub Wall. Climb a faint crack to a short bulge, TR, PR leading to a small roof. Traverse 4m right to a PB. Abseil.
A.Sharp, R.Powles 20.05.1988

23. **Hocus Pocus**   21m   E5,6a
Serious. Start 3m right of All Those Years Ago, beneath the remains of a PR at 4m. Climb the short wall, PR, to small ledges above a bulge, then up to a second PR. Traverse 3m left (crossing All Those Years Ago) and move up to a sloping ledge. Climb diagonally left to a ledge, then move up right to the top, belay well back.
J.Harwood 11.08.1974
FFA P.Littlejohn, A.Davies 1982

24. **Focus**   12m   E3,5c   *
Start 3m right of Hocus Pocus. Climb the bulging wall to a PR at 9m, traverse 3m right to a PB. Abseil.
P.Lewis, A.Sharp, J.Harwood 17.06.1986

Area Above Rainy Day Arete (Central Section)
The following two routes are on the headwall above Rainy Day Arete.

25. **Hot Moon**   24m   E3,4c,5c
A serious climb up the crack in the head wall gained from P1 of Rainy Day Arete, PR. Finish to the right.
T.Penning, P.Cresswell 20.11.1983

26. **Crime Minister**   21m   E2,4c,5b
From P1 of Rainy day Arete, move right to the start of a crack and up it to the top of the cliff. Tree belay high up.
T.Penning, C.Court, P.Littlejohn, J.Harwood 10.04.1984

The Red Bay
The quality end of the crag starts with a poor route - The Rib, forming a well defined arm. Right of this is a slabby wall which runs to a point just before the huge red corner of Gladiator.

27. **The Rib**   30m   S   ●
A lethal route up the arm of the buttress. Ab off or finish at will, after writing your own.
J.Noel 00.00. 1960

28. **Red Square**   24m   E4,6a
Scramble up the gully right of The Rib to a ledge at 18m. Climb the crack in the wall, PR, tree belay.
A.Sharp, R.Powles 07.03.1988

29. **Organised Chaos**   21m   E4,6a   *
A good route, with fine technical climbing up the flowstone wall. Start on a pedestal 4m right of The Rib, BB. Climb directly past 4BRs to a small vertical slot. Traverse left to finish as for Red Square.
A.Sharp, P.Lewis, A.Swann 12.03.1988

30. **Ye Old Campaigner**   40m   E5,6b   *   \
The right-trending corner and wall right of Organized Chaos. Start from BBs on the ledge by the Red Square slab.
M.Crocker, J.Harwood 12.07.1992

31. **Crowman**   42m   E6,6a   *
A bold and strenuous route taking a central line up the wall right of Ye Old Campaigner. Some poor rock at the top. Start from a tree belay on a grass ramp under the line of overlaps high up. Climb up then right, PR, to black flowstone, climb this, PR, move 1m left then up to a poor TR. Go over the bulge above then left and up to finish.
P.Littlejohn, T.Penning 05.07.1983

32. **Painted Bird**   42m   E5,6a   **
Climb the crack up the flowstone right of Crowman, TR, then up the flowstone directly to the top.
P.Littlejohn, T.Penning 12.07.1983

The line of BRs to the right is a project. Several bolt lines now follow.

33. Unnamed #1   30m   E5,6b   Fr7a+   **
Climb the flowstone wall some 10m left of the pillar at the right end of the wall.
G.Gibson 00.09.2003

34. **Melting Man**   30m   E5,6a   *
A sustained pitch taking the wall to the right. The old start to Ghenghis Khan followed this route to BR 2.
M.Crocker, J.Harwood 12.07.1992

35. **Ghengis Khan**   30m   E4,6a   Fr6c+   **
The new direct start takes the centre of the red bulgeat the lowest part of the wall. Finish Direct.
A.Sharp, P.Lewis 00.00.1985, Direct-G.Gibson 00.09.2003

36. Taurus Bulbous   30m   E3,6a   Fr6c   *
Climb the vague scoop right of Ghengis Khan to a hard move left. Step back right and finish direct.
G.Gibson 00.09.2003

37. Unnamed #2   20m   VS,4c   Fr4+   *
Climb the centre of the pillar just right of Taurus Bulbous.
R.Thomas 00.09.2003

38. Unnamed #3   15m   E1,5b   Fr6a
Climb the wall to the right.
R.Thomas 00.09.2003

To the right of Ghengis Khan is an area of rock steps leading up to the base of the red corner of Gladiator. This is the start of The Red Bay Proper and where you will arrive if following the access notes for it.

Left Of Gladiator (Red Bay Proper)

39. **No Name**   26m   VS,4b,-
A good first pitch. Start by scrambling up the rock steps to a comfy ledge about 10m left of the angle of the wall (8m right of Ghengis Khan) and about 9m up the cliff. Move left and up to a corner/groove, then up and step left to the bottom of a slab, PR. Climb the slab and the shallow groove above to reach a final steep v-groove, PR.

Follow the groove to a large ledge and tree belay. Abseil. For those wanting a wild experience it is possible to climb up leftwards across grass ledges and unstable rock until a final wall is climbed to tree belays.
Unknown 00.00.1960

40. Unnamed #4   30m   E3,6a   Fr6c
Start from the comfy bay of No Name, BB and climb the left hand bolt line.
G.Gibson 00.08.2003

41. **Christendom**   30m   E4,6a   Fr7a   **
The wall above the BB at the comfy Stance of No Name.
M.Crocker, R.Thomas 03.02.1989, G.Ashmore – Direct 26.05.2002

42. **The Angel Of Mons**   30m   E3,6a   Fr6c   *
The slab right of Christendom to join Chistendom at its final bolt.
G.Ashmore 28.05.2002

43. Decimus Maximus   30m   E3,6a   Fr6c   *
As for The Angel of Mons, but break out right and climb the slab right of the corner.
G.Gibson 00.08.2003

44. **Gladiator**   57m   E3,- ,5c   ●
A dose of death. The obvious red corner has suffered severe de-stablisation high up and is best avoided.
T.Penning, P.Cresswell 10.07.1983

45. Unnamed #5   15m   E3,6a   Fr6c   *
From the belay on Decimus Maximus, swing right and climb the wall right of the corner.
G.Gibson 00.09.2003

The wall to the right is a project.

Right Of Gladiator (Main Bay Proper)
To the right of Gladiator, the routes as far as Southern Entry are either start from Western Traverse, or finish on it. Western Traverse is described first, then the routes above it. The descriptions then start again at ground level.

46. **Western Traverse**   45m   HS,4b
1. 21m Start up Gladiator, then from the belay move right onto a ledge which runs along the crag for the next 20m. Belay on the BB under an overlap nest the start of the ledge.
2. 25m Continue along the ledge, then step right and move along a higher ledge, PR. Climb down to ledges and past a rib. Climb up to a metal spike belay, abseil.
Unknown Pre-1973

Routes Above Western Terrace (Red Bay Proper)
These routes start from one of the belays, which can be reached by any of the routes below, although most logically from Gwesty Cymru or Look Over Yonder. Sugar Bullets and Scram start from the left-hand BB, Rancho La and New Day Today from the right-hand belay. Note that a 60m rope will NOT enable you to lower to the ground, but you can, with care reach the lower offs above Western Terrace.

47. **Sugar Bullets**   30m   E6,6b   Fr7b+   ***
A brilliant route up the bulging walls right of the Gladiator Corner. From the left-hand BB, pull over a small overlap and climb a blunt rib to a fractured ledge. Pull over the bulge and continue up the rib via intricate moves as the rock improves to a bulge and large pocket. A difficult sequence leftwards leads into the superb black wall where continuous difficulties lead to the crux bulge right at the top. BB, Abseil. Hard for the grade.
G.Gibson, R.Thomas 05.06.1993

48. **Scram** 30m E6,6a Fr7b **
The more obvious of the two long sports routes taking an undercut groove, wall and rib in a spectacular position with some snappy holds. From the BB, step right and up into the undercut groove. Climb the wall above then the arete and a BB on the right, abseil. The original route wombled up the ramp leftwards to abseil off a twig.
M.Crocker, R.Thomas 29.01.1989

49. **New Day Today** 25m E4,6a Fr7a
Start at the right-hand belay. Pull up to a vague crack and from this climb the wall slightly right, BB.
G.Gibson, R.Thomas 11.05.1991

50. **Rancho La Cha Cha Cha** 25m E3,6a Fr6c *
Start at the right-hand belay and traverse rightwards for 2m. Gain a big jug, then follow a line of bolts leftwards to join New Day Today at the slab. Abseil. The route just to the right is the top section of Ulrika Ka Ka.
M.Crocker, R.Thomas 11.02.1989

Routes Below Western Terrace (Red Bay Proper)
The other routes are described from ground level. Underneath and right of the Gladiator corner is a slabby buttress.

51. Unnamed #6 21m HVS,5a Fr5
The left hand side of the slabby buttress.
G.Gibson 00.07.2003

52. **Gwesty Cymru 7" Mix** 21m E2,5c Fr6b **
A delightful pitch up the slabby buttress, following the line of ring bolts. Harder than it looks. BB, LO.
G.Griffiths 00.00.2001

53. Unnamed #7 21m E4,6a Fr7a
The first bolted line just right of Gwesty Cymru.
G.Gibson 00.08.2003

54. **Daggers** 20m E3,6a Fr6c *
The first bolted groove right of Gwesty Cymru.
M.Crocker, R.Thomas 22.01.1989

55. **Look Over Yonder** 20m E4,6a Fr6c+ *
Climb the technical groove just right of Daggers.
M.Crocker, R.Thomas 22.01.1989.

56. **Wet Afternoon** 20m E5,6b Fr7a+ **
As for Look Over Yonder, but at the base of the groove, pul right and follow the flowstone up the wall to the right.
G.Gibson, R.Thomas 28.06.1992

57. **Southern Entry** 24m E1,5c
A redundant route that started up the groove right of Wet Afternoon then wandered off right into Western Traverse.
P.Watkin, C.Jones 00.00.1960, FFA P.Littlejohn, J.Harwood 04.09.1977

58. Unnamed #8 20m E2,5c
Climb the awkward groove right of Wet Afternoon to a chain below the terrance.
Unknown 00.00.2002

59. **The Id** 30m VS,4c
Start 8m right of Southern Entry at a tree stump. Climb to a ledge at 3m, then a crack until it is possible to move right onto a sloping ledge, PR. Climb up and right onto a doubtful looking block under an overhang and then gain the ledge above, PR, possible belay. Climb the groove behind the tree and gain a ledge on the left, continue left

more easily and then up to a tree just above the belay on Western Traverse. Abseil off.
M.Fairlamb, G.Ashmore 00.00.1967

60. Ulrika Ka Ka Ka   40m E4,6a Fr6c+ *
The groove to the right. Warning! check your rope length before the lower!
G.Gibson 00.08.2003

To the right, is a rib of rock forming the left-hand side of a buttress with some overlaps at 8m. In the centre of the rib is the prominent groove of No Beer, No Fear.

61. Unnamed #9   20m E1,5b Fr6a+
The barrel shaped rib.
R.Thomas 00.08.2003

62. **Good Gear, Good Cheer** 20m E2,5c Fr6b *
Climb the rib left of the prominent groove.
R.Thomas, N.O'Neill 01.06.2002

63. **No Beer, No Fear**   24m E2,5c Fr6b *
Gain and climb the obvious groove in the buttress.
R.Thomas, M.Learoyd 00.00.1990

64. Not My Fault!   20m E4,6a Fr6c+
Squeeze up the wall right of No Beer, No Fear.
G.Gibson 00.08.2003

65. **Foot And Mouth**   18m E2,5c Fr6b
The wall right of Not My Fault.
Unknown 00.00.1967, FFA A.Sharp, J.Harwood 17.10.1979

66. Unnamed #10   20m E2,5c Fr6b *
The wall right of Foot And Mouth.
R.Thomas 00.00.2003

67. Unnamed #11   15m E2,5c Fr6b
The groove to the right.
R.Thomas 00.00.2003

68. **Get Thee Hence**   12m E3,6b Fr6c+
Climb up onto a broken pillar right of Foot and Mouth, then climb directly up a blunt rib on small holds.
M.Crocker, R.Thomas 11.02.1989

69. Unnamed #12   10m E3,6a Fr6c
The short slab right of Get The Hence.
M.Hirst 00.07.2003

70. Unnamed #13   9m E3,6b Fr6c+
The short slab right again.
M.Hirst 00.07..2003

71. **Talk About False Gods** 24m E6,6b
Follow one of the last few routes and climb the wall above.
M.Crocker, R.Thomas 12.02.1989

TAFFS WELL WEST

GR123827 to 125825
By Goi Ashmore

BOLTING POLICY: Retro-bolting permissible with first ascensionist's permission. Replacement of worn fixed gear on a point for point basis with bolts is permissible. New sports routes allowed.

PREAMBLE

Taff's Well West is an easily accessible sports climbing area, only 2 minutes drive from the M4.. The back wall is an impressive sheet of vertical limestone. Unfortunately, it is in need of re-equipping and often damp. The North Wall, is well equipped and has climbing of a very unusual and strangely satisfying nature. It can seep, but otherwise it stays dry in the rain. At the time of writing all the routes on the North Wall have recently been cleaned. The slabs, in contrast to the main crag are very open, providing some good technical climbing.

ACCESS

From the J32 of the M4 turn onto the A470 in the direction of Merthyr Tydfil. Take the first turnoff (Radyr/Taff's Well) to reach the roundabout below the main Taff's Well crag. Turn left to Radyr, then right at the next roundabout. Just over ½ mile along this road is a blocked off quarry track on the left, just where the road starts to rise. Park in a small housing estate on the right. From the blocked off quarry track, continue up the road for 100m to an obvious track leading up into the woods. Follow this to a T-junction at a wider track. Turn left here, and continue for 200m to a clearing with a small pinnacle. The quarry is the box shaped hollow behind the pinnacle. To reach the slabs, continue up the same track for 150m to reach a grassed over spoil heap. Strike rightwards up the hill to reach the obvious slabs.

The South Wall of the main crag is reached from the top of the spoil heap. The North Wall is reached by walking a few metres back from the pinnacle, to reach a leafy path running down the north side of the quarry. Routes on the Back Wall can also be reached from this direction, but an easier approach is to abseil down from big trees above the crag (follow a good path up behind the North Wall).

DESCENTS: Descents for all routes are by abseil.

South Wall

This is the short diamond-shaped wall down and left of the pinnacle with a central leaning groove line.

1. **Bristol Beat**   8m   E5,6b
    Start 6m left of the central groove line, halfway up an earth slope. Step onto the wall below a BR, trend right past a pocket BR. Mmake difficult moves up the blunt rib until an easier traverse can be made rightward, PB. Abseil.
    A.Sharp, P.Lewis 03.04.1988

2. **Screaming Neutrinos**   13m   E6,6b   *
    A short, power packed pitch up the central leaning groove line, BRs.
    M.Crocker, G.Gibson, M.Ward, R.Thomas, J.Bullock 13.12.1987

3. **It's a Black World**   13m   E4,6b   *
    The fine black wall right of Streaming Neutrinos. Start below the central groove. Trend rightwards above vegetation then move up to a borehole, BR, to gain good holds on the left, BR. Step left and go over a bulge to better holds, BR, continue directly to a ledge and PB. Abseil.
    G.Gibson, M.Ward, M.Crocker, R.Thomas, J.Bullock 13.12.1987

Back Wall

The best appoach is to abseil in from the top to belay above the veg. Towards the left end of the wall is a prominent undercut. The old undercut fell down so caution is advised, particularly as many of the BRs have been stolen!

4. **The Quartz Bicycle**   16m   E4,6a
    Climb to the prominent undercut flake a few metres left of its right-hand end, TR. Undercut left for 3m and pull onto the wall, BR. Technical moves lead straight up, BR, to a large quartz hole, hex. Trend rightwards on cleaned

rock to a small shelf, PR and climb the headwall to a tree, TR and exit.
G.Gibson, R.Thomas 20.04.1991

5. **You Never Can Tell**   18m   E4,6a   *
A fine wall pitch. Start just right of The Quartz Bicycle BR, to gain 2TRs. Press on via a trio of good pockets, to reach good holds above and slightly left, BR. Technical moves lead to better holds, BR, and a direct exit to a tree.
G.Gibson, R.Thomas 14.10.1990

6. **Palm Springs**   18m   E5,6a   **
Start below a short ramp. Climb up pockets, TR, until a hard move gains the ramp, BR. Palm up the ramp to good finger jugs in the bulge above, PR. Continue direct, BR, step left and then finish direct, BR, on good finger holds.
M.Crocker, R.Thomas 30.05.1989

7. **A Million Destinies**   18m   E5,6a   **
Climb the wall right of Palm Springs leftwards on pockets and balls, to reach the first BR. Climb the wall via an intricate move, PR, then leftward to the final BR. Move left to exit up Palm Springs.
M.Crocker, R.Thomas 30.05.1989

8. **Stay Hungry**   15m   E5,6b   *
The crack to the right of A Million Destinies. From a tree climb up on good pockets to a PR. Technical climbing past 2PRs leads to a good hold and BB.
A.Sharp, P.Lewis 00.07.1987

9. **Digitorum Brevis**   18m   E5,6b   **   \
A great wall climb, high in the grade. Start by abseiling into a stake below the right side of the wall, or better still, climb the easy-angled slabs to the same point. Swing up and left to crystalline pockets, then climb the smooth wall, via a weird pocket, to reach a bucket at an undercut. Pull straight up onto the wall above, then continue directly until moves left past a sapling lead to a root exit. Lots of in-situ gear.
G.Gibson, R.Thomas 14.10.1990

The North Wall
The north wall forms the right side of the quarry. The climbing is unusual for limestone, being insecure but with powerful cruxes involving undercuts. All the routes have good bolts and lower offs apart from Scream For Cream.

10. **The Creaming Dream**   18m   E4,6a   Fr7a
The slabby left-hand end of the wall.
G.Gibson 21.03.1998

11. **Ice Cream Sunday**   18m   E4,6b   Fr7a+
Climb the vague line up the wall 3m right of The Creaming Dream to a desperate move over an overlap. Once established, mooch up the wall to a large prominent flake, finishing slightly left to the BB.
G.Gibson, R.Thomas 14.10.1990

12. **Scream For Cream**   18m   E5,6b   Fr7a+   *
Start down and right of Ice Cream Sunday. Climb directly up to and through the overlap.
M.Ward, M.Crocker, G.Gibson 13.12.1987

13. **Trailblazer**   21m   E5,6b   Fr7b   **
Takes the centre of the wall from the lowest point. Step right to the BB.
M.Crocker, M.Ward, R.Thomas 06.12.1987

14. **Sink Or Swim**   21m   E5,6a   Fr7a+   *
The wall right of Trailblazer. Run out low down.
G.Gibson 21.03.1998

15. **Security Plus**   21m E5,6b Fr7b *
Powerful, well protected climbing, giving the hardest route on this wall. Start at the lowest point of the wall under a shelf at 2m. Gain the shelf and a quarry spike, then proceed up the wall to good undercuts. A very powerful move to more undercuts leads to a shakeout. A final difficult move leads to the lower off.
G.Gibson, R.Thomas 20.09.1990

16. **Norman Normal**   18m E5,6b
Start 4m left of where the diagonal crack meets the ground. Gain a borehole then move up right to a ledge. Go straight up past 2BRs and an overlap to a vague rib, Follow the rib and finish by moving right to a ledge and BB.
G.Gibson, R.Thomas, M.Crocker, M.Ward 06.12.1987

17. **Taffy Duck**   18m E3,6a **
Start as for All's Well. Move up for 3m before traversing left to meet a crack past a bush. Climb the crack, stake, BR to gain Trailblazer, stake and sapling. Continue across the crack, BR, PR and a high BR in Scream for Cream to gain the chain belay on Ice Cream Sunday.
G.Gibson 28.04.1991

18. **All's Well**   18m E3,5c
Start just right of the diagonal crack/ground junction. Climb the cleaned slab to an obvious overlap at 9m, pull out right and up a shallow groove, PR, to gain a ledge. Step left to PB, BB, lower off.
G.Gibson, R.Thomas, M.Ward M.Crocker 06.12.1987

19. **Any Old Iron**   15m E3,6a ● \
Start at a cleaned strip, 27m to the right of All's Well. Take a direct line up the slabby lower wall, stake runner, 2PRs, to a good break, take the headwall directly, BR, PR.
R.Thomas, J.Bullock, M.Ward, M.Crocker, G.Gibson 13.12.1987

20. **Rag And Bone**   18m E2,5c Fr6b
The wall to the right of any Old Iron.
R.Thomas 07.10.1998

21. **Knacker's Yard**   18m E2,5c Fr6b+ \
The wall to the right of any Old Iron.
R.Thomas 00.00.1998

The Slabs
The slabs are about 5 minutes walk further on up the path (see access notes).

22. **Can The Can**   21m E4,6a
The left line of the slab, 3BRs. Move right to join Palm at its third BR.
A.Sharp, P.Lewis 00.04.1987

23. **Palm**   21m E4,6b *
Takes the centre of the slab. Climb a shallow orange groove to small ledge, move up and right, BR and continue to a deep slot, move left, BR and finish directly, BR, PR, BB.
A.Sharp, P.Lewis 00.04.1987

24. **Neil Kinnock's Last Stand**   23m E4,6b *
As for Palm but move right at the slot. Continue up the headwall, BR. Traverse left at the top to the BB of Palm.
G.Ashmore, R.Lawrence 10.07.1992

25. **Chinese Whispers**   24m E3,6a
This route climbs the right-hand edge of the slab. Start as for Palm and climb rightwards to a small ledge at 9m, move back left and climb the slab, 2BRs, PR (poor) to a BB.
A.Sharp, P.Lewis 00.06.1987

TWYNAU GWYNION

GR065105
By Goi Ashmore

BOLTING POLICY: No bolting.

PREAMBLE

Twynau Gwynion quarries lie on the hillside above Taf Fechan Quarry and provide some magnificent views of the Brecon Beacons. The routes were probably climbed by the same teams active at Taf Fechan in the 1960s. For many years it has been the secret location for many outdoor centres who wanted to avoid the crowded and polished crags of Morlais. It is an ideal crag for the middle grade climber who wants some seclusion and is not tempted by the delights of Taf Fechan

ACCESS

By car, turn off the A465 'Heads of The Valley's Road' at Dowlais roundabout (Asda superstore). Miss the superstore's entrance and turn left, left again and then right and park. Follow the road/track through the buildings and horse boxes and turn right to follow a pot holed track for 10 minutes to reach some boulders. Continue into the quarry. It is also possible to scramble up directly from Taf Fechan, which is probably quicker.

DESCENTS: It is relatively easy to walk down either side of the quarry.

Bay One
The smallest bay, glimpsed through the spoil heaps on the right of the track when coming from Asda superstore. It is an 11m high wall of rough white rock and 30m in length.

1. **White Groove**   11m   HS,4b
   The front of the clean buttress on the south end of the wall. Move left to finish.
   Unknown Pre-1991

2. **Spare Rib**   11m   HS,4b
   The arete forming the right angle.
   Unknown Pre-1991

Bay Two
150m north of Bay One is Bay Two forming a right angle and facing northwest. An obvious feature is the arete of Corrugation. The routes are described from right to left.

3. **Short Crack**   9m   HS,4b
   The first crack.
   Unknown Pre-1973

4. **Black Crack**   9m   VS,4b
   The crack immediately right of a rounded groove, with an overhang at 6m, finish up the groove.
   Unknown Pre-1973

5. **Flowstone**   9m   HVS,5a
   Start 1m left of two trees low down. Climb the flowstone wall direct to the top.
   Unknown Pre-1973

Next are two cracks.

6. **Two Half Quids**   9m   VS,4c
   The right-hand crack.
   Unknown Pre-1973

7. **Two Fingers**   9m   VS,4c
   The left-hand crack.
   Unknown Pre-1973

8. **Cystitis Eat Your Heart Out**   9m   VS,4c
   Start 3m right of a left-hand corner with a tree low down below a curving crack. Follow it to the main horizontal break, step left then follow a crack left of a small roof.
   Unknown Pre-1991

9. **Suns Going Down**   9m   VS,4c
   Start just right of the left-hand corner and follow a crack to the top.
   Unknown Pre-1973

10. **Corrugation**   11m   E1,5b   *
    The wrinkled arete of the great block climbed on its right up the shallow groove.
    Unknown Pre-1973

11. **Frontal Wall**   11m   S,4a   *
    The front wall of the block has two cracks high up. Climb either one, the right-hand one being harder.
    Unknown Pre-1973

12. **Hawthorn Chimney**   6m   D
    The obvious chimney above a tree.
    Unknown Pre-1973

Bay Three

45m north and at a lower level than Bay Two is Bay Three. It has a single north facing wall, its right-hand end is two tiered and its left-hand section contains some fine crack lines. The lower wall of the double tier contains a number of problems 5m high.

13. **Staircase**   5m   2a
    Unknown Pre-1973

14. **Painful Crack**   5m   4a
    Unknown Pre-1973

15. **Short Cleft**   5m   4a
    Unknown Pre-1973

16. **Wide Crack**   5m   3a
    Unknown Pre-1973

17. **Grooves**   5m   2a
    Unknown Pre-1973

18. **Finger Line**   5m   5b
    Unknown Pre-1973

19. **Thin Crack**   5m   5a
    Unknown Pre-1973

20. **The Reach**   5m   5a
    Unknown Pre-1973

The first real route is:

21. **Pete's Finish**   12m   E1,5b
Just left of where the tiers merge. Follow a crack which is obvious high up past a number of horizontal breaks.
J.Harwood 17.05.1987

22. **Nut Wall**   12m   VS,4c
Follow the obvious line diagonally left to a ledge with trees. Climb the crack for 3m then move 2m left to a thin crack, which leads to a ledge.
Unknown Pre-1973

23. **Nut Wall Direct**   12m   E1,5c
Thin moves gain a ledge and tree at 3m, carry on up a crack to a large grassy ledge. Move left to Finish.
G.Evans, K.Wood 00.00.1974

24. **Unnamed**   12m   E1,5b
Climb thin discontinuous cracks in the slabby wall.
J.Harwood 17.05.1987

25. **Friends In Need**   12m   HVS,5a
Start 4m left. Difficult moves gain a crack line at 6m.
Unknown Pre-1991

26. **Little Owl**   12m   VS,4c
The distinct crack.
J.Harwood 12.05.1987

27. **Pleasurance**   12m   HS,4b
Climb the wide crack.
J.Harwood 17.05.1973

Bay Four
The largest of the bays. The following routes lie on its south-facing wall.

28. **Balance**   9m   VS,4c
A crack on the left wall gives more trouble than anticipated.
Unknown Pre-1991

29. **The Block**   10m   VS,4c
To the right is a block, climb it.
Unknown Pre-1991

WENVOE WHITEHALL QUARRY

GR115735
By Roy Thomas

PREAMBLE
This slabby quarry is now a landfill site and so will be lost in the near future. Nevertheless the routes names are recorded here, mainly to add weight to the guidebook for added inconvenience when climbing at Ogmore.

THE ROUTES

All these routes are defunct and are included as a matter of historical interest only.

Rubble Rouser E2,5b (R.Thomas, S.Walsh 1987), Clean Sweep E2,5b (R.Thomas, G.Royle 1987), Left On Ice E2,5b (R.Thomas, G.Royle 1987), Here Comes The Sun E1,5b (R.Thomas, E.Thomas 1986), Horses Mouth HVS,5a (R.Thomas, S.Walsh 1987), Before I Go E3,5b (R.Thomas, G.Royle 1988), East Clintwood E3,6a (D.Meek, etc. 1986), The Way We Were E1,5a (G.Lewis, H.Griffiths 1987), Filoo E2,5c (R.Thomas, G.Royle 1987), The Gingerman E2,5c (R.Thomas, G.Royle 1987), That's My Line E2,5c (R.Thomas, G.Royle 1986), The Meek, The Mad And The Ugly E3,6a (G.Lewis, S.Lewis, D.Meek 1986), The Meek, The Mad And The Ugly Direct (R.Thomas, G.Royle 1989), Highly Strung E3,6a (M.Crocker, R.Thomas 1986), The Big Leek E2,5b (M.Crocker, R.Thomas 1986), Slow Seduction E1,5b (M.Ward, R.Thomas, M.Crocker 1986), Terminal E1,5a (H.Griffiths 1986), Statement Of Age E2,5b (H.Griffiths 1986).

Sandstone

SOUTH EAST WALES SANDSTONE

By Goi Ashmore

TIDAL STATUS: Unfortunately there are no sandstone sea cliffs.

BOLTING POLICY: Unlike other crags, the bolting policy for sandstone is simple.

NATURAL SANDSTONE: No bolting.

QUARRIED SANDSTONE: Retro-bolting permissible with first ascensionist's permission. Replacement of worn fixed gear on a point for point basis with bolts is permissible. New sports routes allowed.

DESCENTS: Almost all routes are equipped with abseil bolts. For other routes, it is fairly straightforward to walk down either side of the crag.

ABBEY BUTTRESS

GR790884

PREAMBLE
This is the obvious crag above the steelworks, easily visible from the M4. It has awesome views of one of the last remaining pieces of heavy industrialisation in South Wales, somewhat akin to a 1960s black and white film about the working man. It is somewhat exposed, but has a sunny aspect from 11am onwards (though you would not know this if you turned up after sunset, when it looks like something out of Bladerunner..... or was it Roadrunner)? Seepage is only a problem on the extreme left-hand side of the main wall. The rock quality is exceptional. For routes without lower offs, stake belays are in place, sensibly situated at the top of the crag.

ACCESS
Approach by leaving the M4 at J40 and follow the signs to the steel works. Turn left at the traffic lights, and continue to the Old Surgery pub. Take the left turning opposite the pub and follow a road back under the motorway to some bungalows. Park here, treating the grass with care. Left of the first bungalow is a gate. Pass through this and proceed up the hill to a track. Turn right and continue until below the crag, finding a suitable way up.

THE ROUTES

1. **Bargaining Counter**   25m   E1,5b
   A left to right girdle along the horizontal break. Start up Closed Shop and finish up Writings On The Wall.
   G.Evans, L.Moran 26.10.1986

2. **Closed Shop**   16m   E2,5c
   Start at a left-trending ramp, 3m right of the left-hand corner of the main face. Proceed up the ramp to a horizontal break. Pull onto the upper wall, to gain and finish up a thin crack.
   R.Thomas, J.Bullock, G.Evans, L.Moran 26.10.1986

3. **Restrictive Practice**   16m   E3,5c   *
   As for Closed Shop, but pull out right up a thin crack to gain the break. Once on the headwall, move right to a good nut placement, then move back left to finish.
   R.Thomas, G.Royle 30.09.1986

4. **Crack Basher**   18m   E2,5c   ***
   A classic, with a couple of hard cruxes. From the foot of the left-trending ramp, climb up a niche to a glacis. Pull onto this and plod up easily to a hard move up the final crack, TR.
   R.Thomas, G.Royle, 28.09.1986

Abbey Buttress

Photo: Garl Ryan

5. **Sign Of The Times** 18m E4,6a *
    Start slightly right and pass a PR to gain a prominent crack. Follow this to a big, bendy PR and make a hard move up and slightly right, to gain the break. Finish more or less direct, PR.
    R.Thomas, J.Bullock, M.Learoyd 1pt 00.09.1986
    FFA M.Crocker 18.10.1986

6. **PR Job** 18m E4,6b
    A route which sports several PRs of some form, not all of which are runners! Start just right of Sign Of The Times under the initials 'PR'. Climb the crack past a real PR and move left. Move slightly back right to gain the finish of Urban Development.
    M.Crocker, R.Thomas 18.10.1986

7. **Urban Development** 18m E4,6b **
    Start to the right of PR Job and slightly left of a slanting groove at half-height. Climb past 2PRs to a hard move out left to a flake. From the horizontal break follow the crack on the left to the top.
    R.Thomas, G.Royle 1pt 00.00.1986
    FFA M.Crocker, R.Thomas 18.10.1986

8. **Writings On The Wall** 18m E3,5c
    Start as for Urban Development. At the first PR move right to gain the base of a hanging groove. Climb this to the break, passing a leaf of rock on the way to the top. Can also be started direct.
    G.Royle, R.Thomas 00.09.1986

9. **Split The Equity** 16m E2,5b
    The steep flake line down and to the right. Reach the small cave below and right of the small tree. Now pull out and follow the flake.
    R.Thomas, G.Royle, J.Bullock 00.04.1988

10. **Hot Mill**   16m   E5,6b   Fr7a+   *

SE Wales answer to The Quarryman. Between the last route and the tower of Industrial Relations is an innocuous looking groove starting at 6m. Gain, then battle up this! The gear is OK after the first clip, which can be protected by a couple of small friends. The BB is set well back.
R.Thomas 00.00.1995

11. **Industrial Relations**   18m   E1,5b

Start below the tower toward the right-hand end of the crag. Climb the corner and follow a crack splitting the tower to a small ledge and the final wall. PB and stake.
G.Royle, R.Thomas 00.09.1986

12. **Cold Rolled**   10m   E3,6b   Fr6c+   *

A tricky little boulder problem up the slab/wall at the right-hand side of the crag.
R.Thomas 00.00.1995

13. **Nether Edge**   9m   E3,6c   Fr7b

The arete to the BB of Cold Rolled with a desperate move at half-height.
E.Travers-Jones 00.00.1997

ABERCYNON HIGH BUTTRESS

GR078958

PREAMBLE
A series of natural sandstone buttresses on the hillside overlooking Abercynon. All the current routes are either on a rectangular buttress above 'the tree line, or the buttress immediately above it.

ACCESS
The best approach is probably from The Gap (see The Gap for details). From the left-hand side of the lower quarry, go up the banking and across the plateau. Carry straight on when the ground starts dropping down, taking care not to fall over the top.

THE ROUTES

Lower Buttress

1. **Eagle**   9m   VS,4c   \

The crack, overhang and wall on the rectangular buttress.
S.Richardson, C.Shorrock 00.09.1991

Upper Buttress

There are a couple of unrecorded Severes and:

2. **Girdle Traverse**   15m   S,4a   \

As the name suggests.
C.Shorrock 00.09.1991

BARGOED

GR006153

PREAMBLE

A small quarry consisting of two walls seperated by an arete. West facing, sheltered during the winter, but a suntrap in the summer. Lichen can be a problem at times, though is easy to remove and it is not as bad as the burnt rubber coating at Penrhiwceiber. Some care is needed with the remaining loose rock. Most of the routes could just about be described as sports climbs, but without belay bolts. There is a good telegraph pole about 20m back from the top of the crag, but watch out for the goat. There is also a tip at the left-hand end to add to the general Valleys ambience of the place (Beware).

ACCESS

From Bargoed town centre, follow the B4511 northwards to a steep right hand bend ¼ mile beyond the town centre. Park on the left. On foot, alight at Bargoed railway station, take the east exit and turn left to reach the same spot. Walk 100m up the hill and turn into Quarry Row on the left hand side. Proceed 100m down to the track to the obvious quarry on the right.

THE ROUTES

1. **Mr. Gorrilla's Got A Big Nose**   9m   E3,6b   Fr7a   *
   The slab at the left-hand side of the wall left of the central tower. Desperate. BR, PR.
   M.Crocker, R.Thomas 04.03.1989

2. **Pepperatzi**   14m   E2,5b
   The obvious corner left of the main arete.
   L.Foulkes, M.Learoyd 00.00.1989

3. **Blowing For Tugs**   14m   E4,6b   Fr7a+   *
   The route of the crag. The wall left of the main arete has a desperate and somewhat baffling move to pass the BR (hint, a heelhook/footlock is needed). The wall above is somewhat easier and possesses a mega-bong.
   A.Sharp, P.Lewis, J.Harwood 29.01.1989

4. **Hawk's Cheep**   14m   E2,5c
   The corner to the right.
   P.Lewis, A.Sharp, J.Harwood 29.01.1989

5. **Our Man In Bargoed**   6m   E2,6b   Fr6c+
   The wall to the right currently only climbed to a good hold above the BR. It is inadvisable to continue to abseil off the pegs at 14m, as they have now fallen out.
   A.Sharp, P.Lewis, J.Harwood 29.01.1989

6. **Black Dog**   12m   E2,6a
   To the right is a sloping ramp at 3m. Gain this, move up a few metres, then step left to a BR. Climb the groove and crack above, PR.
   A.Sharp, P.Lewis, J.Harwood 29.01.1989

7. **Up For Grabs**   12m   E3,6a
   Gain the same ramp, but move right to a PR. Continue up the groove past further PRs. Finish on the shelf above.
   M.Learoyd, L.Foulkes 00.00.1989

Gary Gibson - The Big Time (First Free Ascent) (E6,6c) Dinas
(Page 316) Photo: Hazel Gibson

Gary Gibson - Wet Afternoon (1st Asc) (Fr7a+) Taff's Well
(Page 371) Photo: Hazel Gibson

BLAENLLECHAU

GR004969

PREAMBLE

Although it looks impressive from Ferndale, the crag is disappointing, holding lichen and having few unbroken areas. Actually to be quite honest its abag, without merit and probably the worst crag in the area, apart from Penrhiwceiber.

ACCESS

Take the A4233 to Ferndale and follow the signs to Blaenllechau on the other side of the valley. Follow the hairpin road into the village and take the first right (very sharp bend into the minor road to Penrhiwceiber). Follow this road for ½ mile to a track and a lay-by over on the right. Park here and follow the track down into the quarry which is not visible from the road. If on foot, buses run from the railway station at Ystrad Rhondda and Porth. Alight at the last stop in Ferndale and follow the Blaenlleachau signs as before.

THE ROUTES

In the left bay of the quarry is a pillar.

1. **Electrolux**   18m   VS,4b
    The right hand arete of the pillar.
    S.Coles 08.02.1992

Further right is another pillar and a short steep wall.

2. **Possessed By The Mind Of A Hoover**   9m   HS,4a
    The centre of the pillar left of the short steep wall.
    S.Coles 08.02.1992

The final routes are on the short steep wall.

3. **Away With The Mixer**   12m   E3,5c
    Follow the flake line up the centre of the wall past worthless RP placements to a harrowing final move.
    A.Sharp, P.Lewis 22.10.1988

4. **Away With The Fairies**   12m   E3,6a
    The crack/seam immediately to the right.
    A.Sharp, P.Lewis 22.10.1988

CEFNPENNAR

GR034013

PREAMBLE

A good, if limited crag, which is quite sheltered despite its high position. It has breathtaking views of the once scenic cokeworks and Frank Whitehead's old house. There is a very good left wall and some shorter more broken slabs along the long low right wall. The main wall seeps for quite some time after rain.

ACCESS

From the A4059 at Mountain Ash, take the minor road signposted to Cefnpennar at the roundabout. Follow this road (bearing up the hill at the hospital turn off), then turn left along an uneven track at the fork at the top of the hill. Continue to a lay-by by a TV aerial, parking here to avoid blocking the field entrance. Walk down to the end of the track, go through a gate, then climb over the fence to the left to arrive at the top of the quarry. If on foot, take the train to Mountain Ash, from where it is possible to catch a bus to Cefnpennar and then follow the directions above.

THE ROUTES

Left Wall
The belay for all these routes is the telegraph pole behind the main wall.

1. **Old Gringo**   11m   E1,5b
   The crack at the left-hand side of the wall. Take care with gear placements in the friable rock.
   R.Thomas, M.Learoyd 00.00.1989

2. **Pickpocket**   12m   E3,5c   *
   The route of the crag. Start just right of Old Gringo and follow a line of holds up the steep wall, passing a couple of prominent pockets. 2PRs and good RPs.
   M.Learoyd, R.Thomas 00.00.1989

3. **Bring On The Spring**   12m   E5,6c   Fr7b+   \
   The wall to the right has some hard moves low down (Friend 1) and then it gets really hard, 2BRs. The final jump out right has proved impossible for all but Crockola to date.
   M.Crocker 02.04.1994

4. **Root 66**   11m   E1,5b
   The obvious crack to the right PR, which is blocked by a tree at the top (possible abseil).
   M.Learoyd, R.Thomas 00.00.1989

5. **Wackaday**   9m   E3,6b
   The short wall to the right, passing 2PRs.
   M.Learoyd 00.00.1989

Right Wall

6. **Walking On Coles**   9m   HS,4a
   Some 50m to the right of Wackaday is a set of broken steps leading up to the top of the crag. Just right of this is a prominent overlapping slab. Take the centre of the slab.
   S.Coles 29.03.1992

7. **Masterfool**   7m   E2,6a   Fr6b+
   Over to the right is a short steep arete, with 2BRs and no BB.
   M.Crocker 02.04.1994

8. **Tory Bloating Floater**   7m   VS,4b   \
   The corner between Masterfool and Valerie Singleton is loose and fit only for those who have ticked everything (except for Penrhiwceiber of course).
   D.Irving, M.Hirst 28.03.1997

9. **Valerie Singleton**   8m   E1,5c
   To the right is a narrow slab, set back from the previous face and blessed with 2PRs and a belay stake.
   R.Thomas Pre-1991

CEFNSTYLLE QUARRY

GR571964

PREAMBLE
A small and very obscure sandstone quarry near Gowerton, with routes up to 11m.

ACCESS
Take the B4295 west along the North Gower from Gowerton for about 1 mile to an umarked road on the left by a telephone box and a row of houses. Follow this road up past the houses to a track leading off right. Follow this track for 100m to arrive at the quarry on the left. If travelling by public transport the #17 bus runs from Swansea city centre to Gowerton, then proceed as above.

THE ROUTES

1. **Winky's Amazing Technicolour Tracksuit**　　11m　　E3,6a
   A line past 1BR.
   M.Richards 00.00.1996

2. **An Old Bolt Line**　　11m　　E2,5c
   No details supplied.
   Unknown Pre-1996
   FFA M.Richards 00.00.1996

3. **Rock A Block**　　11m　　HVS,4c
   The diagonal breakline to a lower off.
   M.Richards 00.00.1996

4. **Peg Scare**　　11m　　HVS,4c
   No details supplied.
   M.Richards, J.Brown 17.06.1996

CILFYNYDD NAVIGATION QUARRY

GR086937

PREAMBLE
A quality slabby crag with the odd steep section, which cannot be seen from the main road. Formerly the glittering prize in the sandstone crown, being one of the first quarries to be developed, but since superseded by the Gap, Llanbradach, Mountain Ash and most other places. The quarry is basically a huge box, with nearly all the routes taking lines up the wide, tall back wall. There is little vegetation on the main face, although the odd shale layer and occaisional loose hold can be a nuisance. Bolt and spike belays are available at the top of the crag. Some of the routes in the centre of the crag have individual bolt belays. It is in a somewhat exposed position, so can be windy despite the enclosed nature. However, as a bonus, some sections do dry out very quickly as it gets any sun going and is one of the more aesthetically pleasing sandstone crags.

Unfortunately many of the PRs used to protect the original ascents have been stolen. Please accost peg thieves and devise suitable punishment.

ACCESS
From the south either turn off the A470 at Pontypridd and take the A4054 up to and through Cilfynydd, or quicker, drive

up the A470 to the roundabout beyond Abercynon and go back down the A4054. Just by the first set of traffic lights encountered from the north (or first out of Cilfynydd coming from the south) is a lay-by and a gate. Park here. Go through the gate and follow the track and path up the hill to reach the quarry in 10-15 minutes (obvious). If on foot take the train to Abercynon. If deposited at Abercynon South, walk up to Abercynon North (yes that's right, the platform 100m up the track). From Abercynon North, take the path out of the station, go left and left again, to pass under a bridge. Turn right and go over the bridge over the dual carriageway to the same set of traffic lights as described above.

THE ROUTES

The main interest is the Main (back) Wall. This starts as a large slab on the left, with a second slab round an arete before the steep and obvious Western Front wall. Right of this the rock of the lower section deteriorates, but the rock of the upper section remains good. The first routes are on the left retaining wall of the quarry.

Left Wall

1. **Expanded Mole Groove**   21m   HVS,5a   ●

   A rather overgrown pitch which Percy Thrower would probably rate as a three star classic. Percy Thrower is, however, dead. If you wish to follow suite, start 3m left of the left hand corner of the crag, climb up and move into the Savanna. Climb the left-hand veldt, sorry groove, then up through pampas to finish. According to the SWMC 1985 supplement 'A climb that should improve with traffic' - try diverting the M4.
   G.Lewis, C.Hurley 00.00.1984

2. **Gold Block**   21m   E2,5b   ●

   As for the previous grasslands and climb up to a large thread in a small groove at 5m. Gain the arete above and follow it boldly to a large ledge at 15m Step left to finish up a steep groove and crack.
   G.Lewis, M.Learoyd 00.00.1984

3. **Kestrel Groove**   21m   HVS,4c   ●

   As for Gold Block, but step off right at 16m to a large ledge. Finish Up a loose crack.
   G.Lewis solo 00.00.1984

Main Wall

This starts off with a broad slab, capped by a grassy terrace at 18m. Rising up from the grassy terrace is a steeper wall, with a prominent scoop (the finish of Geeny). Left of the prominent scoop is Elastic Retreat.

4. **Elastic Retreat**   11m   E4,6b   *

   Climb the steep wall left of the Geeny scoop PR, to a an overlap. Place good Friends in pockets above the overlap and overcome it, via a rock up using a couple of very thin pulls on razors.
   G.Barker 00.07.1989

The rest of the routes in the quarry start from the floor.

5. **Code Of The Road**   25m   E1,5a

   Start from the pedestal on the slab to the right, and follow the obvious line to a grassy ledge. Finish up the chossy corner, or better, as for the next routes.
   M.Learoyd, C.Hurley 00.00.1984

6. **Rockover Beethoven**   25m   E1,5a

   Follow a vague line up the slab to the right, to finish as for Geeny.
   R.Brewer 00.00.1988

7. **Where Did You Get That Bolt?** 25m E2,6b *
Right again is a pocket next to a retro-BR (bahaus probably). Gain this dynamically, then make a second large dyno up right for a flat edge. Move up to the hole on Geeny, finishing as for that route. Frequently soloed.
A.Sharp, P.Lewis 11.02.1989

8. **Geeny** 25m E1,5b
Start just right of the last route and move directly up to a step left at 6m to gain a hole. Continue up, then move left into a notch and mantle onto the grassy terrace. Make good moves up the scoop behind the terrace to finish.
G.Lewis, G.Barker 02.07.1989

9. **Squash Match** 25m E1,5b
The line up the slab between Geeny and the corner, finishing as for Geeny.
G.Lewis, M.Learoyd, L.Foulkes 00.00.1983

10. **Deathwish** 25m E1,5a
The arete bounding the slab on the right and the wall above on big hidden holds. Exciting.
M.Learoyd solo 00.00.1984

11. **Fly Me To The Moon** 25m HVS,5a *
Right of Deathwish is a slim buttress with diagonal cracks running up it. Gain and follow these to the roof. Either haul directly over the roof on jugs, or awkwardly step right, to finish up a corner.
G.Lewis, S.Blackman 00.00.1982

12. **A Blank Abstract** 25m E3,6c
The slab immediately right of Fly Me To The Moon, with a very difficult pull past a BR. Run it out up the slab to join Fly Me To The Moon at the roof. Finish as for Fly Me To The moon.
G.Ashmore, R.Lawrence 10.01.1992

13. **Man Or Mouse** 25m E4,6b Fr7a *
The true line on the slab. Start right of A Blank Abstract and make unlikely looking rockovers past a BR, to a lunge up to gain the shale band. Step up, BR, to gain a slot and follow the slab above, passing another BR with hard moves to gain a ledge. Step left and finish as for Fly Me To The Moon.
A.Sharp, P.Lewis 11.02.1989

14. **Let Me Play Amongst The Stars** 25m E2,5c **
Take the flake crack to the right of Man Or Mouse to a ledge, then take the right-hand of the two parallel cracks right of Man Or Mouse, BR, crux. Finish up the centre of the slab above via some shot holes and a good horizontal wire in an old peg slot.
G.Lewis, S.Blackman, C.Heard 00.00.1982

15. **Black Magic** 25m E3,5c
To the right of Let Me Know What Life Is Like at a thin crack splits the lower slab. Start up this crack and follow a direct line through Ladybird.
T.Foster 00.00.1988

16. **Ladybird** 27m E3,5c
Many of the PRs have gone missing. Start right of Black Magic. Wander up the groove past a PR. Follow a crack out leftwards, until a traverse line leads back right to a small ledge. Step up to a PR and go for the groove in the left side of the overlap to finish.
L.Foulkes, G.Lewis 00.00.1983

17. **Relax** 27m E2,5b
A contrived and rather pointless expedition. From where Ladybird saunters off left, move up to a BR, then left following a line of jugs across Great Expectations, then up and right into Western Front to finish.
A.Richardson, G.Lewis 00.00.1984

18. Great Expectations   25m   E4,6a   Fr6c+   *

Better. Take the continuous wall directly, avoiding an easier sequence out left at two-thirds height, BB.

M.Learoyd, G.Lewis 04.11.1988

19. Western Front   27m   E3,6a

The original version was peg protected and gained the upper crack of Western Front Direct by traversing in from the right, just below the main overlap of Eastern Bloc Rock.

M.Learoyd, G.Lewis 00.00.1983

20. Western Front Direct   25m   E5,6a   Fr7a   **

Start directly beneath the obvious thin crack splitting the upper wall. Gain it from directly below by a couple of interesting moves. Low in the grade, with nothing too tricky, but quite sustained, BB.

M.Crocker, R.Thomas 29.10.1988

21. Eastern Bloc Rock   25m   E5,6b   Fr7a+   *

Takes the big, open wall high up on the crag right of the upper crack of Western Front. Climb a vague groove by easy but bold climbing to gain the first BR. The protection now improves. Surmount the overlap by a series of pulls which are hard to on-sight. Climb the wall more easily to an overlap and the top.

M.Crocker, R.Thomas 29.10.1988

22. Tears For Smears   30m   E1,5b

Another route that wanders round the quarry like a beer-nasty Valley Commando. Climb the wall right of the start of Western Front to land in the main groove of Let Me Know Etc. Follow this for 6m then pull out right to finish.

G.Lewis, R.East 00.00.1984

23. Goblin Girl   25m   E3,6a   Fr6b+   *

Follow Let Me Know What Life Is Like to the large shelf, then follow the groove in the wall out left, BR. Finish directly over the overhang, BR.

G.Barker, G.Lewis 02.07.1989

24. Let Me Know What Life Is Like   25m   HVS,5b   *

The rather obvious corner in the centre of the crag has a hard finish.

G.Lewis, Steve Blackman 00.00.1982

25. Evening Light   25m   E2,5c

The right arete of Let Me Know What Life Is Like, PR, finishing just to the right of the arete.

G.Lewis, H.Griffiths 00.00.1984

26. Save A Mouse, Eat A Pussy   25m   E3,6a   *

As for Evening Light to the tree. Move up to the base of the slab and grope over to a hidden bore hole. Swing right, BR, then climb the tricky scoop, BR. Climb the easier slab to the top, but watch out, it slopes.

G.Lewis, A.N.Other, G.Barker 00.06.1989

27. The Owl And The Antelope   25m   E2,5b   **

One of the best traditional routes on sandstone taking the fine slab high up on the crag. Start immediately below the left side of the obvious inverted staircase roof. Climb up to this and pull straight up to a borehole and thread runner (not in situ). Pull up again to the apparent wilderness of the upper slab. Instead of panicking, move up and slightly right to find a hidden slot (Friend 1 and Friend 1½). Climb up on the right-hand side of this slot to a ledge. Step left to finish up a groove.

G.Lewis, C.Heard, M.Learoyd 00.00.1983

28. On Jupiter And Mars   27m   E1,5b

The obvious overhanging inverted staircase at the right hand side of the crag, PR.

G.Lewis, S.Blackman 00.00.1982

29. **Crash Landing**   25m   E2,5b
Start below a shallow groove at 20m, about halfway between On Jupiter And Mars and Ol' Blue Eyes. Gain this and leave it with trepidation to gain the finishing slab of On Jupiter And Mars.
G.Lewis, D.Renshaw 00.00.1983

30. **Ol' Blue Eyes**   25m   E3,6b
Right of Crash Landing is a prominent boss of rock, with a BR at 12m. Gain the boss and make a very long move up to good holds. Finish direct with poor gear.
G.Barker, M.Kidd 00.06.1989

31. **Heart Throb**   25m   E2,6a
Right again is a corner at 12m. Climb directly up to this on loose rock to a BR. Swing left onto slabs to finish.
G.Lewis, D.Hart 15.01.1989

32. **Sheepbone Wall**   25m   HVS,4c   ●
Horrid. The groove above the tree to the right of Heart Throb.
G.Lewis, M.Learoyd 00.00.1983

33. **Feeling Sheep**   8m   E3,6c   Fr7b
A perverse activity up the bulge right of Sheepbone Wall. One very hard move, without much merit. BRs to tree.
G.Ashmore 18.10 .1997

34. **Big Spider Groove**   18m   HVS,5a
Looser and less appealing than Caroline Street. The obvious and once clean corner on the right wall of the crag.
G.Lewis, L.Foulkes 00.00.1983

35. **Acid House Trip**   30m   E2,5c
Follow Heart Throb, then move left into On Jupiter Etc. at its final overhang. Pull over to a hole (Friend 3½), move down and traverse the lip to the slot on The Owl Etc. Go down to a ledge then round to the BR on Save A Mouse etc. Swing round the arete to the ledge on Let Me Know Etc. Finish up this or as for The Gang Of Four.
G.Lewis, D.Hart, G.Barker 00.07.1989

36. **The Gang Of Four**   30m   E3,5b
From the tree on Let Me Know What Life Is Like move left to where the PR on Tears For Smears should be. Continue up and left, PR, then descend to a crack, PR. Up Ladybird to the ledge then keep going left to finish diagonally left of a faint crack in the headwall.
M.Learoyd, G.Lewis, C.Pound, T.Jordan 12.09.1985

CLYDACH QUARRY

GR971932

PREAMBLE
There is one recorded and unstable route in this quarry.

ACCESS
Follow the A4119 to a roundabout the start of Tonypandy proper. Turn left at the roundabout to Clydach and take the fourth right after the Church (1 mile). Drive to the end and park. Head up hill to the obvious quarry in about 5 minutes.

THE ROUTES

1. **Escape From The Bogmonster**   10m   S
The only sharp arete in the quarry. Good photos are apparently possible.
M.Salter Pre-1998

COEDELY

GR021856

PREAMBLE

From the road this crag looks awful. However, it is a good small crag, the gently leaning main wall being of particular merit and probably the ideal evening crag for passing visitors. There are some belay stakes at the top and some routes have in situ thread belays. The bolts at the time of writing are still 8mm expansions, but generally seem in reasonable condition. This normally indicates they will fail without warning, but hey, if you want to make it safe, bring that paddling pool to simulate deep water soloing in Tiger Bay.

ACCESS

Follow the A4119 to the roundabout on the north side of Tonyrefail. Take the right hand turning if coming from the south and continue into the village, turning right up any of the side streets to gain a parallel road running back right (Gladys Street). Park as near to the right-hand end as possible and follow the gate into the field beyond. Cut uphill to a track and follow this rightwards to the crag. There are buses from Llantrisant.

THE ROUTES

Left Wall

1. **Monkey Business** 8m VS,4c
   The left hand line on the wall, left of the first BR.
   H.Griffiths 00.00.1989

2. **Lager Lout** 8m VS,4c
   The line just right of the crack of the last route, BR.
   D.Viggers, E.Alsford, P.Donnithorne 15.06.1991

3. **The Pure Way** 8m VS,4c
   The crack line immediately right.
   H.Griffiths, J.Harwood, A.Sharp, P.Lewis 04.03.1989

4. **Alements** 8m HVS,5b Fr5+
   Follow a direct line past a BR and PR. Take care with loose earth at the top.
   P.Donnithorne, E.Alsford 00.00.1991

5. **Scandal** 9m E3,6a
   To the right is a BR, just right of a caveman cannabis leaf painting. Climb up to the BR and make a hard move left to a small hold and the break, Friend. Continue up (loose) or sidle off left to Alements. Poor.
   A.Sharp, J.Harwood 21.02.1989

6. **Bush Wacker's Crack** 14m HVS,4c
   Over to the right is the first of two grooves. Climb this - but be warned, it is a little loose. Move right at the top to abseil off a tree.
   G.Lewis, M.Allely 00.00.1989

7. **My JCB's Exploded** 14m VS,4c
   Similar stuff up the next groove along. Abseil.
   G.Lewis, D.Hart, S.Blackmore 00.00.1989

Main Wall

8. **Tall Dark And Handsome** 14m E3,5c Fr6b+ *
   Start on the slim pillar forming the left hand side of the main wall. Climb up a flake to sloping ledges and tackle the leaning wall above via its arete, TB.
   A.Sharp, P.Lewis, J.Harwood, H. Griffiths 04.03.1989

9. **Tall Dark And Handsome Direct**   14m   E3,6a   Fr6c   *
    As for the parent route, but avoid the arete. Dynamic and more fun in trainers. TB.
    A.Sharp, P.Lewis 07.03.1989

10. **Campaign For See Through Bikinis**   14m   E2,5b   *
    A route up the narrow flake crack to the right, PR. Move left or right at the top to a tree.
    G.Lewis 04.03.1989

11. **Young, Free And Single**   14m   E4,6b   Fr7a   *
    The left-hand bolt line on the main wall. The crux is the start, the finish is hard to work out.
    A.Sharp, P.Lewis, J.Harwood 04.03.1989

12. **The Uninvited**   14m   E4,6a   Fr6c+   **
    The best route on the crag. The central bolt line, with continual interest. 3BRs. Wires are required for the top
    crack, TB.
    A.Sharp, J.Harwood 19.02.1989

13. **Behind The Lines**   12m   E3,6a   Fr6c   **
    Hard for the grade. Watch out for the poorly placed BRs. Start below the bolt line right of The Uninvited and pull
    directly up to a big pocket. Continue past the second BR, to a hard move right for the last BR. Pull up on a small
    pocket (crux) to finish, TB.
    A.Sharp, J.Harwood 21.02.1989

14. **Buffalo Hunter**   11m   HS,4a
    A loose and unremarkable route up the groove on the right of the main wall.
    J.Harwood 04.03.1989

15. **Girdle Traverse**   16m   E1,5c
    From the base of Buffalo Hunter, gain the shelf leading all the way along the main wall, and foot traverse this
    leftwards to finish up My JCB's Exploded. The BRs on other routes provide the protection, TB.
    Unknown Pre-1992

CRAG GRAIG FAWR

GR799867

PREAMBLE

A good, if small crag situated above Margam Abbey. It is part quarried and part natural, but the rock is generally sound with some surprisingly strong and clean lines. There is an old BB at the top and a PR and some threads set well back for back ups.

ACCESS

From Junction 38 of the M4, follow signposts for Margam Abbey and park on the forestry track at the base of a hill. Walk up the the path leading up the hill to the ruined chapel, then follow a path off left into the woods for about 5 minutes to reach the crag. Public transport is not really practical. Access is a sensitive, so a low profile is recommended.

THE ROUTES

1. **Silf**   11m   HVS,5a
   Takes the obvious rightward-curving crack on the left wall of the crag. From the half-height ledge follow a crack just left of the arete.
   P.Boyd, A.Freem 00.00.1986

2. **Left Edge**   11m   E1,5b
   Follow the square-cut arete on the left of the main face on its right-hand side for 8m then step left into Silf to finish.
   A.Freem, P.Boyd 00.00.1986

3. **Quercus**   14m   HS,4a
   Climb the crack containing an oak sapling and follow the groove behind to finish, PB.
   A.Freem, A.Freem 00.00.1986

4. **Antonia's Route**   14m   VS,4c
   Climb up the crack right of Quercus to join Owl Groove at the top overlap.
   A.Freem, A.Freem 00.00.1986

5. **Owl Groove**   14m   VS,4c   *
   Follow the impressive central groove, left of the leaning wall.
   A.Freem, D.Owens 00.00.1986

6. **Derbyshire Hiraeth**   14m   E2,5b
   Right of Owl Groove is a jutting block at 2m. Use this to gain al v-groove, then a leftward-trending crack.
   A.Freem 00.00.1982

7. **The Orangery**   14m   E1,5b
   The straight crack to the right of Derbyshire Hiraeth.
   A.Freem, N.Gould 00.00.1986

8. **Gorsedd Groove**   14m   S
   The right-facing corner, capped by a small roof which is negotiated on the right.
   A.Freem, D.Owens 00.00.1986

9. **Gibbon**   14m   VS,4b
   Start 3m right of Gorsedd Groove and climb directly up via various cracks.
   P.Boyd, D.Owens 00.00.1986

10. **Ivy Tilsley** 14m HVS,5a
The arete right of The Gibbon.
N.O'Neill & The Old Harrovians 00.03.1993

11. **Brian Tilsley** 12m VS,4c
The cracks in the wall to the right of the arete.
N.O'Neill & The Old Harrovians 00.03.1993

CROSSKEYS QUARRY

GR223932

PREAMBLE
A small quarry with a couple of reasonable routes.

ACCESS
From J28 of the M4, follow the A467 to a roundabout where the A4048 carries on and the A467 swings right. Follow the A467 to a second roundabout, take the right exit and turn right again. Take the second left into an estate and keep following this road up to the top branch of the estate, parking near the bend in the road. From the bend in the road, follow a path up and left into a field. Continue along this track for 200m, to reach the quarry on the right.

THE ROUTES

1. **Pick Locks** 14m E3,5c Fr6b
The first substantial buttress on the left side of the quarry.
R.Thomas 17.10.1999

2. **Skeleton Key** 12m E1,5b Fr6a
Gain and climb the faint crack right of the black arete.
R.Thomas, P.Hadley 00.07.1999

3. **Locksmith** 12m VS,4c
The crack to the right of Skeleton Key.
N.O'Neill, R.Thomas 00.07.1999

Over to the right is another buttress, with an abandoned project up a blunt never-dry arete.

4. **Five Lever** 12m E3,5c Fr6b+
The wall to the right of the blunt arete, starting up a thin cracks. Some nuts are needed.
R.Thomas 00.00.1999

5. **Petersman** 12m E3,5c Fr6c
The wall to the right of Locksmith gives sustained climbing on small holds.
R.Thomas, N.O'Neill 00.07.1999

6. **Wreckernoitre** 14m VD
Start in the hollow left of the obvious crack at the back of the quarry. Gain and follow the ramp to finish up the slab at the end of it.
C.Shorrock solo 09.05.1995

7. **Wreckernoitre Direct** 9m S
The direct start to Wreckernoitre with a tricky mantle to reach the gangway and slab.
M.Hirst solo 09.05.1995

8. **Radovan Karadijc**   8m   E4,6a   Fr7a
The centre of the obvious thumb on the right-hand wall of the quarry.
G.Ashmore 17.10.1999

CWMAFAN

GR769914

PREAMBLE
A minor crag high on the hillside.

ACCESS
From J40 of the M4, head for the lovely steelworks and turn right at the traffic lights. Follow the main road past the railway station (if on foot get the train to here) and continue round the roundabout following signs to Cwmafan. Continue down the road by the high wall, until a set of steps can be seen up the wall. Park about ¼ mile further down the road on a lay-by on the left hand side (avoid the parking space in the lane between the steps and the lay-by, as there is a sloping forehead type who gets very narky, as the world won't see his hideously bedecked and modified Cavalier if you park in front of it). Walk back up to the lay-by, pointing and laughing at the aforementioned vehicle. Climb the stairs to reach a path that leads up rightward to the crag. Summer visits will probably be impossible, due to seasonal vegetation.

THE ROUTES

1. **Amicable Settlement**   8m   E3,5c
The short crack at the left-hand end of the main crag.
R.Thomas, G.Royle 00.00.1990

2. **Slack Alice**   15m   E1,5a
The Brown's Eliminate of Sandstone! The arete of the slab down and right, gained from the left.
G.Royle, R.Thomas, M.Learoyd 00.00.1990

CWMCARN

GR221940

PREAMBLE
A worthwhile crag in a forested area, which dries quickly and catches any sun (as opposed to one of the crags in the previous guide, which attracted the sun). Why bother going all the way down to Andalusia for Christmas?

ACCESS
Transport yourself on the A467 to the right hand turning to Cwmcarn ½ mile north of Crosskeys. Turn right at the Cwmcarn pub into Park Street, then take the next left to a parking spot. Follow a lane up between some garages to a path trending leftwards, which leads to the crag. Public transport is impractical..

THE ROUTES

1. **Where There's A Killer**   18m   E3,5c   ⟍
A serious route. Take the first arete left of the words 'Killer Wall'. Go up a short rib to a ledge and continue up the right-hand side of the main arete to pull on a sapling and gain a small ledge. Continue until it is possible to move left into a corner to finish.
M.Crocker 27.12.1990

2. **Face The Rap**   18m   E2,5c
More of the same, but slightly better. Climb the left-hand arete, PR, studiously avoiding the pillar on the right.
M.Crocker 27.12.1990

3. **Rap Crap**   18m   E3,5c
Start in the centre of the face at the initials 'MC' (Captain Crocker). Clamber up ledges to gain some cracks which are followed to a ledge and a long span up the final headwall.
M.Crocker 27.12.1990

4. **Squeaking Bats**   11m   E1,5b   \
To the right is small steep red wall. Gain the ledge at 5m via the short arete at the left hand end. Follow the slim corner to a BB.
M.Crocker 27.12.1990

5. **Red With Rage**   11m   E3,5c   \
Climb the wall right of Squeaking Bats past two horizontal slots to reach a long layback edge. Follow this until jugs lead to a BB. Using the large ledge on the right is strictly for cheats and will result in exile to Penrhiwceiber.
M.Crocker 27.12.1990

CWMAMAN

GR007993

PREAMBLE
This is primarily an E3-E5 sports climbing crag. The left wall is steep and very fingery even for sandstone. It is a good suntrap, although seepage is generally quite bad, so take a blow torch. Most of the routes were in the process of being re-equipped as the guide went to press. There are some belay stakes for a back up rope if required, although they are set well back in the bracken and consequently are hard to find.

ACCESS
From the A4059 Mountain Ash to Aberdare road take the Cwmaman (Aberaman) turn off and follow this road to a T-junction. Turn left and follow this road to The Shepard's Arms on the left. Take the obvious side road forking off left just before the estate. Follow this past a prominent row of houses, until a gravel track leads off left by a substation to two houses. Follow a track off left and park, taking care not to block the forestry road bending back right. Follow the track for 100m, then take a steep path up the hill to arrive in the quarry. If on foot, regular buses run to Cwmaman itself from Aberdare and Mountain Ash.

THE ROUTES

Left Wall

1. **Rab/The Numbers Game**   30m   E5,6a   **
A long and exhausting traverse. Start up Good Tradition, and move across to the break on Mother Of Pearl. Move up and across to the PR on Two For Tuesday and across the loose corner onto the arete. Climb this for a few feet to the PR, then traverse the obvious break as far as Innuendo, which is followed to finish. BB.
A.Sharp, P.Lewis 05.11.1988

2. **Good Tradition**   9m   E2,5c
The leftmost line on the small left hand section of the wall, 2PRs.
P.Lewis, A.Sharp 05.11.1988

3. **A Clear Head And A Blow Lamp**   11m   E3,6a   *
The crackline to the right has a superb starting move and is hard higher up, 2PRs.
A.Sharp, P.Lewis 05.11.1988

4. **A Clear Conscience And A Blow Job**   14m   E3,6a
As for A Clear Head And A Blowlamp until just below the top, then step out right onto the wall to finish.
N.Davies, A.Meek 00.00.1994

5. **Unnamed**   14m   E5,6b   Fr7b
Now heavily chipped. A direct approach to the finish of A Clear Head And A Blow Job.
A.Sharp 00.00.1995

6. **Mother Of Pearl**   14m   E4,6b   Fr7a+   **
The centre of the wall to the right with a very thin crank at half-height.
A.Sharp, P.Lewis 05.11.1988

7. **Two For Tuesday**   21m   E4,6a   \
A poor loose line just left of the arete of the higher section of the main wall, PR.
A.Sharp, P.Lewis, J.Harwood 08.05.1989

8. **The World Is My Lobster**   20m   E4,6a   Fr6c+   *
The right-hand side of the aforementioned arete. PRs to BB.
A.Sharp, P.Lewis, J.Harwood 08.05.1989

9. **Propaganda**   20m   E5,6a   Fr7a   ***
A superb very on-sightable route at the lower limit of its UK grade. Start right of the arete, and make a hard move
up past a two finger pocket, BRs. Continue up the wall between breaks, PRs, to join The World Is My Lobster
at its final PR, BB.
A.Sharp, P.Lewis 07.11.1988

10. **Science Friction**   20m   E5,6b   Fr7a+   *
A harder proposition to the right of Propaganda. At the high bong, move left to the BB of Propaganda.
A.Sharp, P.Lewis 05.11.1988

11. **La Rage**   20m   E5,6b   Fr7b   **

An utterly desperate move from the lower break gives way to sustained climbing and a hard move near the top. Start by a step in the banking, below a PR. Pass this BR, to a very hard move up to a sloping jug and the break. Continue direct to a BB.

A.Sharp, P.Lewis 16.05.1989

12. **Innuendo**   20m   E5,6b   Fr7b   *

The final line of in-situ gear on the wall. It rarely dries out.

M.Crocker, R.Thomas 14.05.1989

Long Back Wall

13. **Instead Of This**   12m   E1,5b

The loose looking wall on the back wall right of Innuendo, past a visually stunning ring bolt of immense size and another BR, BB.

G.Gibson, R.Thomas 16.06.1990

14. **Zoo Time**   12m   E2,5b

The line immediately to the right to the same belay, BR, PR. Take care with the wobbly flakes, erm... actually, not any more.

R.Thomas, G.Gibson 16.06.1990

15. **Crack Line Man**   12m   VS,4c

The crack line in the loose blocky buttress to the right.

SWMC 00.00.1989

The Side Wall

After a gap of 50m, is a slightly slabby square-cut buttress. The left wall faces back towards the main left-hand wall of the quarry.

Cwmaman Side Wall   Photo: Carl Ryan

16. **Hot Beef Injection**   12m   E3,6a   Fr6c   *
The left-hand route on this slab is tricky. A wire is needed to thread the first PR. BRs, old BB.
M.Crocker, R.Thomas 13.11.1988

17. **Spam Javelin**   14m   VS,4b
The loose crack in the centre of the slab to the BB of Neo Maxie Zoom Weenie.
R.Thomas, E.Travers-Jones 00.00.1990

18. **Neo Maxie Zoom Weenie**   14m   E3,6a   Fr6b+   *
Just to the right is a short thin crack (wires). Follow this up onto the slab, and climb the slab past 2PRs to a BB.
M.Crocker, R.Thomas 13.11.1988

19. **Pork Sword**   15m   E2,5c   Fr6a+
The right-hand side of the arete, swinging round left to the BB on Neo Maxie Zoom Weenie.
R.Thomas 15.03.1998

20. **Anniversary Walk**   15m   HVS,5b   Fr5+   *
The wall just right of the arete, BB.
R.Thomas, M.Crocker 13.11.1988

21. **Hey Mister**   15m   E1,5c   Fr6a
The wall right again, BB.
R.Thomas, M.Crocker 13.11.1988

22. **Buff The Happy Lamp**   15m   E1,5c   Fr6a
The wall right again, then follow a rising traverse to the belay of Pork Sword, BB.
R.Thomas, P.Hadley 00.08.1999

23. **Yank Plank**   15m   E1,5b   Fr6a
The wall right again to a BB.
R.Thomas, P.Hadley 00.08.1999

24. **Evil Ways**   15m   E1,5b   Fr6a
The wall right again to a BB.
P.Hadley, R.Thomas 00.08.1999

CWMAMAN WEST

GR002992

PREAMBLE
The crag consists of a slab and arete, that are in the shade when the main crag is unbearably hot. Seepage is not really a problem. Although residual dampness lingers, this is only on the easier sections of routes. Not a particularly interesting crag in itself, only being worth a visit in conjunction with another.

ACCESS
This is the crag on the other side of the road to Cwmaman. Follow the directions for Cwmaman, but park up rather than turning off along the gravel track. Turn right about 50m further on, and walk down to a gate on the left. Go through this to a path leading up an embankment to the crag.

THE ROUTES

1. **Cwm To Papa**   9m   HVS,4c
   The left arete of the slab is unprotected. BB.
   R.Thomas, G.Gibson 10.06.1990

2. **Cwm To Mamma**   12m   E1,5c
   The obvious line up the slab to the right, to gain the BB.
   G.Gibson, R.Thomas 10.06.1990

3. **Cwm Mammon**   12m   E2,6a   Fr6b+
   The best of the bunch. The rightmost line with a hard start, to the same BB.
   G.Gibson, R.Thomas 10.06.1990

CWMPARC STREET

GR956958

PREAMBLE
Somewhere up over by there is a crag. No-one apart from Chris seems to have the navigation skills to find it. So unknown, but said to be quite good.

ACCESS
Drive past Ton Pentre railway station on the A4058 and turn left at the bridge. Turn right at the Spar and follow the road, taking the second turning on the left, by the police station. Park at the top of the hill. Walk up the mountain track to a mast, enter the forest and walk up to a fire break and follow this until it forks rightward to the crag (quite some distance).

THE ROUTES

1. **Unnamed #1**   9m   E3,6a
   Start 9m from the right-hand end of the crag and climb up the slab past BRs and a PR.
   C.Evans 00.00.1993

2. **Unnamed #2**   9m   E2,5c
   Some distance to the right, follow the slab past PR and Friend placements to a BB.
   C.Evans 00.00.1993

CYMMER (PUNK ROCKS)

GR019907

PREAMBLE
Four quarries situated on the SE face of Mynydd Cymmer. The left hand (first) quarry contains the easier routes and there is some loose material on their top outs. However, there is virtually no seepage in this quarry. The second quarry, the main one, is a very sheltered and slightly overhanging wall of excellent orange rock, containing the majority of the worthwhile routes, although this section is affected by seepage. The third quarry is on loan from Penrhiwceiber with no routes of any substance. The final quarry is two-tiered, with a long, low wall containing a number of bays. There is some potential for bouldering on the lower tier. Belays can be a problem and a back up rope is handy for fixing belays.

ACCESS
Take the A4233 from Porth into Cymmer. Take the first right after the Rickard's Arms. Take the third road on the right to the end and park. Take the concrete track and subsequent dirt track up the hill to arrive at the Second Quarry.

Cymmer

If on foot, take the train to Porth, then take the road leading directly out of the station. At the cross roads take the far left hand turning (signposted to Cymmer) and turn right up the track leading off from the uphill side of the Rhondda Pub. Follow this track right up the hill to arrive at the Fourth Quarry.

THE ROUTES

First Quarry

1. **James Bond**   15m   E1,5b
    Beneath the highest point of the quarry is a shelf at 5m. Gain this awkwardly by a thin crack below its right end. From the shelf follow a vague groove slightly right and then back left to finish.
    L.Foulkes, M.Learoyd 00.00.1989

2. **Eddy Edwards**   12m   HVS,5a
    The crack to the right has a downward-pointing spike near the bottom. Climb this gingerly and continue, stepping slightly right to finish.
    M.Learoyd, L.Foulkes 00.00.1989

3. **Edwina Curry**   12m   HVS,5b
    A somewhat contrived right-hand start to Eddy Edwards up the thin crack just to its right.
    L.Foulkes, M.Learoyd 00.00.1989

4. **Black Looks**   10m   E2,5b
    The wall to the right of Edwina Curry, PR.
    M.Learoyd, L.Foulkes 00.00.1989

5. **To Distant Friends**   10m   VS,4c
    The obvious crack 4m right of Edwina Curry.
    M.Learoyd, L.Foulkes 00.00.1989

Second (Main) Quarry
Belays are available by using the stile on the fence some distance back.

6. **Intravenous Suffragette Injection**   8m   E2,5c
    To the left of the main face proper is a shorter wall. Take the wall left of the arete via a pocket, then make a hideous exit up a scoop to finish. Descend to the right.
    G.Ashmore, A.Senior 18.01.1992

7. **The Scoop**   9m   VS,4c
    The chimney-crack at the extreme left of the main face of the second quarry.
    M.Learoyd, L.Foulkes 00.00.1988

8. **Dai Swasticka**   12m   HVS,5a
    The first crack on the main wall proper, PB.
    M.Learoyd, L.Foulkes 00.00.1988

9. **Call My Bluff**   12m   E2,5c
    The thin crack to the right, PB.
    M.Learoyd, L.Foulkes 00.00.1988

10. **Mona Lisa**   14m   E4,6b   Fr7a+   *
    A good route at last! The wall to the right, with superb fingery climbing that is a touch easier for the tall. BB.
    A.Sharp, P.Lewis 07.03.1989

---

11. **Completely Punked**   14m   E1,5b   *
The central jamming crack speaks for itself, although most people probably swear at it. Move left at the top to the BB of Mona Lisa.
L.Foulkes, M.Learoyd 00.00.1988

12. **Waiting Game**   14m   E3,5c
The wall to the right, finishing up a thin crack PRs, to PB. Worthwhile, but not as good as it looks.
M.Learoyd, L.Foulkes 00.00.1988

13. **Ferret Wall**   14m   E1,5c
Past some unclimbed cracks is a corner. This route takes the wall left of the corner.
M.Learoyd, L.Foulkes 00.00.1988

14. **Amen Corner**   16m   VS,4b
Up the corner to the ledges. Step left and finish up a vague scoop.
L.Foulkes, M.Learoyd 00.00.1988

15. **Broga-y-Meirow**   8m   HVS,5c
Short but sharp. Right of the corner is a short overhanging face at right angles to the main wall. Take the hairline crack and from the second pod, move out left to finish up the short crack in the centre of the wall. Scramble off right to finish.
G.Ashmore, A.Senior 18.01.1992

16. **The Entrepreneur**   12m   E1,5b
The cracks in the wall round to the right, just before the next quarry.
L.Foulkes, M.Learoyd 00.00.1988

Third Quarry

17. **False Protection**   14m   E3,5c   \
The obvious jam crack dominating the bay, passing a loose band to gain the headwall, BR. Move left onto the arete to finish.
G.Lewis, M.Learoyd 00.00.1989

Fourth Quarry

18. **Window Shopping**   9m   HS,4c
Towards the left-hand end of the quarry is a square recess. Take the thin layback crack in the groove on the right-hand side of the bay and the chossy wall above.
G.Ashmore, A.Senior 18.01.1992

19. **Left Hand Start**   5m   HS,5b
Reach the large ledge on the previous route by a dynamic move up the wall to the left.
G.Ashmore, A.Senior 18.01.1992

20. **Syd B'Arete**   6m   HS,4c
The short clean arete at the extreme right-hand side of the crag.
G.Ashmore, A.Senior 18.01.1992

DAN DICKS

GR022933

PREAMBLE

A long wall in the quarry behind the village of Ynyshir on the west side of the valley. Lots of potential. Watch out for the Llama (this is not a wind up).

ACCESS

Follow the A4233 for about 1 mile out of Porth passing a Post Office on the right. Turn back sharply left about 100m on to reach a T-junction and park. Follow a path almost immediately opposite the T-junction and turn right behind the houses. The crag is about 150m further on.

THE ROUTES

There are currently two E2's and an E4, following lines of situ gear, but full details are not available.

THE DARREN

GR070913

PREAMBLE

An utterly transformed venue since the bolting up of Terminal Overhanging Wall, which gives some superb routes on very steep rock. The quarry contains two large bays split by a smaller recess. The older routes in the left-hand bay need a good brush. BAT wall does dry very rapidly after rain, whereas Terminal Overhanging Wall can provide shelter from heavy rain until it seeps.

ACCESS

If travelling by car, steps need to be taken to avoid travelling up the one way system in reverse. Approaching from Pontypridd town centre on the A4223, follow the road into the town centre, then follow signs to Graigwen to reach St. Catherine's church on the right (obvious). Turn right immediately in front of the church and follow the road over a metal bridge. Turn right, then left, signposted White Rock Estate to reach Griagwen place, take the next right and proceed up the hill to White Rock Close. If on foot, from Pontypridd station, turn left and proceed up to the roundabout. Turn right under the bridge then take the exit up the hill more or less to the top, where it is possible to turn into White Rock Close.

In both cases, take the first road left, and the first left again, then follow the track into the woods between the bungalow and the house about 200m down the road on its left-hand side. Go through the gate, turn right, and follow the higher track into the quarry in about 300m.

THE ROUTES

Left Hand Bay

1. **Striking Twelve**   11m   E3,6a   *
   The steep wall on the left immediately upon entering the quarry, via a huge pocket (Friend 3½), and a PR. The top usually requires a good brushing, but it is worth the effort.
   A.Sharp, P.Harding, T.Foster 23.04.1989

2. **Midnight Express**   12m   E2,5b   ●
   Unjustifiable. The gnarly offwidth to the right, gained by an initial move up the corner.
   G.Lewis, T.Penning 00.00.1980

3. **New Sensations**   12m   HVS,4c   ●
    The large corner is not only rancid, but as filthy as P**rh*wceib*r.
    T.Penning, J.Harwood 04.05.1982

4. **Return Of The Dodo**   12m   E1,5b
    The crack between New Sensations and My New House.
    M.Richards, J.Harwood 00.05.1997

5. **My New House**   12m   E2,6a   Fr6b+   *
    The slab to the right, BB.
    G.Ashmore, R.Lawrence 02.05.1992

6. **Uphill Walker**   12m   VS,4b
    The first crack on the right-hand wall of the bay.
    T.Penning, G.Lewis 00.00.1980

7. **Sheik Yerbouti**   12m   E1,5b
    The crack and overhang immediately to the right.
    A.Sharp, P.Harding, T.Foster 23.04.1989

8. **Trillian Crack**   12m   HVS,5a
    The next crack.
    H.Griffiths, G.Lewis, C.Heard 00.00.1980

9. **Behind The Bikesheds**   11m   E3,5c
    Bold. The wall to the right.
    T.Foster 23.04.1989

Middle Alcove

10. **Unnamed**   8m   E3,6a
    The cleaned arete on the left side of the alcove.
    A.Sharp Pre-1994

11. **Lotta Bottle**   9m   E2,6a
    The thin crack to the right is gained from the left. A direct start is available at the same grade, but seems easier.
    Abseil from the scaffold.
    A.Sharp 00.00.1983
    P.Lewis – Direct 09.06.1990

12. **Smack**   14m   E3,6a   *
    The prominent overhanging arete to the right. Excellent moves, BB.
    A.Sharp, P.Lewis 24.06.1989

13. **Hear No Evil, See No Evil**   20m   VS,4c
    The big crack in the back of the alcove.
    G.Lewis, S.Mundy, J.Card 00.00.1980

14. **Reach For The Sky**   20m   E2,5b
    Follow the flake to the right, until it is possible to swing right onto the bulging slab (small Friend useful). From the
    top of the slab, PR, follow the short finishing flake on the right.
    C.Heard, G.Lewis 00.00.1980

There is a boulder problem traverse round the bay at 5b.

Terminal Overhang Wall

This is the left-hand wall of the bay. Previously akin to overhanging Weetabix, the wall has been well trundled and bolted to give a good quality venue.

15. **Arizona Stan**   14m   E5,6b   Fr7a+   *
    Climb the wall right of the arete via a huge reach off an undercut pocket. Swing onto the arete and rock left to a BB. A little redundant since the advent of Capstan.
    A.Sharp, P.Lewis 09.06.1990

16. **Capstan**   18m   E5,6b   Fr7b   ***
    Stunning! As for Arizona Stan, but instead of swinging onto the arete, carry on up the bulging right-hand side to a BB.
    A.Sharp 00.00.1997

17. **Basildon Slapper**   17m   E5,6b   Fr7b
    Start just left of a thin crack splitting the clean lower wall right of Arizona Stan. Follow a direct and strenuous line up the overlaps to a BB under the final (loose) roof.
    A.Sharp, etc. 00.05.1997

The Darren - Terminal Overhanging Wall
Photo: Carl Ryan

18. **Alive And Kicking** 18m E5,6a ●
An appalling route of the basest quality. Follow the thin crack splitting the clean wall right of Basildon Slapper. This is actually quite enjoyable. Move diagonally up and right (BR), to gain a jam crack. Climb this to enter a niche (gross and filled with self-regenerating dust, coal and general filth). Gain an imploding jam crack, pull over the roof and step left to the BB of Basildon Slapper. The worst hard route on sandstone.
T.Penning, J.Harwood 21.06.1989

19. **Round Are Way** 18m E5,6b Fr7a+
Start just left of a prominent crack in the middle of the lower wall, below a square-cut groove. Make a very tricky entry into the groove and follow steep ground directly to a BB.
A.Sharp, P.Lewis, J.Harwood 08.05.1997

20. **Rise** 18m E5,6a Fr7a *
Start up the prominent crack in the middle of the wall and make awkward moves up to a rattling jug at two-thirds height. Make a monster lurch up the wall to fingery climbing up the headwall.
T.Foster, P.Harding 00.00.1990

21. **Sharpy Unplugged** 18m E6,6b Fr7b+ ***
Brilliant climbing up the wall to the right of Rise.
A.Sharp 10.05.1997

22. **Enter The Darren** 17m E4,6a
Right again is a short slabby arete. Climb this to the overhanging crack, providing the substance of the route, PR.
P.Lewis, A.Sharp 24.06.1989

23. **Night Train** 24m E5,6a Fr7a+ *
Start up Arizona Stan and traverse right along the break to reach and finish up Sharpy Unplugged.
M.Richards 00.00.1997

24. **Niart Thgin** 24m E5,6a Fr7a+ *
A counter-traverse. natS anozirA pu hsinif dna deggulpnU yprahS pu tratS. This is not the proper name by the way.
M.Richards 00.00.1999

B.A.T. Wall
The right-hand wall of the main bay. Most routes finish by abseiling from trees near the top.

25. **Autumn Leaves** 21m E3,6a
Just right of the corner is a small roof. Surmount this and follow a crack PRs. From this either step left to finish up a blunt rib, or gain a tree on the left and abseil.
T.Penning, J.Harwood 12.06.1990

26. **Kosovo** 21m E2,5c Fr6a+ *
The slab right of Autumn Leaves.
A.Sharp 00.00.1999

27. **Sorry Lorry Morry** 21m E2,5c Fr6a+ **
The prominent groove to the right of Kosovo, pulling straight through the overlap to gain a thin crack to finish.
A.Sharp, P.Lewis 08.01.1989

28. **La Grande Crise** 21m E2,5b
As for Sorry Lorry Morry, but pull out right at the strip roof, surmount it, then step back left. No longer worthwhile, but was the original (and unbolted) route up the wall, with PRs.
G.Lewis, M.Harber, L.Foulkes, S.Blackman 00.00.1982

29. **Juvenile Justice**   21m   E4,6b   Fr7a+   *
The narrow slab to the right of Sorry Lorry Morry is accessed directly. The first clip is awkward, but can be protected by a Friend ½ in a slot slightly down and right. Pull onto the slab with some difficulty and climb its centre past BRs. Abseil from the final BR or finish at will.
A.Sharp, P.Lewis 07.01.1989

30. **Alfred's Variation**   •   21m   VS,4b   *
As for Boulevard De Alfred Turner (1926) to the tree. Step left to finish up the left-hand narrow crack, which is slightly loose.
T.Penning, P.Cresswell 00.00.1981

31. **Boulevard De Alfred Turner (1926)**   21m   VS,4c   **
The central groove of the wall with the carved inscription at its base. From the tree at the top of the groove, move right to gain the right-hand thin crack. Finish up this. Possibly the best route on Sandstone at this grade.
G.Lewis, H.Griffiths 00.00.1981

32. **Andrew The Zebra**   21m   E2,5c
Just right again is a thin crack splitting the leaning wall. Gain this via a bold heelhook and follow it direct to the ledge, finishing at will.
G.Lewis, C.Heard, S.Robinson 00.00.1981

33. **Calling Card**   18m   E4,6b
The groove to the right, 2PRs, is deceptively hard. From the ledge, finish up a thin crack.
T.Penning, J.Harwood, P.Lewis, A.Sharp 12.06.1990

34. **Stow Crack**   18m   HVS,5b
The large layback flake. Wander up the rotting wall above to finish.
G.Lewis, C.Heard 00.00.1980

35. **Shaken Not Stirred**   11m   E3,6a   Fr6c
The wall to the right. A Friend 4 in the pocket and a Rock 2 in the slot take all the fun out of the crux dyno before the BR. PR in the easy upper wall.
A.Sharp, J.Harwood, P.Lewis 15.01.1989

36. **Madame X**   11m   E3,6b   Fr7a   *
The short hanging arete to the right provides a superb power problem involving a hard rockover and two imaginative dynos.
A.Sharp, J.Harwood, P.Lewis 15.01.1989

37. **Antelope Migration**   16m   HVS,4c   \
The (rather pointless) girdle of B.A.T wall. Start up the groove right of Madame X and wander along the big terrace, until a flake crack is reached. Climb this to some ledges and traverse left across to a tree. From here step left and climb a crack to a hole. Gain another tree over to the left and finish up the groove above.
T.Penning, G.Lewis 00.00.1981

DERI

GR129012

PREAMBLE

An utterly transformed venue, providing a summer time rival to The Gap (i.e. it is in the shade), with some really superb wall climbs. The quarry has two walls either side of an arete, a slightly scrappy left-hand one and a superb right-hand one. Belaying can be exciting due to the slope of the banking. Unfotunately some of the bolts are missing at the moment.

ACCESS

The crag is located between Deri and Bargoed and is quite awkward to get to. Either drive towards Deri from Bargoed, until the crag can be seen up on the left, park and walk in, or take a shorter but easy-to-get-lost way in. This involves taking the left fork just before Bargoed high street starts to drop down and taking a steep road to a right turn immediately before Heolddy Comprehensive School. Go over the first cattle grid to a second, then turn right. Follow this road for about a mile, until a grassed-over spoil heap can be seen on the right about 200m before a small stream valley with a marked footpath. Park, go over the fence and follow the path leftwards contouring round the hill to arrive at the crag. If on foot, forget it. The landowners (Parc Cwm Darren) have requested that climbers phone them on 01443 875557 when intending to use the crag.

BIRD BAN: A pair of Peregrine Budgies have nested here and the crag should be avoided from 31st March through to 31st July. Re-direct them to Penrhiwceiber.

THE ROUTES

Left Wall

1. **Ace In The Hole**   9m   E1,5b   Fr5+   ☙
   The short wall on the left of the crag, finishing through some slaty overhangs.
   R.Thomas, G.Gibson 08.10.1994

2. **Two Of A Kind**   9m   E3,6b   Fr7a+   ☙
   The short wall to the right is characterised by a scoop above the starting overhang. Climb this either by means of a hit and miss jump (6c) or a stylish heelhook and rockover. The wall above is straightforward.
   G.Gibson 04.09.1994

3. **Mine's A Pair**   9m   E3,6a   Fr6b+   ☙
   A short tough route with a horrible reach for the chain. Guaranteed to skin shins in the event of a missed clip! Right of Two Of A Kind is a short groove, which is gained and left by some difficult moves. Climb the wall above to a gnarly swing left to the chain.
   G.Gibson 08.10.1994

4. **Joker In The Pack**   14m   E3,6a   Fr6c   ☙
   A worthwhile number up the more continuous wall to the right. Pull over the overhang by means of a good rockover and follow the fingery wall above.
   R.Thomas, G.Gibson 04.09.1994

5. **House Of Cards**   14m   E4,6a   Fr7a   *   ☙
   The central arete of the crag is climbed on its left throughout.
   G.Gibson, R.Thomas 01.09.1994

Right Wall

6. **Kicking Ass And Taking Names** 15m   E5,6a   Fr7a   ** ☙
   Cleaning and re-equipping have rendered this route an excellent proposition, which is actually much easier for the short despite long reaches! The big central arete on its right throughout.
   A.Sharp, P.Lewis, T.Foster, P.Harding 27.03.1989

7. **Chattery Teeth**   14m   E5,6b   Fr7a+   ***   ঝ

The best route at the crag, which follows the wall right of Kicking Ass And Taking Names past a couple of massive rockovers. Move left at the top to the BB of the arete.
G.Gibson, R.Thomas 08.10.1994

8. **Olympic Doctor**   12m   E4,6b   Fr7a+   *   ঝ

Right of Chattery Teeth is another bolt ladder, which is climbed past a hard start and a desperate finish.
A.Sharp, P.Lewis 00.00.1993

9. **Deri Made**   20m   E3,6a   Fr6c   **   ঝ

Further up the banking is a sustained pitch with superb protection. Start up the pod-cum-crack and move out onto the wall following the BRs to the break (watch out for loose shale here). From the break continue up a crack to final hard move for the chain. BB.
R.Thomas, G.Gibson 01.09.1994

10. **Steroid John**   20m   E4,6a   Fr6c+   *   ঝ

The wall to the right with a hard start is another Deri pumper.
P.Lewis, A.Sharp 00.00.1993

11. **Coffee Shop**   18m   E4,6a   Fr7a   ঝ

More of the same to the right, but with blind moves to finish.
G.Gibson 01.09.1994

12. **Full Dog**   14m   E5,6b   Fr7b   *   ঝ

At the top of the banking is a corner and a prominent blunt arete. Climb the arete direct, with a huge span at 8m, which can be a bit of a stopper.
G.Gibson, R.Thomas 01.09.1994

13. **Menage A Chien**   14m   E5,6b   Fr7b   *   ঝ

The original (but better equipped and cleaned) version of Full Dog. Start up Mister Foothold to a square overlap, then make a hard move along a thin horizontal slot to gain the arete of Full Dog.
M.Crocker, R.Thomas 13.05.1989

14. **Mister Foothold**   14m   E4,6a   Fr7a   **   ঝ

Right of the arete, below an obvious coal slot is a faint square-cut groove. Climb this to get the coal slot, move out of this (crux), then move up the pumpy headwall on hidden jugs.
A.Sharp, P.Lewis 00.00.1993

15. **Troilism Trouble**   12m   E2,5c   ঝ

The jam crack to the right. Trad, but has a BB.
R.Thomas, M.Crocker 13.05.1989

DERI PARK

GR123033

PREAMBLE

This is a mediocre crag, possibly worth a visit by locals when the waterfall dries up (high summer only). Only really worth visiting in conjunction with Deri Crag Proper, but still better than anything in Pembroke (sorry, meant to say Penrhiwceiber). The sports routes on the left wall are the main attraction, but the rock remains a bit brittle.

ACCESS

This is the small quarry around the pool in the upper reservoir of Deri Park (Parc Cwm Deri), which lies 1½ miles past Deri village and is clearly signposted. Possibly SE Wales first drive-in crag, although to do so may upset the local warden. The best approach when coming from Deri is to turn right down the track at the pub just before the park on the right. Drive down the track and up the hill to the quarry entrance and then park. The landowners (Parc Cwm Darren) have requested that climbers phone them on 01443 875557 when intending to use the crag.

THE ROUTES

1. **Athabasca Falls**   11m   E4,6a   Fr7a   *
   The left-hand line on the left wall of the quarry is the best route here.
   M.Crocker, J.Harwood 16.04.1994

2. **High Force**   11m   E3,6a   Fr6c+
   The wall to the right.
   M.Crocker, J.Harwood 16.04.1994

3. **What Happened Then?**   11m   E3,5c
   The dirty cracks to the right are trad.
   M.Crocker, J.Harwood 16.04.1994

4. **Heron Egg Poacher**   8m   E3,6b   Fr7a
   A problem for a sick mind, with arse scraping bramble potential before the first clip. The centre of the tower at the left hand side of the right wall. Frustrating and currently completely overgrown.
   M.Crocker, J.Harwood 16.04.1994

5. **Lakeside Shuffle**   8m   E3,5c
   The wall below a large tree 100m right of the waterfall on the right hand side of the quarry. Step up into a shot hole, climb the smooth right hand side of the face, PR, to grapple with the tree.
   M.Crocker, J.Harwood 16.04.1994

DIMBATH

GR947902

PREAMBLE
The Yosemite of South East Wales. The crag consists of a natural rift that has been quarried in some parts to form two distinct areas. The lower rift is more extensive in size and height and has some routes on natural sandstone.

This is a very good crag, unfortunately plagued by lichen. At the time of writing, however, all the routes have recently been cleaned and are in good condition. A little more traffic should keep them in a reasonable state. (Someone appears to have taken this literally and has driven a car over the top of the upper rift). Some routes remain dry in the rain, even after a prolonged spell, but seepage can be a problem, particularly during the winter. Midges are a real pain in summer after 7 pm. Take midge cream, a heavy smoker, or an alarm clock that only has 6 hours on it to confuse the little sods.

ACCESS
Follow the A4061 from the M4 at Sarn through Bryncethin to Blackmill. Turn right along the A4093 towards Gilfach Goch and follow this road for ¹/₂ mile until Glynllan estate is reached. Turn left into Dimbath Avenue and follow it through an estate, continuing down a country lane until a ford is reached. Park here. This point can also be reached by travelling westwards along the A4093 from Tonyrefail and turning right opposite the church in Glynogwr.

Having parked at the ford, walk up the river following the path on the true right bank for ¾ mile, until a gravel forest track doubles back rightwards and up the hill. Follow this until the track straightens after a left-hand bend, where there is currently a tree covered in white paint. Follow a path up into the forest to arrive at the lower lift. There is no possibility of arriving at the crag if relying on public transport.

THE ROUTES

Lower Rift

1. **Across The River**   8m   VS,4c
   Immediately upon turning right to enter the main rift is a prominent short arete on the right side.
   R.Thomas, G.Royle 00.00.1990

2. **Into The Trees**   8m   VS,4b
   6m to the left is another obvious cleaned arete of natural sandstone.
   R.Thomas, G.Royle 00.00.1990

3. **Groucher**   8m   VS,4c
   The rounded arete to the left.
   R.Thomas 00.00.1990

4. **Midget Gem (Whinger)**   8m   HVS,5a   *
   6m to the left is a scoop running from a ledge to a prominent tree.
   E.Travers-Jones 00.00.1990

5. **Moaner**   5m   VS,4c
   Left again is a steep wall with a PR at 5m and an arete to its right. Start on the ledge to the right of the arete and layback the sharp arete facing left, passing a useful Friend slot en route.
   R.Thomas 00.00.1990

6. **Teaching Granny**   9m   E1,5c   *
   Climb the steep wall past the PR, trending right to finish.
   R.Thomas, G.Royle 00.00.1990

7. **Huff And Puff**   9m   HVS,4c
   The next arete to the left.
   R.Thomas, G.Gibson 09.06.1990

8. **Sucking Eggs**   12m   E3,6a   ***
   Tackle the strikingly obvious leaning sharp arete to the left, PRs. Perhaps the best route on natural sandstone in the area. BB.
   R.Thomas, G.Royle 00.00.1990

9. **At Your Convenience**   12m   E3,5c   Fr6b+   *
   Climb the overhanging wall to the left past 4PRs to the BB of Sucking Eggs.
   R.Thomas, G.Royle 00.00.1990

10. **Phil's Ammonia**   18m   E1,5b
    Over to the left is a blunt arete forming the left-hand side of a gully. Start at the base of the mossy slab and wander up this to gain the arete. Climb the arete, 2PRs, to a large ledge and either top out or lower off a pre-placed rope.
    R.Thomas, G.Davies 00.00.1990

11. **Sal's Ammoniac**   15m   E2,5c
    To the left are two vague towers. This route climbs the front face of the left hand tower, with a tricky start, PR and the spectacular overhang above, PR, to a BB.
    R.Thomas 00.00.1991

12. **Teddy Bear's Picnic**   15m   E1,5a
    Climb the large left wall of the corner directly up its centre passing 2PRs. A Friend 2 proves useful.
    R.Thomas, G.Davies 00.00.1990

13. **Coming On Strong**   21m   E5,6b   ***
Brilliant albeit somewhat overshadowed by its neighbour. Climb the overhanging crack past a wide niche, PR and a situ wire to the overhang. Thug through the roof and up the overhanging crack (Friends ½ and 1½), BB.
A.Sharp, P.Lewis 06.05.1990

14. **Where The Power Lies**   21m   E6,6b   ***
Awesome, spacious and decidedly uphill. Climb the blatantly obvious crack starting from a ledge at 2m, to a baffling move through the roof. Shakeout, crank up for a good jug and finish by jug hauling and a couple of jams to the chain. Several PRs.
A.Sharp, P.Lewis 21.04.1990

15. **Haven't A Clue**   15m   E5,6b   Fr7a+   **
Incorrectly called 'The Knowledge' in previous editions. The obvious and deceptively powerful blunt arete down and to the left, passing 4BRs to a BB out to the left. A bit run out in the central section.
A.Sharp, P.Lewis 29.04.1990

16. **If You Go Down To The Woods Today**   15m   E4,6a   **
The thin cracks in the wall to the left contain a couple of long, powerful locks, with shaky gear in the central section. Friends are useful to protect the exit onto the upper slab, and a Friend ½ is very useful at 10m. BB.
P.Lewis, A.Sharp 21.04.1990

There is a project up the wall to the left (Recurring Pantomime).

17. **Big Surprise**   15m   E1,5b
The 'offwidth' to the left.
R.Thomas, G.Davies 00.00.1990

18. **Day Of The Mastodon**   15m   HVS,5a   *
Climb the obvious flying arete at the extreme left hand end of this section of wall before the larger bank and the upper rift.
R.Thomas, G.Gibson 09.06.1990

19. **Burdizzo**   9m   E1,5b
Opposite Phil's Ammonia on the other side of the rift is a small scoop with some painted graffiti. Climb the scoop direct past a PR, to finish direct.
R.Thomas Pre-1991

Upper Rift
Up and left from the Lower Rift is the Upper Rift.

20. **Trickie**   8m   VS,4b
An obvious small buttress, overhanging on its left-hand side just left of a grass col provides this route, which climbs onto the obvious small ledge, moves up and then traverses right under the overhang to finish.
G.Lewis 00.00.1990

21. **Trieksodeephobia**   9m   HVS,5a
Climb onto the small ledge as for Trickie, but continue direct to finish (The finish can be reached directly, via a boulder problem through the overlaps).
G.Lewis, A.Burke 00.00.1990

22. **No. 7 Climb**   12m   VS,4c   ●
Climb the filthy groove 9m to the left until a step left can be made onto a slabby wall. Probably best left to the lichen.
G.Lewis, A.Keward 00.00.1990

23. **Consuming Passion** 18m HVS,5b

Around to the left is a fine wall with a prominent right to left ramp up its centre. Climb the prominent crack to the right of the ramp, finishing direct.

H.Griffiths, L.Travers-Jones 00.00.1990

24. **Unnamed** 16m E6,6b

The chipped wall to the left (the first ascensionist was not responsible for the chips), to gain the finish of Never Mind The Bollocks, Share The Knowledge.

J.Sykes Pre-1999

25. **Never Mind The Bollocks, Share The Knowledge** 18m E3,5c **

Climb the prominent diagonal ramp (good wires) until level with the underside of the capping roof. Step right, and follow a series of slots over the overhangs to finish direct up the centre of the buttress (crux).

A.Burke, E.Travers-Jones, H.Griffiths 00.00.1990

26. **Wild Pussy** 15m E2,5b

Start by some graffiti 5m left of the last routes. Climb the conspicuous left-trending blocky faultline into a niche and finish direct to the left of an obvious tree. A difficult start.

H.Griffiths,E.Travers-Jones 00.00.1990

27. **Grit Expectations** 14m E4,5c

Climb the recessed wall 8m left of 'Wild Pussy' direct via a break, a blind flake (poor Rock 2) to a rounded break, poor Friend. Make crux moves upto the overlap and finish more easily.

E.Travers-Jones, H.Griffiths 00.00.1990

28. **The Creaming Codpiece** 12m E2,5c

The prominent slab to the left, with an undercut base, PRs.

R.Thomas, G.Ashmore 04.10.1997

29. **Bitter End** 14m E1,5b *

Climb the wall to the left starting up an overhanging groove and finishing direct past a PR.

R.Thomas Pre-1991

FERNDALE

GR994969

PREAMBLE

The crag possesses a somewhat dismal aura, except in the early morning, although there are some good lines nevertheless. The quarry has steep walls on both sides, separated by slabs and the obvious central pillar. It can be cold in winter as it faces east, and can still be greasy even in moderately good weather. Belay stakes are in place and most of the routes have been recently re-equipped.

ACCESS

Enter Ferndale on the B4277 Porth road and follow it to a very obvious junction in the middle of town. Turn left here and drive up past the Working Men's Club to the end of the houses on the left. Park here and follow a zig-zag track up the hill to a gate in the fence on the left. Go through this then follow the path leading steeply up the hill to the top, where there is a short scrappy quarry over to the right. Skirt round to the left to come to the main quarry in 150m.

If on foot buses run up from Porth and the railway terminus at Ystrad Rhondda. From Ferndale follow the description above.

THE ROUTES

On the right of the quarry is a clean wall with a clean crack. The routes are described from right to left.

1. **Gregoires Island Lodge** 15m E2,5b *
The wall right of the crack, 2PRs and BR.
M.Crocker, R.Thomas 15.01.1989

2. **Sea Shells On The Seychelles** 15m E1,5b *
The crack.
M.Crocker R.Thomas 15.01.1989

3. **La Digue** 15m E3,6a *
The wall left of the crack is climbed by a couple of steep rockovers to the second BR. Step left into the centre of the wall, and continue steeply to the break. Climb past a very small sapling to the unfortunate top out, or sneak off left to a birch tree and abseil.
M.Crocker R.Thomas 15.01.1989

4. **One Size Fits All** 8m E3,6b
Just left is a ledge just above half-height. The route gains this via some disgracefully chipped holds just right of the corner, BR. The prize contender for the most pointless route on sandstone.
T.Foster 18.04.1989

5. **Nine Green Bottles** 18m E3,6a
Currently bold due to the loss of a PR. Best to clip the second BR on By Apppointment Only. On the large pillar left of the last route, climb the left side until jugs lead out left to the BB of the next routes.
P.Lewis, A.Sharp 08.04.1989

6. **By Appointment Only** 18m E3,6a Fr6c *
Start underneath a niche below a small roof at 8m. Climb the groove to the roof, pull straight over it and go up the wall to finish.
A.Sharp, P.Lewis 01.04.1989

Ferndale Photo: Carl Ryan

7. **Physical Presents**   18m   E5,6b   Fr7b   *

There are a couple of very hard moves on this route. Start as for the last route, but at the huge staple, move out left to another line of bolts. Make a very trying sequence up to a BR and better holds, stepping right to the BB of By Appointment Only.

A.Sharp, P.Lewis 08.04.1989

8. **Rhondda Born, Rhondda Bred**   18m   E2,5c   *

The protection before the BR looks good, but is in a loose block. Start left of the last trio by some grassy steps leading up to a terrace. Climb the right-hand side of an arete to big loose holds on the right wall under a BR. Climb to the BR and pass it (quite hard). Finish up the slab and arete.

P.Lewis, A.Sharp, P.Harding 15.04.1989

9. **Blondes Have More Fun**   18m   VS,4b

On the back wall of the quarry is another pillar. Follow a vague line up this on grass (in future you might be able to skin up this little number on slatey holds. It might be protected with a couple of bongs, or some bolts with resin). Belay on fenceposts.

G.Lewis, F.Barrett, G.Barker 00.00.1989

10. **The Loony Left**   12m   E3,6a   *

On the left wall of the pillar is a slim groove. Climb the slab and groove to a BR, then make a hilarious couple of moves left to good holds and a small tree. Abseil with trepidation, or use a back up rope.

A.Sharp, P.Lewis, P.Harding 15.04.1989

Left again is another grassy terrace at 6m. The next two routes start from this and are easily accessed by a grassy scramble.

11. **Silent Movies**   11m   HVS,5a   *

The thin finger crack in the centre of the slab. Abseil.

A.Sharp, P.Lewis 01.04.1989

12. **Race You Up The Wallbars**   12m   E4,6b   Fr7a+   *

A thin series of cranks and smears up the slab to the left is a little easier now the flake has snapped off. Climb up the slab slightly left of the first BR to a very hard move up for the next one. Step left to a vague sentry box, and finish direct past a PR. Abseil.

A.Sharp, P.Lewis 08.04.1989

13. **Culture Vulture**   12m   E2,5c   Fr6b

The wall to the left of the terrace. The route is slightly harder (6a) if started direct.

A.Sharp, P.Lewis 15.04.1989

14. **Just Good Friends**   8m   E2,5c

A short route up the thin crack starting halfway up the descent gully, BR. The belay stake is hidden in the grass.

A.Sharp, P.Lewis 18.04.1989

15. **The Rhondda Roraima**   18m   E2,5b

Climb the front of the pillar bounding the crag on its left hand side to a PR. At the PR swing round onto the right arete to finish.

W.Gladwin, S.Robinson 00.00.1996

Goi Ashmore - Where Did You Get That Bolt? (E2,6b) Cilfynydd
(Page 389) Photo: Phil Brent

Goi Ashmore & Adam Senior - Young Free & Single (Fr7a) Coedely
(Page 393) Photo: Simon Coles / Rich Lawrence

THE GAP
GR080963

PREAMBLE
Without a doubt the most important and best crag on sandstone. The British equivalent of Smith Rock. It is virtually fully re-equipped, and is the social centre of South East Wales climbing on summer evenings. Its kickin' man, just like Ibiza. Outside spring and summer though its bloody freezing.

ACCESS
Take the A470 to the large roundabout after Abercynon and take the Ystrad Mynach exit. Turn left at the next roundabout (signposted to Treharris) and follow this for 1 mile to a narrow left turning over a bridge immediately before a pelican crossing. Follow this road steeply uphill, and over a railway bridge, then take the first right. Follow this road until the crag becomes visible up on the left. Turn left underneath the larger lower quarry. Park here for the lower crag. Be warned that there have been car break ins and thefts from here. The upper quarry and natural edge to its left are best reached by turning up the track leading out from the gravelled car park of the lower quarry. The best way to reach the quarries from each other is to walk along the top of hill on which the crags are situated.

If on the train, stop at Abercynon. If stopping at Abercynon South walk 100m up the track to Abercynon North. Turn left on exiting the station, and left again under a bridge where there is a T-junction. Turn left, and walk up to the first proper right hand turning into an estate. Walk up this road until it is possible to take a left hand turn up a bumpy track past a farm/garage. Walk up this road for ½ mile to a left hand fork just before a bridge over a dual carriageway. Take the left-hand fork, and walk down this to the crag (½ mile). The approach time is about 30 minutes.

THE ROUTES

Lower Quarry

Left Wall

1. **As It Was**   8m   VS,4c   Fr4+
   Once upon a time Roy had some special pegs, but then people got fussy and wanted sexy pegs. So there were some special pegs left and I wonder where they could be? The short wall on the extreme left-hand end of the wall. Abseil from the scaffold.
   R.Thomas 00.00.1994

2. **Kabuto Mushi**   9m   E1,5c   Fr6a+
   The small wall to the right. 2PR, BB.
   R.Thomas, E.Travers-Jones, A.Japanese 00.00.1993

3. **Yikes**   9m   E2,6a   Fr6b+
   The wall to the right is a sly piece of retrobolting. However, it is also a not so sly piece of retro-chipping.
   M.Crocker, R.Thomas, M.Learoyd 25.03.1990

4. **So Uncool**   12m   E3,6a   Fr6c   **
   Right of a little broken rock is a steep wall bisected by a ramp. Follow the problematic lower wall BR, spotters recommended, to the ramp. Pull awkwardly up, clip the immense bong and smoke up to a lower-off on the right. The route of the wall.
   G.Gibson, R.Thomas 06.02.1993

5. **Just Hanging Around**   12m   E1,5b
   The crack to the right to the BB of So Uncool.
   R.Thomas, G.Royle 00.00.1990

The following two routes replace the unpopular Bluster (P.Donnithorne, E.Alsford 1991), which climbed the left-hand line to the old Troll 8mm at 6m, then stepped right to finish as for Fluster.

6. **Bluster**   14m   E2,5c   Fr6a+   *
A seriously improved route, which is no longer green. The wall to the right of Just Hanging Around.
R.Thomas 00.00.1993

7. **Fluster**   14m   E2,5b   Fr6a+   *
I think that you need to solve that puzzle for yourself.
R.Thomas 00.00.1993

8. **Marlin On The Wall**   14m   E2,5b   Fr6a+   *
Much better than first appearances suggest and tastefully decorated with useful household implements. From the banking follow the BRs past an industrial strength poker, BB.
R.Thomas 00.00.1993

9. **Sumo No Shiro**   15m   E3,5c   Fr6b+
Not without interest. Just left of the corner is a small sandy cave at 9m. Climb up to this and pass the lip with some difficulty, before bombing up the wall to a BB. The grouted PR is more of structural support than a piece of protection.
R.Thomas, E.Travers-Jones, A.Japanese 00.00.1993

Main Wall
The left hand side of the main wall has received a highly productive Roy Thomas face lift. The first three routes are centred around the big cave.

10. **Canine League**   17m   E2,5c   Fr6a+
Climb the wall just right of the large corner to a big ledge. Continue directly to an exciting flake and finish directly over the roof, using a handy borehole, BB.
R.Thomas, S.Coles 22.09.1994

The Gap - Left Wall   Photo: Carl Ryan

11. **Sleeping Dogs Lie**   18m   E3,5c   Fr6b+   ***
Formerly the Ivy League area of the crag, the big central section of the cave has been stripped and renamed the University of Glamorgan. Politics (or black comedy) aside, follow the huge handrail out to the lip of the first roof. Amble up the dirty wall to the right hand end of the roof (Grouted ring peg ****, which makes the bolts at Buoux look feeble and amateurish and probably used to be the mooring ring for the QE2). Swing round the roof to a shelf.
R.Thomas 00.00.1993

12. **Generation Gap**   17m   HVS,5a
The slab, rib and flake to the right. 2PRs. Not all that well protected. BB.
G.Royle, R.Thomas 00.00.1993

13. **Mr. Farady**   17m   E1,5b
Just to the right is an obvious flake crack at 5m. Gain it, pass a BR, then continue up a faint pillar, PRs to a BB.
R.Thomas 00.00.1993

14. **Poker In The Eye**   17m   E2,5b   Fr6a+   **
There is a series of stepped roofs, with someone's GCSE metalwork project (they failed!) hammered into it just to the right of the start of Mr. Farady. Climb directly through the overlaps and follow more BRs up to a BB.
R.Thomas 00.00.1993

15. **Grout Expectations**   17m   E1,5b   Fr6a   *
The roof and groove right again.
R.Thomas 00.00.1993

16. **Shackles Of Love**   17m   E1,5b   Fr6a   *
A similar line to the right.
R.Thomas 00.00.1993

17. **The Frightening Looking Flake**   18m   E2,5c   ●
Obvious. According to the first ascensionist 'It's more of a bag than a route'. TR, BB, AO, RIP.
R.Thomas 00.00.1992

18. **Ring Of Confidence**   18m   E2,5c   Fr6b   *
Formerly a poorly protected frightener, now a good route which is tough for the grade. The 'stuck on flake' down to the right of The Frightening Looking Flake is followed to a ledge. Interest is maintained on the upper slab. I do not really have a word for the lower off.
R.Thomas 00.00.1993

19. **Get Flossed**   17m   E4,6b   Fr7a+
Climb the wall right of Ring Of Confidence (note that it is cheating to climb the flake of Ring Of Confidence for 5m and step out right), BR, to a desperate move for a 'fish box' hold. Make another hard move up to a flake and finish as for the upper part of Ring Of Confidence. BB.
G.Gibson 18.06.1994

20. **Loctite**   17m   E5,6c   Fr7b   *
Right of Get Flossed wall is a blank-looking wall with a pillar above. Make a very difficult pull up on micro edges to eventually gain the ledge and follow the tower above, BB. The hardest technical move at the Gap.
A.Sharp, P.Lewis 15.07.1989

21. **Land Of The Dinosaurs**   15m   E3,5c   Fr6b
Up the cracks to the right to a chain at 15m.
R.Thomas, G.Davies, M.Learoyd 00.00.1990

The Gap - Lower Quarry

Photo: Carl Ryan

22. **A Momentary Lapse Of Reason**   17m   E6,6b   Fr7b+   *
A controversial route, currently without a finish. Climb the slim wall right of Land Of The Dinosaurs, sustained and fingery, to a spike, ledge and rest. Move up to the roof, and make an awkward move on big slopers to a BR above the roof. Abseil. Used to avoid the roof by going round to the left and really needs a proper finish.
T.Foster, P.Harding 00.06.1989

23. **Rattle Those Tusks**   18m   E3,5c   *
The second big crack on the right is climbed past a TR and a hidden BR above the roof. BB. The tusk sadly met its demise in late 1994.
R.Thomas, M.Learoyd 00.00.1990

24. **Mad At The Sun**   20m   E6,6c   Fr7c   **
Climb the corner right of Rattle Those Tusks to a small roof. From here, make a very intricate sequence of moves out left to a good two finger hold (crux). Move up and left to a slot, then follow the much easier upper wall to a rest below the roof. Above the roof used to be the mother of all jugs, which rattled like the exhaust pipe on a T-Reg Ford Fiesta. Pull gingerly over on the remains of this to a superb move up the headwall and the BB.
M.Crocker, R.Thomas 08.04.1990

25. **Salmon Running, Bear Cunning**   14m   E4,6a   Fr7a   *
The right-hand side of the blunt arete to the right is harder than it looks. The original route lowers off a staple from the ledge at the top of the arete. The continuation is described below.
P.Lewis, A.Sharp 17.06.1990

26. **John West**   20m   E5,6b   Fr7b
As for Salmon Running, Bear Cunning, but continue past 2BRs and a hefty stretch for the chain.
E.Travers-Jones 00.00.1992

27. **Anything You Can Do**   15m   E5,6b   Fr7b   *

To the right of the arete a line of BRs goes up past some shot holes, with some seepage generally present in the first 6m. The move through the thin roof at 11m is hard as is the headwall. Land up on a ledge and either walk over to the BR on Salmon Running and abseil or do the direct finish.
A.Sharp, P.Lewis 17.04.1990

28. **I Can Do Better**   20m   E5,6b   Fr7b   *

A more logical, but quite nasty direct finish to Anything You Can Do. Feels insecure although is reasonable for the grade (6a).
G.Gibson, R.Thomas 28.06.1992

29. **Encore! Magnifique!**   21m   E6,6b   Fr7b+   ***

Most people's candidate for the best route on sandstone. Held to be easier by several people, all of whom are very tall. Start right of Anything You Can Do below a strip roof at 5m Climb straight up to the left-hand side of the overlap and hand traverse to its right-hand end. Make a thuggish move up, then gain good slopers and a shot hole. This section feels run out, but the holds are big. From good jugs, make a huge rockover at full stretch for a jug, then tackle the unhelpful flake to pockets, edges and the top. Drop back down onto the belay from the top.
M.Crocker, R.Thomas 25.03.1990

30. **Pleasant Valley Sunday**   18m   E5,6b   Fr7a+   **

Climb the wall left of the obvious arete at the right-hand side of the main wall. If lanky, make a big stretch from the square pockets to big jugs. If normal make an unbelievable cross through out left to a flake which is followed back right to the same point. Make an awkward move up followed by easy 5c moves up to the chain.
A.Sharp, P.Lewis 18.07.1989

31. **One Track Mind**   18m   E5,6a   *

Bold. The impressive right-hand arete of the main wall climbed on its right. The gear is rather a long way up, PR. Belay well back on a scaffold stake. Rarely done, abseil cleaning advised.
A.Sharp, P.Lewis 11.07.1989

32. **Greased Balls**   18m   E2,5c   Fr6b

The wall right of the arete. Top out.
R.Thomas 00.00.1994

33. **Rain And Tears**   18m   E1,5b

The rarely done corner groove and crack, PR.
R.Thomas, M.Learoyd 00.00.1990

34. **Full Bag**   18m   E2,5b

A much better route than it looks! Start up the groove right of the corner and head for the crack. PR, BB.
R.Thomas, M.Learoyd 00.00.1990

35. **Controlled Emission**   18m   E2,5c   Fr6b   **

A popular route. Start right of the last groove at a faint upside down scoop taken by a line of staples. Follow this (crux) up and right to a ledge and finish up the fingery wall above to a BB out right.
P.Donnithorne, E.Alsford 00.00.1993

36. **Sperm Wail**   18m   E5,6b   *

Very rarely done. Quite worrying if the BR on Controlled Emission is avoided as on all the early ascents. Start in the centre of the rectangular lower wall, and follow a vague scoop past a big hold (Friend 4). From the big ledge (possible Friend 2½) undercut up to a PR. Climb the 'overhanging slab' past these to another PR, which is passed via a very difficult move, that should not be underestimated. Finish on brittle holds to the BB of Controlled Emission.
M.Crocker, R.Thomas 11.04.1990

37. **Scrotum Oil**   18m   E3,6a   Fr6c   **
    Good. Follow the right hand arete of the rectangular wall to a rest at the ledge, then follow the faint scoop on hammered holds to a BB at the top.
    R.Thomas 00.00.1994

38. **Naked Truth**   18m   HVS,5a
    The traditional crack to the right feels wobbly.
    R.Thomas, G.Gibson 12.08.1990

39. **Pick Up The Pieces**   18m   E2,5c   Fr6a+   *
    The wall and diagonal flake to the right.
    R.Thomas 00.00.'991

40. **Retro Butt In**   17m   HVS,5a
    Start left of the obvious cave, and climb the corner, 2BRs until it is possible to step out right (just where Eugene Jones pulled off a block on the second ascent, ripping a road spike and landing on his head) to a crack. PR, wires. Finish up this to the BB on the next route.
    R.Thomas 00.00.1992

41. **Perfect Scoundrels**   15m   E3,5c   Fr6b+   **
    Very good, but not as good as when it used to follow the right-hand side of the arete. Start in the back of the cave and follow jugs out to the lip. Pull up onto a flat ledge via an arete, TR, and follow the left-hand side of the arete to a BB. Delightful, with no particularly hard moves.
    T.Penning, P.Lewis, A.Sharp 00.00.1990
    G.Gibson - Direct 18.06.1994

42. **As It Is**   6m   HVS,5b   Fr5+
    A short route up the arete bounding the right-hand side of the lower quarry.
    R.Thomas 00.00.1994

43. **Traverse**   35m   E3,6a
    For people who have done everything. Start up Ring Of Confidence, then hand traverse the ledge clipping various bits of in situ gear. Continue in the same line into Land Of the Dinosaurs, then move right onto an incut edge on A Momentary Lapse of Reason, which is followed to the iron spike and big sloper. Step right and down to the TR on Rattle Those Tusks, then move across and up the easy section of Mad At The Sun. Pull worryingly up onto the ledge at the top of the Salmon Running, Bear Cunning arete, clip the BR above, then walk across (with serious rope drag) to the finish of I Can Do Better, BB.
    C.Evans 04.08.1994

The Edge

200m up to the right of the Lower Quarry is a series of natural sandstone buttresses, which become more continuous as the Upper Quarry is reached on the right. The first notable feature is a gully. The first route is situated on the stacked green blocks well to the left of the gully.

44. **Chapeau Vert**   8m   VS,4c
    The centre of the stacked green blocks.
    R.Thomas 00.00.1992

45. **Blockbuster**   8m   HVS,5a
    The centre of the blocks on the left side of the gully, taken more or less centrally.
    R.Thomas 00.00.1992

46. **Always A Molehill**   6m   HVS,5b
    The left arete of the right side wall of the gully, climbed on the right throughout. PR near the top.
    R.Thomas 00.00.1992

47. **Once A Molehill**   8m   HVS,5a
    The wall round to the right between two wide cracks.
    R.Thomas 00.00.1992

To the right is a high quality rectangular face.

48. **Personal Stash**   9m   E3,6a   *
    The left arete of the front face of the wall up a crack, then climb the arete direct to finish (large Friend at top). There
    are poor wires available in a pocket round to the left, but they are hardly worth placing.
    D.Meek 00.00.1985

49. **Luddites**   9m   E3,5c   *
    The left-hand set of naughty drilled PRs on the front face of the rectangular buttress defines this line.
    M.Learoyd 00.05.1992

50. **Trouble At Mill**   9m   E3,6a   *
    The right-hand set of naughty drilled PRs defines this fingery route.
    M.Learoyd 00.05.1992

51. **Then There Is A Mountain**   8m   E3,6a
    Climb the wall left of the right arete of buttress to a finger jug at 6m. Make a hard move out to the right arete and
    finish up it. Unprotected, but with a reasonable landing.
    M.Crocker 04.03.1990

52. **Juggery Pokery**   5m   E1,6a
    A poor route over the centre of the roof on the short natural buttress round to the right Any deviation from the centre
    makes things considerably easier than 6a. A large sling is needed for protection.
    D.Viggars, P.Donnithorne 06.06.1991

Round to the right is a more continuous wall, which runs into the Upper Quarry. Towards the left side of the wall is
a wide crack (Old Dog).

53. **Thompson Bank Watch**   6m   E1,6a
    Scrapes the bottom of the barrel. Climb the narrow wall left of the wide crack without any deviation to either side.
    Very contrived. 2PRs.
    Gwent MC 00.00.1995

54. **Old Dog**   6m   VS,4c
    The apparent offwidth is taken by a series of satisfying jug pulls.
    R.Thomas, M.Learoyd 00.00.1990

55. **New Tricks**   8m   E1,5b
    Gain the arete to the right of Old Dog and follow it to a PR. Move slightly left to finish on good holds (poor Friend).
    R.Thomas, M.Learoyd 00.00.1990

56. **Tall Story**   12m   E2,5b
    Start at the left end of the roof to the right, then undercut right the way round it. Poor gear.
    P.Thomas, T.Hall 00.00.1987

57. **In Over My Head**   11m   E3,6b   *
    Spectacular and committing. Start below the centre of the big roof on an uncomfortably tall boulder, PR. Climb
    past a PR (hard), to a rest on undercuts under the roof. Lean off a flake in the roof and hope that the PR is in good
    shape. This can be backed up with a Friend ½ and 1. Pull spectacularly up to finish. Throw a rope down the
    back of the roof to belay from the floor!
    M.Learoyd, R.Thomas 00.00.1990

58. **Mister Natural**   9m   E2,5c
To the right is a pod-like groove. Take this all the way up (harder than it looks) to an easier finish up the slab.
R.Thomas, M.Crocker, M.Learoyd 00.00.1990

59. **Surprise, Surprise**   9m   E1,5c
Immediately right is a blocky crack. Up this, PR, moving slightly left and up to a hidden flake. Move up and step back right to finish up a groove.
M.Learoyd, R.Thomas 00.00.1990

60. **Audio Pornography**   9m   E3,5c
Start up the quarried wall to the right, PR. Finish directly up on natural holds (good Friends) to a sloping top out. Belay well back on a large boulder.
M.Crocker, M.Learoyd 04.03.1990

The Upper Quarry
Good, but often cold. All routes belay on the boulders set well back.

61. **Gladwyn Tidings**   8m   HS,4a
The offwidth at the extreme left-hand side of the quarry.
Gwent MC 00.00.1995

62. **Newton's Apple**   11m   HVS,5a   Fr5   *
A very popular route up the slab to the right. PRs.
R.Thomas, G.Royle 00.00.1990

63. **Dirty Gerty**   12m   VS,4c   *
The obvious rounded crack to the right.
G.Royle, J.Bullock etc. 00.00.1990

64. **Acceleration Due To Gravity**   12m   HVS,4c
The thinner crack to the right.
G.Royle, J.Bullock, R.Thomas etc. 00.00.1990

65. **It's A Sine**   12m   E1,5c   Fr6a+
The bolted slab right again, with a long rockover. 3BRs, no belay.
R.Thomas 05.05.1995

66. **Tangent**   12m   E3,5c   ●   \
The slime infested and vegetated corner to the right. A PR may or may not be in situ.
P.Thomas 00.00.1988

67. **Scared Seal Banter**   14m   E4,6b   Fr7a+   **
The wall right of the corner is awkward to on-sight. Top out.
M.Crocker, R.Thomas, M.Learoyd 04.03.1990

68. **The Mastic Mick**   14m   E3,6a   Fr6c
Climb directly up onto the jug above an overlap and left of the central offwidth of the quarry. Make a stiff pull up to a big pocket, then finish quite easily up the headwall.
M.Crocker, M.Learoyd 04.03.1990

69. **Cled's Crack**   14m   HVS,5a
Rubbish climbing on big loose jugs up the central offwidth of the quarry. Much easier than it looks.
P.Thomas, T.Hall 00.00.1987

70. **The Grout Of San Romano**   12m   E3,6a   Fr6c   **
Sandstone's first polished route! The wall right of the offwidth has a very hard start, with interest well maintained above. There is a possible Friend 2½ placement to protect the second clip.
M.Crocker 04.03.1990

71. **Brush Up**   12m   HVS,5a
The corner to the right.
R.Thomas, G.Royle, G.Royle 00.00.1990

72. **Step Up**   12m   E1,5a
The slab right of the corner, via a thin crack. Large Friend low down and PR.
M.Learoyd, R.Thomas 00.00.1990

73. **The Godfather**   12m   E1,5b   *
The right arete of the quarry. Gain the shelf on its right and teeter up (PR, sling). Swing left and finish up the arete.
G.Lewis, H.Griffiths 00.00.1990

74. **Up Yours**   11m   E1,5b   **
The arete 3m right again is a superb jug trip, 2PRs.
R.Thomas, M.Learoyd 00.00.1990

75. **Smoothie**   6m   HVS,5c
A trivial problem up the front of the wall to the right. PR.
M.Learoyd, J.Bright, G.Royle etc. 00.00.1990

76. **Windy Edge**   8m   E1,5b   *
Good. The last arete just round to the right from the quarry, PR. Check out the scenic views down and right.
M.Learoyd, R.Thomas 00.00.1990

77. **Mortar Life**   8m   HVS,5a
The short wall immediately right, past a poorly cemented PR.
R.Thomas 00.00.1992

78. **O Solo Mio**   8m   HVS,5b
Directly facing Windy Edge on the other side of the gap that gives the crag its name, is a short, square buttress. On the left-hand side of its main face is a thin crack, defining this route.
M.Learoyd 00.00.1990

79. **Chips With Everything**   8m   E1,5c
A double helping up the wall right of O Solo Mio, PR.
M.Learoyd 00.00.1994

GELLI

GR983947

PREAMBLE

From the road this crag resembles Trebanog. However, it is not as good. The crag is fairly exposed and catches the wind, but it does dry out quite quickly. The rock is sounder than at many nearby crags, but does get quite lichenous after prolonged rain (all rain in South-East Wales is prolonged). Belays can be a problem and it may be useful to take a spare rope to tie onto the fenceposts, which are quite a long way back.

ACCESS

This is the crag immediately above and south of the entrance to the tipping site just south of Gelli on the B4293. Park with respect to tip users ('May I park here most noble and illustrious refuse disposal site user?') and take the obvious trail up the slag heaps to reach the crag in about 400m.

If on foot the best bet is probably to take the train to Ystrad Rhondda and walk up to the crag through the Gelli Industrial Estate. Such a trajectory would be fraught with danger at night, but anyone who indulges in climbing at night is quite mad anyway and therefore oblivious to hazards such as Glue Sniffers. In fact they are probably on glue themselves anyway.

THE ROUTES

1. **Green Arete**   11m   HS,4a
   The green arete at the left-hand side of the crag.
   G.Lewis 00.00.1989

2. **K.E.S.**   12m   HVS,5a
   The slabby wall to the right, PR.
   M.Learoyd, R.Thomas 00.00.1989

3. **Wot No Metal**   9m   E1,5c
   The y-shaped crack on the left edge of the red wall is tricky and quite intense.
   R.Thomas, G.Royle 00.00.1990

4. **Little Treasure**   9m   E1,5c
   The scooped wall to the right, BR.
   M.Learoyd, R.Thomas 00.00.1989

5. **Toil**   9m   HVS,5a
   The thin crack on the left-hand edge of the red wall, skilfully avoiding the corner crack.
   G.Lewis 00.00.1989

6. **Galvanised**   9m   E1,5c
   The curving crack to the right is followed to a ledge. Move out left onto the upper wall, 2PRs.
   R.Thomas, G.Royle 00.00.1990

7. **Titanium Man**   9m   E1,5b
   Down and right is another red wall. Climb the steep crack in it to the right of the grassy chimney.
   G.Royle, R.Thomas 00.00.1990

8. **Tobacco King**   9m   E2,5c
   The cracks just to the right of the arete.
   M.Learoyd, R.Thomas 00.00.1989

9. **Cigarillo**   9m   E3,6a
   The wall to the right, climbing directly up past the BR.
   M.Learoyd, L.Foulkes, R.Thomas 00.00.1990

10. **Down Under**   15m   VS,4c
    The slab down to the right stepping out to gain and finish up the arete.
    R.Thomas, M.Learoyd etc. 00.00.1989

11. **Little Taff**   12m   E1,5a
    Climb a thin crack in the centre of the wall to the right, PR. Power on up to the overhang at the top and surmount it directly.
    R.Thomas, L.Foulkes, M.Learoyd 00.00.1990

12. A Little Something I Prepared Earlier   12m   E1,5b
The wall to the right immediately left of a grassy gully, 4PRs.
R.Thomas, M.Learoyd 00.00.1989

13. Unearthed   12m   HS,4b
Climb the crack in the left of the side wall to a ledge. Finish up the groove above.
R.Thomas 00.00.1989

14. Ice Station Gelli   12m   E2,5c
The steep wall 4m right of the 'Buzzy' graffiti, taking a direct line up the upper section. 3PRs.
M.Learoyd, G.Lewis 00.00.1989

15. Send In The Specials   12m   E1,5b
Start 3m to the right and step off the grassy ledge to gain the wall and a PR. Finish up the steep wall past 2 more PRs.
R.Thomas, G. Royle 00.00.1990

16. Hole In One   12m   HVS,5a
Start from the grassy ledge above and right of the last one, step left to a pocket/hole and threaded PR. Move diagonally right to finish past 2 more PRs.
G.Lewis, M.Learoyd 00.00.1990

GLYNFACH

GR029904

PREAMBLE
The crag consists of two main sections. The first is a long broken and semi natural bay on the left, with no recorded routes. The second is a sheltered, taller bay on the right. This main bay dries pretty quickly.

ACCESS
Above the village of Glynfach, SW of Cymmer. Follow the A4225 out of Pontypridd, heading for Porth. Pass through Trehafod to a roundabout by the Rhondda Heritage Park Hotel. Continue straight onto Porth, but where the road veers right, bear left. About ½ a mile further on, the main road bears right, but bear left. The road swings steeply left up a hill and past a metal bridge. Immediately after the bridge, turn left into Glyn Street. After 100m, turn right and park. A path leads up to the right of some flats, eventually arriving at the crag. If on foot, get the train to Porth, walk over towards Cymmer, and follow the directions as above.

THE ROUTES

1. Fach Roo   10m   E2,5c   Fr6a+
The short tower at the left of the crag, 3PRs. There is a spike belay hammered into the wall behind.
R.Thomas 17.04.1999

2.)Killer's Arete   16m   E4,5c   *
The arete of the pillar in the left-hand bay, gained from the left. A Friend 3½ is useful. 2 PRs.
A.Sharp, P.Lewis 22.07.1990

3. Dai Hard   16m   E5,6c   Fr7b   *
The wall to the right of Killer's Arete has a dynamic move off some edges for a distant flake.
G.Ashmore 29.04.1999

4. Moses Supposes His Toeses Were Roses   16m   E3,5c   Fr6c   *
To the right is a Sperm-Whale-like flake of rock. Gain this directly and take the wall above direct to a BB.
P.Lewis, A.Sharp 22.07.1990

5. **Nervous Nineties**   18m   E4,6b   Fr7a
Follow Moses Supposes His Toeses Were Roses to the thin break above the Sperm Whale. Make a hard move right, then go directly up to the BB.
A.Sharp, P.Lewis 22.07.1990

6. **Fach Roo Too**   15m   E2,5c   Fr6a+   \
The tower just the other side of the corner to the right of Nervous Nineties.
R.Thomas 00.00.1999

7. **Fach When**   14m   HVS,5a
The baggy crack to the right.
R.Thomas, E.Travers-Jones, Old Harrovians 00.00.1999

8. **Psychotherapy**   11m   E5,6c
The white wall to the right.
A.Sharp, P.Lewis 22.07.1990

9. **Fach This**   7m   VS,4b
The left-hand of the two twin cracks right of Psychotherapy.
R.Thomas 18.04.1999

10. **Fach That**   8m   VS,4c   \
The crack to the right.
R.Thomas, E.Travers-Jones, Old Harrovians 00.00.1999

11. **Yak's Back**   9m   HVS,5a   \
A route up the slab the the right.
G.Henderson, J.Obradovitc 22.07.1990

12. **Little Kurd**   9m   E1,5b   Fr6a
Up the bolted line.
R.Thomas, E.Travers-Jones, Old Harrovians 00.00.1999

GOLF CLUB CRAG

GR085910

PREAMBLE

A hole in the ground, this might be, but worthless it certainly is not. Whilst tucked way behind trees, it is not lichenous. There are some shorter routes on the left and right walls, but pride of place goes to the steep main back wall, with a sandstone classic. The exact seepage situation is not known as most of the development took place during the very dry summer of 1995. The bag of dead chickens will eventually decompose, which is a shame given their generally uplifting perfume. Please keep quiet when entering the quarry as you pass round the back of someone's garden.

ACCESS

Leave the A470 at the Pontypridd junction and take the Glyntaff exit from the roundabout. Go straight on at the cross roads and up the steep hill to a pillar box on the right. Turn left here off the main road and drive out of the built up area for about $^1/_4$m until there is a track on the right leading off to the golf course. Ignore this track, and park about 100m further down on the left in a blocked off track. Walk down left with care to enter the quarry.

THE ROUTES

Left Hand Wall

1. **Unnamed #1**   9m   E2,5c
   The wall left of the short left arete of the left wall.
   R.Thomas 00.00.1995

2. **Caddy-Lack**   9m   E1,5c   Fr6a+
   The arete itself on its left-hand side, with a desperate knee lock to clip the BB.
   R.Thomas 00.00.1995

3. **Poisonous Little Toad**   11m   E3,6c   Fr7b
   Just round the arete is a prominent perched block. This used to be a heavily chipped 'project' of someone else, but was 'repaired' before the first ascent. One very hard move only and not really worthwhile.
   G.Ashmore 06.05.1996

4. **Muck And Germs**   11m   HVS,5a   ◆   \
   The offwidth to the right.
   S.James, S.Jones 00.00.1997

The wall just right of Muck And Germs is a project.

Main Wall

5. **Golf Syndrome**   11m   E4,6a   Fr7a   *
   After the recessed bay is a short arete marking the left-hand side of the main wall proper. Start just right of this under a v-groove. Climb the lower wall to the v-groove and make hard moves up to gain a jam over the top. Pull through the roof to a BB.
   R.Thomas, M.Hirst 00.00.1995

6. **Golf Bag**   12m   E4,6a   Fr6c+
   The thin lower wall to the right, the complex groove through the roof and the final rib.
   R.Thomas 06.07.1996

7. **Fairway To Heaven**   17m   E3,6a   Fr6c
   Start just to the right under the widest section of the overhang. There may be a pram in situ. Climb the wall up-to the roof and surmount this to a diagonal crack, crux. If successful, saunter up the slab above this.
   M.Learoyd, L.Foulkes 00.00.1992

8. **Time For Tee**   18m   E3,6a   Fr6c   ***
   A sandstone classic, which is well sustained through a series of small overhangs. Start right of the last route, and climb the tricky lower wall through the roof. Continue upto a left-facing groove below the capping overhangs and take a pumpy line straight through them to a BB.
   R.Thomas 13.05.1995

9. **Money**   18m   E5,6b   Fr7b
   The wall between Time For Tee and Chip And Putt. The route is without much substance until the headwall and unfortunately detracts from Time For Tee, but the difficult sequence on the headwall makes the route worthwhile.
   G.Gibson 30.06.1996

10. **Chip And Putt**   17m   E3,6a   Fr6c
    An outrageous route on big hammered buckets, starting 5m up the banking.
    M.Learoyd 00.00.1992

---

11. **Golf-Whore**   12m   E3,5c   Fr6b+   *
Some 5m further up the banking is a left-facing shallow, square-cut groove. Climb this awkwardly to the easier upper wall.
R.Thomas 00.00.1995

12. **Unnamed #2**   14m   E2,5c
The original route up this wall, now largely superseded. Start at the right facing flake corner right of the last route. Climb this to a junction with and finish as for Golf Whore, BR, BB.
L.Foulkes, M.Learoyd 00.00.1992

13. **Bunk-Her**   12m   E3,6a   Fr6c   *
A good route with one very hard move. Start up the flake corner as for the previous route, but continue straight up and slightly right to a powerful move and an easier upper wall.
R.Thomas 00.00.1995

14. **Unnamed #3**   12m   HVS,5b   ●   \
The thin crack to the right to a TB.
L.Foulkes, M.Learoyd 00.00.1992

15. **Unnamed #4**   9m   E1,5c
A route up the pocketed wall at the top of the banking. 3BRs to BB.
L.Foulkes, M.Learoyd 00.00.1992

16. **Nibble My Niblicks**   9m   E1,5c
A pleasant little route up the obvious jam crack and wall on the final section of rock before the path. 2PRs, top out and belay.
R.Thomas 06.07.1996

HENLLYS QUARRY

GR255944

PREAMBLE

A loose, grassy, east-facing crag, consisting of one large central buttress and some smaller chossy lumps on either side. Only the central buttress is worth bothering with, but be warned – the grassy ledges near the top are in fact full of soil. According to Mr. Duncan Dangerous Powell, the famous surfer, these 'do not offer any protection' (sic). Or any holds. Allegedly it has nice views.

ACCESS

From the M4 at junction 26, drive up to a roundabout (2 miles), turn left up the A4051 to the next roundabout. Turn left at this roundabout, and left again at the next roundabout. At the next roundabout turn left and follow the road round to Henllys, if not feeling too dizzy by this stage. Turn left just before some overhead cables, and go up the hill to park by Henllys Chapel. Take the footpath up the hill, to where the quarry is soon visible.

THE ROUTES

1. **The Exiles' Line**   10m   D
The 'slabby thing' over left from the left-hand crack on the central face.
M.Salter 00.00.1994

2. **A Tale Of Two Farmers**   12m   S
The left-hand crack on the central face of the quarry. Watch out for the chossy grass ledge. An escape left can be made from the ledge. Or better still, the floor.
M.Salter 00.00.1994

3. **Farmyard Frolics** 12m S
The central crack.
M.Salter 00.00.1994

4. **Castell Henllys** 12m HVS,4c
The face immediately to the right, with a bad landing and no gear (please note that Mark is a paratrooper).
M.Salter 00.00.1994

5. **The Female Of The Species Is More Deadly...** 14m S
Than The Male
The face approximately 5m right of the last route, left of a large crack. Climb the groove exiting left at its top, and then finishing direct.
M.Salter 00.00.1994

LEWISTOWN
GR926880

PREAMBLE
A small crag above Ogmore vale, which seeps heavily in all but the driest weather. However, it will see future development.

ACCESS
Leave the M4 at J36 and follow the A4061 to Lewistown. Distinctive low budget housing will be seen on the left. Pass the Pant-Y-Awel pub (on the right) to a sharp left-hand bend and immediately afterwards take a sharp left-hand turning. Bear right at the first fork, then right again to a rough track. Follow the rough track for 20m and park on the right. Walk 100m up a grassy bank to gain the quarry and do not leave valuables in the car!

THE ROUTES

The current routes are on a slabby wall.

1. **Five Knuckle Shuffle** 12m E2,5c Fr6b
The left-hand line starting from the ledgey corner.
N.O'Neill & Old Harrovians 00.00.2001

2. **Kleenex Man** 12m E2,5c Fr6b
The right-hand line.
N.O'Neill & Old Harrovians 00.00.2001

LLANBRADACH

GR146895

PREAMBLE

This is a vast quarry of mixed quality brittle sandstone. It is a very impressive place nonetheless. The floor of the lower (main) quarry is rather similar to a poor quality Vietnam War film and is full of appropriate booby traps (marsh holes, car and rusty sheet metal). On the back right-hand wall of the main quarry is the huge Expansionist wall, with the obvious arete of Caerphilly Contract dominating the scene. Over to the right and facing this wall is the steep Pool Area. On the far left is Contraband Wall. The upper tier contains a higher concentration of routes on various prominent towers and can be accessed by tracks leading up bankings either side of the entrance area. Drainage in the quarry is odd, much of the lower tier stays dry except in the heaviest of rain, but once seepage starts to come down from the upper tier it takes a long time to dry out. Some of the routes on the lower tier could do with re-gardening.

ACCESS

If coming by car, follow the A469 to the start of the village and park beyond the traffic calming measures. Walk back past the traffic calming measures until a railway bridge is visible on the uphill side of the road. Pass under the railway bridge, turning left at the track junction. the quarry mouth is 150m down the left-hand track. If on foot, get the train to Llanbradach and walk south (Cardiff direction) along the side of the tracks, until it is possible to break out right onto a track, which leads to the quarry mouth in about 300m.

THE ROUTES

The Lower Tier

Routes are described from right to left (anti-clockwise) as approached as far as Loss Leader Wall. The routes on the left (south) side of the quarry (from Bas Chevaliers Area onwards) are described from left to right as approached. If this upsets anybody's sense of order, then they want to try and walk right the way round the quarry floor to regain their sense of proportion.

Pool Wall

Llanbrach Lower Tier
Photo: Carl Ryan

Expansionist Wall

Caerphilly Contract (36)

Loss Leader Area

Sub Contractors Wall

Cascade Walls

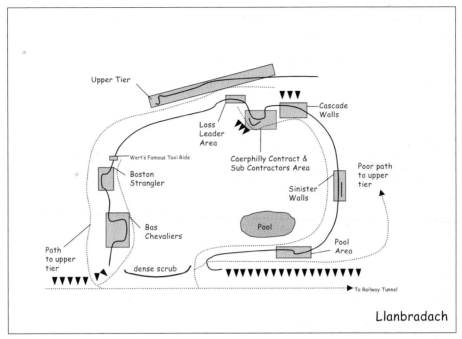

Llanbradach

From the quarry entrance, follow the track leading rightwards round the edge of the pool to a recess bounded by a prominent arete on its right. The first route is 20m before this area.

1. **Sadness**   14m   E1,4c
    On loan from Penrhiwceiber. A bag. The filthy left facing groove 20m right of the prominent blunt arete of Slipping Into Luxury, PR, BR.
    G.Jenkin, R.Thomas 06.11.1988

The wall to the left of Sadness has a prominent overlap.

2. **Internal Reflection**   11m   E1,5c   Fr6a
    This cheesy route takes the right-hand side of this wall.
    R.Thomas, G.Gibson 07.04.1996

3. **Luxury Gap**   12m   E4,6a   Fr7a
    A similarly cheesy route up the wall to the left, with hard moves up from the block to the BB.
    G.Gibson 30.03.1996

4. **Slap Of Luxury**   15m   E3,6a   Fr6c   *
    Start down and left under the blunt arete and make a difficult couple of moves up to gain the slab right of the arete. Follow the slab and tricky wall above to a BB.
    R.Thomas, G.Gibson 30.03.1996

5. **Slipping Into Luxury**   17m   E2,5c   Fr6b   **
    Good and very well protected. Start below and left of the prominent blunt arete and climb the wall to a ledge. Climb the upper arete direct.
    M.Ward, G.Jenkin, R.Thomas, M.Crocker 06.11.1988

Llanbradach

6. **Slip Into Something Sexy**   17m E5,6b Fr7a+ **
The leaning wall left of the corner is very impressive.
M.Crocker, R.Thomas 12.11.1988

There is a project (NHS Waiting List) up the steeper wall to the left, left of a pair of incipient cracks.

7. **Shadow Of The Sun**   14m E4,6a Fr7a **
The steep little wall up the banking futher left.
R.Thomas, G.Gibson 29.06.1996

The Sinister Walls

Further round to the left, before the start of the Expansionist buttress are a series of short, leaning walls at the top of a banking. These are currently home to a number of routes. The routes which continue onto the higher tier are described first. These are normally accessed by either Dreaming In Colour or The Evil Eye. There is a project up the wall above The Evil Eye.

8. **Snapper**   18m E3,6a Fr6c **
The crack above The Evil Eye belay.
G.Gibson 29.06.1996

9. **Overleaf**   12m E2,5c Fr6a+ *
The wall above Dreaming In Colour. Watch out for the very wobbly flake!
R.Thomas 05.07.1996

Returning to the ground and just left of a prominent corner is:

10. **Sinister**   15m E5,6b Fr7b **
Start below an obvious flake at 3m. Gain this with difficulty (crux) and leave it with a monster stretch. Climb up with less interest, but with a gathering pump on brittle flakes, to a final couple of good moves up the flake crack.
G.Gibson 04.05.1996

11. **Abbatoir And Costello**   15m E6,6b Fr7b+ ** \
The wall to the left of Sinister has lost a big hold low down and may now be harder.
G.Gibson 29.06.1996

12. **In Blood, Of Life, Of Sin**   15m E5,6a Fr7a+
The wall to the left is climbed on good holds to a pocket. Reach blindly up and pull round the lip, sauntering up the slab to finish. Often wet, blind and hard to on-sight.
G.Gibson 28.04.1996

13. **The Evil Eye**   12m E4,6a Fr7a
The broken groove on the left, to a step out right onto the wall at a pocket. Pull over the overlap (crux) and saunter up the slab to a BB.
G.Gibson 28.04.1996

Further right, the wall loses height.

14. **Dreaming In Colour**   11m E3,6a Fr6c *
The right arete of the wall.
R.Thomas, G.Gibson 28.04.1996

15. **Letters Of Life**   11m E4,6a Fr7a **
Left of the arete is another bolt line. Climb it by a superb series of rockups and snatches.
R.Thomas, G.Gibson 28.04.1996

16. **Giving It All Up**   11m   E4,6b   Fr7a+   *
The next bolt line right. Some very tricky moves.
R.Thomas, G.Gibson 05.05.1996

17. **Host**   11m   E3,6a   Fr6c
The wall just left of the central drainage streak/cheesy section.
R.Thomas 01.07.1996

18. **Food For Parasites**   11m   E5,6b   Fr7a+   **
The left-hand line on the wall is thin, with a hard crux and pumpy climbing thereafter.
R.Thomas, G.Royle 00.12.1996

Expansionist and Cascade Walls

Further round to the left is the very obvious Expansionist crack, splitting the buttress high up. The Expansionist Wall is bounded on the left by the prominent arete of The Caerphilly Contract. A vague corner runs down from the foot of the Expansionist crack and there is a large slabby ledge splitting the Expansionist area at 15m. The area right of the corner and under the ledge is known as The Cascade Wall. The area above the half-height ledge is known as the Expansionist Wall. The short clean wall left of the corner and directly below the upper arete of The Caerphilly Contract is The Sub-Contractor's Wall.

Cascade Walls

The Cascade Walls are split by a prominent stream emerging from a hole at 3m above which is a left-facing corner (Sphagnum 45). The first route starts from the lowest slab right of the stream.

19. **Bathtime**   15m   E2,5c   Fr6a+
The centre of the lowest slab.
G.Gibson 05.04.1996

20. **Splash It On All Over**   15m   E3,6a   Fr6c
The slab and wall to the left is thin above the ledge.
G.Gibson 05.04.1996

21. **Right Of Spring**   15m   E2,6a   Fr6b
The slab immediately right of the stream, starting up a blunt nose.
G.Gibson 30.03.1996

Left of the hole from which the stream emerges:

22. **Sphagnum 45**   14m   E2,5c   Fr6a
The groove and faint flake above the stream.
G.Gibson 05.04.1996

23. **Cascade**   12m   E4,6a   Fr7a
A worthwhile route up the wall left of Spaghnum 45, passing a prominent overlap.
G.Gibson 03.02.1996

24. **Total Recoil**   15m   E3,6a   Fr6c   *
Starting from a slight platform, climb the broken groove to a good jug at 6m, then step airily out right to the slab. Saunter up to the base of a square cut arete. Swing round this into the groove, then pull back left at the top of the arete and move left to the BB.
G.Gibson, R.Thomas 16.03.1996

25. **Splashdown**   14m   E3,6a   Fr6c

As for Total Recoil, but continue up the groove and its left arete to a hard swing back right to a ledge. Step right to the same BB as Total Recoil.
G.Gibson, G.Ashmore 16.03.1996

26. **Falling Freely**   14m   E5,6a   Fr7a+

A sustained route up the wall to the left of Splashdown.
G.Gibson 17.03.1996

Sub-Contractor's Wall

The rather obvious clean orange wall to the left overhangs very slightly, staying quite dry in light drizzle.

27. **Too Keynes By Half**   12m   E3,6a   Fr6c   *

The right-hand arete.
R.Thomas, G.Gibson 05.04.1996

28. **Post Expressionist**   12m   E2,5c   Fr6b   *

The superb flake line splitting the centre of the wall, stepping right at the top to the same BB.
R.Thomas, G.Gibson 31.03.1996

29. **Simple Addition**   11m   E3,6a   Fr6c+   *

The pocketed wall to the right is hard for the grade.
R.Thomas, G.Gibson 05.04.1996

30. **Sub Contraction**   11m   E4,6a   Fr7a

An unusual route up the right-hand side of the left arete of the wall to the BB of Simple Addition.
G.Gibson 07.04.1996

Expansionist Wall

This is effectively a 'middle-tier' of the quarry, lying above Cascade and Sub-Contractors Wall. The normal approach (apart from The Caerphilly Contract and Little White Lies) is from Total Recoil/Splashdown and up The Link Pitch. The Caerphilly Contract and Little White Lies are normally started via Too Keynes By Half.

31. **The Link Pitch**   8m   VS,4c   Fr4

From the BB of Total Recoil/Splash down, mantle onto the ledge and climb the fin, BR to a BB.
G.Gibson 05.04.1996

32. **Giant Sand**   25m   E4,6a   Fr6c+   **

An excellent trip up the rightmost line on the wall right of the obvious crack of The Expansionist.
G.Gibson, R.Thomas 31.03.1996

33. **Grit Box**   25m   E5,6b   Fr7a+   ***

An awesome route up the steep wall just right of the Expansionist crack. Climb direct, with a hard start to sustained jug pulling that eventually gains the base of a shallow right-angled corner. From the top of the corner make a superbly exposed swing out onto the right arete to gain the belay above.
G.Gibson 05.04.1996

34. **The Expansionist**   60m   E3,5b   *   \

The first route to be done in the quarry, nearly ten years before anything else, is the very striking jam crack splitting the centre of the wall above the chossy corner separating the Cascade and Sub-Contractors walls. It is not known whether this route has ever been repeated. It used to start up the manky corner and pull through 6m of shale to gain the crack, but the corner is now fully vegetated and the shale has gone, therefore access the crack from the Link Pitch stance.
P.Littlejohn, J.Harwood, C.Horsfield 25.05.1978

To the left of the Expansionist Crack are:

35. **Little White Lies**   24m   E3,6a   Fr6c   **
The wall left of the upper crack of Expansionist gained from the former route, or by abseil. Superbly positioned climbing, with one tricky move.
M.Crocker, R.Thomas 27.11.1988

36. **The Caerphilly Contract**   55m   E6,6c   Fr7b+   **
Regeared and now totally direct. Start up Too Keynes By Half and from the belay, climb the nose to the base of a wall (The original route wandered up the grooves round to the right of Subcontractors Wall to gain this point). Clip the BR, pull up the crack out right for one move, then step boldly back left to climb the centre of the wall, 2BRs, to end up on a slabby section below the arete. Move up the arete and stretch right for good holds leading up to an obvious undercut and shakeout right on the arete. Now the fun begins. If over 6ft. make one hard move up the flake to a jug. If normal, make a surprisingly contrived and difficult sequence to leave the top of the flake. If successful, romp up the easy upper section to a BB at the top. Double abseil descent.
M.Crocker, R.Thomas, M.Ward 06.11.1988

Loss Leader Area
This area is back on ground level, situated above the banking left of Sub-Contractors Wall. There is a project up the wall above the sycamore in a crack halfway up the banking.

37. **Acatalepsia**   17m   E2,5b   Fr6a+   *
The wall left of the obvious crack on the long wall at the top of the banking.
R.Thomas 03.06.1996

38. **Insomnia**   17m   E3,6a   Fr6c   *
The wall to the left with a very hard move to gain the ledge and some good rockovers on scabs thereafter. Take care with the final flake.
G.Gibson 05.05.1996

39. **Amnesia**   17m   E4,6a   Fr7a
The wall left again to the same BB.
G.Gibson 05.05.1996

Bas Chevaliers Area and Contraband Wall
The routes are described from left to right, i.e. as encountered walking round the quarry clockwise. Bas Chevaliers Area is the first area of rock encountered on the left-hand side of the quarry, when following the path in from the left-hand banking.

40. **Horns A Plenty**   18m   E1,5b   Fr6a+
The left-hand line on the buttress, taking the sharp groove and crack.
R.Thomas 03.05.1998

41. **Magellan's Straight**   21m   E3,6a   Fr6c
To the right of Horns A Plenty, is a cave at ground level. Pull out of the left hand side of the cave past some interesting structural engineering and climb the overlapping wall above.
R.Thomas 07.05.1998

42. **Maurice Chevaliers**   21m   E4,6a   Fr7a
Start in the centre of the roof right of Magellan's Straight. Climb this awkwardly to a semi-rest on the arete, then swing out under the overlap. A powerful move from the jug on the lip leads to a ledge. Wander up the groove in the front face of the buttress, then swing left to gain the BB of Magellan's Straight.
G.Ashmore 05.04.1999

43. Bas Chevaliers   21m   E3,5c

A good pitch loosely based around the right arete of the buttress. Climb the slabby right wall, until it is possible to swing out onto the groove of Maurice Chevaliers. Move up to just below the 'fang' roof, swing right and climb the right wall, PR, making a long stretch left for a jug on the arete. Move back right, and up to a good nut slot, then back left to the BB.
M.Crocker, R.Thomas 26.11.1988

44. Moutton Dagger   18m   E3,6a   Fr6c   *

The best route up the buttress, taking the wall to the right of Bas Chevaliers.
R.Thomas 01.05.1999

45. Peel Back The Flaps   18m   E2,5c   Fr6b   \

The ledgy, dirty, cheesey chimney and tower.
R.Thomas, Old Harrovians 01.11.1999

46. Jam One In   18m   E1,5b   \

The jam crack to the right and just left of Hush Money.
R.Thomas, Old Harrovians 01.11.1999

The next routes are on the striking vertical wall to the right (Contraband Wall). There is a bolt belay on the terrace.

47. Hush Money   12m   E4,6b   Fr7a+

To the right is an impressively steep 'sheet wall'. Climb the left arete of the wall with some very hard moves past the overlap. Do not wander off right at the crux. Originally given E3!
M.Crocker 11.12.1988

48. Contraband   18m   E6,6c   Fr7c   ***

A fingery and reachy masterpiece up the centre of the wall. Start in the centre of the wall, and undercut to a two finger edge. Make a desperate lunge left for a very thin edge, and gain the break. Leaving this is problematical, but the wall above is easier. Still considered to be the hardest route on SE Wales sandstone.
M.Crocker, M.Ward, R.Thomas 11.12.1988

Boston Strangler Area

Following the path further to the right, is a bay with a prominent rectangular wall, normally marked by a waterfall.

49. Boston Strangler   21m   E5,6b   Fr7b

Boston Strangler climbs the corner for 6m to avoid the waterfall at the base, then steps out onto the left wall, to gain and climb the centre via tricky, hard to on-sight moves.
M.Crocker 00.00.1990

50. Exhumation Corner   20m   E2,5c

A 'never-dry' route up the obvious angled, slabby corner. Probably better as an ice route.
R.Thomas, M.Learoyd 00.00.1989

51. Balance Sheet   21m   E1,5b   Fr6a

The centre of the slab forming the right wall of the corner is delicate and enjoyable.
R.Thomas, M.Learoyd 00.00.1989

52. Expense Account   24m   E3,5c

Follow a faint groove in the right-hand side of the slab, to gain a thin diagonal crack. Follow this leftwards to join the finish of Balance Sheet.
M.Learoyd, R.Thomas 00.00.1989

53. Cashflow Crisis   25m   E2,5c   Fr6a+
The right arete of the wall, climbed on its right above the ledge at 18m. It can be made harder and better, by avoiding the use of the holds on Balance Sheet at the top.
G.Ashmore 03.05.1998

The next route lies in a bay at a higher level. It can be accessed from the start of Cashflow Crisis. Trend right across a ledge and under a roof. Continue for a few metres to gain a bay up on the left.

54. Open Project   8m
The left-hand line on the right wall of the bay.

55. Wert's Famous Taxi Ride   8m   E2,5c   Fr6b
A good route taking the crack just left of the right arete of the bay.
G.Ashmore 01.05.1999

The Upper Quarry
Described as approached from the left-hand banking of the quarry entrance. About 100m into the tier is an awesome tower (resisting the obvious Frank Zappaism, we continue), which contains Desert Storm. There are some shorter buttresses leading up to this tower and a large slabby wall. The first routes, however, start in the small bay right at the start of the tier.

56. Hedge Of Time   8m   S
The short arete at the start of the upper tier, PR. BB.
R.Thomas 07.05.1997

57. Conan's Boil   8m   VS,4c   Fr4+
The short wall immediately upon entering the tier, PR, to the visually stunning lower off.
R.Thomas 07.05.1997

58. The Lapse   8m   E1,5c   Fr6a+
The wall and flake right of the corner.
R.Thomas 07.05.1997

59. Roraima   9m   E3,6a   Fr6b+   *
A good, short route up the centre of the little tower up and right of The Lapse.
R.Thomas, G.Gibson 23.03.1997

Futher right is a clean wall above a terrace.

60. Three Men In A Goat   12m   E3,6a   Fr6c   *
The left-hand route on the terrace, keeping out of the crack to the left.
R.Thomas 02.04.1997

61. Once Bitten   12m   E1,5c   Fr6a
The centre of the wall to a tree.
R.Thomas, M.Crocker 00.00.1991

62. Twice Shy   12m   E1,5b   Fr5+
The right-hand line on the terrace wall.
R.Thomas, G.Gibson 23.03.1997

Up in the trees, 6m to the right is a short arete.

---

63. **Hollow Feeling**   12m   E2,5c   Fr6a+
The arete proves quite exciting at the moment! 3BRs, PR, BB.
M.Learoyd, R.Thomas 00.00.1991

64. **Practice What You Preach**   12m   E3,5b   \
Climb the centre of this wall to the same BB. Why do the anti-bolters not do this route?
M.Crocker, R.Thomas 00.00.1991

Just to the right is a large slabby wall, forming the first area of rock to run the full height of the tier.

65. **Pampered**   20m   E2,5c   Fr6a+   *
The left-hand arete of the slabby wall
R.Thomas 14.04.1997

66. **You Change Me**   27m   E3,6a   Fr6c   *
The centre of the slabby wall. No longer bold, but a little harder than the original version, having shed holds and gained an optional problem start by avoiding use of the banking on the left. At the top of the arete swing right to the belay out on the slab.
M.Crocker 00.00.1991

67. **Nappy Rush**   27m   E2,5c   Fr6b   ***
The line to the right of You Change Me is absolutely brilliant with good holds all the way up.
R.Thomas 00.00.1997

There is a never-dry project up the corner right of Nappy Rush. A large sandstone tower now rears up from the quarry floor.

68. **Torch The Earth**   24m   E5,6c   Fr7b+   *
A route with a real stopper move. The tall can dyno, the short have to make a horrendous static move Sounds unusual, but you will soon see why. Start at the left arete of the tower and climb to a borehole and TR. Climb the slab to a couple of tricky moves up a crack and a good rest. Rock up the wall to the undercuts. Fall off repeatedly, go away and grow 6" then come back to complete the monster stretch to the easier upper wall. There is no lower off at present so abseil off the tree or top out - both are exciting! TR, PR, BRs.
M.Crocker, R.Thomas 27.01.1991

69. **Dirty As A Dog**   24m   E2,5c   Fr6a+   **
Start below the left arete of the tower and follow it with interest to brilliant moves left of the capped niche to a BB, in a splendid position. It is possible to start up the slab to the left of the starting groove at 6a.
R.Thomas, G.Royle, M.Learoyd 00.00.1991

70. **Desert Storm**   24m   E5,6a   Fr7a+   ***
A stunning route, sustained though never too hard, but the crux is at the top. The leaning, orange, right-hand wall of the tower. Start at a vague triangular niche and follow the wall directly to a good shakeout just before the crackline. Make hard moves up the slanting crack and swing right to a good shakeout jug. From here, step left and make a massive rock up back left to the BB. The top BR may now be missing as someone took the staple out before it was glued.
M.Crocker, R.Thomas 27.01.1991

To the right of the tower containing Desert Storm is a more moderately angled wall:

71. **Twenty Second Chance**   18m   E4,6c   Fr7a+
To the right of a loose corner is a steep face. Climb the blunt arete directly, with a very tricky move at 5m, then finish easily up the arete to a sapling and a BB out on the right.
M.Crocker, R.Thomas 26.01.1991

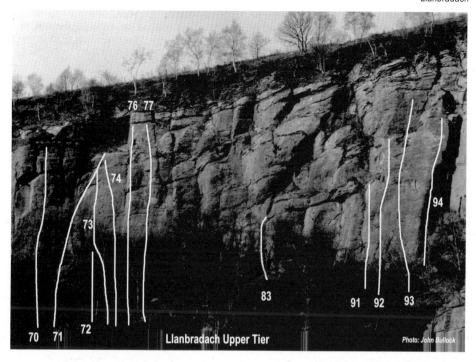

Llanbradach Upper Tier

Photo: John Bullock

72. **Sixty Second Go See**   21m   E4,6a   Fr7a   *
The wall to the right of the arete offers short but brilliant tips pulling. Finish up Roaring Forties.
M.Crocker, R.Thomas 26.01.1991

73. **Roaring Forties**   21m   E2,5c   Fr6a+   *
Start up the shattered flaky groove to the right and follow a curving flake onto the easy upper slab and the common BB.
R.Thomas, J.Bullock 00.00.1989

74. **Between The Lines**   21m   E3,5c   Fr6b
Climb directly up the wall right of Roaring Forties to an undercut and straight up the wall above, making a slight detour onto a flake out left at 14m. At the last BR, move left to the BB.
R.Thomas, G.Royle 00.00.1991

75. **Dirty Day Out**   21m   E3,5c   ● \
The groove on the right. The situ gear is currently missing.
J.Bullock, R.Thomas 00.00.1989

The rock now becomes more complex. To aid location, the next slightly slabby arete is Harrowed Harrovians, the obvious tall blunt arete to the right is Blinded By Love and much further on, the last big slab contains You Are What You Is.

76. **Harrowed Harrovians**   27m   E3,6a   Fr6b+   *
The big, slabby arete.
R.Thomas, Old Harrovians 00.00.1998

77. **Saboo** 27m E3,6a Fr6c
The big slab to the right has an obvious capped groove at 18m. Climb boldly up the slab to gain the niche, then either move left (the original finish), or right (harder), round the roof to the ledge. Make a hard move up off the ledge to gain the BB.
M.Learoyd 00.00.1989
G.Ashmore, J.Tracey - Direct 17.06.1997

78. **Dandelion** 27m E2,5c Fr6a+
To the right is a slim corner groove before the corner proper. Climb this to a BB below the roof.
M.Hirst 08.04.1997

79. **Burdoch** 25m E2,5c Fr6a+
The wall to the right of Dandelion.
M.Hirst 06.06.1997

80. **Blinded By Love** 21m E3,5c Fr6b+ **
To the right is a damp corner followed by an arete. Climb the arete from its bottom left-hand side to an awkward top out to the tree belay. Sustained and well worthwhile.
R.Thomas, G.Royle, M.Learoyd 00.00.1991

81. **The Laughing Policeman** 27m E3,5c Fr6b
The square-cut groove immediately right of Blinded By Love only dries out to an acceptable state in mid-summer, which is a shame, as the upper groove is good. Take care with the monster loose block.
R.Thomas 13.07.1997

82. **Fair Cop** 25m E2,5c Fr6a+ *
The next groove to the right. Take care with the flake at 18m and take a lot of quickdraws.
R.Thomas, G.Gibson 24.05.1997

83. **Aptitude Test** 12m E4,6b Fr7a *
The blunt arete 3m to the right.
M.Crocker 00.00.1991

84. **The Merthyr Infill** 12m E3,6a Fr6c
The wall right of Aptitude Test.
G.Gibson 23.03.1997

85. **My Blue Bell** 12m E1,5b Fr5+
The groove to the right of Aptitude Test.
G.Gibson, R.Thomas 18.05.1997

86. **All Sand Together** 18m E4,6a Fr6c+
The blunt arete to the right of My Blue Bell, stepping right at the third bolt to finish up Red 'Erring.
G.Gibson 18.05.1997

87. **Red 'Erring** 18m E3,5c Fr6b+
Straight up the wall right of We All Sand Together, with a bold finish.
G.Gibson, R.Thomas 18.05.1997

88. **Plaque Attack** 12m E2,6a Fr6b+
To the right is a corner, followed by a slab leading up to a roof. Follow the left-hand bolt line on the slab to the BB below the roof.
G.Gibson, R.Thomas 00.00.1997

---

89. **Incidentally**   12m   E2,6a   Fr6b+
   The slab and arete just right to the BB of Plaque Attack.
   G.Gibson, R.Thomas 23.03.1997

The next feature is an impressive slab, containing the best of the routes at this end of the tier, including an original sandstone classic.

90. **Cop The Lot**   11m   E4,6b   Fr7a
   The blunt rib on the far side of the dirty groove right of Incidentally.
   G.Gibson 24.07.1997

91. **The Caerphilly Cop Out**   11m   E4,6a   Fr6c+
   The blunt rib and short wall just right of Cop The Lot.
   G.Gibson 24.05.1997

92. **I Am What I Am**   18m   E2,5c   Fr6b   **
   The longer line to the right of The Caerphilly Cop Out, starting up the flaky groove.
   G.Gibson, R.Thomas 24.05.1997

93. **You Are What You Is**   21m   E3,6a   Fr6b+   ***
   The line right the way up the slab, just right of centre. Superb. A maturing sandstone classic from the late Giles Barker. The top BB is not glued at the time of writing - use the BB on I Am What I Am for the time being.
   G.Barker, R.Trevitt 00.00.1989

94. **Is It What You Are That Is**   21m   E3,6a   Fr6c   **
   The impressive arete bounding the right-hand side of the slab, on its overhanging side to half-height, then the left hand side thereafter. Sustained and pleasantly exposed.
   G.Gibson, R.Thomas 18.05.1997

LLANTRISANT DRUGSCLIFF

GR0448377

PREAMBLE
A very sheltered and fast drying little crag, albeit of somewhat limited scope. Worth a visit in conjunction with Coedely or Trebanog.

ACCESS
This is the small quarry, the top of which is just visible to the east of the A4119 on Llantrisant Common. Although there is an easier way in through the housing estate, this is harder to describe, so take the described approach on your first visit, and walk out right via the path to the estate to find the best way for any subsequent visits. Park in the superstore complex and walk back up and turn down the A4119 (Rhondda) road. Walk down this for $1/_4$ mile to just before a roundabout. Cross the road (E6 in bad traffic) to a footpath sign by a tarmac area. Follow the zig zag path up the hill to reach the quarry in 5 minutes,

THE ROUTES

1. **Something To Do With Drugs**   12m   E2,5c   Fr6a+
   The left-hand bolt line in the quarry.
   Llantrisant Deal Team 00.00.1991

Llantrisant

2. **After Effect**   9m   E1,6a   Fr6b+
   The slab to the right has a hard start, but is easy thereafter.
   Llantrisant Deal Team 00.00.1991

3. **Drugs Make You Fall Off**   12m   E2,6a   Fr6b+
   As for After Effect to the second BR, then move left to the second BR on Something To Do With Drugs, finishing as for that route.
   Llantrisant Deal Team 00.00.1991

4. **Virgo Intactae**   9m   HVS,5a   Fr5   *
   The crack at the right hand side of the face. 2PRs, BB.
   Llantrisant Deal Team 00.00.1991

5. **Ant Hill Mob**   11m   E1,5c   Fr6a+
   A route up the arete to the right, climbed on its right hand side. 2BRs, PR. There is no lower off and the PR is in cheese, so it is better to climb back down.
   The Ant Hill Mob 00.00.1992

6. **Unnamed**   9m   VS,4a
   The wall in the bay to the right. Quite loose and muddy. TB.
   Llantrisant Deal Team 00.00.1991

7. **Crackola**   9m   VS,4a   \
   Climb a vague rib 4m right of the corner to a tree belay. Abseil.
   M.Crocker solo 25.10.2000

LLWYNYPIA

GR993938

PREAMBLE
A reasonably good crag in a nice setting. Unfortunately it does get pretty lichenous and retains moisture more effectively than Oil of Ulay. The main section of the quarry is on the far side of the obvious pool, but there are some buttresses and a small natural section about 100m left of the entrance to the complex. The right-hand end has a lot of potential for new routes including what looks like a couple of old aid routes (no details). Some 25 routes are alluded to in the 1973 SWMC guide, but details seem to have been lost for all but the eight described in it, which would otherwise yield a staggering 38 lines.

ACCESS
Go through Llwynypia via the A4119 or B4293, to a steep right hand bend, with the prominent new Magistrates Court on the left. Turn left in front of the court and park on the road. Go into the woods on the right via a gate and follow the obvious track up the hill for about 300m to enter the quarry. If on foot, the railway station is right next to the court building.

THE ROUTES

Left Hand Section
Located about 100m left of the path leading to the quarry entrance.

1. **Led Astray**   9m   E3,6a
   At the far end of the left section are two buttresses forming a right angled bay. This is the central face of the left-hand buttress, passing 2 stacked PRs.
   E.Travers-Jones, A.Sharp, P.Lewis 16.04.1992

2. **Ylide**   9m   E1,5c
The arete to the right of Led Astray climbed on the left side throughout.
S.Coles 05.04.1992

3. **Nowhere Man**   8m   HVS,5b
The same arete climbed on the right side.
R.Lawrence 05.04.1992

4. Perverted By Language   9m   E4,6c   Fr7b
The right-hand buttress leans slightly. At its left end is a faint groove. Climb this desperately past a BR and PR. Blood blisters are compulsory.
G.Ashmore 05.04.1992

Main Section
The Main Section is dominated by a pool. Routes can be reached by walking over the small dam wall. Behind the dam is an obvious buttress and a diagonal terrace at a higher level.

5. **Bathtime**   12m   HS,4c   \
A nice line on rotten rock up the steep crack at the top of the diagonal grassy terrace.
Unknown Pre-1973

6. **Bernard's Balls Up**   12m   E3,6a   *
The wall immediately left of the obvious offwidth behind the pool, PR, finishing up a flake crack 1m below the top. A good fingery number.
M.Crocker, R.Thomas 08.04.1989

7. **Maz**   26m   VS,4c
The obvious offwidth and the overgrown corner above and left.
Unknown Pre-1973

8. **Greet Whoppin Jugs**   12m   E4,6b
To the right of Maz and directly above the dam is an obvious arete. Climb this to a PR, then step left and climb the technical upper slab.
C.Evans, A.Jenkins, P.Green 00.00.1992

9. **Calling The Shots**   12m   E4,5c   **
The excellent arete above the little dam. The PR on Greet Whoppin Jugs is not clipped at this grade. The start of the route is currently problematic due to the tree.
M.Crocker, R.Thomas 08.04.1989

10. **Well Heeled**   12m   VS,4c
The crack in the centre of the slab down and to the right of Calling The Shots.
R.Thomas, M.Crocker 08.04.1989

11. **Calcaneum Crunch**   12m   E2,5c   *
Above Well Heeled is a grassy terrace. This route climbs a faint groove in the right hand side of the slab, past a low PR which is the only gear. Committing and airy.
R.Thomas, M.Crocker 08.04.1989

12. **Free Wales Army**   15m   E1,5b   *
The arete down to the right of Calcaneum Crunch, starting on the left is better than it looks, PR. Hard for the grade.
M.Crocker, R.Thomas 08.04.1989

The exact line of the next three routes is not known for sure.

13. **Whatah**   12m   VD   \
The layback crack up the corner to the right of a small arete to a grass ledge. Finish up the wall, with a move out left.
Unknown Pre-1973

14. **Scream**   12m   S   \
To the left of Whatah, climb the corner and fractured crack to the grass ledge on Whatah. Take the crack at the back of the ledge to the top.
Unknown Pre-1973

15. **Phil's Arete**   15m   D   \
The arete to the right of Scream. Poor, with loose rock.
Unknown Pre-1973

16. **Harbour Wall**   15m   S   \
The centre of the prominent red wall.
Unknown Pre-1973

17. **Alibi**   15m   E2,5c   \
The central wall in the penultimate bay of the quarry.
M.Crocker, R.Thomas 08.04.1989

18. **The Brawl**   12m   E3,6a   \
The crack to the right.
M.Crocker, R.Thomas 08.04.1989

MOUNTAIN ASH

GR057985

PREAMBLE

A good, popular crag. Basically the quarry is a large overgrown box, although all but a few of the routes are vegetation free and in cleared areas. Apart from the routes in the main left-hand bay the routes dry quickly and are slime free. The rock is mostly very good except for the trad routes in the central section. All the sports routes are well equipped, although some have only a single BB at present so topping out/abseiling from trees is strongly recommended. The left-hand section is a series of orange walls and a good sun trap in winter. The right-hand section by contrast is shady and can be damp, but does stay dry in light drizzle due to the trees. Between these two sections are some short easy slabs for the novice sports climber and a short terrace - the Sports For All Wall. There is also a poor natural sandstone edge, up and left from the quarry proper and a recently re-discovered better one some 300m to the right. Please stop stealing lower-off crabs from this crag.

ACCESS

If on foot, take the train to Mountain Ash, and leave the station onto the first road encountered. Turn left, and follow the road out of the town for about 400m to a track crossing through an old works. Go through this and continue over a footbridge. From the end of this footbridge cross the road and walk straight up to the main road (A4059). Turn right and proceed for about 400m to the last few houses in Mountain Ash. Turn left onto the estate and immediately left again, then take the first right to an obvious track leading uphill past some garages. Where the track veers off right, scramble up the bank to a path and follow this rightwards to enter the quarry.

If coming by car, simply follow the A4059, and take the first turning right after the first few houses to reach the same spot. If you pass a garage on the left you have gone too far. It is possible to park on the estate.

THE ROUTES

Mountain Ash Northern Natural Buttress

The natural buttress running leftwards from the left-hand side of the quarry. Starting in a small bay in the centre of the natural section.

1. **Spittle Jacuzzi**   8m   HVS,5b
   Climb the overhanging crack on the front left-hand face.
   Cardiff University MC c.1975

2. **Fist In Vice**   8m   HVS,4c
   The crack on the left-hand side of the bay proper.
   Cardiff University MC c.1975

3. **20 Years In Llangattock**   8m   E1,5c
   Climb the starting crack of Getting Fatter, but pull left to climb the wall on slots.
   G.Ashmore, R.Thomas 27.05.2003

4. **Getting Fatter**   8m   VS,4c
   A left hand start to the chimney starting up the jam crack.
   Cardiff University MC c.1975

5. **The Spam Tree**   8m   S
   The large chimney.
   Cardiff University MC c.1975

6. **Another Toss Gobbler**   8m   VD
   Climb the centre of the square wall in the back of the bay.
   Cardiff University MC c.1975

7. **Crocker's Pot**   8m   S
   The centre of the buttress to the right.
   Cardiff University MC c.1975

8. **Pork Pie Driller**   8m   S
   The arete just to the right of the overhangs.
   Cardiff University MC c.1975

The Quarry Proper

At the extreme left end of the quarry are some broken walls.

9. **What's The Arc De Triomphe For Then?**   9m   E1,5c
   Left of the main section of this orange wall is a section of poorer rock, guarded by vicious brambles in summer. At the extreme left is a short slab with one hard move past a BR and no real belay.
   J.Williams 00.00.1992

10. **The Old Firm**   18m   E3,6a   *
    Follow the centre of the rib/pillar to the right to a wide terrace, BR, PR. Follow the short crack above to finish, PR. PB, but it is better to belay on the tree above.
    C.Evans 00.00.1992

11. **Coggers Lane (John You Prick)**   9m   E2,5c
    To the right is an overlap, which is climbed past a BR to the terrace. Finish up The Old Firm or belay and walk off right.
    C.Evans, P.Green 00.00.1992

12. **Beef Tasting Strawberries**   6m   S
Unbelievably poor. The short square pillar just left of the good orange wall, climbing past an extremely poor bolt.
A.Jenkins 00.00.1992

The Orange Walls
The prominent orange walls and aretes at the left hand end of the quarry are superb and a real suntrap in winter.

13. **Outspan**   11m   E4,6b   Fr7a+   **
At last, a real quality route, although a retro-chip has made things a bit easier than before. Takes the left-hand line on the orange concave wall. Very fingery and a bit committing to start.
M.Crocker, R.Thomas 25.09.1988

14. **Ripe And Ready**   14m   E5,6c   Fr7b+   *
Unbelievably hard for those with a short ape index (E4,6b for the tall). Start just right and follow the corner (easier) or climb direct to the second BR. Either way arrive at the third BR and make an absolutely massive dyno from a poor egyptian to good holds and an easy finishing wall.
M.Crocker, R.Thomas 27.10.1988

15. **Pastis On Ice Direct**   12m   E4,6b   Fr7a+   *
The striking arete starting from a lower level on the right is gained from below and slightly right. It has a very powerful move from a book-like flake at the top.
E.Travers-Jones 23.05.1995

16. **Pastis On Ice**   14m   E4,6b   Fr7a+   *
The original way, coming in from the right to the obvious ledge.
M.Crocker, R.Thomas 25.09.1988

17. **Cointreau**   12m   E5,6b   Fr7a+   ***
Classic. The obvious, pocketed, orange wall to the right.
M.Crocker, J.Harwood 17.04.1994

18. **Choice Cut**   8m   E2,5c
Up right, just left of a black lichenous wall, is a thin, short crack. Poor.
P.Donnithorne, A Price 07.11.1988

19. **Blacker Than Black**   6m   E3,6b   Fr6c+
The bolted boulder problem just right. Poor.
M.Crocker, J.Harwood 17.04.1994

At at lower level in front of the last routes are some shorter walls.

20. **Branch Manager**   6m   E3,6c   Fr7a
Starting from the quarry floor is a steep wall forming the left hand side of a cleared bay. Left of the main orange section is a single bolt marking this route (use a clip stick)!
R.Thomas 31.03.1996

21. **Totally Stumped**   8m   E2,6b   Fr6c+
A naughty chipped route up the vague scoop left of the rounded arete.
R.Thomas 21.03.1995

22. **Molybdenum Man**   8m   E3,6a   Fr6c   *
A splendid little problem up the aforementioned rounded arete. Deceptively hard.
M.Crocker, R.Thomas 27.10.1988

Gary Gibson - Mother of Pearl (Fr7a+) Cwmaman
(Page 398) Photo: Hazel Gibson

Goi Ashmore - Mad at the Sun (Fr 7c) The Gap
(Page 420) Photo: Carl Ryan

23. **Ferndale Revisited**   9m   E5,6b   Fr7b   *
A horrendously technical wall, just right of the arete, which has got considerably harder since the loss of some holds. Wimping out left along the scoop near the top reduces the grade.
A.Sharp, P.Lewis 22.04.1989

24. **Dusk**   11m   E4,6b   Fr7a+   *
Another short problem just left of the main corner. BB right over the sloping top. This route has become progressively harder since the first ascent as loose flakes have dropped off.
E.Travers-Jones 21.03.1995

The Slabs

25. **I Came**   12m   E2,5c   Fr6a+   *
Right of the angle of the corner is a slab with a headwall. This route takes the left-hand side of the slab and subsequent headwall.
R.Thomas 22.03.1995

26. **He Sawed**   6m   VS,5a   Fr5
A short but worthwhile line up the shorter section of the slab just right.
R.Thomas 22.03.1995

27. **Into The Valley Of Death**   6m   S,4c
Right again is a long continuous section of short slabs, separated from the last route by an earth-filled chimney. This route mantles awkwardly onto the right-hand arete of this chimney, then steps up and left along a natural line of ledges for 3m before finishing direct. Unprotected.
G.Ashmore 26.03.1995

28. **I Conkered**   5m   E1,5c   Fr6a+
The first bolted line to the right, 1BR.
R.Thomas 22.03.1995

29. **Taking The Pith**   5m   S
A route up the slab to the right.
R.Thomas 22.03.1995

30. **Bring Back The Birch**   6m   VS,4c   Fr4
The slab 6m to the right, 1BR.
R.Thomas 22.03.1995

31. **Under The Axe**   9m   E2,6a   Fr6b+
Just to the right is a prominent v-groove at the top of the slab. Climb the rib down and left of this past 2BRs, stepping into the v-groove at the top. BB.
R.Thomas 22.03.1995

32. **No Barking Up This Tree**   8m   VS,5a   Fr4+
The wall just to the right with one tricky move. 1BR, BB.
R.Thomas, P.Donnithorne 23.03.1995

33. **A Sight For Saw Eyes**   9m   E1,5c   Fr6a+
The wall at right angles to the main slab has a dynamic start. BRs, BB.
R.Thomas, Paul Donnithorne 23.03.1995

34. **Carpet Bombing** 9m VS,4c
Just to the right is the square arete of Tragedy. This route takes the slab left of Tragedy to the same BB, passing some chopped BRs. Please do not replace these as they interfered with the unprotected (and better) Tragedy. Llantrisant Deal Team 00.00.1995

35. **Tragedy** 9m E1,5a *
The square-cut arete to the right is unprotected and rather good. BB.
M.Crocker, M.Learoyd, R.Thomas, P.Lewis 09.10.1988

36. **The Future Holds** 11m E5,6b Fr7b *
The wall immediately right, with a tricky middle section and a horrific rockover to pass the top bolt.
M.Crocker 16.10.1988

Central Section

37. **Belgium** 27m VS,4c
The loose and vegetated groove system bounding the big slab in the centre of the quarry on its left. David Bellamy might approve, but you won't.
M.Capron, G.Lewis 00.00.1987

38. **Narcissi** 27m E1,5b *
The line of the following route has never been particularly obvious, so watch out. Climb Belgium for 8m, then move right to a groove in the centre of the slab, PR. Move up left to a crack, which is followed to the upper slab. Gain the final v-groove from the left. Worthwhile, but watch out for loose rock moving up to the final groove.
G.Lewis, J.Boyle 00.00.1987

39. **Rising Sap** 26m E2,5b Fr6a+ **
One of the longer clip-ups on sandstone and at a reasonable grade. Start just right of the centre of the slab. Follow the obvious bolted line to finish up the right arete of the Narcissi groove.
R.Thomas 00.00.1995

40. **A Clip Round The Year** 9m E5,6b Fr7a+
Some odd holds have 'disappeared' to create a harder and better proposition. 50m right of Rising Sap, before the obvious Sport For All terrace is a corner, with a steep left hand wall, split by a diagonal crack low down. Climb the wall left of (but using) the crack, past 3BRs, crux. Instead of following the holds out right, pull straight up on a couple of big crumbly pockets past a poor PR to a BB.
A.Sharp, P.Lewis 03.03.1991

41. **No Chips Round Here** 17m E5,6b Fr7b **
Better. As for the last route, but follow the bolts out right on superb but widely spaced buckets to a BB.
G.Ashmore 12.07.1995

42. **Helmet Man's Day Off** 11m S
The left line up the slabs at right angles to No Chips.
M.Hirst 13.07.1995

43. **Ant Frenzy** 11m S
The right line.
M.Hirst 13.07.1995

44. **Homebase** 25m E1,5a
Right again and just before the start of the Sport For All Terrace is clean slatty arete. Climb this (creaky in places) to a meadow. Scramble off up the back wall somewhere.
G.Lewis, G.Barker 00.00.1989

Sport For All Terrace

Just right is the start of Sport For All Terrace, a ledge starting 6m above the quarry floor. Rising from it is a short fingery wall, South Wales answer to Mur Zappa! There are BBs at the start of some routes.

45. Little Polvier   25m   VS,5a

The corner bounding the left end of the terrace and the subsequent crack.
G.Lewis, A.Keward 00.00.1989

46. Slap Happy   9m   E4,6a   Fr6c+

The first route starting from the Sport For All Terrace. Take a thin left-trending crack past BRs to an awkward step right to the BB.
A.Sharp, P.Lewis 11.04.1991

47. Sport For All   9m   E5,6c   Fr7b+   *

The 'blank' face to the right is not as blank as it at first appears, especially given the strangely jagged 'solution' pocket high up. Quite thin.
A.Sharp, P.Lewis 31.03.1991

48. Sporting Supplement   9m   E2,5c   Fr6a+   *

A smart pitch up the scoop to the right, with a devious finish.
P.Lewis, A.Sharp 13.04.1991

49. Sunday Sport   9m   E3,5c

The thin flake to the right has a bold start, 1PR.
A.Sharp, P.Lewis16.04.1991

50. Abdominal Showman   9m   E3,6a   Fr6b+

The flake left of the corner. This is supposedly Fr7c if climbed directly, but this is too really too contrived. The arete to the right is the top section of the next route.
A.Sharp, P.Lewis 13.04.1991

Main Bay

Back down on the quarry floor, is the obvious right-angled main bay, with some long, quality routes, as well as some dross.

51. A Certain Peace   14m   E2,5c   Fr6a+   **

Named in memory of Bob Powles who was found dead near the bottom, having slipped off when setting up an abseil. Start from the quarry floor, below the arete that separates Sport For All Terrace from the main bay. Climb the wall under the arete, to gain the arete, which is followed to its end. Finish up a short crack to a BB.
R.Thomas, M.Crocker 27.10.1988

52. Misadventure   14m   E4,6a   Fr7a   **

A superb, rather well cleaned route up the wall to the right of the arete and left of the diagonal crack, is climbed awkwardly to the BB of A Certain Peace.
R.Thomas 12.07.1995

53. A Far Cry From Squamish   15m   E4,6a

The diagonal crack. The rock is not exactly perfect.
M.Crocker 22.07.1990

54. The Theory And Practice Of Glue Sniffing   17m   E4,6a   Fr6c+   •

Follow Jetlagged for 5m, then swing left below the ledge to gain an arete. Slap up the blunt arete to gain a ledge and slim corner, then follow the slim corner and continuation flake to the top.
G.Ashmore 12.07.1995

55. Jet Lagged   17m   E3,6a   Fr6c   *
A bouldery crux section up the wall left of the main corner, gives access to a large resting ledge. Finish easily up the wall above.
M.Crocker 22.07.1990

56. Sennapod Corner   21m   HVS,5a   *
The big right-angled corner crack is usually overgrown, but worth a star when clean. Step left at the top to avoid poor rock.
P.Thomas 00.00.1970

57. Whiter Than White Wall   18m   E5,6b   Fr7a+   *
The wall right of the corner has one very hard move (a dyno) that is much easier for the tall. Good.
M.Crocker, M.Ward 21.05.1988

58. A Load Of Rubbish   20m   E2,5b   *
The series of cracks right of Whiter Than White Wall, PRs. Better than it looks.
A.Richardson, A.American 00.00.1984

59. Valleys Initiative   20m   E5,6a   Fr7a   **
The best route up this wall. Follow a line of pockets and coal breaks to a hard finishing section. Hard to on-sight.
A.Sharp, J.Harwood 04.10.1991

60. Ain't As Effical   20m   E3,5c
The dirty crack to the right. Not as stable as it looks. A couple of PRs might be handy!
M.Crocker, M.Ward, G.Jenkin 21.05.1988

61. Grave Concern   18m   E2,5c   Fr6a+
The wall to the right.
R.Thomas, E.Rees 00.00.1998

62. Final Plot   18m   E2,5c   Fr6a+
The wall right again.
R.Thomas, E.Rees 00.00.1998

63. The Entrepreneur   18m   HVS,5a
Climb the ramp and wall 6m to the right. PR, tree runner. Abseil from the tree.
M.Ward, M.Crocker, G.Jenkin 21.05.1988

Moutain Ash Southern Natural Buttresses
There are a couple of rediscovered edges about 300m south of the quarry. To gain them, follow the path up the right bank of the quarry, then follow a fence and path off right until opposite the first of three red factory buildings on the valley floor. The first buttress is directly below, the second about 50m further on.

The first buttress is a small, square lump with an undercut front face.

64. Dr. Foster And Confused Of Gloucester   7m   VS,4b   ⟍
The left side wall of the buttress.
G.Ashmore, R.Thomas 27.04.2003

65. Vertical Drain   7m   HVS,4c   ⟍
The left-hand side of the arete.
G.Ashmore solo 27.04.2003

---

66. **20,000 Llangattocks Under The Sea**   7m   HS,4b   ↖
    The undercut crack on the right.
    G.Ashmore solo 27.04.2003

The second buttress is a much more impressive pillar of rock. Reach the base by descending left, walking around the front, then climbing down a tree.

67. **Once More Off To The Beach Dear Friends**   20m   HVS,5a   *   ·
    As for Angel Flakes to the ledge, then climb the wall left of the blunt arete past some good micro-friends. Now I bloody well will be after finishing this ******g guide.
    G.Ashmore, R.Thomas 26.05.2003

68. **Angel Flakes**   20m   VS,4c   **
    Climb the blunt arete from bottom to gain the mid-height ledge. Leave this taking care with some flakes and continue up the arete to finish up a short wall. The right (overhanging) arete can be used as an alternative start at HVS,5a.
    M.Crocker Pre-1978

NEATH ABBEY QUARRY

GR724985

PREAMBLE
A big bramble infested quarry similar to the upper tier of Llanbradach but steeper. There is quite a bit of seepage. Most of the routes are sports routes, but the gear consists of 8mm bolts in a grid iron at exactly the same interval, making clips awkward. The PB lower offs are dubious. Some of the routes may not have been done yet. Access is a major problem and it is highly probable that one of the residents, a stipendiary magistrate, will insist that you leave.

ACCESS
The large quarry above Neath Abbey visible from the M4. Leave the M4 at J44 and follow signs to Birchgrove (B4291). At the first church turn right, drive along this road for about 2 miles and where the road contours right, park just beyond a wooded area. Head up through new estates to reach a path which is followed to eventually reach the quarry.

THE ROUTES

Grid Iron Wall

1. **Unnamed #1**   21m   E6,6b   Fr7b+   **   ↖
   The left-hand bolt line, passing a big pocket.
   A.Sharp etc. 00.00.1994

2. **Unnamed #2**   21m   E6,6b   Fr7b+   **   ↖
   The central line.
   A.Sharp etc. 00.00.1994

3. **Unnamed #3**   21m   E6,6c   Fr7c+   **   ↖
   The right-hand line. Said to be very hard.
   A.Sharp etc. 00.00.1994

4. **Unnamed #4**   12m   E4,6a   Fr7a   ↖
   The wall at right angles to Grid Iron Wall.
   A.Sharp etc. 00.00.1994

5. **Unnamed #5** 20m E3,6a Fr6c

Round to the right is a capped groove containing a BR. Climb up the crack to this and move left and up (crux). Pull round the roof, and onto the slab, which is climbed past BRs and PRs to a BB.

A.Sharp etc. 00.00.1994

PENALLTA

GR138948

PREAMBLE

A good quality sandstone outcrop, probably the first scene of early sandstone exploration. The friction is excellent and the crag dries rapidly after rain. Protection can be a bit sparse on the harder routes and some of the flakes in the 'Scabs' and 'Klingon' area are a little brittle.

ACCESS

If on foot, from Ystrad Mynach train station proceed down onto the main road, turn left, and walk up the road for 200m. The crag is now visible over on the right and is accessed by the obvious track leading leftwards across the fields. If approaching by car from Ystrad Mynach, pass under the railway bridge on the A472 and take the first right which leads into a housing estate. Take the first left into Griffith Street and park on the rough road on the right-hand side at the end of the street. An obvious path leads left across the fields to arrive at the crag in about 300m.

THE ROUTES

The crag has a somewhat scrappy middle section, left of which is the prominent undercut pinnacle taken by Scabs. This pinnacle splits the two upper amphitheatres. Right of the central section is big slabby face capped by a large roof. Left of the pinnacle is a sharply undercut buttress and a final small bay. The routes are described from left to right, starting from this bay.

Penallta
Photo: Carl Ryan

Far Left Hand Bay

1. **Limbo**   8m   VS,4c   *
The short arete at the extreme left-hand side of the crag, on its left.
Unknown Pre-1973

2. **The Leap**   8m   HVS,4c
The wall immediately right of the arete, finishing up the left-hand side of the arete.
Unknown Pre-1973

3. **Cornflake**   11m   HVS,5a
The wall immediately to the right.
Pre-1978

4. **Afterthought**   14m   HS,4b
The obvious overgrown corner, swinging left into the crack at the top, which provides the only real difficulty.
Unknown Pre-1978

5. **Cadet's Route**   12m   VD
The wall just right of the corner, exiting via a crack in the wall above.
Unknown Pre-1978

6. **The Wolery**   14m   S
Start immediately left of Spiney Norman and climb the wall just left of the crack, to finish up a crack just left of the chimney.
I.Jones Pre-1973

7. **Spiney Norman**   14m   HS,4c   *
Round to the right is an undercut buttress, at the left-hand end of which is a large boulder. Make a bold rockover, and continue up the slab to a generous terrace, stop for a picnic, then finish up the large chimney at the left-hand edge of the shelf.
I.Jones Pre-1973

8. **Anarchia**   20m   E2,5b
The overhang on the left side wall of the buttress, just right of the Wolery, bold. Finish up on shelves just right of the chimney.
C.Parker 00.00.1983

9. **Rhymney And Cocaine**   6m   E4,6c   *   \
A very powerful boulder problem up the vague flake halfway along the upper terrace (gained from Y-Fronts) PR, with long sling.
G.Ashmore 28.09.1997

Lower Left Hand Amphitheatre

10. **Y-Fronts**   21m   S
The right-hand side of the undercut buttress marks the start of the lower left hand amphitheatre. There is an obvious chimney in the left-hand wall. Climb the slab which forms the left side of the chimney until an obvious traverse line leads out left onto the terrace. Finish as for Spiney Norman.
I.Jones 1973-1978

There are several good boulder problems in the roofs around this area.

11. **Split Crotch Variation**   18m   E1,5b   *
Climb the corner right of Y-Fronts directly to the roof and a very wide bridge (the Third Severn Crossing). Swing out left above Y-Fronts, then take the wall above the right hand end of the terrace to an exciting finish on slopers.
C.Hurley 00.02.1978

12. **Maginot Line**   9m   E1,5b
A poor line. Start up Split Crotch Variation and reach a pocket in the right wall. Use this to swing right to the top of Klingon.
A.Sharp 00.00.1976

13. **Klingon**   8m   E2,5c   *
The blunt arete to the right has a hard start, little if any gear and a dyno off loose flakes to a good flat topped ledge. Slide off into the Upper Amphitheatre to finish.
S.Lewis 00.00.1976

14. **Eeyore's Gloomy Place**   15m   VD
Very apt. The dense tropical forest just right of Klingon. Finish up the unpleasant chimney at the left-hand side of the upper amphitheatre.
I.Jones Pre-1973

15. **Pinnacle Chimney**   15m   D
Start below the tree growing out of the centre of the bay. Follow the steps up to the upper amphitheatre and finish up the chimney directly behind.
Unknown Pre-1973

16. **Dinsdale**   15m   S
The obvious crack in the right wall. Finish up the right-hand chimney of the upper amphitheatre.
I.Jones Pre-1973

17. **Too Risky**   15m   VS,4c
As for Dinsdale for 5m to the break, then traverse right to a ledge. Climb up to the huge ledge above the front face of Scabs, and finish either left or right with little interest.
T.Penning Pre-1985

Upper Left Hand Amphitheatre

18. **Hell For Pleasure**   9m   E1,5b
The left-hand wall of the amphitheatre.
C.Court 00.00.1984

19. **Sheer Pleasure**   9m   E1,5b
The face immediately right of the righ- hand chimney.
T.Penning Pre-1985

Pinnacle Area

20. **Stitches On Scars**   12m   E5,6b   *
Right of Too Risky on the left hand side of the lower part of the Scabs pinnacle is a jug by a prominent PR held in with 6" nails. Stick Clip this, as many of the holds in the roof are now much looser. Make a huge dyno for the jug, then make hard moves right and up to finish,
M.Crocker, R.Thomas 04.03.1989

21. **Stitches Direct**   12m   E6,6a   *
Start up Scabs, but pull left to gain the base of the arete and finish up this. Very bold.
G.Williams 00.00.1997

22. **Scabs**   12m   E3,5b   **
The most famous route on the crag. Start directly below the main overhang and power up to a tricky step right
to a horizontal flake. Move up and left to finish. Please do not place protection this route - the gear will not hold
and the crucial flake will be destroyed.
P.Littlejohn solo 00.00.1982

23. **Shriekback**   12m   E5,6a
Horrid. The roof right of Scabs, via two pockets and a wafer thin flake, to a blind jump for a hold just left of a
protrusion just above the lip of the overhang. Slap up again, then move left to finish up Scabs.
C.Parker 00.00.1983

24. **Shag Rat**   21m   E1,5b
Easy for the grade with the crux low down. Start from a rocky platform on the right of the pinnacle and climb the
wall directly behind on good pockets. Mantle out right to land in the upper right amphitheatre, then follow jugs
directly up the leaning wall, keeping as near to the left-hand arete as possible.
P.Thomas 00.00.1976

Upper Right Amphitheatre

25. **The Last Waltz**   12m   D
From the corner of the amphitheatre, traverse left out along the ledge to the front of the pinnacle and finish direct.
Unknown Pre-1973

26. **Bold Finger**   6m   VS,5b   *
A superb one move wonder. Take the obvious finger crack through the overhang to exit on the left wall of the
amphitheatre.
A.Sharp 00.00.1976

27. **The Sighting**   9m   VS,4c
The fist-sized crack just left of the corner, surmounting the overhang on a very loose flake.
J.Harwood solo 05.04.1978

28. **The Gibbon**   14m   S
The large corner-crack of the bay, which is better than first appearances suggest.
Unknown Pre-1973

29. **Sheer Hell**   14m   E2,5b   *
The obvious wall to the right, with an awkward undercut start and a grassy finish. Technical Friend and small
RPs useful for the start, Friend 4 useful for the top.
J.Harwood 03.10.1975

Central Section

30. **Sennapod**   25m   HS,4b
Follow the runnel leading into the right hand amphitheatre from the base of the crag. Step out right onto a grassy
ledge, then climb the arete above.
L.Parsons, I.Jones Pre-1973

31. The Horticulturalist 25m S,4a

To the right is a short crack, which is followed to a ledge. Douse the whole area liberally with Agent Orange. Proceed up the wall above and head for a tree over on the right. From the tree climb the arete just to the right, taking care with the rock.
Unknown Pre-1973

32. The Herbiculturalist 25m S ●

Climb the wall just right of the initial crack of the previous route to a ledge and move left over a bulge to surface at a larger ledge. Climb the corner above, finishing either right or left as the mood takes you. The mantle onto the ledge at 5m is currently under a heap of slag.
P.Watkin Pre-1973

The Big Slab

33. Free Wall 25m S

Climb the wall just right of the obvious flake crack passing a bulge to reach the large ledge (The Prow). Finish up the corner.
I.Jones Pre-1973

34. Devils In Hell 25m VD

The obvious flake crack leading up to The Prow. Finish up Free Wall.
Unknown Pre-1973

35. Direct Finish 9m VS,4c *

From the Prow, make a hard swing up the short right-hand arete. Finish directly up the slab above.
I.Jones Pre-1973

36. Western Roll/Free World 27m E1,5b **

Climb the centre of the buttress between the two flake cracks at the base of the crag. Continue straight up to the big ledge under the roof. It is possible to wimp out left here (HVS,5a). Old BB. From the BB, make a hard move up left into a groove, 2PRs and climb easily through the roof to a hard move round the lip. Finish direct.
M.Crocker - Free World 00.00.1975
G.Lewis - Western Roll 00.00.1975

37. Arse Trad Mynach 6m E3,6a

Straight over the roof to the right passing a very old BR and a bendy PR.
M.Crocker – A2 Route A2 Pre-1978
FFA G.Ashmore 28.09.1997

38. Aaron The Amorous Aardvark 24m S

Start right of Western Roll and climb the wall to the first ledge. Stomach traverse through Western Roll, to join Devils In Hell. Follow this for 5m until it is possible to move right into a diagonal crack. Follow this to a sloping ledge, then go up and right to gain the ledge below Free World. Wander off right.
I.Jones Pre-1973

39. Pushover 20m VS,4b

To the right are two obvious cracks at 5m. Take the flake crack below and follow the left-hand crack. Gain the finishing ledge via a thinner crack slightly to the left.
P.Thomas Pre-1973

40. The Pusher 20m HVS,5a

The right-hand crack is tougher. From the top, step right to finish up the obvious crack.
I.Jones Pre-1973

41. **Alley Crack**   18m   S,4a   *
Up and to the right of The Pusher is a pair of less prominent cracks. Gain the left-hand crack via the flake crack right of The Pusher and overcome the intervening bulge.
M.McMahon Pre-1973

42. **Alley Oop**   18m   S,4a   *
The right-hand crack, gained via the short wall below.
Unknown Pre-1973

43. **Thin Chimney Finish**   5m   HVS,4c   *
The way gnarly grim reaper on wheels finish from the large ledge, via the thin chimney to the right of the roof of Free World. Not recommended for bloaters. The reversal of this route is quite hard.
Unknown Pre-1973

44. **Giggler's Arete**   18m   E1,5b
Climb the arete to the right of Alley Oop, placing some gear and using the crack of Alley Oop just before the top. Very contrived.
J.Harwood 05.04.1978

45. **Rainmaker**   30m   VD
Takes the easiest line on this section of rock. Usually done in two pitches. Start at the extreme right-hand edge of the crag below the obvious dirty gully. Swing onto the small ledge and traverse left to the final corner of Pushover. Climb the wall to the left to a large hole and move left to mantleshelf onto the sloping ledge. Belay on the Prow, or continue up the easy corner moving right at the top. Largely superseded by The Higher The Fewer.
Unknown Pre-1973

46. **The Higher The Fewer**   35m   HVS,4c
A girdle. Climb Alley Oop to the base of the crack, then traverse off and left into the corner. Continue to a tree, then go up to a large ledge and belay. From the belay climb up to a holly, then cross the wall of Sheer Hell, via the obvious break. Finish up The Gibbon.
I.Jones Pre-1973

There is also a low level traverse of the crag, from the right hand side as far as Y-Fronts at 5b. This can be extended to the end of the crag at 6a, with the crux being to get past Y-Fronts without trailing your feet on the ground or getting your underpants dirty.

PENRHIWCEIBER QUARRY (CEIBER PASS)

GR053978

PREAMBLE
Censored. The place is also a rubbish tip, and on the checking visit we found half a dead dog in a plastic bag, with its guts hanging out. Even this valleys culinary delicacy could not persuade us to stay.

ACCESS
From the A4059, take a left turn over a railway bridge signposted to Abercynon, until the end of the one way system. Turn right at the Mount Pleasant Inn and follow the road up the hill until it finishes. The crag is reached by following the dirt track up the hill (obvious). Warning - do not leave anything in your car. If on foot, walk from Penrhiwceiber Station to the Mount Pleasant Inn. Warning – Do Not Go, this place makes Gandamak look like a spa town.

THE ROUTES

Penrhiwceiber

1. **Pickhead Arete**   18m   E1,5b   \
Start 3m left of the arete bounding the left-hand side of the crag, and scramble up towards it, PR. Climb the arete on its right for 5m, before swinging back round left to finish. BB.
E.Alsford, P.Donnithorne 00.00.1991

2. **Edgeware**   17m   E4,6b   \
Start just right of the grassy left-hand corner of the crag, beneath a blocky groove. Climb this groove until it is possible to move directly up the slab passing 3BRs. PB, BB over on the right.
P.Donnithorne, E.Alsford 00.00.1991

3. **Landfill Project**   18m   E3,5c   \
As for Edgeware to the grassy ledge, then move right, PR and go along another grassy ledge until below the second line of BRs. Climb the slab past 2BRs until it is possible to move left to a common belay with Edgeware.
P.Donnithorne, E.Alsford 00.00.1991

SIRHOWY

GR974955

PREAMBLE
The Rust Curtain is perhaps the best sandstone wall in the area. This is quite a large quarry of rusty sandstone with a heavily overgrown floor, although given the good path round its base, this is not so much of a problem as with other quarries out west. At the extreme left-hand end of the crag is the impressive unbroken Rust Curtain, which dries rapidly, providing the seepage season is over. About 100m to the right is another smaller wall, containing the rest of the routes, which unfortunately seeps quite badly.

ACCESS
Leave the M4 at J27, and follow the A467 towards Risca, then the A4048 towards Abercarn. Just before the industrial estate is a roundabout. At the roundabout carry straight on (signposted 'Sirhowy Country Park') and park up. Follow the track into the park to reach the crag on the left-hand side 250m beyond the visitor's centre. It should be mentioned here that there is no official access at present. However, visits after park closing time (5.30-6.00pm) have not caused a problem, provided that climbers understand that they climb at their own risk and keep a low profile. The crag is not really accessible via public transport.

THE ROUTES

The Rust Curtain

1. **Gott In Himmel**   12m   E4,6b   Fr7a   *
The left-hand bolt line on the wall proves technical. It is harder and more interesting than first appearances suggest.
R.Thomas, S.Coles 09.05.1996

2. **Butcher Heinrich**   14m   E5,6b   Fr7a+   *
The line up the vague groove at the left-hand end of the Rust Curtain. Fingery, with a massive reach at the crux.
M.Crocker, R.Thomas 00.00.1989

3. **Strange Little Girl**   14m   E3,5c   Fr6b+   **
Start 3m to the right. Climb a discontinuous and sustained crack.
R.Thomas, M.Crocker 00.00.1989

4. **King Ada**   15m   E5,6b   Fr7b   **
The wall to the right. Start at a square-cut groove under an overlap. From the roof swing left to a good flake. A line of spaced jugs up the wall yields best to a moderately dynamic style, leading to a shakeout below a PR. The finish involves a gigantic reach off a small pocket for a rounded break.
G.Gibson 07.04.1996

5. **Skanderbeg**   14m   E6,6b   Fr7b+   **
The hardest route on the crag. As for King Ada to the overlap, then out right on a flake to a very difficult move out right. The climbing relents slightly around the cheesy break, then a trying and thin sequence leads to the upper sloping break. Head right on disposable rock to the top.
M.Crocker, R.Thomas 11.06.1989

6. **King Zog**   14m   E5,6b   Fr7b   *
Climb the crack to the right, which cuts through the roof on jams. Continue direct.
M.Crocker, R.Thomas 11.06.1989

7. **Face**   14m   E5,6b   Fr7b   *
To the right is an obvious square-cut jug in the overlap taken by Mawr, Mawr, Mawr. This is the line to the left, which proves thin in its upper reaches.
G.Gibson 06.04.1996

8. **Mawr, Mawr, Mawr**   14m   E4,6a   Fr6c+
Climb to the square-cut jug, make a long rock out right to a vague crack and follow this to the top horizontal break. Clipping the BB is desperate.
G.Gibson 06.04.1996

9. **The Crimson King**   14m   E4,6a   Fr7a   *
The wall to the right of Mawr, Mawr, Mawr and left of the thin tree.
G.Gibson 06.04.1996

10. **VIP Lunge**   12m   E3,6a   Fr6c   *
The wall to the right of the sapling is climbed via technical moves out from the hollow flake. Step left to square-cut jugs and move up to the horizontal break for another desperate BB clip.
R.Thomas, G.Gibson 06.04.1996

11. **Hostility Suite**   12m   E3,6a   Fr6c   *
A technical number keeping just left of the arete of the wall. The top stretch for the belay is absolutely miles - if you do not know about the jug on the arete out right.
R.Thomas, G.Gibson 06.04.1996

The Western Walls

12. **Deaf As A Post**   12m   E4,6b   \
At the right-hand end of the quarry is a blind crack in a friable wall. Start below the centre of the wall, scramble up to the highest ledge to just below an overlap. Pass this via a huge reach, BR, to a short crack. From the top of the crack swing left to good holds and an ab-station. This route could not be located during guidebook checking, due to ivy growth.
M.Crocker, R.Thomas 00.00.1989

TON PENTRE (YSTRAD)

GR974955

PREAMBLE

A small quarry with surprisingly good rock, especially on the mildly leaning wall taken by most of the routes. It dries quickly and is sheltered. There are some lower offs, but it is advisable to back them up with a rope from fenceposts at the top. Many of the PRs are missing, although all the routes have been repeated in their current state.

ACCESS

Pass through Ystrad on the A4058, then turn right by a disused church with a prominent fountain. Drive up the hill, bearing right to a terrace overlooking Ton Pentre. Park here. Walk through the gate, cross the fence to the right and contour round this to reach the quarry in about 100m. If coming on foot take the bus or train to Ton Pentre and follow the same description as above.

THE ROUTES

1. **Alone And Blue**   11m   E3,5c
    The left-hand side of overhanging back wall, just left of the first crack, (missing PR - use Friend 1½) to a break. Finish up a slight crack to a PB.
    R.Thomas, G.Royle 00.00.1990

2. **Help The Aged**   12m   E1,5b
    The crack immediately to the right.
    R.Thomas, M.Learoyd 00.00.1990

3. **The Road To Nowhere**   12m   E2,5b
    The crack to the right, TR, proves bolder than expected, and is slightly loose in places.
    R.Thomas, M.Learoyd 00.00.1990

4. **April Fool**   12m   E3,5c
    Used to have 5PRs (not an April Fool Joke), but now has only one. 3m right is a vague crack, followed to a shelf. Move up and left, then up the headwall to a BB out left.
    M.Learoyd, R.Thomas, L.Foulkes 00.00.1990

5. **Spirit Of Ystrad**   12m   E4,6a   *
    Mean and fingery. Start up the wall to the right, RP and Friend ½. Make hard moves up onto the shelf, PR. Move up and slightly right, 2PRs, crux, to a BB.
    M.Learoyd, R.Thomas 00.00.1990

6. **Shins**   12m   HS,4a
    Climb the slatty wall at right angles to the last route, then move out right along the huge ledge. Finish direct from its right hand end.
    A.Eggleton solo 14.05.1995

7. **Tom Tom Club**   15m   E2,5b
    Start in the large depression in the bay right of the wall housing all the other routes. Climb the prominent tower, with a hard and quite bold start, then finish more or less direct. Only one of the original 3PRs remains.
    R.Thomas, E.Travers-Jones 00.00.1990

TREBANOG

GR013903

PREAMBLE
A moderately good, pretty solid, low-lying crag, with a sunny aspect and many routes in the lower grades. It can occasionally be windy. Unfortunately, there is a lot of broken glass at the bottom of the crag, and visits with dogs are probably not wise for this reason. There are plenty of concrete fenceposts to belay on at the top of the crag. Due to its relatively easy angle and climbing and solid rock, a large number of extremely trivial filler ins have been claimed. As many of these as possible have been included, but you will need two plumb balls, some string and a ruler to climb them independently.

ACCESS
Take the A4233 to Trebanog, taking the Tonypandy turn off at the traffic lights in the centre of the village. The crag is 200m down the road on the right hand side, above the obvious parking space. If on foot buses run up from Porth.

THE ROUTES
At the left-hand end of the crag is a short wall with a sharp left-hand arete.

1. **Howell's Arete**   6m   HVS,5a
   The arete at the extreme left hand side of the crag is climbed on its left.
   T.Howell 00.00.1988

2. **Howell's Arete Right**   6m   HVS,5c
   A good extended boulder problem up the arete on its right-hand side.
   T.Howell 00.00.1988

3. **Pete's Boulder Problem**   6m   E2,6c
   The brushed wall to the right of the arete.
   P.Lewis 00.00.1995

4. **Loose Stuff**   6m   VS,4b
   The vague line of slightly broken cracks at the right-hand side of the sheet of solid rock. Poor.
   Unknown Pre-1990

5. **To The Left**   6m   VS,4b
   Another poor line slightly to the right.
   Unknown Pre-1990

Bolted Overhanging Wall
This is the first substantial area of rock enocountered.

6. **One Upmanship**   6m   E1,5c
   On the left-hand side of the wall are some thin cracks. Climb them with more difficulty than might be expected.
   M.Learoyd, C.Nash, G.Lewis 00.00.1988

7. **March Of Progress**   12m   E5,6b   Fr7a+   *
   The blankest section of rock left of the central hairline crack, is gained directly and climbed with a hard crux BR, 2PRs. Using holds in For Your Hands Only reduces the grade to E4,6a.
   A.Sharp, P.Lewis 00.00.1990

8. **For Your Hands Only**   12m   E3,6a   *
   The central crackline. The top section is protected either by an RP4 or a Friend 3!
   A.Sharp 00.00.1984

Trebanog Left
Photo: Carl Ryan

9. **Banog's Barmy Army**   12m   E4,6a   Fr6c+   *
Straightened out since the first ascent. Start right of For Your Hands Only, gain the ledge and then move right,
BRs, PRs. Swing left over the overhang to finish on huge holds.
A.Sharp, P.Lewis 00.00.1990

10. **Grab Some Tree And Follow Me**   12m   E4,6a   Fr7a
Start to the right of Banog's Barmy Army and left of the corner. Avoid bridging the corner. Climb to a break at 3m,
crux, poor PR, then pull up to a BR under an overlap. Pull left round this, then make a committing stretch for a
poor jug and a PR. Finish direct.
A.Sharp 00.00.1991

11. **Aunty Pasty**   12m   HVS,4c
The unlovely corner to the right.
G.Lewis, H.Griffiths 00.00.1988

12. **Unnamed #1**   12m   E1,5a   \
The wall to the right of the corner, swinging right past a missing PR to finish up Airplay.
J.Harwood 17.03.1990

Main Area

13. **Air Play**   12m   VS,4b   *
The arete to the right and the crack directly above.
G.Lewis, H.Griffiths 00.00.1988

14. **Playing Away**   12m   HVS,5a
The wall immediately to the right and the overhanging headwall immediately above the ledge.
H.Griffiths, SWMC 00.00.1988

15. **Bushbaby** 12m HS,4a
Start in a hollow immediately to the right and climb a line up the left hand side to the top.
Unknown Pre-1990

16. **Skull Orchard** 12m VS,4c
A vague line somewhere to the right.
R.Lawrence, S.Coles 12.07.1992

17. **Twenty B&H And A Packet Of Rizlas Please** 11m HVS,5a
The centre of the buttress to the right.
S.Coles, R.Lawrence 06.12.1991

18. **Simon's Crack** 11m S
The crack to the right.
Unknown Pre-1990

19. **S.S.R.** 11m D
The chimney.
C.Shorrock 24.02.1992

20. **Jaffa Buttress** 9m HVS,5a *
The centre of the buttress to the right.
H.Griffiths, G.Lewis 00.00.1988

21. **Terry's Crack** 9m VS,4b *
The overhanging crack to the right.
T.Howell 00.00.1988

22. **Heatherette** 9m VS,5a
The bounding right-hand arete of Terry's Crack provides a couple of almost independent moves.
C.Shorrock, T.Darlow 26.11.1994

23. **Howell's Horror** 9m D
A nondescript line up the corner of the bay to the right, containing the prominent Flat Wall.
T.Howell 00.00.1988

24. **Tankard** 9m VS,4c
The crack to the right of the corner.
C.Shorrock, J.Whitford 24.02.1992

25. **Blagdon** 11m VS,4c
The shallow corner bounding the left-hand side of the obvious Flat Wall.
P.Hamer, R.Smith 00.00.1984

Flat Wall
The obvious rectangular wall, with an obvious sentry box in the centre.

26. **Firewater** 11m E2,5c
The left-hand side of the wall. Contrived.
A.Sharp, R.Smith 00.00.1984

27. **Hair Of The Dog** 11m E5,6a *
Dangerous. Climb direct up from the sentry box.
A.Sharp 00.00.1983

28. **Ethanol** 11m E3,5c
From the sentry box, head right and follow a line of flakes directly up.
J.Harwood 26.03.1990

29. **Unnamed #2** 11m VS,4c
The cracks to the right.
Unknown Pre-1990

To the right of the Flat Wall and as far as the nose (Ledge Climb) where the crag starts to double back towards the Black Chimney Area, are a number of short routes.

30. **Barlamb Abuse** 9m D
The first groove to the right of the Flat Wall.
Unknown Pre-1990

31. **Shteep** 11m VD
The cracked arete seperating Barlamb Abuse from Gambolling Groove.
C.Shorock, J.Whitford 24.02.1992

32. **Gambolling Groove** 11m M
The second groove.
C.Shorrock 02.01.1994

33. **Vaughan** 11m S *
Rather good. The vague blunt arete 6m to the right, starting on the left and traversing across to the right and a tricky finishing move.
A.Eggleton, C.Shorrock 02.01.1994

34. **Even Cheesier Than Barrow In Furness Bus Depot** 11m HVS,5a
To the right of Vaughan, climb the slab and the bulging wall directly above it.
C.Shorrock, M.Chapman 05.11.1994

35. **Even Sleazier Than Barrow In Furness Bus Depot** 11m HVS,5a
The slab to the right, then step right onto the prominent horizontal platform. Stretch up past a slot to finish.
G.Ashmore 26.04.1998

36. **Ledge Climb** 12m VD
To the right is the arete bounding the area. Go for it, coming in from the left.
Unknown Pre-1990

Big Black Chimney Area
Round the corner is a horrid soot-blackened chimney.

37. **Sunday Swing** 12m VS,4c *
Climb the wall just right of the arete of Ledge Climb to a horizontal break. Traverse right to an enjoyable swing right up a good crack above the apex of the chimney. Using the start of the next route is a better option with no change in grade.
G.Lewis 00.00.1988

38. **Out With The Boys** 11m VS,4c
Originally given E2,5c! Climb the thin crack in the left wall of the chimney, just left of where the soot starts. At the juggy break swing slightly left and finish direct on big greasy holds.
L.Foulkes, G.Lewis, M.Learoyd 00.00.1988

39. Fire Down Below   14m   E2,5a   ●
Bridge up the extremely dirty chimney, until a handrail of loose jugs leads left to the finish of the last route. Probably unrepeated in its current state.
G.Lewis, T.Howell, H.Griffiths 00.00.1988

40. Kiwis Can't Fly   12m   E1,5c
The thin crack in the right-hand wall of the chimney, finishing up the right-hand crack of Sunday Swing. Another poor route.
L.Foulkes, M.Learoyd, C.Nash 00.00.1988

41. I Spy Arete   11m   HS,4a   *
At last a worthwhile route! The arete to the right of the chimney.
M.Learoyd, SWMC 00.00.1988

42. I Spy Direct   9m   E1,5b
The wall to the right. Hidden RPs are available behind the flake above the half-height ledge.
M.Learoyd, SWMC 00.00.1988

43. High And Dry   10m   E1,5a
The crack line just right.
J.Harwood, R.High 17.11.1996

44. Eastend Groove   9m .   HS,4a
The crack in the left wall of the bay to the right.
H.Griffiths 00.00.1988

45. Blood   9m   E1,5b
An extremely contrived route up the wall between Eastend Groove and Mick's Little Viper, avoiding gear and holds on either of those routes.
T.Darlow 00.00.1995

46. Mick's Little Viper   9m   HVS,5a
The crack in the centre of the right-hand wall of this bay.
M.Learoyd 00.00.1988

47. Eastend Crack   9m   HS,4a
The next crack to the right.
Unknown Pre-1990

48. Desperate Arete   9m   S
The arete to the right.
Unknown Pre-1990

To the right is another bay.

49. Descent Route   9m   D
The cracks in the left wall of the bay.
Unknown Pre-1990

50. Hard Death Rain Down   9m   HS,4b
The wall and overhang to the right of Descent Route.
C.Shorrock, M.Chapman 05.10.1994

51. **Jo**   9m   VS,4c   *

In the right wall of the bay and left of the arete is a curving crack which is followed until it is possible to pull out left into a scoop. Continue up the headwall via a protruding block. Good stuff.
C.Shorrock, A.Eggleton 02.01.1994

52. **Last Arete**   9m   HS,4c   **

Obvious by name. Simply superb and probably the best route in the entire quarry.
Unknown Pre-1990

53. **Penultimate**   9m   HVS,4c

The wall immediately right of last arete. Bold with fragile holds.
G.Williams, J.Harwood 26.09.2002

THE SECRET TREBANOG (EDMONSTOWN QUARRY)

GR011904

PREAMBLE
A recent development by a power mad psychopath from the Lake District. The quarry is extremely poor, fairly loose and belays and loose earth are a problem. Obviously a typical high quality venue of the future. Only really attractive for people who like to get as dirty as possible.

ACCESS
This is the small quarry at the end of the track running leftwards from the top of Trebanog proper, see that crag for more details.

THE ROUTES
Are described from right to left as approached.

1. **Third Arete**   8m   D

The third arete from the right-hand side of the massif.
C.Shorrock, M.Hirst 04.02.1995

2. **Chocwert Orange**   8m   S

The cracked arete just left on its left-hand side. The top block is terminally wobbly.
M.Hirst 04.02.1995

3. **Greasin' Ma Bearings**   8m   HS,4a

The thin crack to the left.
M.Hirst 04.02.1995

4. **Hand Job**   8m   HVS,5a

The face left of the previous route is probably the best thing here. A hand placed peg is used for protection.
M.Hirst 04.02.1995

5. **Cheeter**   8m   VD

The poor loose wider crack to the left.
C.Shorrock, M.Hirst 04.02.1995

6. **Ji**   8m   VS,4c

The face and crack to the left, finishing direct.
C.Shorrock 04.02.1995

7. **Fungus Face** 9m D \
    The face right of the open book corner in the natural crag above the quarry.
    C.Shorrock, M.Hirst 04.02.1995

8. **Crank Extractor** 9m HS \
    The overhanging arete left of the open book corner.
    M.Hirst, C.Shorrock 04.02.1995

THE SECRET TREBANOG UPPER TIER

GR006907

PREAMBLE
An exposed natural edge, apparently of better quality than the Edmonstown Quarry.

ACCESS
The edge is usually reached by following the track leftwards along the skyline from Trebanog proper (above the Edmonstown Quarry area).

THE ROUTES
These are described from left to right when viewed from the base of the crag.

Pyramid Buttress
This is the first substantial buttress, with an obvious pyramid/conical form on its left-hand side.

1. **Scope For A Slope** 5m D
    The north-facing slab up and left of the pyramid.
    C.Shorrock 12.03.1995

2. **The Pyramid** 6m M
    The rounded left-hand arete of the buttress.
    C.Shorrock 01.03.1995

3. **Up And Over** 9m VD
    The crack in the centre of the overhanging wall to the right to a slabby finish.
    C.Shorrock, A.Potter 12.03.1995

4. **Two Tier Slab** 9m D
    The leaning crack and groove to the right, followed by the two-tiered slab above.
    C.Shorrock 01.03.1995

Square Walls Sector
Some 50m right of Pyramid Buttress lie two square walls. The left-hand one is virgin, the right-hand one contains the routes described below.

5. **Depression Arete** 8m HS,4b
    The left-hand arete of the wall.
    S.Coles 14.06.1995

6. **Enough Is Enough** 8m VS,4c
    The left-hand line on the wall.
    S.Coles 14.06.1995

7. **No More**   8m   VS,4c
The central line on the wall.
S.Coles 14.06.1995

8. **Fire Up Above**   8m   VS,4c
Start left of the right-hand arete, then follow this to finish left of the arete.
M.Salter, C.Shorrock 11.04.1995

9. **Cracking Up**   6m   VD
The crack in the side wall.
C.Shorrock 01.03.1995

Firecracker Buttress
Right of the Square Walls Sector lies a series of buttresses. Initially there are some short slabs, before the overhanging, ivy-covered wall.

10. **Laid Back But Slack**   9m   D
Left of the overhanging wall is an easy angled pillar.
C.Shorrock 01.03.1995

11. **Alpha 7 Hazard**   9m   HVS,4c
Climb the aforementioned overhanging wall and continue to the top.
S.Coles 14.06.1995

12. **Ash Tray**   9m   S
The right-facing arete 5m right of Alpha 7 Hazard.
S.Coles 14.06.1995

13. **Empty Plate**   9m   VD
The wall left of the prominent crack 5m right.
C.Shorrock 11.04.1995

14. **Firecracker**   9m   VD
The aforementioned crack.
C.Shorrock 11.04.1995

15. **Too Pooped To Scoop**   9m   S
The cracked, scooped wall 2m right of Firecracker.
C.Shorrock 11.04.1995

Main Slabs Sector
Well to the right of the last routes, the Main Slabs Sector is the obvious series of steep quarried slabs, identified by the fence at its left-hand end.

16. **Dismounting**   8m   M
The right arete of the square, scrappy buttress approaching from the fence.
C.Shorrock 11.04.1995

17. **The Pillar Rock Shock**   8m   VD
The small buttress set up and back from the others.
C.Shorrock 11.04.1995

18. **Chim Chiminee**   6m   M
The deep chimney 3m to the right.
M.Salter, C.Shorrock 11.04.1995

19. **Anchorage Slab**   11m   S
The main slab starting at a metal stake.
M.Salter 11.04.1995

20. **Columnar Joint Tin**   11m   HVD
The column of rock and subsequent slab above the bend in the main slabs.
C.Shorrock, M.Salter 11.04.1995

21. **Twisting Groove**   21m   D
The obvious twisting groove up the front corner of the prow.
C.Shorrock, M.Salter 11.04.1995

22. **Mini Groove**   9m   S
The slab and shallow groove right of the start bay of Twisting Groove.
M.Salter 11.04.1995

The Top Secret Trebanog - Hidden Overhang Buttress

Up and right of The Prow lies a low steep buttress with a large horizontal flake at its right hand end.

23. **Mantle Master**   5m   VS,4c
Climb an obvious niche on good holds to a vague crack finish.
J.Whitford, A.Potter 12.03.1995

24. **Tree Time Trundle**   5m   S
The niche with a tree at two-thirds height, via a crack in the overhangs.
C.Shorrock, A.Potter 12.03.1995

25. **Elbow Exit**   6m   HVS,5a
The niche to the right, passing through the overhangs to a hard finish.
J.Whiford, A.Potter 12.03.1995

26. **Green Bullet Drama**   6m   HVS,5a
The pillar to the right, finishing through overhangs. The last move is the crux.
S.Coles 14.06.1995

TREHAFOD

GR045911

PREAMBLE

Trehafod is a short, well sheltered, sunny and not very good little crag. On the positive side it takes little seepage, and stays dry even in light drizzle. The rock consists of a brittle skin of cheese-cake-like sandstone and is bolted. All the bolts are in the wrong place and at exactly the same height. This is a direct result of the height of the Ant Hill Mob's step ladder. There are PB lower offs on most routes although they are not very secure. A pre-placed abseil rope is strongly advised.

ACCESS

This is the crag behind and to the north of Trehafod railway station. If on foot take the train there and take the path leading out from the north side of the station. After 150m, a metalled road is reached, turn right to reach the crag more or less immediately. If in a car take the Trehafod exits off the A4225 carriageway. If coming from the south turn right just before the Industrial Heritage Park at the north side of the village, go under the railway bridge and park immediately under the crag (plenty of space). If coming from the north use your brains to read the directions in reverse or go back to school and take a GCSE in geography.

THE ROUTES

1. **Roaches Revisited**   11m   HVS,5b
   The crack at the left side of the crag. I hope it has a good lawyer for the forthcoming libel suit by the Roaches.
   C.Evans solo 00.00.1992

2. **Chris Evans, Baked Bean Superhero**   11m   E3,6a   *
   The wall to the right, 3PRs.
   C.Evans 00.00.1992

3. **Rave Crave**   11m   E3,6a   Fr6c   *
   12m to the right is prominent undercut buttress. Gain the centre of the wall above the overhang by a traverse in from the right, and climb the centre of the wall direct. 2BRs, BB. Anyone less than 6ft. had better have a good dental insurance scheme - the second bolt is in a daft place and a fall will result in an unintentional attempt to eat sandstone. The clip is semi-protectable with a small Rock.
   C.Evans, A.Sharp, P.Lewis 00.00.1992

4. **Rhubarb Lets Fly**   9m   E3,6a   Fr6c+
   The direct start to Rave Crave can be achieved by a stylish manoeuvre, although a massive lurch is more usual. Spotters advised.
   A.Sharp, C.Evans 00.03.1992

5. **Free Wales**   8m   VS,4b
   The crack at the left-hand side of the main wall, above the graffiti of the same name.
   M.Herbert, J.Carter, C.Evans 00.00.1992

6. **Missing Link**   11m   E3,6a   Fr6c
   The first bolt line to the right.
   C.Evans, I.Austin 00.00.1992

7. **Demi Moore**   11m   E3,6a   Fr6c
   The next one.
   A.Sharp, P.Lewis 08.02.1992

8. **Gorki's Zygotic Mynci**   11m   E3,6b   Fr7a
   The next one is the best and hardest on this wall.
   C.Evans 00.00.1992

9. **Unnamed**   11m   E3,6a   Fr6c   \
   The next one.
   Ant Hill Mob 00.00.1992

10. **Just Another One Move Wonder**   11m   E3,6a   Fr6c
    The last bolt line before the crack. The ring peg is dodgy.
    A.Sharp, R.Chard 16.02.1992

11. **Traverse**   18m   E5,6b   \
    There is a traverse along this main section starting up either the left or right bolt line and finishing up its counterpart. Exact details are not known. Clip the BRs en route.
    Ant Hill Mob Pre-1995

12. **Nasty Norman**   9m   VS,4c
Not bad. The large central offwidth on this wall.
J.Carter, M.Herbert, C.Evans 00.00.1992

13. **Sniffing Debrah's Pocket**   11m   E2,5c
Gain the large ledge to the right of the offwidth. Climb the wall above.
C.Evans, R.Chard 00.00.1992

14. **Cenotaph Norm Carter**   15m   E2,5c
Start above the 'Andi Capp' graffiti and gain the BR. Step up and right, traverse right to the BR on Discount Included In The Price and follow the same finish.
C.Evans, R.Chard 00.00.1992

15. **Discount Included In The Price**   15m   E2,5c   Fr6a+
The central line up the highest section of the wall.
P.Lewis, A.Sharp, C.Evans 08.02.1992

16. **Baldy Walks To Ponty**   15m   E2,5c   Fr6a+
Follow the groove 3m to the right, PR, then make an awkward move out left to a BR. Finish direct.
L.Ashton, R.Chard, C.Evans 00.00.1992

17. **Michelle Pfieffer**   12m   E3,6a   *
The best route on the crag. Follow the thin seam in the wall right of the angled corner with a hard start, PR. Continue up to a second PR (loose). There is a better wire down and right. Swing round the arete to a PB.
A.Sharp, P.Lewis, C.Evans 08.02.1992

18. **Beef Curry And Chips**   12m   HVS,5b
The arete itself climbed on its right-hand side, PB.
C.Evans, A.Sharp, P.Lewis 08.02.1992

TREHERBERT QUARRY (RHONDDA PILLAR)

GR934981

PREAMBLE
A great crag in a stunning position (especially if facing away from Treherbert). Not recommended in winter due to its exposed position. Plenty of scope for new routes. Some bolt belays are now available to replace/supplement the former belays (tied off earth mounds). The stake on the top is very shallow and should not be relied on as anything other than a rope guide for lowering off. The BB is hidden down the back of the pillar.

ACCESS
The crag lies up the mountainside above Treherbert railway station - a convenient way of arriving if on foot. If coming by car drive to the same place and park. Cross over the track to the far side of the railway, and follow a track left across a stream, then take the track up right. Continue up this for $^1/_4$ mile, until a trail breaks off left after a couple of bends where the track starts to flatten out. This track leads directly up to the crag in about 5 minutes.

THE ROUTES

Main Pillar
From right to left (as approached) and left of a free standing blocky pillar:

1. **Nailbiter**   18m   E4,6a
The leaning wall right of the obvious crack in the wall, 1BR, PR.
M.Crocker, R.Thomas 02.07.1989

2. **Thumbsucker**   18m   E4,6a   ***
   The classic finger jamming crack. The Mau Mau and the Heaven Crack of sandstone!
   M.Crocker, M.Ward 31.12.1988

3. **Nosepicker**   18m   E5,6b   **
   The arete to the left, 2PRs, BR.
   M.Crocker, R.Thomas 02.07.1989

4. **Bizarre Geetar**   18m   E3,5c
   The crack/wall/arete round the corner. PR (missing).
   M.Crocker, M.Ward 31.12.1988

5. **Lamb Leer Disease**   18m   E1,5b
   The dirty crack on the front face of the pillar.
   M.Ward, M.Crocker 31.12.1988

Main Bay

6. **Baker Day**   9m   HS,4b
   Over left from the pillar is a short wall rising from a ditch at the top of the banking. This route takes the chimney on the right-hand side of the crag.
   R.Thomas, M.Learoyd 00.00.1989

7. **Submerged By Blubber**   8m   E2,5b
   The crack and roof to the left.
   M.Crocker, R.Thomas 02.07.1989

8. **Little Big Ego**   9m   E2,6a
   The crack to the left stepping in from the boulders.
   M.Crocker, R.Thomas 02.07.1989

Back Crag
Round the back of the quarry, and over to the left is another pillar.

9. **Lynch 'Em**   12m   E5,6a
   This routes takes the leaning, unprotected groove in the south face of the pillar.
   M.Crocker, R.Thomas 02.07.1989

10. **Exterminate All Bolt Thieves**   12m   E4,6a
    A bold line to the right.
    M.Crocker, R.Thomas 02.07.1989

TROEDYRHIW

GR019078

PREAMBLE
An extensive and generally broken set of natural sandstone crags overlooking Troedyrhiw. There are a number of pleasant VS climbs up the centre of each buttress done by John Harwood, without fully recorded details. There is a buttress at a lower level at the right-hand end which comprises of a smooth slab on the left, and a bulging tower.

ACCESS
Approach the crag from the 4054, travelling northward, by taking the first (acute) righthand turn immediately before

Troedyrhiw and parking on a parallel unmetalled road after a left turn. The crag is 60m up the hillside, above a small reservoir.

THE ROUTES

1. **Solo Para Tos Zapatos**   12m   E4,5c
    Take a direct and unprotectable line up the centre of the tapering slab. A long stretch for a crux at the top but the rock is perfect.
    M.Crocker 26.12.1991

2. **Snow Jest**   12m   E6,6b   *   \
    The bold, bulging tower. Ascend a crack to an off-balance shelf. Launch out left (superb Rock 5 placement in a slot) and turn the arete to gain small fingerholds in the left-hand face. Make a committing crank for the horizontal crack and pull out right onto the arete to finish.
    M.Crocker, J.Harwood 04.04.1994

TYLE-Y-COCH QUARRY

GR214 957

PREAMBLE
This is a newly-developed quarry with some new sports routes and a fair amount of scope. The climbing is good although it is surrounded by trees and it may be necessary to abseil down to remove leaf debris before climbing the routes.

ACCESS
From J28 of the M4 take the A467 dual carriageway as far as the Halfmoon (Sirhowy/Crosskeys) roundabout. Take the third exit signposted A467 to Newbridge. Follow this road taking the third turning on the left after the mini roundabout at Pontywaun, into the village of Westend (not signposted). Drive through the village passing The Crown pub on the left. Approximately $^1/_3$m after passing all the houses a long lay-by is reached on the left. Park here.

From the parking area, follow the road back toward Westend for about 20m. Just before a wooden post on the right-hand side of the road, take a small track up to the right leading on to a broad incline of forested land. Walk along this until you come out on to a disused rail line (passing the painted arse on the left and then a small tunnel on the right just before exiting). The quarry is directly opposite you. It should take you less than five minutes to walk from the car.

THE ROUTES
The routes are described from right to left.

First Wall

1. **Lilly Of The Valleys**   8m   S   Fr3+
    A slabby line up a groove at the right-hand side of the crag. A Friend 2 protects the one awkward move.
    S.Abbott, J.James, W.Gladwin, D.Jones 04.02.2001

2. **Jumping Jack Flash**   7m   VS,4c   Fr4+
    Climb directly up the short orange wall, passing two bolts to the belay.
    S.Abbott, J.James, W.Gladwin 14.05.2000

3. **Enema Of The Affair**   12m   E3,6a   Fr6c   **
    Climb the arete via several tricky moves.
    J.James, W.Gladwin 14.05.2000

4. **High Moon**   12m   E2,5c   Fr6a+   *
   A good face route 2m left of the arete, with a good rockover at 10m.
   J.James, W.Gladwin 00.12.1999

5. **Suppose A Tree**   12m   VS,4c   Fr4+
   Climb the corner on the left side of the pillar, stepping left on to the wall at 8m. Climb the small overhang to finish.
   W.Gladwin, J.James 08.07.2000

6. **Buen Culo**   11m   VS,4b   Fr4
   Start 2m to the left of Suppose A Tree. Climb a short steep wall continuing up the narrow slabby wall above, trending slightly left to the belay.
   W.Gladwin, S.Abbott, J.James 13.05.2000

7. **Mal Culo**   11m   VS,4b   Fr4+
   Start in a shallow corner 2m to the left of Buen Culo. Climb the shallow corner, moving over the small overhang on the right. Continue directly above on the short slabby wall and small overhang to finish.
   W.Gladwin, J.James, J.Keyhole 07.05.2000

8. **The Ring**   10 m   S   3+
   Climb the same shallow corner as Mal Culo, but continue straight on to the overhanging prow of rock, turning this on its right. Step left to the belay.
   W.Gladwin, J.James 16.07.2000

9. **Bore Hole**   10m   S   3+
   Again climb the shallow corner of Mal Culo, but move left to follow a line of bore holes to the belay.
   W.Gladwin, J.James 16.07.2000

The Second Wall

10. **Cheeky Arete**   8m   S   \
    The short arete is started on the right. Move on the left side, PR and finish by scrambling left up the narrow ramp towards the belay.
    S.Abbott, J.James, W.Gladwin 14.05.2000

11. **The Big Tissue**   11m   E2,6a   Fr6b+
    Start 2m left of Cheeky Arete of Peachy. Climb and mantle over the overhang with difficulty. Easier climbing up the wall leads to a thin finish.
    J.James, W.Gladwin, D.Jones 13.05.2001

12. **Peachy**   12m   E3,5c   Fr6b+   **
    Start 2m left of the Big Tissue and make a tricky move onto a jutting hold to gain a bore hole. Move up with some difficulty and continue past an awkward overlap to finish at the top of a narrow ramp.
    J.James, W.Gladwin 14.07.2000

13. **Mislivings**   14m   E4,6a   Fr7a   **
    Start as for Peachy, but at the large borehole traverse left with feet below the small overhang and hands above. Climb the leftward-trending line from the edge of the overlap to a final roof and crux finish. A sustained route.
    J.James, W.Gladwin 22.06.2001

14. **Paradise Row**   15m   E4,6a   Fr6c+   **
    A sustained wall climb, with the crux at the top. Start 5m left of Mislivings and climb through an overlap to reach a break. Swing right to join Mislivings at its crux and follow this to finish.
    G.Gibson, R.Thomas 23.09.2001

15. **The Pink Lady**   11m   E3,5c   Fr6c   *

Start in the centre of the wall under a vague crack line. Ascend with difficulty to the small roof, where improving holds lead to a BB in the centre of the headwall.
G.Jenkin, W.Gladwyn, G.Gibson 16.09.2001

16. **A Cleft Stick**   15m   E4,6a   Fr7a   *

Follow The Pink Lady to the second BR. Step left and up to the overlap, pull through it to gain the break and finish up the headwall.
G.Gibson 23.09.2001

17. **Belly Up**   10m   E5,6b   Fr7b   **

Start 5m left of A Cleft Stick and follow a tricky initial crack to gain the overlap. Pull through this rightward to gain a hole and wide break. Swing left and finish up the tricky headwall.
G.Gibson, A.Jenkin, J.James, W.Gladwyn 16.09.2001

18. **Root Canal**   13m   E1,5b

The corner is climbed on natural gear to the belay.
J.James, T.Williams 23.07.2000

19. **Rump And Scoop**   12m   E1,5b   Fr5+   *

Ascend the arete 3m left of the corner.
J.James, S.Abbott, W.Gladwin 08.10.2000

On the face to the left of the arete are:

20. **The Black Circular Cat**   15m   E3,5c   **   \

Start at the left-hand end of the face, directly below the left end of a narrow ledge at 3m. Climb to the ledge with difficulty. Walk right along this and ascend a ramp, leading to a corner and overhang. Arrange gear and break out right using a very thin ramp line for feet, eventually gaining a good hold and the top.
J. James, S. Abbott, W. Gladwin 04..03.2001

21. **The Postman**   14m   E2,5c   \

Start as for the above route. Move along the ledge until reaching a thin crack. Use this and continue up right across the face to the corner. Follow this moving left to the top. Large Friends are handy.
J.James, J.Steer 20.05.2001

22. **Pecker Patrol**   12m   E1,5b   \

Start 1m left of the Postman. Climb the left hand edge of the wall to a PR. Pass this and move up and right to the large ledge.
J.James, S.Thompson, D.Williams, W.Gladwyn 16.09.2001

UPPER MOUNTAIN ASH

GR054002

PREAMBLE

Not the best crag in the world but worth a quick visit. It should have a pleasant sunny aspect on a good day and has a superb Chew-valley-esque outlook. However, it can be a wind tunnel. The crag dries quickly and takes minimal seepage. There is only one trad route here, but the sports routes have no lower offs, hence the need for a back up rope. Alternatively it is common place to jump back down the bolts.

ACCESS

From the traffic lights in Mountain Ash on the A4059 road, turn right as for Cefnpennar. Turn left at the T-junction, but then take the first right again. Follow this road uphill, to a right-hand turning, then take one of the left-hand turnings up a cul-de-sac ending in a very obvious cemetery. Park here, unless you have walked up (following signs for Cefnpennar when walking northwards from Mountain Ash station). Take the path running up the outside right of the cemetery wall, and overlooking a stream valley. Continue up the path for around 15 minutes to come across a 1m wide gravel track. Follow this rightwards for 400m or so up the hill until a large boulder is spotted down to the right of the path, exactly level with the start of a prominent stone wall on the other side of the valley. Leave a situ rope over this for belays. The crag still cannot be seen from here! Walk down and left from this point for 30m, until it is possible to double back right to enter the quarry.

THE ROUTES

1. **Co-Conspirator**   9m   E2,5b
Not bad. The jamming crack to the right of the right-hand arete of the quarry. There is a lower off tat round a sapling at the top, but a back up rope would be wise.
M.Crocker, R.Thomas 07.05.1994

2. **Stretch People**   11m   E5,6b   Fr7b   *
Good climbing up the prominent blunt arete on its left-hand side. The best thing here.
M.Crocker, R.Thomas 07.05.1994

3. **Irn Bru**   9m   VS,4b
The painfully obvious chimney offwidth in the centre of the wall left of Stretch People.
D.Irving etc. 28.09.1997

4. **Masai**   9m   E1,5c   Fr6a
A worthwhile little number with an awkward crux low down, following the clean wall 9m left of the arete, just before the corner.
R.Thomas 24.09.1994

5. **Chumbawumba**   9m   E3,6b   Fr6c+
A bit of a bag. A one move wonder up the short wall facing Masai.
M.Crocker, R.Thomas 07.05.1994

6. **African Head Charge**   11m   E5,6a   Fr7a   *
Not bold after the first clip, which is reached after a couple of pulls on rattly flakes. The wall round to the left of the last route, is conquered by a repetitive series of 6a finger cranks, which are blind, making it hard to on-sight, 3BRs. The top BR is a Bristol one. After the top BR, step left to a flake crack to finish.
M.Crocker, R.Thomas 07.05.1994

YNYSBOETH CRAIG-Y-SIOMI

GR077954

PREAMBLE
Possibly the most obscure crag on sandstone. The quarry that can easily be seen from the Abercynon to Aberdare road up on the hill behind the Gap proves a little disappointing if you are (un)lucky enough to find it. It does dry quickly and there is room for a couple more VSs and has the only graded jump in the area.

ACCESS
As for the Gap. Park or walk to the upper quarry and follow a vague track leading directly down from the Gap proper into the forest. Cross the fence, and go straight down through the trees following a direct unmarked line to come to a clearing after about 300m. Turn right, and proceed 100-200m to reach the quarry.

THE ROUTES

1. **Hallucinogenic Road Works**   9m   E2,6a
   The blunt arete on the left of the quarry, climbed on its right throughout, BR. No belay. Jump off right (J2).
   G.Ashmore, S.Coles 30.03.1992

2. **Stay At The Gap**   9m   VS,4c
   To the left is a narrow slab, located by the BB at the top. Start up a groove below this, then move left out on to
   the arete, skilfully avoiding the rocking block. Step right at the top, BB. Aptly named.
   G.Ashmore, S.Coles 30.03.1992

YNYSYBWL LADY WINDSOR QUARRY

GR053951

PREAMBLE
Superb little crag, now mostly underground. There used to be 18 routes here including the classic Paws For Thought
E3,5c**), Tickled Pink E3,6a*) and Ten Fingers On The Fender E4,6b**). These had their tops blown off and their
bottoms filled in (painful) in December 1991. RIP.

THE ROUTES

All these routes are defunct and are included as a matter of historical interest only.

Noddy's Revenge E1,5b (M.Hamilton, G.Lewis 1988), Monkey's Uncle E1,6b (A.Sharp, P.Lewis, P.Harding 1989),
Echo Man HVS,5a (G.Lewis, D.Hart 1989), Vote Wave Power HVS,5a (G.Lewis, D.Hart, A.Sharp, P.Lewis 1989),
The BMC Man's Groove VS,4c (Gwent M.C. 1989), Tickled Pink E2,5c (A.Sharp, P.Lewis, J.Harwood, G.Lewis
1989), You Are What You Is E3,5c (T.Foster, P. Harding 1989), Paws For Thought E3,5c (P.Lewis, A.Sharp,
P.Harding 1989), Fairweather E2,5c (G.Lewis, Dave Meek 1989), Ten Fingers On The Fender E4,6b (A.Sharp,
P.Lewis, J.Harwood 1989), Rent Boys E2,5c (A.Sharp, P.Lewis etc. 1989), Worker's Playtime E3,5c (T.Foster,
D.Hart 1989), Heartless Folly HVS,5a (D.Taylor, S.Cashmore, G.Lewis 1989), Lady Windsor E2,5b (G.Lewis,
D.Taylor, Other 1989), Chimney Sweep S (J.Custance 1989) and I've Got Your Nads HVS,5a (J.Davidge, D.Hart
1989)

YNYSYBWL UPPER QUARRY

GR054954

PREAMBLE
Pleasant sheltered crag, with sound rock, although there is frequent seepage on routes off the main slab. Protection
is sparse so dig out your gritstone head. The belay is frightening (a wobbly sapling in a collapsing shale bank) on the
routes off the main slab.

ACCESS
From the centre of Pontypridd take the Ynysybwl turn off by the main Police Station (B4273). Continue into Ynysybwl
and pass the post office on the right hand side. Take the gravel track 300m further on the right and follow this (remains
of Lady Windsor Quarry on the right) to a gate on the right, behind a new estate development. Park up. Follow the path
leading on, and climb over the fence into the field on the uphill side. Follow any of the vague paths up the hillside to
the obvious square-cut quarry. Buses also run from Pontypridd to Ynysybwl.

THE ROUTES

1. **For Pete's Sakes**   12m   E1,5a   *
   The left-hand line up the obvious central slab. Abseil from the tree.
   A.Sharp 02.02.1991

Ynysybwl Upper

2. **You Drip**   12m   E1,5a
The right-hand line on the slab. Abseil from the tree.
A.Sharp, P.Lewis, J.Harwood 02.02.1991

3. **Ass-Slider**   9m   E2,5c
The centre of the wall at right angles to the main slab, BR.
P.Lewis, A.Sharp, J.Harwood 02.02.1991

4. **Snowman**   8m   E3,5c
The short arete to the right on creaking flakes.
P.Lewis, A.Sharp, J.Harwood 02.02.1991

Goi Ashmore - Encore Magnifique (Fr7b+) The Gap
(Page 421) Photo: Carl Ryan

Gary Gibson - Giant Sand (Fr6c+) Llanbradach
(Page 436) Photo: Hazel Gibson

BOULDERING

Unfortunately, there is not too much scope for an extensive bouldering section in the guidebook and more information is best sourced from the web. By far the most popular and extensive sites are Coed Goitre for sandstone, the Trench at Ogmore and Box Bay. Here is a rough indication of what's available in stripped down format

Sandstone

Area	Grid Reference	Location	# Problems	UK Grades	Notes
Coed Goitre	085958 - 0779961	Above Abercynon.	120+	4a-6b	Extensive low sandstone outcrops.
Gap Boulder	079964	Just round from the Upper Quarry and on the Natural Bit.	10-15	4a-6a	Limited.
Not Navigation	084944 - 087940	Above the quarry itself.	30	4a-6b	Several areas scattered around the hillside.
Penallta	137948	Round the base of the cliff and on the boulders above.	30	4a-6a	Long low level traverse. Inventive footless things below Y-Fronts.
Ponty Common	077904 - 083902	By the football area and under the memorial.	20	4a-6c	Good, but limited with some inventiveness required.
White Rock	064911 - 056917	Runs along the hillside well west of The Darren.	60+	4a-6c	Extensive series of small boulders and edges of variable quality.

Gower

Area	Grid Reference	Location	# Problems	UK Grades	Notes
Caswell	587874 - 590874	As for Caswell in Gower Section.	30	4a-6b	Odds and sods
Graves End East	572864	As for Graves End East in Gower Section.	20	4c-6b	Good sheltered bouldering round the base of the routes with good landings.
Limeslade	625869	Just west of Mumbles below an ice cream parlour.	15	4a-6b	Decent little crag with reasonable landings (Not *that* Ice Cream van).
Oxwich	505860	Underneath Oxwich Quarry.	30	4a-6b	Half a dozen tidal boulders Normally better used for sunbathing.
Rotherslade	605870 - 612872	Approach from Langland Bay	25	4c-7a	Best bouldering on Gower.

Inland Limestone & Bridgend Area

Area	Grid Reference	Location	# Problems	UK Grades	Notes
Box Bay	587874 -	As for Caswell in Gower Section	30	4a-6c	Best bouldering in area. Loads of potential on the frozen wave.
Dinas	913081	The underside of Kennelgarth Wall	30+	5c-7a	Powerful overhanging stuff, with Tom Starkes Fr8b/+ thing.
Ogmore Estuary	867761	About 5 minutes walk down the river from the car park at the west of Ogmore village.	5	5b-6b	Good long traverses. Grade depends on height taken.
The Secret Beach	860751	Tucked away down on the beach, gain from Craig-Y-Eos Rd.	10	6a-6b	Very low level traverses on fat slopers.
Southerndown	883732	The long low roofs to the west of the car park at Southerndown.	5+	4c-5c	Mostly 5b traversing on big jugs which have an alarming tendancy to fail.
Sully Island	167760	The south side of the tidal island at Sully.	10+	4a-6b	Long easy traverses and a couple of harder things.
The Trench	866743	About 1/2 mile west of the start of the main crag at Ogmore	40	4a-6c	Well known area with lots of problems and a sandy landing.

SPORTS ROUTES GRADED LISTS

Limestone

Fr8b+
The Route Of All Evil

Fr8b
Inferno

Fr8a+
Masada
Black Wall

Fr8a
Three Turd Slab
Bloody Sport Climbers!
Palace Of Swords Reversed
Maesteg-A-Saurus
Dai Laffin
Sansarete
Hydraulic Lunch

Fr7c+
Fin
Senser
Welsh Fargo
Powers That Be

Fr7c
Durbin Two, Watson Nil
Totally Clips
The Regulators
Crock Of Gold
Thieving Little Scrote
The Morgue The Merrier
Grow Up!
Help, Help Me Rhondda
Whey It Up
Turkey Lurking
Chives Of Freedom
Hawaiian Chance
The Milkier Way

Fr7b+
Still Life
Bitchin'
Senser Part I
Rotbeest
Sport Wars
Subversive Body Pumping
Hypocritical Mass
Edge-More
The Uninvited Guest

Skull Attack
Skin 'Ed
Spore Wars
Time To Dai
Piss In The Sink
This Cod Is Mine
Two Of A Perfect Pair
Red Letter Day
Edge-Hog
Ambrosia Mountain
Incidentally X
Harlem
Red Snapper
The Oxwich Blobby
Power Struggle
The Overlook

Fr7b
Forty For Three
Kennelgarth
Rain Dance Dance
Pioneers Of The Hypnotic Groove
Staple Diet
Shot Yer Load
Straining At The Leash
Cannar Canard
Fings Ain't What They Used To Be
Dr. Van Steiner
Plus Ca Change
Settin Stone
Llandfill-A-Gogoch
Written In Red
Tortilla Flats
Security Plus
Crawling King Snake
Pour Marcel
Munsterosity
Trailblazer
The Sharp Cereal Professor
Its Tufa At The Bottom
Plum Duff
Danny La Rue
Red River Rock

Fr7a+
Ik Kan Mijn Ei Niet Kwijt
Runnel Vision
Beware of Poachers
Berlin
Missin' The Drink
Scream For Cream
Matt's Groove

Red With Rage
Leave It To The Dogs
The De-Regulators
Jezebel
Totally Pants
Ma's Strict
Before The Beak
Museum Piece
In Search Of Bedrock
Bask Seperatist
Jump The Sun
Sink Or Swim
Resin D'Etre
When Push Comes To Shove
Mars Attacks
Say Cheese Please
Voice From The Pulpit
Ducky Lucky
The Inflated Roundhead
Twisted To Fit
Ice Cream Sunday
Foaming At The Gussett
Out Come The Freaks

Fr7a
Joy De Viva
The World vs Gibson
Big Cheese
Old Slapper
Panteon Shot
The Millennium Thug
The Running Man
Its Tufa At The Top
Down Under Deborah
The Raven
Helmut Cheese
Glue Year
Liassic Lark
Flick The Frenulum
Jump Over My Shadow
Tragic Moustache
I'm Sika This
Wandelanden Tak
Sweet September
Eugene Genie
Christendom
Pugsley
The Cool Crux Clan
Rob Roy
Puss Off
Tribulations

Graded List

Red October
Sverige
Pinch The Helmet
Jury's Out
The Creaming Dream
The Oxwich Bobby
Caught Mid-Shot
Conglomeration
By Proxy
Picking Berries
Tump Jumper
Look Over Yonder
Epoxy Clips Now
Reign Of The Deer
Resination
Skedaddle

Fr6c+
Deborah
Geef Onze Fietsen Terug!
Inspector Glueseau
Thinner
Brazilian Blend
Cordoba Express
Five O'Clock Shadow
Chicken Licken
Stoeipoesje
Tufa Tennis
Ride The Funky Wave, Babe Direct
Tufa Joy
There's Life In The Old Dog Yet
Stoned Dates
Ride The Funky Wave, Babe
Screaming Lampshades
Rancho La Cha Cha Cha
For Sportsmen Of The Epoxy Clips
Thousand Yard Stare
Welcome to Royston Vasey
Double Dutch

Fr6c
El Camino Del Roy
Goose In Lucy
Cujo
Ponty Pandy
Squeal Like A Hog
The Minchkins
Hanging By A Thread
Call a Spade a Spade
Academy Awards
Big Ears Takes Flight
The Last Arete
The Angel Of Mons
Angela's Ashes

The Clampetts
Crock Block
Sniff That
Breakout
Kissin' The Pink
Debauching Deborah
Each Way Nudger
Deadly Nightshade
Swim With The Sharks
Totally Invalid
Going Down On Deborah
Anal Retention
Banal Pretention
Standing On A Beach
Teasing The Zits
Charlie's Rusks
Technitis

Fr6b+
Wij Zitten Nog In Een Sneeuwstorm
Croeso-I-Gymru
Totally Radish
Pinheads
Anchors Away
The Day The Sky Fell In
Sideburn
I Can I Can't
Triple Sigh
Dream Academy
Miss You
Ladder Of Desire
Weak Lemon Drink
Pipsqueak
Knacker's Yard
Cast Adrift
Barry Freight
Pubic Enema
Open Roads

Fr6b
Opening Shot
Open Verdict
Pinch The Helmet
The Trainspotter
Special Stuff
Rag And Bone
Illegal Congress
Precious Things
Treading The Grapes
No Beer No Fear
The Wake
Her Helmut Schmutt
Broken On The Rocks
Fringe Benefits

The Dumbfounded Dunderhead
Pis En Lit
Beyond The Fringe
South West Guru
Bob's Birthday Party
Marooned
Squash The Squaddie
The Deflated Dickhead
Magic Touch
Cheesy Rider
Gary's Talking Climbs
Top Cheese
Drip Free

Fr6a+
New Zawn
Steel Yourself
Family Values
Miss Alto
Don't Jis On My Sofa
The Dove From Above
Tapping The Keg

Fr6a
Gentlemen's Relish
Red Leicester
Rusty Roy
Pantyliner
Pelagic Mush
Bottom Cheese
Stinking Of Fish
Red With Age
Jap's Eye
Connect One

Fr5+
Pantyhose
Blight At The End Of The Funnel
Spear The Bearded Clam
Slurp The Savoury Oyster
Fromage Frais
Scraping The Barrel

Fr5
Voyage Of The Zawn Treader
Pinch A Minch
Cheesy Flaps

Fr4+
Telefunken U47

Sandstone

Fr7c
Contraband
Mad At The Sun

Fr7b+
Sharpy Unplugged
Encore! Magnifique!
The Caerphilly Contract
Skanderbeg
Torch The Earth
Bring On The Spring
Sport For All
Ripe And Ready
Abbatoir And Costello
A Momentary Lapse Of Reason

Fr7b
La Rage
Dai Hard
Loctite
Innuendo
King Ada
King Zog
Capstan
Physical Presents
I Can Do Better
Unnamed (Cwmaman)
Face
Ferndale Revisited
Anything You Can Do
John West
Sinister
Full Dog
Boston Strangler
Basildon Slapper
The Future Holds
No Chips Round Here
Menage A Chien
Stretch People
Money
Perverted By Language
Feeling Sheep
Poisonous Little Toad
Nether Edge

Fr7a+
Haven't A Clue
Butcher Heinrich
Science Friction
Food For Parasites
A Clip Round The Year
Cointreau

Whiter Than White Wall
Pleasant Valley Sunday
Niart Thgin
Mother Of Pearl
Arizona Stan
Chattery Teeth
Desert Storm
Round Are Way
Night Train
Slip Into Something Sexy
Olympic Doctor
Eastern Bloc Rock
Falling Freely
Grit Box
Twenty Second Chance
Get Flossed
Hush Money
Outspan
In Blood, Of Life, Of Sin
Race You Up The Wallbars
Juvenile Justice
Scared Seal Banter
Giving It All Up
Mona Lisa
Blowing For Tugs
Dusk
Pastis On Ice Direct
Pastis On Ice
Two Of A Kind

Fr7a
Hot Mill
Rise
Western Front Direct
Propaganda
Valleys Initiative
Kicking Ass And Taking Names
The Evil Eye
African Head Charge
Salmon Running, Bear Cunning
Gott In Himmel
Grab Some Tree And Follow Me
Young, Free And Single
Madame X
A Cleft Stick
The Crimson King
Man Or Mouse
Aptitude Test
Cop The Lot
Golf Syndrome
Gorki's Zygotic Mynci
Maurice Chevaliers
Letters Of Life
Nervous Nineties

Coffee Shop
Shadow Of The Sun
Sub Contraction
House Of Cards
Cascade
Radovan Karadijc
Mister Foothold
Amnesia
Athabasca Falls
Luxury Gap
Sixty Second Go See
Misadventure
Branch Manager
Heron Egg Poacher
Mr. Gorrilla's Got A Big Nose

Fr6c+
Great Expectations
The Theory And Practice Of....
Slap Happy
Steroid John
Giant Sand
Golf Bag
Banog's Barmy Army
Mawr, Mawr, Mawr
The Uninvited
The World Is My Lobster
All Sand Together
Cold Rolled
The Caerphilly Cop Out
Simple Addition
High Force
Chumbawumba
Totally Stumped
Blacker Than Black
Rhubarb Lets Fly
Our Man In Bargoed

Fr6c
Behind The Lines
VIP Lunge
Fairway To Heaven
Is It What You Are That Is
Shaken Not Stirred
Hostility Suite
Demi Moore
Jet Lagged
Scrotum Oil
Total Recoil
Host
Time For Tee
Dreaming In Colour
Deri Made
Chip And Putt

Moses Supposes His Toeses...
You Change Me
So Uncool
The Mastic Mick
Missing Link
Rave Crave
Enema Of The Affair
Molybdenum Man
Three Men In A Goat
Bunk-Her
Snapper
Little White Lies
Unnamed @ Trehafod
The Merthyr Infill
Insomnia
Splashdown
Hot Beef Injection
Moutton Dagger
The Grout Of San Romano
Slap Of Luxury
Just Another One Move Wonder
Joker In The Pack
Tall Dark And Handsome Direct
By Appointment Only
Magellan's Straight
Splash It On All Over
Too Keynes By Half

Fr6b+
Perfect Scoundrels
Saboo
Blinded By Love
Strange Little Girl
Abdominal Showman
Roraima
Golf-Whore
Sleeping Dogs Lie
At Your Convenience
You Are What You Is
Neo Maxie Zoom Weenie
Sumo No Shiro
Yikes
Peachy
Plaque Attack
Red 'Erring
Mine's A Pair
The Big Tissue
My New House
Tall Dark And Handsome
Harrowed Harrovians
Incidentally
Masterfool
Under The Axe
Drugs Make You Fall Off

Cwm Mammon
After Effect

Fr6b
The Laughing Policeman
Greased Balls
Land Of The Dinosaurs
Between The Lines
Controlled Emission
Nappy Rush
Ring Of Confidence
I Am What I Am
Right Of Spring
Slipping Into Luxury
Culture Vulture
Pick Locks
Wert's Famous Taxi Ride
Post Expressionist
Peel Back The Flaps

Fr6a+
Canine League
Fair Cop
Pampered
Dirty As A Dog
Baldy Walks To Ponty
A Certain Peace
Discount Included In The Price
Sporting Supplement
High Moon
Grave Concern
Something To Do With Drugs
Dandelion
Cashflow Crisis
Acatalepsia
Hollow Feeling
Overleaf
Rising Sap
I Came
Burdoch
Marlin On The Wall
Roaring Forties
Fluster
Pick Up The Pieces
The Lapse
Bathtime
Poker In The Eye
Bluster
Kosovo
Sorry Lorry Morry
Fach Roo Too
Final Plot
Caddy-Lack
Fach Roo

Ant Hill Mob
Pork Sword
Kabuto Mushi
Horns A Plenty
A Sight For Saw Eyes
It's A Sine
IConkered

Fr6a
Spaghnum 45
One Bitten
Masai
Grout Expectations
Internal Reflection
Mr. Farady
Buff The Happy Lamp
Shackles Of Love
Balance Sheet
Hey Mister
Yank Plank
Evil Ways (Cwmaman)
Little Kurd

Fr5+
My Blue Bell
Anniversary Walk
Ace In The Hole
Rump And Scoop
Twice Shy
As It Is
Alements

Fr5
Virgo Intactae
Newton's Apple
He Sawed

Fr4+
No Barking Up This Tree
As It Was
Conan's Boil

Fr4
The Link Pitch
Bring Back The Birch

Index

Index

Index

Index

Index

Index

Index